Functions of
Varied Experience

Functions of Varied Experience

Donald W. Fiske

and

Salvatore R. Maddi

with contributions by

James Bieri

William N. Dember

Joe Kamiya

John R. Platt

Austin H. Riesen

Theodore Schaefer, Jr.

William R. Thompson

W. I. Welker

Robert W. White

1961

THE DORSEY PRESS, INC.

HOMEWOOD, ILLINOIS

First Printing, September, 1961

Library of Congress Catalogue Card No. 61–17207

PRINTED IN THE UNITED STATES OF AMERICA

Preface

*T*HIS book is about varied experience, its effects on organisms, and the functions it serves. Variation in experience comes from the changes occurring from moment to moment in the environment, both external and internal. These changes are produced not only by external forces but also by the behavior of the organism. Variation is the normal condition. It is so ubiquitous that its significance is often overlooked. Indeed, most psychological theory ignores it and most psychological experiments are designed to minimize its unwanted effects.

The purpose of this book is to consider the functions that this experienced variation serves in the organism's development, in its interaction with the environment, and in the affective experience of man. Some of the topics in this volume are rather familiar: for example, the variability of behavior seen in exploring and alternating responses. Examples of less familiar topics are sleep and aesthetic appreciation. It is our conviction that, in spite of this marked diversity, each chapter is relevant to the notion of varied experience.

The list of subjects examined in the different chapters is itself quite varied. In addition, the nature of the problem considered by each chapter and the state of knowledge in that area has in part determined the particular approach taken by its author. The multiple authorship has increased the heterogeneity still further by introducing a range of styles and technical levels. As the reader progresses through this book, we trust that the variation he encounters will contribute to his interest and enjoyment, especially as he notes the common elements and themes underlying the diversity. Since this volume is intended for people with some knowledge of psychology, the uniformity of style desirable in an introductory textbook has been given up in favor of the diversified individual styles of the specialists who have contributed chapters.

The wide range of topics included should not lead the reader to expect a comprehensive account of behavior. The book is not a treatise in general psychology but rather a consideration of those aspects of behavior pertinent to variation in experience. (Thus certain relevant problems in development and motivation are considered, but there is no systematic analysis of topics such as learning or the several classical drives.)

We are grateful to the American Psychological Association for permission to reprint the article by Dr. Robert W. White which originally appeared in the *Psychological Review,* and for permission to use Figure 3-2 in Chapter 3; to Dr. Arthur Hess and the *Journal of Comparative Neurology* for permission to reproduce Figure 3-1 of Chapter 3; and to the Association for Research in Nervous and Mental Disease for permission to reprint Table 4-2 of Chapter 4. We want to express our appreciation to Mrs. Joan Adams and Miss Birute Petrulis for their careful and patient typing and retyping of drafts and manuscript. Miss Petrulis was also of great assistance in preparing the bibliography. This work was supported by a grant from the Ford Foundation Behavioral Sciences Fund made by the Social Science Research Committee of the University of Chicago.

We are deeply indebted to Dr. Howard F. Hunt for his scholarly and incisive editorial suggestions and for his advice and encouragement throughout our work on this volume. Dr. Donald W. Taylor also contributed a valuable critique for which we are grateful. Our biggest debt is to Barbara P. Fiske and Dorothy-Anne Maddi for their devoted help and sympathetic understanding through the many months of our preoccupation with this book.

D.W.F.

S.R.M.

Table of Contents

Chapter 1

The Forms of Varied Experience

DONALD W. FISKE and
SALVATORE R. MADDI
University of Chicago

*W*HY does an animal approach and explore a new object encountered in its familiar environment? How can we account for the playful behavior of lower animals, human children, and even adults? Why do we like to listen to a song that we heard some time ago, but not to one that we have just heard several times? Why do artists prefer asymmetrical line drawings to drawings with marked symmetry? Why does a rat which has just taken one route through a maze tend to take a different one when immediately returned to the starting box? Why should healthy young men dislike resting all day in a dark, quiet room?

These are some of the problems to which psychologists have recently devoted increasing attention. These questions suggest the range of phenomena discussed in this book. The answer to each of the questions seems to involve the dimension of temporal variation in an organism's experience. While variation in stimulation may be produced by changing events in the external world, or by changes within the organism, it may also result from the responses of the organism.

SOME BACKGROUND RELEVANT TO VARIED EXPERIENCE

Scientific psychology emphasized simple things first. It started by working on consistent aspects of behavior. It investigated capacities which do not change much from time to time: How rapidly can a person react? How do individuals differ in ability to solve problems? How small a physical difference between two stimuli can a person detect?

Psychology looked at separate functions and mechanisms, one at a time. It determined the conditions for memory. It studied the struc-

1

ture and process by which we see or hear, and it examined perceptions and misperceptions. The typical strategy was to investigate a particular kind of response by manipulating the relevant stimuli and other conditions. These studies emphasized the regularities in behavior.

In contrast, more pertinent to this book are the investigations of phenomena showing rapid change over time, such as the elusive matter of attention. In Pillsbury's classic book on this topic (1908), he deals with many of the problems considered in the present volume, such as the contribution of changing stimulation to attention.

But along with the study of separate processes and discrete classes of responses, and more relevant to this book, there has been a persisting interest in general characteristics of organismic functioning. For example, as early as the 1860s, Bain (1868) wrote about spontaneous activity and the craving of the senses for stimulation. An outstanding early example of this approach in physiology is Cannon's classical work on homeostasis. A later landmark is Kleitman's analysis of the cycle of existence (1939) with his proposal of a wakefulness center.

More recently, neurophysiological research has produced concepts and findings whose pertinence to the topic of varied experience will be developed in Chaper 2. The work of such men as Magoun and Jasper has brought out the activity of an arousal system which receives excitation from afferent neural pathways as well as feedback from the cortex. A review of current thinking about the complex mechanisms by which the active nervous system regulates behavior has been provided by Pribram (1960).

Also relevant is the work relating physiological activity to performance, particularly the studies of muscular tension which came into prominence in the 1920s (see Courts, 1942) and are still receiving attention today. The same problem has been given increasing emphasis from the more psychological side. For example, Duffy (1941, 1957) has steadfastly urged her colleagues to consider the broad general dimension of behavior which she has called intensity. This concept parallels that of physiological arousal.

These several currents from rather different directions have come together in the work of Hebb (1949), and especially in his classical discussion of the conceptual nervous system (1955). He has brought out the contribution of the nonspecific effects of stimulation to level of arousal and has provided a conceptual basis for the suggestion that optimal performance is associated with the middle range of the arousal function. More recently, Malmo (1959) has presented a systematic exposition of the neuropsychological concept of activation. Parts of the same trend are the notion of an optimal level of excitation (Hebb and Thompson, 1954) and the concept of optimal stimulation (Leuba, 1955).

In the area of motivation the significance of varied experience has been intermittently recognized. About 40 years ago, when instincts were popular, a "desire for new experience, for fresh stimulations" was proposed by W. I. Thomas as the first of four basic wishes (see Volkart, 1951). But in systematic psychology, the unfruitful concept of instinct was superseded by drive theory. Such drives as hunger and thirst lent themselves readily to experimental investigation and manipulation. Recently, many psychologists have found this viewpoint unsatisfactory and incomplete. It cannot account for motivational drift as a function of the familiarity of stimulation (Hebb, 1949). It does not handle the tendency of organisms to alternate responses (see Chapter 8), a disposition first observed more than 30 years ago and given increasing experimental emphasis in the last decade.

A major problem for the classical concept of drive is the interpretation of exploratory behavior. Reactions to unfamiliar stimuli have been investigated and conceptualized by a growing group of workers, including R. Butler, Glanzer, Harlow, Montgomery, Walker, and Welker (see Chapter 7). Berlyne and others have contributed to the current experimentation on exploration in human beings (see Chapter 9). At a more abstract level, Goldstein (1939) and Maslow (1943) have advocated the concept of self-actualization to account for aspects of human motivation that classical drives cannot handle. Much of this broad but articulated area has been analyzed by White (Chapter 10; 1960) and integrated by his conceptualization of competence and effectance motivation, the tendency of the organism to seek to produce effects in the world about it in a manner which increases the efficacy of its behavior at later times. A theme common to the several parts of this trend is familiarity as a dimension of external stimulation.

This rapid overview has mentioned only a portion of the background contributing to the topic of varied experience. We feel that the area has been relatively neglected even though this concept has relevance for several classical and intensively explored problems. Thus in attempts to explain illusions, little attention has been paid to the fact that they are most marked when first presented and tend to disappear with repeated exposures. Much of the work on learning has concentrated on the acquisition of a fixed response, using conditions designed to counteract the disposition toward variation in successive responses. Such variability is more difficult to analyze, to manipulate experimentally, and to conceptualize than regularities in responses. Again, the response to novelty is not repeatable, except with a new stimulus. And the equating of novel stimuli presents serious difficulties because the term novelty is difficult to define precisely. Finally, the exploratory response is itself complex and of varying strength.

Among other relevant problems are the following: The roles of dissimilarity among stimuli and among prior experiences in learning; sensitivity to changing frames of reference; rigidity of reaction when the nature of the problem changes; the biases in subjective conceptions of random sequences. Subsequent chapters will add still further areas. While varied experience, variation in stimulation and in response, is not a new problem in psychology, its many facets have usually been considered separately. This volume brings them together so that their common basis can be determined.

THE PLAN OF THIS BOOK

The chapters in this volume fall into two large classes. The bulk of the book is the set of twelve chapters on specific topics pertinent to varied experience. These are framed within three chapters written jointly by the editors. Between this chapter and that central core, Chapter 2 presents a formulation by which we seek to account for some of the contributions of varied experience to behavior. The closing chapter offers our appraisal of this conceptualization: How well does it handle the phenomena considered in the several intervening chapters? For which of the reported observations does it provide a reasonable interpretation? Which are beyond its scope? Does it offer leads for further investigation?

We began our development of the conceptual formulation in Chapter 2 with the intuitive feeling that behind the trends considered earlier in this chapter and underlying the topics of the subsequent chapters was the core notion of variation in stimulation and in response. As we thought about the means by which such variation contributed to the behavior of organisms, we became convinced that the neuropsychological concept of activation had to be given a central role. Activation is produced by aspects of stimulation, including changes in stimuli. Activation is fundamental not only as a condition for effective behavior but also in its effects on the ongoing processes of living organisms. Thus level of activation plays the major part in Chapter 2. The term variation is mentioned in only one of the eight propositions because variation makes its contributions to behavior through activation.

In the main section of the book, the several chapters contributed by our colleagues were requested because we feel that they demonstrate the far-reaching, if not ubiquitous, implications of varied experience for behavior. These chapters were not written to support our argument. Each author was asked to write about a topic in which he was known to have had a prior interest, and about which he was already well informed. In several cases, in addition to the reprinted paper, the work had been completed before this book was conceived. We are convinced that each chapter is a significant contribution in its own right, whatever its relevance to the general theme or to our argument. We are bringing them together because we believe each considers material which is best understood in the light of the phenomena and concepts presented in other chapters.

The order of the chapters on specific topics (Chapters 3-14) is somewhat arbitrary. In general, the earlier chapters deal with areas permitting more experimental manipulation and control. For this reason, the several chapters emphasizing work on animal subjects occur in the first half. Most of the later chapters consider correlational and observational studies of human subjects.

Some contributions of varied experience to development are considered in Chapters 3 and 4. (Growth and development are also mentioned in Chapters 7, 10, and 13.) Chapter 3 reviews the evidence for the effects of stimulation on the ontogenetic development of sensory mechanisms and perceptual processes. In these experiments, the standard procedure is to minimize or eliminate certain aspects of stimulation, particularly in the visual modality.

The effects of early stimulation upon later functioning are examined in Chapter 4. Included are studies dealing with the amount, type, and pattern of stimulation experienced by animals in their early life.

Strictly speaking, these two chapters deal with the range of stimulation experienced by the developing animal. The first discusses animals deprived of patterned visual stimuli for a sustained period from birth. The second reports work restricting the variety of stimulation below that normally experienced. While the notion of varied experience is certainly appropriate for this material, it should also be noted that the concept of temporal variation in stimulation is also relevant. Animals reared in the dark or exposed only to diffuse visual stimulation can experience little or no change in such stimulation from one moment to the next. Animals that have been raised in a limited environment will later encounter more new and strange objects than the normal animal and will be exposed to more extreme shifts in stimulation than those previously met.

Two types of restricted stimulation with adult subjects are reviewed in Chapter 5. One is the vigilance task in which a subject watches for a standard signal. The conditions are monotonous, with even the signals being repetitious. These experiments indicate the difficulties in maintaining performance when variation in stimulation is restricted. The second type are the so-called sensory deprivation experiments. In these, the subjects are deprived not of sensation but of stimulation which has meaning, intensity, and variation. As the hours pass, normal functioning becomes disturbed. Thus the chapter demonstrates temporary effects from relatively brief periods of experimentally restricted and homogeneous stimulation in mature persons.

Sleep is a normal state with curtailment of sensory input and minimal variation in external stimulation. Chapter 6 considers the growing body of experimental work on this topic, with special attention to the intriguing phenomena of dreams. In this state of low but varying activation, there is considerable, if not continuous ideational production (see Chapter 11); between the several dream periods, there appears to be discrete imagery which is less fanciful than dream content.

The next group of chapters deals with behavior by which the organism insures variation in its stimulation. Organisms react to moderately novel stimuli not just by attending but also by approaching: they explore and manipulate new objects. The voluminous literature on exploration and play in both higher and lower animals is reviewed in Chapter 7. (See also Chapter 10.) The data and interpretations of alternation behavior form the subject of the next chapter. In experimental work, it has been repeatedly noted that animals tend to make a response which is different from the one they made on the immediately preceding trial; by varying their response, they vary the stimulation they experience.

Man also explores and seeks variation. Research on some of the variables influencing these tendencies is discussed in Chapter 9. In addition, the usefulness of conceptualizing the need for variation as a personality variable is suggested.

Unlike the preceding chapters, Chapter 10 is not a review of a single topic but instead it advances an interpretation derived from several independent lines of thought. Attempts to explain exploratory behavior, manipulation, and play by a drive concept or by an instinctual force are critically examined. The concept of effectance motivation is then proposed.

Chapter 11 presents evidence for viewing behavior as basically variable. The limited consistency in responses is associated with the organism's efforts to cope with particular sets of conditions. Variability in responses not only facilitates the acquisition of new adaptive responses but also provides variation in stimulation.

The disposition to perceive objects as complex rather than simple is analyzed in Chapter 12. Also considered are studies of differences in preference for complex stimuli. Such stimuli offer greater variation in experience from moment to moment (see discussion in Chapter 2). This relatively new research area provides one approach to the study of individual differences in the tendency or need to seek varied experience (see Chapters 8 and 9).

Moderate unexpectedness in stimulation is associated with positive affective tone, while low or extreme unexpectedness is not. With this viewpoint, Chapter 13 introduces the role of varied experience in feelings of pleasantness and unpleasantness. It emphasizes the importance of interpreting variation not merely as objective change in stimulation but also as departure from the pattern perceived in the preceding sequence of events.

The following chapter argues that an essential characteristic of outstanding works of art is a pattern that contains the unexpected. This position is developed from evidence that evolution has produced organisms with nervous systems that respond to patterns or regularities in stimulation but also require variation in pattern. Variation in stimulation is necessary even to our aesthetic enjoyment.

This book describes and interprets facets of behavior pertinent to varied experience. In addition to psychological observations, physiological findings are brought in by various of its authors where such data contribute to an understanding of the behavior with which we are concerned. However, the explanatory concepts invoked by us (in Chapter 2) and by the other authors are essentially psychological. This point applies particularly to the concept of activation, which is mentioned frequently throughout the book. While the word has been taken over from physiology, it is construed for present purposes in a basically psychological sense. Even though relevant physiological measures may sometimes provide convenient experimental operations, our primary emphasis is on the marked psychological significance of activation, on its roles in behavior. While we hope for an eventual *rapprochement* between the physiological and the psychological approaches to the behavior considered in this book, the concepts utilized in these chapters are fundamentally psychological and their evaluation must rest on their explanatory power and fruitfulness for psychological theory, and not on their congruence with physiological knowledge today.

The Limits of This Volume

The purpose of this book is to provide an overview of its topic, not a comprehensive encyclopedia. It is too early to delineate the full scope and ramifications of varied experience. The subjects we selected for inclusion in this volume characterize but do not exhaust the domain of potentially relevant phenomena. The chapters might well have included one on the satiation and adaptation observed with continuing stimulation. Many perceptual phenomena change with continuous, unvaried exposure. In addition to illusions which were mentioned earlier, there are the familiar autokinetic effect, as well as the reversability of visual figures and the abrupt shifts in the perceptions of repeated auditory stimulation (see Warren, 1960). A considerable experimental literature has been stimulated by the pioneering work of Köhler and Wallach (1944). McEwen (1958) has provided a comprehensive review of the problem, and other contributions are available in Spitz (1958) and in Sagara and Oyama (1957). In every sensory area that has been investigated, some satiation effects have been found. Although small in magnitude, these effects have been demonstrated to occur very rapidly.

Humor might also have been given a chapter by itself (but see Chapter 14). This pleasant phenomenon requires a stimulus that varies from the expected; a joke is never quite so amusing the second time it is heard. An analysis of humor from a viewpoint related to that of this volume has been made by Berlyne (1960; Chapter 9).

Since understimulation characterizes much of the material in this book, the reader may wonder why there is no chapter on overstimulation, or stress. Very strange and quite unexpected stimuli can be highly stressful, and a history of such stimulation, especially early in life, has important consequences for later behavior (see Chapter 4). Yet stress is primarily a function of the intensity or meaning of stimulation. After the onset of the stressful conditions, the contribution of temporal variation is minimal. Therefore the study of stress seems to add little to the understanding of varied experience.

In keeping with the limited objectives of this volume, we have not attempted to include a systematic exposition and critique of other conceptualizations and theoretical positions which may be seen as more or less pertinent. Berlyne's analysis (1960) of many of the phenomena considered in this book is clearly different from ours. There are also Helson's Adaptation Level theory (1959) which may appear related to our concept of impact, the psychoanalytic concepts of constancy and stimulus hunger (see Fenichel, 1945), and Glanzer's suggestion (1958a) that each organism has a standard, preferred rate of information flow from his environment. While each of these latter three might serve as the starting point for a conceptual framework applicable to the topics examined in this volume, such comprehensive analyses have not yet been made. The reader may wish to consider the applicability of these positions, as well as the one we present in the next chapter, to the various phenomena and problems discussed in the subsequent chapters.

Chapter 2

A Conceptual Framework

DONALD W. FISKE and
SALVATORE R. MADDI
University of Chicago

PURPOSE

*T*HE main body of this volume is a series of chapters on a wide range of topics. While each chapter is a distinctive contribution, a significant entity in its own right, it was not included solely for this reason. The editors believe that each of these separately treated and diverse topics adds to the understanding of a central theme in the functioning of organisms. Hence, the major purpose of the book is to bring these topics together in one place so that the common features and underlying principles can be more easily seen. Although each of the chapters by invited contributors was prepared independently, the editors indicating only the broad area, the commonality of concepts and of the experimental studies cited is striking and significant.

This chapter presents a broad conceptualization offering concepts and propositions which we believe to be applicable to some or all of the various phenomena. We have chosen to place this exposition here, rather than at the end, not only to provide one possible orientation to the reader but also to permit him to assess the usefulness of such a formulation as our own, while he explores each specific topic. At the least, we trust that our efforts at a synthesis will stimulate the integrative efforts of the reader.

The set of interrelated concepts and propositions expounded below may be a preliminary step toward the development of a more formal theory. Some of the concepts are familiar ones. Some of the propositions are principles which have been stated by others or are generalizations from empirical findings that are already known. Among the authors who have proposed conceptualizations or interpretations similar to or overlapping those presented below, the following can be taken as representative: Bindra (1959a), Berlyne (1960), Goldstein (1940), Hebb (1955, 1958b), Leuba (1955), Lindsley (1951), D. C. McClelland (1956), Malmo (1959), and Morgan (1959). The work of these men is considered later in this chapter or elsewhere in the book.

The other concepts and propositions are more novel, and their utility must be determined in the future. The main contribution of this chapter is the juxtaposition and integration of the various constructs, many of which have obvious value in their own right, but all of which take on, we hope, additional value from their location within an integrated framework. The comprehensiveness and the fruitfulness of the formulation will be weighed in the final chapter.

VARIED EXPERIENCE AND ITS FUNCTIONS

In this chapter, we will tend to use the terms "varied experience" and "variation in stimulation" interchangeably. This usage requires comment. As will become clear in later discussion, the concept of variation in stimulation refers to the extent to which stimulation at a particular moment differs from that which preceded it, or to the average degree of such moment-to-moment changes. (Occasionally, variation may be used to refer to the relative range or heterogeneity of the stimulation which an organism has experienced; for example, we may characterize an organism's experience as homogeneous and having little variation. This usage to describe the distribution of prior experience is not inconsistent with our primary meaning because a greater range of experience ordinarily involves a larger amount of variation from moment to moment.)

However, it is not only the well-known exteroceptive stimulation which is of concern in this chapter; interoceptive, and even cortical, stimulation receive considerable attention. It is primarily this broad definition of stimulation which has led us to use the term varied experience.

Once it is recognized that internal as well as external stimulation is to be considered, then the value of the broad connotations of the term varied experience becomes clear. Variation in stimulation can occur not only when the external environment changes but also when the organism itself behaves. And even the reaction to an externally produced change in stimulation provides new stimulation or experience. The reader should keep in mind that although the term variation in stimulation will be used repeatedly in this chapter, it is meant to have the broad connotations of the term varied experience.

The functions of varied experience which are delineated in this book are contained in three empirical generalizations. First, variations in stimulation contributes to the normal development and also to the functioning of organisms. Much evidence concerning the developmental role of variation is included in Chapters 3 and 4. The next chapter considers the contribution of variation to the adequacy and effectiveness of ongoing behavior in adulthood.

A second function of varied experience is that it is oriented toward and sought out for its own sake. Evidence for this statement is provided by Chapters 7 and 9, which analyze the exploration, play, and variation-seeking of lower animals and man. Also relevant is Chapter 8, which discusses the more specific tendency of rats to alternate or vary the stimulus environments available to them.

Finally, varied experience is one factor contributing to the affective state of human beings. The relationship between unexpectedness and affective tone is analyzed in Chapter 13, and the next chapter considers the contribution that variation in patterning makes to aesthetic preference. The evidence suggests that moderate degrees of variation in stimulation produce positive affect.

AN OVERVIEW OF THE CONCEPTUAL FRAMEWORK

These three points indicate that at least some variation in stimulation is sought out by organisms and may be required for normal development and functioning. How does varied experience serve these functions? In attempting to answer this question it is important first to consider the effect of variation in stimulation on the organism. Imagine a situation with a minimum of variation, such as a series of repetitions of the same stimulus, a stimulus with weak intensity and no special meaning. The organism experiencing such a repetitive situation will become adapted to it; alertness will decrease. Now suppose a new or different stimulus occurs. This variation in stimula-

tion immediately increases alertness and the vigor of ongoing behavior.

Variation has arousing effects upon the organism. But aside from
variation, a stimulus may have arousing effects primarily because it
has high intensity or is very meaningful. We have chosen the term
impact to refer to the activating effect common to these three properties of stimulation: intensity, meaningfulness, and variation.

For a complete description, stimulation from exteroceptive, inter-
ceptive, and cerebral sources must be considered; a loud noise, a
sharp pain in the chest, and a disturbing thought all have impact.
Stimulation from each of the three sources can be characterized by
variation, intensity, and meaningfulness. While it may be useful at
times to speak of the impact of a single stimulus element, we will
ordinarily use the term to refer to the total of the nonspecific effects
of all stimuli from all sources at a point in time.

This composite impact produces its observable manifestations
through its contribution to the organism's level of activation. Activation is a basic dimension referring to the common core in such variables as alertness, attentiveness, tension, and subjective excitement.
It is a postulated central nervous system phenomenon which affects
other parts of the organism. We use the term arousal to refer to the
somatic correlates of activation, to its effects on the circulatory system, the muscular system, etc. These effects in turn produce stimulation with impact that sustains activation. Under most circumstances,
this contribution to impact is smaller than that from other sources.

Thus far in our attempt to understand the functions of varied
experience, we have considered the contribution of variation in stimulation to impact, which in turn determines level of activation. In
order to obtain the complete answer to the question, it is now necessary to consider in greater detail the behavioral significance of level
of activation. There are two types of conditions, that in which the
specific qualities of the stimulation direct and force behavior and
that in which behavior is not constrained in this way. While many
situations represent intermediate degrees, one or the other condition
is predominant for any given brief period of time and this fact
justifies considering them as separate. The first condition, in which
the organism has specific motivation, has been emphasized heavily
in psychological research; for example, the organism with a drive

for food or water, or the organism that is threatened by its environment. When flight or fight is required, the organism must be mobilized. Activation prepares it for vigorous response. In the case of such drives as hunger or thirst, and even when the demands of the situation are as moderate as those of the usual experimental task or test, an organism must be sufficiently aroused to perform adequately.

An organism with such a specific drive or motive engages in instrumental responses which, if successful, reduce tissue tensions or cope with external pressures. In all such instances, but especially when a difficult response or series of responses is required, the effectiveness of the instrumental behavior is a function of the approximation of the current level of activation to the appropriate optimal level, that is, that level which most facilitates coping with the task or conditions at hand. When there is a large discrepancy between current level of activation and the optimal level or range for the given situation, the organism will typically engage in behavior designed to increase or decrease impact and thus to shift activation to reduce the discrepancy, thereby making effective instrumental responses more possible. For example, the organism may increase muscle tonus to augment activation level or it may act to eliminate sources of stimulation that have raised activation and distracted it from the task at hand.

It should be clear that we are not attempting to explain the specific instrumental responses which will occur in any given situation where drive-states are present. These specific responses are a function of the specific information contained in the stimuli. It should be noted, however, that such instrumental behavior can contribute to impact in various ways, including the variation in stimulation that it produces.

This major class, specifically motivated behaviors, has been thoroughly studied. While we are not attempting a new explanation of them, our formulation does seem to provide a framework which can apply to them as well as to the second general condition, in which there are no imperative demands upon the organism, either from internal tissue needs or from external threat or imposed task. What is the significance of level of activation for behavior under these freer conditions?

Evidence suggests that there is a characteristic level of activation for each organism depending upon the time of day, or more precisely, depending upon the stage of its sleep-wakefulness cycle. There is reason to believe that an organism maintains its activation at a value close to this norm. Any large discrepancy results in behavior which modifies impact in the direction which will reduce the discrepancy. When external stimulation and internal tissue needs provide low levels of impact, the organism typically orients toward or seeks out new or different stimulation. The resulting variation in stimulation furnishes increased impact and serves to sustain activation near the characteristic or normal level. The organism may also seek stimulation possessing sufficient intensity or meaningfulness to generate appropriate impact. Thus some behavior is not tension-reducing but tension-increasing.

Some conditions may produce degrees of activation above the norm. In these instances, the responses of the organism that reduce the drive or remove the threat also lower the level of activation toward the norm. To take a specific example of another sort, when the organism is ready for sleep, it will seek out conditions with minimal variation and low intensities, so that its level of activation can decline appropriately.

To a considerable extent, affect is a function of the discrepancy between actual and characteristic levels of activation. Large discrepancies are ordinarily associated with negative affect, while positive affect usually is experienced when such discrepancies are reduced: for example, when there is relief from tension or situational pressure. There are exceptions, of course. Some motives and drives (for example, sexual) may produce states of high arousal with positive affect.

Other factors contribute to the quality and intensity of affect, such as activation itself (at least at very high levels). Again, even when activation is near its characteristic level, affect is influenced by the meaning of stimuli, by their specific cue-function.

The general outlines of our answer to the question concerning the functions of varied experience have been presented. In brief, that answer is that the organism's level of activation will decline when stimulation does not change very much and when there also is no pressing task or strong need which can sustain a high level. In such situations, the organism must maintain activation at the level characteristic for it at that point on its sleep-wakefulness cycle if it is to remain alert and is to avoid negative or displeasurable feelings. A particularly effective way of maintaining characteristic level of activation is to seek out or produce variation in stimulation. Variation is effective because, like the intensity and the meaningfulness of stimulation, it has impact and hence contributes to level of activation.

Our interpretation of the roles of varied experience has considered only its roles in affect and the ongoing functioning and behavior of organisms. We have not attempted to account for the function of varied experience in the development of the organism. This matter will be discussed in Chapter 15.

In answering the question posed earlier, we have devised a conceptualization portraying an active organism, in continuous interaction with its internal and external environments. It is activated not only by the specific content of the diverse types of stimulation it receives but also by such nonspecific aspects as the mere variation in stimulation from moment to moment. The organism we describe is more than simply reactive: it behaves in such a way that it receives stimulation with impact appropriate for the level of activation required by the particular situation demanded or by its own organic functions. But because the impact of unchanging stimulation will diminish with time, an active organism also seeks variation in stimulation.

EIGHT PROPOSITIONS

From the preceding brief overview, let us turn now to a more complete exposition of our conceptual framework structured in terms of propositions which are literally proposals. The three propositions forming the first subset introduce basic concepts pertaining to all behavior. The next pair, Propositions IV and V, apply to an organism in which a specific drive or motive is operating. The final triad consider the condition where no very specific motivation exists at the particular moment.

Impact and Activation

The first three propositions serve to define impact, activation, and arousal. These concepts and propositions have general relevance for all behavior. While the phrase "varied experience" does not appear in these propositions, variation will be shown to be a major factor in impact, which in turn determines activation.

I. *The impact of a stimulus is its momentary contribution to the activation level of an organism.*

This proposition is essentially definitional. It indicates that the property of the stimulus which affects activation level shall be called impact. Although the concept of impact will not be discussed in detail until Proposition III, it should be kept in mind during the following discussion that the variation, intensity, and meaningfulness of the stimulus determine its impact. Examples of stimuli which ordinarily possess a considerable degree of impact are a bright, flashing light, a sharp pain, and a feeling of guilt.

Level of Activation. While the major theoretical and empirical work on the concept of activation has been done only recently, it has roots in the classical idea of attention (for example, Pillsbury, 1908) and is related to alertness. Our use of the term activation is very close to that of Malmo in his recent review (1959), although his usage is somewhat broader. In a footnote on the first page of the article, he indicates that activation refers to "the intensive dimension of behavior." Later, it seems to refer to the general state of the organism. We prefer to restrict the term to the degree of excitation of a postulated center in the brain, reserving the concept of arousal for the peripheral, somatic manifestations of such activation.

Thus we locate activation in a "conceptual nervous system" (Hebb, 1955). Since it is a so-called neuropsychological concept, it is not necessary for our purposes to delineate the exact neuroanatomical structures involved in activation. However, the reticular formation is certainly implicated (see Samuels, 1959; Jasper, 1958; O'Leary and Coben, 1958). It is quite possible that activation level as we are using the term will be found to apply to the degree of excitation in the diencephalic component of the activating system, which Sharpless and Jasper (1956) found to be more sensitive to slight changes in the quality of stimuli and to be characterized by more specific habituation. We speculate along these lines because, as Proposition I indicates, we consider activation to be a fairly sensitive gauge of the impact of particular stimuli. Thus, for our purposes, activation level must be considered to shift from moment to moment under certain conditions. This matter will be discussed under Proposition II.

Summary. We use level of activation to refer to the state of excitation of a brain structure, probably the reticular formation. Impact is that property of a stimulus which can affect activation level, and its sources are the variation, intensity, and meaningfulness of the stimulus.

II. An organism's level of activation varies directly over time with the total impact of current stimulation.

This proposition is crucial for our formulation because it relates two of our central concepts. At the present time, it is best viewed as an assumption. The further development of measuring operations will make it possible to test it empirically.

Much of this proposition has already been implied in the preceding one. However, where the previous proposition was concerned with the impact of discrete, specifiable stimuli, this one concerns the summation of impact from all stimuli impinging on the organism at a point in time and the determination by this total impact of level of activation.

Sources of Stimulation. What sources of stimulation are important in this discussion? Our answer to this question follows from the association of activation level with the relevant structures in the reticular system. Hence, any route by which these reticular structures can receive stimulation is a potential source of impactful stimulation. In addition to the usually considered exteroceptive stimulation, we recognize interoceptive stimulation (for example, stimuli from muscles and organs) and cerebral stimulation. The evidence that exteroceptive and interoceptive stimulation can reach the reticular formation is clear (see Samuels, 1959; Lindsley, 1956) and need not be detailed here. That cerebral stimulation, such as ideas, images, and thoughts, can influence the reticular formation can be argued on the basis of the extensive feedback system between the two brain structures (Hebb, 1955; Magoun, 1958; Bremer, 1954). This evidence bolsters the intuitively reasonable conclusion that thoughts can be powerful activators.

Moment-to-Moment Changes in Level of Stimulation. Activation level provides an index of the gross energizing effect of stimulation on the organism. Since stimulation has diverse origins, it seems reasonable to expect that total impact can vary both widely and rapidly, and therefore that activation level can also change from moment to moment. Certainly some stimuli have abrupt, marked effects upon activation level. One example is the jump of activation associated with the startle pattern following an unexpected gunshot. In our concern with momentary changes in activation level, we differ slightly from Malmo's emphasis upon activation as "a phenomenon of slow changes, or drifts in level with a time order of minutes (even hours) not of seconds or fractions thereof" (Malmo, 1959, p. 385). While it appears that level of activation for him is a smoothed curve of the rate of discharge from the ascending reticular activating system, our formulation implies a measure which can vary from second to second.

At first thought, our assertion of precise covariation between total impact and activation may seem inconsistent with observations that indices of arousal (such as heart rate and galvanic skin response) tend to rise precipitously but fall off more gradually. It is true that activation may continue to be elevated after termination of an external stimulus. However, we must remind the reader that activation varies with total impact from both external and internal stimulation. A momentary external stimulus (for example, a gunshot or a sudden blow) may have impact during its duration but also resultant effects within the organism which themselves act as stimuli, which continue to have impact and hence to support activation. Another example is the chain of associations set off by glimpsing a person who looks like an old friend. Since these residual effects last beyond the termination of the external stimulus itself, the maximum rate of increase in activation is greater than the maximum rate of decrease and, typically, the rate of increase will be higher than the rate of decrease.

We are postulating a covariation between total impact and level of activation. For any brief period of time, activation level reflects impact in a precise fashion. But rather than use one term for both, we distinguish total impact and activation for two reasons. First, it is useful to have one term with a clearly stimulus referent and one with a neuropsychological central referent. The term total impact permits us to state the commonality existing among three aspects of stimulation: variation, intensity, and meaning. The term activation permits us to refer to the effects of this common aspect. In addition, insofar as different operations for measuring these two variables can be specified (see the section "Further Considerations" below), it is desirable to retain the different labels. Finally, it is possible that although two temporal periods might show the predicted covariation, the absolute levels of activation might be different for sequences of stimulation with comparable values of impact. When the organism is fatigued, it is possible that there is some constant dampening or even some blocking so that the covariation still is present even though activation is at a generally lower level.

Activation and Arousal. Activation is associated with arousal. We are restricting the term activation to mean the state of a catalytic and energizing mechanism in the central nervous system and using the term arousal to refer to manifestations of activation in various parts of the organism. Thus a high level of activation may be reflected in the functioning of internal organs, such as the heart and lungs, in the tonus of muscles, and perhaps even in sensory receptor mechanisms (Malmo, 1959; Duffy, 1957). It may also be manifested in other parts of the central nervous system itself. (See Bindra, 1959a, Chapter 8.)

The distinction between activation and arousal is useful for several reasons. Arousal can take varied forms: anger, preparedness for physical effort as in an athletic contest, and intense concentration on the writing of a technical paper may be distinguished on the basis of physiological and behavioral indices even though they may present patterns of neural excitation which cannot be distinguished by current techniques such as the electroencephalogram (EEG). (See Lacey, 1959, pp. 195-198.) It is also desirable to allow for the possibility that a given level of activation may manifest different degrees of arousal as a function of particular types of fatigue or other somatic states. Finally, we conceive of activation as a process common to all higher organisms. In principle, levels of activation for different organisms can be compared, although we shall be emphasizing intraindividual comparisons for different points in time. In contrast, arousal is manifested in different ways in different organisms. Interindividual correlation between indices of arousal are typically low (Malmo, 1959; Duffy, 1957; Lacey, 1959).

Although we are using arousal to refer to side effects of activation, we do recognize its importance. Such aspects as muscle tonus contribute to the subjective experience of alertness. The peripheral manifestations of arousal may also lead to an increased or decreased sensitivity to external stimulation. For example, reticular stimulation has been shown to decrease the potential in the cochlear nucleus evoked by a click. The effect stems from contraction of muscles in the middle ear (Hugelin, Dumont, and Paillas, 1960). Thus arousal contributes to activation by feedback, by modifying the impact of other stimulation, and by providing impact through interoceptive channels from the muscles and other participating organs.

Activation and Drive. Our concept of activation appears to be essentially the same as Hebb's concept (1955) of arousal or level of "arousal function." He equates arousal with general drive state. In such an equation, we believe drive must be viewed as Hebb discusses it in that article: drive is not simply a state, the decreasing of which is rewarding. At high levels, the reduction of drive is rewarding; but at low levels, an increase may be rewarding (see Proposition VIII). As some of our other propositions assert, the organism may behave so as to reduce activation or to increase it, depending upon the circumstances. There are particular conditions, such as the sexual drive, which require a high level of activation for consummation and subsequent tension reduction.

The apparent congruence between activation and drive stems from one particular definition of drive. When general drive is construed as having certain properties attributed to such specific drives as hunger and thirst, the concepts are distinctly different. If drive is a general state with no steering function or specific goal and if its reduction is not always rewarding, it is very similar to activation, as Malmo (1959) points out. Because drive may have irrelevant connotations stemming from the theoretical contexts in which it has been embedded, it seems best to use the term activation in the present context.

Summary. Total impact determines activation level at any point in time. As a consequence, activation level can shift from moment to moment as total impact varies. The intensity, meaningfulness, and variation of stimulation reaching the reticular formation from exteroceptive, interoceptive, and cerebral sources must be taken into account in the determination of total impact. The somatic and peripheral manifestations of activation level, some of which are readily observable, are called arousal.

III. The impact of a stimulus is derived not only from the intensity and meaningfulness of the stimulus but also from the extent to which it provides variation from prior stimulation.

Intensity and Meaningfulness as Sources of Impact. Let us consider first the immediate and direct contributions to impact provided by intensity and meaningfulness. At the moment of onset, the intensity of a stimulus contributes to impact. Other things being equal, an intense stimulus, one with considerable physical energy, has more effect on the organism than a weak one. Examples are a very loud noise, a bright light, a muscular cramp.

Another aspect of stimulation making a direct, almost instantaneous contribution to impact is the degree of meaning possessed by a stimulus. The role of meaningfulness is rather complex. At onset, any auditory stimulus can provide impact as a function of its intensity. But a stimulus which is recognized as human speech has more impact. If it is a word in a language known to the listener, it has greater impact. Finally, the sound may have even higher impact as a function of the implications of the word for the perceiver. For example, if a person reading a book hears someone shout "Coming!" this stimulus will have much less impact than the shout of "Fire!" Thus there are many levels of meaning from simple recognition or identification through perceptions with increasing significance for the organism to such extremes as stimuli signifying a vital emergency. Each of these successive degrees of meaningfulness has a larger contribution to impact.

As we are using the term, meaningfulness includes what Hebb (1955) has identified as the cue function of a stimulus. His proposal suggests that the meaningfulness of a stimulus contributes to activation by an excitation pathway leading from the sensory receptor through the cortex to the activation center.

In addition to their immediate effects, intensity and meaningfulness also make indirect contributions to impact. A sudden loud noise of brief duration may evoke a startle response producing a number of physiological changes within the organism. Even if the source of the sound is identified as an accident with no resulting damage (perhaps a book falling flat from a high shelf), the physiological proc-

esses mobilized by the external stimulus may continue to provide
internal stimulation with considerable impact and thus sustain activation at an elevated level. In somewhat parallel fashion, the meaningfulness of a brief stimulus may have continuing effects. The
shout of "Fire!" leads to a sequence of behavior effecting escape.
The glimpse of a symbol or a word may set off a chain of associations
which produce a sustained or even increasing level of activation.

For continuing stimuli, the direct contribution of intensity to impact is typically of limited duration: an organism habituates more
or less rapidly to all but the strongest stimuli. The direct contribution of meaningfulness is harder to specify, but it also would appear
to decline. When steadily fixated, a word quickly loses its usual
meaning. Therefore continuing stimulation has steadily decreasing
effects and cannot provide sufficient impact to maintain activation.
Change or variation in stimulation is necessary to sustain activation.

Variation as a Source of Impact. The preceding section attempted
somewhat unrealistically to analyze the contribution to impact from
the intensity and meaningfulness of a given stimulus taken by itself,
without regard for preceding conditions. But the fact that even these
effects are strongest at the moment of onset indicates that the change
provided by a stimulus plays a primary role in its effectiveness. The
impact of a stimulus is very largely a matter of the extent to which it
differs from preceding stimulation. We are using the term variation
to encompass several kinds of difference.

First, a stimulus can differ from the one preceding it. This difference can be in intensity or meaning. Both the onset of a bell and
the cessation of a motor's hum have impact derived from the change
in intensity. The larger the difference, the larger the contribution to
impact from this source. A stimulus of low intensity following one of
high intensity will have more impact than the identical stimulus
coming after one of similar intensity. The difference in meaning between a stimulus and the one just before it also contributes to its
impact. Thus one aspect of variation is the extent to which a stimulus
differs from that which immediately preceded it.

A second aspect of variation is the extent to which the given stimulus differs from the entire range of previously experienced stimuli.
This aspect can be called the novelty of a stimulus, although novelty
should be viewed as relative because a wholly new and strange stimulus is quite rare. It is indeed exceptional for a mature organism to

experience a stimulus with a degree of intensity which it has not previously encountered. It is also unusual for a sensory quality to be entirely new. Hence this aspect applies primarily to meaning. The degree of similarity in meaning between a stimulus and all prior stimulation is a complex matter. Thus the first sentence in any newspaper story presents words in a sequence which is probably entirely new in the reader's experience. Yet the words themselves are all familiar and even the message ordinarily bears some degree of resemblance to previous messages.

But the degree of relative novelty is not simply a function of the size of the difference between a given stimulus and all previously experienced stimuli. Also important is the time which has elapsed since the previous experience with those stimuli which are similar in some degree to the given one. The greater these time intervals, the more the impact of the given stimulus. The determination of degree of relative novelty of a stimulus becomes extremely difficult when both the factors of similarity and of interval-since-previous-experience are considered: while a long period may have elapsed since the occurrence of an essentially identical stimulus, there may have been recent experience with somewhat similar stimuli.

The last aspect of variation is the degree to which the given stimulus departs from the pattern or regularity of the preceding sequence of stimuli. If such pattern exists, and is recognized in some sense by the organism, an expectancy develops. Hence, the degree of departure of the given stimulus from the pattern built up by prior stimulation may be called the unexpectedness of that stimulus. We presume that there is a direct relationship between degree of unexpectedness and impact. Thus, the appearance of a circle where a square was expected has more impact than does the appearance of a rectangle. It should be emphasized that in our view this aspect of variation in stimulation is significant only when some patterning of successive stimuli exists and has somehow been recognized by the organism so that it is reasonable to consider the predictability of the various stimuli.

Unexpectedness applies to both intensity and meaning. The loud chord following the quiet phrases in the "Surprise" Symphony not only departs from the intensity of the preceding note but also from the expectation built up by the prior passage. In most instances, however, the impact contributed by the relative intensity of a stimulus is probably better construed in terms of its departure from the intensity of the several preceding stimuli, that is, in terms of the first two aspects of variation discussed above, rather than in terms of unexpectedness. On the other hand, the variation provided by the meaning of the present stimulus can appropriately be conceptualized in terms of unexpectedness.

In addition to its dependence on the degree of departure constituted by the given stimulus, unexpectedness is also a function of the strength of the expectancy built up by prior experience. In this dimension, the degree of patterning of prior stimulation is of most importance. In general, the greater the order or regularity in the preceding sequence, the greater the unexpectedness and impact when the given stimulus departs from that order. Stated in other words, the stronger the expectation that a given stimulus will appear, the greater the effect of some other stimulus. Thus, when a series of stimuli has the pattern, A A A A A, a K will have considerable impact. A 4 would have even more impact because it would be even more discrepant from the strong expectation built up by the series of A's. At the other extreme, another A would have minimal impact because it would be strongly expected. However, if the series of preceding stimuli had been A B D G H, then no precise expectation would have built up. At this point, a K would have little impact and an A only slightly more. But now consider a series such as S C M V P F. At this point, any letter would have about the same impact. A K here would have less impact than it had in the first series because it would not constitute a departure from any pattern. But a second F would have some impact because the repetition would probably be unexpected, even though a repeated stimulus ordinarily has less impact the second time it is experienced.

This account has not exhausted the possible types of unexpectedness which can be identified. Particularly worthy of note is the occurrence of a familiar stimulus in an unusual context of more or less familiar stimuli, that is, the unexpected juxtaposition of well-known elements: a political candidate is photographed in an Indian headdress; a friend known in one social context is found in an entirely different one; a well-known industrialist has been observed to combine tuxedo with tennis shoes. These events may be identified as spatial unexpectedness, parallel to the notion of temporal unexpectedness discussed above. (See also Chapters 9 and 14.) It is important to recognize that the impact from this unexpectedness of spatial context, like the direct contributions from the intensity and meaning of a stimulus, is greatest at its onset.

Our present opinion is that each of the aspects discussed must be considered in the analysis of variation in stimulation. In general, then, variation is a term which refers to the extent to which each successive stimulus departs from stimulation which the organism has previously experienced, especially from the stimulation experienced most recently, and from the temporal pattern in which it may be embedded.

In the preceding discussion, we have used the term meaningfulness even though it is broad and imprecise. At some future date, it may be possible to replace this term by the more precise technical concept of information as employed in information theory. At the present time, it seems impractical to attempt to measure the contribution to impact from a complex stimulus or a configuration of stimuli in terms of information. While this variable would handle the unexpectedness aspect of variation, it appears to be less satisfactory for the direct contribution from the significance of a stimulus for the organism and it could not cope adequately with the indirect and delayed contributions.

The Three Sources and Total Impact. The separation of the three sources of impact, made for heuristic purposes, is somewhat artificial. While both intensity and meaningfulness can be viewed as making direct contributions to impact, their effects are not completely independent. A very intense stimulus is meaningful if it is recognized as a threat to the functioning and structure of the organism. The meaningfulness of a verbal stimulus may be derived in part from its intensity. And as we have seen, both intensity and meaningfulness have their strongest effects at the onset of a stimulus, that is, when there is a change in stimulation.

Variation has been introduced because the impact from a new stimulus is determined not merely by its intensity and its meaningfulness for the organism but also by the extent to which it differs from preceding stimulation. Yet such differences involve either intensity or meaning. Hence there is an intricate interdependence among these sources of impact. This fact is one of the reasons why we need the concept of impact which comprehends all three sources and their interactions and combinations.

For clarity of exposition, Proposition III and this consideration of sources of impact have been stated in terms of a single stimulus. The discussion has tacitly implied that this stimulus was the most prominent one in the entire configuration being experienced at a given moment. While a stimulus with such prominence ordinarily supplies a major portion of the total impact from current stimulation, other stimuli also contribute and the same analysis applies to them.

In different situations, we find very different relative contributions from variation on the one side and from intensity and meaningfulness on the other. Thus the impact may be almost entirely derived from the intensity or meaningfulness of a configuration, regardless of variation. Even when a loud noise is expected, it has great impact. Even when the stimulation is part of a perceptible sequence, if it is potentially threatening to the organism, its occurrence has impact. The sight of the dentist's chair is not appreciably less striking because its appearance has been anticipated down to the minute.

On the other hand, impact may be almost wholly determined by the degree of variation between previous and immediate configurations. Thus, if we hear that a masochist says to a sadist "Beat me!", the impact of the sadist's "No!" is not a function of the word but of the degree to which it is unexpected. The climax has little effect the second time we hear the story.

Again, there is the familiar example of the person who wakes up when a steady noise stops. The fascination of watching the ocean and of gazing into an open fire comes in large part from the continuous variation in the visual stimulation, even though the intensity and the range of hues may be relatively constant. Variation plays a major role in total impact when the ongoing stimulation is not especially intense or meaningful.

In our view, the concepts of variation, intensity, and meaningfulness can be used to characterize any stimulation from exteroceptive, interoceptive, or cerebral sources. Total impact is an additive function of the contextual and inherent properties of stimulation from all three sources at a point in time. There is the possibility, however, that impact from one source may make a larger relative contribution when impact from another source declines. When one diminishes exteroceptive stimulation at night by turning off the radio and the light, and by lying down on the bed, activation may nonetheless remain high if the impact from cerebral stimulation increases as an unsolved problem comes to mind. The return of the problem to the center of attention may be a result of the reduction in the impact from exteroceptive stimulation. It is also reasonable to consider the possibility that stimulation from one source may have less impact than usual, if another source is contributing stimulation with very great impact. For example, an ache may have no discernible effect when one is totally absorbed in a movie or a book. Again, it has recently been suggested that white noise may serve as an analgesic (Gardner and Licklider, 1959).

The relative contributions of variation, intensity, and meaningfulness of stimuli appear to vary with the organism's current level of activation. While intensity is important at all but perhaps the very highest levels, its relative contribution may be greatest at low levels, for example, when the organism is barely awake. Meaningfulness is also important at almost all levels. In contrast, variation can contribute to impact only for low to moderate values of activation. When the activation level of an organism is elevated beyond some absolute point (perhaps near the highest point which it normally reaches during a day), variation has little or no effect.

There is, however, one exception. The intensity and meaning of pertinent external or internal stimuli can produce a drive state. If this state leads to avoidant behavior, activation will be high and more variation in stimulation adds no appreciable increment to impact. In contrast, variation may make a difference if the drive is appetitive. The consummatory behavior associated with such a drive continues longer when one appropriate goal-object is replaced by another, than it does when only one and the same appropriate object is continually present. Grunt and Young (1952) have shown that sexual activity can be restimulated in a male guinea pig after ejaculation by replacing the first female with a second, even if the second is not in estrus. In human beings, the amount of food intake is probably increased by providing a variety of foods in each course of a meal, and by having more than one course. Thus variation in stimulation can contribute to the production and maintenance of behaviors associated with drive states.

Complexity as Variation. If a stimulus configuration does not change for a period of time, its impact and its contribution to activation level will ordinarily decline steadily. The rate at which impact diminishes is very likely a function of the complexity of the configuration. A fairly simple stimulus, such as the whir of a ventilating fan, will have impact at its onset but will be adapted to rapidly, so that it will have little impact after a short period of time. However, a complex configuration, like a painting, may have undiminishing impact, or even increasing impact during the first few seconds of presentation. But what is happening? When a person looks at a painting, or any other complex stimulus, his visual image changes as his fixation point jumps from one spot on the canvas to another, even though the gross physical relationship between himself and the painting remains relatively unchanged. Thus, a complex stimulus provides functional variation in stimulation within the period of unchanging physical relationships. Even if the exposure is very brief, the recall of the image may permit variation as the person thinks of first one part and then another. (See Dember, 1960b, Chapter 10; Bindra, 1959a, Chapter 8; Berlyne, 1960, Chapter 2.)

Complexity attenuates the effects of context. The greater the complexity of the configuration, the less the reduction in impact from continued exposure, repeated presentation, experience with similar patterns, and the predictability of its occurrence.

Summary. Total impact, and hence activation level, is determined by the variation, intensity, and meaningfulness of stimulation from exteroceptive, interoceptive, and cerebral sources. Variation refers to the extent to which a given stimulus differs in intensity and meaning from the immediately preceding stimulus, from all previously experienced stimuli, and from the pattern of preceding stimuli. The impact of a complex visual stimulus is attributed to its providing greater opportunity for the functional variation in stimulation concomitant with scanning the visual field.

Performance and Activation Level

The preceding propositions have implications for all of the ongoing functioning of organisms with nervous systems that are sufficiently developed for the concept of activation to be relevant. In order to develop further the significance for behavior of the concept of activation, it is necessary to distinguish between two general organismic conditions. In the first of these, the organism is motivated to a considerable degree to achieve a specific goal state. If the goal is successfully achieved, the specific motive decreases in intensity for some period of time. The second condition is that in which no such specific motivation is evident.

The following two propositions apply to the first condition. In order to achieve the specific goal state, the organism must interact in a particular way with the environment in which he finds himself. A hungry rat in a maze must search successive portions of it if he is to obtain food. An achievement-oriented person must compete with his fellow workers even at the boss's cocktail party to create the impression of superior ability. A frightened child must run in order to escape from the suspicious-looking stranger. The nature of the transaction required to achieve the same goal differs from situation to situation. In any situation, the specific transaction required to attain the sought-for goal state will be called the *task*. It is obvious that we are defining this term somewhat more broadly than its usual meaning.

IV. For any task, there is a level of activation which is necessary for maximally effective performance.

This proposition brings out a significant application of the notion of activation level: namely, that the effectiveness of goal-oriented performance is not independent of the activation requirements of the particular transaction undertaken by the organism.

Activation Level and Performance. It is currently fairly well accepted that activation level is an important determinant of effectiveness of performance. The function relating the two variables is typically considered to be an inverted **U**. Hebb (1955) presents his version of this function as the relationship between "arousal function" of stimulation and potential or actual level of "cue function" of stimulation. Duffy (1957) and Malmo (1958, 1959) discuss the function and cite such relevant investigations as that of Stennett (1957), who obtained better performance on an auditory tracking task under a "learning" instruction that produced moderate levels of skin conductance and muscular tension than under two other instructions that yielded higher and lower levels on the physiological measures. Also pertinent is Courts' review (1942) of work relating muscular tension and performance. It must be pointed out that, in general,

these authors and the experimenters they cite do not restrict themselves to the narrow, specific conception of activation which is being
developed in this chapter. However, the measures that have been
used involve either external conditions affecting level of activation
through impact of stimulation or indices of arousal that reflect activation level.

The significance for performance of the U-shaped relationship
mentioned above is as follows: at low levels of activation, the organism may be inattentive, easily distracted, and not concentrating
fully on the task. At somewhat higher levels, the organism is alert
and attentive; it mobilizes its resources and is oriented toward coping
with the situation. It performs to the best of its abilities. Still higher
levels of activation are associated with excessive tension or hyperactivity. Anxiety and other strong emotional states appear, and behavior is less efficient.

There is considerable evidence on the effects of too high a level
of activation. (See Malmo, 1958.) Harlow, Harlow, and Meyer
(1950) have observed that increases in the hunger drive were associated with decreases in the effectiveness of performance in a
puzzle-solving task involving fairly complicated manipulations. We
would speculate that, if the task had been a much easier one for his
monkeys, the increment in hunger (and hence activation) would not
have produced a decrement in the effectiveness of performance of
the task because their activation level would not be beyond the maximum for adequate performance.

An example of an effect similar to that observed by Harlow *et al.*
is provided by an experiment reported by J. Miller (1959). Subjects were trained to press the appropriate button for each of a series
of stimulus alternatives which were presented at a rapid rate, one
to four stimuli being presented at a given moment. As the rate of
presentation rose (as the task of responding appropriately became
more difficult), response rate rose and then leveled off. Still faster
presentation rates had the primary effect of producing more omissions of response, that is, there were more stimuli to which the subjects did not respond. When the subjects were then rewarded for
reducing their number of omissions, the precision and accuracy of
their performance fell off. It would appear that the reward produced
a level of activation too high for the task at hand, a task which could

be performed better without this complicating motivational factor.

Poor performance associated with low activation levels is presumably due to a lack of sufficient cortical arousal to permit relevant response processes to continue at a normal rate (Hebb, 1955). In the extreme, the organism goes to sleep. Two related explanations of the decline in performance associated with higher levels of activation have been offered. There is the possibility of competing responses: very high levels of activation may increase the strength of responses which are incorrect or maladaptive as well as the strength of more adaptive ones. Hebb (1955) has favored the possibility that high activation levels impair cortical control or selectivity of response. Thus decline in performance reflects a relative disorganization of response processes.

The preceding discussion has implied that there is a narrow range of activation level within which maximally effective performance can occur. This position requires qualification. There is probably a relationship between the narrowness of this region and the difficulty of the task: while maximally effective performance on very difficult tasks can occur only within a limited zone of activation values, adequate and economical performance on simple tasks may be possible over a wide range of such values. A difficult task can be defined as one with several necessary conditions for successful performance. Thus success on a difficult intellectual task may require the possession of certain skills and knowledge gained from prior experience, certain innate capacities, an appropriate orientation of motivation, and appropriate activation level. In this connection, success refers to the close approximation of the individual's actual performance to his potential performance, that is, to the extent to which he does as well as he can. We need not be concerned here with tasks which a person cannot do.

Even on relatively simple tasks, a level of activation within the wide band of appropriate values is a necessary but not a sufficient condition for maximally effective performance. A hungry rat in an unfamiliar maze may have a level of activation appropriate to running through the maze to the food but still must learn the correct path in order to read the food efficiently.

Bindra (1959a, Chapter 8) presents a viewpoint similar to that embodied in Proposition IV. He also goes on to suggest that with practice and a consequent increase in habit strength, the optimal range of activation for a response is increased. His formulation emphasizes the single response and its occurrence or nonoccurrence, as well as the total activity or performance on a task.

The Activation Requirements of Different Tasks. While the exact function relating performance to level of activation must be worked out empirically for each task, some preliminary indications are available, such as the narrowness of the plateau for difficult tasks. It is likely that a given level of activation will often be within the optimal zone for several easy tasks and for one or more difficult ones.

It is also probable that different types of task have different activation requirements, that is, that there are different ranges of activation which are optimal for the effective performance of different tasks. While this possibility is by no means conclusively supported by experimental evidence, it is strongly indicated by everyday experience. A routine, repetitive task requiring no thought may be performed better at a relatively low level of activation; a challenging intellectual problem may best be solved at a higher level; maximum exertion of physical energy, as in running a foot race, would appear to call for a still higher level.

As early as 1908, Yerkes and Dodson demonstrated that the optimal level of motivation was lower for learning a difficult discrimination than for learning a simple one. The motivation utilized was the avoidance of shock; in terms of previous discussion, it can certainly be considered to be a rough indication of level of activation.

While Freeman (1940) indicates that fastest reaction times occur within a particular intermediate range of skin conductance that is associated with a subjective report of feeling aroused and tense, Schlosberg (1954) demonstrates that the optimal level of skin conductance for a steadiness task is higher than that for reaction time. In an earlier paper, Freeman (1933) reported that higher levels of muscular tension reduced accuracy on a manual pursuit task but did not reduce speed of finger oscillation. Later (1938), he found that as muscular tension increased rate of finger oscillation first increased and then decreased. Furthermore, the optimal tension for this task was above that for mirror-drawing. Although in each of these citations the compared tasks may differ in the width of the band associated with most effective performance, the evidence indicates that they also differ in the location of the band and of the optimal point.

Summary. The evidence that we have cited clearly supports the view that performance on a given task is a function of level of activation, that for almost any task there is an intermediate level or range of levels of activation associated with effective performance and extreme regions of high and low activation associated with poor performance or inability to respond at all. Among the conditions necessary for effective performance on a difficult task is a level of activation within the narrow band of appropriate values. The locus of that thin band appears to vary with the nature of the task: intellectual and skilled tasks probably have optimal levels of activation below those for tasks requiring physical exertion.

V. *The behavior of an organism tends to modify its activation level toward the optimal zone for the task at hand.*

This proposition is an interpretation based primarily on observation of behavior and introspection. We believe that, in most instances, an organism motivated to seek a specific goal-state by the performance of a particular task will, if necessary, attempt to shift its level of activation toward the optimal zone by engaging in impact-modifying behavior.

This proposition introduces the notion of a different type of instrumental behavior. While it is well known that an organism will behave so as to relieve certain tissue needs (for example, those associated with hunger or thirst), it appears that the organism's behavior can also be instrumental in preparing the organism for performing specific goal-oriented activity. Behavior which serves to alter activation level by modifying total impact is also of major significance for conditions where no specific drive or motive is strong, as we shall see in the next set of propositions.

Impact-Modifying Behavior and Activation Level. We implied previously that arousal phenomena can themselves influence activation level. In this feedback, the bodily manifestations of arousal supply interoceptive stimulation possessing considerable impact.

In addition, there is the very plausible possibility that some behavior may have the primary function of modifying impact and hence influencing activation level. Such behavior may increase the impact from stimulation by causing momentary or more long lasting variation in visual, tactual, olfactory, or gustatory stimulation. Also, new and varied thoughts or daydreams may be engaged in. The stretching and preliminary movements of an individual who has just waked up serve to increase his activation level. Kleitman (1939) notes that a person who has been awake for a longer-than-normal period of time can sometimes continue to remain awake only by walking around or engaging in other gross physical activity. As suggested by some of these examples, impact can also be modified by behavior which increases the intensity or meaningfulness of incoming stimulation. Thus, an individual may turn the lights up more brightly, or search for a television program with more important content.

The organism's behavior can also serve to reduce impact. For example, by lying down and closing the eyes, a person reduces the intensity and variation of kinesthetic and visual stimulation (Kleitman, 1939). Impact can also be reduced by seeking insignificant stimulations such as late-evening TV fare.

The discussion indicates that impact-modifying behavior may be initiated quite intentionally. Such activity need not be consciously determined, even though the organism may have learned the utility of the behavior from past experience.

Impact-Modifying Behavior and Optimal Activation. Proposition IV suggests that classes of tasks can be characterized by the level or band of activation which they require for maximally effective performance. The present proposition indicates that when a discrepancy exists between activation level and this optimal activation for the task, the organism will ordinarily attempt to decrease the discrepancy by engaging in impact-modifying behavior. This behavior may or may not overlap with the means or instrumental behavior serving to bring the organism to the goal.

Running a foot race to the best of one's ability is an example of a task which requires a rather high level of activation. From our point of view it is not mere accident or superstition that runners warm up for such a remarkably long time before the race. One function of this procedure is to increase the amount of impact from stimulation, and hence, to increase activation level.

Sometimes the existing level of activation will be too high for optimal performance. By comparison with running, a task requiring less energy output but more precise movements and considerable concentration (for example, surgery) is probably best performed with a somewhat lower level of activation. If the surgeon's activation level is too high, there are a number of things he can do in an attempt to reduce it. He can seek a place free of extraneous stimulation in which to rest. In an attempt to relax, he may try listening to soothing music or lying still for a period of time before working.

One implication of this proposition is clear: when the organism is unable to modify its level of activation toward the optimal zone for the task at hand, its efficiency or effectiveness will be reduced. Thus, if the individual in the example above is not successful in lowering his level of activation to within the optimal range, he may not be able to carry out a surgical operation which demonstrates maximal utilization of his abilities. This holds not only for excessive degrees of activation but also for deficient levels. On such monotonous tasks as being a lookout or monitoring a radar screen, performance may decline over time when the task requirements do not permit behavior which would be sufficient to maintain the necessary level of activation. (See Chapter 5.)

Summary. Since the behavior of an organism provides stimulation, behavior can modify impact and alter activation level. When confronted with a task, the organism can maximize the effectiveness of its performance by taking advantage of this potentiality. This capacity of an organism to modify its level of activation makes a major contribution to its flexibility, adaptability, and efficiency.

Affect and the Maintenance of Normal Activation Level

For heuristic purposes, we have divided behavior into two broad categories: that in which a specific motive involving a specific goal-state can be identified, and that in which no such specific motivation is obvious. The preceding two propositions deal with the former category, while the following three deal with the latter category.

An organism with specific motivation attempts to perform the task (the transaction with the particular environment in which it finds itself) which will serve to bring it closer to its goal. An organism without specific motivation of significant intensity does not exhibit such behavior. However, such an organism is not devoid of any behavior. It plays, it explores and investigates, it enters into a wide

variety of activities and varies its responses. Although these behaviors do not indicate the performance of any particular task, or
the seeking of any very specific goal, we will argue that they are
nonetheless motivated behaviors. The need they serve is a pervasive,
ever-present characteristic of living, even though its effects may not
be very apparent when any other, more specific motive is prepotent.
This pervasive need is nonspecific in the sense that it can be met in a
wide variety of ways, in contrast to specific drives that are reduced
by a comparatively small class of consummatory responses. (See
Chapter 10.)

These two categories of behavior, that with specific motivation and
that without, have been distinguished for heuristic purposes. A more
complete statement would refer to these as extreme prototypes which
occur only occasionally in their pure form. Any actual behavior
usually resembles one extreme more than the other and hence can
reasonably be placed in that category. However, any given segment
of molar behavior may have aspects appropriate to both classifications. Thus a rat running a familiar maze with food at the end may
pause momentarily to investigate some small modification in the
structure of the maze. A human adult seeking food at his typical din-
ner hour will select not just any food but rather food which is different from that which he has most recently eaten. The preference for
variety in food cannot be explained directly by the hunger motive.

On the other side are instances in which some specific motivation
is present but of low intensity and the behavior is largely determined by the organism's seeking for new or varied experience. A
person who is not particularly thirsty may welcome an opportunity
to try a new carbonated beverage, a rare wine, or a recently in-
vented cocktail.

*VI. For each stage in an organism's sleep-wakefulness cycle,
there is a characteristic or normal level of activation.*

Given an appropriate measure of activation, this proposition is
subject to empirical testing. It is strongly supported not only by in-
formal observation and everyday experience but also, more or less
indirectly, by a large body of experimental studies cited in the references given below.

While Proposition IV postulates a level of activation which is a
norm specific to each task, Proposition VI establishes the concept of

a general norm independent of the immediate external demands on the organism. This general norm is dependent upon the continuing requirements of an active, living organism, requirements which have been incorporated by Kleitman (1939) into the concept of the sleep-wakefulness cycle, or the "cycle of existence."

The Sleep-Wakefulness Cycle and Activation Level. The cycle of sleep-wakefulness has a single major rise and fall during the wakefulness segment. After waking, higher organisms typically show an increasing degree of alertness, then a relatively long period with a gradual rise and later a gradual decline, and, finally, a sharper decline toward drowsiness and a return to the sleeping state. A number of diverse variables covary with alertness during wakefulness (Kleitman, 1939, Chapters 15 and 16). Body temperature rises on waking and falls on becoming drowsy. Not only heart rate (Kleitman and Ramsaroop, 1948) but also reaction time and performance on several mental tasks show parallel curves. During the sleep period, the cycle of sleep-wakefulness appears to have a series of troughs of progressively less depth, all the crests being at about the same level. Since the wakefulness portion of the cycle is of major interest here, we shall simply note that Kleitman, after quoting the suggestion of Sidis (1908) that sleep is caused by a "diminution in the variability of the volume of sensory impressions," goes on to say "we must define sleep to mean a suspension or decrease of the somatic activities that bring the organism into relation with the environment. . . ." (1939, p. 500). (See Chapter 6.)

The relating of activation to the organism's state on the continuum from deep sleep to maximum wakefulness is almost a matter of definition. Activation is sometimes discussed in terms of drowsiness and alertness (for example, Lindsley, 1952; Hebb, 1955; Malmo, 1959). We have implied above that the observed degree of alertness may prove useful as an index to level of activation. Duffy (1951) has considered a continuum of energy mobilization from deep, undisturbed sleep through such intermediate degrees as light sleep, the state associated with familiar situations, and the state accompanying work on difficult problems, to the extreme of the startle response or intense excitement. In a later paper (Duffy, 1957), she refers to this continuum by the phrase "arousal or activation." Activation as we are using the term certainly parallels her continuum.

The characteristic or normal level of activation associated with a given stage of wakefulness is an inferred quantity which can be approximated by averaging the actual activation curves for an organism during a number of wakefulness periods. For any one period, we assume that the curve is quite irregular in shape even though its gross form shows a gradual rise and a subsequent decline. This irregular shape is not surprising in the light of our contention that activation level fluctuates from moment to moment with the impact of stimulation. However, the important points for the present discussion are that the averaging of records for many periods of wakefulness shows a general rising and then falling modal curve, and that this curve defines the normal level of activation associated with various stages of wakefulness. Thus one can roughly specify the level of activation normal for a given higher organism at various times during the day, with the curve varying somewhat from organism to organism.

The Origins and Course of the Diurnal Cycle of Activation. There is extensive evidence for 24-hour cycles in animals and man (Harker, 1958; Webb and Brown, 1959; Halberg, 1960). These have been observed for activity, metabolism, circulatory processes, and blood components, among other indices. While various theories have been offered (see preceding references), these cycles are not fully understood. At least in man, the length of the cycle is undoubtedly influenced by such exogenous factors as the physical cycle of day and night, but social and cultural influences seem to be even stronger (Kleitman, 1949). In the individual person, previous experience and habituation certainly play a major role.

Consider the transition from sleep to wakefulness. There are probably individual differences in the mean hour of waking up, together with some variation around this value from day to day. On a given day, the time at which a particular person wakes up is determined in part by an increase in the intensities of external stimulation (for example, in the degree of illumination, and in the amount of noise generated by other people's activities) and in part by internal stimulation (such as from the bladder). But it seems also to be determined by habituation; some people wake up at the same time each morning regardless of the time they went to sleep and of the day of the week.

The course of the diurnal cycle and the interrelationships among the factors influencing it are described concisely in the following quotation:

> Practically from the day of birth . . . the baby is subject to "acculturation" with the social environment, light, warmth, noise, etc., impinging on it during the day. All these stimulate activity, and thus metabolism, during a fixed fraction of the 24-hour period. Muscular activity raises temperature, which increases the activity of the nervous system, the latter in turn augmenting muscular activity. In the older child and the adult there are established cortico-muscular circuits, or "feedback" mechanisms, to use a popular term, which operate like a vicious circle. Both muscular activity and nervous activity (metabolism, body temperature, efficiency of performance, etc.) keep on rising. As the muscles get tired, not only from overt work, but from postural or tonic activity inherent in being awake, the trend is reversed. This reversal is aided by the onset of darkness, the lowering of the air temperature, and the abatement of noises, characteristic of evening in the social routine of living. When the reversed trend of activity and metabolism has reached a certain low ("drowsiness level"), it becomes harder to remain awake. Sleep occasions a further drop in all the variables, until the diurnal minimum is reached, but proprioceptive impulses from the muscles, cramped by prolonged maintenance of certain positions, increase from more frequently "turning over" as the night goes on. When aided by visceral impulses (from stomach, urinary bladder, etc.), and environmental influences inherent to the advent of morning, it becomes more and more difficult to remain asleep (Kleitman, 1949, pp. 25-26).

In the dozen years since this passage appeared, a mechanism has been observed which makes it possible that, toward the later part of the normal period of wakefulness, the potential impact of sensory stimulation is reduced by some interference in transmission beyond the level of the receptor mechanism itself. Bruner (1957b) cites a number of studies that clearly favor the view that not all signals from sense organs reach the cortex. It seems reasonable to entertain the speculation that due to transmission difficulties, a given configuration of stimulation may have less impact, less effect on level of activation, at later stages of wakefulness, perhaps as an indirect effect of muscular fatigue.

Summary. On any one day, an organism's level of activation tends to vary with the stage of its sleep-wakefulness cycle. Activation level rises as the organism wakes up and becomes fully alert; during the later part of a period of wakefulness, activation declines. The curve for a given day is in part a function of particular conditions: the general physical and psychological state of the organism and the events impinging on it from the environment. But the curve is also a function of the characteristic or normal curve of activation for that individual organism, this norm being developed from past experience by habituation and perhaps originating in some fundamental physiological rhythm. The acquisition and maintenance of this characteristic curve is influenced by the impact not only of external stimulation but also of interoceptive stimuli, with muscular tonus and fatigue playing a central role. This norm is more or less closely approximated during any given cycle.

VII. *In the absence of specific tasks, the behavior of an organism is directed toward the maintenance of activation at the characteristic or normal level.*

This proposition indicates one major application of the concept of characteristic level of activation which was introduced in the preceding proposition. In the absence of specific motivation requiring the performance of some specific task, the organism is still active. This activity can be viewed as motivated in the sense that the organism is faced with the need to maintain the level of activation normal for its particular stage of wakefulness.

Impact-Modifying Behavior and Normal Activation Level.   When there is no specific motive or task, internal drives and external stimuli are of low intensity and thus level of activation will ordinarily be rather low. If this level is below normal, the organism tends to increase activation. To accomplish this end, it can behave in such a way that ongoing stimulation provides the requisite amount of impact.

This relatively nonspecific need to maintain normal activation level is more commonly manifested in these conditions where intensity and meaningfulness are low. On the other side, there are some situations in which the impact from external stimulation or from cerebral sources produces a level of activation well above the comparatively small value characteristic for that particular time: for example, at the end of a period of wakefulness. At such a time, a person may dip into a mildly interesting but not exciting book or may listen to soothing music. By withdrawing from stimulation with considerable impact, the organism can reduce activation toward the level characteristic of the presleep period. Another example is the waking up period, during which human adults can be observed making efforts to avoid stimulation with such substantial impact that activation would be raised above the low level characteristic of this stage.

At other stages of wakefulness, above-normal levels of activation can occur only when there is a specific motive with enough strength to orient the organism toward the achievement of a particular goal-state. Such a motive is evoked by exteroceptive or interoceptive stimulation with high impact. Proposition VII does not apply to such conditions. It should be emphasized that the demands of a specific task ordinarily take precedence over the need to maintain the characteristic level of activation.

In the absence of specific tasks, the organism can sustain or increase impact by behaving so that the intensity and meaningfulness of stimuli are increased. The available evidence suggests, however, that variation is more likely to be utilized than these other two sources of impact. Of course, the three sources are not wholly independent of each other; a new stimulus has some intensity and may be more or less different in meaning.

Variation in stimulation may be selectively emphasized because it cannot ordinarily contribute to higher-than-characteristic levels of activation as effectively as can the other two components. Thus the organism does not have to risk raising the level of activation to above the normal level. In any event, we believe that this proposition explains, among other things, such phenomena as play, exploration, curiosity, and behavioral variability or alternation (see Chapters 7-10). When not motivated by some more specific, prepotent need, the organism is attracted to new, changing, interesting stimulation, and may indeed attempt to produce such stimulation itself.

One mechanism by which an organism sustains activation is orientation. Organisms tend to orient toward or attend to the source of stimulation providing the highest impact at that moment. This behavior maximizes the amount of impact and thus supports the level of activation. On the other hand, if activation is above the normal level, or if it is raised above that level by the impact of the stimulus to which the organism orients itself, the organism will subsequently act to reduce the total impact. One possible response is a change in orientation away from the object with high impact, as in turning away from a bright light or a gruesome accident.

Normal and Task-Appropriate Levels of Activation. Thus far we have stressed one aspect of the significance of characteristic or normal level of activation: if the actual level is below normal, the organism will attempt to increase that level by increasing the impact of stimulation. We also believe that the organism will attempt to decrease overly high levels to that which is normal for the particular stage of wakefulness in question. It is important for the moment to recognize that we choose to define what others have called the optimal level of activation in terms of the sleep-wakefulness cycle.

While a number of writers have considered the possibility of an optimal level of activation, none has defined this term very extensively. Hebb and Thompson, for example, suggest that organisms "act so as to produce an optimal level of excitation" (1954, pp. 551-552). Very similar is Leuba's concept of optimal stimulation: "The organism tends to acquire those reactions which, when overall stimulation is low, are accompanied by increasing stimulation; and when overall stimulation is high, those which are accompanied by decreasing stimulation" (1955, p. 29). He emphasizes the idea of total stimulation. Since he views his concept as furthering the integration of learning theories, he stresses the change in level of stimulation and does not elaborate his perception of what is "optimal;" he does indicate that it must be defined in terms of the state of the organism and its environment.

Berlyne expresses a view which is very similar to Proposition VII but is stated in terms of his conceptual framework: ". . . for an individual organism at a particular time, there will be an *optimal influx of arousal potential. . . .*" He goes on to say ". . . the organism will thus strive to keep arousal potential near its optimum . . ." (1960, p. 194. Italics his). While his definition of optimum is not explicitly developed, he too relates it to the ongoing functioning of the organism and indicates that the optimal value is found at an intermediate point on the continuum.

Although these writers do not define "optimal" very clearly, they all suggest that it has to do with the arousal state of the organism and with ongoing functioning. We feel that the optimal degree of and with ongoing functioning. We feel that the optional degree of "excitation," "stimulation," or "arousal potential" can be more precisely understood as the normal or characteristic level of activation. This interpretation suggests that during the waking-up and approaching-sleep segments of the curve of normal level of activation, the term optimal refers to a lower value than it does during the middle portion of the curve. The writers cited above seem to have restricted themselves to the central portion of the wakefulness period. The concept of characteristic level is part of a broader, more comprehensive view, which embraces systematic variation over a period of wakefulness.

We considered earlier the condition in which activation is higher than even the upper ranges of characteristic level that occur during the middle of the wakefulness period. Such overly high levels are typically produced by strong, specific motivation, which leads the organism to perform the appropriate task in order to reach the appropriate goal-state. In such instances, the same behavior which is successful in reducing the specific need also lowers level of activation. Thus the achievement of specific goals aids in maintaining normal activation level.

But the optimal level of activation for maximally effective performance of the task relevant to an existing, specific motive will often be different from the normal level for that particular stage of wakefulness. At such a time, in an attempt to perform the necessary task effectively, the organism may engage in impact-modifying behavior which temporarily produces a discrepancy between normal and actual levels of activation. When the task is performed and the goal has been reached, this discrepancy, of course, would be reduced. This mechanism whereby temporary discrepancies from normal activation level can be achieved in order to permit performance of specific tasks probably works only within limits. For some tasks, the optimal activation requirements are probably too high to be well performed immediately upon waking or just before falling asleep.

The factors determining the organism's normal level of activation and the mechanisms for sustaining it may come to be better understood from continuing work on the self-stimulation of the brain. The rate of such self-stimulation can be influenced by food deprivation, androgen level, and drugs (Olds, 1958b). The stability of the preferred intensity of the stimulating current has been demonstrated by Stein and Ray (1959).

Summary. Organisms manifest a need to maintain their normal level of activation. This motive is nonspecific in the sense that any of a wide range of behaviors may be utilized to furnish stimulation with appropriate impact. When no specific motive is present, the organism commonly attempts to sustain activation by seeking or producing stimulation with variation; it may attend to complex stimulation, it may explore, or it may play.

VIII. *Negative affect is ordinarily experienced when activation level differs markedly from normal level; positive affect is associated with shifts of activation toward normal level.*

This proposition has been placed here because it is particularly relevant to the condition where no specific motive is present. Affect occurs in other conditions for which this proposition may have some relevance.

Proposition VII outlined one of the major applications of the concept of normal level of activation, and this proposition indicates the other. We are concerned here with the implications of activation level for affective tone. We distinguish negative affect, which is a set of internal sensations experienced as unpleasant, from positive affect, which is a set of internal sensations that are pleasant.

Negative Affect and Overly High or Low Levels of Activation. This proposition can be viewed as providing the source of the motivation to maintain normal level of activation. Certainly the organism is not ordinarily aware of its level of activation, but it can be aware of the somatic concomitants of that level. Through experience, the organism learns to avoid markedly high or low levels of activation under most circumstances, because they are accompanied by unpleasantness. An extremely high level of activation is typically unpleasant because it is associated with such states as inability to concentrate, anxiety, rapid heart beat, or a sinking feeling in the stomach. The decrements in the effectiveness of performance associated with high levels of activation (see Proposition IV) may also be a factor in the negative affective tone. Affect is also likely to be negative when the impact of stimulation is low, as in reading a dull book.

Some manifestations of the concomitant low level of activation may be boredom, drowsiness, and apathy. (See McReynolds' discussion [1956] of ennui as a function of low rate of obtaining and assimilating new percepts.)

However, the relationship between affect and the size of the discrepancy between actual and normal level of activation is complex and rather weak. Extremely negative affect probably occurs only with very high levels of activation. Moderately negative affect can occur when activation is relatively high or relatively low, but not when it is at the normal level.

This complex and weak relationship between level of activation and quality of affect is understandable when we recall that level of activation varies with the impact of stimulation, and that impact has several different sources. When stimuli are very intense (and activation is consequently high), discomfort or pain is experienced. Again, negative affect can have its origins in the specific meaning of the stimulus, as in the case of a frightening object. It seems reasonable to consider that unusually high levels of activation, well above the normal level, are typically associated with negative affect (see Hebb, 1955). Some of the apparent exceptions to this statement probably involve raised but not extreme levels; for example, some unexpected good news can increase activation above the normal level, but only moderately. One interesting implication of our approach is that stimulation with substantial impact may produce negative affect when the normal level of activation is relatively low, but need not produce the same result at a point in the sleep-wakefulness cycle characterized by a higher level.

Very low levels of activation can occur only under certain conditions: the intensities of both external and internal stimuli must be rather low; the stimulation must have little significance for the organism; finally, the configurations of stimuli must be familiar and must occur in a relatively unvarying or in a highly predictable sequence. All of these conditions must occur together, since any exception (high intensities, marked significance, etc.) by itself, can contribute substantially to the impact of stimulation. Situations meeting these conditions for low level of activation are monotonous, and except at the beginning and end of the wakefulness period when normal activation is comparatively low, they are likely to produce large discrepancies between normal and actual levels. In such situations, a person may well feel uncommonly drowsy, lethargic, and ineffective. It seems reasonable to consider that these situations will often be associated with negative affect.

If, in such a situation, the person does nothing to increase the impact of stimulation, sleep may be the result. However, he may not be ready for sleep, or it may be inconsistent with a task which must be performed. While experiencing boredom, he may also wish to obtain stimulation with greater impact. He may be able to produce greater impact by varying his behavior, as the subjects in a satiation experiment did by elaborating the moon face they were instructed to draw over and over again (Karsten, 1928). A subject may also stimulate himself by making responses irrelevant to the task, such as singing, humming, or daydreaming (see Fenichel, 1951). These various activities initiated by a person increase activation not just by raising the intensities and perhaps the meaningfulness of stimuli but also, and perhaps largely, by producing some variation.

Another kind of resolution appears frequently when the person feels constrained so that he can neither leave the situation nor readily increase impact by varying his behavior. Such frustration produces irritation, a state with considerable impact. A student who is bored by a dull lecture in a required course may effectively keep himself awake and attentive by taking a critical attitude toward the lecturer. If the resulting level of activation is near normal, we have an instance in which the characteristic activation level is associated with negative affective tone.

It should be emphasized that this proposition is not intended to provide a complete explanation of affect. There are other determinants of affective state, among which the meaning of stimuli has prime importance. Under some conditions, levels of activation well above normal may be accompanied by positive affect (as in the case of sexual activity) or by complex, probably mixed states (as in situations when risk is intentionally sought out).

Positive Affect and Shifts Toward Normal Activation. When the health of an organism is good and when its environment is fairly typical, its level of activation will follow its characteristic course. The normal level of activation is probably associated with the mildly positive affective tone involved in the feeling of well-being. However, the affective tone associated with normal activation is by no means always positive or, for that matter, very strong.

The most clear-cut experiences of positive affect are probably associated with shifts in activation toward the normal level. This part of Proposition VIII is similar to Leuba's conceptualization (1955) of the reinforcing value of changes toward optimal stimulation: the organism acquires those responses which tend to shift the level of stimulation away from extremely low or extremely high levels. We are adding to his development the specification of the optimal level as that which is characteristic for the organism's stage of wakefulness, and a more clear-cut emphasis upon the underlying hedonic mechanism. Our formulation permits understanding of the occurrence of impact-modifying behavior aimed at maintaining normal level of activation.

It should be apparent that this proposition implies that a given configuration of stimulation may be associated with positive affect at one point in the wakefulness period and with negative affect at another. This happens because the normal level of activation varies during wakefulness. Similarly, a particular shift in level may be pleasant or unpleasant, depending upon the time at which it occurs.

Summary. The concept of characteristic level of activation has relevance for affect. Marked discrepancies from this norm are associated with negative affect; positive affect accompanies or follows the process of reducing such discrepancies. On the one hand, acts involved in effective task performance and behavior instrumental to reducing drives shift affect in the positive direction. On the other hand, behavior which merely sustains normal activation accomplishes the same end.

FURTHER CONSIDERATIONS

The Measurement of Impact

Although our concept of impact embraces several aspects of stimulation, it may be amenable to operational specification and hence to experimental investigation. The measurement of impact can be approached from two different directions. We might determine the impact of a particular stimulus or the total impact of the entire set of stimuli impinging on an organism at a point in time, without differentiating the three components of impact. We believe a more fruitful alternative is to assess the impact of a stimulus by separately determining its intensity, its meaningfulness, and the extent to which it provides variation, and then to combine these values by an appropriate function.

The first of these two approaches, the direct measurement of impact as a whole, presents certain difficulties. Impact is that property of stimulation which determines its nonspecific effect on an organism. Since the total impact of current stimulation covaries with activation, measures of activation may have to serve as indices of total impact, at least for the time being. In fact, it appears that total impact can be assessed only through its determination of activation. Perhaps the most relevant index is alertness. However, we shall see when we consider measures of activation that measures of alertness are indirect and approximate.

At the present time, impact and activation can be separated only by studying the organism in different states. The impact values of sets of stimuli could be determined in relative terms for each of several conditions: several hours after waking, late in the evening, and perhaps under some drug. We would predict at least an ordinal relationship between the values for each pair of conditions.

The measurement of the impact of a particular stimulus may be less difficult. For an external stimulus, impact is closely related to attention value. Such measurement will probably have to be in relative rather than in absolute terms. The relative impact of two stimuli can be determined from the division of attention between them when presented simultaneously.

The second approach, assessing the impact of a stimulus by measuring its three relevant characteristics, is at the present time more promising. Our primary interest would be in estimating, for constant background conditions, the impact of the salient feature of experienced stimulation, the figure as opposed to the ground. When the separate effects of intensity, meaningfulness, and variation had been determined, it would be possible to know their relative importance for a particular stimulus under the given conditions.

Of the three properties, intensity presents the least difficulty. Techniques are currently available for determining the intensity of exteroceptive stimuli. Even though there is habituation to stimulus intensity, this source can probably be quantified adequately by measuring the physical energy of stimuli at the point where they impinge on the organism's receptors. The contribution of intensity to impact is presumably a monotonic function of physical energy.

It would appear possible, at least in principle, to measure the meaningfulness of a stimulus. The definiteness of denotation might be approached by having the subject identify the stimulus, and the richness of connotation might be assessed in terms of the spread or polarity of responses on a semantic differential instrument (see Osgood, Suci, and Tannenbaum, *The Measurement of Meaning*, 1957). However, it is likely that only gross differences in contribution to impact could be determined and the results would hardly seem worth the labor. An intriguing lead for the measurement of meaningfulness is suggested by the work of Eckhard Hess (Hess and Polt, 1960). Holding intensity and variation constant, he has found an increase in pupillary size (measured from photographic records) upon presentation of a stimulus picture of special interest to the human or animal subject. In a personal communication, Hess has reported that contraction of the pupil may also be an index of the relative significance of a stimulus. In this work, the observed response is of course a form of arousal.

The measurement of two aspects of variation, the difference between current and immediately preceding stimulation, and the relative novelty of current stimulation, presents certain problems. The use of *a priori* judgments would be unwise except as a very rough first approximation. Thus, the experimenter might assume that for colors of comparable saturation, red and yellow were less different than red and green because they were closer in wave length. But the subject might perceive red and green as less different because they are complementary, or he might be unable to distinguish red and green because he is color-blind. To assess relative novelty, a complete knowledge of the past history of the organism is needed. However, such knowledge is rarely available. One of the most feasible, though admittedly tedious, approaches to assessing these two aspects of variation is the use of psychophysical methods to determine the psychological or subjective distance between each relevant pair of stimulus configurations.

The measurement of unexpectedness is possible at the human level.

One can determine whether there is a difference between what was predicted and what actually occurred, but here again there is the problem of assessing the size of this discrepancy. A number of possibly suitable procedures to determine the subject's prediction of what is coming next are already available (see Rotter, Fitzgerald, and Joyce, 1954; Chapter 13).

While the intensity, meaningfulness, and variation associated with a stimulus may be separately determined as variables in their own right, there is still the matter of the function relating each to impact. Although Proposition III states the relationship as monotonic, it is not necessarily linear. For example, a given difference in intensity may correspond to a large difference in impact at low levels but to a small difference at high levels.

Once we have procedures for assessing intensity, meaningfulness, and variation, we can investigate the function by which these should be combined to estimate the total impact of a stimulus. It might seem that the function is multiplicative because of the possibility of facilitation effects: the impact of a sharp pain in the chest may seem to be magnified many times when it is attributed to cardiac malfunction. It is more likely that the effects are additive. The interpreted significance of the pain may have tremendous impact independent of the experienced intensity. This issue is complicated by the interaction of the three aspects of stimulation. The suddenness and intensity of a shout of "Fire!" contributes to its meaning. If the word is expected or is uttered with normal speaking intensity, it does not signify an emergency.

The Measurement of Activation and Arousal

The earlier discussion of activation implied that activation could be determined from measuring the excitation of appropriate structures in the brain. At this time, we cannot say whether the amount of such excitation is the appropriate indicant: it may well be that the type or patterning is crucial, the activation variable being an ordering of patterns rather than a continuous quantity. In any case, the implanting of electrodes cannot readily be performed with human subjects.

Alternative techniques involve less direct observation. The subject can be asked to report his current state of alertness or the degree to which he feels "energized." More indirectly but less subjectively, observers can estimate the subject's state from behavioral cues. Neither type of index is fully satisfactory, largely because it is indirect and subject to considerable error of judgment.

Within limited ranges of activation, other procedures may prove more adequate. For lower levels, reaction time may be useful for obtaining gross differences. Above that range, the amount of activity or the rate of energy discharge might be amenable to recording, but here again the measure would not be very sensitive.

Most previous work has not attempted to distinguish between activation and arousal. The measures which have been used in research in this area are appropriate to what we are calling arousal; they reflect the effects of activation on other parts of the body. One of these measures is the electroencephalogram (EEG), a highly complex record whose chief usefulness in this context lies in gross differentiations of degrees of alertness in the waking organism and in indicating depth of sleep (see Chapter 6). Other measures include heart rate, respiration rate and pattern, muscle tension, blood volume in the finger, and skin conductance. At the present time, the most satisfactory way to get at activation may well be through these indices of arousal.

The major problem in regard to these measures stems from one of the considerations that led us to differentiate arousal from activation. While a given level of activation can occur in a particular organism at different times and in different situations, this level may be associated with different patterns or profiles of arousal as reflected in the physiological measures listed above (see Lacey, 1959). Compare two stages of wakefulness with the same characteristic level of activation: for example, a person who has just recently arisen from a night's sleep with the same person making preparations for sleep. While activation may be at the same level, muscular tension and EEG pattern may be different. Again, a person might have identical levels of activation when his tooth is being drilled by a dentist and when he has just obtained some surprising research data, although skin conductance, respiration rate, and the pattern of muscular tension were clearly different.

Thus two states of activation may have the same level but different effects. This fact suggests that such states may also have different qualities. From these considerations, it appears probable that our conception of activation will turn out to be oversimplified. Although our view appears to be a reasonable first approximation, it will almost certainly have to be modified sooner or later to include more than one aspect of activation. The development of further knowledge about the functions of the several structures in the reticular formation will require a careful reappraisal of our concept of activation as a unitary intensive dimension of organismic functioning.

In addition to situational effects on arousal, different subjects may show different patterns of reaction to the same situation: the correlations over individuals between pairs of arousal measures tend to be low. Thus a situation with considerable impact, such as impending physical injury, may elicit primarily muscular tension in one person and primarily sweating in another. Both may show rises in both measures, but the relative sizes of the increases may be opposite in the two persons. (See Duffy, 1957; Malmo, 1959; Schnore, 1959; Lacey and Lacey, 1958; Lacey, 1959.) It would appear that two factors contribute substantially to reducing the association between such measures over individuals: different response pattern or different reactivity of the several autonomic functions, and different levels of activation or over-all levels of arousal.

Fortunately the covariation of these measures within an individual seems to be larger than the covariation between individuals. So it appears feasible to use a composite index based upon several physiological measures to assess the general state of arousal in an organism, and such an estimate should provide a satisfactory indirect estimate of activation. This intraindividual covariation indicates that the study of activation and of arousal is best conducted with an experimental design that emphasizes comparisons between different states of the same individual, with replication over individuals.

A Perspective: The Active Organism

The orientation of this chapter, and of this book as a whole, envisages the organism as active, not just reactive. The organism is more than an object equipped with mechanisms which can be activated or released by certain conditions, more than the site of drive-states, as Pribram (1960) brings out in his comprehensive review of current neurophysiological theories and findings. It is an entity within which many processes are continuously going on. To be sure, it reacts to signals from its environment: it interprets some stimuli as warnings of potentially disrupting or dangerous conditions. There is a biological utility in perceiving and reacting to such new stimulation. Yet even when new stimulation imposes no demands upon the organism, it utilizes such stimulation to sustain its internal processes and its activity. For this purpose, it is the stimulation as stimulation which is important, whatever its specific quality or significance. But in addition to the utilization of new stimulation for its internal economy, a higher organism and especially a human being may seek to experience varying stimulation almost as an end in itself.

The need for varied experience can be construed as the need of higher organisms for the environment in which these species have developed. An organism equipped with a variety of broad-spectrum sensory receptors normally experiences new stimulation almost continuously because of physical changes in the surrounding environment and especially because the activity of the organism itself produces changes in its orientation and locus within the physical world. We are arguing that such an organism actually requires such an environment not only to maintain its capacity for adaptation but also to sustain its internal processes. Two billion years of evolution stand behind this "mutuality"—the fitness for and need for the niche to which the organism's evolution has adapted it.

The statement of these propositions in terms of the single organism should be interpreted as an implicit recognition of the presence of differences between individual organisms with respect to such variables as characteristic levels of activation and the impact from a given stimulus configuration. Our immediate interest has been in the search for principles which would be applicable to the behavior of any higher organism. Later chapters will consider some of the ways in which human beings differ with respect to the role that variation in stimulation plays in their behavior.

The eight propositions stated and discussed in this chapter should be viewed as preliminary definitions and hypotheses. We have offered evidence from experimental work and from observation which at least justifies their tentative consideration. Their real value will be determined by their ultimate fruitfulness in generating new ways of interpreting established findings and in suggesting areas requiring further experimental investigation. In the present context, some estimate of their utility can be formed from assessing the extent to which they provide a useful framework for interpreting the material presented in the following chapters. In the concluding chapter, we shall attempt such an evaluation.

Chapter 3

Stimulation as a Requirement for Growth and Function in Behavioral Development

*AUSTIN H. RIESEN**
University of Chicago

$\mathcal{I}$N the developing organism, stimulation is a continuing factor. Because of this, the contribution of stimulation has been difficult to measure except in specific and rather limited cases. Studies with restriction of stimulation at later ages are confirming the conception of a strong interdependence between environmental stimulation and the ongoing capacities of organisms to respond adaptively. (See Chapter 5.) How much and in what manner are neural and behavioral development dependent upon general or specific constellations of sensory activation? This is a question which controlled experimentation is beginning to answer.

For more than 50 years biologists have been reporting scattered experimental studies which support the contention that the development and subsequent maintenance of neural structures are dependent upon functional activation. Landmarks in this area of research are the concepts of neurobiotaxis and transneuronal degeneration. These were applied, respectively, in neuroembryology and in neuroanatomy. It is now increasingly evident that there may be an underlying neurochemical problem that is common to both processes. Both maintenance and development of the nervous system are products of a metabolism that appears to be highly dependent upon afferent neural activation.

---

*Some of the data here reported for the first time were from studies supported by PHS research grant No. B-1590 from the National Institute of Neurological Diseases and Blindness, Public Health Service.

It is almost a truism to say that later function depends upon earlier function. Here the current questions aim to ferret out the numerous and subtle ways in which behavior may reflect variations in early stimulation. Motivational tendencies, perceptual capacities, and complex response skills are separately and conjointly affected by early experiential sequences. The task of summing up all lines of evidence for these effects is a formidable one.

Some day we may be able to describe structural modifications which correlate with the more subtle behavioral variations seen after different kinds of early environmental histories. The structural variations known at present are too gross to provide more than suggestions as to what biochemical processes may underlie learning and memory. Among the studies dealing with structural growth and maintenance of afferent neural systems, those involving rapid and quickly reversible effects of stimulation can be distinguished from those involving more lasting and sometimes irreversible changes.

NEURAL ELEMENTS AND RESTRICTED STIMULATION

To exclude stimulation from any given end organ is difficult. It is even more difficult to exclude activity within the sensory nervous system. Spontaneous firing of nerve cells makes it unlikely that the complete exclusion of such neural activity will ever be achieved. Studies utilizing the sensory deprivation technique must be understood as involving variations in degree of stimulation, as well as in kind. Their interpretation therefore requires consideration of their success in achieving both quantitative and qualitative control over the sensory environment of the experimental organism.

For experiments in which later restoration of function was not essential, the cutting of sensory nerves, deafferentation, has been a particularly useful technique. Deafferentation of the optic nerve of monkeys (Clark, 1932) produced degeneration of cells in the lateral geniculate body, thus firmly establishing that transneuronal degeneration could take place within an afferent transmission system. The more recent study of A. Hess (1958), in which this technique was applied during fetal development, gave such dramatic results that it must surely be followed soon with studies of other sensory systems and at earlier fetal ages.

The hypersensitivity of denervated structures (Cannon's law of denervation) has sometimes been advanced as an argument contrary to the concept of transneuronal degeneration. That the two principles are not necessarily opposed has been ably argued in a paper by Cook, Walker, and Barr (1951). Hypersensitivity may be a stage preceding a clearly apparent degeneration. Both phases of the deafferentation "syndrome" support the general view that the nervous system *requires* activation if it is to maintain itself.

For studies in which sensory deprivation was to be temporary, vision has been the sensory modality of choice. After exclusion of light or patterns, tests of function have been resumed. Changes in structure and function are not peculiar to the visual system, however. This much is clear from a very few studies of somatic sensation (Hamberger and Hydén, 1949; Nissen, Chow, and Semmes, 1951). But strictly comparable data between modalities are not yet available. And even for the visual system, present experimental results only suggest the effects of age at deprivation and of phylogenetic position of the experimental organism.

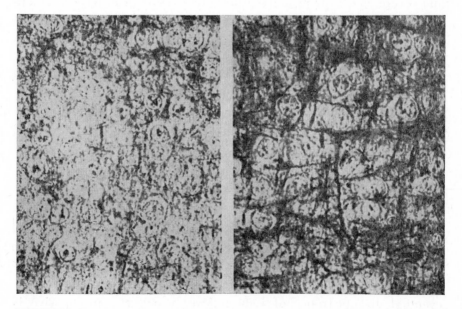

FIGURE 3–1. Arrested growth and degeneration of nerve fibers of the visual cortex after removal of one eye, showing the contrast between the right and left hemispheres of the fetal guinea pig at a gestation age of 50 days. Iron hematoxylin method of Cajal (A. Hess, 1958). Reprinted from the *Journal of Comparative Neurology* with the permission of the publishers and A. Hess.

Effects of Fetal Deafferentation. Arthur Hess (1958) surmised correctly that deafferentation should produce a quick structural arrest and degeneration during the fetal period. He removed one eye from fetal guinea pigs. The effects were apparent not only in the lateral geniculate body but in the reduction of fibers in the visual cortex of the hemisphere contralateral to the enucleation. Figure 3–1 illustrates the difference in the density of nerve fibers four days after removal of the contralateral eye in a guinea pig at a gestation age of 46 days. In the superior colliculus, Hess found a loss of cell bodies in those layers receiving optic fibers from the side of the enucleated eye.

Studies of adult rabbits (Cook, Walker, and Barr, 1951; Lindner and Umrath, 1955), cats (Cook, Walker, and Barr, 1951), and primates (Clark, 1932, 1942) confirm the general fact of a slower transneuronal degeneration in the mature nervous system following removal of the eye. The lateral geniculate body of the primate has a very direct relationship between optic fiber and cell body that permits little "cross-talk" either within or between lamina. A more rapid and severe change is produced in the monkey than in the cat, where one finds many cells with branching axons. This difference between species is considerable: atrophy is detected in the monkey after seven days (Glees and Clark, 1941), compared with one to two months for the cat (Cook, Walker, and Barr, 1951). This comparison is based on studies utilizing the Nissl technique.

Visual Deprivation during Infancy. Withholding light or markedly reducing the degree of visual stimulation during early postnatal weeks has both temporary and long-term effects. The retina is a convenient place in which to study the cytochemical responses of individual cells to varying amounts and different schedules of stimulation.

Studies begun 10 years ago (Brattgård, 1952; Chow, Riesen, and Newell, 1957; Riesen, 1950, 1960a) concentrated on the large ganglion cells of the third nuclear layer of the retina. Pallor of the optic disc, loss of the ribonucleic acid and nucleoprotein, and an eventual disappearance of light reflexes which was progressive in chimpanzees even after the animals were returned to light all give unmistakable proof of atrophy of ganglion cells and their optic nerve fibers.

With stimulation varied in terms of only hours or even fractions of hours, the effects on nucleic acid concentrations in ganglion cells (Bech, 1955) or in the absolute content of pentose nucleotides (Brattgård, 1952) are reported to vary from barely discernible to dramatic. Authors of these studies are not in full agreement regarding their interpretations. Their data, however, make it evident that the changes are easily reversed when stimulation is resumed. Furthermore, there is evidence of optimal levels and durations of stimulation in the ganglion cell response (Carlson, 1902-3) such as has been reported for the cells of Deiters' nucleus in the vestibular sensory system (Hamberger and Hydén, 1949).

When visual stimulation is restricted to an hour or less per day and such restriction is continued over a period of weeks or months, all three cellular layers of the retina are affected. Rasch and co-workers (1961) demonstrated a reduction in cytoplasmic and nucleolar ribonucleic acid (RNA) levels in neurons from receptor, bipolar, and ganglion cell layers of the retinae of cats. They confirmed an earlier observation of Weiskrantz (1958) that the inner plexiform (nerve fiber) layer of the retina of dark-reared cats is thinner than that of normally stimulated controls. There were no changes in the relative frequencies of cell types nor in the thickness of cell body layers.

Chow and co-workers (1957) reported a disappearance of the major portion of the ganglion cell layer of chimpanzees kept in darkness for 16 or 33 months, but in cats no actual disappearance of cells was seen after periods up to 40 months (Rasch *et al.*, 1961).

The Problem of the Reversibility of Effects of Prolonged Deprivation. How long may deprivation continue before irreversible depletion of protein results? Data are incomplete. After total light deprivation from birth to 10 weeks the rabbits of Brattgård's study (1952) exhibited ganglion cells with arrested, but not reduced, levels of protein. When given stimulation in light for three weeks, to the age of 13 weeks, these animals possessed ganglion cells with markedly *varying* amounts of increased protein fractions. Some cells increased hardly at all, and thus were not overcoming the growth lag, whereas other cells reached levels of those from normally stimulated control animals.

Rasch and co-workers (1961) used three groups of rats: light-reared, dark-reared, and dark-reared to 90 days followed by light for an additional 60 days. They obtained intermediate levels of ribonucleic acid in retinal ganglion cells for the third group of animals. This result suggests only a partial or slow reversibility of the early effects of deprivation. These authors report data for cats which indicate that one hour daily of full, indoor visual stimulation given from birth in a lighted laboratory is not sufficient to maintain maximum levels of RNA in retinal ganglion cells. However, the full functional adequacy of eyes and central neural elements after weeks or months of light deprivation is suggested by several behavioral studies of threshold sensitivity or of capacities for visual discriminatory behavior. In some of these animals there must be cellular densities or RNA as low as 50% of normal. These data on visual performance will be considered in more detail below.

STIMULATION REQUIRED FOR BEHAVIORAL CAPACITIES

An extreme condition of retarded neural development or neural atrophy should be associated with behavioral incapacities. This general expectation is verified in a study of the chimpanzee (Chow, Riesen, and Newell, 1957; Riesen, 1958). But there is no close relationship between behavioral and biochemical alterations for intermediate degrees of chronic nucleoprotein depletion (Weiskrantz, 1958; Baxter, 1959; Riesen, 1960a).

The RNA content of nerve cells has greater significance for behavior as an indication of the turnover of the molecular constituents of the cells than as any direct quantitative index of their capacity to function at a given moment. Since the protein molecule is dependent on RNA and RNA is dependent upon stimulus-induced function, the conclusion seems inescapable that molecular transformations of the nerve cells are in some way dependent upon function, with RNA synthesis an intermediate stage in the process. This interpretation supports in a general way such theories as those in Katz and Halstead (1950) and of Watson and Crick (1953), which contend that ontogenetic and phylogenetic "experience" may be stored in the complex protein or DNA molecules. Other work clearly implicates RNA as well as DNA in the replication of complex molecular identities (Rich, 1959).

The further discussion of behavioral development and its specific, partial dependence upon the life history of organism-environment interactions must rest at present upon observations made of behavior as a function of early environmental variations. The more complex an organism's later behavior, the more such behavior depends upon cumulative changes in its earlier behavior. As a general statement this may be quite acceptable, but psychologists are still very far from being able to trace more than crudely the detailed sequences of such cumulative increases in complexity. As the individual organism develops its own peculiar spectrum of behavioral capacities, essential stages must be separated from nonessential bypaths or even from interfering behavior tendencies.

In the remainder of this chapter four general categories of sensory-perceptual and response capacities will be examined, with specific examples, and the nature of the dependence of these behaviors upon early learning will be discussed.

Categories of Adaptive Response in Terms of Antecedent Behavior Required. When we classify behavior, we accept the risk of artificial distinctions in order to sharpen our discrimination of differences and our understanding of essential antecedents. Some artificiality may be necessary. If we recognize, in spite of our Western philosophical tradition, that categories need not be mutually exclusive, our analysis of conditions that lead to a particular behavioral manifestation can be extremely fruitful. Such recognition should also make the endeavor more tolerable to the exploring psychologist, who is seeking order and explanation in a complex array of data.

At least four categories of behavior must be distinguished on the basis of the nature and extent of essential prior organism-environment interactions. Variation in behavior under identical external stimulation accompanies growth and development. Perhaps recognized most clearly, but intimately known only in subhuman species, is the category of so-called *innate responses*. These are sometimes present at birth or they evolve during growth under any environmental conditions. They are not dependent upon a series of improving approximations to a final stimulus-response pattern. None of the laws of learning, such as contiguity or reinforcement, need be operating specifically in the development of such an action pattern. Man exhibits reflexes, certainly, and perhaps some more complex instinctual behaviors which are entirely or primarily members of this class.

A second category includes a type of behavior that demands *sensory preconditioning*. Perception of the environment is initially inadequate. The young organism fails to integrate complex information from the environment without first being exposed to fairly specific stimulus-contiguities. This class can be thought of as one kind of perceptual learning. This category reflects the fact that the appropriately experienced higher organism can instantly structure complex sensory information.

A third category includes those discriminations which are possible to the organism only after previous acquisitions of *sensory-motor and motor-sensory integrations*. Behavior associated with either (or both) a consistent sensory antecedent or a consistent sensory result must have occurred repeatedly in order for the organism to become properly equipped for precise discriminations and responses. The sensory-motor and motor-sensory associative sequences have been combined here. Later in this chapter an argument for their separation will be presented.

A fourth class of behaviorally developed building blocks is what will here be called *motor preconditioning*. The term "response-response" learning has been suggested previously (Riesen, 1960b) as indicative of the kind of contiguous conditioning that is demanded in the development of "pure" motor skills, as distinguished from sensory-motor learning. Most commonly studied skills involve a complex combination of this and the previous category.

Our next task will be to consider some specific examples of the four categories of behavioral building blocks to see how they are developed under proper conditions of environmental stimulation, or, as in some examples of the first category, without such stimulation.

INNATE ACTIVITIES AND RESPONSES

The significance of innately organized neural mechanisms is attested by the classical studies of mammalian postural reflexes, the startle response, nystagmus of vestibular origin, reflexes with autonomic mediation including the arousal reaction, and many specific exteroceptive reflexes such as pupillary, palpebral, and pinna responses.

The primates, including man, exhibit some of these only during early development. Others are functional throughout the life span. Some postural reflexes involve the coordinated participation of widely dispersed effectors. Orientation responses of eyes and head, involving ocular and neck muscles simultaneously, occur in optokinetic nystagmus and in the first response to a moving light source in an otherwise dark field. None of these are entirely impervious to effects of prior stimulation, but they can all be elicited in specifiable form on the first occasion of the requisite impingements on the receptors. They also share the limited modifiability that is known as habituation (reduced response magnitude with repeated elicitation by a stimulus of a given intensity), and they sometimes show the converse change, sensitization, when repeatedly elicited by stimuli of high intensity or during a state of high general arousal.

Stimulus "Generalization" as an Innate Behavioral Mechanism. In addition to the innate stimulus-response mechanisms there are other properties of the genetic neural substrate that assure behavioral regularities. Although the Pavlovian conception of generalization was commonly accepted by American students of behavior (Osgood, 1953, pp. 444-50), Lashley and Wade (1946) gave strong voice to a minority argument against such a mechanism. In a statement that seems odd for Lashley, they proposed that stimulus continua are developed by differential training (1946, p. 74) and that one must not expect to find gradients of generalization in the naive organism. Recent experimentation has put this issue to a test.

The assertion that a response conditioned to a specific stimulus occurs to a lesser degree when a new stimulus is presented has been difficult to verify in an organism for which the test stimulus was clearly new. Using monkeys that had either no light or only white light experience from birth, Ganz and Riesen (1961) trained four experimental animals and four control animals to press a key for liquid reinforcement when a diffused monochromatic light of a given hue flooded the eye, and not to press in darkness. Interference filters were used to produce stimuli at seven spectral points along the continuum between 450 and 630 mμ. The generalized response frequencies were measured under an extinction procedure. Test trials were, of course, given in mixed counterbalanced order to control for effects of sequence.

Both the visually naive and the experienced groups showed gradients of decreasing response frequencies to hues progressively more removed from the color used in training (Figure 3–2).

The gradient for the hue-naive group of animals showed a steeper slope near the training color, and, rather than a linear function, it possessed a significant quadratic component. The experimenters conclude "that generalization in some cases simply follows automatically from the physiological properties of the receptor system involved and does not require previous experience."

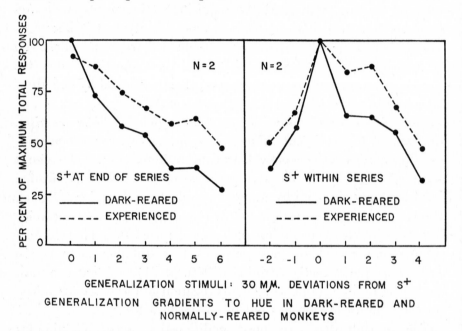

GENERALIZATION STIMULI: 30 M.M. DEVIATIONS FROM S^+

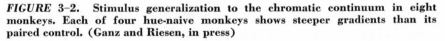

GENERALIZATION GRADIENTS TO HUE IN DARK-REARED AND NORMALLY-REARED MONKEYS

FIGURE 3–2.   **Stimulus generalization to the chromatic continuum in eight monkeys. Each of four hue-naive monkeys shows steeper gradients than its paired control. (Ganz and Riesen, in press)**

From the data of this same experiment, we may now also accept the fact that the four monkeys with prior visual experience exhibited an important consequence of sensory learning: namely, the broader generalization to other stimuli that variegated sensory experience makes possible.

Discrimination and Innate Emotional Concomitants of Response to Novelty.   The implication of steep generalization gradients in the naive primate is that he also discriminates innately. Many observations are on record (Hebb and Riesen, 1943; Hebb, 1949, pp. 242-

245; Riesen and Kinder, 1952, p. 26; Welker, 1956a; Riesen, 1961a and also Chapter 4) to document the proposition that innate emotional disturbances of a fearful or disruptive character result from certain kinds and degrees of novel stimulation. Deviation from familiar stimulation is often more arousing than is complete novelty. The monkeys of the hue generalization experiment cited above gave some evidence of behavioral disruption on the first day of presentation of the novel hues, exhibiting a much depressed response to the training stimuli and consequently a deceptively flat gradient until subsequent days of testing brought return of the normal rate of responding.

PERCEPTIONS REQUIRING SENSORY PRECONDITIONING

Sensory contiguities and sequences form one essential basis for memory and imagery. Both the American tradition of stimulus-response analysis and the Gestalt insistence on a nonanalytic configurationism have unnecessarily impeded the acceptance of sensory preconditioning as a precursor to much of complex learning and concept formation. The recognition of sounds and objects is perhaps universally dependent upon sensory preconditioning. Patterns of auditory, visual, and tactual stimulation, both within and between sense modalities, must recur in a regular manner before the mammalian organism begins to respond to such recurrences predictably. The exceptions to this, in reflex activities, must be recognized as highly significant ecologically. Such important exceptions must not prevent consideration of the ubiquitous sensory contiguity learning that is also essential to the survival of complex organisms.

William James anticipated on primarily introspective evidence the resurgence in America of emphasis on sensory-sensory associations as a fundamental factor in the development of complex perceptual discriminations. In 1890 he wrote: ". . . both sensations and perceptions differ from 'thoughts' in the fact that nerve-currents coming in from the periphery are involved in their production. In perception these nerve-currents arouse voluminous associative or reproductive processes in the cortex; . . . with a minimum of perception, the accompanying reproductive processes are at a minimum too" (*Principles of Psychology*, Vol. II, p. 3 of 1904 edition).

Perhaps few today would quarrel with the position that the identification of place, person, or object is dependent upon prior associative learning. The continuing area of disagreement is the question whether such absolute discriminations are a major part of perception.

George Miller (1956) has most convincingly marshalled the evidence that human subjects are limited to an astonishing degree in their ability to categorize stimuli which are restricted to a single dimension of physical change. Four to nine absolute discriminations is the full range when the various senses are sampled along unitary physical continua. This places a premium on the need for simultaneous utilization of multiple dimensions of stimulation. How, if not through associative integrations of contiguous sensory events, can the real world be apprehended? A re-examination of evidence that this process is fundamental to the perception of identity was contributed most penetratingly by Hebb (1949).

Although Hebb distinguishes between early learning and late learning, he combines sensory and motor learning at each stage. He clearly states that both sensory and motor modifications are implicated in his neuropsychological model of the phase sequence. Recognizing that excellent experimentation must often leave the two kinds of learning inseparably bound together, we have attempted (Riesen, 1960b; 1961b) to make a distinction that can sometimes be experimentally investigated. In the present and following sections of this chapter, we consider those studies which have met with some success in furthering the analysis.

Withholding patterned visual stimulation delays the early learning of both sensory and motor associations having to do with spatial visually coordinated behavior. Where only visual intensity discrimination is involved, the first learning is as rapid as later learning, as shown in dark-reared cats (Aarons, Kitsui, and Riesen, 1960), as well as in cats reared in diffused light (Riesen and Aarons, 1959). Mere orientation toward and approach to the source of light (or, in other animals, the avoidance of same) was required in this experimental behavior, which occurs readily in animals without the striate area of the visual cortex. The visual mediation of this discrimination transfers promptly from a single eye used in training to the contralateral eye even when that eye has never received light stimulation previously.

For movement and pattern vision the results are very different. Both the initial learning and the interocular transfer following monocular training are significantly retarded in animals reared in the dark or in diffused light. Here the sensory information must be integrated over space and through time. The geometric figures, square or circle, are neither promptly utilized as cues in initial learning nor initially effective when viewed through the second eye in tests of interocular equivalence. This ineffectiveness is increasingly apparent in comparative studies from birds (Siegel, 1953; see also Mowrer, 1936) and rats (Gibson and Walk, 1956; Forgus, 1954), to cats (Riesen, Kurke, and Mellinger, 1953), chimpanzees (Chow and Nissen, 1955), and man (Senden, 1932; Weill and Pfersdorff, 1935; Pokrovsky, 1953). The difficulty of discrimination of form is greatly reduced for the visually naive subject if the differences between the stimuli to be discriminated are replicated throughout the figure, as in horizontal vs. vertical striations, or in horizontal vs. vertical rectangles. This is apparent in data for the cat (Balaban, 1959; Riesen, unpublished), and for the chimpanzee, as seen in Table 3–1. In our chimpanzee study eight horizontal vs. vertical stripes of alternating yellow and black, each stripe five cm. in width, were discriminated equally well by animals in the first month *after* diffused light as by those normally reared.

Motion in depth across the entire visual field becomes effective in four to five hours of visual-locomotor experience after kittens have

TABLE 3–1. *FORM DISCRIMINATIONS BY CHIMPANZEES*: Total errors by three experimental (reared in diffused light to age seven months) and three control animals to 18 consecutive errorless trials. The shock-disc required avoidance; the other plaques required approach. Stimuli were present in mixed, balanced sequence, approximately 15 trials per day. The shock-disc was followed after five seconds by shock unless animal turned away; the other four plaques were followed by feeding bottle (Riesen, unpublished data).

Differential Stimulus	Experimentals	Controls
Horizontal	41	41
Red	39	40
Small	68	22
Square	212	43
Shock-disc*	173	59
Totals	533	205

*A large, circular plaque with vertical stripes of yellow and black.

attained the age of 27 days, following normal rearing to day 19 and eight days of exposure to diffused light. A very effective measure of this is by the visual placing response of the forepaws (Munro's experiment reported in Riesen, 1961b). According to Gibson and Walk (1960) the visual cliff is another useful measure of the length of pre-exposure to visual patterns that must be provided to make possible movement discrimination or depth perception based on motion parallax. Their kittens required 10 hours or more of visual pre-exposure over several days, whereas the dark-reared rat exhibits the discrimination almost immediately upon its being permitted to locomote along the edge of the cliff (Nealey and Edwards, 1960). The chimpanzee reared to seven months in diffused light and then brought into daylight for normally patterned visual experience requires about 10 days to respond to an object moving across his visual field. Many more days were required before this motion was discriminated from motion toward the face, as indicated by the protective eyeblink (see Riesen, 1958). In a study of this response with human babies Jones was not sure whether the blinking to a hand moved suddenly before the infant's face "develops by maturation, by conditioning, or by some combination of the two" (1926, p. 561). In her group the first response appeared at 46 days of age and the median was 76 days.

Two newborn chimpanzees were given daily conditioning trials in our effort to bring about this blink response as early as possible. The response appeared in both during the sixth week after birth, following 965 conditioning trials in one infant and 1,100 in the other. Comparing this outcome with the results for our older infant chimpanzees reared in diffused light, we can answer the question raised by Jones in terms of the third of her alternatives: maturation and conditioning must be appropriately combined before the eye closes to the approaching movement.

Perceived form and perceived movement are dependent upon continuities in space and time across populations of retinal receptors. Different continuities must be discriminable. Pattern vision requires that the elements in the retinal mosaic must be related specifically to their projections in the brain and differentially to each other. Perception of a line, or other forms of spatial continuity, occurs only when adjacent receptors may relate to each other during activation in a manner sharply distinct from that of nonadjacent receptors. Orderly arrangement of elements from retina to cortex may be essential to this and may be generally determined by the biochemical mechanisms of hereditary transmission. It is scarcely conceivable that 10^8 elements can be so precisely specified as to provide for the spatial acuities exhibited by the more advanced vertebrate visual systems. There is evidence that they are not. Pre-exposures to pattern are necessary to complete the specification (that is, to refine the *addresses,* to use a term from computer language) of these millions of units. Platt (1958) has given us a most illuminating discussion of how this process might be effected by the rapid succession of stimulation that is produced in adjacent elements during patterned stimulation and in conjunction with movements of the eyes.

Even the adult human subject improves with practice in visual form perception when using retinal areas away from the central foveal region. Testing regions that were 7 to 9 degrees above or to either side of central fixation, Franz and Layman (1933) presented 25 complex forms tachistoscopically for upwards of 1,000 trials. Their learning curves show gradual improvement in accuracy of recognition. Transfer of this improvement is reported for corresponding regions of the contralateral eye and to a lesser extent to new regions of the first eye (Franz and Morgan, 1933).

Pre-exposure of visual forms aids subsequent discriminations based on the same or similar stimuli in the absence of response learning; the same principle holds for a comparable procedure for developing an acquired distinctiveness among complex sounds. Forgus (1958), modifying a method introduced by Gibson and Walk (1956), found that the most effective of several pre-exposure methods was to employ figures that provided familiarity which was then combined in the subsequent test with a degree of novelty. This actually resulted in fewer than chance error scores from the beginning of response training. The moderately novel stimulus attracted an immediate preponderance of responses. Later chapters of this book will clarify the preference shown and its contribution to rapid discriminative behavior.

Using adult human subjects and difficult compound auditory stimuli, Royer (1959) extends into another sensory modality the experimental evidence for associative units to which he applies the term: nonverbal auditory concepts. According to his conclusions, "The results support a postulated primitive, basic learning-process which, as a function of the frequency of exposure to stimuli, affects subsequent learning. This process, conceived of as a modification of neural structures, operates independently of any instrumental response and of any observable, specifiable, experimentally controlled reinforcement" (Royer, 1959, p. 31). Readers with strong auditory imagery will note a familiar ring in these words. There is much evidence in common experience that recognition of a voice comes from the repeated hearing of compound simultaneous and sequential stimuli.

The prompt (often one-trial) learning of place is also dependent upon stimulus pre-exposure, with vision normally taking the major organizing role. Sequential stimulation is of fundamental significance during the early learning of spatial relationships. The organism's movements, both manipulative and locomotor, contribute to the sensory sequences. This makes isolation of sensory preconditioning from sensory-motor and motor-sensory learning technically difficult. Here we may do well to follow Hebb and to treat the typical latent learning of place as a complex process of percept formation. This will be the topic for the next section. First, to quiet any remaining doubts that intramodality sensory preconditioning occurs readily and has functional importance in the subsequent behavior of the mammalian organism, we may examine briefly a recent experiment by Kendall and Thompson (1960).

Within the stimulus dimension of auditory frequency, these experimenters chose pure tones of 250 and 2,000 cycles per second (c.p.s). Presenting the two in immediate succession, the higher pitch for 2 sec. followed by the lower for 2 sec., they gave 20 preconditioning trials to each of 24 cats. Then shock avoidance training was given to the lower 2-sec. tone alone. Tests for generalization of this conditioned avoidance to frequencies between 250 and 8,000 c.p.s. demonstrated a sharply peaked responding at 2,000 and 4,000 c.p.s. A control group showed no responding at 2,000 c.p.s. or above. Comparing their results with other data from the Wisconsin studies of intermodal sensory preconditioning, the authors suggest that "sensory preconditioning may be stronger within a modality than across modalities" (1960, p. 441). They also assert that the speed with which it develops as well as its specificity sets intramodal preconditioning apart from the usual phenomenon of the classical conditioned response. There is a striking parallel between the outcome of this experiment and the implications of the steep generalization curves shown by the hue-naive monkeys of Ganz and Riesen. For those animals there was no previous juxtaposition of stimuli varying along the visible spectrum.

PERCEPTION DEPENDENT UPON PRIOR SENSORY-MOTOR AND MOTOR-SENSORY ASSOCIATIONS

Organisms living in normal environments have very complex skeletal orienting responses to both simple and compound stimuli. An appreciation of the difference between the response of a normal and that of a stimulus-naive organism can be achieved only by carefully controlled and relatively painstaking experimentation. The experimental findings of recent years have brought surprises not only to psychologists with a nativistic bias but also to those with an opposing empiricistic bias. As an example, the contrasting findings for the rat and the cat with the visual cliff test as developed at Cornell University epitomize the point in mammalian phylogeny at which both theoretical camps have had to give ground. These experiments do not permit overgeneralization, however, for they are only one link in a growing body of evidence that demonstrates a considerable contribution from innate factors at so-called "higher" mammalian levels and, conversely, some highly significant modifiability factors in any of the representative vertebrates and even in insects. Behavioral orientation in space is such a complex perceptually determined adaptive process that we find this to be perhaps the richest field of investigation for the study of the problem of interaction between innateness and learning. If questions in this area are to receive empirical clarification they must be phrased specifically and individually both for species and for type of response.

Much of the research on latent learning, on spatial delayed response, and on shifts in egocentric localization can be brought to bear on the problem of the genesis of spatial orientation. This relevance is recognized and partially analyzed in recent discussions of perception (see Thorpe, 1956, pp. 90-134; Dember, 1960b, pp. 235-270). The inability of dogs reared in a homogeneous environment to maintain even for a few seconds a spatial orientation in a delayed response problem was noted by Thompson (1955). He also reported failure of these animals to develop this behavioral capacity later in life.

Cats reared in total darkness to nine months of age and exhibiting normal electrical activity at the visual cortex (Baxter, 1959) also failed initially in tests of orientation in visual space. They were found to improve gradually but with a residual variability of performance in all tests of visually guided spatial discriminations including spatial delayed response. The most improved animals were indistinguishable from normals in delayed response with delays up to 60 sec., in jumping up onto or down from chairs or tables of varying heights and sizes, in visual following and paw striking at swinging strings, and in binocular convergence. A minimum of two weeks to a maximum of many months were required for successful performance on such tests of visuomotor coordination. Some animals failed persistently on some tests, as though competing habits of perceptual adjustment blocked development of the unpracticed coordinations.

A persisting inability of cats reared in unpatterned light to discriminate moving from nonmoving two-dimensional figures (Riesen and Aarons, 1959) has been confirmed with oscillating targets. On the other hand, cats reared with freedom of movement and locomotion in patterned light to five months of age and then put into total darkness for six months discriminate such movement and a variety of complex patterns as well as do normally reared animals. The movement discrimination studies revealed an unexpected inability of animals that only received patterned light stimulation while in a holder preventing locomotion. In spite of excellent ocular coordination, normal pursuit movements with eyes and head, and good orientation to moving persons during bodily restraint, these animals consistently failed to discriminate movement from nonmovement in the two-dimensional figures. They achieved prompt learning of visual intensity discriminations in the same Yerkes alley that was used for the movement problem. It can be concluded that during locomotion toward the choice-point and to the surface onto which the stimuli were projected, these animals were unable to distinguish self-initiated from externally produced movement across the visual field.

But there is also the factor of movement within a stable surrounding square contour. This motion of figure relative to ground, often advanced as the primitive and compelling environmental condition for visual movement perception, seems to require sensory preconditioning. It would be of the intramodality type (see Kendall and Thompson, 1960) and would depend upon patterned stimulation provided by stable visual contours. If this were sufficient, it would belong as a specific example in the category of the previous section of this chapter. Sensory preconditioning is a necessary but not a sufficient condition for movement perception in our experiments. The "holder-only" group (Riesen and Aarons, 1959) did not succeed in making the discrimination. We must call in an explanation in terms of an underdeveloped reafferentation mechanism. Von Holst (1954) has demonstrated that an efferent process (as in locomotion) must be followed by corresponding "normal" sensory information from the external environment, typically by way of visual or proprioceptive stimulation, if the organism is to maintain its orientation in space. This provides an essential registration of information for the discrimination of position and of motion in the environment relative to the position and motion of the organism. Without the coordination of these two factors, perception of real movement would be restricted to times when the organism held its receptors completely still.

Our results imply that some "normal" efferent-sensory coordinations, $R \rightarrow S$ in addition to $S \rightarrow R$, are learned in the cat, at least for locomotion within a visual environment. Held and co-workers (Held and Hein, 1958; Held, 1961) have shown that this motor-sensory association can be modified in human subjects, the relearning being dependent upon movement-produced stimulation over a period of 30 minutes or longer, the active organism receiving concurrent reafferent visual stimulation. *Passive* movement during vision is ineffective. These investigators pointed out the applicability of von Holst's principle of reafferentation to the type of problem here discussed and extended it to include associatively modified feedback.

Distinguishing between sensory priority and motor priority in the associative process may often be impossible and for some purposes quite unnecessary. Adding either or both to a strictly sensory-sensory perceptual learning has been shown to aid in subsequent transfer experiments. Meier and McGee (1959) found that early visual-tactual-motor experience with three-dimensional forms was superior to other conditions of rearing, including visual experience with the same objects, in preparing animals for subsequent discriminative behavior based on food reinforcement. In this example all combinations of central afferent and efferent processes are considered to be interlocked as neural cell assemblies. Reaction time measures have revealed differences when residual effects of early auditory deprivation have been set into competition with those from visual deprivation in stimulus-response latencies for either modality. Latency of response in groups of adult rats was shown (Gauron and Becker, 1959) to increase when the relevant starting cues (either light or sound) were shifted to correspond with the specific modality that had received minimal stimulation during the first month of life. These authors place a new interpretation on the older "competition stress" experiment of Wolf (1943).

ACQUIRED RESPONSE-RESPONSE UNITS

Do response integrations (or motor "cell assemblies") belong in a discussion of the effects of previous stimulation? This is not necessarily a contradition in terms. Skills are developed with initial sensory control which is gradually short-circuited, as becomes apparent in the movement combinations that begin as slow poorly coordinated sequences and end in swiftly executed, accurately timed responses that are controlled as to pressure and amplitude. Initiation of an act such as the playing of an arpeggio, typing of a word, or execution of a punt or drop kick must clearly set off a complex efferent sequence in which sensory feedback could check or modify performance only after much or all of the sequence has been executed. Reinforcement of the more effective execution must here, as in typical operant conditioning, exercise its effect on a subsequent trial, since major components of the action are completed before trial and error can bring about any correction of the error. Response integration progressively reduces the degree of detailed sensory monitoring that is necessary to skilled execution. What happens when the basis for sensory monitoring is reduced before the response system is well integrated?

In the absence of sensory input the motor neurons do not remain quiescent. They become hypersensitive (Cannon and Rosenblueth, 1949), and locomotor sequences may be initiated following minimal excitation and coordinated on the basis of purely internuncial and efferent sequential activity (Weiss, 1941). Where sensory control is deficient or absent during development, motor patterns evolve either in accordance with genetically determined potentialities and restrictions or as a consequence of intrinsic neural oscillatory sequences. Neither of these guarantees the establishment of motor integrations that will be effective under a given set of environmental conditions, including the conditions under which an organism typically lives. We have only limited information that is relevant to this problem. Motor neurons are difficult to isolate completely without producing hypersensitivity and spasticity. With techniques yet to be developed, more informative experiments may be expected, but we may examine what we know.

Cutting off the visual control over eye movements and head postures soon after birth consistently produces in primates and other laboratory mammals such as the cat and the dog (Raudnitz, 1903; Blohmke, 1927) a gradually developing assortment of autonomous movement rhythms of the eyes and head, the head being less consistently involved than the eyes. There are available some descriptive and speculative theoretical articles based on clinical observations of human infants reared in very dimly illuminated surroundings. *Dunkelnystagmus* and *spasmus nutans* are recognized clinical entities (Ohm, 1950) whose explanation has remained both incomplete and faulty.

We have had kittens, monkeys, and chimpanzees under extended observation following early weeks either in diffused light, flickered light, or in darkness. In general, it is clear from reports of other investigators and our own observations that the necessary and sufficient environmental condition for the development of autonomous motor rhythmicities is the absence of pattern upon which the eye may fixate. The rhythmic movements are variable. They are often said to be spontaneous, yet there is a measure of environmental control. Any arousing stimuli tend to increase their frequency or amplitude, which renders them unlike central EEG rhythms. Their rate is typically slower than alpha rhythm, being from three to six per sec. Visual or vestibular stimulation may initiate the rhythms, but neither is necessary. Hebb's suggestion (1949, p. 121) that intrinsic cortical rhythms may be a type of "learning" based on self-synchronized firing sequences of the central nervous system can appropriately be invoked. Here there may be some contribution from the natural frequency of oscillation of the eyeballs and their musculature. Cats are more frequently seen to develop pendular nystagmus, both lateral and vertical, and rhythmic torsional movements of the eyes, whereas the primates typically exhibit jerky nystagmus. This is lateral, diagonal, or vertical (in decreasing order of frequency). Head jerks accompany these jerky rhythms of the eyes in a synchronous manner, *if* they occur at all, and are the *spasmus nutans* of light-deprived human infants. Figure 3–3 shows sample records of jerky nystagmoid eye movements from a monkey that was reared to the age of two years with diffused light stimulation, followed by 800 hours of patterned light stimulation given two hours per day.

The primates require somewhat longer to develop the eye and head movement rhythms than do the cats. Once present the rhythms also persist longer in primates after the animal has opportunity to fixate visual targets. Improvement in fixation and visual pursuit is the essential counterpart to the disappearance of the nystagmoid rhythms. One set of skills is slowly developed under adequate sensory control as replacement for a mixture of random and rhythmic motor patterns that represent maladaptive learning in the absence of sensory input from contours in the visual environment.

RECAPITULATION

The complex interaction of neuropsychological processes that are involved in early stimulus deprivation is nowhere more dramatically documented than in the human studies of congenital cataract (Pokrovsky, 1953; Senden, 1960). Animal studies have verified the complexity of the relevant factors, and, of much more significance, they are now providing controlled observations; these begin to form the basis for a scientific understanding of the sensory, perceptual, and motivational manifestations that result when stimulation is withheld during development.

In this chapter the emphasis has been on sensory and perceptual aspects of early stimulus deprivation. The growth and maintenance of neural structures depend upon the adequacy of functional demands placed on them by stimulation. Related to but also distinct from the

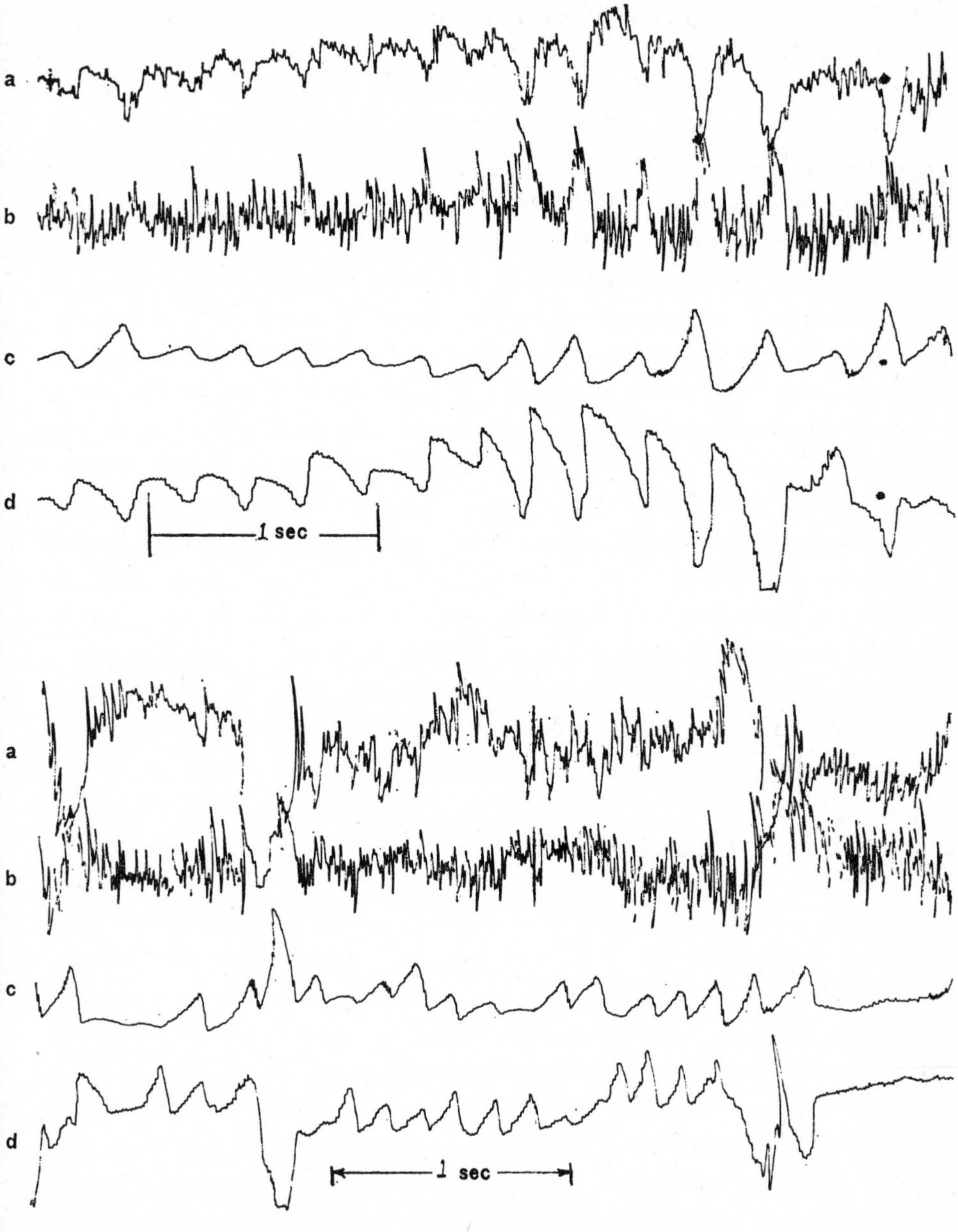

FIGURE 3–3. SPONTANEOUS RHYTHM (NYSTAGMUS) IN THE EYE MOVEMENTS OF A VISUALLY DEPRIVED MONKEY. In each of the two records, the lower pair of lines (c & d) indicate lateral eye movements taken from electrodes at the outer canthi to provide records of corneo-retinal potentials. Occipital (a & b) electrodes reveal muscle "artifacts" showing that neck muscles are active in synchrony with the eye movements. This *spasmus nutans* is only seen occasionally if observation is based on gross head movements. (Riesen, unpublished data; records obtained by Robert L. Ramsey.)

arrest in afferent structural development is the failure of central integrative functions. This must be viewed as multifaceted, for it is clear that at least three or four levels of associative integration are involved in the changed courses of development that various restrictions of afferent input impose upon the nervous system. The capacity to process and unify complex sensory input within the visual modality is markedly inferior when only simplified stimulation is permitted to enter that system during infancy. We have referred to this as an arrest in sensory-sensory integrative capacity, to distinguish it from sensory-motor and motor-sensory functions. Within all of these categories and also in a conceptually distinguishable response-response class of functional integrations, there is behaviorial evidence of genetically determined patterns of activity. In this last group are the genetically determined eye movement patterns which show only crude binocular coordination until sensory control has been established. In many experiments even with animals the effects on more than one type of integration are intermingled. For this reason it will become increasingly important for the researcher to permit normal development of most integrative functions in order to study the role of stimulation during the ontogenesis of others, both singly, and in simplified combinations.

Chapter 4

Early Environmental Stimulation*

WILLIAM R. THOMPSON and
THEODORE SCHAEFER, JR.
Wesleyan University and University of Chicago

*I*N recent years there has been an increasing interest in two lines of research in psychology: the effects of early environmental experience, and the effects of different amounts of stimulation on behavior.

The first of these lines is not a novel one. Indeed, in the early part of the twentieth century, Freud suggested, on the basis of clinical evidence, that early experience played an important role in behavioral development. There is little question that, in terms of therapy and clinical research, this postulate has been a useful one. In experimental psychology, although a number of observations on the role of early experience had appeared sporadically, intensive systematic work commenced in the early 1950s, following the publication of Hebb's book, *The Organization of Behavior* (1949). Hebb's theoretical stress on the importance of early experience was responsible for a large amount of subsequent experimental work, especially with animals, on this topic.

Another important influence on animal research in early experience has been the work of Konrad Lorenz who emphasized the importance of critical periods in development during which certain environmental events have wide-ranging and long-lasting effects on behavior. Lorenz's classic paper on imprinting in birds (1937) and summaries of ethological work by Tinbergen (1951, 1953) present evidence not only of the effects of early experiences on later behavior but also of the effects of rearing animals in isolation or in reduced social stimulation.

The consideration of amount of stimulation as a basic dimension

*The senior author gratefully acknowledges the support of the National Science Foundation and the Guggenheim Foundation.

in experimentation also has a fairly recent origin. For some time, changes in behavior occurring during learning were explained in terms of reduction of drives or needs (Hull, 1943). Later the preferred explanation came to be reduction of stimulation (Hull, 1949; Miller, 1951). More recently *increases* in stimulation have been shown to alter behavior. Again, Hebb (1949) in his book emphasized the importance of stimulation, and experimental evidence was added from quite diverse lines of research, such as that on exploratory behavior in animals (Barnett, 1958c), the effects of sensory deprivation in humans (Heron, 1957), the electrical self-stimulation behavior of rats (Olds and Milner, 1954), and numerous studies, to be discussed later, of the effects of added stimulation in early life on learning in animals.

It is our purpose in this chapter to discuss experimental work that bears on both these lines of research: stimulation and early experience. We will first attempt to define more exactly the terms "early experience" and "stimulation." Second, we will discuss some relevant empirical studies. Third, we will offer some theoretical postulates that may be useful in clarifying the data already at hand, and also in suggesting some new directions for research.

DEFINITION OF TERMS

By the phrase *early experience*, we refer to environmental forces which act on the organism during the period of development extending from conception through puberty or up to maturity when most growth processes, both physiological and psychological, taper off. The duration of this period and the rate of maturation of different functions within it naturally vary from species to species and even from genotype to genotype within a species.

We shall restrict the term *stimulation* to any physical energy impinging on the organism. This stimulation may be specified in terms of the type of energy involved, as well as in terms of a number of quantitative dimensions. In psychology, stimulation usually implies the existence and activation of a sense receptor in the organism. In higher organisms, it is true that most energy input from the external environment is mediated via sensory processes and nervous system activity. But in lower organisms, and in the embryos and infants of higher animals, the nervous system and sense receptors are often poorly developed or nonexistent. Physical energy changes may affect such organisms without being mediated by sensory or nervous mechanisms but rather through more direct action on physical, chemical, or physiological processes. These processes may be more or less permanently modified, producing lasting changes in the behavior of that organism. An example of behavioral modification due to such nonsensory stimulation is the finding (Thompson, 1957) that stressful stimulation applied to the mother rat during gestation has an effect on the adult behavior of her offspring. Since the effect was present even when the offspring were reared by a foster, nonstressed mother, the stimulation must have been effective *in utero* when the nervous system of the fetus was incompletely developed. It is necessary, in working with very young organisms, to consider the role of stimulation in terms of its effects upon the organism through processes other than sensory-neural activation.

Finally, behavioral changes related to early stimulation may be described in terms of a number of parameters. These parameters are listed in the last column of Table 4–1. The first two columns are the relevant stimulus and organismic variables. In our discussion of empirical data in the next section, we will follow this basic scheme as closely as possible.

TABLE 4–1. Main Variables Involved in the Relationship between Early Environmental Stimulation and Later Behavior of the Organism.

Stimulation	*Organism*	*Response*
Type (e.g., light, sound)	Genotype	Type (e.g., emotion, learning)
Intensity	Age or developmental stage	Intensity or magnitude
Onset	Past history	Direction
Duration		Latency
		Permanence
Variability and complexity		Variability
		Range or extent

The physical dimensions of stimulation may or may not be entrained with corresponding psychological dimensions, depending on the organism variables. The same physical intensity may result in more or less intense effects depending, for example, on sensory threshold factors determined by genotype.

EMPIRICAL DATA

Stimulation Variables

We may begin by establishing first the simple empirical proposition that early stimulation does have important effects on later behavior. Data bearing on this point have been obtained for human beings and for a wide variety of species ranging from insects to chimpanzees (Beach and Jaynes, 1954; King, 1958; Thompson, 1955, 1960). Both decreased and increased levels of early postnatal stimulation have been found to have effects. For example, rearing in the restricted environment of an orphanage has been found to produce a number of behavior changes in children, including lack of attentiveness, impulsiveness, lowered cognitive capacity, and diminished ability to relate to others (Goldfarb, 1955). Similarly, in animals, such as the rat, dog, or monkey, restriction of early environmental stimulation can have drastic and enduring effects on such traits as emotionality, learning ability, activity level, social behavior, and perception (Beach and Jaynes, 1954; Thompson, 1955; King, 1958). The exact dimensions of so-called "restriction" which are responsible for the major effects have not yet been fully specified, a problem which we will examine shortly.

On the other side of the coin, we find that an increased level of early stimulation may also have effects. In the case of human beings, the evidence is rather ambiguous. It has been argued that nursery school attendance, for example, can produce desirable changes in young children, and even that special types of enriching experience can produce large increments in IQs of the feeble-minded, but the data on which these assertions are based are by no means conclusive (Thompson, 1954, 1955). Such effects, if they occur, can only be evaluated by contrast with a normal control group. In the case of human children, it is probable that the environment in the normal course of events is almost as stimulating as that provided by any program of enrichment. Consequently, it is not too surprising that the latter should fail to produce marked effects even though the enrichment is devised to offer added diversity and complexity of stimulation. In animals, on the other hand, because conditions of normal laboratory rearing are themselves fairly restrictive, large gains in growth rate, intelligence, ability to withstand stress, and changes in other traits can readily be demonstrated to result from additional early stimulation (Thompson, 1955, 1960; King, 1958).

It should be noted that changes in later behavior may be produced by varying stimulation not only during the postnatal but also during the prenatal phase of early development. While less work has been done on the latter phase from the standpoint of behavior, many studies in endocrinology, pediatrics, and teratology have included behavioral findings. There is now growing interest in the study of prenatal development and later behavior, and what data there are suggest that behavioral effects in offspring can result from stimulation of animal mothers during pregnancy (Montagu, 1950; Thompson, 1955, 1958, 1960). We will consider this work in more detail below.

The proposition that early environmental stimulation is important for later behavior is, in a sense, incomplete. Generally implied is the additional qualification—"more important than later environmental stimulation." Furthermore, what is meant by "important" is also worth consideration. What seems to be meant by most authors is that a more marked behavioral change is produced when an animal is subjected to a given treatment at one age than another. In point of fact, the data purporting to demonstrate this are often inadequate. Many investigators who conclude that a given type of stimulation in early life has a unique effect on later behavior fail to include a control group given the same stimulation in later life (King, 1958).

Using appropriate controls, Wolf (1943) and Hymovitch (1952) both found that restriction of normal laboratory stimulation produced effects on adult behavior of rats only if administered early in life. In well-controlled experiments, E. H. Hess (1959) has demonstrated that in several breeds of fowl a very marked critical period exists at 13 to 16 hours after hatching. During this critical time the presence of a moving object in the young bird's environment results in *imprinting*—the young bird apparently accepting the moving object as its mother, thereafter following that object and chirping contentedly when it is present. The same kind of stimulation after the critical period does not result in imprinting. This phenomenon will be discussed later in the chapter. A fairly large body of evidence has also been accumulated on the effects of early handling. Bernstein (1952) found that in rats increased stimulation by handling for 10 days, starting at 50 days of age, yielded animals whose maze performance was superior to nonhandled control animals. A group similarly handled beginning at 21 days and continuing until testing at 60 days was superior to both. Bernstein suggested, on the basis of these results, that handling at an early age might have a special effect on later behavior. Subsequently, Levine and Otis (1958) tested this early handling hypothesis by comparing rats handled daily before weaning with nonhandled control animals, and animals handled daily for 21 days after weaning. As in Bernstein's study, both the early and the late handled groups were more resistant to the stress of food and water deprivation than nonhandled controls, but the early handled animals were most resistant. More recent evidence for the importance of age on the effectiveness of added stimulation provided by handling will be discussed later. It seems clear, from the studies above, that stimulation early in life is more important than later stimulation for at least three situations: restriction of normal laboratory stimulation, imprinting, and handling.

Comparison of behavioral differences occurring between early and late stimulated groups is not entirely a sufficient criterion for defining "importance." We may be interested in the size or kind of deviation produced and also in its permanence or irreversibility. It is indeed quite possible that even if later environmental stimulation produces as much effect as early environmental stimulation, the reversibility of the effect might be considerably less in the second case. So far, there is little empirical work bearing on this point. One exception is the study of imprinting in which the evidence indicates that the effects are long-lasting (E. H. Hess, 1959). Another is a carefully designed experiment by Woods (1959). This investigator confirmed the conclusion that early sensory and motor deprivation produces deficits in the later learning abilities of rats, but that these losses could be markedly reduced by subsequent exposure to a "free" or enriched environment. In this case, the effects were certainly not irreversible. It would be interesting to learn to what extent the converse is true— that is, the extent to which the effects of early enrichment can be overcome by later restriction.

We may conclude that the proposition that early stimulation has important effects on later behavior is generally a valid one, but, at the same time, is one involving a number of ambiguous aspects that need to be clarified empirically. We will now discuss experimental studies that bear on the more specific dimensions of stimulation that we have outlined above in Table 4–1.

Type of Stimulation. Most investigators have used such general types of enriched or reduced stimulation that it is difficult to identify the exact dimensions responsible for producing effects. This is true for the free-environment rat studies (Hymovitch, 1952; Bingham and Griffiths, 1952; Forgays and Forgays, 1952), the work with dogs reared in restricted environments (Thompson and Melzack, 1956), and much of the analogous work on human children and infants (see the work on vision, Chapter 3). Restriction in motor activity by itself has not been found to be effective (Hymovitch, 1952; Forgays and Forgays, 1952), though this is not to say that *enrichment* in early motor activity may not be crucial in producing differences in adult motor behavior. Manipulation of perceptual rather than motor opportunity seems to have much larger effects, though it is again difficult to specify which dimensions of the broad domain of perception are mainly responsible for the effects produced. At the human level, Ribble's work (1944) suggests that all sensory modalities may be important in providing for what she calls "stimulus feeding" of the infant by the mother. Studies of the effects of early stimulation in rats seem to bear out this contention. There is no question now that tactile stimulation during early life in the rat results in a great many alterations in later behavior, whether the stimulation is produced by handling (Bernstein, 1952; Weininger, 1956), stroking with a camel's-hair brush (W. J. McClelland, 1956), mild electrical stimulation (Levine, Chevalier and Korchin, 1956), tossing the young in the air and catching them (Ader, 1959), or by shaking the nest cage mechanically (Levine and Lewis, 1959b). As Montagu pointed out some time ago (1953), cutaneous stimulation is crucial for normal development in rats and other infraprimate mammals: Tactile stimulation in the genital area is necessary to elicit defecation and urination in infant rats, mice, rabbits, and dogs. The importance of cutaneous stimulation is probably even greater in more advance species, such as primates. Harlow's observations of monkey love (Harlow,

1958, 1959) suggest that this is so, and, in addition, they indicate that the type of cutaneous stimulation is important. Thus surrogate mothers made of a wire-frame covered with terry cloth were found by him to be much preferred by infant monkeys, and much more capable of reducing anxiety in stress situations, than surrogate mothers of uncovered wire. The degree to which such preferences are innate or (in some sense) acquired is at present not known. In general, Harlow's findings do indicate that for the young primate a particular type of cutaneous experience has both immediate effects and some bearing on later behavior.

Changes in the amount of early visual stimulation also appear to be important. Presumably vision has been the crucial modality involved in most of the free and restricted-environment studies with rats and dogs, though in these cases the level of complexity of the visual experience rather than the actual amount of stimulation may have been important. A study by Macdonald and Teghtsoonian (1957) suggests that sheer amount may also affect later behavior. These investigators compared rats reared in total darkness from 22 through 42 days of age with rats given different amounts of light stimulation during the same period, these amounts ranging from 2 to 16 hours a day. Weight differences between the light and no-light groups appeared later, though only after a period of daily exposure to intense light. One might suspect, in this case, that the differences were due to an abnormal reaction to bright light by the dark-reared animals rather than to a supernormal reaction on the part of the light-experienced groups.

Presumably, the physiological effects of stimulation via particular sensory channels are both neurological and endocrinological. We should thus be able to produce such effects more directly by the use of drugs. There is obviously a fruitful field for research here, using drugs that excite or inhibit particular physiological structures. Little work has been attempted along these lines in early postnatal development, but a great deal has been done at the prenatal level. Most of this research has dealt with morphological defects produced in offspring by drug administration to the mother during pregnancy. However, a few studies have been concerned with the behavioral changes produced. Alcohol (Vincent, 1958) and adrenalin (Thompson, unpublished data), for example, given to mother rats during pregnancy have been found to produce effects on emotionality, motivation, and learning ability of the offspring. Similarly, agents that affect brain serotonin concentration also have been found to alter offspring behavior when injected into mother rats during pregnancy (Werboff, 1959). The exact channels by which such chemical substances have their effects are not yet known. Since chemicals can be more easily controlled and manipulated than gross sensory stimulation, it is obvious that their use could prove fruitful in exploring the basic problems of the mechanisms which underly the effects of early experience.

Intensity of Stimulation. A second important property of stimulation is its intensity. In discussing this we will use the term in a physical sense, that is to say, in terms of the actual physical intensity of some stimulating source. Obviously, the same amount of stimulation may affect different organisms quite differently, depending on their genotype, past history, and other factors which will be discussed later. In general, common sense might suggest that mild or moderate stimulation administered to young organisms would have a beneficial effect in terms of such behavior as emotionality, motivation, and stress resistance, while strong stimulation might be expected to have just the opposite effects. Such a model is predicated on the idea that adaptation or habituation occurs up to a certain threshold beyond which breakdown or injury of some kind will occur. Mild added stimulation could operate to raise this threshold, thus extending the range of environmental stimulation the organism can handle (Thompson, 1958).

Experimental work both at the prenatal and postnatal level, with humans and animals, seems to confirm this point of view, though many details still need to be investigated. Denenberg (1959) and Denenberg and Bell (1960) have shown that adult learning in mice varies in a curvilinear fashion with amount of stimulation given at weaning. A moderate amount of shock improves later conditioning to shock as an unconditioned stimulus; a large amount, or none at all, results in poorer learning later in life. Analogous data at the human level are also available. We have already referred to Ribble's report (1944) that understimulation or lack of mothering of human infants may have drastic effects. The implication is, of course, that mild stimulation is desirable. Overstimulation, on the other hand, as sometimes occurs with hyperefficient or unduly anxious mothers, appears to be involved in the etiology of enuresis, according to Bostock (1958), and possibly is also related to feeding problems (Escalona, 1945). In the prenatal phase, the same kind of rule appears to operate. The senior author has found that anxiety undergone by mother rats during pregnancy may produce either hyperactivity or hypoactivity in offspring. There are indications from these data that such a variation depends on the amount of anxiety produced in the mother, as well as on other factors. Vincent (1958), in a study to which we have already referred, found that large dosages of alcohol given to pregnant mother rats produced an increase in emotionality, but deficits in motivation and learning in the offspring; small dosages, on the other hand, produced exactly the opposite effects. Furchtgott and Echols (1958), using prenatal ionizing radiation, and Windle and Becker (1942), using anoxia, have found the same kind of reversal in the effects on activity level of rats and guinea pigs, respectively.

In view of such data, the kind of curvilinear model outlined above relating intensity of stimulation to magnitude of effect on later behavior seems generally valid. At the same time, we know very little as to the model's mode of operation in respect to specific behavior traits or different genotypes. Nor do we understand the kind of physiological mechanisms underlying it.

Onset of Stimulation. It is likely that speed of onset of stimulation has effects mainly through its influence on the functional intensity of the stimulation. Auditory stimulation that has a rapid onset will, other things being equal, produce a greater startle response than the same intensity of sound preceded by an adaptation period of some duration. We already know that sharp sounds of fast onset, such as bells or buzzers, presented several times in early postnatal life (Hall and Whiteman, 1951), or else to the mother during pregnancy (Thompson and Sontag, 1956), affect later emotionality and learning ability. But it is doubtful that the same results would be obtained if some adaptation to the stimulation were allowed.

Duration of Stimulation. Duration, like speed of onset, is another variable that relates to intensity, though it is probable that the relationship is by no means one-to-one. Thus, an increase in length of stimulation may be equivalent to an increase in intensity only up to a point, beyond which habituation may attenuate the effects. We have few empirical data on this precise problem, but a number of studies have yielded some general information of importance. Brooker (1955) handled three groups of weanling rats for 5, 10, and 20 minutes per day for 21 days. All handled groups showed greater weight gains than a nonhandled group. However, the maximal gain was shown by the 10-minute rather than by the 20-minute group. Denenberg and Karas (1960) have reported similar findings: Rats handled daily for 10 days during infancy learned a conditioned avoidance response and survived food and water deprivation longer than rats handled for 20 days and nonhandled control animals. They suggest that handling for 10 days is moderately stressful and produces more stress-resistant adult animals, but 20 days of handling produces an inability to respond appropriately to stress in adult life. Brooker explained his results in terms of "monotony" produced by excessive handling, this having, in Hebbian terms (Hebb, 1949), a disruptive effect on cortical organization. Another explanation might be that when the stimulation was prolonged beyond 10 minutes, it became stressful. It would be interesting to attempt experimentally to test these two alternate hypotheses.

It is interesting that the lower limit of tactile stimulation that can produce effects is apparently minimal. Several investigators (see Bovard, 1958) have reported that merely picking up a young rat and replacing it into its cage is sufficient to increase stress resistance later in life. This finding is perhaps not so surprising. Whatever neural and endocrine responses are produced by a brief stimulation, it is likely that these responses continue to discharge for some time after the physical stimulation has ceased. Consequently, what seems to be a very brief period of stimulation may actually be much greater in terms of the duration of its physiological effects.

In respect to the prenatal phase, we have, as yet, little information about the effects of varying duration of stimulation. Charlesworth and Thompson (Charlesworth, 1958) found some evidence that daily electric shocks given to pregnant mother rats over 11 or more days resulted in offspring showing hypoactivity in an open-field, while 10 or fewer days of shock produced hyperactivity. Since these data were based on small numbers of animals, and duration of the treatment was confounded with the time of gestation during which electric shock stimulation occurred, no firm conclusion is possible regarding the relationship between open-field behavior and number of shocks.

Variability and Complexity of Stimulation. As far as the writers are aware, there are no data bearing exactly on these variables. It is certainly true that what is normally meant by a "rich" environment is one in which both variability and complexity of stimulation are increased. It is clear that such environments produce effects on later behavior, whether the subjects are rats, dogs, chimpanzees, or humans. At the same time it is equally clear that the simplest type of stimulation involving perhaps only one primitive channel, tactile sensation, may also have equally large effects. This may mean that under certain conditions, the addition of sheer stimulation, without regard to complexity or variability, is adequate to produce permanent changes, while under other conditions variable and complex stimulation is necessary. One important variable that must determine what kind of stimulation will be maximally effective is age. From the previously discussed work on rats and other mammals, it is obvious that even before the animal is mobile or can hear or see, tactile stimulation as supplied by the mother's licking may be important in promoting growth and development (Thompson, 1955). At a later age, however, when the senses are functional, it may be the level of variability and complexity of stimulation that becomes crucial. Indeed, it is entirely possible that the behavioral changes produced in rats by handling at the postweaning phase of development have been due at least partly to the fact that new perceptual experience has inadvertently been provided in addition to the simple tactile stimulation. The usefulness of the mammalian mother may be described in terms of two of these dimensions. Both human and animal mothers fondle, stroke, and hold their infant. Later on, they will reward and punish their offspring, serve as some kind of model for it, and generally initiate it into the complexities of the environment. Prolonged absence of the mother at this stage will probably cause severe anxiety reactions on the part of the young animal. This is clearly seen in the behavior of young lambs and kids (Liddell, 1954), for example, and some species of birds, and is well documented in the case of the so-called "separation experience" in human children (Bowlby, 1951).

In general, then, we may state that complexity and variability are probably less important dimensions of stimulation for the younger and more primitive organism, but more important dimensions for the older, more fully developed organism. We will return to this point in the final part of the chapter.

So far we have dealt only with variables relating to stimulation. As mentioned earlier, however, the specification of these variables in any particular case must depend to a large extent on the organism involved. We will now discuss information bearing on this point.

Organism Variables

The three main organism variables which may influence both the manner in which early stimulation has effects and also the extent of these effects are age, genotype, and past history. Let us now look at each of these factors in turn.

Age. The age of the organism on which stimulation impinges is perhaps one of the most crucial variables in terms of influences on later behavior. At least three hypotheses about the relation of age and size of effect seem plausible. These are shown diagrammatically in Figure 4–1. These postulates are not mutually exclusive: it is likely that the applicability of each may vary with the particular target function or process and with the type of organism involved. Let us look at some representative empirical studies bearing on the relationship of age and environmental influence.

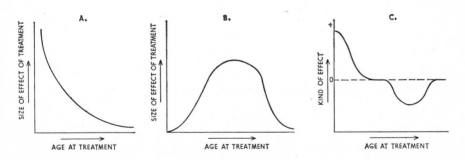

FIGURE 4–1. **Hypothetical relationships between age at treatment and size or type of effect produced. In Figure 4–1a the hypothesis states simply that the effect of stimulation is inversely proportional to age. The hypothesis diagrammed in Figure 4–1b is of the critical period type, stating that there is a specific time during which certain kinds of stimulation will have maximal effect. Figure 4–1c represents the hypothesis that stimulation at the earliest stage of development has an effect which is opposite to the effect of the same stimulation at a later stage of development.**

In the postnatal phase Schaefer (1957) investigated the preweaning age at which handling was most effective in rats. Animals handled daily throughout the three-week period from birth to weaning and those handled on days 2 through 7 exhibited significantly less emotionality in an open field than nonhandled animals. Handling daily during the second week, however, resulted in no change. Figure 1a represents this kind of effect which is inversely proportional to age. Denenberg (1958) and Denenberg and Karas (1959, 1960) found handling during days 1-10 resulted in better avoidance learning and longer survival of food and water deprivation than nonhandling or handling on days 10-20 or 1-20. These studies also implicate a period very early in life as important in the effectiveness of handling as stimulation. The importance of this early stage is further supported by the report of Levine and Lewis (1959a) that rats handled on days 2 through 5 show maturation of the adrenal cortical response to stress as early as 12 days of age, while nonhandled animals, and animals handled at later stages of infancy, do not exhibit maturation of the adrenal response until the 16th day of age.

Further evidence of the special importance of the early days of life in the rat is provided by observations of maternal behavior (Schaefer, 1959). Mother rats having free access to a second cage for food and water spent very little time (1% to 12% of each 24 hours) away from the nest cage during the first three or four days after whelping. At about the fourth day, amount of time away from the pups began to increase gradually until, during the third week of the nursing period, the schedule of maternal absences approximated the prebirth pattern of long absences totalling approximately 40% of each 24-hour day. These data, indicating a gradual change in maternal behavior after the first 3 or 4 days, support the first model in Figure 4–1, since it is likely that maternal behavior has a functional relationship to developmental processes in the nursing offspring. The possibility remains, however, that further experiments, varying the age during the first week, will demonstrate a critical period of maximal effectiveness on some particular day during the first week. Such a finding would support the model in Figure 4–1b. As a matter of fact, E. H. Hess (1959) has published an empirical curve for the maximal effectiveness of imprinting in the mallard duckling which is very similar to Figure 4–1b. Hess's curve, based on a large number of birds for each hour throughout the first several hours after hatching, shows a very sharp critical period at 13 to 16 hours.

Another study, by Seitz (1959) on kittens, tends to support the first model (Figure 4-1a). Seitz separated kittens from their mothers at two weeks, six weeks, and 12 weeks of age. He measured the effects of separation by a series of behavioral tests. The largest effects were found with those kittens separated earliest. They were more randomly active, less able to learn, and more aggressive and fearful than kittens of the other two groups. Seitz, in fact, concluded that his findings correspond with a basic principle of development in embryology, namely, that the earlier some traumatic event occurs in organismic development, the more structures are affected by that event. This conclusion is in line with the model illustrated by Figure 4–1a, but again it must be noted that further experiments, removing kittens from their mothers at different times during the first two weeks, might demonstrate the existence of a critical period as in Figure 4-1b.

The analogy which Seitz made between behavior traits and structures is, of course, a matter of speculation. Gross learning ability, for example, may be made up of a number of components, each of which has a different rate of maturation. Furthermore, it is always difficult to know exactly when a function or structure commences to develop. A substrate of some kind may be in evidence well before the actual structure itself becomes clearly defined. Thus a trauma occurring at what might seem to be the onset of development may actually be occurring at a critical period well after development has started. In the prenatal phase of development much of the work on the experimental production of congenital defects, rather than supporting the notion that the earlier a traumatic event occurs the greater the effect, suggests that there are critical periods in the embryological development of different structures. During such periods the effects of many different agents are maximal (Kalter and Warkany, 1959). The studies of Clark Fraser on the etiology of cleft palate are a good case in point (Fraser, Walker, and Trasler, 1957). Incidence of cleft palate in mice appears to be greatest when mothers are subjected to cortisone treatment starting around the 10th day of the 21-day gestation period. The latter half of the second trimester (days 10-14) is critical for normal palate formation insofar as this is a time of movement of the right and left palatine shelves from a vertical plane on either side of the tongue to a horizontal plane over the tongue followed by fusion. The delicate interaction of a number of forces that contribute to this effect can be upset by various extraneous agents such as cortisone, with the result that the palate does not close, but remains cleft. It should be emphasized, of course, that such a critical period is critical only in a statistical sense. Abnormality may be produced in a lower incidence of cases not only before palate formation but also after it is complete. The latter fact is of particular interest since it indicates that degenerative or regressive changes can occur for this structure.

This work suggests, if we can analogize from embryology to psychology, that a critical period model of some kind (as in Fig. 4-1b) is most feasible in describing the relation of age and size of effect produced. The evidence presented above that the earliest treatment is maximally effective may appear to support Figure 4—1b only because the experiments were not designed to investigate the relationship between treatment and effect at ages within the early stage. Whether one or several critical periods exist in respect to some trait or function will presumably depend on the complexity of that function. However, a good deal of exacting empirical work of the kind Hess has done with imprinting will be necessary before any definitive answers can be given to this problem.

Although there is as yet no good experimental evidence for it, the hypothesis diagrammed in Figure 4—1c exists as a logical possibility. This hypothesis states that the same treatment may have one effect at an early age and an opposite effect at a later age. As the human child matures certain kinds of stimulation which have beneficial effects when administered in infancy might be expected to have quite different and even opposite effects at older ages. Except for Schaefer's (1957) finding that rats handled only during the third week were somewhat more emotional while rats handled during the first week of life were less emotional than nonhandled animals, this hypothesis has not been verified experimentally.

Genotype. A second variable of major importance in determining the action of environment on the organism is the genetic constitution of the latter (see Fuller and Thompson, 1960). Not a great deal has been done along these lines as yet, but we may mention a few interesting studies. Cooper and Zubek (1958) have studied the effect of enriched and restricted environments on the McGill bright and dull strains. These rats were bred selectively (genotypically and phenotypically) on the basis of performance on the Hebb-Williams maze (Thompson, 1954). During selection, they were raised under normal laboratory conditions. Cooper and Zubek found, however, that the differences between them were eliminated by rearing them either in a restricted or an enriched environment. Thus dulls profited much more than brights by additional early stimulation, but brights were affected much more than dulls by lack of it. This finding is supported by another study done in the same laboratory on the effects of glutamic acid given in early life to animals of the same strains (Hughes and Zubek, 1956, 1957). It was found that the maze performance of dulls improved greatly as a result of glutamic acid while that of brights was hardly affected at all. It seems quite clear that adding or reducing stimulation early in life will have differential effects according to the genotype of the animal involved. Ginsburg (1960) has reported that adult aggressivity and emotionality of the C57BL/10 mouse strain is differentially affected by each of three different handling procedures in infancy, while two other mouse strains included in his study were hardly affected at all.

It is well known that genotypic effects occur in the prenatal phase of development. Thus in Fraser's experiments to which we have already referred, incidence of cleft palate in the young was far higher in one inbred mouse strain (A/Jax) than another (C57BL) (Fraser, Fainstat, and Kalter, 1953). The same has been found to apply in the effects of many different teratogenic agents (Kalter and Warkany, 1959).

Past History. As in any behavioral work, here also the past history of the organism is a variable that should always be considered. Provided the organism is old enough to have a history, it will respond to stimulation in terms of its past experience. This point is an obvious one and we present it here more by way of striking a cautionary note than of suggesting a fruitful line for empirical work. At the same time, the relation of the organism's past to its present behavior represents a very basic theoretical issue to which we will return shortly.

Response Variables

It will perhaps be clear from the studies discussed above that a great variety of response systems may be affected by alterations in level of early stimulation. Stimulation by means of environmental changes, by gross stimulation, or by the use of drugs can have an enduring effect on emotionality, motivation, intelligence or learning ability, and social behavior (Thompson, 1955, 1958, 1960). In addition to, and perhaps underlying, such behavioral changes are alterations at the physiological level. Changes in adrenal weight (Weininger, 1956; Levine, 1957), in metabolic rate (Ruegamer, Bernstein, and Benjamin, 1954), in adrenal ascorbic acid depletion following stress (Levine, Alpert, and Lewis, 1958), and even in brain cholinesterase activity (Krech, Rosenzweig, and Bennett, 1960) have been produced by early environmental changes. Furthermore, the extent of change possible through manipulating stimulation is as striking as that produced by manipulation of genotype, at least in respect to one trait—intelligence. This fact is illustrated by the data in Table 4–2. Restriction of early environment can increase error scores on the Hebb-Williams maze about as much as selective breeding for poor performance on this maze. Consequently, it is futile to argue as to the relative importance of nature and nurture. Either can be maximally important, depending on the nature of the population being studied.

TABLE 4–2.   **Comparison of Genotypic and Early Environmental Effects on Rat Intelligence***

	Error Score on Hebb-Williams Maze
Hereditary dull........................	279.5
Environmentally restricted..............	238.2†
Hereditary bright......................	142.8
Environmentally enriched...............	137.3†

*From Thompson (1954). Reprinted by permission.
†Scores based on data of Forgays and Forgays (1952) and Hymovitch (1952).

One final point is worth making in regard to response variables in early experience studies. We have already suggested earlier that when we speak of the *importance* of effects produced by early environmental stimulation, we may refer not only to the magnitude of change (for example, a gain of 10 IQ points) but also the potential reversibility of this change through special treatment or training in later life (see Chapter 3). We may also add two other criteria of importance, both worth closer investigation: the duration of the effect (age to which some difference persists) and the generality of the effect (number of response systems affected). Little is known about the persistence of the effects of early experience though a good deal of evidence does suggest that many of the changes by manipulation of early environment are relatively long-lasting. Hunt and Otis (1955), for example, demonstrated differences in timidity and emotionality in early handled and nonhandled rats when tested for the first time at 339 days of age, quite late for the rat. While we also lack information for the generality of effect, some twin studies (Blewett, 1954; Thurstone, Thurstone, and Strandskov, 1953) indicate that some components or factors of measured intelligence are more easily changed by environment than others. That is to say, concordance is more marked for certain factors than for others. In this case, the problem of generality of effect becomes a problem of differential susceptibility of different traits to environmental influences. This problem in turn will depend on the relation of different traits to each other at different ages. If component abilities or traits differentiate out from the same original source, then some environmental influence affecting this source trait should affect all components that later differentiate out of it. On the other hand, if the traits develop quite separately, we may expect different ones to be affected to a different degree. There are a number of such interesting possibilities that present themselves in connection with the generality criterion of environment-produced response changes.

Another factor determining the generality of the effect of a particular kind of early stimulation is the way in which such an effect interacts with other behavior patterns. Early handling in the rat has been shown to affect maze learning (Bernstein, 1952), conditioned avoidance learning (Levine, Chevalier, and Korchin, 1956; Denenberg and Karas, 1959), weight gain and survival of food and water deprivation (Weininger, 1956; Levine, 1957; Levine and Otis, 1958; Denenberg and Karas, 1959), timidity and emotionality (Hunt and Otis, 1955; Schaefer, 1957). Most authors attribute these diverse effects to an underlying difference in emotional reactivity to novel or stressful situations. Thus an early environmental stimulation which affects some basic behavior or response characteristic can be expected to have a broad generality of effect. Another example of this kind of generality is the phenomenon of imprinting in birds discussed earlier. The early experience in this case determines the object to which the organism will direct all later social and sexual responses and from which it will learn many behavior patterns which may not be typical of its species (E. H. Hess, 1959).

We have discussed in broad outline the main dimensions relating to the effects of early environmental stimulation on later behavior. It remains now to pull together some of the above theoretical suggestions into a more coherent summary form.

THEORY

Perhaps the most basic question that presents itself here is simply this: why are early environmental influences so important? We assume now that they are, in fact, more important than equivalent influences occurring later in life, but the answer to this question is by no means obvious. Let us look at a number of possibilities.

Behavioral Variables

Primacy. The most immediate possibility lies in the fact that early influences occur prior to later influences. Thus an event occurring at maturity has an effect that depends on the state of the organism as already conditioned by events which occurred earlier in life. By this hypothesis, we do not need to assume that the organism has different properties in early life, but merely that any changes that occur then endure for some time and influence behavior in later situations. Early handling could be more important than later handling in the sense that it would influence the effects of a greater number of subsequent events than would late handling. We may contrast with this simple hypothesis several other possibilities, all of which involve the attribution of special properties to the young as opposed to the older organism.

Plasticity. It is fairly common to speak of the young organism as being especially plastic or easily changeable in contrast with the older animal. Although this certainly appeals to general observation and to common sense, it is not a proposition that has been definitely verified by careful experiment. The exact meaning of the term "plastic" is vague. In its broadest sense it simply means changeable. Thus it is likely that some function which is in process of developing is more amenable to change than the same function after it has matured. For example, it is relatively easy to change weight and height at an early age by manipulating hormonal and dietary factors, but it is much more difficult to alter them once the organism has grown up. We should note, however, that although plasticity implies ease of producing changes, it does not necessarily mean ease of producing *permanent* changes. In fact, it is possible that great plasticity may mean greater impermanence of those changes which do occur. Thus the organism might be most definitely influenced (in terms of extent or permanence of changes) at some period of life characterized by only moderate plasticity. This is, of course, an argument in favor of a critical period hypothesis.

Differentiation. Another characteristic often imputed to young organisms is lack of differentiation. It has thus been suggested that in the normal sequence of development, mass action precedes finely differentiated, coordinated activity. Again, this hypothesis is debatable (Carmichael, 1946), but assuming it to be true in some sense, one can argue that events occurring in the early life of an organism will have a more widespread effect than they will later in life. For example, harsh treatment of a 10-month-old child by its father may cause the child to develop a general anxiety to all males or perhaps all human beings. The same treatment of a 10-year-old, on the other hand, might result in anxiety directed only to that particular father. While apparently plausible, this general idea has not been specifically tested. It would perhaps be not too difficult to do so, and any information obtained would certainly contribute greatly to our understanding of the process of development.

Critical Periods in Development. At the beginning of this chapter, we cited Hebb and Lorenz for two theoretical orientations which have guided and instigated much of the work on the effects of early environment on behavior. One of the more striking differences between Hebb's theory of development (1949) and that of Lorenz (1937, 1950) is the way in which the early stages of life may be crucial in determining later behavior. For Hebb the young organism is poorly developed and relatively undifferentiated. Environmental stimulation is necessary for completing development. Both physiologically and behaviorally, differentiation depends on a gradual process of frequent and constant stimulation.

Lorenz conceives of a more fully developed, fairly complete, young organism ready to interact with a normal environment in ways that are characteristic of its species. For Lorenz, the effects of early stimulation must be viewed in terms of the normal stimulus situations for a given organism in the ecological niche in which its species has developed through evolution. Given a normal environment, development proceeds normally, but abnormal stimulation, whether increased or decreased, results in abnormal behavior. Thus demonstrations of the effects of enriched environment on laboratory rats serve only to demonstrate how abnormal is the behavior of normal laboratory rats due to living in an environment which is unnatural for the rat. For Lorenz, the investigation of the effects of early stimulation is important because it permits the study of normal development by producing aberrations in it. The intimate relationship between stimulation and normal behavioral development is analogous to the delicate relationship between the intrauterine environment and normal physical development of the embryo. As in embryological development, behavioral development is characterized by critical periods during which crucial maturational processes can be adversely affected by a wide range of abnormal stimuli. Imprinting, with its very sharp critical period and its almost infinite range of adequate stimuli, is good evidence for this view.

The critical period has been a very fruitful concept in understanding developmental processes in the embryo. Early research in morphological development was characterized by attempts to understand the underlying mechanisms in terms of the kinds of stimuli which could be demonstrated to result in some particular abnormality. It was only after a long, confusing list of stimuli had been shown to be effective in producing similar abnormalities that embryologists began to realize that the time of application was as important as the kind of stimulus. It is conceivable that similar critical periods exist in behavioral development during which a wide range of stimuli are effective in altering development. Experimental analysis of the exact relationship between the effectiveness of stimulation and the age of the organism would then contribute to our knowledge of developmental processes as well as the effects of stimulation on behavior.

The above dimensions—primacy, plasticity, differentiation, and critical periods in development—probably represent the most crucial characteristics of the young organism. It will be noted that examination of them suggests several properties of response change in addition to those we considered earlier. Thus the global term "importance" as applied to early environmental influences must be judged in terms of a number of response variables as follows: (a) extent of change in a particular function; (b) the potential reversibility of the change; (c) the permanence or duration of the change, especially in relation to the initial amount of change occurring; (d) the generality of the change, that is, the number of functions affected. In thinking about early environmental influences, all of these should be given some consideration. In a general way, these indices resemble Hull's (1949) measures of response strength, though they include more than his, and are, perhaps, more useful in the present context. However, it remains to be seen whether the work in the area of early environmental influences can achieve the degree of precision implied by the use of such measures.

The final point we wish to make relates to the physiological aspects of early stimulation.

Physiological Variables

Earlier, we defined stimulation in terms of physical energy impinging on the sensory receptors. We also indicated that such stimulation could be described in terms of gross amount, that is, quantitatively, and also in terms of the meaning it has for the organism, that is, qualitatively. We further suggested that these two aspects of stimulation may have different degrees of importance for development, depending on the age and constitution of the organism involved. Thus the handling received by a one-week-old rat has probably little meaning for the animal. On the other hand, the caress given by a human mother to a 10-year-old child probably has a great deal of meaning, in addition to any stimulating effects it may have. As one of the authors has already pointed out (Thompson, 1958), this duality at the behavioral level may have a counterpart at the neurological level. It is now a well-established fact that there are two main sensory pathways. One is highly organized in the sense that a pattern of stimulation on the receptor is transmitted in a point-to-point manner to the thalamus and thence to a relatively well-defined cortical projection area. Somehow, this pathway must furnish a basis for what we know as meaning. It must have cue value. The second pathway, in which there has been a growing interest in recent years, is the so-called generalized activating system. This path, starting in the brain stem reticular formation, transmits impulses from sensory receptors up to the midthalamus, from which point they are projected to all parts of the cortex. This system is diffuse, massive, and unorganized. It is associated behaviorally with vigilance or arousal, in the sense that stimulation of it may produce marked variations in the attention level and alertness of the animal (Lindsley, 1951; Hebb, 1955; Jasper, 1952, 1958).

Hebb (1955) has speculated that these two pathways together form the neurological basis of drive or motivation. The specific projection system is responsible for the organization of behavior; the generalized activating system, for the arousal or general drive level. One of the present writers (Thompson, 1958) has further suggested that this division has a useful application to the problem of development. Thus, as we indicated earlier, it is likely that the effects of stimulation on the very young animal (or late fetus) occur mainly by virtue of the arousal function produced by such stimulation, this arousal being mediated by the generalized activating system. Later in life, when the animal can perceive the world in an organized and meaningful way, stimulation has effects mainly via the specific projection system. Thus the mother, in terms of stimulation, may be important to the infant in the first few weeks of life because the handling she supplies keeps him aroused and alert through the generalized activating system. This alertness allows opportunity for neural organizations to be built up via the specific sensory pathways. She is important later on, however, mainly as an aid in organizing the child's experience. In this capacity, she guides his behavior by rewards and punishments, provides cues for his behavior, serves as a model for him, and generally gives a focus to his view of the world.

Thus, in a sense, the problem of development is one with the problem of motivation. Efficient behavior in the adult involves a moderate degree of arousal and an organized pattern of behavior. Efficient development occurs by virtue of the same two factors, though their relative importance varies according to the age of the individual. In respect both to motivation and development, the duality at the behavorial level is probably reflected in a duality at the neuro-physiological level. Explications of this theoretical parallel should be worth exploring empirically.

Finally, with respect to these physiological aspects of early stimu-lation, we must remember that stimuli from the environment may act directly on the organism or parts of the organism without being mediated by the nervous system. Thus the amount of light, heat, sound, or mechanical energy impinging on the young organism may influence development by altering the speed or direction of an on-going biochemical process which is involved in structural or func-tional development. As psychologists, we tend to conceive of stimu-lation in terms of sensory stimulation which triggers impulses into the nervous system, but there is evidence that stimulation can have an effect on behavior in the absence of adequate neurosensory mech-anisms. Totally blind, enucleated migratory birds, for example, may still exhibit the typical increased hormonal activity leading to mi-gration in response to changes in the day-night cycle. Experiments by Benoit and Ott (1944) indicate that this behavioral response depends on the intensity and periodicity of light which penetrates the skull and directly stimulates the anterior pituitary and centers in the hypo-thalamus with consequent changes in hormonal and activity levels.

In summary, we may say that the whole area of research on stimu-lation in early development is a very basic one in which there has been a growing interest in recent years. It is our hope that the at-tempt we have made to specify the relevant dimensions involved will be of some value in guiding future experimentation.

Chapter 5

Effects of Monotonous and Restricted Stimulation

DONALD W. FISKE
University of Chicago

WORLD WAR II called attention vividly to the problem of maintaining performance under monotonous, regular stimulation, such as that experienced in prolonged watching of a radar screen. The Korean War evoked an interest in the process of "brainwashing" and led to studies of the effects of marked reductions in the intensities and variety of stimulation. The two problems, the one prosaic and the other exotic, have some features in common.

The last two chapters have reported effects found in developing organisms after extended periods of reduced stimulation. The subjects in those chapters were young animals, and the periods of reduced stimulation were in the order of weeks or months during the development of the animals. In the present chapter, the experimental periods are from minutes to a few days and the subjects are mature human beings; perhaps for these reasons, the effects are reversible, as far as we know today.

The topics of the two sections of this chapter are defined by the experimental conditions. The first section will consider the effects associated with prolonged tasks involving monotonous conditions: the subject is instructed to make a certain kind of response to each of the successive stimuli, or signals, and to keep at it throughout the period of one half hour to several hours; the tasks are typically realistic. The second section will examine studies with the following conditions: the subject is placed in a situation in which external stimulation is reduced to a bare minimum; he is instructed to stay within a small space and may be told to move as little as possible; while he is not required to respond to specific stimuli, he may be asked to report his thoughts and feelings as they occur. While these conditions are also monotonous, their distinctive feature is the restriction of stimulation.

Two aspects are common to these topics. Essentially no new external stimulation is experienced during a session—after the first few minutes, any subsequent stimuli are highly similar to, if not identical with, stimuli which have occurred before. Moreover, the experimental sessions last a substantial period of time so that negative affect is commonly experienced by the subjects. Taken together, these features make the situations stressful to at least a small degree. However, these are not stress experiments in the more usual sense of the term; because the external stimuli experienced by the subjects are not noxious, intense, or fear-inducing, any stress effects come from internal stimulation (including the reactions of the subject) and thus are indirect. No attempt will be made to include research concerned with the effects of directly stressful stimuli, or the psychological and physiological effects of prolonged exposure to such stimuli.

The main differences between studies of monotonous conditions and those of restricted stimulation stem from the dependent variables which must be used. Experiments using monotonous conditions concentrate on measures of performance, of adequacy of response to the stimuli which are successively presented during the experimental condition. Since these test stimuli are highly homogeneous, their presentation provides alternating stimulation but no novelty. In contrast, the operations for measuring the effects of restricted stimulation typically consist of measures of perception and ability which are applied before and after the experimental condition. In some instances, tests are administered during the experiment and constitute an interruption or modification of the experimental condition. Also used are data from self-report both during the experimental condition and immediately afterwards, with some of the most striking effects being observed only in these materials.

Another difference should also be noted. The first set of conditions provides the subject with a task to perform, a task requiring overt responses. The second experimental situation includes no task necessitating coping or instrumental responses but only passive objectives: trying to endure the situation as long as possible and not violating the experimental prohibitions.

MONOTONOUS CONDITIONS

What are the factors associated with quality of performance on a continuous, repetitive task at various points over an extended period of time? In this area, the adequacy of performance refers to the subject's success in responding appropriately to each presentation of the signal. The measure most commonly used is the proportion of such signals to which the subject makes the designated response. Since the occurrence of such responses in the absence of a signal is rare, it is of less interest. We are applying the label "monotonous conditions" because there is no change in the nature of the task or in the nature of the test stimuli and the background stimulation. The main focus of this section will be on change or decrement of performance: how does subsequent performance compare with initial performance? Since the tasks are usually simple ones, acquisition of skill is not a factor. Hence any change in level of performance is typically downward. While we shall be primarily concerned with identifying factors associated with decrement of performance, we shall also consider factors related to level of performance, factors operating at both the initial and later stages of prolonged tasks. More specifically, the tasks used in vigilance experiments are all within the potential capacity of any subject. While a subject is able, in principle, to detect each and every signal, he does not do so even in the first minute or two. The factors accounting for this initial discrepancy between actual and potential performance can be assumed to operate throughout the extended task. It may be that decrement in performance over time can be interpreted largely in terms of the increasing potency of such factors.

Historically, the major problem in this area has been seen as that of maintaining attention and avoiding distraction. In the last decade, under the influence of practical, military considerations and at the suggestion of Mackworth (1950), Head's concept of vigilance has been invoked to identify the topic. Specifically, the performance involved is that of responding rapidly to a signal, the intensity of the signal being typically well above threshold. A related problem is the maintenance of output over a period of time, as in factory assembly work and other industrial situations. This topic will not be reviewed in this paper because there has been less systematic experimental investigation of the problem. In addition, it seems probable that the same factors are associated with level and decrement of performance in both types of tasks: in most human activities, the effects of prolonged work are more psychological than physiological; while performance may decline, the potential capacity to perform can be shown to be essentially unaffected by the continued work.

Although some of the studies in the late 1920s and in the '30s were theory-oriented, much of the work has been directed at applied aspects of the subject. The studies of endurance, of capacity to maintain heavy physical activity, will not concern us here. We shall also not attempt to include the work on fatigue, a vague and subjective concept. (This topic has been reviewed by Bartley and Chute, 1947, and by Bartley, 1957.)

We shall consider and interpret the major studies in this area without attempting complete coverage. The great majority of the literature has been reviewed by Broadbent (1958, especially Chapter 6), Mc-Grath, Harabedian, and Buckner (1959), and Wheaton (1959).

Experiments on vigilance have used a variety of tasks. A classical instrument is the Clock Test of Mackworth (1950), in which the hand or pointer moved once a second over the plain background, one hundred movements being required to complete the full circle. From time to time, the pointer would make a movement twice as long as the standard, the subject's task being to press a response key when this happened. A more complex task is the Twenty Dials Test used by Broadbent (1954) in which the subject is required to turn a knob under a dial as soon as its pointer went beyond a critical point. Less common are mockups such as the Cambridge Cockpit (Bartlett, 1950).

In studies of vigilance, the usual dependent variable is number or proportion of signals detected. Other measures have been examined, such as number of false detections of signal and speed of response. The type of error may also be important in complex procedures such as the Cambridge Cockpit. In the older research on sustained work, the measures included rate of work (amount done per unit of time) and accuracy.

A decline in performance over time has been observed under many but not under all conditions. When such a decline is observed, it typically occurs within 30 minutes but may not be significant until the second or third half-hour period. However, there is evidence that the decline may start within the first few minutes. Ditchburn (unpublished paper cited by Mackworth, 1950) found an increase in reaction time within a few minutes. A lengthened reaction time within a two-minute trial was reported by Singleton (1953). Jerison (1958) has shown that when a decline in performance occurs on the Clock Test, it begins in the first few presentations of the signal.

Because the problem of vigilance has important applied aspects, most of the experimental reports have emphasized measures of performance. The subjective experiences associated with monotonous conditions have received little attention, perhaps because they are difficult to assess objectively. However, we shall see later that these side effects are highly relevant to the interpretation of both decrement in performance and the absence of such decrement. Thus, in addition to decreased output during a 90-minute period on a repetitive task, Barmack (1937) reports boredom, unpleasantness, inattentiveness, fatigue, irritability, daydreaming, increased attention to hunger and aches and pains, and often restlessness. One or more of the items in this catalogue is usually noted, at least in passing, by other authors.

The diversity of these reactions deserves emphasis. Not only is there a shifting of attention away from the task to such internal products of central nervous processes as daydreams and to such interoceptive stimuli as aches and pains, but there are also lethargic feelings and overt reactions of irritability and restlessness. One or another of these somewhat opposed forms of reaction may predominate in a given subject: Davis (1948, as noted by Scott, 1954) found boredom and tiredness characterized an "inert" group while excessive responses occurred in an "over-reactive" group. It would appear, however, that any one subject can show combinations of these several reactions, at least during different stages in the extended time period.

One indirect measure of subjective state has been studied: time estimation. Time judgments appear to grow longer with repetition and continuation of a task (Jerison, Crannell, and Pownall, 1957; Jerison and Arginteanu, 1958). An important hint is provided by Loehlin (1959), who found that time estimates were longer not only when the activity was boring but also when the subject was passive.

In this paper, we are taking the position that any decrement in performance associated with continued work under monotonous conditions is not primarily a function of reduced capacity. Whether sensory acuity declines as a function of time in such conditions cannot be established on the basis of available evidence (see McGrath *et al.*, 1959, pp. 46-49). As we shall see later, recovery of performance can be achieved by a variety of factors which appear irrelevant to capacity itself. When test periods come at intervals during an extended experimental period, "The subject can muster his resources for a test period quite well, as other studies have shown, but he may 'coast' between the test periods unless he is monitored continuously" (Kennedy, 1953). A similar observation has been made by Halstead 1947, pp. 115-116) on anoxic subjects: they can make a short-lasting effort so that little impairment is found on definite, fairly straightforward tasks, even though there is evidence of cognitive and motivational deterioration. On the basis of the available and future evidence, it may turn out that our assertion should be modified as follows: any temporal decrement in performance associated with extended exposure to monotonous conditions can be recovered readily, the speed of recovery being primarily a function of the type of task.

Factors Associated with Decline in Performance under Continued Monotonous Conditions

Characteristics of the Task. A decrement in performance over time has repeatedly been observed in studies requiring the subject to perform a single task for extended periods of time. But such a decrement is not always observed. Our objective in this part of the paper is to identify the factors associated with decrement and with maintenance of performance. It is clear that some aspects of the task requirements play a major role. There is first the length of time that the subject has been working up to the point of measurement. As pointed out earlier, a decline may occur within a couple of minutes or may not appear until a half hour or more has elapsed. Hence time itself is not the crucial determinant, but is rather an index of the state of other variables.

Decrement in performance is not a linear function of time, but rather levels off at some point. Jerison (1958) has suggested that the level of the plateau is constant for different experimental conditions with a given task, although the time taken to reach the plateau and the preceding course of the decline may vary.

Rest periods typically lead to partial or complete recovery. After a 40-minute period, McCormack (1958) found that a 5-minute rest produced partial recovery and a 10-minute rest complete recovery of initial reaction time. A gain following a rest period is also reported by Adams (1956). With alternating half-hour periods of watching and resting, Mackworth (1950) was able to demonstrate recovery after the rest period. The reader should recall that vigilance tasks require minimal activity in the response so that the by-products of muscular work are not involved here.

Of central importance are characteristics of the stimulus signal. Performance is more likely to suffer on vigilance tasks when the signal is harder to detect (Fraser, as reported by Broadbent, 1958, p. 111). Duration of signal appears to be a crucial variable. Signals lasting one second have usually been associated with a decrement but Fraser found no decline with a two-second signal. Broadbent (1953b) has interpreted this effect in terms of the momentary blocking that Bills (1931) observed on self-paced repetitive tasks. No decline in mean response time was observed by Broadbent (1958, p. 114) when the signal stayed on until the subject responded, the subject making up for slow responses by responding more rapidly to subsequent stimuli. With a three-second, easily discriminated auditory signal, Webb and Wherry (1960) obtained nearly perfect performance and no decrement, even over nine-hour trials on five successive days.

Other aspects of tasks are the number of different types of response required of the subject and the number of things to be observed. Simply keeping the subject active by requiring responses to negative stimuli as well as to positive did not prevent a decrement in the study by Wittenburg, Ross, and Andrews (1956). It might seem that giving the subject more to attend to would eliminate a temporal decline in performance. While a decrement was found when subjects watched just one clock, Jerison and Wallis (1957) found that when subjects watched three clocks, there was no decrement, at least after the first few minutes. The percentage of signals detected was higher on the one-clock task and never fell as low as the percentage on the three-clock task. But the absence of a decrement cannot be explained by this lower average level of performance on the more complex task which still left room for such a decline. It seems likely that the variety of stimulation provided by the three-clock task helps maintain performance: the subject attempts to attend to all three clocks, and not just focus on one. It must be noted, however, that the level of performance (proportion of signals detected) on the three-clock test was much lower than with one clock. No one has determined whether it is possible for subject to monitor three clocks with perfect detection, at least for a brief period of time.

The evidence seems to show that the complexity or variety in the stimulation is related to maintenance of performance but complexity of discrimination does not prevent a decrement. While Bakan (1959) obtained better over-all performance when his subjects had a secondary task to perform in addition to the primary one, his graphs seem to indicate a decrement both with and without the secondary task. Similarly, Broadbent (1958, p. 114) cites an earlier study by Bakan and one by Kappauf, Payne, and Powe (1955) showing little decrement for a relatively easy task and more for a more difficult one. In each of these three studies, the stimuli were the same: digits presented aurally, one per second.

The contribution of variety is supported by the finding of E. S. Robinson and Bills in 1926 that performance is maintained better with varied than with repetitive tasks. Other aspects of the stimulus materials also help. The connectedness and the comprehensibility of materials were inversely related to performance decrement in Mary Robinson's study (1938). In fact, no decrement was observed with highly comprehensible material.

Motivation. The temporal decrement in performance under monotonous conditions can be reduced or even eliminated by factors affecting the motivation of the subjects. A telephone call in the middle of a test session, urging the subject to do better on the remaining part of the test, was found by Mackworth (1950) to restore performance for nearly half an hour. The effect was presumably motivational, although it might have been produced simply by the brief interruption of the monotony. In contrast, prior instructions to be particularly alert during an indicated portion of the two-hour test period had no effect. The value of even the mere presence of the experimenter was demonstrated by Fraser (Broadbent, 1958, p. 111). Having the experimenter provide verbal feedback after correct and incorrect responses appeared in Mackworth's data (1950) to prevent the usual decrement on the Clock Test. Providing the subject with an objective indicator of speed of response relative to speed of preceding response, McCormack (1959) greatly reduced, but did not eliminate, the lengthening of response time during the course of the trial. Similarly, Baker (1959b) found a significant decrement with no knowledge of results but a smaller, nonsignificant decrement with knowledge and with feedback (repetition of the signal) until the subject responded.

No temporal effects in responses to multiple dials were observed by Loeb and Jeantheau (1958) under a variety of realistic conditions including heat and the noise and vibration from a moving troop carrier. This maintenance of performance may have been helped by the external stimulation of the outdoor situation and also by the financial incentive of a prize for the best performance. The individual quality of the motivation required to prevent decrement is suggested by Mackworth's report (1950) that during World War II, a study of reported submarine contacts as a function of time on radar watch showed a sharp rise at the beginning of the watch, followed by a sharp fall for watches over half an hour. There is a suggestion that subjects adjust their effort to the expected duration of the task. Subjects expecting a long vigil show a decrement more rapidly than subjects expecting a short (half-hour) watch (Jerison, 1958). Just as a person starts a long walk at a pace below his maximum, so subjects appear to adopt a level of vigilance which they anticipate they can maintain throughout the task.

The effects of motivation on maintenance of performance are not a simple matter. In an experiment by Pollack and Knaff (1958), the task was to detect increments in the momentary and periodic deflections of a meter's needle. A decrement over 30 minutes was obtained under each of three conditions: monetary reward; the blast of a truck horn as "punishment" following failures to detect signals; and the instructions to "do your best" which they consider a "neutral" condition. The best over-all performance was obtained with the horn condition; in addition, it produced the shortest latencies of response but also more false detections. The horn also reduced the decrement in performance of the poorest subjects. The horn blasts may well have functioned more as intense, irregular stimuli disrupting the monotony and alerting the subject, rather than as unpleasant stimuli that the subject tried to avoid. Reward was more effective when the subject was in a lighted room with conversation permitted between subjects and with a radio playing than when the subject was alone and in the dark.

While the differences between conditions make difficult any attempted integration of these findings, it is clear that motivation is a factor in level of performance and probably in sustaining performance over time. For our present purposes, we may note the apparently beneficial effects of conditions providing actual or potential extra and varying stimulation: for example, knowledge of one's success on the task and the presence of the experimenter.

Findings on individual differences, which unfortunately are reported in only a few papers, may help our understanding of the effects of motivation. In the Pollack and Knaff study, punishment was more effective for the subjects with poorer performance, although consistent individual differences were observed under all conditions. Greater decrements in poorer subjects are reported by Bakan (1955) and by Kappauf and Powe (1959), the latter also noting larger decrements for subjects with lower scores on a general aptitude test. The addition of an easier, secondary task was demonstrated by Bakan (1959) to counteract the poorer over-all performance of extroverts; his data also contain a hint that the decrement function may vary with extroversion in interaction with the complexity of the task. (Unpublished work in progress by Jerison, Wing, and Kagan suggests that over-all detection performance may be associated with a descriptive cognitive style.)

One intensive study of the individual differences in performance yielded many pertinent findings (Buckner, Harabedian, and McGrath, 1960; McGrath, Harabedian, and Buckner, 1960; McGrath, 1960b). The tasks required detecting changes, either in the loudness of an intermittent sound presented over headphones or in the brightness of an intermittent light. Each subject had 16 watches (test periods) of each type of task during a four-week period. For each task, stable individual differences were found. These differences were larger during the watch than during a two-minute test under alerted conditions given just before and just after the watch. However, performance was relatively specific to the task, the correlation between the two tasks for the watch period being only .24. Subjects performed better on the task they preferred and on the task for which their discriminatory ability was better. In general, a subject did better when he had had more sleep the previous night, when he did not feel tired, and when he had been doing an interesting job just before the watch.

Interviews with the subjects brought out their lack of interest in the tasks and their tendency to pace themselves rather than to attempt to maintain a high level of attention throughout the hour. Many subjects were unsuccessful at one time or another in their efforts to stay awake, even though they resorted to a variety of behaviors irrelevant to the task.

Of particular interest is the difference between the tasks. While the visual problem required visual fixation, the auditory detections did not necessitate the voluntary attention of the subjects and made it possible for some of them to engage in extraneous activities. The finding of more correlates with auditory performance than with visual performance may indicate that the psychological tests were predicting the differences in the amount of such irrelevant activity.

These findings, together with those from the other studies cited above, suggest the hypothesis that performance on a vigilance task is in large part a function of level of activation, which in turn varies with strength and quality of motivation. In addition to group effects from motivating factors, there are effects associated with the motivational state of the particular subject, resulting from the interaction between the conditions of the experimental task and characteristics of the individual.

In this connection, it should be noted that only low levels of motivation have been explored: would performance be essentially perfect and show no decrement if subjects were paid $10 for each signal detected during a two-hour period?

An Overview of Findings on Temporal Decline in Performance. The research considered above suggests that when a decrement in performance occurs for subjects working under relatively unvarying conditions, it takes place during a period of varying length and location in the temporal sequence. It may commence very shortly after the subject begins work and it may be ended after a few minutes or may continue for an hour or more. The decrement itself, its location, and its duration are complexly determined.

Decrements are greater or are more likely to be observed on tasks involving a simple function, where initial performance is at a high level, and on tasks involving disconnected and less comprehensible materials. Decrements tend to be minimized by stimulation extrinsic to the task proper, such as motivating conditions involving the experimenter or information on adequacy of performance. The precise nature of the variables producing a subject-task interaction needs further investigation.

To assist the interpretation of these findings, some factors associated with over-all level of performance under monotonous conditions should be examined. It is obvious that the strength of a signal affects the probability of its being detected: more intense and longer signals yield better performance. Less obvious is the finding that higher signal rates are correlated with higher proportions of detections (Jenkins, 1958; Kappauf and Powe, 1959); higher rate was associated with both higher level and reduced decrement in the study of Deese and Ormond (1953). Performance on a simple primary task may be improved by setting a concurrent secondary task (Bakan, 1959) and by providing stimulation extraneous to the task (McBain, 1959; McFarland, Holway, and Hurvich, 1942).

Taken all together, these studies permit the speculation that for simple, repetitive tasks, such as signal detection, there is probably a set of conditions associated with maximum performance, these conditions including not only characteristics of the signal and its occurrences but also aspects of the total setting which affect the subject's level of functioning. These conditions appear to be related to and to overlap somewhat with those associated with maintenance of performance as opposed to decrement.

Theoretical Interpretations of Temporal Decrement in Performance. Mackworth (1950) has attempted to interpret performance decrement by means of the concept of inhibition. The criticisms of this position that have been offered by Deese (1955), Broadbent (1958), and McGrath *et al.* (1959) make it unnecessary even to outline this viewpoint. (These references should be consulted for more comprehensive discussion of the several theories and the evidence pertaining to each.)

Another suggestion is the expectancy hypothesis which "states that (a) the observer's expectancy or prediction about the search task is determined by the actual course of stimulus events during his previous experience with the task, and (b) the observer's level of expectancy determines his vigilance level and hence his probability of detection" (Deese, 1955, p. 362). This view seems to be better suited to the interpretation of level of performance at a given point in time than of decline in performance over time. It has been supported by Baker (1959a, 1959b.)

An early explanatory concept was that of blocking: in continuous work, very brief lapses begin to occur, becoming more frequent as the task goes on (Bills, 1931). These blocks can be reduced by an increased rate of work (Bills and Shapin, 1936) and they almost disappeared with automatic pauses in the work (Bills, 1935). This concept has been used to account for the failure to find a decrement with unpaced, or rather self-paced tasks, as opposed to tasks where the successive stimulus presentations are independent of the subject's responses. Broadbent began his interpretation of vigilance findings by using this concept: ". . . attention cannot be maintained steadily on one object for a long period: as time goes by it must change its object and may then return to the task" (1953b, p. 299). He notes that discontinuities or changes in stimulation help to reduce decrement in performance by reducing the number of blocks.

From this beginning, Broadbent (1958) developed his filter theory, a conceptualization with implications well beyond behavior under monotonous conditions. Viewed as a single communication channel, a nervous system has limited capacity, so a selective or filter operation is performed on its input. The probability of a certain class of sensory events being selected is a function of the properties of the events and also a function of the state of the organism. For example, intense and relatively novel stimuli are more likely to be selected; in addition, food has a higher probability of selection for a hungry animal.

The interpretation to be proposed here incorporates certain features of the preceding positions into the activation theory developed in Chapter 2. The earliest application of an arousal viewpoint to performance decrement appears to be that of Scott (1954). After a thoughtful review of earlier work, he summarizes his position as follows:

Besides those immediately relevant to a task, a variety of other stimuli appear to be necessary in maintaining adaptive, organized behavior. . . . in organized behavior there is a nice balance and cooperation between the central processes involved in selectivity (among surrounding stimuli), and peripheral processes providing excitation. But these peripheral events do not merely provide cues; they also have a non-specific or general role in maintaining a relationship between organism and environment without which the organism cannot make the best use of those cues. A stimulus achieves its non-specific effect by the variation it introduces into the sensory environment. The data suggest that lasting exposure to a restricted range of stimuli results in habituation to the variations that *do* exist in such an environment . . . . When 'sensory habituation' takes place, stimuli lose their capacity to maintain the neural organization on which alert, organized behavior depends (Scott, 1954, pp. 27-28).

How do the propositions in Chapter 2 relate to the interpretation of performance under monotonous conditions? From Proposition IV, it follows that for a given task used in a vigilance study, there is a range of activation associated with maximum performance. Jerison's analyses (1958) suggest that this activation level is typically present when the subject begins work, although some studies (Broadbent, 1958, p. 118) have noted a small rise during the first few minutes. This activation level is achieved by the impact of the relatively new stimulation in the task situation together with the subject's internal state as a function of instructions and other motivating factors. After the first few minutes, there is no stimulation which has not been experienced recently: both the negative stimuli and the signals become familiar, and so do the kinesthetic and other stimuli associated with the subject's responses. As times goes on, the impact of these several types of stimuli declines gradually, contributing to a decline in the subject's level of activation. As activation sinks below the optimal range for the task, performance will suffer.

Support for this view is found in the work of McFarland, Holway, and Hurvich (1942). Sensitivity to brightness showed a typical curve of decrement, the rate of decline becoming less as the three-hour period continued. When subjects were given a chance to get up and move around every 30 minutes, partial recovery was observed after each break. From subsequent observations, they decided that this benefit was due not to relief of visual fatigue but to the facilitating effect of increased muscular tonus.

Vigilance performance has been shown to be a function of signal rate. With a Skinnerian orientation and experimental procedure, Holland (1958) finds that observing rate is higher at faster signal rates and interprets this result in terms of more detections providing more reinforcements for observing responses. But Jerison and Wing (1961) has recently shown that detection rate, when independently measured, is uncorrelated with observing rate. Higher signal rates can also be viewed as providing more variation in stimulation, both in the display and in the stimulation associated with responding.

Consistent with the latter view is the finding that the presence of stimuli extraneous to the task may enable the subject to maintain his performance. (See also McGrath, 1960b.) More particularly, any stimulation which supports the subject's motivational state may serve this purpose. For example, knowledge of results or the presence of the experimenter is effective. Thus any factors which sustain the total impact of stimulation will sustain activation, and performance will be maintained. Intrinsic features of the task, such as varied or comprehensible material, will serve. Other external stimuli not related to the signal detection itself can be effective. But most important of all are internal stimuli which perpetuate the subject's motivational state. These may stem from cortical phenomena which result from the subject's reaction to promised rewards or from a desire to do well for other reasons, or they may come indirectly from other internal sources of stimulation. Steadily maintained muscular tension may facilitate performance and decrease decrement on some routine tasks (Bills, 1927). A relation between tension level and performance is indicated in studies cited by McGrath *et al.* (1959), who also point out that the negative relationship that others report between performance and muscular activity is not necessarily contradictory: muscular tension may be generally lower in subjects manifesting restless motor activity.

Pertinent evidence is provided by Baker (1959a, 1960). While his subjects maintained their performance on a clock test for the one-hour period, their measured restlessness increased. Moreover, the second study notes a rise in the proportion of time samples in which they were not observing (for example, were blinking or were looking away from the display). These data suggest that the subjects were providing themselves with more stimulation, and with more varied stimulation.

What is the function of the impact-modifying behavior in which such subjects engage? From Proposition V in Chapter 2, one might expect that subjects were attempting to make their level of activation optimal for the vigilance task. This interpretation is unsatisfactory because subjects typically do not know when they miss a signal and therefore are unaware that their performance is below their potential capacity. It seems more likely that the function of any impact-modifying behavior is primarily to sustain activation at the subject's characteristic level of activation (Proposition VII). In principle, it should be possible for subjects to maintain activation through the impact of mental sets or of muscular activity extraneous to but not interfering with the activity required by the task. In practice, the low involvement of the subjects in the task and their interpretation of the restrictions imposed by the experimenter's instructions often result in spontaneous activity which provides impact but also interferes with maximal performance on the task.

While a drop in level of activation will tend to produce a decrement in performance, a sustained activation level does not necessarily maintain performance. A subject's activation might be kept up by his annoyance with the requirements of the task, by his irritation or sense of inadequacy resulting from feeling his performance is poor or declining, or by the contents of irrelevant mental preoccupations; each of these states might well be detrimental to his performance. Thus an appropriate degree of activation is a necessary but not a sufficient condition for sustaining performance.

The interpretation presented above has attempted to account for the group trends found in the experimental literature. In any explanation of these findings, the role of the particular subject's internal state must be considered crucial. As McGrath *et al.* (1959) point out in their critique, large individual differences are typically found in performance on vigilance tasks, the differences increasing as time at the task progresses. Even more significant is the observation that a considerable proportion of subjects (20% to 50%) show no decrement in performance over time. Since it is unreasonable to assume that these subjects are experiencing considerably more impact from the repetitious stimuli in the task situation, we must conclude that their activation level is maintained by impact from their motivational state, impact from cortical processes, or more indirectly from manifestations of arousal in other somatic components, such as muscle tension.

Several of the other interpretations discussed earlier seem to mesh with and even to strengthen our own. Thus the internal representation of an expectancy of a signal may contribute to impact, especially as the strength of the expectancy varies over time. (See Baker, 1959b.) Certainly Broadbent's designation of not-recently-experienced stimuli as one class likely to be selected as a source of information (1958) is congruent with our viewpoint. Deese's position that ". . . the problem of maintaining vigilance under conditions of monotonous search can better be viewed as a problem in maintenance of a background sensory input. . ." (1955, p. 367) is along the same lines as ours but we would feel it is deficient in neglecting the subject's internal state.

RESTRICTED STIMULATION

While experimental work on the effects of restricted stimulation or "sensory deprivation" began less than a decade ago, there is a mass of earlier literature reporting human experiences during imprisonment, arctic exploration, and solitary sailing trips as well as experiences following shipwrecks. Since reviews and bibliographies are available (Lilly, 1956; Solomon, Leiderman, Mendelson, and Wexler, 1957; Wheaton, 1959), these unsystematic observations will be touched on only lightly in this paper. Experimental studies of restricted stimulation are reviewed by Freedman and Greenblatt (1959) and by Wheaton (1959). (See also the symposium on *Sensory deprivation* [Solomon *et al.*, 1961].)

Extended periods of solitary confinement have been reported to have disturbing effects and obviously can disrupt the organization of behavior. While uncertainty and inability to escape play a role, there is also a reduction in the kinds and variety of stimulation. Bizarre experiences also occur in prolonged isolation, with or without objective risk to life. When isolation lasts a number of weeks, it may well disrupt functioning and produce abnormal phenomena. However, isolation for periods of seven days may have no marked effects: experimental studies such as that reported by Steinkamp, Hawkins, Hauty, Burwell, and Ward (1959) suggest that no aberrant behavior may be observed when subjects have tasks to do and know they are being monitored so that no real danger exists.

The individual differences in reactions to isolation and shipwreck merit particular attention. An inner conviction that one will survive appears to characterize survivors (Lilly, 1956; Wheaton, 1959). Following shipwreck, complete passivity (acceptance of the immediate situation?) seems to help. In other situations, it is apparently desirable to establish routines of little tasks, spending a limited time on each.

The literature of clinical medicine offers many instances of symptomatology associated with restrictions of stimulation. In the comprehensive review made by Leiderman, Mendelson, Wexler, and Solomon (1958), a number of conditions are shown to be conducive to disorientation, delusions, or hallucinations. For example, orthopedic cases may develop psychoticlike states following prolonged immobilization. Hallucinations may be found in cases of deafness and cataract. (See Arbit, 1960.) Disturbances in patients with eyes patched for treatment of detached retinas are noted by Ziskind, Jones, Filante, and Goldberg (1960). Outstanding is the consistency of the finding that outside stimulation may eliminate the abnormal phenomena: for example, a word from a nurse in cataract cases with bandaged eyes (Linn, Kahn, Coles, Cohen, Marshall, and Weinstein, 1953), or removal of the eyepatch from the nonoperated eye.

Similar phenomena are noted in cases undergoing treatment in a tank-type respirator (Mendelson and Foley, 1956; Mendelson, Solomon, and Lindemann, 1958). Symptoms appear in two to seven days and last intermittently for 10 to 15 days; the explanation of their termination remains to be worked out. Most of the experiences take place at night or when there is little activity near the patient. As the latter paper notes, restriction of mobility is common to these phenomena and to the conditions in some experiments on restricted stimulation. (Further evidence for the importance of kinesthetic sensations will be brought out later in considering the experimental studies.)

Restriction of Auditory or Visual Stimulation

Following the report of Ramsdell (see Hebb, 1949, pp. 252-253) on the feelings of perplexity, disorientation, and irritability induced by experimental deafness, Hebb, Heath, and Stuart (1954) induced partial deafness in six subjects for three days. While no extreme effects were noted, there were disturbances of motivation and some mild subjective effects.

Visual effects have also been studied. When subjects view a homogeneous colored field, adaptation produces an achromatic field within 3 minutes (Cohen, 1958). Within 20 minutes, hallucinatory shapes may appear (Hochberg, Triebel, and Seaman, 1951) although some subjects may report no imagery in a 40-minute period (Goldberger, 1961). Rosenbaum, Dobie, and Cohen (1959) found that 5 minutes of total or partial visual deprivation led to lower visual recognition thresholds; 15 and 30 minutes of either type of deprivation did not alter thresholds but instead induced emotional states which interfered with visual efficiency. Subjects in Ormiston's experiment (1958) sat in a chair for 30 minutes with translucent goggles, earplugs, and muffs. This sensory deprivation lowered the lower threshold and raised the upper threshold for apparent movement. In the study by Held and White (1959), subjects were exposed to one of four visual patterns for 30 minutes; an increase in perceived visual speed followed exposure to a hyperstable pattern that was differentiated but fixed, while a slight decrease in perceived speed followed total darkness, with somewhat more decrease after a patternless field, and even more after a noisy field with ever-changing random dots.

The abnormal visual phenomena discovered in the classical McGill studies of restricted stimulation (discussed below) have led to still other experiments with less extended or less restricted conditions. Spontaneous imagery like that described in the McGill reports, but even more vivid and real, have been produced by Pinard (as cited by Freedman and Greenblatt, 1959) with subjects simply sitting comfortably, closing their eyes, and looking into their "mind's eye." After 10 minutes of lying on a bed in a semilightproof room and wearing opaque goggles, subjects were encouraged to describe their visual sensations, in the study by Kandel, Myers, and Murphy (1958). Imagery from simple lines to complex, integrated scenes was reported, positive instructions being associated with more reports and with more complex sensations. Prior verbalization on selected Rorschach cards had no effect. A longer experimental period was involved in Doane's dissertation, 1955 (cited by Goldberger and Holt, 1958). Subjects wearing translucent goggles developed "hallucinations" and other visual phenomena as rapidly as isolated subjects for whom stimulation was also restricted in other modalities.

Taken together, these experiments clearly show that restriction of the patterning and of the temporal variation in visual stimulation can rapidly produce changes in visual functioning and in visual experiences. This restriction may lead to temporary reduction of thresholds. Most significant are the reports of visual imagery when external visual stimulation is reduced or eliminated for periods as short as 10 minutes. It remains to be determined whether these phenomena are experienced only when mobility is reduced or are found whenever visual input is curtailed. Perhaps they are the same kind of phenomena as those reported during sleep (see Kamiya, Chapter 6).

In these studies and also in those considered in the next section, there are serious methodological difficulties. Subjects must feel free to report their experiences, however bizarre and pseudopathological they may seem. In addition, there is the question whether subjects should verbalize their experiences as they occur, with the risk that such overt behavior may modify the phenomena. If the reports are delayed until the experiment is terminated, they will be less complete and detailed. Finally, the experimenter is confronted with the task of classifying the reported phenomena as imagery, illusion, hallucination, etc., in a way which will permit meaningful comparisons between subjects. In the published reports of studies in this area, the reader cannot be certain that these categories are used in the same way by different investigators.

General Restriction of Stimulation

In the research limiting the sensory input for several modalities, the number of relevant factors is large; the diversity of the conditions in the several experiments is so great that only a few general findings can be considered to be established. The available literature will first be presented with a minimum of comment. Later on, interpretations will be offered separately.

An analysis of the types of restriction will provide an orientation to the diversity of the studies. Of primary importance is the number of sensory modalities which are appreciably affected. The preceding section considered studies involving a single modality, vision or audition. In the experiments considered below, two or more modalities were restricted. Of particular significance is the limitation of mobility, with consequent reduction in tactual and kinesthetic experience. In the following review, experiments are roughly ordered in terms of increasing degree of restriction of mobility so that the influence of this condition will be highlighted.

Within each modality which is affected by the experimental conditions, several forms of restriction may be distinguished. In most instances, the average intensity is reduced or there is a restriction of stimulation with moderate to high intensity. Thus hearing may be curtailed by ear plugs or a constant white noise may be introduced.

Such conditions also reduce or eliminate the patterning of stimulation. Primarily as a consequence of this decrease in patterning, the meaningfulness of stimuli is reduced or abolished (Rosensweig, 1959; Davis, McCourt, and Solomon, 1960).

To illustrate the variety of conditions that have been used, two studies may be considered. In a preliminary investigation by Myers, Forbes, Arbit, and Hicks (1957), the subjects had earplugs which greatly reduced auditory input but the experimental room was so situated that subjects could hear trucks and airplanes. Wexler, Mendelson, Leiderman, and Solomon (1958) used a very different condition. Their subjects, confined in a tank-type respirator, could see a small area of screen and ceiling. These authors refer to their conditions as "imposed structuring of stimulation."

Finally, all these experiments involved social isolation. In most studies, there were no signals or other communication from the experimenter to the subject. The exceptions included those in which tests were administered during the isolation period. In every case, the subjects were told or could infer that they were being monitored, so that the isolation was never complete and subjects undoubtedly knew they could be released if necessary. Ordinarily, subjects were told that any communication intended for the experimenter would not be answered, except as toilet needs required.

Let us look first at studies in which the subjects had some freedom to move around. In one program (Ruff and Levy, 1959; Levy, Ruff, and Thaler, 1959; Ruff, Levy, and Thaler, 1961), subjects spent up to seven days in a dark and soundproof chamber. While they were free to move, they were requested to restrict the amount of activity.

Tests of intellectual functions, given within half an hour of release, revealed no striking changes. Almost no hallucinations or perceptual distortions were described. However, a loss of the sense of urgency to think was reported and some subjects did find the experience stressful.

Relative improvement of learning performance during sensory deprivation and absence of aftereffects have been observed in the Princeton studies (Vernon and Hoffman, 1956; Vernon and McGill, 1957). Their subjects wore earplugs and gauntlets during their stay in a lightproof and soundproof room; although they were instructed "to make as little noise as possible" in the first study or "to remain as quiet as possible" in the second study, it is clear in the first report that they were permitted to move about in the 4×9-foot cubicle. The tasks involved 12-item adjective lists. While the data on trials required to achieve the criterion of learning favored the experimental group, the differences are not reported as statistically significant in either study. Significant differences favoring the experimental group were found in the second study for overt errors, fluctuation cycles, and efficiency ratio. In the analyses of the later study, the data from five trials during deprivation seem to have been combined. (The testing during the experimental periods provided an interruption in the conditions; such a change may be welcomed by subjects.) While the evidence for significant improvement during deprivation is not conclusive, it is clear that no relative loss was manifested by the experimental subjects either during or after the experience.

No hallucinations were reported by the four subjects in Vernon and Hoffman (1956). These subjects had patterned vision under dim red light for three meal-periods per day. Working on the hypothesis that hallucinations are associated with patternless rather than "blackout" conditions, both visual and auditory, Vernon, McGill, and Schiffman (1958) placed subjects in a dark cubicle, with meals provided there. There is no indication that movement was restricted, except by the size of the cubicle. One group also had toilet facilities there. Another group was taken to a toilet outside the cubicle; for these excursions, the latter group was blindfolded, but some light leaked in. Of the nine in the second group who stayed 72 hours, six reported hallucinations such as flashes of light or geometric shapes, in contrast to the single hallucination reported by one subject remaining in the dark cubicle. Considering their findings together with the McGill reports of extended hallucinations under diffuse light without pattern vision, Vernon *et al.* suggest that with increasing visual stimulation (from none up to but not including pattern vision) the number and complexity of visual hallucinations increase. However, this finding cannot be considered as established. More systematic and standardized procedures for investigating these visual experiences are required. The frequency and complexity of the imagery varies from experiment to experiment; it is hard to reconcile these findings with those cited above for brief periods of visual deprivation.

Effects on perceptual and motor skills were explored in another study from the same group (Vernon, McGill, Gulick, and Candland, 1959, 1961). Although no decrement was shown on some tests (for example, depth perception), performance on some tests (such as color perception) was affected.

In a preliminary study conducted under the supervision of the Human Resources Research Office (Myers, Forbes, Arbit, and Hicks, 1957), the subjects were members of the professional staff. They were requested to keep their head within a box or "cradle" which was designed to reduce auditory stimulation; although they generally refrained from gross activity, they did move about for food and for toilet needs, and some engaged in calisthenics to induce fatigue and facilitate going to sleep. Because of pinpoint light leaks and auditory cues from trucks and airplanes, the subjects were able to gauge time with considerable accuracy during their four-day stay. In their small group of psychologist subjects, no striking changes were noted for intellectual and learning tests, including auditory tests administered during the experimental period. While most subjects reported flashing of lights, no full-blown hallucinations were noted; any colorful or vivid imagery was ascribed by them to daydreams or nightdreams.

Some work with mentally disturbed subjects has used isolation and moderate perceptual restrictions including translucent goggles, cylinders on arms, but no reduction of sound aside from that accompanying the spatial isolation (Azima and Cramer, 1956; Azima and Cramer-Azima, 1957; see also Azima, Vispo, and Azima, 1961). Half of the subjects experienced a depersonalization state with visual, auditory, and gustatory hallucinations of varying degrees of intensity. In another study using psychiatric patients (Gibby, Adams, and Carrera, 1960; Adams, Carrera, Cooper, Gibby, and Tobey, 1960), significant improvement in symptomatology and in intellectual performance was observed following brief partial sensory and social deprivation. The sizable interval between the deprivation and posttesting, together with the absence of a control group, limits any interpretation of these findings. The schizophrenic patients used by Harris (1959) had a half hour of deprivation on one day and a period of up to two hours on a subsequent day. Some of his subjects reported reduction or cessation of their hallucinations during the experimental sessions.

Following up the observations on respirator patients, a Boston group put volunteers in a respirator (Wexler, Mendelson, Leiderman, and Solomon, 1958). Movement and tactual contact were restricted by cylinders on arms and legs. The motor of the respirator was run to furnish repetitive auditory stimulation but the subjects breathed for themselves. Under constant and minimal artificial light, the subjects could see a small area of screen and ceiling. They were instructed to move as little as possible. Only six of 17 stayed the entire experimental period of 36 hours. Judgments of time in tank were in error as much as 50%. Eight of the subjects reported hallucinations, illusions, or pseudosomatic delusions. A subsequent study (Davis, McCourt, and Solomon, 1960) found similar effects even with the introduction of brief changes in the illumination and tachistoscopic presentations of colored Rorschach cards.

The pioneer experimental reports of "sensory deprivation" came from the McGill group (Heron, Bexton, and Hebb, 1953; Bexton, Heron, and Scott, 1954; Heron, Doane, and Scott, 1956; Heron, 1957; Scott, Bexton, Heron, and Doane, 1959; Doane, Mahatoo, Heron, and Scott, 1959). The first papers labeled the condition "decreased variation in the sensory environment." In this work subjects' motility was restricted more than in most of the previously cited investigations. They had their subjects lie on a bed and wear translucent goggles, gloves, and cardboard cuffs. The intensity of auditory stimulation was restricted and a constant hum masked variations in such stimuli. Almost by accident, it was discovered that the first subjects experienced hallucinatory phenomena; when 14 subjects in a second group were asked to report any "visual imagery," all 14 reported dots and lines, a majority experienced more complex patterns, and some saw isolated figures and even integrated scenes. These experiences tended to become more complex and more frequent as the days passed. Perceptual disturbances were also reported on returning to the normal environment.

Significant decrements in performance (as compared to control subjects) were observed on a variety of cognitive tests given immediately after release from the cubicle. Some tests administered by auditory means during the experimental period also showed significant effects. The experimenters note that the relative decline in intellectual performance did not increase with isolation time, perhaps because the motivation of the control group flagged with repetition of the tests. It must be emphasized that the effects, even when statistically significant, were not extreme, and that small or no differences were obtained on some measures.

Several studies have demonstrated effects from experimental periods of eight hours or less. The subjects used by Goldberger and Holt (1958) had cuffs, gloves, and translucent plastic eyecups. External auditory stimulation was minimized by partial soundproofing and a masking noise was provided through earphones. The subjects were instructed to lie on a couch and not to move unless absolutely necessary. They were taken to the toilet on demand and were fed while sitting on the couch. Comparisons of performance before and after the experience revealed a significant number of subjects showing impairment on only one out of seven cognitive measures; however, no control group was used. Many subjective effects were noted, such as unpleasant affect and disturbances in the time sense. They reach the generalization that such experimental conditions tend primarily "to increase the vividness (intensity) and structure of imagery" (Goldberger and Holt, 1958, p. 111), the effects increasing with time in perceptual isolation. In a later study (Holt and Goldberger, 1960), again without a control group, they found no systematic evidence of impairment on complex or on simple long tests.

One early and well-known experiment (Lilly, 1956) used a technique which few others have tried. The subjects were immersed naked in a tank of water. Vision was blacked out by a mask. The subjects could hear their own breathing and faint sounds from the piping.

They could feel the mask and the supports. The subjects were instructed to inhibit all movements as far as possible. Successive stages could be identified in the experiences of the two subjects during the three-hour period. At first, the day's residues are prominent and the subjects are aware of their surroundings and of recent problems; as they gradually relax, they enjoy the feeling of isolation; but gradually tension develops and hidden methods of self-stimulation are found; if all movement is inhibited, the tension may force the subject to leave the tank; attention is focused solely and almost overwhelmingly on any residual stimulus such as the mask; then reveries of a highly personal and emotionally charged nature appear; finally, there may be projection of visual imagery and forms like those in some hypnogogic states. After leaving the tank, the day seems to start over again.

One of Lilly's associates, Shurley (1960), has continued research with this technique, seeking to determine the effects of simultaneous as opposed to retrospective reporting, and of varying temporal and spatial distance between the experimenter and the subject. Mental imagery phenomena have been invariably found. Of particular interest is his description of the postexperimental state: "Most frequently one observed a peculiar, mixed state characterized by calm, clear mental vigilance, coupled with lethargy, muscular relaxation, and a decided disinclination for exercise, but without any sense or sign of fatigue" (1960, p. 543).

Similar conditions were used by Cambareri (1958) except that subjects read reports of "sensory isolation" experiments before entering the tank. Using a separate set of tests to classify his subjects as more or less suggestible, he arrived at the following tentative conclusions: suggestible subjects appear to be able to tolerate sensory isolation longer, produce more hallucinations and fantasies, and are more tolerant of such "regressive" phenomena; less suggestible subjects are more aware of and more defensive about their intellectual control, are more aware of external factors that reinforce reality, and are more likely to perceive the experiment as a stress situation.

In one of the most systematic studies in this area (Freedman and Greenblatt, 1959; Freedman, Grunebaum, and Greenblatt, 1961), three conditions were compared: (a) nonpatterned visual and auditory input plus social isolation; (b) visual deprivation (blackout), nonpatterned auditory input, plus isolation; and (c) isolation alone. In the first condition, subjects wore translucent goggles; in the second, blackout goggles in a darkened room. Under the first two conditions, the subjects wore gloves and cuffs, heard a constant white noise through earphones, but could hear occasional airplanes and slamming of doors. In all three conditions, they lay on a bed for eight hours with instructions not to move about excessively. While isolation alone had no effects, perceptual and cognitive performance on postexperimental tests was affected by the other two conditions, which had in common a homogeneity of the visual field. Significantly more perceptual distortion was found with the diffuse-light than the blacked-out visual field, a finding which parallels that of Vernon *et al.* regarding hallucinations (p. 128). They make the valuable suggestion that some effects can be detected only with particular tests and careful experimental procedures. Visual and auditory imagery was reported by some subjects under the diffuse light condition and by some under the blackout condition. They stress the resemblance between this visual imagery and hypnogogic imagery. They also note the similarity between their findings and those of the McGill group.

Extreme and prolonged conditions characterize the recent study by Zubek, Sansom, and Prysiazniuk (1960). Sixteen subjects spent at least seven days lying on a mattress in a dark and soundproofed chamber. It was determined that the subjects followed the instruction not to vocalize, and it appeared that they also refrained from physical activity in accordance with instructions. No gloves or other manual restrictions were employed. Food and toilet facilities were provided within the room. At approximately 24-hour intervals, the subject was tested in the chamber with the experimenter remaining outside. Some trends but no significant differences from a control group were obtained for rote learning and some conventional intellectual tests. Significant impairment was demonstrated for a test of perceptual ability (cancellation), a test of dexterity, and tests of recall and recognition of nonsense syllables. Some impairment persisted for 24 hours, especially on these latter memory tests. In view of the subjects' reports, the experimenters interpreted the effects as primarily perceptual. Impairment of ability to think normally, to sustain thought on a given topic, was reported by some but not by all subjects. The authors suggest that the elimination of visual and auditory stimulation may have a less disorganizing effect than the low and unvarying illumination and noise used in some of the other studies.

Perceptual tests were also administered to these subjects before and immediately after isolation (Zubek, Pushkar, Sansom, and Gowing, 1961). Although the experimental group did worse than the control group on several tests, the only clearly significant difference was in performance on a modified Mackworth Clock Test. A majority of the subjects tested showed changes in EEG activity and the experimenters suggest that the nature of these changes may be related to amount of individual effect from the experimental conditions. Hallucinatory activity was reported by 11 of the 16 subjects. Postisolation disturbances in motivation, some of which were quite marked, were found for half the group.

Overview of Findings on Restricted Stimulation

We have presented this array of studies in some detail because the area is relatively recent and unfamiliar and because the number of possibly relevant factors is large. It is regrettable that each laboratory seems to have used a set of conditions which is not precisely duplicated in any other place, so far as the reader can tell from the often limited expositions of the conditions and of the actual behavior of the subjects. Also, as in studies of dreams (see Chapter 6), there are serious methodological difficulties, some of which have already been noted. (See Kubzansky and Leiderman, 1961.) One is that imagery and hallucinatory experiences can be known only from the subjects' reports. Again, any testing during the deprivation period obviously changes the immediate conditions; moreover, it has frequently been noted in studies of anoxia, alcohol, and sleep deprivation that human subjects have a remarkable capacity to pull themselves together and to mobilize their resources so that they can perform with little apparent decrement on some tasks for brief periods.

Even though these limitations make it unwise to attempt relating specific effects to specific conditions, it is possible to point out certain effects which have been observed under one or another type of sensory restriction or deprivation. Both clinical and experimental evidence indicates that disturbances of functioning can occur with restriction in a single sensory modality. Thus it is clear that visual imagery is readily and rapidly produced by restricting at least the patterning, both spatial and temporal, of visual input. While such effects should ordinarily not be construed as pathological phenomena, the clinical reports suggest that temporary and reversible personality effects can also occur.

Some experimental work with conditions restricting stimulation in several modalities has revealed no impairment of performance on intellectual tests. Indications of some impairment are found in the studies at Manitoba (Zubek *et al.*, 1960) and McGill (Scott *et al.*, 1959), but even here the effects are of limited degree. The suggestion that such performance may actually improve (Adams *et al.*, 1960) must be checked in more controlled studies, and the finding that rote learning is more efficient after 24 and 48 hours of deprivation (Vernon *et al.*, 1956, 1957) calls for replication, especially with the permitted extent of the subjects' physical movement being varied. By systematic exploration of the manifold range of aptitudes, it may be found that some functions decline and some actually improve after a period of deprivation.

Less is known about the effects on objective tests of perceptual functions. The most intensive study (Freedman and Greenblatt, 1959) showed trends but few reliable differences, the most striking being in perceived distortions in simple forms. Other studies also suggest impairment. In this area also, further work and procedural ingenuity are needed to delineate more precisely what, if any, effects are produced.

In contrast with the limited influence of restricted stimulation on objective tests are the striking reports of subjective experiences under this experimental condition. Most subjects find the situation unpleasant. While a few subjects may enjoy it (for example, Scott, 1954; Freedman and Greenblatt, 1959) and while the experience may not be unpleasant in some early stages (Lilly, 1956), the typical subject clearly dislikes it and would not wish to undergo it again. Furthermore, in many of the experiments (for example, Wexler *et al.*, 1958; Goldberger and Holt, 1958), some subjects have asked to be released, often within the first few hours. (The reported rise in secretion of epinephrine and norepinephrine provides further evidence that the experience is generally stressful [Mendelson, Kubzansky, Leiderman, Wexler, and DuToit, 1960].)

We have encountered only one exception (Zubek *et al.*, 1960) to the report that after the first few hours, the subjects find that they cannot sustain their attention on a problem or topic, and cannot maintain logical thought. Hebb (1958b) observed in the McGill subjects a lack of energy to work on tests. Also noted is a loss of the desire to think. Related to this point is the observation that the imagery and other unusual phenomena experienced during deprivation are for the most part beyond the subject's control: he cannot produce or eliminate them.

While the reports of vivid imagery, illusions, and hallucinations are the most striking finding from these studies, these reports occur only in a few experiments, and not in all subjects in any single study. This topic presents difficult methodological problems. Not only are the terms used differently by the various experimenters but there is also the matter of obtaining adequate reports from subjects. There is the question whether it is better to have the subject report them as they occur or to obtain the reports hours afterward, at the end of the confinement period. Finally, it is apparent that the experimenter must know what the phenomena are like and should encourage the subject not to withhold such reports (see Kandel *et al.*, 1958). The range of time of onset for a given type of phenomenon, as reported in different experiments, appears to be great: for example, from a couple of hours or less, to three days. Such differences probably stem from variations in general conditions, in instructions to subjects and procedure for reporting, and also in the classifications used by the several experimenters.

While few studies have obtained reports from subjects for the period following isolation and deprivation, it appears that any perceptual or cognitive effects are readily dissipated but that disturbances of concentration and motivation may last for several hours if not longer. Bexton *et al.* (1954) found that some subjects experienced feelings of confusion and minor physical symptoms such as fatigue for as much as 24 hours afterwards.

Individual Differences in Effects. We have already noted that some subjects may like the deprivation experience while others cannot endure it for more than a couple of hours. Holt and Goldberger (1959, 1961; Goldberger, 1958) have carried out two studies, using students in one and unemployed actors in the other. In each study, they identified one adaptive syndrome and one maladaptive syndrome on the basis of the subjects' reactions to the experiment. The common variables in the two adaptive syndromes (one from each study) were: unimpaired secondary process thinking, controlled and accepted primary process, imagery, self-stimulation, and exploration. In the maladaptive syndromes, only unpleasant affect and quitting or preoccupation with terminating the experiment were common. The two adaptive syndromes had somewhat different patterns of intercorrelations with a large number of variables derived from a separate personality assessment. But in each experiment, this syndrome had a substantial positive correlation with Barron Ego-Strength and a large negative correlation with MMPI Hypochondriasis. Dissimilar patterns of intercorrelations were also found for the two maladaptive syndromes. Holt and Goldberger appropriately conclude that individual reactions to restricted stimulation show different personality correlates in different populations.

The ability to endure sensory restriction may be a function not only of adaptive capacity but also of the intensity of the effects for a given subject. The independence of these factors is suggested by the finding of no relationship between estimated ego-integrity and relative extent of imagery and other effects (Grunebaum, Freedman, and Greenblatt, 1960). These effects may be less disturbing, less stressful, for subjects with relevant previous experience; Freedman and Greenblatt (1959) offer a preliminary finding that a disposition toward hypnogogic imagery is associated with reports of imagery in their deprivation subjects.

Wexler *et al.* (1958) found some variables that correlated with length of stay in the respirator. Relative error in estimating time in the respirator and number of somatic complaints showed a negative relationship, as did the need for Exhibition as measured by the Edwards Personal Preference Schedule. Positive associations (significant at or near the .10 level) were obtained for the needs for Affiliation, Succorance, and Nurturance. Subjects with less tolerance for the deprivation showed greater effects of sensory satiation, in terms of loss of apparent size of a test object after three or five minutes of stimulation (Petrie, Collins, and Solomon, 1958). As noted earlier, Cambareri (1958) came to the tentative conclusion that suggestible subjects are more tolerant of deprivation.

From these various discrete findings and from other reports (for example, Solomon *et al.*, 1961, Chapters 6, 7, 8) no definite conclusion can be considered established. It is clear, however, that some subjects are more able to tolerate severe restriction of external stimulation. Perhaps their neurophysiological functioning is less disrupted in the relative absence of sensory input from external sources. Perhaps their psychological integration is less dependent upon normal contact with the external world so that they can adapt to the abnormal experimental conditions without experiencing anxiety. Perhaps they are also less disturbed by the imagery, fantasy, and similar subjective phenomena which are experienced as being beyond voluntary control. (See the interpretation in terms of ability to handle the primary process, offered by Holt and Goldberger, 1959.)

Interpretations.   In the various experiments presented above, seven days of social isolation in the laboratory seems to have no appreciable effects. Of course, the subjects know that they can terminate the experiment at will and feel in contact with people because they are being monitored, even if no interpersonal communication actually occurs. The importance of being able to terminate the condition, or at least of knowing the planned duration of the experiment, is emphasized by Levy *et al.* (1959). In contrast, prolonged isolation under stressful conditions can be disruptive. Solomon *et al.* (1957) point out a common denominator in the anecdotal literature: control of external stimulation is imposed from without. This factor is especially true for solitary confinement.

Most writers on the topic of restricted stimulation appear to accept the proposition that the normal and efficient functioning of the human organism depends upon external stimulation (for example, Solomon *et al.*, 1957). The concept of impact developed in Chapter 2 is pertinent. Restricted stimulation involves a reduction in the intensity of external stimulation in one or more modalities, the reduction being not only in the average intensity but also in the maximum levels of intensity. But it is not only intensity which is curtailed: the uncontrolled stimuli which the subject is permitted to experience are stimuli with little or no meaning; they are not stimuli which disturb the homeostatic state and require the subject to respond to restore equilibrium; they furnish no information of inherent value to the subject. Davis, McCourt, and Solomon (1960) argue that the brain needs meaningful stimulation, not just stimulation, for normal functioning.

But this restriction of stimulation has another aspect at least as important as the reductions in intensity and in meaningfulness. The temporal variation is very severely limited. With a homogeneous visual field, a change of fixation point no longer produces a change in sensation as it normally does. There is ordinarily no variety in the auditory input, at least for long periods. Thus the amount of impact from external stimulation is lowered to a very minimal level.

The experimental work in this area has usually emphasized the restriction of visual and auditory stimulation. With such deprivation, other sense modalities become relatively more important. Explicit mention of taste and smell is not made, presumably because it is obvious that these senses are more or less restricted by the confined conditions, with smoking being prohibited or permitted only after meals.

Kinesthetic stimulation becomes of central significance. Lilly (1956) provides a graphic description of the almost overwhelming urge to move a finger, in order to have some sensation. Evidence has been marshalled by Freedman, Grunebaum, and Greenblatt (1961) to show that hallucinations are reported in experiments where motility was restricted but not in those that permitted some physical movement (with one partial exception: Vernon *et al.*, 1958). The reader may have noted that in the preceding overview of the experimental literature, reports of hallucinatory experiences were absent or less common in the studies discussed first, and more frequent in those considered later, their occurrence tending to increase as the degree of permitted motility was reduced. But restriction of motility appears to be related to the observation of effects other than amount of imagery and hallucination. Deprivation for four to seven days may have little or no measurable effect, as the studies by Levy *et al.* (1959) and Myers *et al.* (1957) found, provided some motility is permitted. In contrast, disturbances of perception occurred within eight hours in the experiment by Freedman *et al.* (1961), and severe subjective effects appeared in even less time for subjects of Wexler *et al.* (1958) and Lilly (1956). (See the finding of Goldman [1953] that immobilization increased the autokinetic effect.)

Although the evidence clearly demonstrates the role of immobility which is concurrent with deprivation in other modalities, the effects when restriction of kinesthetic stimulation is the sole condition are less well known. This control condition in Freedman and Greenblatt's work produced no effects in eight hours. However, the clinical literature suggests that immobilization for longer periods may produce symptomatology, although other variables may be contributing factors here. It seems likely that severe restriction of kinesthetic stimulation for several days may disrupt normal functioning as much as a similar degree of restriction in either the visual or the auditory sphere alone.

Rapid effects from immobility are suggested in the observation which Page (1959) found in *The Arctic Year*. When an Eskimo is hunting seals, he may have to remain motionless for hours. If the sea is calm and reflects the sun, the hunter feels sleepy and then dizzy. He gradually forgets everything around him, cannot move, and may feel that his kayak is sinking and the water is rising around him. This condition may be relieved only by the rippling of the water or a shove from another hunter. It can apparently be an unpleasant, even traumatic experience.

When the intensity of external stimulation is markedly reduced, the sense receptors become more sensitive to stimuli of very low intensities. Thresholds are lowered (Rosenbaum *et al.*, 1959; Ormiston, 1958; Doane *et al.*, 1959; Vernon and McGill, 1961). Thus "the sensitized organism may be brought into contact with an underlying field of weak tactual, kinesthetic, even auditory and visual stimuli or system noise . . ." (Davis, 1959, pp. 313-314). Davis goes on to suggest that these weak inputs could be the basis for hallucinatory responses.

As time goes on, even these weak stimuli have little meaning and very limited impact for most subjects. A few may indulge their hypochondriacal inclinations. But the typical subject will focus his attention increasingly on his own mental processes. In the first stages of deprivation experiments, subjects who do not simply relax and go to sleep typically try to think about some problem. Their success in this endeavor is quite limited, as one would expect from everyday experience in attempting to sustain thought on a topic in the absence of external stimuli such as books, notes, or conversation. The more nearly complete the elimination of visual, auditory, and kinesthetic stimulation, the more rapid is the onset of a state in which the subject's experiences are essentially beyond his control. Thoughts, images, and affective states may come and go. As time goes on, the subject is no longer able to use his mental processes as a source of "stimulation" but can only passively experience whatever occurs.

The conceptual scheme in Chapter 2 would predict a decline in level of activation during the first stages of deprivation. With the impact from external and kinesthetic stimuli severely curtailed, other interoceptive stimuli and cerebral processes are the only available sources of appreciable impact. Somatic states do come into greater prominence, as the study of Wexler *et al.* (1958) indicates, but their usually low intensity, significance, and variation produce only limited impact. As a consequence, the major potential source of impact is the nervous system itself, especially cortical states. Unless the subject's thoughts and imagery have considerable impact, his activation level necessarily declines. This prediction or interpretation is supported by the observation that many subjects do become less alert and daydream or fall asleep.

What evidence is available on the level of activation during restricted stimulation? In addition to the subjective reports and the indirect evidence provided by overt behavior such as sleep, there are two findings on measures of arousal. In the McGill work (Heron, 1957), the EEG records show that deprivation produced a tendency toward a sleeplike pattern and toward slower frequencies in the alpha range. In another study (Vernon *et al.*, 1961), a drop in galvanic skin resistance was found. We shall have to wait for further experimentation before we can trace the course of arousal during deprivation.

Two suggestions seem appropriate. As discussed above, there are marked individual differences in reaction to these experiments. In those subjects who relax and sleep, it can be inferred that level of activation is generally low. In contrast to them, some subjects become upset, anxious, and may even seek forcibly to free themselves from the situation (see Wexler *et al.*, 1958). It seems reasonable to infer that their level of activation is clearly elevated, the increase stemming from the impact of stimuli arising from their mental distress, increased muscular tension, and other internal sources.

But even this picture is oversimplified. We cannot meaningfully talk about a subject's level of activation for an extended period except in terms of gross characteristics such as mean level. It is more pertinent to consider activation at different points in the temporal sequence. From the overt behavior of the subjects, it seems safe to infer that activation level changes during the experiment. While a subject may become drowsy and even sleep for a while, he wakes up sooner or later, and his level of activation presumably rises at this point. While awake, the subject may seek stimulation in various ways: In one experiment (Myers *et al.*, 1957), subjects explored their surroundings with their arms and whistled into the microphone; subjects may sing to themselves (Goldberger and Holt, 1958). These behaviors produced changes in stimulation which should have had temporary effects on activation. Changes in the content of the mental processes presumably have similar effects. It therefore seems safe to predict that future studies which measure arousal during restricted stimulation will reveal not only differences in mean levels between subjects but also fluctuations over time for any given subject, fluctuations which may be of large magnitude in those subjects who find parts of the experience to be disturbing or threatening, and especially in subjects who are driven to terminate the experiment at an early time.

A similar view is taken by Berlyne (1960, pp. 186-192). He points out that under conditions of restricted stimulation, subjects experience periods of irritability and unpleasantness similar to the more constant but increasing reactions of subjects engaged in monotonous activities. He argues that the feeling of boredom is associated with a rise in arousal.

The interpretation that we have offered above attributes the observed effects principally to the restriction of external stimulation. Although social isolation can be ruled out as a factor, other aspects of the experimental conditions that are consequences of this primary manipulation may merit empirical investigation. There are the strangeness of the situation and the elimination of the usual routine, of the common patterns of activities, and of the tasks and goals in everyday life. It is not likely that such factors, by themselves, have direct effects since their influence would be observed primarily at the onset of the experimental conditions. However, there may be incidental characteristics of the setting with cumulative effects, for example, the reduction or elimination of smoking.

Alternative Interpretations. Psychoanalytically oriented interpretations have also been offered for the phenomena of restricted stimulation. Rapaport (1958) suggests that stimulus deprivation interferes with the relative autonomy of the ego from the id, an autonomy supported by the motor, perceptual, and other apparatuses involved in adaptedness to the environment. Lilly (1956) also discusses the dependence of the healthy ego on exchanges with the external world. Goldberger and Holt (1961; also Goldberger, 1958) emphasize the role of reality contact in the maintenance of secondary process (adaptive, rational) thinking. Similar views are held by Ruff and Levy (1959) and by Rosensweig (1959), who emphasize the lack of meaning in the stimuli received during these experiments.

These views appear to complement or extend the interpretation that has been outlined above. When the impact of external stimuli is minimal, spontaneous cerebral productions become predominant. Disturbing thoughts and images associated with residual unresolved tensions emerge. The conditions make it difficult or impossible for the subject to cope with this material by the means he usually employs under normal circumstances.

Jackson (1960) has argued that the role of suggestion must be considered. He based his view on his own study in which the experimental subjects were given a set of expectancies regarding experience during sensory deprivation and the effects of such conditions upon test performance. The suggestion was reinforced by administration of a "drug" (actually a placebo) which was said to have similar effects. As compared to a control group given neither suggestion nor isolation, no effects were found on any of ten different tests.

During the one-hour period of isolation, Jackson's subjects experienced many of the phenomena reported in other studies. Since he did not have a group who had the restricted stimulation but no suggestion, it is difficult to evaluate the contribution of the suggestion. However, in view of the brevity of his experimental period, it would appear that suggestion probably contributed to the type and frequency of experiences reported, if not to the actual experiences. (See Kandel *et al.*, 1958; Cambareri, 1958.) On the other hand, it is unlikely that suggestion can be viewed as the major factor producing the results that have been found in other studies using periods of three to eight hours, or several days. Another study (Cohen, Rosenbaum, Dobie, and Gottlieb, 1959) used highly permissive instructions suggesting unusual experiences and also obtained the usual kind of imagery in a one-hour period, but these hallucinatory reactions were less developed and idiosyncratic than the ones reported for longer periods of isolation.

FEATURES COMMON TO MONOTONOUS CONDITIONS AND RESTRICTED STIMULATION

In this chapter, we have examined the findings for two sets of experimental conditions: first, the confinement of subjects to a single, unchanging task for minutes or hours; second, the deprivation of normal intensities and fluctuations in stimuli for one or more sensory modalities. Both situations are marked departures from the everyday experience of most people and both involve greatly reduced temporal variation in stimulation.

In the vigilance studies, performance typically declines over time, presumably because normal functioning is somewhat disturbed by the continually monotonous conditions. Markedly restricted stimulation clearly disrupts normal functioning and probably impairs task performance to some degree. In both types of experiment, the most marked effects are to be found in conditions with the greatest reduction in temporally varying stimulation. Conversely, any external stimulation that varies over time will reduce the probability of occurrence of performance decrement or disturbances of normal functioning.

In the two sets of conditions, it has also been observed that subjects will, as much as permitted, attempt to increase the impact of stimulation, and especially the amount of variation. Marked individual differences have also been noted. Some subjects are able to adapt by providing themselves with stimulation having an appropriate degree of impact. Others cannot cope with the situation. In the vigilance task, their performance suffers. In the studies utilizing restricted stimulation, they are likely to quit soon after the experiment begins.

These findings indicate that the extent of the observed effect is somewhat subject to internal control by the organism, that is, that organismic variables are involved. We believe that adaptation to these experimental conditions occurs when subjects are able to maintain an appropriate level of activation.

Perhaps the most unexpected finding is the association between immobility and magnitude of effect. Under more usual conditions, kinesthetic stimulation is always available to the organism and yet is rarely prominent. The findings described above suggest that physical movement ordinarily provides the organism with a potential source of stimulation which it can utilize to counteract the effects of unvarying stimulation in other sensory modalities. In addition, the production of such stimulation by the organism can serve its needs for experiencing stimuli with impact and yet will not interfere with concurrent orientation toward a task. Although the kinesthetic modality has received little emphasis in psychology, it seems to play a steady, unobtrusive, but significant role in the maintenance of the organism's readiness for action and in the organism's effective interaction with the ever-changing physical environment.

Chapter 6

Behavioral, Subjective, and Physiological Aspects of Drowsiness and Sleep *

JOE KAMIYA
University of California Medical Center

*E*XCEPT for the current reawakening of interest in dreaming, research on sleep has been relatively neglected by psychologists in recent years. Kleitman's *Sleep and Wakefulness* (1939), an extensive review of data and theory in the field with many contributions of direct psychological interest, has not stimulated nearly as much research among psychologists as might have been expected. With few exceptions, studies done in the last decade have received little attention. It is significant that, in the 11 years of publication of the *Annual Review of Psychology* up through 1960, the subject of sleeping is listed in the index pages only twice.

Why the neglect? Perhaps one reason is that we have implicitly taken the transition from waking life to sleeping as a natural boundary for the study of behavior. We seem to have assumed that sleeping is behaviorally empty. Another reason, coupled with the first, is that somehow sleeping has appeared to be more "physiological" than psychological. Given the tendency among psychologists to ignore the physiological, such a view naturally leads to the neglect of sleep. Perhaps still another reason is that our strict behavioristic heritage has led us to ignore one of the most salient features of the sleep of humans, dreaming. If we ignore dreaming we need not inquire about the conditions under which it thrives.

*Research presented in this chapter was supported by Grant M-2116 from the National Institute of Mental Health while the author was at the University of Chicago.

Although these reasons may account historically for at least part of psychology's neglect of sleeping in recent years, they do not seem very valid theoretically. In the first place, it is evident that behavioral properties do not vanish as one goes to sleep. Even in the deepest normal sleep, a person retains some degree of behavioral responsiveness to external stimuli. Just exactly how responsive he is, how his responsiveness varies with different kinds of stimuli (conditioned or unconditioned, positive or noxious, etc.) are questions that can only be answered by behavioral study. As of this time, available answers to these and many other behavioral questions about sleep are very sketchy.

In the second place, in opposition to the view that sleep is more physiological than psychological, it is perhaps well to reflect that sleeping, and its absence, waking, are in the last analysis defined by such *psychological* criteria as degree of behavioral responsiveness to the outer world and qualities of awareness. Questions concerning whether subjects are "really" asleep are answerable only by such methods as determining the strength of stimuli needed to elicit a predefined response or by obtaining a subjective judgment following awakening. Physiological indicators of sleep (for example, the electroencephalogram) derive their validity only from their covariation with psychological criteria. Just as "lying quietly awake with eyes closed" refers to specific psychological attributes, so sleeping refers to certain additional psychological attributes of unresponsiveness to stimuli, or retrospective reports of unawareness of the immediate environment. Sleeping is in this sense no more physiological than talking, thinking, or fighting. While it may be more essential for life survival than any of these, this fact is irrelevant to the defining attributes of sleeping.

But recognition of sleeping as a descriptive term at the psychological level does not at all justify ignoring its physiological concomitants and mechanisms in our efforts to understand it. On the contrary, it seems rather clear in the light of recent advances in neurophysiology that an understanding of the physiological mechanisms is becoming increasingly useful for ordering the behavioral and subjective aspects of sleeping.

Finally, the methodological difficulty of coping with dreams and other events observable only to the subject cannot forever justify our ignoring or avoiding them. Private events like dreaming, for all their privacy, are still events; psychology simply cannot be complete without encompassing them in its theory.

In keeping with the above considerations, this chapter attempts an assessment of both the behavioral and subjective aspects of the low end of the activation scale, beginning with drowsiness and proceeding downward through increasing depths of sleep. Physiological concomitants and mechanisms will be considered along the way in the hope that the alignment of phenomena from each of the three realms —behavioral, experiential, and physiological—will stimulate their eventual theoretical integration.

DROWSINESS

If the concept of a continuum of arousal or activation is to be more than a fiction, we need at least to know its properties at a minimum number of points. But this may be easier said than done. Any point along the scale is likely to be easily influenced from one moment to the next by external circumstances (for example, social stimulation, variation in stimulation, and conditions provoking fear or anger). This dependency of arousal level upon the momentary situation leads to measurement difficulties not only because arousal level is so transitory but also because the very conditions imposed on the subject in the attempt to measure his arousal level are likely to affect it. Fortunately, at least for the drowsy range of the scale, the difficulties can be minimized sufficiently for most purposes by proper experimental procedures.

Behavioral and Subjective Measures of Drowsiness

Each of the several possible ways of conceiving of drowsiness has its own measurement methods and problems.

(1) *Readiness to Fall Asleep.* Certainly the drowsier the person is, the more rapidly he should fall asleep under favorable conditions. This idea of drowsiness is close to its everyday meaning, and the method to be used in applying it is self-evident, assuming some previously established criterion of sleep onset. One of its difficulties as an assessment procedure, at least at the human level, is that subjects must be made comfortable and be thoroughly familiarized with the

test setting. Moreover, the method obviously is not well suited to continuous or frequent determinations of drowsiness. It has some utility as a measure of that drowsiness which just precedes normal sleep at the usual hours, but otherwise it is not very practical.

(2) *Reduced Activity Level.* The drowsier the individual, the less he interacts with the environment, by responding to it and by making it respond to him. This is a drive, or energic, conception of drowsiness. The activity wheel and open field tests as used in animal research are examples of methods embodying this idea. At the human level, since much of man's activities are symbolic rather than overt, the assessment of the total activity level for purposes of indexing drowsiness becomes correspondingly more difficult. However, we shall see that reliable and valid ratings by judges are possible, at least for the more extreme forms of drowsiness.

(3) *Attenuation of "Best Effort."* The idea here is that drowsiness is accompanied by deterioration of performance on assigned tasks, even under "maximal" effort on the part of the subject. Sensory functions, motor coordination and strength, and symbolic capacities are thought to be impaired by drowsiness. Typical tests are reaction time, motor steadiness, and mental arithmetic. In the method for this commonly used approach the subject is instructed to "do his best." The method therefore permits sources of performance variation other than sheer capacity, inasmuch as the response of the subject under these conditions is a function of his cooperativeness, his attitudes toward success and failure, and his own conception of what the "best effort" involves. These clearly are motivational in nature because they have to do with the effectiveness of the social reinforcer used to obtain the behavior, or how much the subject will *arouse* himself to perform the tasks. From the point of view of obtaining an over-all index of arousal level, this approach is useful insofar as degree of motivation is conceptually a part of arousal, but it does not necessarily permit inferences concerning the specific components of drowsiness.

(4) *Introspective Report.* The subject is simply asked to report, usually on a rating scale, how drowsy he feels. The assumptions are that drowsiness is accompanied by internal stimuli, that these are discriminable to the subject, and that they can be reported to the experimenter. This method is simple and direct; it does not require

familiarization beyond definition of points along the rating scale; and it does not unduly influence the level of drowsiness. However, it does permit extraneous sources of variance: contributing to the response are not only the stimulus compound associated with the particular level of drowsiness but also the previous training given the subject in discriminating and describing it, as well as the social experimental conditions under which the report is given.

However drowsiness is measured, the method should involve comparisons among measurements of the same subject on different occasions. It seems essential to use repeated observations on the same subject over a representative range of the arousal scale, and to take such precautions as thoroughly familiarizing the subjects with the test setting before taking measures, training him to a plateau on performance tests, and standardizing test conditions.

Although there is general agreement among the results from the different measures, there are also frequent disparities. An example of the latter is reported in an experiment on sleep deprivation by Murray, Williams, and Lubin (1958): When observers' ratings of subjects' sleepiness (based on general activity level, including social interaction) were compared with the subjects' own ratings of sleepiness, it was found that during the first 90 hours of sleeplessness the subjects tended to rate themselves as less sleepy than the observers did, but in the eight remaining hours of the vigil the subjects began to agree with their observers. The authors' interpretation of this difference as reflecting an adjustment mechanism for maintaining wakefulness is in accord with the expectation noted above that self ratings can be a function of the social experimental setting.

Discrepancies can also occur among different procedures within a single type of approach, as Williams, Lubin, and Goodnow (1959) showed in another study of sleep deprivation. They found that in performance tasks requiring subjects to give their best effort, the results are a function of whether the tasks are paced by the experimenter or paced by the subject himself. In tasks that were paced by the experimenter, the occurrence of lapses or blocking led to failures to respond, and hence errors were increased. In subject-paced tasks, responses were deferred until these lapses were over, and hence speed was the measure affected. (For a related finding concerning performance under monotonous conditions, see Chapter 5.) Their work shows that identification of the sensitive aspect of performance is the crucial problem in the performance test approach, and they suggest that previous apparently inconsistent results should be re-evaluated in light of their findings.

Extreme Drowsiness from Sleep Deprivation

Behavioral Aspects.   To turn now to defining drowsiness more precisely, we may begin by noting that the milder forms of drowsiness characteristic of everyday life have been studied less than the extreme forms of drowsiness induced by prolonged sleep deprivation covering several days. In one study of the everyday form, Kleitman (1939) undertook the determination of the course of drowsiness through the day-night cycle. He used a battery of performance measures administered every two hours throughout the waking period. His tests included dealing and sorting cards, mirror tracing, code transcription, multiplication, hand steadiness, and reaction time. In terms of both speed and accuracy there was a well-marked diurnal rhythm in performance with minima early in the morning and late at night, and a maximum in the middle of the day. The early morning performance was usually poorer than the late night performance. The last result was also observed in our Chicago laboratory, particularly in reaction time and in strength of manual grip.

Total performance level during drowsiness appears to suffer not so much because of a generalized performance decrement over all trials, but because of an increase in number and duration of "blocks," or periods of no response (Bills, 1931; Kleitman, 1939). Although subjects can perform efficiently for brief periods of time, they appear to be unable to maintain attention as long as they can when not drowsy.

Under prolonged sleep loss, the blocks in performance increase in both frequency and duration (Kleitman, 1939; Williams, Lubin, and Goodnow, 1959; Bjerner, 1949). The nature of the tasks does not affect the occurrence of these blocks although, as indicated earlier, it does determine the specific aspect of the performance that is affected by the blocks. Kleitman found that, beginning from about the second night of deprivation, subjects showed a repeated inability to count their own pulse for as long as a minute. Williams, Lubin, and Goodnow report impaired performance on simple visual reaction

time, addition, concept attainment, a communication task, memoriza-
tion of short items of information, and a vigilance task in which the
subject is required to distinguish a critical signal from other signals.

Kleitman reports a diurnal fluctuation in performance level dis-
torting the picture of a progressive decline over the entire deprivation
period. Specifically to avoid these variations, Williams, Lubin, and
Goodnow took their performance measures once each day at the same
time. Therefore, although their charts, drawn by interpolating between the observations, show a monotonic decrease in performance
level with increased hours of deprivation, the uniformity may be
more apparent than real.

Another consequence of prolonged deprivation appears to be
slowed eye movements in a visual fixation task. Corrective movements
are larger and less exact and subjects can not hold fixations well. The
eyes drift slowly with a rolling type of movement, in sharp contrast
to the usual saccadic adjustment (Miles and Laslett, 1931).

Subjective Aspects. The subjective feeling of drowsiness accompanying prolonged sleep deprivation is not only a function of the
total hours of deprivation but is also dependent on the time of day.
During a 98-hour deprivation period, Murray, Williams, and Lubin
(1958) found a daily fluctuation of sleepiness (rated by observers as
well as by the subject themselves) superimposed on an approximately
linear increase of sleepiness throughout the entire period.

Contrary to earlier suggestions of Kleitman (1939) and of Tyler,
Goodman, and Rothman (1947), irritability of mood or disposition
does not seem directly attributable to sleep loss. In the study of
Williams, Lubin, and Goodnow (1959) and by Eagles, Halliday, and
Redfearn (1953), incidents of anger and irritability were rare. Apparently the specific social conditions of the experiment can influence
the observations.

There is general agreement that prolonged sleep deprivation results
in the development of hallucinatory experiences. These have been
reported by several investigators (Katz and Landis, 1935; Kleitman,
1939; Hauty and Payne, 1957; and Morris, Williams, and Lubin,
1960). The last-named authors report that the perceptual anomalies
of extreme drowsiness seem to follow a course similar to that of
performance on the tests. They appeared sporadically during lapses.
Their frequency, duration, and intensity covaried with performance

loss. Subjective images and intrusive thoughts became confused with external events. Later motor activity would slow and stop and if not aroused, the subject seemed to fall asleep. The lapse usually ended spontaneously after a few seconds and following this some subjects recalled dreams while others consistently reported blank periods.

From observers' ratings on visual misperception, temporal disorientation, and cognitive disorganization, it was determined that perceptual anomalies became more frequent with greater sleep loss. The visual misperception scale had the following five points: (1) Eyes itching, burning or tired, blurred vision; (2) visual illusions; (3) labelling of illusions but with no doubt concerning their illusory character; (4) labelling of illusions with some doubt concerning their reality; (5) labelling of illusions with, for a time at least, belief in their reality. The authors state that if some subjective belief in the reality of the false perception is used as the criterion, then 12 of the 26 subjects could be said to have hallucinated and four of the 12 had two hallucinations. A correlation of .59 is reported between the occurrence of dreams during lapses and the later development of visual hallucinations.

These hallucinatory dream-like effects are particularly interesting in light of Dement's (1960) findings on "dream deprivation" (to be discussed later), which suggest that the hallucinatory effects here noted may be due not to the total amount of sleep deprivation but rather to deprivation of certain parts of the sleep cycle.

Physiological Aspects of Drowsiness. Among physiological concomitants of drowsiness, the electroencephalogram will be considered first because it is particularly sensitive to variations along the lowest end of the arousal scale, including deep sleep. The EEG recorded from the occipital area of relaxed, nonsleepy subjects with eyes closed typically shows intermittent trains of a rather regular wave form with a frequency of about 10 cycles per second. This wave is the well-known alpha rhythm. The trains of waves vary from moment to moment in duration and in proportion of time they are present, but the average per cent of time they are present in any particular individual in the relaxed waking state is a fairly stable characteristic. This alpha rhythm becomes disrupted and is replaced by irregular, lower amplitude waves under two conditions. One condition is any stimulation that attracts the attention of the relaxed but not drowsy subject. The disruption is most noticeable upon initial presentations of the stimulus, and it diminishes or fails to occur upon repeated presentations (Darrow, Vieth, and Wilson, 1957). The other condition is increased drowsiness, as is seen most clearly in subjects shortly before they fall asleep. Using a variant of the introspective technique discussed above), one group (Davis, Davis, Loomis, Harvey, and Hobart, 1938) instructed sleepy subjects to give a signal whenever they felt a spell of drowsiness. Most of these signals were preceded by depressions of alpha. In subjects who are deprived of sleep, the per cent time of alpha declines progressively until it is nearly absent in most subjects after 50 hours of deprivation (Armington and Mitnick, 1959).

Thus the *presence* of alpha rhythm during drowsiness is very decidedly indicative of a relatively aroused level and is associated with performance tasks requiring attention. This is the reverse of the relationship found in the normal nonsleepy state when tasks requiring attention give rise to a *disruption* of the alpha rhythm. Thus the alpha rhythm is characteristic of an intermediate stage of arousal. In the Armington and Mitnick study, the alpha rhythm was more prevalent when the sleep-deprived subject was instructed to add "seventeens" than when he was merely instructed to keep his mind blank. In the study by Williams, Lubin, and Goodnow (1959), errors of omission in an auditory vigilance task were accompanied by the lowest amount of alpha activity. The alpha measure returned to base line level 24 hours after termination of deprivation.

Body temperature has been found by Kleitman (1939) to be a good indicator of arousal. He reported a close covariation throughout the day between body temperature and performance on the tasks described earlier, higher task efficiency being related to higher body temperature. He believes that body temperature is in part a reflection of generalized muscle tonus, as seen in another study by him and Doktorsky (1933). If subjects who have been standing for one hour assume a horizontal position, thereby making possible a great reduction in muscle tonus, the oral temperature falls during the next hour. These temperature decreases were associated with an increase in reaction time. Several experiments in which the subject first lay down and then stood up resulted in a rise in temperature and an accompanying decrease in reaction time. More recent work by Kleitman and Ramsaroop (1948) shows that the diurnal temperature cycle is closely followed by heart rate.

The previously mentioned study by Murray, Williams, and Lubin supports Kleitman's hypothesis relating body temperature to drowsiness. Their study of a 98-hour period of sleep deprivation shows clearly that throughout the deprivation period there was a progressive decrease in temperature, on which was superimposed a diurnal variation. In their data, sleepiness ratings of the subjects by observers were negatively correlated with body temperature even with hours of sleep deprivation partialled out.

Heart rate decreases during performance lapses induced by sleep deprivation (Bjerner, 1949). This finding supports the general idea gained from EEG and body temperature data that deprivation leads to reduced physiological activation level.

Malmo (1958, 1959) has challenged this interpretation. He reports progressive upward changes in skin conductance level and respiration rate over a 60-hour period of sleep deprivation. Normally such a trend indicates increasing arousal. Reconciling his data with the others may not be impossible, however. His measurements were taken during a task (tracking), while those in the other studies were taken under more quiescent conditions. It is possible that the apparent increase in activation following sleep deprivation in Malmo's data is attributable to the fact that at the time his measures were taken the subjects were actively fighting sleepiness in doing the task. In other words, he may have been measuring the degree of effort the subject exerted in performing the task, and not the degree of activation prior to the task.

But the picture is not completely clear. Earlier work by Kleitman and by others, reviewed by Kleitman (1939), showed inconsistent changes or no changes at all in many variables frequently used as indicants of arousal level, including respiration, blood pressure, skin resistance, knee jerk, and pupillary responses. Perhaps some of the disparities would be eliminated by considering differences in procedure, such as the time of day the measures were taken, the total number of hours of deprivation, and the method of keeping the subject awake.

SLEEP ONSET

Where drowsiness stops and sleep begins is an arbitrary matter, depending on the psychological indicator used, the point along the indicator scale designated as the boundary, and the inclusion of a transition or drifting period. The task at hand is not the choice of these points, for that is a terminological matter, but rather the ordering of the behavioral and subjective attributes along the arousal scale and the study of their relationship to physiological concomitants.

Criteria for Sleep

Physiological Measures. As indicated earlier, there is need for more precise specification of the behavioral and subjective dimensions of sleep. Investigations of the physiological concomitants or indicators of sleep have tended to neglect these dimensions. There appears to be a tendency to use physiological indicators, especially the EEG, as the *criteria* of sleep rather than to investigate more precisely the dimensions of behavior and experience that lead us to recognize sleep in the first place. Besides the EEG the following physiological measures have been among those used in attempts to define sleep, either in terms of its onset, its depth, or both: heart rate, blood pressure, body temperature, secretion of gastric juice, knee jerk, pupillary diameter, electrical skin resistance, respiration, and muscle potential (see Kleitman, 1939, Chapters 9 and 11). Correlations among these measures are not always high or, as in the case of palmar skin resistance (Titelbaum, 1938) and EEG (Dement and Kleitman, 1957a), somewhat opposite trends may occur through the night. Any conclusions about sleep from such data (for example, that sleep onset or depth is too elusive to measure or that one measure is better than the other) would surely be unwarranted in the absence of studies linking these measures to sleep itself.

Also, the use of these measures as criteria of sleep leads to confusion when they are found to be at variance with psychological properties. For example the EEG, being generally well related to sleep and to states of consciousness, has increasingly come to be regarded as the criterion of sleep. But under conditions of extreme sleep deprivation, the EEG can indicate "deep sleep" when the subject is awake, at least by all the usual standards—talking, responding to instructions, etc. (Blake, Gerard, and Kleitman, 1939). Such dissociation between behavior and the EEG can also be produced pharmacologically or surgically. Cats (Bradley and Elkes, 1957) and dogs (Wikler, 1952) injected with atropine, and cats with rostral thalamic lesions (Meyer and Hunter, 1952; Knott *et al.*, 1955; and Chow *et al.*, 1959) similarly are wakeful (showing orienting responses, locomotion, etc.) while showing what is normally an EEG of deep sleep. It would be confusing to reconcile these differences by distinguishing between "behavioral sleep" and "physiological sleep." They merely indicate imperfect validity of the physiological indicator.

Behavioral Criteria. The most common behavioral criterion of sleep seems to be the responsiveness of the subject to auditory stimuli. To determine the time course of the onset of sleep with this measure, Mullin and Kleitman (1938) made determinations of the intensity of 10-second bursts of 60-cycle sound required for the subject to respond verbally, "I hear it." The bursts were presented 10 seconds apart at steadily increasing intensities, beginning at various intervals after "going to sleep." This was defined as the point at which the subject no longer retained his grasp on a sheet of paper placed in his hand, allowing it to fall. The maximum threshold values were reached about 30 to 35 minutes after this arbitrarily set zero time. This was followed by a downward turn to lighter sleep.

O. R. Lindsley (1957) has also used response to sound as an indicator of sleep onset, but in a rather different manner. His method, using operant technique, utilizes escape from high intensity sound as a reinforcer and thumb-pressing on a hand switch as the response. The sound is delivered to the subject's ear by earphone. The volume of this sound is controlled by the subject's rate of operation of the switch. If he does not respond at all, the volume climbs to a maximum in a few seconds. This is normally so noxious to a waking person that he operates the switch with the necessary rapidity (about 30 times a minute) to keep the volume at a tolerable level. Lindsley found that in the early part of the evening when the subject was still awake, a rather constant rate of responding was maintained. But this period was followed by a few minutes of steadily decreasing rate as sleep approached, and then the responses stopped altogether. Later, responding occurred only in very brief bursts, usually accompanied by gross body movements.

While the auditory awakening threshold method may be thought of as more akin to a sensitivity threshold, Lindsley's technique may be thought of as providing a threshold for *tolerance* of a steady noxious stimulus. The intensity value on the sensitivity curve corresponding to the point where the subject stops responding in the Lindsley procedure is not known. Two other studies, however, provide a basis for prediction. EEG records were taken by Blake, Gerard, and Kleitman (1939) in a study utilizing the same technique of having the subject hold an object in his hand as used by Mullin and Kleitman in the study described above. They found that the object (a spool held between the thumb and forefinger) usually dropped between 0.5 to 25 seconds after the alpha rhythm disappeared. In our laboratory we are currently conducting a study using EEG recordings in conjunction with Lindsley's procedure. We are finding that as alpha is replaced by the low voltage, random pattern of drowsiness, the rate of thumb pressing declines often to zero. Hence it would seem reasonable to predict that if both spool holding and thumb pressing were compared in a two-handed experiment, the thumb press rate will either be already at zero or have begun declining by the time the spool drops. It is doubtful that thumb pressing would occur very far into the subsequent 30- to 35-minute interval required for the auditory awakening threshold to reach a maximum.

In light of the elevated auditory thresholds that characterize sleep onset it is not surprising that subjects show no recall, upon awakening, of low intensity auditory stimuli presented during sleep. Simon and Emmons (1956b) presented tape recorded verbal stimuli (questions and answers) to subjects at five-minute intervals throughout the night, while continuously monitoring the EEG. Testing for retention (method of recall and recognition) was conducted in the morning upon awakening. A significant degree of learning took place only on those occasions when alpha waves occurred in close temporal contiguity to the stimulus (within a period from 30 seconds before the stimulus to 10 seconds afterward). Since alpha waves disappear with drowsiness and sleep, it seems that learning of complex verbal material cannot occur after sleep onset.

Eye Movements. We have already referred to the nature of eye movements in a visual fixation task under conditions of extreme sleep deprivation. The slow rolling movement that occurs when the subject can no longer fixate was thought by Miles (1929) to indicate sleep onset, in spite of the fact that the eyes remained open. The same sort of movement occurs during normal sleep onset and for a few minutes thereafter (Aserinsky and Kleitman, 1955). It is perhaps worthy of mention as a historical note that this relationship was first predicted via the introspective method by George Trumbull Ladd (1892). In the course of an introspective analysis of visual dreams at the subjective onset of sleep, Ladd noted a relationship between the images accompanying sleep onset and muscular tension in the eyes. "I am inclined to believe," he observed, "that the eyeballs move gently in their sockets" (p. 304).

Electrical recording methods now permit precise and continuous measures of eye movement through the closed lids, thus eliminating the need of lifting the lids for direct inspection. Using these techniques in conjunction with the EEG, Aserinsky and Kleitman (1955) observed two distinct types of eye movement in the sleeping subject. The first was the slow rolling movement just mentioned, which usually required three to four seconds for completion, was frequently binocularly asymmetrical, and was observed at sleep onset (as indicated by the EEG) and at irregular intervals thereafter for varying periods of time throughout the night's sleep. These movements were frequently initiated by a gross body movement and would decline gradually back to quiescence. The second type of movement was characterized by rapid jerky motions of relatively short arc. These did not occur at sleep onset. Further discussion of these will be postponed until we turn to the consideration of dreaming, with which rapid eye movements have been implicated.

Subjective Phenomena and the EEG. The subjective phenomena at the beginning of sleep were studied by Dement and Kleitman (1957b) in conjunction with the EEG and eye movements. They interrupted their subjects for subjective reports when they were showing a "drowsy" EEG (see Gibbs and Gibbs, 1950; Loomis *et al.*, 1937; Simon and Emmons, 1956a). In this brain wave pattern, the alpha rhythm has become diminished or has disappeared entirely, being replaced by a low voltage, random pattern with some fast frequencies. This pattern does not show the "sleep spindles" (brief bursts of 12-15 cycle per second waves) which characterize the next stage of sleep (Dement and Kleitman's Stage 2). In all instances, their subjects felt that the mental content, although often "dream-like," was distinctly different from an actual dream. They invariably stated they were not asleep and that the mental imagery was not as organized or "real" as that occurring in dreams. A variety of images and sensations were described, such as "floating," "drifting," and "flashing lights."

As part of a large-scale study of dreaming and its electrophysiological concomitants, data from which are yet to be published, we obtained judgments from subjects on whether they had been awake or asleep and whether any dreaming had been occurring. A bell was rung at the first appearance of sleep spindles (Stage 2), the point usually taken as definite indication of sleep onset. Since both the spool technique (Blake *et al.*, 1939) and the operant technique (O. R. Lindsley, 1957) suggest sleep in the prior stage (Stage 1), one might expect most subjects would report having just gone to sleep or at least have been drifting off to sleep at this point. However, out of 47 reports from 20 subjects, there were 19 reports of having been awake and thinking, 4 reports of imagery, and 12 reports indicating uncertainty of the subjective state, or drifting. Only 12 awakenings resulted in reports of having been asleep, 11 of which were accompanied by reports of dreaming. No rapid eye movements occurred prior to any of the awakenings. (Awakenings in Stages 3 and 4 almost always resulted in reports of having been asleep, as Teplitz [1943] also found.)

Comparing these results from early Stage 2 awakenings with those of Dement and Kleitman from State 1, three observations may be made: (1) Stage 1, when it occurs in going from wakefulness to sleep, is always associated with subjective reports of wakefulness. This is noteworthy inasmuch as the two behavioral indicators of Blake *et al.*, and Lindsley would suggest sleep had started with Stage 1. (2) Even Stage 2, at least its very beginning, is frequently associated with subjective reports of wakefulness. (3) If subjects feel they were asleep at the beginning of Stage 2, they are likely to report they had been dreaming. The absence of rapid eye movements is noteworthy, as will be seen later.

Several problems of research methodology seem important here. First of all it is probable that terms like awake, asleep, imagery, thinking, and dreaming as used by the subjects to describe their subjective experiences have somewhat different meanings among different subjects. Second, the availability of these experiences, which may in part be due to the subjects' previous experiences in discriminating them, may differ from subject to subject. Third, the experience accompanying some common indicators of sleep onset, such as muscular relaxation, behavioral cessation, and onset of spindles, may actually be different from subject to subject, following different courses in time for each individual. A great help in future research in this area would be the use of repeated observations for single subjects, to obviate extraneous sources of variance arising from individual differences.

In conclusion, it seems that the EEG is a fairly good indicator of sleep onset, in spite of its limited usefulness in the nonnormal conditions of extreme sleep deprivation and pharmacological or surgical intervention that produce dissociation between the EEG and behavior, and in spite of its less than perfect relation to subjective reports at sleep onset. Additional evidence of its utility in assessing the depth of sleep will be presented below. Because of its general promise, and because it can provide a continuous measure over time without disturbing the arousal level of the subject, it is understandable that the EEG has come increasingly to be regarded as the criterion of sleep. Reflecting this trend, in this chapter we frequently use the word "sleep" to mean EEG-indicated sleep. However, we must be mindful that this usage may be premature or not sufficiently specific. What we need very much is a clearer picture of what specific behavioral and experiential attributes are associated with each differentiable EEG pattern, and under what conditions.

VARIATIONS IN THE DEPTH OF SLEEP

We have already mentioned that after the subject can no longer continue holding objects placed in the hand there follows a period of progressive deepening of sleep as evidenced by the increasing intensity of sound required for awakening. This is accompanied by a progressive change in the EEG patterns grossly discernible by direct inspection. After the low voltage, essentially random pattern (Stage 1) of drowsiness, and the subsequent appearance of sleep spindles (Stage 2) as previously described, there appears an irregular low frequency (.5-2 cycles per second) component ("delta") mixed with the spindles. This low frequency wave gradually gains in amplitude and in relative preponderance over other frequencies. When delta is only moderately represented in the total pattern, the record is designated Stage 3, and when the record consists almost entirely of delta, it is designated Stage 4. If the EEG pattern is decomposed into its components by Fourier analysis, the "stages" would be seen as arbitrarily selected regions of a rather regular progression of mixtures of frequencies (Knott *et al.*, 1942).

The most recent evidence linking these stages to the depth of sleep is in unpublished work by Lentzner and Rechtschaffen. They show a high predictability of auditory awakening threshold from the EEG, stage by stage. Another validating study, by Coleman *et al.* (1959), showed that reaction time to sound is a direct function of the amplitude of the EEG.

The EEG of the sleeping subject responds to external stimuli with a transient arousal pattern called the "K-complex." This response is useful as another indicator of the depth of sleep, since the depth of sleep determines the probability of occurrence of the response, as well as its magnitude. Of particular psychological interest is the fact that this EEG response occurs selectively to previously learned stimuli. For example, Toman (1958) and Oswald *et al.* (1959) have shown that sleeping subjects are more likely to show the EEG response to the calling of their own names than of other persons' names, even in the absence of an overt behavioral response. Also, Christake (1957) has shown selectivity in EEG arousal during sleep to conditioned emotional stimuli.

Dement and Kleitman (1957a) have published a graph of the EEG-derived depth of sleep curve, based on 126 nights from 33 subjects, which indicates that the initial decline to maximum depth takes an average time of about 25 minutes. This is essentially confirmed in our data based on 25 subjects who were recorded for 10 nights each. This time required for the decline to maximum depth according to the EEG is quite similar to the determinations made by the earlier behavioral methods of Mullin and Kleitman (1938).

The subject changes his depth of sleep rather frequently during the night, moving from deeper to lighter sleep and back to deeper sleep again, sometimes as often as 50 to 60 times and usually at least 10 or 15 times. The recurrent upward changes toward lighter sleep are of two different types: (1) the transient shifts, usually associated with gross body movements, and (2) the longer lasting changes associated with rapid eye movements at the high points. The first are quite brief, typically lasting only a few seconds at their peaks and then declining to the initial level within three or four minutes. Frequently, the EEG records of these peaks are indistinguishable from relaxed wakefulness. The onset of these peaks usually follows the body movement with which they are associated, giving the appearance of being caused by the movement. They occur more frequently as the night progresses. They do not show any regularity in time of occurrence, except that they frequently occur at the onset or the end of a period of ocular motility.

The second type of change toward lighter sleep is more periodic and longer lasting (from a minute to an hour or more, with an average of about 15 minutes). Since the EEG pattern for this period is not distinguishable (at least by gross inspection of the raw tracing) from the Stage 1 pattern discussed previously, it also is called Stage 1. But Dement and Kleitman (1957a) showed that Stage 1 of drowsiness and sleep onset was associated with lower auditory thresholds than the same stage occurring later at night. In this period, sleep is also deeper than in the momentary peaks accompanying the larger body movements. Such movements often occur during this stage.

As the night proceeds, the durations of the successive recurrences of this state usually get longer. Their onset usually precedes by one or two minutes the rapid eye movements associated with them. They occur fairly regularly, showing a periodicity of about 80 to 110 minutes between their onsets. The rapid eye movements rarely or never occur outside these periods of lightened sleep. Finally, in the intervals between these Stage 1 periods, the troughs in the sleep curve get progressively shallower.

In other words, depth of sleep during the entire night is characterized by a slowly undulating "sleep cycle" whose crests are rather flat and of constant height and whose troughs get progressively shallower and briefer during the night. Superimposed on this basal pattern are many transient peaks which frequently resemble wakefulness and which recur irregularly but more often as the night progresses.

Transient Changes and Gross Body Movements

There can be no doubt that the gross movements of the sleeper indicate a shift from deeper to lighter sleep and back again, however brief this shift may be. It is commonplace, of course, that movement instigated by external stimuli is a frequent accompaniment of arousal. Movements occurring in the absence of known external stimuli also indicate arousal. Accompanying the larger movements, particularly when two or more large movements occur within a few seconds of each other, the EEG patterns of sleep are replaced by the waking alpha wave for at least a few seconds. If the subject is not aroused to the point where alpha persists for about 15 seconds or longer, he will then return to deeper sleep considerably more rapidly than during the first onset of sleep (often within a half a minute). If the alpha persists, it indicates a level of arousal that by most criteria would be judged as wakefulness: the subject would say he was awake if asked, would follow instructions, etc.

On the occasions when alpha lasts only a few seconds, there is room for debate concerning whether the subject is awake or asleep. On the one hand he is likely not to recall the body movement or any external stimulus that may have caused it, especially if he is not asked about it until the end of the night's sleep. Even if the subject is awakened for a report after only a minute or two has elapsed since the short-lived alpha period, he may still be unable to remember. On the other hand the switch-pressing operant previously described often occurs for a brief time at these occasions. Even though this behavior (probably of the same sort as sometimes occurs in turning off bedside alarm clocks) is also forgotten, there is no doubt of its awake-like quality. Also, the auditory threshold is at or very near the waking level, as was shown by Mullin *et al.* (1937). The threshold rises again with the return to deeper sleep.

Alpha does not accompany all body movements. The smaller movements and those occurring during the deeper phases of the sleep cycle tend to show lesser degrees of EEG arousal than the alpha pattern. The degree of alpha present during a body movement was shown by Simon and Emmons (1956b) to be related to the likelihood of immediate reporting of tape-recorded verbal stimuli and to their subsequent recall in the morning.

What gives rise to these body movements is not very clear. Apparently there is some gradually increasing physiological activation. Jackson (1942) observed, in one subject, a gradual acceleration of the heart rate, beginning from as much as six minutes before body movement. Muscular discomfort from lying too long in one position is probably important. Wada's work (1922) suggests gastric contractions are associated with body motility during sleep.

These transient disturbances of the depth of sleep take on special interest because of their close association with "sleep talking." We have observed quite consistently from subject to subject that whenever sleep talking (groans, mumbling, or brief articulate speech) occurs, it is usually accompanied by body movements. Among 98 instances of these spontaneous vocalizations, 70 accompanied body movements. And it is of further interest that among these 70 combinations of body movement and vocalization, 64 (91%) occurred during the deeper phases of the depth-of-sleep cycle. (Among all the 98 vocalizations, 86 occurred during these deeper phases.)

Do these vocal episodes occur during dreams? We do not have enough awakenings immediately following vocalizations to be very sure, but present indications are that they are not accompanied by the experience of dreaming. In cases where reports of dreaming are given following the vocalization, the two are not related in content. This clearly needs more investigation, for it seems natural to expect dreaming to accompany sleep talking.

Subjective states accompanying those body movements which are not associated with vocalization are also in need of investigation. Dement and Wolpert (1958) have studied these during the light sleep (Stage 1) phases of the sleep cycle. They concluded that each gross body movement marks the end of one dream sequence and the beginning of another. This interpretation was based on the observation of a greater frequency of long continuous dream reports from those periods of Stage 1 and rapid eye movement in which no body movement occurred, while fragmented dreams were more likely to be recalled if the periods were marked by body movements. Also, when dream reports were brief, body movement had recently occurred. However, the body movement apparently does not have a counterpart in the activity experienced by the dreamer. That is, gross body movements do not signal corresponding movement in the dreamed activity.

Also worthy of attention is the fact that body movements during sleep trigger off slow, rolling movements of the eyes, in the same manner as during sleep onset. Aserinsky and Kleitman (1955) observed these to last an average of four minutes following a body movement after a long period of inactivity. Not all periods of slow eye movements are traceable to body movement, but the latter always give rise to slow eye movement.

These general findings are confirmed by our own observations. Using improved equipment designed to respond to the slowest eye movements as well as to those movements rapid enough to be detected by the conventional EEG equipment used in their studies (and in all subsequent ones), we have been able to get a much more detailed picture. Preliminary analysis shows that "slow" and "fast" as previously used to describe eye movements are too coarse to handle the gradations in between. Perhaps most important for the present discussion is the fact that the slower eye movements often build up in magnitude and speed, sometimes over a 5- or 10-minute period, into the rapid eye movement periods. Also, the slow eye movements do not cease upon the onset of the rapid ones. On the contrary the rapid eye movement period is really a period of heightened slow eye movement as well as rapid eye movement.

These periods of slower ocular activity may turn out to be important in settling ambiguities that have developed recently in determining the time of occurrence of dreaming. Recall that the observation of ocular activity started the recent studies on dreaming. At the least, more precise specifications of this indicator should result from the recognition of the possibility that "slow" and "fast" may be a coarse dichotomy produced largely by the time constants built into the available recording equipment.

The Longer-Lasting Changes

The onset of Stage 1 following deeper stages of sleep may or may not occur with a gross body movement. For this reason, and also because the time of the onset of Stage 1 is relatively constant despite variations in rate of body movement, the mechanisms controlling the two phenomena must be at least partially independent. Also, the duration of Stage 1 is greater than the duration of the lighter sleep following a body movement. In the study by Dement and Kleitman

(1957a), the average durations of the first, second, third, and fourth periods of Stage 1 were 9, 19, 24, and 28 minutes, respectively.

Whatever the mechanism underlying this cyclic course of the depth of sleep, it seems to be rather basic; it is apparently universal in man. Moreover, it is found in species other than man. Dement (1958) and Grastyan (1959) have observed the fluctuations in the cat. Our preliminary observations of the EEG of sleeping monkeys in the laboratory of Dr. K. L. Chow reveal the same cyclic property.

In the later occurrences of Stage 1, Dement and Kleitman (1957a) showed that the auditory threshold is higher than in Stage 1 just prior to sleep onset, and Lentzner and Rechtschaffen (personal communication) found that the threshold is lower than in Stage 2, 3, and 4. The Lindsley thumb operant does not occur here unless there is a gross body movement. According to Dement and Kleitman (1957a), gross body movements happen less frequently during Stage 1 than in other stages, but our data fail to show this difference.

According to physiological measures other than EEG, Stage 1 is usually a more active state than the other stages. Brooks *et al.* (1956) and Aserinsky and Kleitman (1955) showed that light sleep was usually associated with higher heart rate. The latter investigators also showed that respiration rate was higher in light sleep. Our own observations on heart rate and respiration rate confirm these findings, there being an average increase of 5.3% in heart rate and 5.9% in respiration rate from the 15-minute interval preceding Stage 1 to the period of Stage 1, taken either to its natural termination or to the point of an awakening by the experimenter. Basal skin resistance measures do not show any consistent differentiation of sleep depth, except that resistance always rises at sleep onset. Wolpert (1960) found that muscle potentials from the wrist increase during Stage 1. This stage of lightest sleep is possibly that which Max (1935) encountered in the dreams of deaf-mutes in his successful pioneering effort to develop a physiological indicator of dreaming.

Perhaps the most important concomitant of the light sleep phase of the cycle, and certainly the most widely known, is the rapid eye movement or REM. REMS, intermingled with slow eye movements, are distributed throughout the light sleep or Stage 1 phase, varying in intensity and frequency from a few barely discernible ones in an entire period of 5 to 10 minutes of Stage 1 EEG to as many as 200 or 300 large, quick movements, sometimes coming in bursts of two or three per second for four or five seconds at a time. REMs rarely occur outside periods of Stage 1, and if the Stage 1 lasts more than just a few minutes, REMs nearly always occur.

In summary, the depth of sleep varies many times during the course of the night. One source of the variation appears to be associated with gross body movements. These occur irregularly but more frequently as the night progresses. They represent at least a partial arousal, and they are followed by a few minutes of slow eye movements. Sleep talking occurs most frequently in conjunction with body movements. A second source of variation is the more regular and slower change associated with the "sleep cycle." This longer rhythm has a period of about 80 to 110 minutes between the onset times of the light sleep phases. The duration of the light sleep phase tends to lengthen progressively over the course of the night. Rapid eye movements are associated with this phase of the sleep cycle.

DREAMING

Aserinsky and Kleitman (1955) at the University of Chicago suspected that the rapid eye movements were indicative of dreaming. They therefore systematically awakened subjects both during periods of such movements and during periods of no movement, and asked whether dreaming was recalled, and if so, asked the subjects to describe in a few words the dream content or any visual imagery which could be remembered. Twenty out of 27 replies yielding detailed dream descriptions were obtained from individuals awakened after rapid eye movements had been observed. In contrast, 19 out of the 23 negative replies were given by persons awakened in the absence of eye movements. Follow-up studies by Dement and others at the University of Chicago confirmed and extended these findings, as summarized below.

Dement and Kleitman (1957b) found that (1) roughly 80% of the awakenings from rapid eye movement (REM) periods resulted in reports of dreaming, while only about 7% of awakenings from non-REM periods resulted in such reports; (2) if subjects are awakened either 5 or 15 minutes after the onset of REMs and asked to choose one of these two intervals as more nearly representing the time they

spent dreaming, their choices significantly favor the corresponding
REM time; (3) the length of the narrative is correlated positively
with the duration of the REM period; (4) the pattern of the REMs
was related to the visual imagery reported in the dream.

Dement and Wolpert (1958) found that (5) the greater the degree
of ocular activity ("active" *vs.* "passive"), the more actively did
the subject report participating in the events of the dream; (6) body
movements seemed to signal a termination of a dream sequence.

The very first of these findings, the differential frequency of reports of dreaming upon awakening from REM and non-REM periods,
will be the major concern of what follows, for it is on this point that
ambiguities have arisen on the basis of more recent work using the
same EEG and EOG (electroculogram) recording procedures. Further, the validity of rapid eye movements as an indicator of the occurrence of dreaming must be based largely on this observation.

Dream Recall and the Definition of Dreaming

Analyzing our own data on 25 subjects run for a total of 10 nights,
Orlinsky (unpublished study) has found them in substantial agree
ment with Dement and Kleitman's findings concerning the frequency
of reports of dreaming following awakenings from REM periods: our
percentage is 85 as compared with their 80. However, our data differ
in the frequency of reports of dreaming from non-REM periods.
Whereas their study found that only 7% of all awakenings from the
non-REM periods resulted in reports of recall of dreaming, our figure
is about 27%.

Perhaps one source of the disparity is the differences in the criterion used in categorizing the verbal report as "dreaming" or "not
dreaming." In Dement and Kleitman's study, subjects were considered to have been dreaming "only if they could relate a coherent,
fairly detailed description of the dream. Assertions that they had
dreamt without recall of content, or vague, fragmentary impressions
of content were considered negative" (Dement and Kleitman, 1957b).
Rather than the dichotomy, dreaming *vs.* not dreaming, Orlinsky
applied an eight-point rating scale. Its points were defined as follows:
(0) Subject cannot remember dreaming; no dream is reported on
awakening. (1) Subject remembers having dreamed, or thinks he
may have been dreaming, but cannot remember any specific content.

(2) Subject remembers a specific topic, but in isolation: for example, a fragmentary action, scene, object, word, or idea unrelated to anything else. (3) Subject remembers several such disconnected thoughts, scenes or actions. (4) Subject remembers a short but coherent dream, the parts of which seem related to each other: for example, a conversation rather than a word, a problem worked through rather than an idea, a purposeful rather than a fragmentary action, etc. (5) Subject remembers a detailed dream sequence, in which something happens, followed by some consequence, or in which one scene, mood, or main interacting character is replaced by another (different from [3] either in coherence of change or in the development of the several parts of the sequence). (6) Subject remembers a long, detailed dream sequence involving three or four discernible stages of development. (7) Subject remembers an extremely long and detailed dream sequence of five or more stages; or more than one dream (at least one of which is rated 5) for a single REM period.

Of 400 non-REM awakenings, 57% could be placed in one of the "dreaming" categories (1-7). Combining only categories 2 through 7, the percent of "dreaming" reports fell to 46%. For categories 3 through 7 only, it fell further to 32%. For categories 4 through 7, which appear perhaps most similar to Dement and Kleitman's criterion, the percentage of reports of dreaming from the non-REM period awakenings is judged to be 27%, the figure given above. Continuing up the scale, categories 5 through 7 yield 13%; and 6 through 7 yield 7%. Clearly, the validity of ocular motility as an indicator of the occurrence of dreaming is very much a function of what one chooses to call a dream. But whether the data from the two studies can be reconciled on this basis is doubtful: it would seem unlikely that Dement and Kleitman (1957b) would have labeled as dreams only those reports with the complexity of categories 6 and 7, which is what we would need to do to arrive at their figures of recall for non-REM reports; furthermore, the application of such a stringent criterion would probably produce a discrepancy between the two values for REM awakenings.

The data of Goodenough *et al.* (1959) raise the same problem. Their study, utilizing the same techniques, was principally devoted to examining differences in dream recall rate between subjects who claimed that they dreamed almost every night and those who claimed that they dreamt less than once a month. The "dreamers" showed 93% recall of dreams from eye movement periods and 53% recall from non-REM periods. The "non-dreamers" showed recall of 46% and 17% for REM and non-REM periods respectively. The criterion for recall *vs.* nonrecall was whether the subject "recalled in some detail." Both percentages for non-REM recall are higher than Dement and Kleitman's. When dreamers and nondreamers are pooled, the average recall rate is 35% from non-REM awakenings and 70% from REM awakenings. With a sample of subjects whose aggregate recall rate for REM awakenings is lower than in Dement and Kleitman's, there is a considerably higher rate for non-REM recall than in the Dement and Kleitman study. To interpret the high incidence of recall, Goodenough *et al.* suggest that dreams reported from a non-REM period "may refer to dreams which occurred earlier in the night during eye movement periods, or even to the recall of thoughts which the subject might have had while falling asleep." One of the difficulties of this suggestion is that the same logic underlying it can be applied to dream reports from any part of the sleep cycle, calling into question the time of occurrence of dreams reported from REM awakenings as well. Furthermore, it leaves unanswered why their study shows more frequent recall from non-REM awakenings than the study by Dement and Kleitman.

Mental Activity during Sleep. Given the data from our study and from that of Goodenough *et al.*, a reasonable interpretation would seem to be that dreaming or some form of mental activity occurs without rapid eye movements as well as with them. A study completed recently in our laboratory by Foulkes (1960) bears rather directly on the issue. While he obtained 88% recall of mental activity from REM awakenings, a percentage similar to previous findings, the recall rate from the non-REM awakenings was 74%. To test the possibility that the non-REM recall was to be attributed to dreaming earlier in the night, during prior REM periods, he compared the frequency of recall in those non-REM awakenings following prior uninterrupted REM periods with those non-REM awakenings following no REM period at all or following a REM period that had been interrupted for a dream report. There was no difference in recall frequency between these two types of awakenings. Hence it seems that previous REM dreams, persisting in memory until a subsequent non-REM awakening, cannot account for non-REM recall in any simple way.

Four reasons are advanced by Foulkes to account for the difference between his and the other studies in the incidence of recall outside periods of Stage 1 REM activity: (1) The use of a more stringent criterion of recall by others. (2) The use by others of an overly restrictive subject set. (In Foulkes' study the subject's task was to describe anything that had been "going through his mind," rather than describe only his "dreams.") (3) Failure by others to insure continued subject arousal after awakening. (His interview of the subject in deep sleep awakenings, where drowsiness can easily influence the report adversely, typically covered at least three or four minutes of intensive probing.) (4) The nature of the content to be recalled.

The second and fourth points are particularly important. Directing the subject's attention to all mental activity prevailing at the time of awakening, and not just to dreaming, helps to avoid reports influenced by the subject's conception of what a dream is. With this broader approach to phenomenal qualities during sleep, Foulkes found a rather large proportion of recalls reporting mental activity that resembled waking thought drawn from the subject's everyday activities and was free of the distortions so frequently cited as characteristic of dreaming. Such activity was not as readily describable in terms of visual or auditory imagery, and was more difficult to recall. Perhaps most important in relation to the incidence of recall from the other studies, his data show that there is a much higher proportion of such "thinking" reports from deep sleep than from REM periods. During the latter, dreaming reports were found in 82% of the awakenings, and "thinking" reports in 6% (giving the 88% above reported). But during non-REM periods (Stages 2, 3, and 4) "dreaming" was obtained 54% of the time, and "thinking" 20%.

Hence, mental activity of some sort appears to occur outside of periods of Stage 1 and rapid eye movements, as well as within such periods. The terminological problem is obvious: if we choose to label any mental activity during sleep as "dreaming," then eye movements are virtually nonpredictive of it. If, however, we choose to limit the meaning of the term dreaming to the more distorted, imagery-laden scenes that correspond less directly to normal waking activity, then Stage 1 and eye movements are more predictive, although not as much so as the study of Dement and Kleitman suggested.

Foulkes' findings bring to mind similar earlier attempts to link the EEG to dreaming. His data are a striking confirmation of the results of the most systematic of those prior studies, that of Teplitz (1943). Teplitz concluded that dreams were most likely to be reported from Stage 1, but that they could occur in all stages of sleep. Reports of having dreamed were obtained in 63% of 78 spindle and delta awakenings.

What are we to conclude from these observations? Tentatively, it seems to the writer that perhaps there is some mental activity occurring at all times, in wakefulness and sleep, but that the kind of activity is a function of the depth of sleep, and that the discriminability or "availability" of the residues (memory traces) of the activity is greater in the lighter periods of sleep, either by virtue of their quality (perhaps their bizarreness or their emotional significance) or by virtue of the subject's greater alertness.

Why the eyes should move at the peaks of these periods of mental activity is uncertain, but that they do so may turn out to be of first importance in understanding memory processes, perhaps specifically recognition and recall. The suggestion that the subject is watching the events in his dream (Dement and Kleitman, 1957b) may indeed be true for the dreams that occur during REM periods. This notion would seem to be the direct internalized analogue of the "observing response" (Wyckoff, 1952). Some of the older introspective literature is both provocative and supportive along these lines. We have already cited Ladd (1892). Moore (1903) says that sensations from eye movement play a predominant role in the control of the memory image. Perky (1910) in the second half of an article (the first half of which describes the widely known study on how imagination is influenced by a sort of "subliminal perception") presents data that should perhaps be equally widely quoted. He observed that when subjects are asked to "project images" of specific objects on a screen, two types of imagery occur. One kind Perky found to involve abstract imagery—a sort of vague generic composite of all previously experienced perceptions. The other, termed by him "memory images," consisted of more concrete instances of objects remembered from a specific perceptual experience of the subject. These were more vivid and, most important, were accompanied by eye movements. (The latter he detected by having the subject fixate a point during the task; if markers placed just outside the periphery of the visual field came into view, eye movement was inferred.) This experiment ought to be repeated with the aid of the electroculogram, under the instructions in the original study, and also under conditions of more spontaneous imagination, as in daydreaming or the hallucinations of reduced stimulation described in Chapter 5. It is possible that the relationship of mental activity to ocular motility can be studied more easily in the waking state (with its increased alertness) than during sleep.

The Periods of Rapid Eye Movement. Two additional studies may throw new perspectives on the role of eye movements. Both of them can be seen as interesting instances of research inspired by the introspective methods of the study of dreaming, but do not themselves require introspection for validation, for the rapid eye movements have become the dependent variable. In the first of these, Dement (1960) interrupted the rapid eye movements by awakening the subject as soon as they became discernible to the experimenter. If these interruptions are repeated throughout the night's sleep, and are continued over several successive nights (Dement used five), the subjects appear to show a deprivation effect. On subsequent nights of undisturbed sleep, the total per cent of sleep time that is spent in the REM periods is increased, for at least a few nights, over the normal level. Control nights in which the subject is awakened an equal number of times but outside of REM periods do not result in such increases. In light of the above discussed frequency of dreaming outside REM periods, it may be premature to think of this phenomenon as demonstrating "dream deprivation" and a "need to dream." Yet the data certainly suggest some special functional properties of the light sleep, eye movement phase of the cycle. Further work in this area opened up by Dement may well have the widest implications for psychological theory.

The second experiment, by Stoyva, is still in progress in our laboratory. Its results thus far seem to show that experimental control of the duration of REM periods can be achieved in quite a different manner from that of Dement. Stoyva began his study as an inquiry into the effects on dreaming of posthypnotic suggestions to dream. He suggested specific actions that the subject would dream about, in every dream of the night. He then let the subject go to sleep and awakened him for a dream report later in the night, at the third or fourth REM period. One unexpected result was that if the subjects reported dreams in accordance with the suggestions, the first two REM periods were shorter in duration than on control nights with no suggestions. In other words, REM activity can be influenced by social control, at least in the form of hypnotic suggestions. This is interesting in view of the universality and relative intraindividual stability in the occurrence and temporal distribution of ocular activity during sleep under normal conditions.

FINAL REMARKS

Looking back over the course of this chapter, one can see that, largely due to the efforts of Kleitman and his associates, sleeping is now on the psychological map in a rather secure way. The research activity spurred by the recent work on dreaming, especially by Dement, is now expanding rapidly. From the point of view of a general psychology, one cannot help but feel that research on the psychological properties of sleeping will have far-reaching effects on the theory of behavior and experience.

Meanwhile, we may look forward to increased stimulation and clarification from neurophysiology. Lindsley's excellent review (1960) of the neurophysiological systems mediating attention, consciousness, sleep, and wakefulness provides evidence that we may expect soon a more unified understanding of the behavioral, experiential, and physiological aspects of arousal.

Chapter 7

An Analysis of Exploratory and Play Behavior in Animals *

W. I. WELKER[†]
University of Wisconsin

INTRODUCTION

*A*NIMALS that enjoy a relatively helpless and behaviorally limited infancy pass into a phase of early life when their behavioral repertory expands rapidly and they come in contact with or attend to discrete environmental stimuli in a variety of ways. Thus emerge the complex and fascinating phenomena of exploration and play. These behaviors are of fundamental importance not only because of their early appearance in ontogeny but also because of their crucial roles in adaptive learning and in maintaining alert contact with the environment. The following sections are intended as a conceptual dissection of the phenomena of exploration and play in an attempt to identify the factors, forces, and mechanisms of which they are composed.

We shall begin by suggesting tentative descriptions of exploration and play. These descriptions briefly summarize the salient characteristics which have been assigned to these behavior categories in the literature (Welker, 1954). *Exploration* consists of cautiously and gradually exposing the receptors (by biting, licking, sniffing, touching, looking, listening, and moving) to portions of the environment. The goals or incentives consist of sensory stimulation, and novel stimuli in any modality are especially important. *Play* consists of a wide variety of vigorous and spirited activities: those that move the organism or its parts through space such as running, jumping, rolling

---
*This project was supported in part by research grant M-2786 (C1), National Institutes of Health, Public Health Service.
†Kenny Foundation Scholar.

and somersaulting, pouncing upon and chasing objects or other animals, wrestling, and vigorous manipulation of body parts or objects
in a variety of ways. The goals and incentives of vigorous play
consist of certain patterns of variable or changing stimulation of the
sensory surfaces. In mammals and birds, both play and exploration
occur in relatively familiar surroundings. Both arise early in ontogeny whenever these animals are comfortable and free from internal
tissue needs (food, water, hormone, and temperature imbalances)
or environmental stresses. There are four prominent features of
play and exploration: (1) heightened interest in novel stimuli, (2)
habituation of interest with continued exposure, (3) recovery of responsiveness during unstimulated intervals, and (4) preferences and
aversions for certain stimuli.

It is obvious that a great variety of specific act sequences may
be classed as exploration and play, and that a number of variables
can affect them. Moreover, it will be necessary to pay particular attention to an intimate relationship between curiosity and fear. Such
issues will be raised in due course. Most of the experimental studies
to be considered below have concentrated on exploratory behavior,
and some of the important concepts derived therefrom have been
the subject of excellent reviews (Barnett, 1958c; Berlyne, 1958c,
1960; Butler, 1958a; Dember and Earl, 1957; Glanzer, 1958a; and
White, Chapter 10). Where necessary, for adequacy of coverage,
reference will be made to observational studies, especially with respect to play phenomena, which have not been examined experimentally.

In Part I, below, the phylogeny and ontogeny of exploration and
play will be traced first and then stimulus-response components of
exploration will be examined. Relationships to learning and to physiological states are discussed in Part II, along with consideration of
pertinent neural mechanisms. Part III takes up problems of measurement and definition, and problems of interpretation.

I. AN ANALYSIS OF THE PHENOMENA

Phylogenetic Considerations

Throughout the animal kingdom, exploratory-like behaviors may
be observed (Fraenkel and Gunn, 1940; Thorpe, 1956; Washburn,

1936). Both the extension and retraction of pseudopodia by *Amoeba* as it makes its way among the objects and surfaces of its environment as well as the probing by head and antennae of insects and arthropods appear similar in a general way to the commonly observed exploratory actions exhibited by birds and mammals. The exploratory actions of invertebrates as well as vertebrates appear to be induced by novel stimuli and to manifest not only habituation but also recovery phenomena (Darchen, 1952; Grosslight and Ticknor, 1953; Lepley and Rice, 1952). That the neural mechanisms involved cannot be the same in such divergent forms is obvious (Pantin, 1952). One possible difference between exploration in invertebrates and in mammals is that the former explore presumably only under the stresses of food deprivation, excessive stimulation, temperature imbalance, etc., whereas the latter may explore when not under such duress. Vigorous play activities probably do not exist in invertebrates, or even lower vertebrates such as fish (Breder, 1932), cyclostomes, amphibia, and reptiles, although courtship and aggressive displays may be misinterpreted as such in these forms. Vigorous play activities are commonly observed in young birds and mammals. Excessive concern with mutually exclusive and rigorous definitions will not carry us far, however, especially with the meager experimental data at hand. Rather, full effort must be given to careful description of the various behavior sequences and their determinants in animals within each of the taxonomic groups.

A survey of the literature has disclosed numerous observational accounts of play and exploration in a variety of animal types. References to a few of these reports are listed in Table 7-1. Descriptions of play and exploration were not found for the following mammalian orders: Monotremata, Dermoptera, Edentata, Pholidota, Tubulidentata, Hyracoidea, and Sirenia. These exceptions can probably be attributed to the limited study of behavior of animals in these groups. The purpose of Table 7-1 is complementary to the main analysis to be presented later. It has been prepared to indicate the taxonomic range of the behaviors commonly designated as exploration or play. The reader may turn to these references to obtain descriptions of these behaviors in the various animal types.

As we shall see in later sections, most of the experimental studies

TABLE 7-1. Animal Groups for Which Play and Exploration Have Been Described

Class Mammalia*

Order	Family	Genus	Common Name	Play	Exploration
Marsupalia	Phalangeridae	Trichosurus	phalanger		Adey et al., 1956
Insectivora	Soricidae	Neomys	shrew	Lorenz, 1952	Lorenz, 1952
Chiroptera	Vespertilionidae	Myotis	bat	Dubkin, 1952	Dubkin, 1952
Primates	Lorisidae	Galago	galago	Lowther, 1940	Lowther, 1940
	Cebidae	Alouatta	howler monkey	Carpenter, 1934	Carpenter, 1934
		Ateles	spider monkey	Carpenter, 1935	
		Cebus	cebus		
	Callithricidae	Callithrix	marmoset	Fitzgerald, 1935	Klüver, 1937
	Cercopithecidae	Macaca	rhesus	Foley, 1934	Fitzgerald, 1935
				Hines, 1942	Foley, 1934
					Hines, 1942
	Pongidae	Papio	baboon	Benchley, 1942	
		Hylobates	gibbon	Carpenter, 1940	Carpenter, 1940
		Pan	chimpanzee	Hayes, 1951	Hayes, 1951
		Gorilla	gorilla	Yerkes, 1927	Yerkes, 1927
		Pongo	orangutan	Schmid, 1939	
Lagomorpha	Ochotonidae— Leporidae	Ochotoma	pika		Loukashkin, 1940
		Lepus	hare	Seton, 1929	Seton, 1929
Rodentia	Sciuridae	Sciurus	squirrel	Klugh, 1927	Klugh, 1927
		Eutamias	chipmunk	Jaeger, 1929	Gordon, 1943
		Citellus	ground squirrel	Linsdale, 1946	Linsdale, 1946
		Glaucomys	flying squirrel	Svihla, 1930	
	Castoridae	Castor	beaver	Leighton, 1933	Leighton, 1932
	Cricetidae	Neotoma	woodrat	Richardson, 1943	Richardson, 1943
	Muridae	Rattus	rat	Small, 1899	Small, 1899
				Tilney, 1933	Tilney, 1933
					Williams et al., 1953
		Mus	mouse		
	Erethizontidae	Erethizon	porcupine	Shadle, 1944	
	Caviadae	Cavia	guinea pig		King, 1956

*Classification after Simpson, 1945.

Order	Family	Genus	Common name		
Cetacea	Delphinidae	Tursiops	porpoise	Essapian, 1953	Essapian, 1953
		Globicephala	pilot whale	Kritzler, 1952	Kritzler, 1952
Carnivora	Canidae	Canis	dog	Scott et al., 1950	Scott et al., 1950
			coyote	Russell, 1936	———
			wolf	Fichter, 1950	———
		Vulpes	fox	Schmid, 1939	———
		Speothos	bush dog	Seitz, 1950	———
	Ursidae	Ursus	bear	Bates, 1944	
	Procyonidae	Procyon	raccoon	Volmar, 1940	Whitney et al., 1952
		Nasua	coati mundi	Whitney et al., 1952	Richter, 1925
	Mustelidae	Mustela	weasel	Pearce, 1937	Aldous, 1940
			ferret	Aldous, 1940	
			mink	Svihla, 1931	
		Martes	marten	Remington, 1952	Remington, 1952
		Meles	badger	Eibl-Eibesfeldt, 1950	Eibl-Eibesfeldt, 1950
		Mephitis	skunk	Stegeman, 1937	Stegeman, 1937
		Spilogale	skunk	Gates, 1937	Gates, 1937
		Lutra	river otter	Liers, 1951	
		Enhydra	sea otter	Fisher, 1940	
	Felidae	Felis	cat	Lorenz, 1955	Tilney et al., 1924
			lynx	Lindemann, 1950	
		Panthera	leopard	Benchley, 1945	
			lion	Cooper, 1942	Cooper, 1942
	Otariidae	Callorhinus	fur seal	Bartholomew, 1959	Bartholomew, 1959
		Phoca	seal	Benchley, 1945	
Proboscidea	Elephantidae	Elephas	elephant	Inhelder, 1955b	Benchley, 1945
Perissodactyla	Rhinocerotidae	Rhinoceros	rhinoceros	Inhelder, 1955b	
Artiodactyla	Hippopotamidae	Hippopotamus	hippopotamus	Noble, 1945	Darling, 1937
	Cervidae	Cervus	red deer	Darling, 1937	Linsdale et al., 1953
		Odocoileus	mule deer	Linsdale et al., 1953	Altmann, 1958
		Alce	moose	Altmann, 1958	Skinner, 1922
	Antilocapridae	Antilocapra	antelope		

TABLE 7-1 (Cont.)

Class Aves*

Order	Family	Genus	Common Name	Play	Exploration
Pelicaniformes	Sulidae	Sula	gannet		Griffin, 1953
Anseriformes	Anatidae	Somateria	eider duck	Roberts, 1934	
Falconiformes	Falconidae	Falco	kestrel	Battersby, 1944	Thorpe, 1951
		Buteo	buzzard	Battersby, 1944	
	Accipitridae	Haliaeetus	American eagle	Herrick, 1934	
		Accipiter	goshawk	Bond, 1942	Bond, 1942
Galliformes	Phasianidae	Gallus	chicken		Fantz, 1954
Cuculiformes	Musophagidae	Turacus	plantain eater	Moreau, 1938	Herrick, 1910
	Cuculidae	Cuculus	cuckoo		
Coraciiformes	Bucerotidae	Lophoceros	crowned horned-bill	Ranger, 1950	Ranger, 1950
Passeriformes	Corvidae	Cyanocitta	bluejay	Moreau, 1944	Rand, 1937
		Corvultur	raven	Nice, 1943	
	Fringillidae	Melospiza	song sparrow	Howard, 1907	Nice, 1943
	Sylviidae	Acrocephalus	sedge warbler		

Class Pisces†

Order	Family	Genus	Common Name	Play	Exploration
Acanthopteri	Gobiidae	Bathygobius	goby		Breder, 1950
	Pomacentridae	Pomacentrus	beau gregory		Breder, 1954
	Cyprinidae	Brachydanio	"zebra fish"		Breder, 1950
	Gerridae	Eucinostomus	common Mojarra		Breder, 1954
					Breder et al., 1946
					Welker et al., 1958

*Classification after Wetmore, 1940.
†Classification after Breder, 1948.

of exploration and play have been carried out with primates, carnivores, and rodents. Very few truly comparative studies have been made, however, and knowledge concerning species differences with respect to these behaviors has been largely observational. Nevertheless, several facts have emerged from such studies. It is known, for example, that each animal group has exploratory and play actions that are peculiar to itself (Inhelder, 1955a). Thus, cattle frisk and butt (Brownlee, 1954), whereas cats pounce and wrestle (Lorenz, 1955). The rate and vivacity of playful actions also varies considerably from one group to another (Groos, 1898). Closely related animals may exhibit quite dissimilar modes of exploration. In the raccoon, for example, the forepaws explore ceaselessly, whereas the coati mundi probes the environment predominantly with its snout (Welker, 1959a). Moreover, there are species differences in the types of stimuli which elicit exploration and play. Thus, visual details are primary excitants for the gray squirrel, whereas tactile stimuli are more important for moles and auditory stimuli for bats. Such variations as these are often obvious even to casual observation and reflect certain differences in body size and structure or in anatomical and functional organization of the receptors and nuclei of the central nervous system. To such problems we shall return.

Several authors have suggested, explicitly or implicitly, that play and exploratory behaviors show a comparative increase in variety and complexity in the phylogenetically more advanced groups. Nissen (1951) has discussed such a relationship at some length. He suggests that less exploration and play occurs in animals whose repertory of perceptions is determined by innate organization present shortly after birth than in animals whose perceptual organization is primarily acquired during longer periods of immaturity. Evidence for this view is also discussed by Schneirla (1959) and Schiller (1952). According to Yerkes and Yerkes (1929), within the primate series there is a greater diversity of play and exploration (curiosity) in the more advanced forms. Since novelty, an important determinant of exploration, is a function of the degree of contrast of present perception with past experience, it seems clear that animals having a capacity for an extensive range of past experience would be able to perceive a greater number of novel stimuli than those with only short-term memory or meager learning ability. It would follow, therefore, that animals of the former type would find greater incentive for exploration.

In experimental studies Kish and Antonitis (1956), McClearn (1959), and Thompson (1953b, 1956) have found differences in amount of exploratory behavior between mice strains in novel situations. Barnett (1956) demonstrated that wild rats are less likely to approach a particular novel stimulus configuration than are rats bred for the laboratory. Mahut (1958) demonstrated breed differences between dogs in the tendency to approach or avoid novel stimuli. These experiments represent first attempts to identify genetic determinants of exploratory behavior. The data of both McClearn and Thompson suggested polygenic influences.

As we shall see below, novel stimuli elicit both approach and avoidance, depending upon their degree. Barnett suggests that a certain ". . . combination of exploring and avoidance with learning is elegantly adapted to giving a rat the maximum of information about the resources and dangers of its environment, in the safest possible way. . ." (1958c, p. 302). The particular balance achieved between curiosity and fear varies, however, from one species to another and the mechanisms responsible for different aspects of these behaviors may be presumed to have evolved differentially in various animal populations.

Further work should be directed at determining the genetic influence on particular aspects of exploratory behavior, such as responses to various degrees of novelty in various contexts, habituation, recovery rates, and preferences and aversions. Concurrently, attention could also be profitably directed at identifying the skeletal, muscular, and neural correlates of the interspecies behavioral differences.

Ontogenetic Changes

We shall now turn to an examination of evidence concerning ontogenetic trends in exploration and play. During the early development of animals there are a number of striking changes in reactions to external stimuli. Riesen (1960b) has grouped these changes into four successive stages as follows: (1) a period during which there is little or no response to stimuli, (2) a period of gradually increasing familiarity and attention, (3) a period when the animal becomes emotionally disturbed when stimulus patterns deviate from the familiar, and (4) a period of increasingly active exploration.

Although many mammals such as the guinea pig (Allen, 1904) and moose calf (Altmann, 1958) are relatively advanced in their behavioral development at birth and manifest exploration almost immediately, many others have a relatively limited post-parturitional response repertory. For example, in puppies (Scott and Marston, (1950) or raccoons (Welker, 1959d) before eyes and ear canals open, the response repertory consists entirely of reflexes and simple reactions associated with hunger, bowel and bladder tensions, temperature imbalance, and sudden or strong vestibular, olfactory, gustatory, contactual, or thermal stimuli. Waking time is spent almost entirely in essential regulative activities such as sucking, eliminating, or movements to achieve optimum body temperature or postures (Welker, 1959d).

During this period, there are none of the approach reactions to novel stimuli which characterize later exploratory behavior. At some point in development, however, the neonate mammal begins to show signs of attentive reactions to external stimuli when it is awake and also is comfortable with respect to the stresses which previously had activated it. It gently contacts stimuli with its nose, bites them, or paws at them. When they first occur, these exploratory actions may appear both before and after eating and are thus independent of mild hunger and thirst states (Welker, 1959d). Vigorous play actions do not occur during this early phase. After the eyes and ear canals open and the first teeth have erupted, an increasingly greater variety of stimuli are reacted to in an ever-greater number of ways and for progressively longer periods of time (Harlow, Blazek, and McClearn, 1956; Mason, Harlow, and Rueping, 1959; Scott, 1958b). As behavioral differentiation proceeds, there is an increasing vigor in some of these act sequences (Rosenblum, 1961), and the concept of play is appropriately applied to them. It is conceivable that the mechanisms which prompt some vigorous play activities are different from those motivating cautious exploration. Thus observations of infant monkeys (in the study by Rosenblum) and rats (Tilney, 1933) show that at an early phase of ontogeny these mammals exhibit sudden leaps and starts which are soon transformed into vigorous social play sequences. Rosenblum (1961) has also shown that infant monkeys' early exploratory interest in one another is similar to, and develops parallel with, exploratory interest in inanimate objects. These early preplay responses appear to underlie the later, more complex social play patterns.

When exploration first appears, the animal makes contact with stimuli only in the immediate vicinity of the home nest or region. Gradually the animal's horizon is extended (Altmann, 1958; Carpenter, 1934; Fitzgerald, 1935; Hines, 1942; Jacobsen *et al.*, 1932). This territorial expansion is presumably due to (*a*) a mounting habituation to the familiar elements of the nest, and (*b*) the development of approach reactions to the more novel stimuli at the periphery of the home territory, such stimuli becoming less novel with continued exposure and consequently eliciting less avoidance.

Initially, the act sequences exhibited in play with objects or other animals are simple and of short duration. With continued experience (and probably neural maturation), however, these early acts become elaborated, new acts appear and all are woven into more involved, extended, and cohesive sequences, and elaborate "games" thereby evolve (Foley, 1934; Herrick, 1934; Hines, 1942; Jacobsen, Jacobsen, and Yoshioka, 1932; Rand, 1937; Rogers, 1932; Rosenblum, 1961; Schiller, 1952). Although observational evidence indicates that novelty, habituation, and recovery from habituation are involved in vigorous play sequences as well as in the more cautious exploratory acts, no experimental investigations have analyzed these important, interesting, and complicated activities in animals.

The frequency of occurrence of play and exploration reaches a peak sometime during childhood; each animal type having its own maximal age period (Carpenter, 1934; Cooper, 1942; Riesen and Kinder, 1952; Tilney, 1933; Welker, 1956a, 1956b; Yerkes and Yerkes, 1929). With advancing age, external stimuli gradually lose their potency for initiating activities of this sort. Some evidence has shown that such age effects are expressed as different degrees of reaction to novelty, habituation, or recovery (Welker, 1956a, 1956b).

Little is known about the character of responses to various degrees of stimulus novelty after the period of maximal play and exploration has passed. Adults occasionally indulge in brief bouts of vigorous play (Linsdale and Tomich, 1953; Noble, 1945; Thorpe, 1951), but generally spend considerable time in overt idleness. The relatively rapid development of the ability to locomote and to maintain stable postures in the neonate may account to some extent for the early sudden spurt in play and exploration. The decline in these activities as childhood recedes may in part be attributed to the growing concern with sexual affairs. The decrease in vigorous play may also be conditioned by pain and discomfort induced by the biting and roughhouse that increase in severity with approaching adolescence (Carpenter, 1934; Tilney, 1933). The rate of development of exploration may also be under parental influence, the exact nature of which is a function of species. Thus the moose-cow tends to curb the exploratory wanderings of its calf (Altmann, 1958). The chimpanzee mother does this but she may also assist her young in its early exploration and attempt to stimulate it in ways that induce it to play (Yerkes and Tomilin, 1935). Studies of the locomotor activity in albino rats have shown that it reaches a maximum between 80 and 120 days of age (Slonaker, 1907). It is not clear whether this peak of activity coincides with the assumed peak of exploration and play or whether these activities are even motivationally related. So far, there have been no systematic experimental attempts to examine the development of exploration or play throughout the life span of any animal.

As will be discussed later, whether animals will approach or avoid a novel stimulus is determined by its degree of novelty: strongly novel stimuli are avoided and only mildly novel stimuli are approached. Although detailed evidence is not yet available, perhaps fear reactions to novel stimuli appear at about the same time that mildly novel stimuli can be distinguished from strongly novel stimuli, and are approached. Fear reactions to strange objects are very prominent in chimpanzee infants (Hebb and Riesen, 1943; Riesen and Kinder, 1952; Welker, 1956a) and appear to diminish during childhood (Welker, 1956b). Bernstein and Mason (1960) have shown that the initial fear responses of infant rhesus monkeys (1-3 months) to novel stimuli are quite generalized, whereas those of older animals (16-25 months) are directed with respect to the stimuli. More complex stimuli elicited more emotional responses in animals of all ages and were more effective in eliciting avoidance in the older (16-25 months) animals. No approach reactions were observed under the conditions of this experiment. Haslerud (1938) has reported that young adult chimps (9-16 years) are more cautious about approaching novel nonmoving stimulus objects than are chimpanzee children (1-4 years). Schiller (1952) found that adult chimps exhibited greater fear of live moving snakes than did infant animals. The fact that the older chimps in both these studies were jungle-born may have influenced the results. Further research is required to confirm the hypothesis that fear of novelty increases with age. Careful control of past experience and of degree of stimulus novelty is required in such studies.

The evidence clearly demonstrates that experiential factors are involved in the generation of the age trends which have been observed. To a young and inexperienced animal, the great majority of external stimuli will be strongly novel. First reactions to these will be aversive, cautious, and hesitant, yet positive interest will be shown in only slightly novel stimuli. Gradually the range of experience increases to a certain undefined point beyond which the number of stimulus patterns which are very novel would be expected to diminish. The animal would thus show less interest in the environment.

This conception of the course of reactions to novelty during ontogeny is undoubtedly oversimplified. As we shall see, a novel stimulus is defined by its degree of contrast with a familiar context. It is possible that during early infancy when the experiential background is limited, a particular stimulus would be perceived as less novel than it would in adulthood when viewed against a more elaborate experiential context. This possibility needs to be explored experimentally.

Explanation of the observed age trends in terms of past experience is probably not the whole truth, however. Anyone familiar with animals of different ages is aware that older, more experienced animals are not as able to adapt to "new" surroundings as are younger animals (Hediger, 1955). The childhood of animals appears to be a time of special plasticity and flexibility. If one desires a wild animal for a pet, best results are obtained by acquiring an infant before it has developed fear responses to novel stimuli. Such an animal will become exceedingly tame or adapted. The older a wild animal is when brought into captivity, the more difficult does taming become because the novel situation evokes exaggerated fear responses (Hediger, 1950). A study by Thompson and Heron (1954) apparently contradicts this conclusion. They found that when dogs raised in restricted surroundings during infancy were subsequently allowed access to strange environments they explored as much or more than normals. However, these animals may not have been beyond the proposed period of enhanced curiosity and play when given their freedom. Luchins and Forgus (1955) found that rats reared during childhood in broader, more varied environments exhibited greater activity in Y mazes when tested at maturity than did restricted rats. The experimental group also exhibited greater variability during problem solving. Ehrlich (1959) and Montgomery and Zimbardo (1957) did not find an effect of differential early environments although Ehrlich found that handled rats explored more than unhandled rats. Only further research can explain such contradictory results. In order to determine the importance of experience during the maximal period, restricted and nonrestricted animals should be tested some time beyond this period. First, however, the age range of the period of maximal exploration must be determined. It is necessary to recall that the period of maximal exploration and play may occur only in those cases where the animal exists in relatively familiar and safe surroundings where the novel stimuli available are not too strong. If early environmental stimulation is too intense and prolonged, then chronic avoidance, freezing, or bizarre behavior patterns may appear. Although animals with restricted early experience may be poorly adapted when released into a broader and more varied environment, the same is true of mature free-ranging animals brought into confinement (Hediger, 1950): in neither case do the animals attain a full and free behavioral repertory. Wild animals do, of course, live in a type of environment that must be considered restricted, in view of all the available situational possibilities. The important point here is that drastic changes in stimulation are disruptive of behavior organization (Hebb, 1949). It should be added that the particular effect obtained may depend on the species: domesticated animals adapt more readily to captivity and certain animals like the giant sea cow became extinct apparently because they did not fear the strange men who easily slaughtered them in large numbers (Hediger, 1955). There are many examples in natural history of species differences in docility, curiosity of strangers, adaptability to novel conditions of captivity, etc., in adult animals. Only direct experiment can provide answers regarding the exact nature of these differences.

These various lines of evidence indicate that there is a critical period during childhood for the occurrence of play and exploration: a period during which the central nervous system (CNS) is especially involved in acquiring knowledge about the external environment. After this maximal period has passed, the organism attempts to maintain the organization so achieved. To what extent the CNS changes involved are experiential or maturational is unknown.

Four Fundamental Phenomena

Having examined various lines of evidence concerning the widespread occurrence of a variety of behaviors classed as play and exploration, we must now proceed to a more specific analysis of the behavioral details and their environmental and organismic determinants. Both the experimental and observational literature point to the powerful influence of stimulus novelty in eliciting not only approach but avoidance as well. It has been proposed (Barnett, 1958c; Berlyne, 1950; James, 1904; Montgomery, 1955; Thorpe, 1956) that whether one or the other is elicited depends upon the degree of stimulus novelty, strong novelty eliciting avoidance, and mild novelty evoking approach. In attempting to gain a full understanding of the dynamics of exploratory behavior, it is essential to examine these contrasting effects. Attractive and repellent factors often coexist and it is clear that both may influence exploratory behavior in novel situations.

In attempting to discover and analyze the factors involved in exploration, four fundamental phenomena have been identified. These will be characterized here as (a) responses to novelty, (b) habituation, (c) recovery, and (d) preferences and aversions. After considering some of the evidence for these four general factors, an attempt will be made to indicate how they function in the generation of the known variable sequential aspects of exploration and play.

Responses to Novelty. We shall begin by examining the evidence regarding behavioral effects of novel stimuli. Depending upon the degree of stimulus novelty, these effects may be of several varieties, all of which will be briefly considered here. The concept of novelty is a crucial one for the field of motivation. The task of defining the degree of novelty of any stimulus is, as will be shown (see p. 220), an intricate and difficult one. Initially, however, in order to facilitate movement over some admittedly rough ground, let us defer problems of definition and accept the simple notion that a novel stimulus is in some degree new, unusual, strange, odd, or different, and its antithesis is old, familiar, usual, or common. In the discussion that follows we shall arbitrarily distinguish the arousal effects of novel stimulation from the subsequent act sequences that are directed with respect to it.

Behavioral Arousal.   Novelty, or stimulus change, is a potent impetus to behavioral arousal (Sharpless and Jasper, 1956). There may be two sorts of arousal phenomena: one diffuse or general, and the other specific or focused (Dell, 1958; D. B. Lindsley, 1957). A startle response, awakening from sleep, and cessation of ongoing actions (for example, "freezing") are diffuse arousal effects, whereas an orienting "reflex" (Pavlov, 1927), such as turning the eyes and head in the direction of the stimulus, is a specific form of arousal or alerting. In a lucid discussion of problems of arousal, Bindra (1959a) has indicated that there are autonomic, muscular, and neural arousal effects, and that these are not always positively correlated. Even in the case of behavioral arousal effects as considered in this section, various muscular groups are differentially aroused to action (Bindra, 1959a).

There have been few experimental attempts to study the effects of stimulus parameters on specific aspects of behavioral arousal. Observational evidence suggests that the degree of arousal depends not only upon the degree of novelty of a stimulus change but also upon the concurrent activity or set of the organism, and upon the innate or learned preference or aversive value of the stimulus (see below). Bindra has suggested the tentative generalization that the ". . . greater the novelty (and intensity) of a stimulus pattern, as compared with a completely familiar situation, the greater will be the increase in arousal level above the base level" (1959a, p. 235). This assumes that set and preference or aversive factors are equated. In the present context the behavioral effects of stimulus intensity will be classed as preference or aversive phenomena. That certain qualities and intensity ranges of stimuli have differential arousal potency is common knowledge. This group of factors will be discussed in a later section. It is obvious that the current state or set of an animal determines the capacity of a stimulus for behavioral arousal. Thus, a sleeping or copulating animal would be less subject to stimulus arousal than an alert animal or one not so occupied. The role of set or internal state in arousal of animal behavior is another area for which experimental evidence is meager.

The degree of specificity or orientation of an arousal response also depends to some extent upon the degree of novelty. There is probably an optimal level of behavioral efficiency in this respect, with both slight and strong novelty eliciting poorly oriented or disorganized responses (Bindra, 1959a; Hebb, 1955; Schneirla, 1959). In an unpublished study of the cat's orientative responses to spatially discrete clicks, R. Thompson and Welker found that initially the cats made a rapid sweep of head and ears toward the stimulus source. With repeated presentation of the same stimulus over a period of several minutes, however, the rapidity and accuracy of the head orientation decreased. Eventually only the ears were pricked toward the stimulus and, finally, there was no observable response. Thus as the novelty wore off, the responses became smaller and less well directed. Other evidence of habituation of arousal with repeated presentation of a stimulus has been summarized by Bindra (1959a).

The particular muscular apparatus summoned to action during arousal depends upon the modality of the novel stimulus, and, therefore, upon the body locus of the receptors stimulated. Typically a visual, auditory, somatic, or olfactory stimulus brings the head and neck musculature into specific orientative action. However, each receptor surface commands a postural sequence which is more or less peculiar to itself. Overt behavioral arousal is usually accompanied by autonomic (for example, glandular, vascular) actions which are not outwardly visible. Internal biochemical changes so induced may in turn alter behavioral arousal thresholds. Such effects will be considered below.

Behavioral Sequel. After the initial arousal or attentive reactions have occurred, several other actions may quickly follow. Although the evidence is not equally secure regarding the several possibilities of action, the general hypothesis will be advanced here that the particular response sequences which are selected will depend not only upon the relative degree of novelty of the several stimuli of a configuration but also upon the spatial distribution of the stimuli with respect to the animal. We shall first consider the effects of various degrees of novelty on an animal that is in, or has access to, a familiar or preferred locale. Strongly novel stimuli at close range may evoke alarm calls, defensive and aggressive reactions, hiding and freezing, or watching of the stimuli from a distance (Andrew, 1956). Which actions occur depend upon the species (Hediger, 1955) and probably upon subtle temporal characteristics of the stimulus novelty. Several studies indicate that strong novelty elicits avoidance reactions initially (Bernstein and Mason, 1960; Haslerud, 1938; Welker, 1956a). On the other hand, mild novelty, induces approach and contactual behavior (Haslerud, 1938; Hudson, 1950; Welker, 1956a, 1956b, 1956c; Menzel, Davenport, and Rogers, 1961). There is probably a relatively wide range of novel stimuli that elicit approach and contact and within this range the more novel or complex stimuli receive greatest interest (Berlyne and Slater, 1957; Montgomery, 1954; Welker, 1956b, 1956c). A familiar environment is probably necessary for the occurrence of vigorous play actions, but the specific initiating factors of these activities are not known. Maximal familiarity with a stimulus typically yields no overt reaction but only boredom and disinterest (Welker, 1954). Prolonged exposure to highly familiar stimuli, however, results in aversive and discomfort reactions (Bexton, Heron, and Scott, 1954; Heron *et al.*, 1956). If physically possible, the animal tends to leave such a situation, or to seek out more novel stimuli if it has learned how (see "Exploratory Behavior and Learning," below). The fact that both very strong novelty and strong familiarity induce aversive reactions while mild novelty is approached has given rise to the concept that animals have a drive or need for optimal levels of stimulation. This concept will be examined in a later section.

If an animal is in a situation where there are *no* familiar stimuli, the effects are different in certain respects from those listed above. If the novelty of the aggregate is uniformly mild the animal moves about in headlong fashion (Montgomery, 1952b; Welker, 1957, 1959b); the animal exhibits freezing, grooming, and immobilization if the novelty is stronger (Bindra and Spinner, 1958; Denniston, 1959; Patrick, 1931); finally, if over-all stimulation is too strong or extensive it makes vigorous escape (Kawai, 1954; Montgomery and Monkman, 1955; Southern, 1954) or aggressive and defensive movements. In strongly novel stituations the animal may show little or no reaction to a specific mildly novel stimulus which, under familiar conditions, would elicit considerable individual attention (Appel and Hurwitz, 1959; Davis, McDowell, and Deter, 1956).

Nevertheless, in totally novel environments, rats may explore and approach these stimuli. It has been suggested (Welker, 1959b) that these exploratory actions may represent mild motives to escape since rats may choose to leave such a situation if given the opportunity. A variety of situational factors may affect behavior in strange situations (Broadhurst, 1957), but the results are often conflicting. Some of the confusion may be eliminated if stimuli involved are varied parametrically through a wide range of intensity of novelty. Such systematic analyses are necessary to test the validity of the hypotheses proposed here.

These data suggest that, following arousal, the reactions to novel stimuli depend not only upon the degree of novelty of a particular stimulus but also upon the spatial distribution of the novel or familiar stimuli and upon the animal's location with respect to this array. When familiar stimuli are present, they act as a frame of reference or "home base" from which exploration of small novelties may proceed. Familiar stimuli are thus preferred in a context of strongly novel stimuli. From these considerations it becomes evident that the approach behavior called exploration is only one aspect of a complex matrix of possible responses to novel stimuli. It has been necessary to examine all these response possibilities associated with novel stimulation since it has sometimes been assumed that novel stimuli are determinants only of exploration. The evidence is by no means complete, but the hypothesis is proposed here that each degree of over-all novelty has command of a particular set of responses. Considerable observational evidence indicates that by simply advancing a novel object closer and closer to an animal the entire gamut of reactions involving first cautious approach, then mild avoidance, flight, hiding, and "freezing," and finally defense or aggression may occur in close temporal order. Bernstein and Mason

(1960) have examined such progressive changes in avoidance behavior of monkeys. This general hypothesis can be reduced to a
number of specific testable hypotheses which take into account (*a*)
the degree of novelty of a specific stimulus, (*b*) the relative degrees
of novelty of all other stimuli within the situation, and, *(c)* the animal's spatial location with respect to these stimuli.

Habituation. Associated with, and implicit in, the concept of
novelty is that of habituation, and the related terms satiation and
adaptation. These concepts refer to the fact that repeated or continued
exposure to the same physical stimulus influences both its arousal
potency and its effect on the acts which follow. With habituation, the
stimulus loses novelty or becomes more familiar.

Effects on Arousal. With repeated or prolonged presentation,
mild stimuli which once elicited behavioral arousal gradually fail
to do so (Bindra, 1959a; Glanzer, 1953a; Harris, 1943; Hinde,
1954a; Sharpless and Jasper, 1956). In the case of extremely strong
or novel stimuli, however, arousal to repeated presentation may persist until exhaustion.

Effects on Behavioral Sequel. With repeated or prolonged stimulation, the character of the change in the response sequences depends upon the initial degree of novelty of the stimulus. If the initial
stimulus was too strongly novel, avoidance and/or aggressive reactions may persist for long periods of time and approach responses
may never appear. If the stimulus novelty was great enough to be
avoided initially, but yet not too great, the animal gradually comes
to increase the exposure of its receptors to the stimulus (Haslerud,
1938; Hudson, 1950; Montgomery, 1955; Thompson and Solomon,
1954; Welker, 1956a, 1957). This change is often called adaptation
and if the stimulus situation persists the next phase of habituation en-
sues. This consists of a gradual loss of interest in the stimuli (commonly called satiation; Berlyne, 1950; Glanzer, 1953b; Montgomery,
1953a; Welker, 1956b). With continued exposure to familiar stimuli the animal either shows little overt response, becomes inattentive,
inactive, or falls asleep. If the subsequent monotony is too prolonged,
the animal either develops ways of stimulating itself, or makes attempts to avoid the situation. Habituation is thus a process which
alters the degree of novelty of a stimulus.

The rate of habituation of arousal, or of subsequent responses, depends upon the initial strength of the novelty (Bindra, 1959a), and therefore upon the exposure history as expressed in terms of duration, frequency, and recency. If a particular novel stimulus is repeated regularly, habituation is typically negatively accelerated over time (Glanzer, 1953a; Harris, 1943). Habituation rate also depends upon concurrent contextual factors such as the presence of some familiar stimuli (other animals, home cage, etc.) which in effect influence the degree of novelty of the total situation. Habituation, like response to novelty, is an exceedingly general phenomenon. It is apparent in simple reflexes as well as in complex sequential activities although the neural mechanisms involved are not in every case the same (see "Neural Mechanisms" below). Depending upon the degree of novelty of the stimuli, as well as other relevant factors, habituation may be an extremely rapid process, becoming evident with brief exposures, or it may be slow and gradual. Several studies have shown that the habituation effect is more pronounced the shorter the interval between successive exposures (Heathers, 1940; Zeaman and House, 1951). It has also been shown that the more complex the stimulus, the slower the habituation (Welker, 1954, 1956c). This latter effect is presumably due to the fact that complex situations manifest a greater number of novel stimuli, each of which must undergo habituation before the total configuration is ignored. In familiar situations, or in situations into which the animal goes by free choice, habituative effects have been typically observed. In many instances such habituation may be persistent enough to be regarded as a form of learning (Montgomery, 1953a; Thompson and Solomon, 1954; Welker, 1956b, 1957). But more of this later.

Recovery. In the absence of stimuli to which habituation has developed (for example, during periods between successive presentations), there is some degree of recovery of the initial reactivity, regardless of whether the first reactions were approach or avoidance in character (Thompson and Solomon, 1954; Welker, 1956b, 1957). That is, there is a return toward the initial novelty value of the stimulus. The degree to which such recovery occurs probably depends upon the recency, duration, and frequency of previous exposures as well as upon the initial degree of novelty of the stimulus. The longer the time since previous stimulation, the greater the recovery of the initial reactivity (Butler, 1957b). There is some suggestion that recovery of the initial reactions is more complete in situations in which animals are forced to reside and which contain many novel elements (Butler and Alexander, 1955). Such situations elicit mild avoidance tendencies which cannot be consummated. If the animal can freely approach such a situation on its own initiative from out of a familiar context, avoidance reactions readily habituate and are replaced by approach and exploration (Welker, 1957).

Stimulus Preferences and Aversions. In referring to the attentive or arousal value of novel stimuli we have deliberately ignored the similar potency associated with stimuli as a function of learning, conditioning, or innate predisposition. Such stimuli may be avoided or approached because of their quality and intensity, regardless of their degree of novelty. Thus, stimuli within a particular range of temperature, intensity, wave length, or shape may be preferred, whereas others may be avoided. Preferences and aversions exist for particular parameters of stimulation in all sensory modalities. The existence of food (Maslow, 1933) and brightness (Jerome, Moody, Connor, and Ryan, 1958; Roberts, 1954; Robinson, 1957) preferences is well established. In the case of brightness preferences, rats have been shown to avoid zero (Robinson, 1957) and intense illumination (Jerome *et al.*, 1958), preferring mild degrees of illumination (Girdner, 1953; Kling, Horowitz, and Delhagen, 1956; Marx, Henderson, and Roberts, 1955). Similar phenomena probably exist in olfactory, auditory, and tactual (Harlow and Zimmerman, 1959) modalities.

Some cases of preferences may be found upon analysis to be instances of attraction to novelty or changeability. Thus, the preference for wood or paper as against plastic or metal objects may be due to the fact that wood and paper can be torn or bitten and thereby changed (Carr and Brown, 1959b; Cho and Davis, 1957). Study of natural preferences and aversions in mammals has only just begun. A considerable body of literature has accumulated regarding the existence of these phenomena in invertebrates (Fraenkel and Gunn, 1940) and birds (Fantz, 1957; Hess, 1956; Rheingold and Hess, 1957). The innate specific preferences and aversions demonstrated in invertebrates and lower vertebrates are typically involved in courtship and mating, predator-prey relationships, temperature regulation, etc. Only a few studies have indicated that specific preferences play a role in the act sequences of exploration and play (Mason and Harlow, 1959; Welker, 1956b).

It must be added that preferred or avoided stimuli may also be more or less novel, and reactions to such stimuli will be colored by reactions to novelty in ways outlined above. Therefore, reactions to the novelty characteristics of stimuli blend with learned and innate approach or aversive reactions. Habituation to preferred or aversive stimuli may also occur, but is slower than that to neutral stimuli and probably recovers from habituation more rapidly (Young, 1940). It is not crucial for the present discussion whether preferences or aversions are learned or inherent. Since maturational factors play an important role in the development of natural preferences and aversions, it would be expected that the animals' age is an important determinant of the stimulus qualities and intensities approached or avoided. This field of inquiry is in its infancy and only the barest outline of the role of stimulus preference and aversion factors in sequential behavior can be suggested. That these factors are of immense importance in the elicitation and patterning of behavior can no longer be doubted.

Role of the Four Phenomena in Sequential Behavior

The four general phenomena outlined above have been abstracted from several lines of inquiry. In this section an attempt will be made to show how these phenomena can be conceived to generate the variable sequential behavior typical of exploration. Glanzer (1953a) and Lepley (1954) have emphasized the importance of the problem of behavioral variability and the present account draws upon suggestions made by these authors.

One often gains the impression from experimental reports that the important stimuli for an animal are the single, simple, and gross patterns under experimental control. It cannot be overemphasized that, depending upon the degree of elaboration of the sensory systems of a particular animal, the slightest irregularities or changes in the spatial-temporal stimulus flux may be sufficient to capture attention even for a fleeting instant. Since many of such stimuli are fortuitous and therefore uncontrolled, much of the moment-to-moment behavior change which they induce is unpredictable. Most of the data regarding reactions to novelty, habituation, and recovery have been obtained under just such grossly controlled situations in which not only slight stimuli but correspondingly slight responses are ignored or overlooked. The principles governing the generation of sequential acts outlined below are meant to apply to these more delicate moment-to-moment changes as well as to the more obvious and gross act sequences.

Since animals usually encounter relatively complex situations, let us first consider the hypothetical case wherein the animal is confronted by a constellation of spatially discrete stimuli of *equivalent* degrees of novelty. If all the stimuli are very strongly novel, then the entire array will be avoided and differentiated response will not occur to particular items of the assembly until avoidance reactions habituate with continued exposure. If the stimulus array is mildly novel, however, attention is drawn to one or another of the stimuli. Habituation develops to this stimulus and it loses its attractive power while an adjacent stimulus, then relatively more novel, captures attention. Habituation develops to this one too and this sequence of events continues in saltatory fashion resulting in a series of orientations during which the entire configuration may be eventually surveyed. Throughout these sequences some recovery to each item occurs during periods when it is not being attended to. Such recovery may be sufficiently complete that the several stimuli in the array will be re-examined or repeatedly scanned during a single session until habituation is strong and persistent enough to raise the threshold of response to the entire aggregate. If all the stimuli in the array are physically similar, habituation to one results in partial habituation to the other similar, though spatially discrete, stimuli (Lubow, 1959; Welker, 1956c). This may be considered as an instance of generalization or transfer of effect (Glanzer, 1953a). The greater the number and kinds of stimuli in the configuration (that is, the more complex and thus more novel), the more frequent are the shifts in reaction from one to another of the elements (Witkin, 1941), and the longer will be the time spent with the total array, that is, the slower the over-all habituation (Welker, 1956c). The concept of complexity is itself complex and requires careful analysis of the sort achieved by Berlyne (1957b).

The sequential reactions to a stimulus aggregate which consists of several discrete stimuli *varying* in degree of novelty will be differentially directed with respect to the several stimuli. If some stimuli are very strongly novel, avoidance reactions to them may preclude reactions to other adjacent and less novel stimuli which might otherwise have received attention. If there is no avoidance of any portion of the array, the approach or contact reactions are differentially directed so that the more novel stimuli receive the greater frequency and duration of attentive responses. If preferred or aversive stimuli are incorporated within an array, the distribution of attention to the elements of the array will be modulated accordingly.

If a particular stimulus is in motion or otherwise changing, its effect on attention is more potent than an identical stationary or unchanging one (Berlyne, 1951; Carr and Brown, 1959c; Welker, 1956b). A stimulus that changes in position or in intensity eludes habituation, refreshes or maintains its novelty value, and consequently has a greater effect on behavior than a comparable stationary or unchanging stimulus (Welker, 1956b). Nevertheless, if the changes or movements are regular and cyclical, attention to them habituates, and more rapidly so than it does to irregular or variable changes.

When the entire sensory-motor apparatus of an animal is taken into account, the sequential events in behavior can be expected to exhibit an even more complex character. An animal exploring its environment may contact novel stimuli with olfactory, gustatory, somatic, visual, and auditory receptors. Most stimuli are complex in their constitution and are potential sources of a variety of stimulus energies or aspects which may reach several types of receptor either simultaneously or successively. An animal's attention may be attracted to a configuration via only one modality, but it typically investigates the stimulus complex further so that other modalities may also become sequentially involved. Thus, an object may first be perceived visually; it may then be approached, touched, scratched, lifted, sniffed, bitten and tasted, and perhaps whacked so that its acoustic properties are also perceived. In this manner an animal can create additional changes, with the stimulus patterns taking on new meaning accordingly. In a young inexperienced animal such induced changes may come as a surprise and perhaps even elicit avoidance for a time. With continued experience of this sort, however, it learns to produce various novel or preferred changes under conditions of monotony. After habituation of response develops to a stimulus pattern, the animal may discover some novel aspect which will elicit renewed interest. This sort of thing may occur during early childhood when new response sequences appear or are discovered. In such cases the animal "practices" each new act sequence (for example, somersaulting, rolling, pouncing, jumping, etc.) intensively until it too becomes stale. In this manner the four fundamental phenomena are conceived as involved in the generation of various patterns of sequentially variable behavior.

By simple observation of behavior in certain animal types, one can often tell whether the animal utilizes visual, olfactory, auditory, or somatic modalities in exploration. In other cases, however, easy identification is difficult or even impossible because two types of stimuli (for example, visual and auditory in the cat) may elicit similar orienting actions (head turning). Experimental controls become necessary in such cases. In some animals, such as the rat, the situation is even more complicated. For example, sniffing (polypnea) and vibrissae movements which accompany exploration may be aroused not only by olfactory and tactile stimuli, but by visual and auditory stimuli as well. Moreover, these actions persist after interruption of olfactory and tactile input from the snout (Welker, 1958). The mere occurrence of sniffing and vibrissae movements is thus no guarantee that the rats are attending to olfactory and tactile stimuli.

One receptor may be used to guide another into closer contact. Thus a spatially discrete sound induces a cat to orient its eyes in the appropriate direction. By means of vision, the animal may then approach the object and make subsequent contact with olfactory, gustatory, and somatic receptors. Although the sequences involved in this example may be complex to casual observation, they can be understood in terms of the phenomena discussed above. For example, once the cat visually orients the stimulus object, habituation begins. This process slackens when the animal approaches the object and thereby increases its retinal image size or achieves a novel angle of regard. When the animal stops at close range, however, visual habituation again develops. Now tactile impulses, being at this moment more novel, capture attention. By means of head, jaw, tongue, and sniffing movements, several successively novel aspects of the object come to be appreciated. In these sequences, the novel stimulus which is attended to shifts from one modality to another. With time, habituation to all receptor input from the object gradually occurs and it is then abandoned. The greater the number of stimulating possibilities, the greater and more sustained the interest. All the data suggest that by means of a form of saltatory scanning, the degree of novelty of afferent input among the several sensory modalities is continuously controlled and evaluated. No comparative studies have been made to determine in what specific ways the various sensory modalities differ with respect to response to novelty, habituation, or recovery.

In a previous section we have seen that a wide variety of responses may be elicited by novel stimuli of various degrees. For each subrange of intensity of novelty there seems to be an appropriate group of responses. Habituation, by altering the degree of novelty, brings a new set of responses into play. Since habituation may be a relatively rapid event, behavior may exhibit a series of aversive *and* approach reactions in rapid sequence. By approaching a particular stimulus too closely, an animal may boost its novelty value into an aversive range (due to an increase in number of perceptible aspects, increase in retinal size, etc.). Subsequent retreat reduces the intensity of this novelty again to a range favoring approach. The over-all outcome of such temporal sequences would be the vacillatory, hesitant, or skittish actions commonly noted of animals in strange situations (Hinde, 1954b; James, 1904).

The operation of the factors of novelty, habituation, recovery, and preferences and aversions may not always be obvious in complex situations. In the normal life of animals, complete control of stimulus conditions is not possible and the fortuitous intrusion of stimuli of uncertain degrees of novelty or preference is inevitable. In addition, even recurrent stimulus patterns are never physically identical when they occur on successive occasions outside the laboratory. Moreover, there is typically great irregularity in the temporal sequence of successive stimulus presentations in nature. Laboratory experiments, by reducing the impact of these uncontrolled parameters, have dissected the sequential activities of exploratory behavior. It is suggested here that the four basic phenomena so derived are sufficient to account for the major variable sequential characteristics of such behavior. Although the experimental evidence is sketchy regarding this conceptualization of behavior, the several specific hypotheses implied therein and outlined above are subject to experimental test.

We must now bring another aspect of exploration into focus. This concerns the role that these behavior sequences play in the growth of the animal's adaptive grasp of its environment.

II. FURTHER PHYSIOLOGICAL AND BEHAVIORAL CONSIDERATIONS.

Exploratory Behavior and Learning

Learning invariably occurs in any situation that evokes exploratory behavior. A theory of behavior would be seriously prejudiced if it referred to only the motivational effects of external stimuli. It is becoming increasingly clear that it is during the early exploration and play of young animals that fundamental learning regarding the environment takes place. While it has long been known that novel stimuli are powerful determinants of attention (Pillsbury, 1908), the extent to which learning occurs relative to such stimuli has only recently been clarified. It is now evident, however, that novel stimuli play a crucial role in learning. A number of facts bear on this problem. Studies of latent learning (Thistlethwaite, 1951) have shown that the opportunity to explore a novel situation results in learning relevant to that situation. Studies of the effect of early experience on later behavior also demonstrate the importance of early perceptual learning (Beach and Jaynes, 1954; King, 1958; Riesen, Chapter 3). The evidence is now conclusive that mere attentive perception of external stimuli can produce learning changes regardless of whether or not internal tissue needs are present (Birch, 1945; Montgomery, 1954; Thompson and Solomon, 1954; Woodworth, 1947, 1958).

During an animal's initial exposure to a novel situation, each of the many aspects of that situation are attended to according to the rules discussed in the previous sections. During the initial exploration of the situation the attraction to novelty and subsequent habituation and recovery result in a series of attentive responses to a variety of the stimuli present (Dennis, 1939; Maier, 1930, 1939). The behavioral variability so engendered assures a relatively complete assay of novel aspects of the environment regardless of whether it is a problem or non-problem situation. If a hungry animal is induced, by the setting of a problem (for example, presence of food behind barriers), to attend to certain portions of the situation, efficient progress from the experimenter's point of view cannot begin until responses to irrelevant stimuli have habituated (Bindra, 1959b), and it is probably the reactions to these stimuli which account for the errors committed during the early phase of problem solution. The duration of this initial period depends upon the number, intensity, and degree of novelty of the various stimuli in the configuration and is usually called the period of adaptation or familiarization. If there is a solution to the problem, only those S-R sequences that are successful in achieving food persist eventually, whereas reactions to the other irrelevent stimuli habituate. Habituation, or learning not to respond to irrelevant stimuli, is thus one important aspect of learning in problem situations (Sharpless and Jasper, 1956). With ingestion of sufficient quantities of food, of course, habituation also develops to the relevant stimuli, and responses to other irrelevant stimuli may subsequently reappear.

We have seen that the initial responses in mildly novel situations are directed to various specific stimuli. The character of these response sequences indicates that these stimuli are incentives or goals in and of themselves (Nissen, 1954b). After such initial reactions habituate, however, any further responses to these stimuli are instrumental. That is, the animal, by responding to them, produces certain changes (for example, food, stimuli associated with food, or other preferred or novel stimuli). In this connection several experiments have demonstrated that monkeys (Butler, 1953a, 1954b, 1957a; Butler and Harlow, 1957; Harlow and McClearn, 1954; Symmes, 1959a), rats (Arnold and Cho, personal communication; Myers and Miller, 1954; Montgomery and Segall, 1955), cats (Miles, 1958; Wenzel, 1959) and raccoons (Thackray and Michels, 1958) can learn to make discriminative instrumental responses of this sort in order to produce novel or preferred stimulus changes. By means of such learning, therefore, a wide variety of instrumental sequences may become incorporated into the behavioral organization. Thus, an animal may consolidate into a long chain a number of stimulus-response fragments which were previously incentives in themselves, but which now lead to other goals that may or may not be physically present. In this manner the animal can learn to explore *for* or *seek* novelty if it is not immediately present (Glanzer, 1958a) just as it can learn to explore *for* food, water, and a sexual partner. Instrumental avoidance reactions would be organized in similar fashion.

The increase in complexity of the response repertory during child-hood is presumably due partly to such learning changes.

Once an animal has begun to focus on the relevant aspects of a problem, the efficiency of learned responses also depends upon novelty, habituation, and recovery factors. Thus learning is more efficient if a certain degree of change of the familiar relevant stimuli is periodically introduced. Numerous studies have shown that massed practice usually does not foster as efficient learning or performance as does some pattern of spaced practice, and learning set experiments nicely illustrate the importance of variation in the relevant stimuli for the development of more efficient learned performance (Harlow, 1949). Havelka (1956) and Snygg (1936) have shown that rats prefer to solve maze problems that involve variable paths to the goal. And Walker and Paradise (1958) have shown that learning is more rapid in maze situations that elicit greater variability. Changes in a situation probably must be relatively mild for optimal learning, however, since introduction of strongly novel stimuli may distract from efficient learned performance by inducing curiosity (Bindra and Seely, 1959; Patrick and Anderson, 1930; Sutherland, 1957; Thiessen and McGaugh, 1959) or fear (Patrick, 1931). If no changes occur in a problem situation, attentive responsiveness to specific stimuli in the situation lags (boredom), further learning is impaired, and performance deteriorates as the subject attempts to escape from the situation or becomes easily distracted by irrelevant (although at the moment more novel) external stimuli or thought sequences.

All these data indicate that reactions to novelty, habituation, and recovery form the basis of the response sequences in any situation, whether or not a problem is present. They exert a strong influence on the rate of learning as well as on the efficiency of performance after a problem has been learned. Even in situations which do not contain a problem, learning occurs and mere attentive perception such as that induced by novelty is sufficient for it to take place.

Role of Physiological States

So far we have considered the exploratory behavior of animals—stimulus-oriented behavior which may appear when animals are presumably not prompted to action by states of internal stress or physiological imbalance. The purpose of this section is to show that the

four phenomena which characterize exploratory behavior also underlie the action sequences associated with physiological tissue imbalances and that animals under such stresses also may explore or
play. Perhaps because of the obvious importance of physiological
states in regulating behavior, a drive classification of behavior
has obscured the general significance of the four phenomena outlined
above. Unfortunately, little is known about the influences of various
physiological factors on specific characteristics of responses to novelty, habituation, recovery, or preferences and aversions. A few experiments will be cited which suggest, however, that such effects do
exist. It is known, for example, that temperature imbalances (Welker,
1959c), food and water deprivation (Campbell, 1958; Campbell and
Sheffield, 1953; Hall, 1956), hormonal excesses (Dell, 1958), as well
as certain drugs (Elkes, 1958) are capable of selectively altering an
organism's arousal thresholds to certain classes of external stimulation.

It has been shown that the responses to novelty, habituation, and
recovery which characterize exploration occur not only in satiated
animals but also in animals deprived of food and water (Adlerstein
and Fehrer, 1955; Carr, Overall, White, and Brown, 1959; Dashiell,
1925; Nissen, 1930). Food deprivation may have an effect on these
phenomena, although also influential are sex, degree of deprivation
(Thompson, 1953a), degree of familiarity or complexity of maze
situation (Adlerstein and Fehrer, 1955), and free opportunity to
explore a novel situation from out of a relatively more familiar context (Fehrer, 1956; Zimbardo and Miller, 1958). In lever-pressing
situations with light onset as reinforcement, food (Davis, 1958) and
water (Clayton, 1958) deprivation have been shown to increase response frequency. Hurwitz and De (1958) found decreasing and
then increasing response rate with increasing food deprivation. Further research is obviously needed to clarify the nature of interaction
of sex, need, stimulus, and situational factors.

Whether a hungry or thirsty rat eats or drinks when first allowed
access to food and water depends upon the novelty of the situation.
Thus, when such rats are placed in strange situations they do not
eat or drink immediately; rather, they explore the novel surroundings (Chance and Mead, 1955; Lowney, 1958; Welker, 1959b;
Zimbardo and Montgomery, 1957). Strange objects introduced into

familiar situations may also inhibit eating (Barnett, 1958b; Shorten, 1954). Responses induced by novel stimuli thus successfully compete with those induced by deprivation state and food stimuli. With continued exposure these reactions to novelty habituate.

Some evidence has shown that behavioral variability decreases when the animal is subjected to increased hunger (Harlow, 1953), thirst, or shock stress (De Valois, 1954). Moreover, considerable observational evidence suggests that play and exploratory behavior occur primarily in satiated and comfortable animals, and are interrupted by stress states and the presence of food (Davis, Settlage, and Harlow, 1950; Harlow, Harlow, and Meyer, 1950). The hypothetical mental state of rats thrust bodily into totally strange situations may be different from that of rats exploring the same situation leisurely and at their own initiative out of safe, familiar or preferred surroundings (Welker, 1957, 1959b). Certainly the behavior sequences are different in the two cases (see Hayes, 1960). The literature on rat exploration consists almost entirely of studies of behavior under the mildly stressful conditions of a totally strange environment. More thorough examination must be given to the rat's exploration of mildly novel stimuli from its familiar home surroundings.

With respect to food motivation, it should be emphasized that food stimuli have more than just nutritional value. Novelty, habituation, recovery, and preferences and aversions play an important role in the diet of animals and man. If possible, a varied diet is chosen. If preference value is equated, novel foods are ingested instead of familiar ones (Welker and King, 1961; Wilder, 1937), although this is not true for rats deficient in vitamin B when eating a diet containing this vitamin. Such rats were not attracted to novel foods (Harris, Clay, Hargreaves, and Ward, 1933). Specific food preferences, if very strong, may also overshadow the novelty effect (Barnett, 1956). Habituation to the same old food, and recovery of its palatability with prolonged abstinence are common phenomena (Siegel and Pilgrim, 1958). Indeed, these factors probably influence the animal's first interest in food objects. There is a period during the early explorations of neonatal mammals and fledgling birds, for example, when a great variety of objects of preferred size are gnawed, grasped, held in the mouth, tasted, and even ingested (Mason and Harlow, 1959; Nice, 1943; Tilney, 1933). Inedible as well as edible substances receive this treatment, and attractiveness to novelty as well as stimulus preferences and aversions probably play an important role here (Fantz, 1954; Mason and Harlow, 1959). In general, response to nonnutritional substances habituates more rapidly (Welker and King, 1961), probably in part because of distressing intragastric effects. Preferences persist into adulthood, however, not only for the many foodstuffs which are utilized in tissue metabolism but also for some nonnutritional substances (Campbell, 1958).

It should be added in this connection that in all studies where internal state is modified by food deprivation, there is also a coincident deprivation of sensory input from the usual food substances. This sensory deprivation allows for some recovery of novelty value of the food. In view of this, part of the avidity of subsequent ingestion may be due to the exaggerated novelty of the associated stimulus input (pre- and/or postingestional). The periodicity in *ad lib.* feeding may, therefore, be partly governed by novelty, habituation, and recovery factors. Grossman (1955) has summarized evidence that stimulation of receptors of the tongue, mouth, and esophagus during eating does play a role in the habituation of eating.

Evidence from studies of sexual behavior in rats (Fisher, 1958), guinea pigs (Grunt and Young, 1952), cattle (Almquist and Hale, 1956) and man (Kinsey, Pomeroy, and Martin, 1948) indicate that novelty of the partner has an important influence on sexual behavior, especially of the male. In addition, the early development of sexual behavior in rats (Beach, 1942b; Kagan and Beach, 1953; Stone, 1922), as well as in chimpanzees (Bingham, 1928; Nissen, 1954a) and man, is exploratory in nature. Some evidence (for example, Winkelmann, 1959) suggests that in humans the density of innervation of genitalia increases markedly at puberty, a factor which may contribute to the increased preference for play involving these receptors durings the closing phases of childhood.

We have seen above (pp. 191–96) that avoidance behavior in which altered physiological states are presumably involved (for example, in strangely novel situations) also possesses novelty, habituation, and recovery characteristics. Moreover, the appearance of aggressive behavior in mice (Scott, 1958a) and rats (Barnett, 1958a) has been shown to be elicited by novelty of the stimulus animal. Many partially inborn activities such as mobbing in chaffinches (Hinde,

1954b) and hoarding in rats (Bindra, 1948; Lowney, 1958) also involve these factors.

Cyclical running has typically been considered together with behavior having a physiological basis, and will for convenience be discussed here. The relationship between exploratory activity and running activity (as measured in activity wheels) is not quite clear. Montgomery (1953b) has shown that depriving rats of the opportunity to run in wheels did not affect their subsequent exploratory activity in a Y maze. If exploration in strange places is escape rather than simply novelty-approach oriented (Welker, 1959b), then the influence of activity deprivation upon such approach behavior has not been adequately tested. Hill (1956) has shown that activity wheel deprivation increases subsequent running and that activity habituates within sessions. It is possible that novelty of afferent input from muscle, joint, and vestibular receptors may constitute the incentive for such running activity so common to many rodents. Walker, Dember, Earl, Fawl, and Karoly (1955) have demonstrated that rats show a preference for a maze alley that permits the execution of a novel response pattern. However the clocklike activity cycles exhibited by rodents like flying squirrels (DeCoursey, 1959) does not show habituation over time. Moreover, incidental observations do not indicate that activity deprivation enhances subsequent activity level in such animals. There are species differences in these running phenomena and the kind of measuring apparatus influences the result (Eayrs, 1954; Reed, 1947). It is possible that spontaneous running activity is motivated differently from that of exploration and play as Hill (1956) has suggested, but the problem requires more thorough study.

It must be concluded that the four phenomena outlined in previous sections contribute to the spatio-temporal organization of many classes of activity, being apparent in sexual, eating and drinking, escape and aggressive, as well as in exploratory behavior. Each of these behavior types has distinguishing features, of course, especially with respect to the kinds of stimuli that are preferred and to the response classes elicited, but all exhibit responses to novelty, habituation, recovery, preferences and aversions. These findings, added to the ontogenetic, phylogenetic, and problem-solving data, further attest to the fundamental significance of these phenomena in the elicitation and patterning of behavior. With respect to exploratory and play behavior very little experimental work has been directed at determining the effect of altered physiological states on specific parameters of these activities. A study by Beach (1957) is an excellent prototype of such studies. By appropriate controls he showed that morphinized rats explore novel stimuli more than normals. He stresses the inadequacy of drive conceptions and suggests that the phenomena be conceptualized in terms of altered threshold, arousability, and adaptation levels.

Stimulus Motivation

That behavior, at least of a simple sort, may be elicited by mere activation of peripheral receptors has long been obvious. There are, for example, a great variety of protective, postural, adjustive, and orientative reflexes. These reflexes occur in response to stimulation of specific groups of receptors by certain forms of stimulus energies. Such reflex figures usually involve brief and coordinated muscular actions, and in various combinations form the substructure of action out of which the more prolonged and complex integrated action sequences are constructed. The simple reflexes themselves exhibit reactions to novelty, habituation, and recovery (Lehner, 1941; Prosser and Hunter, 1936). However, such recovery does not show long-term memory effects as do the more complex act sequences discussed in the previous sections.

Superimposed on these simple responses to stimuli lies the bulk of the complex behavior repertory which may also be elicited by simple external stimulus events. Although many of these action sequences are operant (or active) as well as respondent (or reactive) in nature, it is a common assumption that all complex behavior is motivated by its immediate sensory consequences or feedback characteristics. This seems to be the case with many of the activities discussed under the rubric of exploration (Butler, 1958a) as is suggested by the studies of Walker and his collaborators (Walker, Dember, Earl, and Karoly, 1955; Walker, Dember, Earl, Fliege, and Karoly, 1955; Walker, Dember, Earl, Fawl, and Karoly, 1955; Kivy, Earl and Walker, 1956), but there are certain exceptions to this generalization which merit some consideration. It is probably not true, for example, of the initial arousal responses to novel stimuli.

the so-called orienting reflexes. These would be considered as respondent behaviors (Keller, 1954). Moreover, some of the characteristics of rat exploratory behavior occur regardless of sensory feedback. Thus, sniffing (polypnea) and vibrissae movements occur regardless of whether olfactory or tactile nerves are intact (Welker, 1958). Weiss (1955) has summarized embryological evidence which indicates that the developing central nervous system is capable of producing a finite repertory of simple act sequences before it receives control from afferent impulses.

It has also been shown that in learned tasks which involve very rapid sequential movements, or in which sensory feedback is prevented by denervation (Knapp, Taub, and Berman, 1958; Lashley, 1917), movements do indeed occur which are not regulated or directed by receptor feedback effects. Such sequences are initiated and programmed centrally. Twitchell (1954) has shown that the movements obtained in denervated limbs are "associated" movements which are brought into play by reflex action. Nevertheless, his monkeys with a denervated forelimb learned to control the tonic neck reflex so that the associated forelimb's movements could produce appropriate visual feedback effects in climbing or defense. Studies of cyclical running behavior (for example, of flying squirrels: DeCoursey, 1959) suggest that such behavior is not directly motivated by its stimulus consequences. These facts, together with those discussed in the next paragraph, suggest that it is the particular patterning of neural firing within the central nervous system which is the important goal or incentive in any act sequence (Hebb, 1949) and not just sensory or receptor stimulation *per se*.

The view has been advanced that animals have a need for certain optimal levels of stimulation (Bindra, 1959a; Hebb, 1955; Leuba, 1955). If the animal is stimulated to excess of this optimum, it tends to behave so as to reduce the stimulation. On the other hand, if the level of afferent stimulation is too low, the animal will behave so as to increase the level of over-all stimulation. Studies of approach to mild novelty and avoidance of strong novelty in animals attest to the importance of optimal levels of stimulation. The stimulus level which is sought, however, is dependent upon previous experience, for animals raised in restricted environments are less prone to approach particular stimuli than are those with wide previous experience

(Mahut, 1958; Melzack, 1952; Riesen, Chapter 3). An obvious reason for such experiential differences is that for the restricted animals
a given set of stimuli are far more novel than they are for animals
with wider experience, and thus avoidance reactions predominate.
Glanzer in referring to these experiential differences has suggested
that the organism functions ". . . as an information processing system
that requires certain amounts of information per unit time" (1958a,
p. 311). He postulates that an ". . . organism's information requirements are set by its past experience. An organism that has had a high
flow of information directed at it in the past would have a high requirement or standard. The organism would respond in terms of the
difference between its individual standard and the amount of information furnished by the situation" (1958a, p. 312). Thompson
(1958) has expressed similar views.

Studies on light-reinforced behavior indicate that rats or mice
will push levers that produce slight changes in illumination—either
increases or decreases (Barnes and Kish, 1957; Forgays and Levin,
1957; Hurwitz, 1956; Kish, 1955; Roberts, 1954; Roberts, Marx,
and Collier, 1958). Moon and Lodahl (1956) demonstrated similar
phenomena in monkeys. In some cases it was found that only increased intensity changes were preferred (Hurwitz, 1956; Robinson,
1957). Thomas, Appel, and Hurwitz (1958) found that rats would
press more readily for illumination changes if larger levers were
used. Premack, Collier, and Roberts, (1957) found that rats would
press a bar to turn on a weak light more frequently when they had
been deprived of light stimulation for a longer time.

Results from experiments with blinded rats have been taken as
support of the notion of optimal stimulation. Thus blinded rats have
been reported to explore more in novel illuminated situations (Glickman, 1958) or to consume greater volumes of nonnutritive saccharine
solution than normal rats (Rhodes and Wyers, 1956; Garcia and
Kimeldorf, 1958). The blinded rats are said to be making up for visual deficit by increased afferent stimulation via other modalities.
However, it is likely that blinded rats are more active in novel illuminated surroundings because they are not inhibited by general illumination as are normal rats (Keller, 1941; Welker, 1959b). Moreover,
the increased saccharine consumption may be related to metabolic
and hormonal disturbances suffered by peripherally blinded rats

(Browman, 1940). Thus anophthalmic rats manifest anorexia and decreased body weight, as well as alterations in preference for taste stimuli (Welker and King, 1961).

In view of the total weight of the evidence, however, there can be no doubt that animals tend to produce or seek certain levels of stimulation. The optimum sought is the over-all expression of interest in certain levels of novelty as well as in specific qualitative and quantitative stimulus characteristics which are preferred or avoided on an innate or learned basis. The optimal level is influenced by experience, age, and physiological factors, and it shifts through wide ranges of absolute stimulation over time. Diurnal shifts from sleeping to waking implicate one type of cyclical factor. A great deal of research is required to establish firmly the specific nature of the hypothetical optima and the factors which influence them.

Neural Mechanisms in Exploratory and Play Behavior

An attempt will be made in this section to summarize data from experiments which point to the neural mechanisms involved in the phenomena of exploration and play.

It must be realized at the outset that all extended behavior sequences that consist of locomotion and attentive sensory orientation to specific environmental stimuli involve the integrated function of several levels of the neuraxis (Denny-Brown, 1960; Eldred, 1960). Considerable evidence indicates that even the relatively simple postural reflexes which enable an animal to maintain stable bodily contact with supporting surfaces involve the spinal cord, medulla, cerebellum, midbrain, thalamus, basal ganglia, and cerebral cortex (Eldred, 1960). The task facing the neuropsychologist, therefore, is that of determining in what ways these various neural masses contribute to the organized patterning of overt behavior. Several lines of evidence give partial answers to this general question with particular reference to phenomena of exploratory behavior.

Comparative studies of the cerebral cortex of mammals have shown that there is a positive correlation between the degree of elaboration of cortical sensory areas and the degree to which particular sensory surfaces are used in the exploration of the environment (Welker and Seidenstein, 1959). Thus, the rooting pig has a much larger cortical snout area than does the grazing sheep (Adrian, 1943;

Woolsey and Fairman, 1946). The spider monkey with a prehensile tail has an exaggerated cortical somatic and motor tail area (Chang, Woolsey, Jarcho, and Henneman, 1947; Coxe, Hirsch, Benjamin, Welker, Thompson, and Woolsey, 1957). Rodents in which the snout is prominent in exploration (rat, guinea pig, pocket gopher, capybara) have enlarged face areas (Campos and Welker, 1960; Woolsey, 1952; and unpublished studies by DeCoursey and Welker, and by Zeigler and Woolsey), whereas in certain carnivores (raccoon) and primates (spider, squirrel, cebus, and rhesus monkeys, chimpanzee and man), the cortical hand area has become relatively greater. The raccoon, which manifests an exaggerated use of forepaws in its exploratory activities, has proportionally the largest cortical hand area of any animal yet studied (Welker and Seidenstein, 1959). The coati mundi, on the other hand, with its prominent probing snout has a greater cortical face than hand area (Welker, 1959a). Although such studies have been concerned primarily with the somatic-sensory system, similar evidence of differential cerebral enlargements are known for the auditory, visual, and olfactory systems (L. Edinger, 1899; T. Edinger, 1955).

Brain-behavior correlations have also been reported with respect to motor centers of the brain (Herrick, 1924). In all sensory systems studied, the differential enlargement or elaboration of cortical neural masses is parallelled by similar thalamic, bulbar, spinal, and sensory-receptor elaboration. Thus an entire sensory system, or a portion thereof at each level, may become elaborate or diminutive. It is uncertain just how these systems are involved in motivational mechanisms which prompt exploratory behavior using a particularly enhanced modality. Perhaps the greater number of nerve cells within the enlarged areas are effective in lowering thresholds of reception to external stimuli and permit a greater number of different stimuli to excite the animal to action. Although the specific functional roles played by enlarged neural masses are not known, it is evident that the differential development of certain sensory or motor systems predisposes each species to certain forms of attentive action.

Another line of investigation which has provided information relative to our central topic has involved ablations of various parts of the brain. Total decortication of cats (Bard and Rioch, 1937) and monkeys (Travis and Woolsey, 1956) renders these animals inattentive to discrete stimulus patterns. They become somewhat lethargic and do not attend to or investigate discrete changes as they did before operation. A great deal of this inattention is probably due to the loss of pattern perception and of the memory for patterns which is mediated by the afferent areas of the cerebral cortex.

Krechevsky (1937a, 1937b, 1937c) has shown that the tendency of rats to vary their movement through a simple maze is diminished when bits of cortical tissue of sufficient size are removed bilaterally. Normal rats tend to vary their explorations on successive exposures to simple mazes, and it has been shown that such behavioral variability is due to the tendency to approach novel and avoid familiar stimuli (Glanzer, 1953a). Morgan and Wood (1943) demonstrated that lesions of frontal cortex in the rat were more effective than parietal or occipital lesions for reducing the degree of such variability in the T maze.

Studies by French and Harlow (1955) and French (1959a, 1959b) have shown that bilateral removal of frontal cortex and especially of area 9 in monkeys renders the animals hyperactive. Strangeness of the test situation was thought to be a factor inducing hypermotility. Probably because of this hypermotility, these animals exhibited less bar-pressing behavior and less general curiosity about specific aspects of the cage interior than did animals with bilateral area 6 lesions. Hagamen, Lance, Ungewitter (1959) studied the reactions of cats to visual, auditory, and tactile stimuli after unilateral or bilateral removal of frontal lobe cortex. They found that following unilateral frontal lobe removal, the cat's attention did not readily habituate to stimuli applied ipsilaterally. They suggest that each frontal lobe normally exerts an inhibiting influence on attentive responsiveness to ipsilateral stimulation. Symmes (1959b), using visual exploration techniques, found that following bilateral and anterotemporal cortical ablations, monkeys did not show the interest in novel visual stimuli shown by normal animals and even by those devoid of frontal cerebral cortex. A study by Butler and Harlow (1954) suggested similar findings. A study by Dember, Brodwick, and Roberts (1960) has shown that the hippocampal formation is involved in habituation of responses of rats in a T maze. Thus, exploratory behavior of rats with bilateral hippocampal lesions did not habituate as rapidly as it did in normals. Moreover, the operated rats did not tend to alternate choice of alleys as do normal rats on the second of two closely spaced free trials in the T maze. The authors interpret these results as indicating that the hippocampus can indirectly influence exploratory behavior by preventing habituation through control of mechanisms of recent memory.

Except for the study of Dember, Brodwick, and Roberts (1960), in none of these ablation studies have systematic attempts been made to study novelty, habituative, or recovery effects parametrically. Although considerable experimental analysis will be required to assay the role of frontal cortex in behavior, the results reviewed above suggest that in rats, cats, and monkeys, this cortex is in some manner involved in the normal habituation of orientation toward repeated stimulation of initially novel stimuli.

Another group of ablation studies have shown that certain rhinencephalic nuclei function in normal cautious reactions to novel external stimuli. Lesions in the temporal lobe, and those which involve the basolateral amygdaloid nuclei in particular, produce animals that exhibit enhanced exploration (oral and manual) of objects and surfaces in the environment, many of which are normally avoided or feared (Adey, Merrillees, and Sunderland, 1956; Gloor, 1960; Jameson, 1956; Klüver, 1958; Schreiner and Kling, 1953, 1956). Moving stimuli are especially potent in arousing such attention. This operation also produces marked alterations in sexual and eating behavior. In studying the effects of bilateral amygdalectomy on locomotor behavior, Schwartzbaum, Wilson, and Morrissette (1961) suggest that operated animals do not habituate as rapidly as normals to novel stimuli. Further investigation is required to parcel out the roles played by various rhinencephalic nuclei and to analyze in greater detail the behavioral effects.

A number of important results have been obtained by recording neural activity in unanesthetized animals. Such experiments in conjunction with ablational and brain-stimulation studies have provided some information regarding the locus and activity of neural masses associated with overt response to novelty, habituation, and recovery. Hernández-Peón and his collaborators (Hernández-Peón and Scherrer, 1955; Hernández-Peón, Guzmán-Flores, and Fernández-Guardiola, 1956; Hernández-Peón, Scherrer, and Jouvet, 1956), Galambos, Sheatz, and Vernier (1956), and Sharpless and Jasper (1956) have shown that a novel external stimulus (visual, auditory, somatic) will not only produce behavioral arousal but will also induce changes in the frequency and voltages of ongoing electrical activity in several nuclear masses. Cerebral cortex (Galambos *et al.*, 1956), thalamus (Sharpless and Jasper, 1956), hippocampus (Green and Arduini, 1954), septal nuclei, caudate nucleus, dorsal cochlear nuclei, and thalamic reticular nuclei show such electrical alterations during behavioral arousal (Galambos *et al.*, 1956). Repeated presentation of a particular physical stimulus results in habituation of such electrical activation effects, whereas novel stimuli reinstate them (Sharpless and Jasper, 1956). Other studies have shown that stimulation of brain stem reticular nuclei (Monnier and Tissot, 1958) and of amygdaloid nuclei (Gloor, 1960) arouses a sleeping animal and produces a general alerting of behavior in an animal already awake.

Anatomical and physiological evidence summarized by D. B. Lindsley (1957) indicate that the midbrain reticular system receives collaterals from ascending visual, somatic, auditory, and visceral afferents. These projections do not show sharp localization as do the sensory afferents to the thalamus or cerebral cortex. Microelectrode studies demonstrate convergence of afferents from distinct modalities upon single cells. This evidence, along with that from stimulation and ablation studies, suggests that the midbrain reticular system is intimately involved in generalized arousal and attention induced by stimulation of any sensory modality. Some evidence indicates that portions of the reticular system are differentially sensitive to adrenaline, which alters arousal thresholds (Rothballer, 1956). Moreover several studies suggest that physiological changes effect behavior primarily by altering excitability of particular neural masses (Bradley and Elkes, 1957; Elkes, 1958).

The relevancy of these neurophysiological and neuroanatomical studies to behavioral studies has been repeatedly expressed (for example, Samuels, 1959). Sharpless and Jasper (1956) have suggested that the reticular system mediates habituation of response to repeated external stimulation. That habituation represents an active inhibition has been indicated by Wendt (1931). Sharpless and Jasper (1956) present evidence that the midbrain reticular system is involved in long-term habituation, whereas the diffuse thalamic system is concerned with sort-term habituation. It is important to keep in mind that central habituative processes may be supported by peripheral phenomena which are capable of modulating sensory input. Thus, receptor adaptation may affect short-term habituation as may the attenuation of input produced by the tympanic reflex to loud sounds.

In a series of stimulation studies (unpublished), Albino found that stimulation of the septum and cingulate cortex in unanesthetized rats induces exploratory behavior. In studies of self-stimulation, Olds (1958a) found that rats with electrodes in septum or amygdala exhibited more pronounced habituation of lever pressing than did those with electrodes in the hypothalamus.

In summary of these various lines of evidence, it must be restated that in normal sequential activities involving coordinated, attentive reaction to discrete environmental stimuli, all levels of the nervous system participate. In order for a discrete novel stimulus pattern to be judged as such, its receptor effects must be transmitted to the cerebral cortex (in mammals), although some degree of discriminative capacity exists at subcortical levels. The degree of this novelty is in some way assessed but we know not how or where. We have seen that the character of the subsequent act sequences is related to the degree of novelty. The decision which is made regarding the degree of novelty is organized in some unknown way to activate the entire cerebrospinal machinery, resulting in the act sequences characteristic of fear and escape, curiosity and exploration, or boredom and disinterest. The thalamic and midbrain reticular systems may be responsible for the generation of over-all alertness, habituation, and recovery, but their functioning in this respect is under the control of both the cerebral cortex, which identifies complex stimuli, and the lower sensory relays which are capable of distinguishing simpler patterns or qualities. The fact that response to novelty, habituation, and recovery effects have been observed in certain reflexes of spinal animals suggests that these fundamental phenomena operate within several neural masses of the central nervous system. In addition to the roles played by the cerebral cortex and reticular system in arousal to novelty, habituation, and recovery, the participation of frontal cortex, amygdala, and septal nuclei in the patterning of these phenomena must also be acknowledged. The specific manner in which these various neural masses cooperate in the delicately tuned and timed sequential activities of exploration and play remains a mystery which only further research can solve. Neuroanatomical studies of the brains of infant animals would be of particular interest, especially with regard to discovering whether there are obvious changes in neural maturation at the time when exploration of the environment first begins.

III. PROBLEMS OF ANALYSIS AND INTERPRETATION

Problems of Measurement

In the study of behavior the experimenter usually finds it necessary, for practical or theoretical reasons, to measure only certain responses out of the many which actually occur. Moreover, he also makes a decision regarding the time intervals to be covered by his measurements. In studies of reactions to novelty, habituation, and recovery, as shown by several types of animals, a variety of different response measures have been recorded at varying intervals of time in markedly differing stimulus situations with the result that the data from several experiments exhibit apparently incompatible results. For example, various studies of behavior in novel situations have found either no change in activity level over time (Butler, 1958b; Butler and Harlow, 1954), a decrease (Berlyne, 1955; Hall, 1934a; Schoenfeld, Antonitis, and Bersh, 1950), an increase (Fehrer, 1956; Hudson, 1950; Jenkins, 1953; Welker and Welker, 1958), or an increase followed by a decrease (Carr and Brown, 1959a).

Six main explanations are readily apparent to account for such differences.

a) The Use of Various Durations of Presentation and Intervals between Successive Presentations of the Stimuli. Durations of single presentations of stimuli have varied from 15 minutes (Fehrer, 1956) to 30 seconds (Butler, 1953b). Intervals between successive presentations have varied from one day (Schoenfeld *et al.*, 1950; Welker, 1956b) to 30 seconds (Butler, 1953b). Several studies have shown that the longer an animal is exposed to an unchanged situation, the more pronounced will be the decrement in responsiveness to that situation (Riley and Shapiro, 1952; Rothkopf and Zeaman, 1952; Zeaman and House, 1951). Likewise, the longer the interval between successive presentations, the greater will be the recovery of responsiveness to the previous level when re-exposed to the stimuli (Heathers, 1940; Ladieu, 1944; Montgomery, 1951b; Riley and Shapiro, 1952; Zeaman and House, 1951). Clark (1958) and Danziger and Mainland (1954) have shown that exploration of an open field habituates more rapidly in massed than in spaced trials. Davis and McDowell (1953) found similar results with respect to manipulation of puzzles by monkeys.

b) The Use of Differently Spaced Observations of the Behavior. The frequency of observations of exploratory behavior or of its effects has varied from several spot checks per day (Harlow, 1950) through once every 30 seconds (Butler, 1953b) to once per second (Welker, 1957). Several studies have shown that the more closely the successive observations of behavior in simple situations are spaced, the more likely will a response decrement be found (Harlow and McClearn, 1954; Schoenfeld *et al.*, 1950; Welker, 1956b).

c) The Use of Various Measures of Behavior. The several experiments have used a variety of measures of exploration. Among these are: crossing of a line by the fore paws (McClearn, 1959), or by the nose and eyes or by the total body (Welker, 1957); number of bar presses per unit of time (Murray, 1953); running time (Chapman and Levy, 1957); latency of response (Butler, 1953a); number of different objects contacted (Welker, 1956c) or of different alleys entered (Montgomery, 1952b); number or frequency of head orientations (Montgomery, 1955); frequency of electrified grid crossings (Nissen, 1930); number of puzzle disassemblies or solution (Gately, 1950); duration of contact, or number of contacts (Welker, 1956c). In some cases where several different measures were taken in a given experiment, the several measures did exhibit different temporal trends (Butler and Alexander, 1955; Rueping, 1956).

d) The Use of Different Degrees of Novelty (or Complexity) of the Stimuli Presented, or of the Environments within Which the Animal is Observed or Tested. It has already been documented that the type of response sequences exhibited depends upon the degree of stimulus novelty. In some of the studies, the animals were tested in their home cages (Harlow, 1950; Harlow and McClearn, 1954; Hudson, 1950; Montgomery, 1955; Welker, 1956a, 1956b, 1956c). In others, the animals were forced into situations variously graded in strangeness (Adlerstein and Fehrer, 1955; Berlyne, 1950; Butler and Harlow, 1954; Harlow *et al.*, 1956; McClearn, 1959; Welker, 1957). Thompson and Heron (1954) found that dogs exhibited different activity trends in familiar and unfamiliar environments. It has been demonstrated that whether one finds increasing or decreasing temporal trends in activity depends upon whether or not the animal is allowed freedom of choice to approach or avoid a totally strange situation (Welker, 1957). Thus animals forced to occupy a very strange situation show a response decrement with time (Berlyne, 1950; Montgomery, 1953c; Welker, 1957), whereas a response increment may be found if freedom of choice is allowed (Montgomery, 1955; Thompson and Solomon, 1954; Welker, 1957). Since strange environments have been shown to elicit mild avoidance reactions it is possible that the responses in such situations are to some extent anxiety or escape motivated (Ehrlich and Burns, 1958; Segall, 1959). That they show habituation, recovery, and novelty effects in no way obviates this possibility since fear or avoidance tendencies as well as novelty-approaching tendencies involve these phenomena.

e) The Presentation of Complex Changing Rather Than Constant Stimulus Situations. Since several studies of exploratory behavior have shown that changing stimulation is attended to in preference to nonchanging stimuli, it would be supposed that in a situation where new changes are periodically, sporadically, or unexpectedly occurring (Butler and Alexander, 1955), decrement in response would be less likely to appear, the behavior elicited being maintained at an over-all high rate. The over-all response rate of chimpanzees (Welker, 1956b) and monkeys (Carr and Brown, 1959c) is sustained as long as changes in stimulations are periodically introduced.

f) The Use of Animals of Different Ages. There appears to be an optimum age at which young animals explore certain classes of external stimuli to a maximal extent. Younger as well as older animals have been shown to be less reactive and to exhibit different activity trends (Harlow *et al.*, 1956; Hudson, 1950; Liu, 1928; Welker, 1956a, 1956b).

It must be concluded that reactions to novel situations do not invariably consist of simple temporal trends. Any factors (such as *a, b, d, e,* and *f* above) which influence the degree of novelty of the stimulus will surely influence the corresponding response trends.

Problems of Definition and Conceptualization

Throughout the preceding pages, little attention has been devoted to defining some important concepts. An attempt will be made in this section to identify some of the conceptual problems which are met in discussions of exploration and play. The concept of *novelty* is the most difficult of all to define. This term has been used to represent the fact that an animal's reactions to a particular stimulus are different when it is new than after repeated or prolonged exposure. Novelty is not, of course, a physical stimulus attribute and its degree can be specified only in terms of an animal's past experience with a stimulus (Bindra, 1959b). Stimulus novelty is thus a relative and experiential matter, and therein lies the difficulty of easily specifying its degree. Broadly considered, a novel stimulus is one that has changed with respect to past (immediate or distant) experience. The greater the degree of such change, the greater the novelty. Indeed, the notion of "stimulus" itself implies change (Nissen, 1953b), and accordingly every stimulus is novel or changed to some degree, and is defined in part by its novelty characteristics.

Stimulus changes may be spatial, temporal, or both. If stationary stimuli which have spatially discrete boundaries are scanned by the receptor, the contours of the energy distribution move across the receptor surface. In such a case, spatial changes are translated into temporal ones as far as the sensory systems are concerned. True spatial changes may be perceived, however, as in the stabilized retinal image (Riggs, Ratliff, Cornsweet, and Cornsweet, 1953). Temporal changes consist of appearance or disappearance, increase or decrease in intensity, or movement of a stimulus with respect to the receptor elements.

For practical purposes, the strength or degree of novelty possessed by a stimulus can be, and usually is, specified in terms of the intensity, the frequency, the duration, and the recency of its previous presentations. However, there are several reasons why such specification will not be completely satisfactory: (1) It is difficult to know the complete past experience of an animal with respect to a particular stimulus. (2) There may be unknown degrees of generalization to a test stimulus from stimuli which are similar to it (Montgomery, 1953a), or associated with it in certain respects. In the latter case, a stimulus object, say a yellow box with a closed lid, may be mildly novel and elicit approach and contact. If this object suddenly emits noise as its springed innards pop out, then it becomes more novel by association (see Hudson, 1950). (3) Since it seems that the CNS is able to block (or attend to) input from its receptors selectively, the criterion of mere exposure of receptors is no guarantee of a stimulus being perceived so as to affect behavior. This is a problem of set. For example, attention and interest in one class of stimulus-response events (for example, copulation) may preclude interest in an irrelevant novel stimulus which might be reacted to playfully at other times. The influence of set or expectation on attentive response is also seen when a familiar stimulus is discovered in a novel context. (4) Because the animal may attend to a stimulus in a fluctuating or irregular manner, the exact duration of attentive exposure to it may be difficult to ascertain. (5) An animal's general level of arousal will obviously influence whether it will respond to any stimulus. Although novelty in strong degrees will affect arousal level, a drowsy or sleeping animal is not so readily influenced.

Common sense, as well as some experimental evidence, indicates that these several factors influence the novelty impact of stimuli, but further experiment is required to identify their specific nature. Until then, measurement of parameters of intensity, frequency, duration, and recency of previous exposures must suffice. The problem is no less important because identification of the degree of novelty of a stimulus at a particular instant in time is difficult.

The fact that repeated stimulation results in a gradual loss or change of response in a wide variety of situations has resulted in semantic confusion. Satiation, refractory phase, negative adaptation, just plain "adaptation," extinction, and action decrement, as well as habituation, have been used to refer to such decremental changes in response. The type of responses and the conditions under which they have been observed to change or disappear have undoubtedly been responsible for the shades of meaning invested in these diverse terms. There is not yet sufficient reason to believe that these several concepts implicate fundamentally different neural mechanisms although each of several different levels of the central nervous system may have a habituation network of its own. Thus, some of the simple reflexes in spinal animals exhibit habituative phenomena (Lehner, 1941; Prosser and Hunter, 1936), as do the more complex responses which depend upon the cerebrum. In studies of the mobbing responses in chaffinches, Hinde (1954b) found evidence for two decremental mechanisms: one that was response specific, another that was stimulus specific. They exhibited different rates of habituation. Habituation phenomena have been shown to be common throughout the animal kingdom (Harris, 1943; Hinde, 1954a; Humphrey, 1933).

Another problem of terminology is raised by the purely descriptive use of the terms visual, auditory, olfactory, manual (that is, manipulation), or locomotor to modify exploration. They are intended to indicate which sensory modalities are involved in exploratory behavior, a fact which (as pointed out above) is not always easily established from direct observation. Nevertheless, it is likely that animals are aroused to action by novelty, and that they habituate, recover responsiveness, and exhibit preferences and aversions with respect to all sensory modalities. Although it is unlikely that the several afferent systems differ in any fundamental way with respect to these characteristics, this question can be answered only by further experimentation.

The term play is often used in conjunction with, or in place of, the term exploration. In some cases, no differentiation is made between play and exploration. In other instances, play is used as the generic term, exploration being only one type of play (Groos, 1898). This has been the case especially with reference to the behavior of human children (Mitchell and Mason, 1948). Generally, it appears to have been more common to refer to the more vigorous locomotor activities (including social activities) as play, whereas the unhurried or cautious approach reactions to novel or strange stimuli are usually designated as exploration. Such a distinction is not always readily made, however, since all degrees of vigor may characterize these behavior sequences. Likewise, the degree of caution exhibited in exploratory behavior may be more or less pronounced (Welker, 1954). Similar difficulties are met when one attempts to distinguish either play or exploration from other behaviors involving similar act sequences. Thus play and serious fighting may be difficult to distinguish, as may exploratory actions motivated by search for either novelty or food. Such is the fate of most attempts at clear and parsimonious categorization of complex events, and the general definitions of exploration and play proposed in the introduction must suffice. At present these categories are useful in referring to stimulus-response relationships which have been glossed over by classical motivational concepts. Schlosberg (1947) has suggested that facts subsumed under the concept of play may be conceptualized more effectively in S-R terms, a view towards which the present writer is partial. Empirically, the task is clear: we must seek a greater degree of specificity in describing not only behavior sequences but also the various conditions under which they occur. Until this has been achieved, the stability and validity of classifications of behavior will remain uncertain.

A common technique used to categorize behavior is that which attempts to identify a particular class of internal state (hunger, sex, fear, or thirst) by inference from either deprivation schedules or from the type of goals which seem to terminate a group of behavior sequences. Such an identification of internal state requires the utilization of proper controls. Thus, in situations where all stimuli are essentially novel, behavior which would seem to be novelty-approaching may really be escape-oriented (Welker, 1957; Welker, 1959b) or anxious behavior (Symmes, 1959a). Such observations indicate that the identification of mental states in animals must use experimental conditions which permit differentiation between alternative interpretations.

It is an undisputed and important fact that behavior sequences of an orderly and integrated sort may become organized with respect to a specific class of stimulus incentives which are not immediately present. It is thus useful, in describing learned goal-oriented behavior of experienced higher animals, to say that they *explore for* or *seek* food, water, a sexual partner, nesting materials, a route of escape, as well as novelty *per se* (Berlyne, 1958c; Schneirla, 1959). Such teleological conceptions are necessary in referring to purposive striving of many adult animals. Although the goals sought may not be physically present, they are undoubtedly present as neurological or mental phenomena at the onset of a goal-seeking sequence. These internal surrogates guide long-term sequences until the physical matching stimuli have been directly perceived. The validity of this sort of neurologizing has yet to receive experimental test. Various goal stimuli may terminate the sequences although the activity preceding achievement may exhibit similar characteristics (Barnett, 1958c). It appears that the searchings and wanderings termed exploration may serve many masters. Yet, to ascribe a single motivating force (drive) to all the activities within a particular set of organized sequences (for example, food seeking) is not really justified. It is very possible that many of the reactions to stimuli in a prolonged goal-seeking sequence are not just instrumental but goal-directed in themselves. Nissen (1953a, 1954b) has argued that every little act in such long sequences may have its own motivation, a view not contradicted by the evidence discussed above. To what extent this is true in any case must be determined by experiment.

Brief mention should be made here of the concept of attention. Not all sensory stimuli affect behavior. Although an animal's sensory receptors are constantly being bombarded by stimuli, the nervous system is capable of selecting for action from a massive flux certain classes of stimuli and effectively shutting out others. The neural mechanisms which result in responses to novelty, habituation, recovery, and preferences or aversions are selective in this manner. These facts are extremely common and necessitate a concept of attention in some form (Berlyne, 1951; Dell, 1958; Hebb, 1949; Livingston, 1960).

The comments in the above paragraphs should serve to illustrate the several problems which persistently besiege attempts at conceptual clarity. Too commonly the source of confusion lies in inadequate definition or delineation of the phenomena to be represented by a concept. Added to this, of course, is the real complexity of the events themselves. These problems require persistent and careful attention by the experimenter and theorist.

Theory and Explanation

Any comprehensive explanation of the motivation of exploratory and play behavior, or indeed of any form of behavior, must account for the following points:

1. Stimulus novelty as a potent arousing agent.
2. Differential effect on behavioral sequences of varying degrees of novelty.
3. Habituation of responses with increased exposure to stimuli.

4. Recovery from habituation during intervals between successive exposures.

5. Stimulus preferences and aversions.

6. A capacity to react selectively (attend) to particular types of stimulus changes.

7. Effects of altered internal biochemical conditions on the above phenomena.

8. Age differences in the above factors.

9. Phylogenetic (genetic) differences in these factors.

Various explanations of exploratory and related behaviors have called attention to one or more of these phenomena (Dember and Fowler, 1958). None have adequately considered all; yet all these factors are important in the elicitation and patterning of behavior sequences. Several authors have called attention to the effect of novelty on both approach and avoidance behaviors (Berlyne, 1950; Glanzer, 1958a; Montgomery, 1955; Welker, 1956a). Glanzer (1953a) has emphasized the role of habituation (satiation) phenomena. Dember and Earl (1957) have pointed to the importance of the concept of attention. White (1959 and Chapter 10) has suggested the use of the terms competence and effectance to refer to the variety of activities of animals and man which keep the organism in informative touch with the environment. It does not seem to the present writer that these latter terms will be useful in promoting a more detailed analysis of behavior, however. The term "conflict" (Berlyne, 1954, 1957b, 1960), like that of novelty, is also too general and only further experimental study such as that begun by Berlyne (1957b) can lead us to more specific and fruitful concepts. Some have postulated hypothetical exploratory or play drives, but this device has not proved to be a substitute for careful experimental analysis (see Bolles, 1958; Harlow, 1953; Hinde, 1959; Littman, 1958; White, 1959 and Chapter 10). The inadequacy of explanations of play behavior have been pointed out elsewhere (Beach, 1945; Welker, 1954).

Any theory of behavior is deficient unless it acknowledges the fact that behavior is labile and dynamic, shifting in orientation or direction from moment to moment. It has been the purpose of this paper to bring into focus these sequential characteristics of behavior as well as to highlight a variety of other behavioral phenomena of which the theorist must remain cognizant.

CONCLUSION

Responses to novelty, habituation, recovery, and preferences or aversions characterize the behavior of animals throughout the phylogenetic series. In birds and mammals, and especially within the primate series, these mechanisms have become elaborated and integrated in such a manner and with such potency that they have become prominent forces that motivate and direct sequential behavior even at times when survival is not a matter of immediate concern. In the more advanced animal forms, these mechanisms are responsible for the variable and dynamic acts which characterize exploration, play, adaptable problem solution, and invention. When an animal is exposed to physiological or environmental stresses, these mechanisms modulate behavior in particular ways that increase the probability of appropriate homeostasis. They reach their prime function during the childhood of animals that have a dependent infancy. They automatically serve to enlarge the young animal's store of perceptions and behavioral repertory in a manner that increases its probability of survival when it becomes necessary for the animal to set out upon its own. But with some modification, these mechanisms also function throughout life, promoting an alert and adaptive contact with an environment forever in flux. They prevent the beast from lapsing into inattentive inertia. They force it to acknowledge changes, some of which may prove important and threaten or enhance its very existence. Genetic selection in diverse ecological settings has yielded animal types which exhibit vast differences in the differential employment of these mechanisms.

This is a picture of which the studies discussed above offer a glimpse.

Chapter 8

Alternation Behavior *

WILLIAM N. DEMBER
University of Cincinnati

*T*HE topic of this chapter, alternation behavior, is a phenomenon of utmost simplicity. Despite this, or perhaps because of it, alternation provides a rich source of insight into the behavior of organisms. In particular, the concepts that emerge from the study of alternation behavior seem basic to the understanding of the motivational processes that underlie many more complex behavioral phenomena. In addition, alternation promises to serve as a useful indicator response for the investigation of other processes, such as perception (for example, Dember and Millbrook, 1956) and memory (see Dember, Brodwick, and Roberts, 1960).

The motivational implications of alternation are most pertinent to the purposes of this volume, and therefore they will be stressed in the present chapter. However, in the course of uncovering these motivational implications, it will be necessary to allude to the various nonmotivational features of the behavior.

What is alternation behavior? This can best be answered by reference to a hypothetical experiment. Place a rat in the starting alley of a T maze. Allow it to enter one of the two goal arms. Remove the rat from the arm it first enters, say the left arm, and replace it in the starting alley for a second trial. On this second trial the rat can re-enter the left arm, or it can enter the right arm. Re-entry into the left arm would constitute a *repetition,* entry into the right arm an *alternation.*

More abstractly, if there are two alternative behaviors, R and L, and two trials, on each of which either behavior can occur, then four behavior patterns are possible. Two of these patterns will be repeti-

---

*This chapter is based in large part on a previous review of the alternation literature by Dember and Fowler (1958).

tions—R-R and L-L—and two will be alternations—R-L and L-R. If the two alternatives, R and L, are equally likely to occur, and if the behavior on the second trial is independent of that on the first, then the probability of alternation is 2/4, or .50. In practice, then, alternation will be said to have occurred only if it occurs with a probability that is significantly greater than .50. For this reason, alternation behavior must be studied either with large groups of subjects, or with several tests on the same, relatively few subjects.

When there is a strong preference for one alternative, then .50 is too high an estimate of the chance level of alternation. Dember and Fowler (1958) have discussed this problem and have proposed a better, though by no means ideal, way of estimating the chance level. See also Iwahara (1959) on this problem.

Tolman (1925) and Dennis (1935) are responsible for the discovery of alternation in rats. Since their early observations, there has been a steady output of research on alternation, much of it directed at the question: "Why does alternation behavior happen?" This general question, in turn, is typically resolved into a more specific one: "What is it that the subject is alternating?" or "What is the *source* of the alternation?"

The meaning of the latter questions will become clear in the section that immediately follows, in which the major theories of alternation are described. Empirical tests of these theories are discussed in the next section of this chapter. In the final section, a brief resume of the motivational implications of alternation behavior is given in the context of the author's own view of alternation and motivation.

All of the experiments cited in this chapter use rats as subjects. Alternation behavior would still be interesting, though perhaps less so, if it were confined to that one species. There are, however, several experiments that demonstrate spontaneous alternation behavior in other animals, including man. These experiments, so far, add little that is theoretically crucial, but they do reveal the phylogenetic generality of the phenomenon.

At the infrarodent level, there is indication of response alternation in paramecia (Lepley and Rice, 1952), in the meal worm (Grosslight and Ticknor, 1953), the earthworm (Wayner and Zellner, 1958) and in the pill bug (Watanabe and Iwata, 1956; Iwata and

Watanabe, 1957), though the explanation of the behavior in these animals may not require the same concepts that apply to alternation in higher organisms. Alternation in the cockroach has also been reported (Iwahara and Soeda, 1957).

There seem to be no relevant data for animals between rat and man, but the occurrence of the alternation pattern in man is fairly well documented (for example, Bakan, 1960; Iwahara, 1959; Lawless and Engstrand, 1960; Wingfield, 1943).

THEORIES OF ALTERNATION BEHAVIOR

When Dennis (1935) observed the alternation pattern, it was obvious to him that the rats were alternating maze alleys. This general position, which was to reassert itself a few decades later, was for some time supplanted by an account of alternation that relied on the concept of reactive inhibition.

Reactive Inhibition

Reactive inhibition (Ir) is a Pavlovian concept that was taken over and elaborated by Hull (1943) in his theory of behavior. It was originally developed as a means of explaining both experimental extinction and spontaneous recovery. In essence, Hull's theory postulates that each occurrence of a response produces an increment in Ir, a hypothetical quantity. Ir has the property of decreasing the tendency to repeat the response by which it was generated. During reinforced training trials Ir builds up to a lesser extent than does habit strength, or sHr. However, when reinforcement ceases, elicitation of the learned response continues to increase the amount of Ir, even though sHr is no longer growing. Eventually, Ir reaches a magnitude that is sufficient to override the excitatory effect of sHr, and the learned response is no longer made. That is, extinction has taken place.

Reactive inhibition has a further property. It spontaneously dissipates over time. An extinguished habitual response will therefore spontaneously recover, following a sufficiently long time interval after the extinction trials. To account for permanent extinction, which of course does occur, it is necessary in Hull's theory to add another concept, conditioned inhibition, or sIr.

Through the reinforcement attendant upon the spontaneous dissipation of Ir, a new habit is established, the habit of "not responding." This habit, sIr, is in direct conflict with sHr, or more strictly speaking it conflicts with sEr, the excitatory potential associated with sHr. Being a habit, sIr is permanent. Thus, once sIr is of sufficient magnitude, extinction is complete and, in the absence of further experimental manipulations, permanent.

To summarize the above, Ir temporarily inhibits the recurrence of a response; sIr permanently inhibits its recurrence. It should be easy to see how such concepts might be applied to the alternation situation.

Consider Ir. A right turn in a T maze produces a certain quantity of reactive inhibition that is specific to the right-turning response. This right-turning Ir will slightly decrease the tendency to repeat a right turn on a subsequent trial. Hence the animal, by default, will turn left at the choice-point. For Ir to be of sufficient strength to have this effect, it is of course essential that the animal initially be relatively indifferent as between the two goal arms. In this case, the small amount of Ir generated by a single response may be enough to tip the scales in favor of the alternative response. (The applicability of the Ir concept to the alternation situation is challenged by Iwahara, Matsubara, and Washiyama (1958), who claim that Ir represents only a tendency not to respond, rather than a tendency not to repeat a particular response, for example, a right turn. A close reading of Hull, however, does not bear out their interpretation: Ir is response-specific, though of course its effects may generalize to other responses.)

Among the reasons that the sIr concept has not seriously been invoked to account for alternation, two stand out: *(a)* the fact that alternation does not occur over long intertrial intervals indicates a temporary, rather than a permanent, effect of the first response; *(b)* if it is assumed that sIr is a habit, then, like most habits but unlike the alternation pattern, it should require several trials for its development.

The Ir account thus locates the source of alternation in the response process itself. That is, the animal is alternating with respect to its own output. This approach to alternation is in clear opposition to the one originally proposed by Dennis, whose rats were alternating input, that is, maze-arm stimulation, not turning-responses.

Stimulus Satiation

An approach derived from that of Dennis has been formalized by Glanzer. The basic postulate in Glanzer's theory of alternation reads as follows:

Each moment an organism perceives a stimulus-object, or stimulus-objects, A, there develops a quantity of stimulus satiation to A (1953a, p. 259).

The key concept in this postulate is stimulus satiation, or sI, which, according to the theory, "reduces the organism's tendency to make any response to A" (1953a, p. 259). The source of alternation is in external stimulation, not in turning-responses. In this sense, the Ir and sI theories are in complete disagreement. But note the formal similarity between the two theories. In both, the animal's second-trial behavior is, genotypically, an *avoidance* of the repetition of a previous event, whether a previous response or a previous stimulus-object. Alternation is not conceived of in either theory as an *approach* to a new event.

It would not be incompatible with the theory to assume that satiation can develop with respect to response feedback. With this assumption Glanzer's theory could incorporate findings that fit the Ir model. In his original statement of stimulus satiation theory, however, Glanzer failed to treat response feedback as an important source of alternation.

Stimulus Change

A third account of alternation, developed by the author in collaboration with Robert W. Earl (see Dember and Earl, 1957), views alternation as one manifestation of the general and basic motive to optimize amount of stimulus change or complexity. In contrast with the two theories described above, this one emphasizes the approach aspect of alternation behavior. The animal is not simply avoiding repetition of a previous event; it is approaching an event that is positively attractive. Since it represents the author's own interpretation of alternation, the stimulus change theory is further elaborated in the final section of this chapter.

Action Decrement

The stimulus change theory differs from Ir and sI theories in another respect: it is essentially *centralistic*, while both of the others are *peripheralistic* in focus, Ir emphasizing the output end of the behavioral system, and sI stressing the input end. The fourth and last of the major theories to be described, the one constructed by Walker (1958), is, like the stimulus change theory, explicitly centralistic.

The main concept in Walker's theory is action decrement, symbolized as I_c, where the c refers to the presumed central locus of inhibition. The core of the theory is given in the following quotation from Walker (1958, p. 130):

> *Any psychological action is followed by an action decrement—a lowered capacity for rearousal of the same event. The action decrement is a direct manifestion of the process of perseverative consolidation which is necessary for retention and subsequent performance. The action decrement persists for a limited time and then dissipates. Under many circumstances the dissipation of the action decrement is followed by an action increment which is learning or habit strength.*

The biological function of the action decrement is to prevent disruption of the consolidation process, a function very similar to that of reinforcement in Guthrie's learning theory. In this way, Walker ties the problem of alternation to the problem of learning. The two areas are further related by a postulate that describes the complex interaction among alternation, motivation, and time. The specific implications of this postulate are discussed in the next section.

One final aspect of the theory should be noted. In line with its centralistic orientation, the theory makes no basic distinction between stimuli and responses as sources of alternation. The relative importance of any source of alternation is simply a function of its relative discriminability. This idea, also, is elaborated in the second section.

Other Approaches to Alternation. In addition to the types of explanation summarized above, there are others that have been suggested. One, for example, makes of the alternation pattern a learned, general mode of responding. From this point of view, alternation is an acquired strategy (Estes and Schoeffler, 1955). Another approach might be that alternation represents avoidance of a previous event resulting from punishment or frustration associated with that event. While each of these explanations may very well apply to some particular instances of alternation, neither appears to have as general application as the four presented above. What follows, then, is a more detailed examination of theories of alternation, restricted to the types identified by the four concepts: reactive inhibition, stimulus satiation, stimulus change, and action decrement.

DERIVATIONS FROM AND TESTS OF THE MAJOR THEORIES

The one feature all theories have in common is the prediction of alternation behavior under standard testing conditions. To assess the relative validity of the theories it is necessary to examine the more specific deductions that can be made from each theory. As will become apparent, only a few of these deductions are "crucial" in distinguishing among theories.

Derivations from Ir Theory

Despite its apparent simplicity, the Ir theory generates several testable hypotheses about specific aspects of alternation behavior.

Intertrial Interval. From the Hullian assumption about the manner in which Ir spontaneously dissipates in time, it is predicted that probability of alternation will be a negatively accelerated, decreasing function of the time between trials, or the intertrial interval. Illustrative of experiments that have been devoted to testing this hypothesis is one by Heathers (1940). Using intertrial intervals ranging from 15 to 120 seconds, Heathers found an inverse relation between length of intertrial interval and amount of alternation. The data are not extensive enough, however, to establish the exact form of the relation.

The most thorough attempt to test this same hypothesis is contained in an experiment by Walker (1956). Here, 21 values of intertrial interval were employed, covering a range from about 1 to 300 minutes. There was no evidence in this experiment of a monotonically decreasing relation between length of intertrial interval and amount of alternation. Rather, amount of alternation varied in an apparently random fashion around a value of about 75% for intervals up to about 60 minutes. Between 60 and 90 minutes there was an abrupt drop to a chance level. At the very long intertrial intervals there was some suggestion of below-chance levels of alternation.

Even in this very thorough experiment, the number of observations at each point, 21, was insufficient to generate a smooth empirical curve that would permit a firm conclusion about the form of the function relating intertrial interval and amount of alternation. Furthermore, the form of the curve is undoubtedly influenced by the nature of the testing conditions (see Dember and Fowler, 1958, pp. 421-22).

Amount of Work. In Hull's original formulation, magnitude of Ir is an increasing function of the amount of work associated with making the response. This further characteristic of Ir enables the prediction of a direct relation between amount of work and frequency of alternation. Attempts to test this prediction fall into three classes: *(a)* those where the manipulation of the work variable does not seem really appropriate to the Ir theory; *(b)* those where the effect of manipulating amount of work is either slight or inconclusive; *(c)* those where the results are contrary to the Ir prediction.

Illustrative of the first kind is an experiment by Montgomery (1951b). Here, the rats found a bar at the end of either goal arm of a maze. Depression of the bar yielded food reward. Over different groups of rats the amount of work necessary to depress the bar was varied. It was expected that frequency of alternation between the two equally rewarding goal arms would increase with increasing amounts of work required for bar depression. This result was not obtained. However, there is no basis in Ir theory for expecting the Ir associated with bar pressing to influence the pattern of responses at the choice-point of the maze. The work relevant to the latter is the work involved in the choice-point response itself.

Somewhat more pertinent to Ir theory is an experiment reported by Solomon (1948), who observed the alternation behavior of rats with weights strapped to their backs. The assumption was made that the rats with the greater "handicaps" would be generating, with every response, more Ir than the less burdened animals. This manipulation, however, had no apparent effect on frequency of alternation.

A second experiment reported by Solomon (1948) produced results more favorable to the Ir theory. The maze in this experiment had goal arms inclined at an angle of 16° from the horizontal. Rats run in this maze alternated slightly more than did rats run in the conventional flat maze.

Another experiment that yielded slight, positive results was done by Riley and Shapiro (1952). In this experiment, amount of work was manipulated by varying the weight of the doors through which rats had to push in order to obtain food. Heavier doors tended to produce somewhat more alternation than lighter doors.

Finally, there are experiments with results contrary to the Ir prediction. An attempt was made by Walker, Dember, Earl, Fawl, and Karoly (1955) to increase the slight positive effect obtained by Solomon in his inclined-goal-arm experiment. It seemed reasonable that if a 16° angle was slightly effective, then a greater angle would be even more so. Therefore, the angle of inclination of the goal arms of a T maze was set at 45°. But instead of raising the frequency of alternation, this manipulation, if anything, lowered it.

Negative results for Ir theory are also to be found in a study by Jackson (1941). Here, the work manipulation consisted in making one group of rats jump a 15-centimeter gap to enter either goal arm from the starting alley of a maze. The same maze was used for a control group, except that the gap was eliminated, enabling these rats to walk into a goal arm from the starting alley.

The control group showed the typical alternation pattern. The jump group, which can be thought of as doing more work, showed almost no alternation.

To summarize, experiments in which amount of work has been varied have generally not yielded results conforming to prediction from the Ir theory. Indeed, there is some evidence, in the two experiments just above, that too much work may decrease, rather than increase, frequency of alternation.

Forced Repetition of a Response. Increasing work is one way, in theory, of increasing Ir. Another way of accomplishing this is to use massed repetitions of the same response. For example, a rat that is forced to make several right-turning responses in close succession should generate more right-turning Ir than a rat making but one such response. Thus, massed repetitions should increase the alternation tendency. This prediction is borne out in a number of experiments (for example, Estes and Schoeffler, 1955; Zeaman and Angell, 1953; Zeaman and House, 1951). It should be noted, however, that this prediction is not unique to Ir theory. The same result is expected in the other theories of alternation. These data, therefore, are consistent with Ir theory, but not crucial.

Successive Free Trials. Also consistent with, but not crucial to, Ir theory is the finding that when several free trials are given in succession, the alternation tendency declines over trials. An illustrative set of data is provided by Wingfield and Dennis (1934), whose rats were given six free trials in close succession. Between the first two trials amount of alternation was about 80%; this value declined over successive pairs of trials, until the amount of alternation between trials 5 and 6 was only 50%. Similar results can be found in experiments by Sutherland (1957) and Weitz and Wakeman (1941).

This result is to be expected from the Ir theory, as from the others, for the following reason: the more the animal alternates between trials, early in the series, the more equivalent the two alternatives become. This is particularly so when massed trials are used: when trial 3 occurs, the choice is influenced in part by the aftereffect of trial 2 events but also, in almost equal amount, by the aftereffect of trial 1.

The above considerations led Dember and Fowler (1958) to speculate on a way to maintain high levels of alternation over successive trials. The trick is to arrange the experimental conditions so that, for trial n, the aftereffect of trial $n-2$ has dissipated while the aftereffect of trial $n-1$ is still strong. This could be accomplished if the intertrial interval, t, were of such a duration that an interval of t would yield high levels of alternation, but an interval of $2t$ would not. For example, if t were 30 minutes, than $2t$ would be 60 minutes. If 60 minutes is too long an interval for high levels of alternation to take place, but 30 minutes is short enough to yield high levels of alternation, then the problem would be solved: successive trials separated by a 30-minute interval would not show the typical pattern of decline found under massed trial conditions. No experiment has apparently yet been done which would test this analysis and would demonstrate the experimental control over alternation phenomena provided by this theory.

Response Generalization. The concept of response generalization that is contained within Hullian theory, in conjunction with the Ir interpretation of alternation, makes possible two closely related predictions. If it is assumed that Ir is generalized across responses in inverse proportion to their similarity to the Ir-generating response, the prediction follows that amount of alternation will also increase as response similarity decreases. That is, two alternative responses that are highly similar will yield less alternation than two that are dissimilar.

To test this hypothesis, Jackson (1941) used three mazes that varied with respect to the angle separating the two goal arms. One maze had a separation angle of 15°, one of 90°, and one of 180°. The mazes are listed in presumed order of decreasing response similarity. The results of the experiment failed to confirm the hypothesis, with no differences in amount of alternation shown among the three groups.

The second prediction based on the response generalization concept involves the animal's choice among several responses following the occurrence of a given response. Thus, if a rat has made a left-turning response, and is then offered the choice between a straight-ahead response and a right turn, it should choose the latter. This hypothesis has been successfully tested by Zeaman and Angell (1953). Rats were run in a four-arm radial maze. The two extreme arms, separated by an angle of 180°, formed a conventional T maze with the starting stem. Between them were two additional arms, separated from each other by 60°. Thus, each of these arms was separated from one of the T arms by 60° and from the other T arm by 120°. The animals were given 10 forced, reinforced runs to one of the T arms, and then were given a free trial. As expected, the frequency of their free-trial choices was directly related to the angle of separation between forced arm and choice arm.

The difference in outcome between the Jackson and the Zeaman and Angell experiments is quite instructive. Apparently, amount of alternation under conventional two-trial, two alternative testing procedures is relatively stable. As long as the alternative responses are sufficiently different, high levels of alternation will occur, and amount of alternation, as conventionally measured, will not reflect subtle differences in response similarity. However, when the testing for alternation gives the animal a choice among several alternatives, as in the Zeaman and Angell procedure, then similarity of responses will be reflected in the animal's behavior. This same point is reinforced below, where an analogous problem arises in connection with the *stimulus* generalization of alternation behavior.

Summary. In addition to predicting the occurrence of the alternation pattern itself, Ir theory generates at least five other testable predictions. Amount of alternation is predicted to vary with (a) intertrial interval, (b) amount of work, (c) number of forced repetitions of the same response, (d) number of successive, massed, free trials, and (e) similarity between alternative responses. Predictions with respect to variables *a*, *c*, *d*, and *e* are grossly borne out, though in fine *a* has not been, and *e* has been verified only under one of two possible testing procedures. None of these four successful predictions, however, is unique to Ir theory: they all are incorporated into the other theories of alternation to be discussed below.

Prediction *b*, which relates amount of alternation to amount of work, is the only one that is, at least superficially, unique to Ir theory, and here experimental results have been generally unfavorable. Finally, Ir theory has fared not at all well in the many experiments, described below, that were designed specifically to demonstrate its inadequacy for the explanation of alternation.

Derivations from sI Theory

While Ir theory locates the source of alternation in the response system, sI theory identifies stimulation as the main source of alternation. Glanzer's formalization (1953a) of this latter approach has generated several experiments. Some of these directly show the inadequacy of the Ir theory of alternation; some provide empirical tests of other predictions derived from sI theory.

Stimulus vs. Response as Alternation Source.   Both Ir and sI theories predict the occurrence of the alternation pattern, but they offer different explanations of the behavior. Is there any basis for choosing between them? Glanzer (1953b) has answered this question with an experiment that is both elegant and decisive. A very similar experiment was also performed independently by Montgomery (1952a).

Both experiments made use of a cross-maze—that is, a T maze with two starting alleys, one allowing the rat to approach the choice-point region from the south, the other from the north. On the first of two trials, the rat is placed in one starting alley, say the south alley, and the other, the north alley, is blocked. The rat is allowed to enter one of the goal arms. Suppose the arm entered was the east arm. To enter it, starting from the south, the rat must make a right-turning response.

On the second trial, the rat starts from the north alley and the south alley is blocked. Now Ir theory would predict the occurrence of a left-turning response on this trial. But a left turn, with an approach from the north, would take the rat back into the previously experienced east goal arm. The fact that this arm has been experienced recently would, of course, not be of relevance to Ir theory. On the other hand, sI theory would expect alternation of maze-arm stimuli. Exposure to the east arm, on the first trial, should be followed by a choice of the west arm on the second, regardless of the response necessary to effect the choice. Thus, in the cross-maze situation, the two theories make different predictions: Ir theory predicts response alternation and hence maze-arm repetition; sI theory predicts maze-arm alternation and hence response repetition.

The results of both Glanzer's and Montgomery's experiments unequivocally supported the sI prediction: the rats alternated maze arms, not turning responses. Replication of these findings has since been achieved by others (for example, Walker, Dember, Earl, and Karoly, 1955; Dember, 1958b).

Intratrial Duration. As elegant and decisive as the cross-maze experiment is another study by Glanzer (1953b) designed to test his sI theory. The main manipulation in this experiment involved confinement of the rat in various parts of the T maze following its first-trial choice. One group of rats was confined to the goal box for 10 minutes; a second group was removed from the goal box after choice and then confined for 10 minutes in the starting box; a third group was confined after choice in the choice-point region.

Note that from the point of view of Ir theory the locus of confinement should be irrelevant. Hence, all three groups should alternate with equal frequency and, in addition, should alternate with a lower frequency than a group given an immediate second trial. According to sI theory, however, the group confined for 10 minutes in the goal box is being exposed to the goal-arm stimuli, and satiation for those stimuli is growing, not dissipating, during confinement. For the group confined in the starting box, satiation for the goal-arm stimuli is declining during the 10-minute period, and for the group confined in the choice-point region, satiation for both alternatives is growing. Obviously, the group confined in the goal box should show the greatest amount of alternation.

Again the two theories are pitted against each other, and again the sI prediction is verified. The group confined in the goal box did show the greatest amount of alternation. Indeed, that group alternated at a higher frequency than did a nonconfined, no-delay group. This latter result is, of course, in direct opposition to the Ir prediction.

Exposure without Choice. It is implicit in sI theory that the ani-

mal need not make an active choice of a goal arm if alternation is
to occur; it need only perceive the stimuli characteristic of that arm.
Thus alternation should occur if the rat is simply placed in the goal
arm, exposed to it for some time, and then given a free-choice trial.
Moreover, the theory can be interpreted to imply that exposure, to
be effective, need not even take place in the maze arm itself. Exposure
to a black object anywhere should generate satiation for "blackness,"
and an animal so exposed should avoid a subsequently offered black
goal arm.

This latter interpretation was tested by Walker, Dember, Earl,
Fliege, and Karoly (1955). Rats were placed in one of three compartments, black, white, or gray, in a box unconnected with the
T maze in which they were later given a free trial. The maze, as
usual, had one black and one white arm. Rats previously placed in
the black compartment were expected to prefer the white goal arm
of the T maze, and those exposed to white were expected to choose
the black arm. This prediction was not confirmed.

A second study was conducted by the same group, but this time
the exposure took place in the goal arms themselves. Again, however,
the expected avoidance of the previously experienced arm did not
occur. On the basis of these results the conclusion seemed warranted
that if alternation is to be observed, the animals must actively choose
one of the goal arms on the first trial; passive exposure to the arm
is not enough.

Of course, active choice does not imply that two alternatives must
be available on the first trial. A forced trial to one arm, with the
other blocked off, will yield alternation. The crucial factor seemed
to be that the animal enter the arm "on its own steam." Thus, while
the source of alternation remains *stimulation*, it appeared necessary
that the animal *respond* to the stimulation if alternation were to
occur.

Whatever the final interpretation of the experiments described
above, they appeared to one reviewer (Estes, 1956) to have cast
serious doubt on sI theory. Since that review was written, however,
four studies have been reported that yielded the predicted effect of
passive exposure.

The first of these, chronologically, is an experiment by Kivy, Earl,
and Walker (1956) that is described in detail below (p. 243). The

exposure in this experiment took place with the rats in the choice-point region of the starting alley, rather than in one of the goal arms. It was concluded by the experimenters that if passive exposure is to be successful, it must occur in the context of the choice-point. The second successful experiment is one by Sutherland (1957), in which rats were placed in one goal box, fed there, and then given a choice-trial. Despite the passive exposure procedure, despite the fact that exposure took place outside the context of the choice-point region, and, parenthetically, despite the reinforcement, the rats tended to alternate on the choice trial. The third of these studies consists of a pair of experiments by Glanzer (1958b) himself, who found the passive exposure technique to be quite as effective in producing alternation as the "active-choice" procedure. However, none of the variables that Glanzer examined (for example, the extent of the animals' familiarity with the maze) seemed to be the source of the difference between his results and those of Walker *et al.* In the Glanzer experiments the exposure took place in the goal arms, and the rats were allowed to wander up to the choice-point region. In contrast, the rats in the unsuccessful study by Walker *et al.* (p. 240) were confined in a goal box, spatially removed from the choice-point area. With that procedural difference and the successful Kivy, Earl, and Walker experiment in mind, Dember and Fowler (1958) speculated that passive exposure would be effective only if the animals had access to the choice-point region during the exposure period.

The fourth experiment favorable to the sI prediction was designed by Dember (1960a) to test this hypothesis suggested by Dember and Fowler. Rats were placed in one of the goal arms of a T maze; the arms themselves were divided into two compartments, one *adjacent* to the choice-point region and one *far* from it. After a one-minute exposure in one of these compartments, the rats were given a free trial. The results showed that locus of confinement *within* the arm made no difference—that is, the Dember and Fowler hypothesis was not confirmed, as might have been anticipated from the results of Sutherland's (1957) experiment. However, a significant percentage of the rats did alternate. The data, then, in gross form replicated Glanzer's findings, showing the effectiveness of passive exposure to the goal-arm stimuli. The failure of Walker *et al.* to obtain this result is yet to be satisfactorily explained.

Similarity between Alternatives. The incorporation of a stimulus generalization postulate into sI theory yields two types of prediction. First, the amount of alternation should vary inversely with the similarity between the alternatives. Second, any decrease in the animal's own ability to discriminate should lower the amount of alternation (see Glanzer, 1953a).

The first type of prediction is analogous to the response generalization prediction of Ir theory, and has had about the same empirical fate. That is, there are experimental situations in which the prediction has not been verified, and some in which it has.

In an unpublished experiment by Walker, the similarity between the arms of a T maze was varied by varying their relative brightness, but there was no corresponding variation in amount of alternation. The previously discussed failure of Jackson (1941) to show a relation between amount of alternation and angle of separation between goal arms is also pertinent here, as is the previously described success of Zeaman and Angell (1953) in finding a direct relation between angle of separation and percentage of *choice* among goal arms after forced exposure to one arm. To repeat a point made earlier, a high level of alternation will generally prevail as long as the alternatives are discriminable on some attribute. The effect of similarity, whether of response or of stimulus, can be shown only through somewhat indirect procedures.

This same explanation probably also accounts for the results of two experiments on alternation in blind rats. In the first (Dember and Roberts, 1958), rats blinded by enucleation alternated as frequently as normals. In the second (Dember, 1958b), blind rats showed the same amount of *stimulus* alternation as normals in a cross-maze situation. Blinding eliminates the rat's ability to make visual discriminations, but leaves intact discriminations in other modalities, on the basis of which alternation can take place. Thus the second type of prediction has so far met only with negative findings.

A successful test of the similarity prediction has been performed by Fowler (personal communication), who, in designing his experiment, took into account the ideas discussed above. Fowler's rats were first confined for two minutes in one arm of a Y maze, the arm being either black or white. Following the exposure period, the rats were removed from the arm, and the maze was rotated through 180° to reduce the possible confounding effects of stimulation outside the maze. A free-choice trial was then given.

Four main groups of rats were run. For group I, the two arms on the choice trial were *identical* in brightness, with either both black or both white. For group II, the two arms were *highly similar*, with either (*a*) one arm black and the other dark gray (for those subjects previously exposed to the black arm), or (*b*) one arm white and the other light gray (for subjects exposed to white). For group III, the two arms were *highly dissimilar*, with either (*a*) one arm black and the other light gray, or *(b)* one arm white and the other dark gray. For group IV, the two arms were *opposite* in brightness, with one black and the other white. It was expected that amount of alternation would increase from group I to group IV.

Eighteen rats served in each of the four groups. The percentages of alternation in groups I through IV were, respectively, 56, 61, 78, and 83. While the Ns are too small to yield significant differences between successive groups, the increasing percentages of alternation with decreasing similarity is consistent with the prediction. In addition, the amount of alternation in group III and IV combined is significantly greater than that in group I and II combined. Incidentally, aside from its direct bearing on the similarity hypothesis, this experiment also provides further support for the effectiveness of the passive exposure procedure.

Summary. sI theory has clearly proven itself superior to Ir theory for the explanation of alternation behavior. It has accomplished this by generating predictions that are either directly contrary to those that Ir theory would have to make, for example, in the cross-maze studies, or that Ir theory could simply not handle, such as the effects of passive exposure to a stimulus and the stimulus generalization of alternation.

Derivations from Stimulus Change Theory

The application of stimulus change theory to the alternation situation was directly motivated by the outcome of the experiment by Kivy, Earl, and Walker (1956) mentioned above. In this study, rats were placed in the starting alley of a T maze. They were allowed to wander freely in the alley for either 1, 15, or 30 minutes. The rats could see into the two goal arms of the maze, but were prevented from entering either arm by glass partitions at the choice-point end of each arm. On a given exposure trial the two arms were either both black or both white. Following exposure, the partitions were removed, and one of the arms was changed in brightness, from black to white or from white to black. The rats were then given a free-choice trial. A significant number in the 15- and 30-minute exposure conditions chose to enter the "nonsatiated" arm. The sI explanation of these results is obvious.

The stimulus change explanation of the rats' behavior points not to their satiation for the previously exposed brightness, but to their attraction to the recently changed arm. Both theories, of course, make the same prediction for the Kivy, *et al.* situation. Up to this point, then, the stimulus change theory is superfluous. Its utility becomes apparent, however, when the original experimental situation is slightly modified.

The modification consists simply in reversing the stimulus conditions that prevailed on the exposure and choice trials of the Kivy *et al.* experiment. The original conditions can be diagrammed as follows, where A and B refer to the brightness of an arm:

		Arm	
Trial		*Left*	*Right*
Exposure		A	A
Choice		A	B

The reversed conditions would be, diagrammatically:

		Arm	
Trial		*Left*	*Right*
Exposure		A	B
Choice		A	A

Now, consider the reversed conditions from the point of view of satiation theory. On the exposure trial a certain amount of sI is built up for brightness A and for brightness B; on the choice trial the rat is offered two arms equal in brightness, that is, both are A. On the basis of satiation alone, no preference should be shown for either arm. The sI theory can make no prediction here. But the stimulus change theory can. While both arms are A on the choice trial, one of them, the right arm in the diagram above, had been B on the exposure trial. On the choice trial that arm, having changed, should be attractive. Thus, the stimulus change theory can predict a preference that satiation theory cannot.

The experiment suggested by the above analysis was done (Dember, 1956) and the prediction verified: 17 of 20 rats entered the changed arm. The apparatus and procedure were much like those of the Kivy *et al.* experiment, except that only a single exposure period, 15 minutes, was used, and, of course, the reversed conditions were employed.

There has been some controversy over the replicability of those results. In a series of experiments, Levine, Staats, and Frommer (1958) and Levine (1958) failed to replicate either the original results of Kivy, Earl, and Walker or the later findings of Dember. Positive replications, however, have more recently been reported by Fowler (1958), Woods and Jennings (1959), and Walk (1960). The reasons for the failures to replicate, if they could be discovered, should prove instructive. In the meantime, the phenomenon seems real, and it reveals a real deficiency in sI theory, at least as originally interpreted.

The stimulus change theory has so far generated only one further prediction in the alternation context. This was a prediction that a forced trial, as typically run, should yield a higher percentage of alternation than a free trial. The rationale behind the prediction is as follows: On a typical forced trial one arm is blocked, usually by a guillotine door; on the subsequent free trial the door is raised, allowing the rat access to both arms. The *change* from door-closed to door-open conditions should attract the rat's attention and thereby should add to the already strong tendency the animal has to alternate and enter the previously blocked arm. This hypothesis has been tested and verified (Dember and Fowler, 1959).

While the two experiments described in this section constitute the only derivations based on the stimulus change concept that have been tested in the alternation context, it should be noted that the theory in which the concept is embedded has been tested in other contexts (for example, Dember, Earl, and Paradise, 1957; Earl, 1957). The theory itself is discussed in more detail in the concluding section of this chapter.

Summary. In a situation for which sI theory could make no prediction but for which the stimulus change theory had a specific prediction, the specific prediction was verified and has since been replicated several times. A second prediction, concerning the difference between free and forced trials, has been verified: a greater amount of alternation follows a forced trial than follows a free trial.

The above constitute the only derivations from the stimulus change theory that have so far been made and tested in the context of alternation behavior. However, the larger theory in which the change concept is embedded has also been successfully tested in the context of other forms of behavior.

Derivations from Action Decrement Theory

As discussed in the previous section, Walker's (1958) theory of alternation points to inhibition that is central rather than peripheral. According to the theory, any central activity yields a decremental aftereffect. The temporal course of this *action decrement* is complex, and in addition it is influenced by conditions of drive and reinforcement. Essentially, the theory seeks to account for the fact that reinforced responses may be alternated temporarily but are ultimately repeated, that is, "learned." Reinforcement has the dual effect of enhancing the initial decrement and the later increment; the greater the reinforcement, the greater the initial decrement and the greater the subsequent increment. Behaviorally, the greater the reinforcement, the greater the amount of alternation with short intertrial intervals, and the greater the amount of repetition with long intertrial intervals.

The primary set of data generated by I_c theory comes from the experiment by Walker (1956) previously referred to in the discussion of intertrial interval. One group of thirsty rats was rewarded with water in either arm of a T maze, while a second thirsty group was never rewarded. Typical alternation testing procedures were followed.

Each rat was tested on each of 21 intertrial intervals. With certain purifications made in the data to remove subject-generated sources of error, and with smoothing, idealized curves were drawn relating percentage of alternation to intertrial interval. At short intervals (up to 30 minutes), the rewarded rats alternated at a somewhat higher percentage than the nonrewarded rats; but at longer intervals, the differences were negligible. These results are consistent with the theory as described above.

A similar relation between motivational variables and alternation is reported by Walker (1958) with strong shock as the drive and shock reduction the reinforcement. In this experiment the shock was administered over the entire maze floor with the exception of the two goal boxes. At a very short intertrial interval the shocked rats alternated more frequently than did the thirsty rats of the previous experiment. This result is consistent with the theory. The rats' alternation behavior at longer intertrial intervals, however, does not fit prediction so nicely. A high level of repetition was expected at the long intervals, but the data points hover about the 50% level.

Even harder to reconcile with I_c theory are the results of an experiment by Fowler, Fowler, and Dember (1959). Here, too, shock was the drive and shock reduction the reinforcement. Five levels of shock were used, one level for each of five groups. Each rat was given six massed, free trials. In this experiment—and herein may lie an important difference in procedure from that used in Walker's shock experiment—only the starting alley was charged; the entire length of both goal arms was free of shock. In both experiments, of course, reinforcement was available in both arms.

According to Walker's theory, the greater the amount of reinforcement, the greater should be the amount of alternation when the intertrial interval is short. But the results of the Fowler *et al.* study reveal exactly the reverse relation: as shock intensity increased, amount of alternation decreased.

A third set of data pertinent in this context are those of Fowler, Blond, and Dember (1959) that show percentage of alternation to vary inversely with amount of food reinforcement per trial. Given the conditions of this experiment, however, the intertrial interval of about 30 minutes may be "long" rather than "short."

Another aspect of Walker's theory of alternation concerns the relation between the discriminability of the alternatives and both the amount of alternation and the ease of learning. According to the theory: *"Any factor capable of producing a big decrement should be capable of producing a big increment or rapid learning"* (Walker, 1958, p. 138).

One likely candidate for such a factor is the discriminability of alternatives. This variable was manipulated in an experiment by Walker and Paradise (1958), the selection of conditions being based on the results of two previous experiments.

In the experiment by Walker, Dember, Earl, and Karoly (1955), the cross-maze technique of Glanzer was employed, with the addition of some variations in procedure that enabled the separation of three potential sources of alternation—that is, S (internal maze stimuli), R (turning response), and P (place, or extra-maze stimuli). One group ran under conditions in which all three potential sources of alternation were combined (SRP *vs.* no change); one in which S and P were combined and pitted against R (SP *vs.* R); a third in which P and R were combined and pitted against S (PR *vs.* S); and finally a group in which P was pitted against the combination of S and R (SR *vs.* P). By noting the amount of alternation associated with each of the experimental conditions, one could infer the relative importance of each of the three possible sources of alternation. In this experiment, the ordering turned out to be S, P, and R, from most to least important. And relative importance, in turn, was interpreted by the experimenters to imply relative discriminability. Thus the response was the least important source of alternation presumably because the feedback from the two responses produced the least discriminable inputs.

In the other experiment, Walker, Dember, Earl, Fawl, and Karoly (1955) attempted to increase the relative importance of response cues by making the two alternative responses more discriminable than usual. This was accomplished by constructing a special cross-maze in which the two goal arms were inclined, banked, and turned, one to the right, the other to the left. In this maze, the turning response did take on a significant amount of importance as a source of alternation. In the conventional flat maze, the response apparently contributed nothing to the alternation tendency.

The previously mentioned experiment by Walker and Paradise (1958) used the eight maze conditions which result from combining the two kinds of mazes, flat and inclined, with each of the four testing procedures: SPR *vs.* no change, SP *vs.* R, PR *vs.* S, and SR *vs.* P. A separate group of eight rats was run under each of the eight maze conditions. For each group, reinforcement was contingent on the rats' consistent utilization of one of the sets of cues. For example, for one group the reinforcement was always in the black arm, but was random with respect to place and response; for another, reinforcement was always in the same place, but random with respect to maze arm and turning response. It was expected that ease of learning, in this experiment, would be positively correlated with amount of alternation produced by each of the eight conditions in the previous experiments. This was the result obtained, both for number of days to reach criterion and number of errors, with only one inversion in the rank order.

Summary. That part of Walker's I_c theory that relates amount of alternation to drive strength, amount of reinforcement, and intertrial interval has received empirical support in an experiment using thirst drive and water reinforcement. However, with shock as the motivating agent, the prediction of a direct relation between drive strength and amount of alternation, with short intertrial intervals, was confirmed in one experiment but not in a second. In that second experiment exactly the opposite relation was obtained: shock intensity and amount of alternation were inversely related. Another experiment, using food reward, also yielded an inverse relation between amount of reinforcement and amount of alternation, but the 30-minute intertrial interval of that experiment might be classified as "long" rather than "short." If so, the results are consistent with the theory. A second aspect of the theory, in which discriminability of the alternatives is related both to amount of alternation and ease of learning, has been experimentally supported.

CONCLUSION: ALTERNATION AND MOTIVATION

In the introductory paragraphs of this chapter, reference was made to the motivational relevance of the alternation phenomenon. This point, however, may have been lost in the course of the ensuing discussion of theories of alternation and tests of these theories. The purpose of this brief section is to re-emphasize the idea that alternation represents, in simple form, the expression of a basic feature of motivated behavior—that is, the *optimization of amount of stimulus variability or complexity.* This idea and relevant studies supporting it have been treated in detail elsewhere (Dember and Earl, 1957; Dember, 1960b, Chapter 10) and need only be summarized here.

The motivational theory of Dember and Earl, which incorporates alternation as a special case, postulates that every stimulus possesses a *complexity value* for each individual who perceives it. Complexity is used to refer to the psychological effects of two broad classes of operations, temporal change in stimulation and spatial change. Temporal change is the operation associated with what is usually labeled stimulus variability or novelty; spatial change is essentially what is often called heterogeneity or complexity. Since the theory regards both classes of operations as having a common psychological basis—that is, *discrepancy* between expectation and stimulation, or, more generally, *information*— a single word, "complexity," is used to cover both cases. (For a similar approach to this issue see Welker, Chapter 7.)

The theory also postulates that at each moment in time and on each stimulus attribute a complexity value can be assigned to every individual. The value associated with an individual is referred to as his *ideal,* following the terminology developed by Coombs (1953). Loosely, the ideal is the maximum amount of complexity in a stimulus that he can comfortably handle at a given moment in his development. The ideal can vary from stimulus attribute to attribute.

Moreover, the ideal can change over time. In particular, in the case of the nonanxious individual, the ideal can only increase, and it does so through the individual's interaction with a special class of stimuli called *pacers*. These are stimuli that have complexity values "just above" the individual's momentary ideal—stimuli that provide what other theories call the "optimal" amount of novelty, variability, complexity, impact, arousal, etc. It is assumed that given free choice the individual will spend the greatest amount of time in contact with a pacer. He will apportion the rest of his time in inverse proportion to the difference in complexity between the pacer and other stimuli in the set containing the pacer.

Now, as mentioned above, the theory postulates that contact with a pacer will lead to an increase in the individual's ideal. In this way, what was once a pacer becomes an ideal, and a new pacer, if one is available, will replace the old one. And, in this way, it becomes possible to exhaust a set of stimuli as potential pacers.

If no pacer is available in a set of stimuli, the individual will stop attending to that set. Forced into contact with a pacerless set, the individual will experience strong negative affect, and will act, given the opportunity, to terminate the contact.

Similarly, given the opportunity, the individual will act to provide himself with stimuli of optimal complexity. This action may involve the simple performance of innately organized or well-learned behaviors, such as looking at one painting rather than another, or entering one arm of a T maze rather than the other. In some cases, the individual may have to learn a new behavior pattern in order to escape from or avoid contact with stimuli of nonoptimal complexity, or in order to gain contact with stimuli of optimal complexity.

In any case, the behavior in question is aroused by the motive to optimize stimulus complexity. What does this have to do with alternation? In situations where alternation is typically observed, the available alternatives are such extremely simple ones as the arms of a T maze. Some degree of complexity can be generated by alternate contact with the T maze arms and this amount, however trivial, is usually greater than that to be experienced from repetitively entering the same maze arm, or from simply remaining still in the starting alley. Thus the alternation pattern can be seen as the rat's way of maximizing, though not necessarily optimizing, stimulus complexity.

It follows from this line of thinking that the alternation pattern can be disrupted by making one of the alternatives by itself more nearly optimal in complexity than the amount generated through alternation of the two arms. Under such circumstances the rat will re-enter the complex arm more frequently than otherwise, or at least until repeated contact with that same arm no longer provides the proper amount of complexity. At this point the alternation pattern may emerge, or the animal may stop running in that maze altogther. Thus the alternation pattern can be disrupted by manipulating the complexity of the alternatives, as has been done, for example, by Montgomery (1954) and by Dember, Earl, and Paradise (1957).

Note, finally, that one very effective way of disrupting the alternation pattern is to bait one arm with a conventional "primary" reinforcer, such as a pellet of Purina Lab Chow. Because of their peculiar effectiveness in producing stereotypy, the conventional reinforcers have taken on special significance within modern learning theories. As pointed out elsewhere (Fowler, Blond, and Dember, 1959), parsimony would make it desirable to incorporate the behavior con-

trolled by the primary drives and reinforcers into a single system
with the behavior controlled by stimulus complexity. A first step in
integrating the two types of behavior has been taken by Fowler,
Blond, and Dember, who argue:

> Hunger, for example, can be considered as a source of intense, persistent,
> little-changing, and very familiar stimulation; as such, it is dealt with by the
> animal in the same manner as any other monotonous stimulation. That is,
> the animal learns and/or performs those responses which are instrumental in
> removing this unchanging, intense stimulation or in providing new stimula-
> tion. In the case of persistent stimulation of external origin, e.g., the familiar
> maze arm, the animal, given the opportunity, seeks novel stimulation, e.g., by
> entering the other arm. In the case of hunger stimulation, the source of which
> the animal carries about with it, the most appropriate instrumental response
> is eating. (Fowler, Blond, and Dember, 1959, p. 613.)

From the point of view expressed here, the conventional reinforcers are no different *in principle* from any other stimuli. And any
distinction, in principle, between the primary drives and the motive
underlying exploration, manipulation, curiosity, and alternation is
artificial and misleading. This, of course, is essentially the point
of view taken by Neal Miller (see Dollard & Miller, 1950), though
his approach points to stimulus *intensity* as the relevant variable,
while the present approach emphasizes stimulus *complexity*.

Chapter 9

Exploratory Behavior and Variation-Seeking in Man*

SALVATORE R. MADDI
University of Chicago

*I*T is generally recognized that exploratory behavior occurs in a wide variety of species, including man. But this generality does not obviate the possibility that the phenomenon at the human level possesses some degree of uniqueness, if only in a quantitative sense. The answers to two questions would help in the evaluation of this possibility. First, in the light of currently available evidence, are there any important differences in exploratory behavior between man and the lower animals? Certainly the gap between human and subhuman species is large enough to justify this concern. Second, does the explanation of human exploratory behavior have any significance for the understanding of personality? Although this question is more specific in some ways, it may turn out to be related to the first, as personality has been considered uniquely human.

The assessment of our current ability to answer these two questions, which is the principal aim of this chapter, has largely determined the selection and treatment of the topics that follow. First, a review of some of the observational and experimental evidence about human exploratory behavior will be presented, so that stock may be taken of current knowledge regarding this phenomenon. There will also be some comparison of results at the human level with those at the subhuman level. Following this review and comparison, a number of possible explanations of exploratory behavior will be discussed. Finally, the implications of one of these explanations for the understanding of a motivational aspect of personality will be

*Some of the research reported in this chapter was supported by funds from Ford Foundation Behavioral Sciences Grant #1-5600-49-2863 (Maddi).

elaborated. Important in this elaboration will be the distinction between behavior aimed at the exploration of already existing stimuli,
and behavior which increases the level of variation in stimulation
available in the environment.

Before proceeding to a discussion of the evidence, an attempt will
be made to delineate the meaning of the term exploratory behavior.
This is a very difficult task, and one which a number of investigators
in the area have not explicitly undertaken. The difficulty seems at
least partly due to our insufficient understanding of the phenomenon,
but it may also stem from the ubiquitous nature of exploratory behavior. Because it is so pervasive, such behavior is difficult to define
in any very meaningful manner. Nonetheless, we will state at least
what exploratory behavior will refer to in this chapter.

Any behavior that indicates interest in, or particular attention to,
one portion, as opposed to the rest, of the surround can be considered exploratory. Such behavior involves the exposure of the sense
receptors to that particular part of the environment (see Chapter 7).
However, this meaning will not be sufficient without a major qualification. Interest in a particular portion of the surround occurs in
conjunction with a wide variety of motivational states. The organism
may exhibit what seems to be exploratory behavior even when occupied with such specific tasks as seeking food, a sexual partner, success, or safety. But the seemingly exploratory behavior that occurs
when strong, specific motives (see Chapter 2) exist is primarily instrumental. In this chapter, we will be concerned with interest in
portions of the environment only where that interest appears to be an
end in itself. Hence, it seems reasonable to restrict the term exploration to behavior that, though indicating the type of interest mentioned above, occurs in the absence of any strong, specific needs.

Three types of exploratory behavior will be distinguished. The
first is the orienting response, which involves slight muscular and
postural adjustments, such as head-turning, neck-stretching, or even
simple ocular movement. It should be clear that such responses
satisfy the description of exploration presented above. The second
type is the investigatory response, which involves more gross adjustments in the physical relationship between the individual and his
environment. Examples include locomotion, and simple manipulation
such as picking something up. When such behavior is directed toward

a particular portion of the surround, it can be considered exploratory. Of course, investigatory responses include orienting ones. (The distinctions and terminology employed in this paragraph are rather similar to those in Berlyne, 1960).

The third type of exploratory behavior is play. Although play may be considered a separate category from exploration, this distinction will not be made for the moment because the two phenomena appear to include such similar types of responses. Indeed, it is often difficult to decide whether one is observing investigatory responses or play. Perhaps the most distinctive feature of play by comparison with the other aspects of exploration is that it ordinarily involves a longer period of interest in one or a few objects than characterizes investigatory and orienting responses. This feature of play may be particularly important in the case of humans, who tend to embellish objects with fantasies and daydreams. Welker (Chapter 7) mentions vigor of behavior as an important feature of play. He lists such behaviors as running, jumping, and wrestling as examples. Especially with humans, however, vigor is likely to be a useful, but not infallible criterion. The child can play with a doll, chalk and slate, or a cardboard box very quietly for hours. It will be sufficient for present purposes to consider play to be a comparatively lengthy, sometimes vigorous interaction with a particular portion of the surround. As play includes orienting and investigatory responses, it is tempting to consider it to be a more complex form of exploration than are these other types.

But exploratory behavior is not always present whenever the organism lacks any very strong, specific motivation. Hence, in order to understand the phenomenon more fully, we should have knowledge of the variables which elicit it. A number of variables have been offered, such as stimulus novelty, complexity, incongruity, and surprisingness. Some writers believe only one or two of these to be important, while others (for example, Berlyne, 1960) stress them all. A novel stimulus is either one which is different from recently experienced stimuli, or one which is to some extent unprecedented in the organism's history. The first type of novelty, which emphasizes stimulus change, is relative, while the second type is more absolute. Whether relative or absolute, novelty is usually considered the most important of the variables influencing exploration. The complexity of a stimulus is a function of the number of distinct elements it contains, and its irregularity. An incongruous stimulus contains elements which are perceived as incompatible with each other on the basis of prior experience with these elements. Finally, a surprising stimulus is one which contradicts or violates an established expectation.

Having roughly defined exploration and a number of the variables which may influence it, we can proceed to a discussion of some of the relevant evidence. The following three sections will be brief, as most of what little pertinent research there is has been ably reviewed recently by Berlyne (1960) and White (1960).

ORIENTING RESPONSES

Anyone who has even casually observed the human infant and adult will have found that objects which are novel, complex, and changing are visually fixated. Such fixation can be considered an aspect of exploratory behavior because it represents an orienting response to a particular portion of the environment.

A number of pertinent experiments have utilized the complexity and incongruity variables. Berlyne (1958a) found that the visual attention of three- to nine-month-old infants was initially directed to the most complex of three simultaneously presented patterns. Similarly, Fantz (1958a) reported that infants looked at a checkerboard pattern longer than at a less complex, solid-color square. In a subsequent experiment with adults, Berlyne (1958b) utilized a procedure of exposing pairs of stimuli for 10 seconds each. One member of each pair differed from the other either in complexity or incongruity. In every pair, the figure that was more complex or incongruous was fixated for a longer proportion of the total exposure time than was the other figure. The experiment was repeated (Berlyne, 1958d) with longer exposure times (two minutes per pair of figures) in order to demonstrate that the results of the prior experiment did not involve the effects of complexity and incongruity on identification time alone, to the exclusion of their effects on visual exploration. The results of the second experiment were similar to those of the original one.

Concerning the novelty variable, we have Piaget's careful observations (1952) that, from the age of five weeks on, the infant looks at somewhat unfamiliar or novel objects rather than at very familiar or very new ones. Interestingly enough, Piaget has treated the novelty variable as continuous, rather than dichotomous. His results suggest the importance of doing the same with other proposed independent variables. Although to this time the other variables have generally been treated as dichotomous, there is one exception in the work which has already been discussed. Berlyne (1958a) used three degrees of complexity and, as indicated earlier, found that the largest degree was most often the object of initial fixation. These results suggest the different effects of the complexity and novelty dimensions, but additional investigation is necessary before any firm conclusion can be reached.

In summary, the evidence, though not very extensive, suggests that stimuli which are relatively high in novelty, complexity, or incongruity are likely to be important determinants of visual fixation in the human being. Caution should be exercised both in considering this a firmly established conclusion, and in generalizing too far from the findings, because the systematic research is fragmentary, and has thus far been restricted to the visual modality.

Pertinent Results at the Subhuman Level

Results at the subhuman level are quite similar to, though more complete than, those discussed above. With rats, monkeys, chimpanzees, and other animals, it has been found that a visual, auditory, tactual, or olfactory stimulus which is relatively novel brings the head into specific orientation toward the stimulus (see Chapter 7). There is some evidence (Fantz, 1958b) that complexity has effects at the subhuman level which are similar to those at the human level. Also, in experiments on learning in dogs, it has been observed that orienting responses are often strengthened by what may be considered surprising changes in the experimental conditions (see Berlyne, 1960, pp. 98-99).

Of all the evidence thus far considered, Piaget's observations on humans stand out as different from the rest. While he found that moderately novel stimuli are the preferred objects of visual fixation, other investigators report that a wide variety of novel, complex, incongruous, and surprising stimuli are effective in producing such fixation in both human and subhuman organisms. But it must be kept in mind that Piaget was concerned with the pattern of visual fixation over an extended period of time. He does not conclude that only moderately novel stimuli are fixated, but that these are the preferred objects of visual exploration.

This suggests the usefulness of distinguishing between the occurrence of an orienting response and its duration. Specific orientation may very well occur whenever a stimulus with any degree of novelty, complexity, incongruity, or surprisingness occurs, but the duration of this response may be a function of the degree to which the stimulus is characterized by any of these variables. For example, a moderately novel stimulus may produce a comparatively long period of fixation, while an extremely novel stimulus may produce an initial fixation which is rapidly terminated and perhaps even followed by avoidance. The orienting response which exposes the sense receptors to the stimulus for a relatively long period of time may be more clearly an indication of exploration, while the orienting response of shorter duration, though an indication of cognizance, may demonstrate fear rather than any other reaction.

INVESTIGATORY RESPONSES

The essential difference between the orienting response of greater than brief duration and the investigatory response is that the latter involves more extensive changes in body position and relationship to the environment. Both types of response expose the sense receptors to one portion of the environment more than to other portions. The investigatory response is more efficient than the orienting response, and will probably occur whenever the organism has the necessary capacity for motility and the situation permits such a response.

Again Piaget (1952) has provided us with careful and detailed observations, this time of investigatory behavior. One has only to couple the vivid image of the child, Laurent, repeatedly investigating the possibilities of making his rattle ring by pulling the string attached to it, with similar observations of one's own to be convinced that investigatory responses occur with considerable frequency in the child. On the basis of Piaget's reports, and other similar ones (for example, Gesell & Ilg, 1943; Levy, 1955), White (1960) has argued compellingly that, in our enthusiasm for the psychosexual stages of development, we have overlooked exploratory behavior as a basic feature of infant and child behavior. Although many observations of investigatory behavior are available, surprisingly few systematic investigations have been done. While the observations do suggest the importance of such variables as novelty and complexity, it is not yet possible to state the precise role that these and other variables play in the elicitation and continuation of investigatory responses.

One of the few pertinent experimental approaches is that of Berlyne (1957b; also 1960, pp. 160-162) on self-stimulation. This term is used here to indicate the occurrence of a voluntary response which exposes the person to a particular visual stimulus. Such behavior can be considered investigatory because it brings the person into contact with some stimulus situation, or aspect of it.

In Berlyne's procedure, the adult subjects could expose themselves to a tachistoscopically presented stimulus for 0.14 seconds by pressing a lever. They were told to press the lever as often as they wished. When they no longer wanted to expose themselves to a particular stimulus in this fashion, another one was inserted into the tachistoscope, and the procedure was repeated. All subjects participated in four separate experiments, each of which was designed to test the effects of a particular independent variable on the frequency of lever pressing or self-stimulation.

The complexity variable was involved in two of the experiments. In one case, the aspect of complexity which emphasizes the number of distinguishable parts of, or the intricacy of, the stimulus was of primary concern. Each of Berlyne's two series of pictures involved the development from a simple circle into a more complex figure. In one series, the complex figure was a clown, and in the other it was a bear. The complexity of each successive stimulus in a series was greater than that of any preceding stimuli. The analysis of results indicates that response total per stimulus increased with increases from lowest degree, to intermediate degree, to highest degree of complexity. It did not seem to matter whether the cards in a series were presented in a meaningful or a random order.

The other experiment dealing with complexity emphasized the redundancy of stimulus configurations. Redundancy, an information theory variable, increases with the regularity and symmetry of a stimulus. The less redundant the figure, the greater the number of responses it elicited.

The experiment dealing with the incongruity variable utilized pictures of animals and birds, some of which contained incompatible elements (such as a camel with a lion's head). The incongruous figures elicited more responses than did the more ordinary ones.

The remaining experiment involved the surprisingness variable. The first few stimuli presented were similar to each other in certain respects (for example, color). Then a stimulus occurred which was different. The next few stimuli were similar to this one, and then the final stimulus was different from these. The two stimuli which were different from the immediately preceding ones were considered to be surprising, and elicited more responses than did the others.

Taken as a whole, this experiment seems to have provided evidence that incongruity, complexity, and surprisingness function to elicit investigatory responses. However, it is necessary to note, as Berlyne himself does (1960, p. 162), that the subjects in this study reported pressing the lever only until positive identification of the stimulus had been made. Hence, this experiment does not seem fully adequate to demonstrate that subjects exposed themselves to some stimuli because they were more interesting, rather than simply more difficult to identify. In order to permit such an unequivocal conclusion, the experiment would have to be repeated with longer exposure times in an attempt to show that even after subjects have been able to identify a stimulus, they want to look at it longer if it is more complex, incongruous, or surprising than are other stimuli. Of course, it may be argued that positive identification is the only goal of exploratory behavior, and, hence, that the objection raised here is trivial. But this argument is inconsistent with the bulk of the evidence currently available.

Being convinced of the potential significance of considering the variables influencing exploration to be continuous, rather than dichotomous, Mendel and Maddi (unpublished study) concerned themselves with the effects of various degrees of novelty on investigatory responses. More specifically, they wished to determine the influence of degree of novelty on choice of play objects in young children. Each child in their nursery school sample was between the ages of three and five, and was tested individually. Every member of the experimental group was permitted to play with an array of eight small toys placed on a table. Following eight minutes of habituation to these toys, the subject was shown some additional arrays of toys. Each of these arrays was composed of eight toys on a table similar to the one encountered during habituation. The subject was asked to choose one array of toys for additional play.

One of the five arrays present during this choice period was identical to that encountered during habituation. The other tables had different proportions of habituated toys to toys not previously encountered in the experiment. The toys not previously encountered can be considered to have short-term novelty, to use Berlyne's term (1960, p. 19). As each of the five choice-period arrays contained a different proportion of novel toys, the arrays could be ordered with regard to degree of novelty. This ordering involves the assumption that degree of novelty of a stimulus configuration can be indexed by the proportion of novel elements to total number of elements (see Bindra, 1959b). The subjects, then, chose from among arrays of 0%, 25%, 50%, 75%, and 100% short-term novelty. In order to insure that the results could be interpreted in terms of the degree of novelty to which children are attracted, randomization was used to control other variables such as size, color, shape, and representational value of toys.

Although some choice on the part of the subject was necessary, the particular one made was essentially voluntary and can be considered an investigatory response because it indicates an interest in, and brings the organism into contact with, a particular portion of the total surround. However, because a choice was required, this study is not strictly speaking relevant to the question of whether an investigatory response would have occurred at all in this situation. It does seem rather likely, though, that a young child would show interest in toys.

As mentioned earlier, a control group was also used. This group was similar to the experimental one in age, sex, and socioeconomic level of parents. The subjects of the control group were also asked to choose which of the five arrays of toys they wished to play with. However, the arrays did not differ in degree of novelty for the control subjects because they did not experience a habituation period prior to making their choice.

Taken together, the arrays of from 25% to 75% novelty were

chosen more frequently by the experimental than by the control group. In contrast, the arrays with 0% and 100% novelty, taken together, were chosen with less frequency by the experimental than by the control group. It would appear that the intermediate degrees of novelty were most effective in eliciting choice or investigatory responses.

An interesting extension of this experiment would involve varying the length of the habituation period. With a shorter habituation period, the more extremely novel arrays should be chosen less frequently than they were, while a longer habituation period should lead to the relatively less frequent choice of the more mildly novel arrays.

Pertinent Results at the Subhuman Level

The results obtained by Mendel and Maddi are consistent with those of a number of studies at the subhuman level. For example, Bindra and Spinner (1958) found that moderate degrees of change in a familiar environment produced such behavior as locomotion and head-turning in rats, while more extreme changes produced grooming and freezing. The former behaviors indicate a positive interest in the surround, while the latter ones may even be indicative of avoidance tendencies (see Chapter 13). This interpretation suggests that Bindra and Spinner's most novel condition was more aversive than was that of Mendel and Maddi. This possibility may be due to a number of variables, including pertinent species differences. A very likely factor is the magnitude of the surround which is varied. Mendel and Maddi actually manipulated quite little of the subject's total environment. The room, the experimenter, and everything but a few small toys were the same during the choice period as they had been during habituation. On the contrary, Bindra and Spinner changed a considerably larger proportion of the surround in producing their most novel stimulus condition.

Hebb (1958a, p. 114) also reported aversive effects of novelty. Chimpanzees exhibited fear and flight in the face of unprecedented events (for example, the model of a human head which was clearly without a body), while similar though less unprecedented events (such as the head of a man standing behind a partition) did not produce such reactions. Again, the avoidance reaction to the unprecedented event is more extreme than anything observed by Mendel and Maddi. However, an explanation of this discrepancy cannot be sought in the magnitude of the surround which is varied. That Mendel and Maddi did not obtain any overt evidence of fear and flight may be due to their having studied relative rather than absolute novelty. The children were undoubtedly familiar with the types of toys utilized in the experiment, while, by contrast, the chimpanzees had never had experience with a seemingly human head that was clearly without a body. Differences in the meaningfulness (see Chapter 2) of the novel stimuli used in the two studies may also be of importance.

Berlyne's study of self-stimulation is reminiscent of the finding (Butler, 1954b) that monkeys will learn particular responses in order to obtain access to variable and complex stimulus fields. While no appreciable learning took place in Berlyne's study, his results, like those of Butler, indicate that complex stimuli have rewarding properties. Although dissimilar in structure to that of Berlyne, an experiment by Welker (1956c) has shown that chimpanzees make more investigatory responses to multicolored, mottled, rectangular blocks than to more simple, uniformly colored blocks. It can be seen that there is evidence at the subhuman level for Berlyne's conclusions concerning complexity.

In general, Berlyne's findings involving surprisingness and incongruity do not have very good counterparts in work with subhuman species. However, there is a bit of evidence which seems contradictory to that reported by Berlyne concerning incongruity. Hebb has reported (1958a) that such incongruous stimuli as an attendant wearing the laboratory coat of another attendant produced fear and flight in chimpanzees. There has not been sufficient investigation of this point to indicate whether differences in species, in the meaningfulness of stimulation, or in degree of incongruity *per se* are of major importance in the explanation of the discrepancy between these findings.

PLAY

Play includes orienting and investigatory responses, and, indeed, can even be considered a continuing sequence of such behaviors. Very often investigatory movements shade over into the more prolonged manipulation and activity called play. There is some observational evidence that play is often produced in the same way as other types of exploration, that is, by the presence of stimuli characterized by novelty or one of the other variables. However, we do not have detailed knowledge on this point for humans. The emphasis of most observational work has been on the ontogenetic frequency and duration of play. While our lack of information concerning the stimulus characteristics eliciting play may be caused partly by a lack of interest in such information on the part of observers, it also suggests an important property of this type of exploratory behavior. Play not only occurs in response to a complex or novel stimulus but also occurs more or less spontaneously. The motivational implications of this possibility will be discussed later. For the moment, a brief summary will be presented of our knowledge of the ontogenetic vicissitudes of play.

Play first occurs early in infancy, and increases in intensity and duration during the first year of life to the point where the one-year-old is playing a total of about six hours a day (White, 1960). Observations indicate that at this age the infant may be at least as interested in playing as in eating at mealtimes (Gesell and Ilg, 1943; Levy, 1955). As he grows older, the child spends more and more time in these prolonged interactions with the environment which are not easily explained on the basis of specific motivation (Gesell and Ilg, 1943; Mittelmann, 1954; Piaget, 1952). White (1960) estimates that play occupies the largest portion of the child's waking time during the 2nd through perhaps the 10th year of life. He argues cogently that the theory of psychosexual stages of development is not adequate to explain fully this type of behavior, which he perceives as more related to the development of competence in dealing with the environment than to the conflicts centering around the anus and genitalia.

The increase in time spent playing, which takes place during the first few years of life, is partially related to the greater and more efficient motility achieved during the second and third years, but may also reflect an increasing difficulty in achieving the satisfactions obtained from play. The continual accrual of experience and knowledge, an important concomitant of aging, indicates that less and less potential experience will seem new as time goes on. Thus, the child may have to increase his efforts as he becomes more sophisticated in order to achieve the satisfactions gained from play and perhaps from other forms of exploration as well.

Observation indicates that there is a decline in the intensity and duration of play starting at about the time of puberty or slightly before. This decline may be related to the upsurgence of sexual interest (see Chapter 7), and to the increase in responsibility in the life of the teenager (see White, 1960), but it may also indicate the replacement of play by other functionally equivalent activities. The latter possibility will be elaborated in the last section of this chapter. In any event, by the time adulthood is reached, play (if it occurs as such) has become restricted to relatively short, circumscribed periods of time, and is much more regulated by such extrinsic variables as social mores, and by such specific motives as that for achievement. The adult plays specific games at specific times with specific people, and does not always derive enjoyment from his participation.

Pertinent Observations at the Subhuman Level

In general, observations of play similar to those at the human level have been made at the subhuman level. As would be expected, the subhuman primates engage in manipulation and vigorous activity more than do animals whose motor capacities are more limited in this regard (for example, rats). However, play is by no means restricted to the primates (see Chapter 7). In the lower animal, as in the human, play increases in intensity ontogenetically until a peak is reached sometime during childhood. From this point on, play decreases in intensity and duration. Observations are not precise enough at this time to permit comparison across species of the rate of decline in play as adulthood is neared. One might speculate that man's rate of decline would be greater, because of his superior conceptual ability and his socialization. Play in the human may be more effectively replaced by other behavior, thought, and fantasy.

SPECULATIONS AND INTERPRETATIONS

Comparison of Human and Subhuman Exploration

It is hazardous at this time to state any but tentative conclusions concerning human exploratory behavior. The findings of systematic research are too fragmentary, and there are simply too many possible interpretations at this stage of our knowledge to justify singling out any one or two of them as the most likely. About the most that can be done is to conclude that novel, complex, incongruous, or surprising stimuli elicit orienting and investigatory responses, and play.

Having stated this conclusion, we must immediately qualify it in the case of novelty. Some evidence indicates that moderately novel stimuli may be more effective in producing orienting and investigatory responses than are more extremely novel ones. Complexity is the only independent variable besides novelty which has been treated as continuous, rather than dichotomous. As far as we can tell at this time, the qualification made concerning novelty is not necessary for complexity. The most complex stimuli utilized appear to have elicited the greatest degrees of exploration. In future research, it would be quite useful to treat the incongruity and surprisingness variables as continuous, and to increase the range of complexity and novelty studied.

Another qualification of our tentative conclusion is necessary, this time concerning the play aspect of exploratory behavior. Although play is often stimulated by some or all of the independent variables considered, it also occurs with considerable frequency either spontaneously, or as a result of other factors not currently studied. As will be discussed later, play which seems more or less spontaneous may be most meaningfully classified as something other than exploratory behavior.

In the light of our fragmentary knowledge concerning human exploratory behavior, it is not surprising that it is difficult to make comparisons with subhuman organisms. Perhaps all that can surely be said is that the findings at the human level have their counterparts at the subhuman level. There is not much evidence that human exploratory behavior is qualitatively different from such behavior in lower animals. Either there are in fact no important differences in this regard or whatever differences exist have not yet been studied adequately. Certainly there must be more research on human exploration before one or the other interpretation can be accepted.

In studying this phenomenon, advantage should be taken of man's verbal ability. The use of instructions and the analysis of spontaneous or solicited verbalizations (see Chapter 13) can contribute to the richness of data obtained and the range of studies possible. Of course, there are also some pitfalls in studying exploration in man which are not particular problems at the subhuman level. For example, the experimental situation itself is very likely to interfere with exploratory behavior in humans by arousing specific motives such as that for approval. In addition, it would be difficult to encourage at least the adult human to act as freely in the experimental setting as he would outside of it because of social mores concerning the appropriateness of behavior in particular situations. Such social constraints are likely to be quite a problem in studying the apparently sensitive phenomenon of exploration.

Overlapping Variables

A methodological difficulty which is dramatized by the experiments cited earlier is that the variables presumed to effect exploratory behavior all seem to covary to some degree. Novelty, complexity, incongruity, and surprisingness can be fairly well defined in the abstract, but when an attempt is made to vary one of them while holding the others constant, the distinctions become blurred. The more complex, incongruous, and surprising a stimulus is, the more likely it is to be novel. The more incongruous a stimulus is, the more likely it is to be complex. On closer scrutiny, incongruity appears to be no more than a special case of surprisingness, special in the sense that it involves the spatial rather than the temporal dimension (see Chapter 2). It should be recognized that in most of the experiments which have been discussed, a certain amount of confounding of these variables must have taken place.

The covariation of these stimulus characteristics suggests that they all have in common some property which is crucial to the occurrence of exploratory behavior. Thus, what appears to be a methodological problem may have considerable theoretical significance.

Interpretations of Exploratory Behavior

Is there one basic variable that produces exploration? Among the current concepts which are comprehensive enough to be considered such a basic variable are *complexity* (Dember and Earl, 1957; Chapter 8), *conflict* (Berlyne, 1957c, 1960), and *variation* (Chapter 2). Each of these concepts is embedded in a theory which interprets exploratory behavior. Although a fully adequate comparison of these points of view must await more precise definition and additional investigation, it will be useful at this time to discuss them in order to determine their similarities and differences, and to identify the aspects of each which may require additional elaboration. It should be made clear that the interpretations discussed here are not the only ones available. Some other relevant conceptualizations are included in this volume (Chapters 10 and 13).

Dember and Earl (1957; see Chapter 8) have offered an interesting approach in which *complexity* is considered to be the basic feature of stimulation capable of arousing exploratory behavior. The organism is assumed to possess a complexity value, or a kind of adaptation level, which determines the degree of complexity that is comfortable, and that can be effectively handled.

Common to organisms is the motivation to optimize level of complexity in the environment. The optimal level is that which is just above the organism's complexity value. Such optimally complex aspects of the environment are called pacers; they receive attention in preference to stimuli that are either more or less complex. Attention to pacers brings about an increase in the organism's complexity value.

On first consideration it is not immediately clear how the concept of complexity can apply to all novel and surprising events. While novelty and complexity do covary to some extent, it is certainly possible to devise a novel stimulus which is less complex than that which preceded it. How can complexity be used in the explanation of the effects of such a stimulus? The difficulty stems from the very special sense in which the term complexity is used by Dember and Earl; they appear to emphasize temporal variation in stimulation. That the central concern of their theory is with such variation is demonstrated by the interpretation of an experiment (Dember, Earl, and Paradise, 1957), considered to be important to the development of this line of thinking, in which rats were put in a maze having alternating black and white stripes that were horizontal in one portion and vertical in the other. The tendency of rats to spend more time in the portion having vertical rather than horizontal stripes suggests that they were attracted by the variable pattern of visual stimulation which could be obtained in that portion by locomoting or by moving the head from side to side. Although Dember and Earl have themselves offered this interpretation, they couch it in the terminology of complexity. But in this context the term complexity seems somewhat confusing. It is not really clear that the vertical stripes were any more complex than the horizontal stripes. However, they did possess a greater potential for temporal variation in stimulation.

If we keep in mind that Dember and Earl stress stimulus variation in their usage of complexity, it seems reasonable to assume that this concept applies to novelty, incongruity, and surprisingness. Each of these characteristics involves change in stimulation (except for certain exceptional cases of surprisingness, which will be discussed later). Complexity, defined in the spatial sense used in the introduction to this chapter, reduces to a special case of temporal variation. The greater the spatial complexity of a stimulus, the more effective will be the organism's scanning in producing moment-to-moment changes in sensory stimulation (see Chapter 2).

If the complexity constituted by a particular stimulus is just above the level which can be readily assimilated by the organism (its complexity value), it will be attended to and perhaps explored further. In exploring, the complexity of the stimulus is not reduced, but rather the organism's ability to assimilate complexity is increased. Later discussion will indicate the differences between this and other conceptualizations of the effects of exploration. But first a pertinent question should be raised. If the organism is most comfortable with levels of complexity which are consistent with its complexity value, why should it attend to and explore levels which are greater than this? It would be useful to have further clarification of the reason why the organism does not seek merely that with which it is most comfortable. Such clarification would probably also bear on the sense in which levels of complexity just above the organism's complexity value are optimal.

Although there is considerable covariation between surprisingness and Dember and Earl's complexity variable, there are instances, as suggested earlier, in which the two do not overlap. The line "a rose is a rose is a rose" violates the nature of our expectations concerning sequences of words. Its very repetitiveness is surprising and attracts our attention. Yet, the line is less complex in the sense of change than almost any other English line that might be normally encountered. Dember and Earl's approach does not seem to apply to such instances of unexpectedness. Evaluation of the seriousness of this limitation would involve determining whether or not relatively simple, but nonetheless surprising, stimuli are explored.

Berlyne seems to believe that the common feature of novel, complex, incongruous, and surprising stimuli is the *conflict* they arouse in the perceiver. Conflict is defined in essentially Hullian terms as the simultaneous arousal of incompatible response tendencies. In his recent writing, Berlyne (1960) has stressed the contribution made to activation level by stimuli that elicit exploration. Activation level involves such neurophysiological systems as the brain stem reticular formation. He subscribes to the idea of optimal level of activation, and explains exploratory behavior as the attempt to reduce activation to the optimal zone by decreasing the conflict aroused by a stimulus. Reduction of conflict is achieved through gaining information about the stimulus.

This use of the concept of conflict raises some difficulty. Why should the organism approach that which creates conflict? It is especially difficult to understand why this should occur because conflict is usually considered to be a punishing state of affairs. Aware of this problem, Berlyne has recently argued (1960, p. 197) that it is not logically necessary to assume that the onset of a state is punishing because its termination is rewarding. Conflict is presumably a state of tension, but not one which is to be considered punishing. Nonetheless, the reduction of conflict is rewarding. Berlyne's argument is elusive, and not very convincing. Although there are some exceptions which Berlyne cites (1960, p. 198), it is certain that most punishing states are avoided. If Berlyne's usage is to appear compelling enough to warrant a redefinition of the affective concomitants of conflict, it must be clearly demonstrated that organisms will explore something which has aroused incompatible response tendencies in them. Some manner of measuring such incompatible tendencies should be devised, and the relationship between that measure and exploration should be investigated.

As can be seen even on the basis of this brief presentation, the points of view of Dember and Earl, and of Berlyne have some similarities in structure and some differences in content. One structural similarity is the assumption of an organismic process important for the understanding of the ability of some stimuli to produce exploration. The content chosen for the organismic variable differs, Berlyne favoring the neuropsychological concept of activation level, and Dember and Earl emphasizing the more purely psychological concept of complexity value.

Another agreement on the formal level is that exploratory behavior is motivated, but again there is disagreement at the content level.

For Dember and Earl, the organism explores a stimulus in order to raise complexity value to the optimal level. In sharp contrast, Berlyne believes that the organism explores in order to lower activation to the optimal level by reducing the conflict caused by the stimulus. In the first conceptualization, exploration is an attraction to a stimulus, while in the second it is an attempt to overcome the aversive aspects of a stimulus.

Let us turn now to the conceptualization which was developed in Chapter 2. This comprehensive approach applies to many behavioral phenomena including exploration. As will become clear in the following pages, our viewpoint shares the formal similarities discussed above, but in content, there are both similarities and differences between each of the positions already presented and our own.

The variable which we believe to be basic to the arousal of exploratory behavior is *variation* in stimulation. Although less similar to conflict than it is to complexity, variation is defined more broadly than the Dember and Earl concept. A stimulus is considered to have variation if it is different from the immediately preceding one, if it has relative novelty, or if it is either temporally or spatially unexpected. Thus novelty and surprisingness, as these terms were utilized in the presentation of the data, obviously constitute variation. Incongruity has variation because it involves spatial unexpectedness. And because a complex stimulus provides greater opportunity for temporal change it too is encompassed by the definition of variation. Any variation in exteroceptive, interoceptive, or cerebral stimulation is considered important because it can produce an increment in level of activation. The physical intensity and meaningfulness of stimulation can also produce such increments, and this shared property of the three dimensions is called impact.

We too have found it necessary to assume an organismic variable. Like that of Berlyne and others, ours is level of activation. However, where other writers use the concept of optimal level of activation, we refer to the normal level which characterizes the various portions of the curve of wakefulness. This is an attempt to define "optimal" in some fairly specific fashion. In any event, we propose that the organism attempts to maintain activation at the normal level because large deviations from this level are typically associated with negative affect.

Important to our explanation of exploration is the assumption that this behavior typically occurs in the absence of strong, specific motivation (for example, viscerogenic needs). Such motivation, because it involves stimulation of considerable intensity and meaningfulness, tends to keep activation at or above normal level. But when intensity and meaningfulness are comparatively low, activation will fall below normal unless there is sufficient variation, or the organism is successful in increasing the impact of incoming stimulation. Orienting and investigatory responses (of the type we have called exploratory) are an attempt to expose the sense receptors to an external stimulus characterized by variation. These responses are consistent with what may be considered to be the organism's *need for variation* in order to sustain normal level of activation. While play may in some cases be subject to this interpretation, it often seems to represent more of an attempt to actually increase the variation in stimulation which is available, rather than merely taking advantage of variation which occurs.

The need for variation encompasses what is for us the motivational significance of exploratory behavior. While we agree with the other theorists on the fact that exploration is motivated behavior, our position is in content unlike that of Berlyne, in which exploration is explained as an attempt to diminish, rather than sustain, level of activation, and is perhaps more similar to that of Dember and Earl even though they do not utilize the concept of activation.

A possible disadvantage of our position is that it provides only a general explanation of exploration. However, this difficulty is at least partially attributable to the considerable comprehensiveness of this approach. It permits explanation of many other phenomena besides exploration, and even in this area leads to hypotheses which do not follow readily from other viewpoints. For example, it can be predicted that the occurrence of intense interoceptive stimulation (for example, pain) will inhibit the occurrence of exploration in situations normally eliciting such behavior. This prediction follows from the assumption that stimulus intensity contributes to impact and hence to level of activation, and that at any point in time the level of activation is determined by the total impact from various sources of stimulation. If level of activation is higher than is normal, exploration of a stimulus having variation should not occur.

THE NEED FOR VARIATION AS A DIMENSION
OF PERSONALITY

Variation-Seeking

In exploring, an attempt is made to satisfy the need for variation by exposing oneself to available stimuli which have some variation. But this need is also manifested in behavior aimed at obtaining more variation than that which already characterizes the environment. Such behavior, which will be called variation-seeking, appears to have significance for the understanding of adult personality.

The type of play that is not so dependent upon the triggering action of stimuli actually possessing variation has some of the properties of variation-seeking, and is perhaps best classified as an early form of this behavior. Then does the decrease in frequency and duration of play which occurs as childhood wanes indicate a decrement in the need for variation? Not at all. It is likely that the stimulus variation achieved by the child in play is gained through other functionally equivalent, and perhaps even more efficient activities in adulthood. The adult reads and writes extensively, vacations, talks about virtually anything to anyone who will talk back, day dreams, plans diversified activities, and even varies his sexual behavior.

As information accumulates about the potential effectiveness of a wide range of activities in the production of variation, the play of the child may well give way to the more complex and sophisticated variation-seeking of the adult. An adult attempting to increase variation enters into activities the effectiveness of which has usually been established by prior experience. While such sophisticated behavior is not entirely absent in subhuman species, it would seem to occur with greater frequency and in more different forms in the adult human.

Individual Differences in the Need for Variation

That the need for variation can be considered an aspect of personality is suggested by observation that individuals show reliable differences in the intensity and quality of their variation-seeking. Some people are simply more interested in, and disposed toward, the occurrence of change, novelty, and the unexpected than are others. That there may also be differences in habitual mode of expression of this need is suggested by an example involving the active-passive dimension. One person may read a wide variety of material, attempting to satisfy the need for variation somewhat passively by entering into an activity which has been associated in the past with the occurrence of variation. However, another person may attempt to satisfy the same need more actively by creative writing, which, if successful, produces novelty by virtue of his own thought processes. This motive is not the sole factor necessary for creative writing, but it has been long recognized that poetry, for example, is to an important degree a means of expressing thoughts and feelings in new and surprising ways (see Chapter 14).

At the moment, there is little evidence upon which to base an explanation of the existence of individual differences in the intensity and mode of expression of the need for variation. Previous discussion suggests that the intensity of the need will be a direct function of the height of the normal curve of wakefulness during the major central part of the period. The height of the curve may be determined by neuroanatomical or hereditary considerations. However, in the absence of any information to the contrary, it is equally possible that factors in early experience can be important. Thus, the adult exposed to a relatively great degree of variation in childhood may have a higher normal activation level than the person who has been more restricted in this regard. The first adult will require more variation than the second in order to maintain normal activation in the absence of strong, specific motivation. Along the lines of this speculation, there is certainly evidence that the more variable of two early environments produces an adult organism that is perceptually and behaviorally more alert, flexible, and able to cope with change (see Chapter 4). Maltzman's discussion (1960) of methods for training originality suggests that the intensity of the need for variation can be influenced by parental training practices. Perhaps parents who elicit and reward unusual responses and introduce the child to a wide range of experience are fostering a high degree of this motive.

Measurement of the Need for Variation

At this time, the major stumbling block to investigation of the need for variation as a dimension of personality is lack of a method of assessing its intensity. However, there is a general procedure for developing measures of motivation, utilized a number of times in the past (Atkinson, 1958; McClelland, Atkinson, Clark, and Lowell, 1953; Shipley and Veroff, 1952; Veroff, 1957), which is applicable in this context. The procedure involves the assumption that stable motivational aspects of personality manifest themselves in fantasy as goal-oriented thought sequences.

Maddi, Charlens, and Maddi (1961) have recently employed this procedure in an experiment designed to permit preliminary development of a set of scoring rules with which TAT stories (that is, fantasy productions) can be analyzed for the need for variation. Before composing TAT stories, the experimental group experienced a monotonous condition in which attention was required. This condition was calculated to increase the intensity of the motive under consideration (see Chapter 5; Karsten, 1928). A control group composed stories to the same TAT pictures without having experienced the monotonous antecedent situation. Instead, they were given a free activity period (controlling for such things as gross motility level), the assumption being that not many members of the group would choose a monotonous activity. An adjective checklist filled out after the experiment by all subjects indicated clearly that, by comparison with the control group, the experimental group experienced monotony and boredom prior to the story composition period.

The general aim of our analysis of TAT stories has been that of differentiating the two groups. However, we have considered it most fruitful to approach this task with some a priori ideas of the manner in which the need for variation can be expressed in fantasy productions of this type. We adopted a definition of the need for variation as *the disposition toward changing, new, or unexpected experiences.* The specific types of imagery which we felt could reasonably be expected to be greater in frequency in the experimental than the control group include (1) dissatisfaction with a monotonous or boring status quo, (2) the wish for novelty, excitement, the unexpected, or change (when change is wanted in order to avoid boredom, or for its own sake), and (3) instrumental activity aimed at producing novelty, excitement, change, or the unexpected.

In a preliminary analysis, a motive intensity score based on the frequency of such types of imagery in the stories has been found to differentiate the groups in the expected direction. At present, other

aspects of the stories which yield differences between the groups are
being investigated.

Correlates of the Need for Variation

The results thus far obtained by Maddi *et al.* (1961) indicate the
feasibility of measuring the need for variation (as a dimension of
personality) by scoring TAT stories (composed under objectively
nonmonotonous conditions) in the manner described above. After
more complete development of the measure according to standard
procedures (see Atkinson, 1958), it will be possible to investigate the
correlates of this motive. A program of research of this type would
involve a process of construct validation (Cronbach and Meehl,
1955), the eventual goal of which would be description and understanding of the behavior and personality of representative individuals
with high and low need for variation.

Mention of several dimensions of behavior which may be influenced by the need for variation will serve to suggest the significance
of this motivational aspect of personality. A person high in this need
should show evidence of behavioral variability, interest in situations
typically associated with variation, or both. The passive appreciation
of environmental variability and the more active attempt to produce such variability through behavior are both consistent with the
satisfaction of this need. Hence, the need may be positively related
to such dimensions as flexibility, idiosyncrasy of response, breadth
of interest, preference for complexity (see Chapter 12), and rate
of decline of performance in prolonged repetitive tasks (see Chapter
5). The reasons for these predictions are simple enough. Flexibility
involves giving many different responses in, or to, the same situation,
and hence indicates behavioral variability. Making idiosyncratic responses may show an orientation toward the unusual and the surprising. Breadth of interest is relevant because it indicates the degree
of openness to new experience, and perhaps also the potential for behavioral change. The proposed relationship involving preference for
complexity stems from the assumption that the more complex the
stimulus, the greater is its potential for temporal change in stimulation, and for spatial unexpectedness. Decline in adequacy of performance over time in repetitive tasks is relevant because it may be par-

tially caused by a concomitant increase in behavior or thought aimed at the production of variation.

This discussion would not be complete unless an important qualification was mentioned. In predicting, we have thus far considered the effects of the intensity of the need for variation on certain aspects of behavior, without attention to the preferred, or habitual, mode of expression. Individual differences in mode of expression may well complicate the search for relationships between motive intensity and behavior. For example, a group of people may seek variation in the vocational area but not in the social one. If the social area alone were studied, no relationship would be found between facets of variation-seeking and the need for variation. An example cited previously is also relevant here; an individual with a particular level of this need may be oriented toward producing unusual things, while another person with the same need strength, but who tends to express it more passively, may only be attuned to appreciating unusualness. It should be clear from these examples that it would be useful to develop some method of assessing preferred mode of expression as well as motive strength.

As information accumulates concerning the empirical relationships between the need for variation and aspects of behavior, it will be possible to determine the type of personality structure within which high and low levels of the motive typically exist. If some of the relationships proposed above are reasonable, a high degree of this need may be rather incompatible with great overt anxiety or rigid defensiveness. Such motivation could then be a sign of vigorous mental health. However, when it is extremely intense, this need may be maladaptive in our society, because it would tend to produce behavioral instability.

Chapter 10

Motivation Reconsidered: The Concept of Competence *

ROBERT W. WHITE
Harvard University

*W*HEN parallel trends can be observed in realms as far apart as animal behavior and psychoanalytic ego psychology, there is reason to suppose that we are witnessing a significant evolution of ideas. In these two realms, as in psychology as a whole, there is evidence of deepening discontent with theories of motivation based upon drives. Despite great differences in the language and concepts used to express this discontent, the theme is everywhere the same: Something important is left out when we make drives the operating forces in animal and human behavior.

The chief theories against which the discontent is directed are those of Hull and of Freud. In their respective realms, drive-reduction theory and psychoanalytic instinct theory, which are basically very much alike, have acquired a considerable air of orthodoxy. Both views have an appealing simplicity, and both have been argued long enough so that their main outlines are generally known. In decided contrast is the position of those who are not satisfied with drives and instincts. They are numerous, and they have developed many pointed criticisms, but what they have to say has not thus far lent itself to a clear and inclusive conceptualization. Apparently there is an enduring difficulty in making these contributions fall into shape.

In this paper I shall attempt a conceptualization which gathers up some of the important things left out by drive theory. To give the concept a name I have chosen the word *competence*, which is intended in a broad biological sense rather than in its narrow everyday

*Reprinted by permission of the author and of the American Psychological Association from *Psychological Review*, 1959, 66, pp. 297-333.*

meaning. As used here, competence will refer to an organism's capacity to interact effectively with its environment. In organisms capable of but little learning, this capacity might be considered an innate attribute, but in the mammals and especially man, with their highly plastic nervous systems, fitness to interact with the environment is slowly attained through prolonged feats of learning. In view of the directedness and persistence of the behavior that leads to these feats of learning, I consider it necessary to treat competence as having a motivational aspect, and my central argument will be that the motivation needed to attain competence cannot be wholly derived from sources of energy currently conceptualized as drives or instincts. We need a different kind of motivational idea to account fully for the fact that man and the higher mammals develop a competence in dealing with the environment which they certainly do not have at birth and certainly do not arrive at simply through maturation. Such an idea, I believe, is essential for any biologically sound view of human nature.

As a first step, I shall briefly examine the relevant trends of thought in several areas of psychology. From this it will become clear that the ideas advanced in this paper have already been stated, in one way or another, by workers in animal behavior, child development, cognitive psychology, psychoanalytic ego psychology, and the psychology of personality. If there is novelty in this essay, it lies in putting together pieces which are not in themselves new. They already lie before us on the table, and perhaps by looking once more we can see how to fit them into a larger conceptual picture.

THE TREND IN ANIMAL PSYCHOLOGY

One of the most obvious features of animal behavior is the tendency to explore the environment. Cats are reputedly killed by curiosity, dogs characteristically make a thorough search of their surroundings, and monkeys and chimpanzees have always impressed observers as being ceaseless investigators. Even Pavlov, whose theory of behavior was one of Spartan simplicity, could not do without an investigatory or orientating reflex. Early workers with the obstruction method, such as Dashiell (1925) and Nissen (1930), reported that rats would cross an electrified grid simply for the privilege of exploring new territory. Some theorists reasoned that activity of this kind was always in the service of hunger, thirst, sex, or some other organic need, but this view was at least shaken by the latent learning experiments, which showed that animals learned about their surroundings even when their major needs had been purposely sated. Shortly before 1950 there was a wave of renewed interest not only in exploratory behavior but also in the possibility that activity and manipulation might have to be assigned the status of independent motives.

Exploratory Behavior

In 1953 Butler (1953a) reported an experiment in which monkeys learned a discrimination problem when the only reward was the opening of a window which permitted them to look out upon the normal comings and goings of the entrance room to the laboratory. The discriminations thus formed proved to be resistant to extinction. In a later study, Butler and Harlow (1957) showed that monkeys could build up a series of four different discriminations solely for the sake of inspecting the entrance room. Butler concluded that "monkeys—and presumably all primates—have a strong motive toward visual exploration of their environment and that learning may be established on the basis of this motive just as it may be established on the basis of any motive that regularly and reliably elicits responses." Montgomery, in 1954, reported a study with rats in which the animals, their major organic needs satiated, learned to avoid the short arm of a Y maze and to take the path which led them into additional maze territory suitable for exploration. Similar findings have been described by Myers and Miller (1954), whose rats learned to press a bar for the sake of poking their heads into a new compartment and sniffing around. Zimbardo and Miller (1958) enlarged upon this study by varying the amount of novelty in the two compartments. In their report "the hypothesis advanced is that opportunity to explore a 'novel' environment or to effect a stimulus change in the environment is the reinforcing agent."

These experiments make a strong case for an independent exploratory motive. The nature of this motive can be more fully discerned in situations in which the animals are allowed a varied repertory of behavior. In 1950 Berlyne published a searching paper on curiosity, a theme which he further developed in subsequent years (1955, 1957a, 1958c). The rats in his experiments were confronted with an unfamiliar space and later with various novel objects placed in it. Approaching, sniffing, and examining were readily elicited by each novelty, were fairly rapidly extinguished, but were restored nearly to original strength when a fresh novelty was added. Exploration on the part of chimpanzees has been studied by Welker (1956b), who put various pairs of objects before the animals and observed the course of their interest. The objects were often first approached in a gingerly manner, with signs of uneasiness, then examined and handled quite fully, then discarded. Introducing a new pair of objects promptly reproduced the whole sequence, just as it did with the rats in Berlyne's experiments. Welker used pairs of objects to find out whether or not the chimpanzees would have common preferences. Bigness and brightness evoked more interest, and greater time was spent upon objects which could be moved, changed, or made to emit sounds and light.

Recent reviews by Butler (1958a) and Cofer (1959) show that a great deal of similar work is going on in animal laboratories, generally with similar results.

Exploration as a Drive

The designers of these experiments have favored the idea that exploration should be listed as an independent primary drive. In all cases the experimental plan calls for the elimination of other primary drives by satiation. It is recognized, however, that a confirmed advocate of orthodoxy might bring up two objections to the proposed enlargement of the list of primary drives. He might claim that exploratory behavior could be explained as a consequence of secondary reinforcement, or he might contend that it is reinforced by reduction of anxiety.

The first argument meets an immediate difficulty in Butler's finding that discriminations learned on the basis of visual exploration are resistant to extinction. When reinforcement of primary drive never takes place in the experimental situation, it is to be expected that secondary reinforcement will not prevent extinction (Miller, 1951). But even in those cases where extinction is rapid, as it was with Berlyne's rats and Welker's chimpanzees, serious problems are raised by the quick recovery of exploratory behavior when a novel stimulus is introduced (Berlyne, 1950). In order to sustain the idea that secondary reinforcement accounts for this fact, we should have to suppose that primary rewards have often been connected with the exploration of novelties. It would have to be assumed, for instance, that the securing of food by young animals occurred with considerable frequency in connection with the investigation of novel objects. This image may seem to fit mature animals who search the environment for their food, but it certainly cannot apply to young mammals before they are weaned. Here the learning process can do virtually nothing to reinforce an interest in novelties. Gratification comes from following the same old cues to the same old consummatory responses, and the animal whose attention strays to some novel variation of the breast will only find himself frustrated. One can say that the whole mammalian pattern of infancy works in the opposite direction. The mother is more active than the young in providing gratifications, and the babies must be pursued and retrieved if they stray from the scene of her ministry. However one looks at it, the hypothesis of secondary reinforcement seems to me to demand improbable assumptions about the relationship in the lives of young animals between exploration and primary need gratification.

The hypothesis that exploratory behavior is related to fear and receives its reinforcement from the reduction of anxiety is at first glance considerably more plausible. It seems justified by the observation that Welker's chimpanzees showed uneasiness on first contact with novel objects, and it fits the behavior of rats in a new maze, as reported by Whiting and Mowrer (1943), where initial terror gave place to an exploration so feverish that the food reward was not eaten. Montgomery and Monkman (1955) have undertaken to challenge this hypothesis by a direct experimental attack. They showed that fear induced in rats before entering a novel situation did not increase exploratory behavior, and that fear induced within the novel situation decreased exploration to an extent correlated with the intensity of the fear. They find it more reasonable to suppose that fear and exploration are conflicting forms of behavior, and this view can also be defended on purely logical grounds. Fear shows itself in either freezing or avoidance, whereas exploration is clearly an instance of approach. There is hardly a more perfect example of conflict between incompatible responses than that of an animal hesitating between investigation and flight. It is clear that exploration can sometimes serve to reduce anxiety, but the proposition that it comes into existence only for this purpose cannot be so easily accepted.

What assumptions have to be made to support the thesis that exploration is motivated by anxiety reduction? It has to be assumed that certain characteristic stimuli arouse anxiety and that exploration of these stimuli is then found to reduce the anxiety. If the characteristics in question are those of novelty and unfamiliarity, we must heed Berlyne's reminder that for the infant all experience is novel and unfamiliar. Berlyne (1950) proposes that the exploratory reaction "may be one that *all* stimuli originally evoke, but which disappears (becomes habituated) as the organism becomes familiar with them." But if all stimuli at first arouse anxious tension, we would have to deduce that all response would consist of avoidance in the interest of reducing that tension. Approaching a stimulus and taking steps to increase its impact could not occur. An exploratory tendency must be there in the first place before it can achieve the function of reducing anxiety. As Woodworth (1958) expresses it, "if there were no exploratory drive to balance and overbalance the fear drive, an animal would be helpless in a novel situation." I find it hard to believe that creatures so liberally endowed with fear could ever achieve a working mastery of the environment if they were impelled toward it only by the pressure of organic needs.

Both hypotheses thus far examined—secondary reinforcement and anxiety reduction—require us to make improbable assumptions. There remains the possibility that exploration should simply be added to the list of primary drives and otherwise treated in orthodox fashion. Myers and Miller (1954) suggest that this is the appropriate course, provided the new drive shows the same functional properties as those already known. "If an exploratory tendency can produce learning like other drives such as hunger, and also show a similar pattern of satiation and recovery, these functional parallels to already known drives would help to justify its classification in the same category." Logically the problem can be dealt with in this way, but we must consider very carefully what happens to the category of drive if we admit this new applicant to membership.

Using hunger as the chief model, the orthodox conception of drive involves the following characteristics: (*a*) there is a tissue need or deficit external to the nervous system which acts upon that system as a strong persisting stimulus; (*b*) this promotes activity which is terminated by a consummatory response with consequent reduction of need; (*c*) the reduction of need brings about the learning which gradually shapes behavior into an economical pursuit of suitable goal objects. In this scheme the tension of an aroused drive is interpreted as unpleasant, at least in the sense that the animal acts in such a way as to lower the drive and becomes quiescent when it is lowered. There are probably no living champions of so simple an orthodoxy, yet the scheme remains pervasive, and it is therefore worth while to observe that the proposed exploratory drive hardly fits it at all.

In the first place, the exploratory drive appears to bear no relation whatever to a tissue need or deficit external to the nervous system. It is, of course, clearly related to certain characteristics of stimulation from the external environment, a source of motivation which Harlow (1953) would like to see restored to a serious place in contemporary psychology; but it certainly cannot be correlated with a visceral need comparable to hunger, thirst, or sex. Considering the pattern of satiation and recovery shown by Welker's chimpanzees, Woodworth (1958) remarks that "what becomes satiated is not the exploratory tendency in general, but the exploring of a particular place or object." It is possible, as Hebb (1955) has pointed out, that the so-called "reticular activation system" in the brain stem creates a kind of general drive state, and this mechanism might indeed be flexibly responsive to changes in sensory stimulation. This interesting suggestion, however, is still a far cry from viscerogenic drives; it commits us instead to the novel idea of a neurogenic motive, one in which the state of the nervous system and the patterns of external stimulation conspire to produce motivated behavior. There is even a good deal of trouble in supposing that the adequate stimuli for exploration are either strong or persistent. Novelty certainly cannot be equated with strength or persistence, and animals seem readily able to disregard the stimuli to exploration when they are weary.

In the second place, exploratory behavior cannot be regarded as leading to any kind of consummatory response. It is usual for the animal's investigation to subside gradually. If the animal at some point turns away and leaves the once novel object we may say that its curiosity is "satisfied," but we do not mean by this that the equivalent of a consummatory response has just taken place. The sequence suggests rather that curiosity wears out and slowly falls to a level where it no longer guides behavior, at least until a fresh novelty comes into view.

Finally, in the case of exploratory behavior there is real difficulty in identifying reinforcement with need reduction. Montgomery (1954), describing the learning of the Y maze, points out that the short arm, essentially a dead end, would tend to reduce the exploratory drive, whereas the long arm, itself a complex maze, would increase it—but the long arm is chosen. If the long arm functions as a reinforcing agent, "the mechanism underlying this reinforcement is an *increase*, rather than a decrease, in the strength of the exploratory drive." In this experiment, as in their natural habitat, animals do not wait to have novelty thrust upon them, nor do they avoid situations in which novelty may be found. Such behavior can be most readily conceptualized by admitting that under certain circumstances reinforcement can be correlated with an increase in arousal or excitement rather than a decrease. A drive which has no consummatory climax seems almost to require this formulation. It is distinctly implausible to connect reinforcement with the waning of an agreeable interest in the environment or with a general progress from zestful alertness to boredom.

If we admit exploration to the category of drive we are thus committing ourselves to believe that drives need have no extraneural sources in tissue deficits or visceral tensions, that they are not necessarily activated by strong or persistent stimuli, that they do not require consummatory responses, and that drive increase can sometimes be a mechanism of reinforcement.

Activity and Manipulation

Exploration is not the only motive proposed by critics of drive orthodoxy, and novelty is not the only characteristic of the environment which appears to incite motivated behavior. Some workers have suggested a need for activity, which can be strengthened by depriving animals of their normal opportunities for movement. Kagan and

Berkun (1954) used running in an activity wheel as the reward for learning and found it "an adequate reinforcement for the instrumental response of bar pressing." Hill (1956) showed that rats will run in an activity wheel to an extent that is correlated with their previous degree of confinement. It is certain that the activity wheel offers no novelty to the animals in these experiments. Nevertheless, they seem to want to run, and they continue to run for such long times that no part of the behavior can readily be singled out as a consummatory response. Perhaps an unpleasant internal state created by inactivity is gradually worked off, but this is certainly accomplished by a tremendous increase of kinesthetic stimulation and muscular output which would seem to imply increased excitation in the system as a whole.

Harlow and his associates (Harlow, 1953; Harlow, Harlow, and Meyer, 1950) maintain that there is also a manipulative drive. It is aroused by certain patterns of external stimulation and reduced by actively changing the external pattern. The experiments were done with rhesus monkeys, and they involve the solving of a mechanical problem which, however, leads to no further consequences or rewards. The task might be, for instance, to raise a hasp which is kept in place by both a hook and a pin; all that can be accomplished is to raise the hasp, which opens nothing and leads to no fresh discoveries. When the hasp problem is simply installed in the living cages, the monkeys return to it and solve it as many as 7 or 8 times over several days. It seems unlikely that novelty can be postulated as the essential characteristic of the stimulus which evokes this repeated behavior. The simplest interpretation is rather that value lies for the animal in the opportunity, as Zimbardo and Miller (1958) express it, "to effect a stimulus change in the environment." This formulation suggests something like the propensities toward mastery or power that have often been mentioned in discussions of human motivation.

The addition of activity and manipulation to the list of primary drives can only make more serious the difficulties for the orthodox model that resulted from admitting exploration. But recent research with animals has put the orthodox model on the defensive even on its home grounds. It has become increasingly clear that hunger, thirst, and sex cannot be made to fit the simple pattern that seemed so helpful 40 years ago.

Changing Conceptions of Drive

In a brief historical statement, Morgan (1957) has pointed out that the conception of drive as a noxious stimulus began to lose its popularity among research workers shortly after 1940. "On the whole," he says, "the stimulus concept of drive owed more to wishful thinking than to experimental fact." When technical advances in biochemistry and brain physiology made it possible to bring in an array of new facts, there was a rapid shift toward the view that "drives arise largely through the internal environment acting on the central nervous system." One of the most influential discoveries was that animals have as many as a dozen specific hungers for particular kinds of food, instead of the single hunger demanded by Cannon's model of the hunger drive. If an animal's diet becomes deficient in some important element such as salt, sugar, or the vitamin-B complex, foods containing the missing element will be eagerly sought while other foods are passed by, a selectivity that obviously cannot be laid to contractions of the stomach. Similarly, a negative food preference can be produced by loading either the stomach or the blood stream with some single element of the normal diet. The early work of Beach (1942a) on sexual behavior brought out similar complications in what had for a time been taken as a relatively simple drive. Hormone levels appeared to be considerably more important than peripheral stimulation in the arousal and maintenance of the sex drive. Further work led Beach (1951) to conclude that sexual behavior is "governed by a complex combination of processes." He points out that the patterns of control differ tremendously from one species to another and that within a single species the mechanisms may be quite different for males and females. Like hunger, the sex drive turns out to be no simple thing.

New methods of destroying and of stimulating brain centers in animals have had an equally disastrous effect on the orthodox drive model. The nervous system, and especially the hypothalamus, appears to be deeply implicated in the motivational process. Experimental findings on hypothalamic lesions in animals encourage Stellar (1954) to believe that there are different centers "responsible for the control of different kinds of basic motivation," and that in each case "there is one main excitatory center and one inhibitory center which operates to depress the activity of the excitatory center." As research findings accumulate, this picture may seem to be too cleanly drawn. Concerning sexual behavior, for example, Rosvold (1959) concludes a recent review by rejecting the idea of a single center in the cerebrum; rather, the sex drive "probably has a wide neural representation with a complex interaction between old and new brain structures and between neural and humoral agents." Nevertheless, Miller's (1958) careful work seems to leave little doubt that motivated behavior in every way similar to normal hunger and normal pain-fear can be elicited by electrical stimulation of quite restricted areas of the hypothalamus. It is clear that we cannot regress to a model of drives that represents the energy as coming from outside the nervous system. Whatever the effects of peripheral stimulation may be, drives also involve neural centers and neural patterns as well as internal biochemical conditions.

What sort of model becomes necessary to entertain these newly discovered facts? In 1938 Lashley expressed the view that motivation should not be equated with disturbance of organic equilibrium but rather with "a partial excitation of a very specific sensorimotor mechanism irradiating to affect other systems of reaction." Beach (1942a) postulated that there must be in the nervous system "a condition analogous to Sherrington's central excitatory state." Morgan, in 1943, undertook to capture the facts in a systematic theory which seems to have been well sustained by subsequent research (Morgan, 1957). He distinguished two types of process which he called *humoral motive factors* and *central motive states*. The humoral factors consist of chemical or hormonal constituents of the blood and lymph, and they are conceived to influence behavior chiefly by a direct sensitizing action on neural centers. The central motive states have several properties: They are partly self-maintaining through neural circuits, they tend to increase the organism's general activity, they evoke specific forms of behavior not strongly controlled by the environment, and they prime or prepare consummatory responses which will occur when adequate stimulation is found. This is a far cry from the orthodox model, but we must nowadays admit that the orthodox model is a far cry from the facts.

In view of this radical evolution of the concept of drive, it is not surprising to find the drive reduction hypothesis in serious difficulties.

The earlier identification of reinforcement with drive reduction has been directly attacked in a series of experiments that were designed to show that learning takes place when drive reduction is ruled out.

In 1950 Sheffield and Roby showed that instrumental learning would take place in hungry rats when the reward consisted not of a nutritive substance but of sweet-tasting saccharine in the drinking water. This finding appeared to be "at variance with the molar principle of reinforcement used by Hull, which identifies primary reinforcement with 'need reduction.' " The authors naturally do not question the vital importance of need reduction, but they point out that need-reducing events may accomplish reinforcement through a mechanism more direct and speedy than the reduction of the need itself. They think that "stimulation and performance of a consummatory response appears to be more important to instrumental learning—in a primary, not acquired, way—than the drive satisfaction which the response normally achieves." Their findings are in line with an earlier experiment with chickens by Wolfe and Kaplon (1941), who used different sizes of food pellets so that the number of pecks and the amount of food received could be thrown out of their usual close connection. The chickens, we might say, would rather peck than eat; learning was more strongly reinforced when four pecks were necessary than when one peck was enough to take the same amount of food.

The substitution of the consummatory response for need reduction as the immediate reinforcing mechanism is a step in advance, but it soon turns out that another step is required. Can it be shown that an aroused need which does not reach consummation has a reinforcing effect? To test this possibility Sheffield, Wulff, and Backer (1951) provided male rats with the reward of copulating with a female, but not enough times to produce ejaculation. This reward was favorable to instrumental learning even though there was no need reduction and no performance of the final consummatory act. The results were supported by Kagan (1955), whose animals showed substantial learning under the same conditions, though learning was still faster when ejaculation was permitted. Sheffield, Roby, and Campbell (1954) have proposed a *drive-induction* theory according to which the property of reinforcement is assigned to the excitement of an aroused drive. We have already seen that some such assumption is essential if exploration is to be assigned the status of a drive. Here it can be added that the whole theory of pregenital sexuality involves motivation without consummatory acts and without any but the most gradual need reduction. And as a final blow to the orthodox hypothesis comes the finding by Olds and Milner (1954) that positive reinforcement can be brought about by direct electrical stimulation of certain areas of the brain. Once again we learn that neural centers are deeply implicated in the plot of motivation. The simple mechanics of need reduction cannot possibly serve as the basis for a theory of learning.

Twenty years of research have thus pretty much destroyed the orthodox drive model. It is no longer appropriate to consider that drives originate solely in tissue deficits external to the nervous system, that consummatory acts are a universal feature and goal of motivated behavior, or that the alleviation of tissue deficits is the necessary condition for instrumental learning. Instead we have a complex picture in which humoral factors and neural centers occupy a prominent position; in which, moreover, the concept of neurogenic motives without consummatory ends appears to be entirely legitimate. Do these changes remove the obstacles to placing exploration, activity, and manipulation in the category of drives?

Perhaps this is no more than a question of words, but I should prefer at this point to call it a problem in conceptual strategy. I shall propose that these three new "drives" have much in common and that it is useful to bring them under the single heading of competence. Even with the loosening and broadening of the concept of drive, they are still in important respects different from hunger, thirst, and sex. In hunger and thirst, tissue deficits, humoral factors, and consummatory responses retain an important position. The mature sex drive depends heavily on hormonal levels and is sharply oriented toward consummation. Tendencies like exploration do not share these characteristics, whatever else they have in common with the better known drives. It is in order to emphasize their intrinsic peculiarities, to get them considered in their own right without a cloud of surplus meanings, that I prefer in this essay to speak of the urge that makes for competence simply as motivation rather than as drive.

THE TREND IN PSYCHOANALYTIC EGO PSYCHOLOGY

Rather an abrupt change of climate may be experienced as we turn from the animal laboratory to the psychoanalytic treatment room, but the trends of thought in the two realms turn out to be remarkably alike. Here the orthodox view of motivation is to be found in Freud's theory of the instincts—they might be known to us as drives if an early translator had been more literal with the German *Trieb*.

Freud's Theories of Instinct and Ego

In his final work, Freud (1949) described instincts as "somatic demands upon mental life" and as "the ultimate cause of all activity." He wrote further:

> It is possible to distinguish an indeterminate number of instincts and in common practice this is in fact done. For us, however, the important question arises whether we may not be able to derive all of these instincts from a few fundamental ones. . . . After long doubts and vacillations we have decided to assume the existence of only two basic instincts, *Eros* and the *destructive instinct* (Freud, 1949, p. 20).

The history of Freud's long doubts and vacillations has been lucidly related by Bibring (1941). Up to 1914 Freud used a two-fold classification of sexual instincts and ego instincts. The ego instincts made their appearance in his case histories in a somewhat moral character, being held responsible for the disastrous repression of sexual needs, but in systematic usage they were conceived as serving the goal of self-preservation, and hunger was generally taken as an appropriate model. In 1914, when he evolved the concept of narcissism and saw that it threatened to blur the line between sexual and ego tendencies, Freud (1925b) still expressed himself as unwilling to abandon an idea which followed the popular distinction of love and hunger and which reflected man's dual existence "as reproducer and as one who serves his own ends." Various facts, particularly those of sadism and masochism, served to overcome his reluctance, so that he finally united self-preservation and preservation of the species under the heading of Eros or life instincts, establishing destructiveness or the death instinct as the great antagonist in a profound biological sense (Freud, 1948). This highly speculative step proved to be too much for some of his otherwise loyal followers, and the earlier orthodoxy did not become entirely extinct.

It is easier to follow Freud's reasoning when we bear in mind the simultaneous development of his ideas about the mental apparatus. Bibring (1941) points out that even in his early thinking a sharp contrast was always drawn between instinct and mental apparatus. Instinct supplied the energy in the form of powerful, persisting internal stimuli; the apparatus guided it into channels which produced organized behavior and eventually put a stop to the persisting stimulation. In 1915 Freud wrote:

> The nervous system is an apparatus having the function of abolishing stimuli which reach it or of reducing excitation to the lowest possible level; an apparatus which would even, if this were feasible, maintain itself in an altogether unstimulated condition. . . . The task of the nervous system is—broadly speaking—*to master stimuli* (Freud, 1925c, p. 63).

During the next decade there was a considerable growth in his ideas about the mental apparatus, culminating in the well known division into id, ego, and superego. The activities of the ego now received much fuller recognition. Freud (1927) assigned to it "the task of self-preservation," which it accomplished through its several capacities of perception, memory, flight, defense, and adaptive action. One can see Freud's thought moving from a mechanical analogy—an engine and its fuel—toward a much more adaptational conception of the mental apparatus. Ego instincts did not wholly disappear, but the decline in their systematic importance was compensated by the insight that self-preservative tendencies were to some extent built into the whole living system. It is significant that as he took this course he came to question the earlier tension-reduction theory. In the last year of his life he declared it to be probable "that what is felt as pleasure or unpleasure is not the *absolute* degree of the tensions but something in the rhythm of their changes" (Freud, 1949).

Freud's tendency to revise his thinking makes it difficult to pin down an orthodox doctrine, but most workers will probably agree that his main emphasis was upon somatically based drives, a mental apparatus which received its power from the drives, and, of course, the multitude of ways in which the apparatus controlled, disguised, and transformed these energies. His treatment of the ego was far from complete, and it was not long before voices were raised against the conception that so vital and versatile a part of the personality could be developed solely by libidinal and aggressive energies.

An Instinct to Master

In 1942 Hendrick proposed that this difficulty be met by assuming the existence of an additional major instinct. "The development of ability to master a segment of the environment," he wrote, and the need to exercise such functions, can be conceptualized as an "instinct to master," further characterized as "an inborn drive to do and to learn how to do." The aim of this instinct is "pleasure in exercising a function successfully, regardless of its sensual value." The simpler manifestations are learning to suck, to manipulate, to walk, to speak, to comprehend and to reason; these functions and others eventually become integrated as the ego. "The central nervous system is more than a utility," Hendrick declared. The infant shows an immediate desire to use and perfect each function as it ripens, and the adult secures gratification from an executive function efficiently performed regardless of its service to other instincts.

Hendrick's procedure in this and two supporting papers (1943a, 1943b) is quite similar to that of the animal psychologists who propose listing exploration as an additional primary drive. The instinct to master has an aim—to exercise and develop the ego functions— and it follows hedonic principles by yielding "primary pleasure" when efficient action "enables the individual to control and alter his environment." It is to this extent analogous to the instincts assumed by Freud. But just as an exploratory drive seemed radically to alter the whole conception of drive, so the instinct to master implied a drastic change in the psychoanalytic idea of instinct. Critics were quick to point out that Freud had always conceived of instincts as having somatic sources external to the ego apparatus, a condition not met by the proposed instinct to master. There was nothing comparable to erogenous zones, to orgasm, or to the sequence of painful tension followed by pleasurable release. Mastery, the critics agreed, could not be an instinct, whatever else it might be.

It is of interest that Fenichel (1945), who definitely rejected Hendrick's proposal, gives us another close parallel to the animal work by attributing mastering behavior to anxiety-reduction. He argued that mastery is "a general aim of every organism but not of a specific instinct." He agreed that there is "a pleasure of enjoying one's abilities," but he related this pleasure to cessation of the anxiety connected with not being able to do things. "Functional pleasure," he wrote, "is pleasure in the fact that the exercise of a function is now possible without anxiety," and he contended that when anxiety is no longer present, when there is full confidence that a given situation can be met, then action is no longer accompanied by functional pleasure. We must certainly agree with Fenichel that anxiety *can* play the part he assigns it, but the proposal that all pleasure in ego functions comes from this source raises the same difficulties we have already considered in connection with exploratory behavior. That we exercise our capacities and explore our surroundings only to reduce our fear of the environment is not, as I have already argued, an assumption that enjoys high probability on biological grounds.

Hartmann on the Ego

A less radical change in the orthodox model is proposed by Hartmann, who, in a series of papers since 1939, often in conjunction with Kris and Loewenstein, has been refining and expanding Freud's views on the ego and the instincts. While the ego is conceived as a "substructure" of the personality, this term is somewhat metaphorical because in practice the ego has to be defined by its functions. The list of functions, which includes grasping, crawling, walking, perceiving, remembering, language, thinking, and intention, covers much the same ground that was indicated by Hendrick, but Hartmann does not attribute their growth to an instinct. On the other hand, Hartmann (1950) early came to the conclusion that development could not be explained, as Freud had seemed to conceive it, simply as a consequence of conflict between instinctual needs and frustrating realities. The instincts alone would never guarantee survival; they require mediation by the innate ego apparatus if they are to meet "the average expectable environmental conditions." He therefore proposed that we conceive of an autonomous factor in ego development, an independent maturation of functions taking place in a "conflict-free ego sphere." Functions such as locomotion ripen through maturation and through learning even when they are not caught up in struggles to obtain erotic and aggressive gratification or to avoid anxiety. As Anna Freud (1952) has pointed out, walking becomes independent of instinctual upheavals a few weeks after its beginning; thereafter, it serves the child impartially in situations of conflict and those that are free from conflict.

Hartmann's idea of autonomous ego development has of course been assumed all along by workers in child psychology, but it is an important step to relate it to Freud's disclosures concerning unconscious motivation. In what now looks like an excess of enthusiasm for his own concepts, Freud (1925a) undertook to explain the outgrowing of the pleasure principle and the substituting of the reality principle as a simple and direct consequence of the frustration of instinctual needs. However, the reality principle contained the idea of postponing an immediate gratification in favor of a future one, and Hartmann (1956) properly notes that the capacities for postponement and anticipation cannot be conjured into existence simply by the collision of frustrating reality and ungratified need. Important as frustrations may be, these capacities must already be available, "some preparedness for dealing with reality" must already exist, before the frustration can produce its momentous educative effect. It can be seen from this example that Hartmann's analysis opens the way for profitable commerce between developmental psychologies inside and outside of psychoanalysis.

Hartmann's emphasis on adaptation permits him to perceive much more that is autonomous about the ego than was ever seriously included in Freud's systematic thought. He allows, for instance, that aims and interests which develop in the beginning as defenses against instincts may later become part of conflict-free spheres of activity— become interests in their own right—and thus achieve "secondary autonomy," a concept very close to Allport's (1937) functional autonomy of motives (Hartmann, 1950). He deals with the possibility that adaptive skills developing in the conflict-free sphere may have a decisive influence on the handling of conflicts. These skills have a history of their own, shaped jointly by the child's abilities and by the responses evoked from parents. As Munroe (1955) has expressed it, they have "a very important role in the development of the conscious and semiconscious psychological self." They may thus have a direct influence upon the outcome when a child becomes involved in conflict. Rapaport (1958) sees Hartmann's ideas on the autonomy of the ego as vital to the proper understanding not only of healthy development but also of psychopathology itself.

In explaining the autonomous growth of the ego, Hartmann makes generous use of the concept of maturation, but he naturally does not exclude learning. Hartmann (1950) entertains the possibility, mentioned casually from time to time by Freud (1916, 1949), that ego functions are supplied with their own sources of energy independent of instincts, and that there is pleasure connected with their mere exercise. However, he makes little systematic use of this idea, relying instead upon a concept more central in Freud's thinking, that of the neutralization of drive energies. Freud (1927) found that he could "make no headway" in accounting for the varied activities of the ego without assuming "a displaceable energy, which is in itself neutral, but is able to join forces either with an erotic or with a destructive impulse, differing qualitatively as they do, and augment its total cathexis." He speculated that the neutral energy came from Eros and could be conceived as desexualized libido. Hartmann, Kris, and Loewenstein (1949) carried the idea forward a logical step by proposing that the energies of aggressive instincts could similarly be neutralized and placed at the disposal of the ego. Neutralized energy contributes to the development of the ego and makes possible a continuing interest in the objects of the environment regardless of their immediate relation to erotic or aggressive needs. Hartmann (1955) finds this concept particularly helpful in unscrambling the confusions that have arisen over the concept of sublimation.

The doctrine of neutralized instinctual energies is a curious one, and we should bear in mind the complex clinical findings that perhaps suggested it. Freud was an unquestioned genius in detecting the subtle operation of erotic urges and aggressive fantasies, along with elaborate mechanisms of defense, behind the seemingly objective or "neutral" activities of everyday life. Remarkable transformations of interest could sometimes be observed in the course of development. For example, a patient's childhood erotic rivalry and aggressive competition with his father might later disappear beneath a strong objective interest in running the family business; then suddenly, on the brink of success, this interest might come to a total halt, paralyzed by anxiety because the underlying instinctual goals came too close to symbolic fulfilment. The reappearance of instinctual preoccupations in such a case lends a certain color to the idea that they have somehow been driving the behavior all the time, even though the daily pursuit of business goals seems utterly remote from instinctual gratifications.

It is worth noticing that Freud's procedure in making the assumption of neutralized instinctual energy is similar to the one followed by orthodox behaviorists in connection with primary drives. These theorists started from the assumption that all behavior was powered by a limited number of organic drives, and then, in order to protect this assumption, they developed further hypotheses, such as secondary reinforcement, to account for motivated behavior that bore no obvious relation to primary goals. At the point where he could "make no headway" without postulating neutralization, Freud could conceivably have made a good deal of headway if he had been willing to assume that neutral energy, neither sexual nor aggressive, was available as a natural endowment in the first place. But he preferred to protect his assumption of two primary drives and to interpret other energies as transformations of these drives. Even so, the concept seems superfluous if we take Freud at his word about the nature of the life instincts. Freud (1949) made it clear that Eros included more than instincts having a sexual aim; its larger goal was "to establish even greater unities and to preserve them thus—in short, to bind together." Under this formula, it would seem possible to include energies inherently directed toward building up the integrated functions of the ego. But Freud did not exploit the full range of his theory of Eros and proposed only that neutral energies should be conceived as desexualized.

The concept of neutralization has in some respects had a good effect on psychoanalytic ego psychology. In Hartmann's writings, as we have seen, and in Rapaport's (1951, 1954) work on thinking, it has encouraged a strong interest in autonomous ego functions and a fresh analysis of their place in personality. Nevertheless, it seems to me an awkward conceptualization, one which in the end is likely to lead, as Colby (1955) has expressed it, to a "metapsychological snarl." The theory requires that instinctual energies can completely change their aims, which makes one wonder what purpose was served in the first place by defining them as having aims. It preserves an image of mobility of energies that seems much out of line with recent research on animal motivation, where energy is being conceived in a constantly closer relation to specific structures. To my mind it thus compares unfavorably with its quite straightforward alternative, which is that the alleged neutralized energies are there in the first place as part of the natural make-up of an adaptive organism. I shall later develop this possiblity by means of the concept of competence in its motivational aspect, and I believe that this concept gains support from certain other lines of work in the psychoanalytic tradition.

Motility and a Sense of Industry

The trend away from instinct orthodoxy is illustrated by the work of Kardiner (1947) on what he calls "the development of the effective ego." Kardiner's reflections arose from his work on the traumatic neuroses of war. In these disorders the main threat is to self-preservation, and some of the most important symptoms, such as defensive rituals and paralyses, are lodged in the action systems that normally bring about successful adaptive behavior. It thus becomes pertinent to study the growth of action systems, to discover how they become integrated so as to maintain "controlled contact" with the environment and "controlled exploitation of objects in the outer world," and to work out the conditions which either favor or disrupt this acquired integration. Thinking along these lines, Kardiner is led to conclusions just about the opposite of Freud's: It is the successful and gratifying experiences, not the frustrations, that lead to increasingly integrated action and to the discrimination of self from outer world. Frustration produces chiefly disruptions and inhibitions which are unfavorable to the early growth of the ego. Children are gratified when they discover the connection between a movement executed and the accompanying and subsequent sensations. They are still more gratified when they carry out actions successfully; this "gives rise to the triumphant feeling of making an organ obedient to the will of the ego." Such experiences build up "a definite self- or body-consciousness which becomes the center and the point of reference of all purposeful and co-ordinated activity." Growth of the ego, in short, depends heavily upon action systems and the consequences of action. The course and vicissitudes of this development have to be studied in their own right, and they cannot be understood as side effects of the stages of libidinal development.

A similar theme is pursued to even more radical conclusions by Mittelmann (1954) in his paper on motility. Mittelmann regards motility, which manifests itself most typically in skilled motor actions such as posture, locomotion, and manipulation, as an "urge in its own right" in the same sense that one speaks of oral, excretory, or genital urges. From about 10 months of age it has a distinctly "driven" character, and there is restlessness and anger if it is blocked. During the second and third years the motor urge "dominates all other urges," so that it is proper to "consider this period the motor level of ego and libido development." The child makes tremendous efforts to learn to walk, and to walk well, and he exhibits joyous laughter as he attains these ends. Restrictions of motility may occur because the parents are anxious or because the child's assertiveness troubles them, and a lasting injury to the parent-child relationship may result. Clumsiness in motor or manipulative accomplishments may lead to self-hatred and dependence, for "the evolution of self-assertiveness and self-esteem is intimately connected with motor development." Motility is of central importance in many of the most characteristic functions of the ego. Partly by its means the infant differentiates himself from other objects, and the child's knowledge of objects depends on an extensive activity of manipulation and examination. "This motility becomes one of the most important aspects of reality testing." Because it is an element in all cognitive behavior, it can also be considered "the dominant integrative function." Mittelmann bases motor development, in short, on an independent urge, and he sees this urge as the really crucial motive behind the development of the ego.

Like Kardiner, Mittelmann does not attempt to formulate in detail the nature of the motility urge. It is likened not to an instinct but to a "partial instinct," and this seems to place it somewhere between Hendrick's instinct to master and Hartmann's dimly sketched independent energies of the ego. This indefiniteness may irk the systematic theorist, but Mittelmann's account of the part played by motility in ego development easily stands as a significant contribution. Even more influential in this respect is the work of Erikson (1953), who has given a highly detailed timetable of ego development. Erikson stays with the libido theory as far as it will go, but he passes beyond its reach in his account of the latency period and some of the later crises of growth. It is clear that something more than the orthodox instincts is involved in the "enormous value" with which the child in the second year "begins to endow his autonomous will." Something more would seem to be implied in the expanding imagination and initiative of the "phallic" child. Certainly more is involved during the school years, when children address themselves to motor, manual, and intellectual achievements and need "a sense of being able to make things and make them well and even perfectly: this is what I call the *sense of industry.*" Erikson's (1952) theory of play is also influenced by the idea that learning to deal with the animate and inanimate worlds is an important preoccupation of childhood: "the playing child advances forward to new stages of real mastery." Action systems, motility, and a sense of industry all direct our attention to behavior which can scarcely be contained in the old bottle of instinct theory.

Glancing back over these trends in psychoanalytic ego psychology, we cannot fail to be impressed by striking similarities to the trend in animal work. Using Reik's familiar metaphor, we might say that those who listen with their two ears and those who listen with the third ear have apparently been hearing much the same sounds. In both realms there is discontent with drive orthodoxy. In both there is persistent pointing to kinds of behavior neglected or explained away by drive orthodoxy: exploration, activity, manipulation, and mastery. Similar theories have been proposed to account for the energies in such behavior: *(a)* they are derived or transformed in some way from the primary drives or instincts (secondary reinforcement, neutralization of drive energies); *(b)* they are powered by the need to reduce anxiety; *(c)* they can be accounted for only by postulating a new primary drive (exploratory drive, instinct to master). When these explanations are considered to have failed, the one remaining course is to work out a different idea of motivation. In his study of action systems, Kardiner prefers to leave the question of energy sources unanswered, but Erikson's sense of industry and Mittelmann's motility urge point to a motivational base which is only remotely analogous to primary drives or fundamental instincts. I believe that the difficulties in this undertaking can be greatly reduced by the concept of competence, to which we shall shortly turn.

RELATED DEVELOPMENTS IN GENERAL PSYCHOLOGY

If a systematic survey were in order, it would be easy to show a parallel drift of opinion in other parts of the psychological realm.

Among theorists of personality, for example, something like drive orthodoxy is to be found in the work of Dollard and Miller (1950), who have translated the main concepts of Freud's psychoanalysis, including processes such as repression and displacement, into the language of reinforcement theory. With them we might put Mowrer (1950), whose searching analysis of fear as an acquired drive has led him to postulate anxiety-reduction as the master motive behind the development of the ego. Discontent with drive orthodoxy has long been expressed by Allport (1937, 1946), who not only argues for a functional autonomy of motives from their infantile roots in primary drives but also seriously questions the law of effect, the very cornerstone of reinforcement theory. Little comfort for the orthodox can be found in Murray's (1938) detailed taxonomy of needs, especially when it comes to needs such as achievement and construction, which can be tied to primary drives only by conceptual acrobatics. Murray and Kluckhohn (1953), moreover, have made a case for pleasure in activity for its own sake, reviving the *Funktionslust* proposed many years ago by Karl Bühler (1924) and recently developed in some detail by French (1952). They also argue for intrinsic mental needs: "the infant's mind is not acting most of the time as the instrument of some urgent animal drive, but is preoccupied with *gratifying itself*." Murphy (1947) takes the view that all tissues can become seats of tension and thus participants in drive; in addition to visceral drives, he postulates two independent forms, activity drives and sensory drives. Then there are workers such as Goldstein (1939) who approach the whole problem with a holistic philosophy which precludes the dictatorship of any isolated or partial drives. Goldstein (1940) assumes one master tendency, that toward self-actualization, of which the so-called visceral drives are but partial and not really isolated expressions, and which can find expression also in an urge toward perfection—toward completing what is incomplete, whether it be an outside task or the mastery of some function such as walking. It has been shown by the Ansbachers (1956) that Adler, never a friend of instinct orthodoxy, in his later years reached an idea very similar to the urge toward perfection. Maslow (1954, 1955), too, belongs with the heterodox. He insists that we should take account of growth motivation as well as the deficiency motivation implied in the visceral drives, and he offers the valuable idea of a hierarchy of motives, according to which the satisfaction of "lower" needs makes it possible for "higher" needs to emerge and become regnant in behavior.

Mention of these names must suffice here to show that the trends observed in animal psychology and psychoanalytic ego psychology are pervasive in contemporary psychological thought. Doubtless the same controversies and problems could be pointed out in child development, in cognitive psychology, and in other fields. But in order to advance to my main theme, I shall select only certain developments which bear directly on the concept of competence.

Needs for Excitement and Novelty

Human experience provides plentiful evidence of the importance of reducing excessive levels of tension. Men under wartime stress, men under pressure of pain and extreme deprivation, men with excessive work loads or too much exposure to confusing social interactions, all act as if their nervous systems craved that utterly unstimulated condition which Freud once sketched as the epitome of neural bliss. But if these same men be granted their nirvana they soon become miserable and begin to look around for a little excitement. Human experience testifies that boredom is a bad state of affairs about which something must be done. Hebb (1949) has been particularly insistent in reminding us that many of our activities, such as reading detective stories, skin-diving, or driving cars at high speeds, give clear evidence of a need to raise the level of stimulation and excitement. Men and animals alike seem at times bent on increasing the impact of the environment and even on creating mild degrees of frustration and fear. Hebb and Thompson (1954) reflect upon this as follows:

Such phenomena are, of course, well known in man: in the liking for dangerous sports or roller coasters, where fear is deliberately courted, and in the addiction to bridge or golf or solitaire, vices whose very existence depends upon the level of difficulty of the problems presented and an optimal level of frustration. Once more, when we find such attitudes toward fear and frustration in animals, we have a better basis for supposing that we are dealing with something fundamental if a man prefers skis to the less dangerous snowshoes, or when we observe an unashamed love of work (problem solving and frustration included) in the scientist, or in the businessman who cannot retire. Such behavior in man is usually accounted for as a search for prestige, but the animal data make this untenable. It seems much more likely that solving problems and running mild risks are inherently rewarding, or, in more general terms, that the animal will always act so as to produce an optimal level of excitation (Hebb and Thompson, 1954, p. 551).

The concept of optimal stimulation has been developed by Leuba (1955), who sees it as helpful in resolving some of the problems of learning theory. Believing that most theorizing about motivation has been based upon "powerful biological or neurotic drives," Leuba bids us look at the much more common learning situations of nursery, playground, and school, where "actions which increase stimulation and produce excitement are strongly reinforced, sometimes to the dismay of parents and teachers." He proposes that there is an optimal level of stimulation, subject to variation at different times, and that learning is associated with movement toward this optimal level, downward when stimulation is too high and upward when it is too low. A similar idea is expressed by McReynolds (1956) concerning the more restricted concept of "rate of perceptualization." Monotonous conditions provide too low a rate, with boredom; excessive stimulation produces too high a rate, with disruptive excitement; the optimal rate yields the experience of pleasure. These ideas are now amply supported by recent experimental work on sensory deprivation (Lilly, 1956; Hebb, 1958).

In recent papers Young (1949, 1955) has argued for an hedonic theory of motivation, one in which affective processes "constitute a form of primary motivation." According to Young's theory, "an organism behaves so as to maximize positive affective arousal (delight, enjoyment) and to minimize negative arousal (distress)." McClelland (1953) has offered a version of hedonic theory which is of particular value in understanding the significance of novelty. Affective arousal occurs when a stimulus pattern produces a discrepancy from the existing adaptation level. Small discrepancies produce pleasant affect and a tendency to approach; large ones produce unpleasantness and a tendency toward avoidance. The child at play, like the young chimpanzee and the exploring rat, needs frequent novelty in the stimulus field in order to keep up his interest—in order to maintain pleasant discrepancies from whatever adaptation level he has reached. Hebb's (1949) theory of the neurological correlates of learning also deals with novelty, though in a somewhat different way. He equates sustained interest with a state of neural affairs in which "phase sequences" are relatively complex and are growing, in the sense of establishing new internal relations. Such a state follows most readily from a stimulus field characterized by difference-in-sameness; that is, containing much that is familiar along with certain features that are novel. If the field is entirely familiar, phase sequences run off quickly, are short-circuited, and thus fail to produce sustained interest. Hebb's theory, which has the engaging quality of being able to explain why we enjoy reading a detective story once but not right over again, expresses in a neurological hypothesis the familiar fact that well-learned, habituated processes do not in themselves greatly interest us. Interest seems to require elements of unfamiliarity: of something still to be found out and of learning still to be done.

It seems to me that these contributions, though differing as to details, speak with unanimity on their central theme and would force us, if nothing else did, to reconsider seriously the whole problem of motivation. Boredom, the unpleasantness of monotony, the attraction of novelty, the tendency to vary behavior rather than repeating it rigidly, and the seeking of stimulation and mild excitement stand as inescapable facts of human experience and clearly have their parallels in animal behavior. We may seek rest and minimal stimulation at the end of the day, but that is not what we are looking for the next morning. Even when its primary needs are satisfied and its homeostatic chores are done, an organism is alive, active, and up to something.

Dealing with the Environment

If we consider things only from the viewpoint of affect, excitement, and novelty, we are apt to overlook another important aspect of behavior, its effect upon the environment. Moving in this direction, Diamond (1939) invites us to consider the motivational properties of the sensorineural system, the apparatus whereby higher animals "maintain their relations to the environment." He conceives of this system as demanding stimulation and as acting in such a manner as to "force the environment to stimulate it." Even if one thinks only of the infant's exploring eyes and hands, it is clear that the main direction of behavior is by no means always that of reducing the impact of stimulation. When the eyes follow a moving object, or when the hand grasps an object which it has touched, the result is to preserve the stimulus and to increase its effect. In more elaborate explorations the consequence of a series of actions may be to vary the manner in which a stimulus acts upon the sense organs. It is apparent that the exploring, manipulating child produces by his actions precisely what Hebb's theory demands as a basis for continuing interest: he produces differences-in-sameness in the stimulus field.

In a critical analysis of Freud's views on the reality principle, Charlotte Bühler (1954) makes a strong case for positive interests in the environment, citing as evidence the responsiveness and adaptiveness of the newborn baby as well as the exploratory tendencies of later months. The problem is worked out in more detail by Schachtel (1954) in a paper on focal attention. Acts of focal attention are characteristically directed at particular objects, and they consist of several sustained approaches "aimed at active mental grasp" while excluding the rest of the field. These qualities can be observed even in the infant's early attempts to follow a moving object with his eyes, and they show more clearly in his later endeavors to learn how objects are related both to himself and to one another. Such behavior bespeaks "a relatively autonomous capacity for object interest." Schachtel makes the proposal that this interest is pursued precisely at those times when major needs are in abeyance. High pressure of need or anxiety is the enemy of exploratory play and is a condition, as every scientist should know, under which we are unlikely to achieve an objective grasp of the environment. Low need pressure is requisite if we are to perceive objects as they are, in their constant character, apart from hopes and fears we may at other times attach to them. Schachtel doubts that "the wish for need-satisfaction alone would ever lead to object perception and to object-oriented thought." Hence an autonomous capacity to be interested in the environment has great value for the survival of a species.

Being interested in the environment implies having some kind of satisfactory interaction with it. Several workers call attention to the possibility that satisfaction might lie in having an effect upon the environment, in dealing with it, and changing it in various ways. Groos (1901), in his classical analysis of play, attached great importance to the child's "joy in being a cause," as shown in making a clatter, "hustling things about," and playing in puddles where large and dramatic effects can be produced. "We demand a knowledge of effects," he wrote, "and to be ourselves the producers of effects."

Piaget (1952) remarks upon the child's special interest in objects
that are affected by his own movements. This aspect of behavior occupies a central place in the work of Skinner (1953), who describes
it as "operant" and who thus "emphasizes the fact that the behavior
operates upon the environment to generate consequences." These consequences are fed back through the sense organs and may serve to
reinforce behavior even when no organic needs are involved. A rat
will show an increased tendency to press a bar when this act produces
a click or a buzz. A baby will continue to investigate when his efforts
produce rattling or tinkling sounds or sparkling reflections from a
shiny object. The young chimpanzees in Welker's experiment spent
the longest time over objects which could be lighted or made to emit
sounds. Skinner finds it "difficult, if not impossible, to trace these
reinforcing effects to a history of conditioning." "We may plausibly
argue," he continues, "that a capacity to be reinforced by any feedback from the environment would be biologically advantageous, since
it would prepare the organism to manipulate the environment successfully before a given state of deprivation developed."

Woodworth's Behavior-Primacy Theory

The most far-reaching attempt to give these aspects of behavior a
systematic place in the theory of motivation is contained in Woodworth's *Dynamics of Behavior* (1958). Woodworth takes his start
from the idea that a great deal of human behavior appears to be directed toward producing effects upon the environment without immediate service to any aroused organic need. "Its incentives and
rewards are in the field of behavior and not in the field of homeostasis." This is illustrated by exploratory behavior, which is directed
outward toward the environment.

> Its long-range value as the means of making the child acquainted with the
> world he has to deal with later, and so equipping him through play for the
> serious business of life, can scarcely lie within the little child's horizon. His
> goals are more limited and direct: to see this or that object more closely, to
> find what is behind an obstacle, to hear the noise an object makes when it
> strikes the floor, to be told the name of a thing or person (Woodworth, 1958,
> p. 78).

More complex play, such as building with blocks, illustrates the
same outgoing tendency and reveals more plainly the element of finding out what one can and cannot do with objects. Even social play

falls into the pattern. Playmates do not chiefly supply affection or satisfy organic needs; rather, they "afford the opportunity to do something interesting in the environment."

Woodworth draws a contrast between *need-primacy* theories of motivation and the *behavior-primacy* theory. The latter holds that "all behavior is directed primarily toward dealing with the environment." It is to be noted that "dealing with the environment" means a good deal more than receiving stimuli and making responses. Stimuli must be taken as indicators of objects in space, and responses must be adapted to produce effects upon these objects. Even the so-called "mental" capacities, such as memory and ideational thinking, become in time high-level methods of dealing with the environment. Woodworth leaves no doubt as to what he considers basic in motivation. "We are making the claim that this direction of receptive and motor activity toward the environment is the fundamental tendency of animal and human behavior and that it is the all-pervasive primary motivation of behavior." Organic drives have to break into this constantly flowing stream of activity and turn it in a special direction. But the goals of drives cannot be achieved without effective action upon one's surroundings. The ever-present, ever-primary feature of motivation is the tendency to deal with the environment.

It may appear to some workers that Woodworth has overshot the mark by making primary what has commonly been regarded as secondary, and by reducing the familiar drives to what sounds a little like a subordinate station. Woodworth's theory, however, like Goldstein's concept of self-actualization, probably should be construed not as an attempt to downgrade the drives but rather as an insistence that they be kept in the context of a whole living organism which during its waking hours is more or less constantly active. Woodworth's emphasis on dealing with the environment makes his theory a point of culmination for many of those driftings away from drive orthodoxy which we have found to be persistent in so many different areas of psychology. It will soon appear that the concept of competence, to which I now turn, represents in many respects a similar way of thinking. It emphasizes dealing with the environment, and it belongs in the trend away from drive *orthodoxy*, but it is not intended to supplant, or even to subsume, such dynamic forces as hunger, sex, aggression, and fear, which everyone knows to be of huge importance in animal and human nature.

COMPETENCE AND THE PLAY OF CONTENTED CHILDREN

A backward glance at our survey shows considerable agreement about the kinds of behavior that are left out or handled poorly by theories of motivation based wholly on organic drives. Repeatedly we find reference to the familiar series of learned skills which starts with sucking, grasping, and visual exploration and continues with crawling and walking, acts of focal attention and perception, memory, language and thinking, anticipation, the exploring of novel places and objects, effecting stimulus changes in the environment, manipulating and exploiting the surroundings, and achieving higher levels of motor and mental coordination. These aspects of behavior have long been the province of child psychology, which has attempted to measure the slow course of their development and has shown how heavily their growth depends upon learning. Collectively they are sometimes referred to as adaptive mechanisms or as ego processes, but on the whole we are not accustomed to cast a single name over the diverse feats whereby we learn to deal with the environment.

I now propose that we gather the various kinds of behavior just mentioned, all of which have to do with effective interaction with the environment, under the general heading of competence. According to Webster, competence means fitness or ability, and the suggested synonyms include capability, capacity, efficiency, proficiency, and skill. It is therefore a suitable word to describe such things as grasping and exploring, crawling and walking, attention and perception, language and thinking, manipulating and changing the surroundings, all of which promote an effective—a competent—interaction with the environment. It is true, of course, that maturation plays a part in all these developments, but this part is heavily overshadowed by learning in all the more complex accomplishments like speech or skilled manipulation. I shall argue that it is necessary to make competence a motivational concept; there is a *competence motivation* as well as competence in its more familiar sense of achieved capacity. The behavior that leads to the building up of effective grasping, handling, and letting go of objects, to take one example, is not random behavior produced by a general overflow of energy. It is directed, selective, and persistent, and it is continued not because it serves primary drives, which indeed it cannot serve until it is almost perfected, but because it satisfies an intrinsic need to deal with the environment.

No doubt it will at first seem arbitrary to propose a single motivational conception in connection with so many and such diverse kinds of behavior. What do we gain by attributing motivational unity to such a large array of activities? We could, of course, say that each developmental sequence, such as learning to grasp or to walk, has its own built-in bit of motivation—its "aliment," as Piaget (1952) has expressed it. We could go further and say that each item of behavior has its intrinsic motive—but this makes the concept of motivation redundant. On the other hand, we might follow the lead of the animal psychologists and postulate a limited number of broader motives under such names as curiosity, manipulation, and mastery. I believe that the idea of a competence motivation is more adequate than any of these alternatives and that it points to very vital common properties which have been lost from view amidst the strongly analytical tendencies that go with detailed research.

In order to make this claim more plausible, I shall now introduce some specimens of playful exploration in early childhood. I hope that these images will serve to fix and dramatize the concept of competence in the same way that other images—the hungry animal solving problems, the child putting his finger in the candle flame, the infant at the breast, the child on the toilet, and the youthful Oedipus caught in a hopeless love triangle—have become memorable focal points for other concepts. For this purpose I turn to Piaget's (1952) studies of the growth of intelligence from its earliest manifestations in his own three children. The examples come from the first year of life, before language and verbal concepts begin to be important. They therefore represent a practical kind of intelligence which may be quite similar to what is developed by the higher animals.

As early as the fourth month, the play of the gifted Piaget children began to be "centered on a result produced in the external environment," and their behavior could be described as "rediscovering the movement which by chance exercised an advantageous action upon things" (1952, p. 151). Laurent, lying in his bassinet, learns to shake a suspended rattle by pulling a string that hangs from it. He discovers this result fortuitously before vision and prehension are fully coordinated. Let us now observe him a little later when he has reach the age of three months and ten days.

> I place the string, which is attached to the rattle, in his right hand, merely unrolling it a little so that he may grasp it better. For a moment nothing happens. But at the first shake due to chance movement of his hand, the reaction is immediate: Laurent starts when looking at the rattle and then violently strikes his right hand alone, as if he felt the resistance and the effect. The operation lasts fully a quarter of an hour, during which Laurent emits peals of laughter (Piaget, 1952, p. 162).

Three days later the following behavior is observed:

> Laurent, by chance, strikes the chain while sucking his fingers. He grasps it and slowly displaces it while looking at the rattles. He then begins to swing it very gently, which produces a slight movement of the hanging rattles and an as yet faint sound inside them. Laurent then definitely increases by degrees his own movements. He shakes the chain more and more vigorously and laughs uproariously at the result obtained (Piaget, 1952, p. 185).

Very soon it can be observed that procedures are used "to make interesting spectacles last." For instance, Laurent is shown a rubber monkey which he has not seen before. After a moment of surprise, and perhaps even fright, he calms down and makes movements of pulling the string, a procedure which has no effect in this case, but which previously has caused interesting things to happen. It is to be noticed that "interesting spectacles" consist of such things as new toys, a tin box upon which a drumming noise can be made, an unfolded newspaper, or sounds made by the observer such as snapping the fingers. Commonplace as they are to the adult mind, these spectacles enter the infant's experience as novel and apparently challenging events.

Moving ahead to the second half of the first year, we can observe behavior in which the child explores the properties of objects and tries out his repertory of actions upon them. This soon leads to active experimentation in which the child attempts to provoke new results. Again we look in upon Laurent, who has now reached the age of nine months. On different occasions he is shown a variety of new objects— for instance a notebook, a beaded purse, and a wooden parrot. His carefully observing father detects four stages of response: *(a)* visual exploration, passing the object from hand to hand, folding the purse, etc.; *(b)* tactile exploration, passing the hand all over the object, scratching, etc.; *(c)* slow moving of the object in space; *(d)* use of the repertory of action: shaking the object, striking it, swinging it, rubbing it against the side of the bassinet, sucking it, etc., "each in turn with a sort of prudence as though studying the effect produced" (1952, p. 255).

Here the child can be described as applying familiar tactics to new situations, but in a short while he will advance to clear patterns of active experimentation. At 10 months and 10 days Laurent, who is unfamiliar with bread as a nutritive substance, is given a piece for examination. He manipulates it, drops it many times, breaks off fragments and lets them fall. He has often done this kind of thing before, but previously his attention has seemed to be centered on the act of letting go. Now "he watches with great interest the body in motion; in particular, he looks at it for a long time when it has fallen, and picks it up when he can." On the following day he resumes his research.

He grasps in succession a celluloid swan, a box, and several other small objects, in each case stretching out his arm and letting them fall. Sometimes he stretches out his arm vertically, sometimes he holds it obliquely in front of or behind his eyes. When the object falls in a new position (for example on his pillow) he lets it fall two or three times more on the same place, as though to study the spatial relation; then he modifies the situation. At a certain moment the swan falls near his mouth; now he does not suck it (even though this object habitually serves this purpose), but drops it three times more while merely making the gesture of opening his mouth (Piaget, 1952, p. 269).

These specimens will furnish us with sufficient images of the infant's use of his spare time. Laurent, of course, was provided by his studious father with a decidedly enriched environment, but no observant parent will question the fact that babies often act this way during those periods of their waking life when hunger, erotic needs, distresses, and anxiety seem to be exerting no particular pressure. If we consider this behavior under the historic headings of psychology we shall see that few processes are missing. The child gives evidence of sensing, perceiving, attending, learning, recognizing, probably recalling, and perhaps thinking in a rudimentary way. Strong emotion is lacking, but the infant's smiles, gurgles, and occasional peals of laughter strongly suggest the presence of pleasant effect. Actions appear in an organized form, particularly in the specimens of active exploration and experimentation. Apparently the child is using with

a certain coherence nearly the whole repertory of psychological processes except those that accompany stress. It would be arbitrary indeed to say that one was more important than another.

These specimens have a meaningful unity when seen as transactions between the child and his environment, the child having some
influence upon the environment and the environment some influence
upon the child. Laurent appears to be concerned about what he can
do with the chain and rattles, what he can accomplish by his own effort to reproduce and to vary the entertaining sounds. If his father
observed correctly, we must add that Laurent seems to have varied
his actions systematically, as if testing the effect of different degrees
of effort upon the bit of environment represented by the chain and
rattles. Kittens make a similar study of parameters when delicately
using their paws to push pencils and other objects ever nearer to the
edge of one's desk. In all such examples it is clear that the child or
animal is by no means at the mercy of transient stimulus fields. He
selects for continuous treatment those aspects of his environment
which he finds it possible to affect in some way. His behavior is selective, directed, persistent—in short, motivated.

Motivated toward what goal? In these terms, too, the behavior
exhibits a little of everything. Laurent can be seen as appeasing a
stimulus hunger, providing his sensorium with an agreeable level of
stimulation by eliciting from the environment a series of interesting
sounds, feels, and sights. On the other hand we might emphasize a
need for activity and see him as trying to reach a pleasurable level of
neuromuscular exercise. We can also see another possible goal in the
behavior: the child is achieving knowledge, attaining a more differentiated cognitive map of his environment and thus satisfying an
exploratory tendency or motive of curiosity. But it is equally possible
to discern a theme of mastery, power, or control, perhaps even a bit
of primitive self-assertion, in the child's concentration upon those
aspects of the environment which respond in some way to his own
activity. It looks as if we had found too many goals, and perhaps our
first impulse is to search for some key to tell us which one is really
important. But this, I think, is a mistake that would be fatal to
understanding.

We cannot assign priority to any of these goals without pausing
arbitrarily in the cycle of transaction between child and environ-

ment and saying, "This is the real point." I propose instead that the real point is the transactions as a whole. If the behavior gives satisfaction, this satisfaction is not associated with a particular moment in the cycle. It does not lie solely in sensory stimulation, in a bettering of the cognitive map, in coordinated action, in motor exercise, in a feeling of effort and of effects produced, or in the appreciation of change brought about in the sensory field. These are all simply aspects of a process which at this stage has to be conceived as a whole. The child appears to be occupied with the agreeable task of developing an effective familiarity with his environment. This involves discovering the effects he can have on the environment and the effects the environment will have on him. To the extent that these results are preserved by learning, they build up an increased competence in dealing with the environment. The child's play can thus be viewed as serious business, though to him it is merely something that is interesting and fun to do.

Bearing in mind these examples, as well as the dealings with environment pointed out by other workers, we must now attempt to describe more fully the possible nature of the motivational aspect of competence. It needs its own name, and in view of the foregoing analysis I propose that this name be *effectance*.

EFFECTANCE

The new freedom produced by two decades of research on animal drives is of great help in this undertaking. We are no longer obliged to look for a source of energy external to the nervous system, for a consummatory climax, or for a fixed connection between reinforcement and tension-reduction. Effectance motivation cannot, of course, be conceived as having a source in tissues external to the nervous system. It is in no sense a deficit motive. We must assume it to be neurogenic, its "energies" being simply those of the living cells that make up the nervous system. External stimuli play an important part, but in terms of "energy" this part is secondary, as one can see most clearly when environmental stimulation is actively sought. Putting it picturesquely, we might say that the effectance urge represents what the neuromuscular system wants to do when it is otherwise unoccupied or is gently stimulated by the environment. Obviously there

are no consummatory acts; satisfaction would appear to lie in the
arousal and maintaining of activity rather than in its slow decline
toward bored passivity. The motive need not be conceived as intense
and powerful in the sense that hunger, pain, or fear can be powerful when aroused to high pitch. There are plenty of instances in
which children refuse to leave their absorbed play in order to eat or
to visit the toilet. Strongly aroused drives, pain, and anxiety, however,
can be conceived as overriding the effectance urge and capturing the
energies of the neuromuscular system. But effectance motivation is
persistent in the sense that it regularly occupies the spare waking
time between episodes of homeostatic crisis.

In speculating upon this subject we must bear in mind the continuous nature of behavior. This is easier said than done; habitually
we break things down in order to understand them, and such units
as the reflex arc, the stimulus-response sequence, and the single transaction with the environment seem like inevitable steps toward clarity.
Yet when we apply such an analysis to playful exploration we lose
the most essential aspect of the behavior. It is constantly circling from
stimulus to perception to action to effect to stimulus to perception,
and so on around; or, more properly, these processes are all in continuous action and continuous change. Dealing with the environment
means carrying on a continuing transaction which gradually changes
one's relation to the environment. Because there is no consummatory
climax, satisfaction has to be seen as lying in a considerable series of
transactions, in a trend of behavior rather than a goal that is achieved.
It is difficult to make the word "satisfaction" have this connotation,
and we shall do well to replace it by "feeling of efficacy" when attempting to indicate the subjective and affective side of effectance.

It is useful to recall the findings about novelty: the singular effectiveness of novelty in engaging interest and for a time supporting
persistent behavior. We also need to consider the selective continu-
ance of transactions in which the animal or child has a more or less
pronounced effect upon the environment—in which something happens as a consequence of his activity. Interest is not aroused and sustained when the stimulus field is so familiar that it gives rise at most
to reflex acts or automatized habits. It is not sustained when actions
produce no effects or changes in the stimulus field. Our conception
must therefore be that effectance motivation is aroused by stimulus

conditions which offer, as Hebb (1949) puts it, difference-in-same-ness. This leads to variability and novelty of response, and interest is best sustained when the resulting action affects the stimulus so as to produce further difference-in-sameness. Interest wanes when action begins to have less effect; effectance motivation subsides when a situation has been explored to the point that it no longer presents new possibilities.

We have to conceive further that the arousal of playful and ex-ploratory interest means the appearance of organization involving both the cognitive and active aspects of behavior. Change in the stimulus field is not an end in itself, so to speak; it happens when one is passively moved about, and it may happen as a consequence of random movements without becoming focalized and instigating ex-ploration. Similarly, action which has effects is not an end in itself, for if one unintentionally kicks away a branch while walking, or knocks something off a table, these effects by no means necessarily become involved in playful investigation. Schachtel's (1954) em-phasis on focal attention becomes helpful at this point. The playful and exploratory behavior shown by Laurent is not random or casual. It involves focal *attention* to some object—the fixing of some aspect of the stimulus field so that it stays relatively constant—and it also involves the focalizing of *action* upon this object. As Diamond (1939) has expressed it, response under these conditions is "relevant to the stimulus," and it is change in the *focalized* stimulus that so strongly affects the level of interest. Dealing with the environment means directing focal attention to some part of it and organizing actions to have some effect on this part.

In our present state of relative ignorance about the workings of the nervous system it is impossible to form a satisfactory idea of the neural basis of effectance motivation, but it should at least be clear that the concept does not refer to any and every kind of neural action. It refers to a particular kind of activity, as inferred from particular kinds of behavior. We can say that it does not include reflexes and other kinds of automatic response. It does not include well-learned, automatized patterns, even those that are complex and highly or-ganized. It does not include behavior in the service of effectively aroused drives. It does not even include activity that is highly random and discontinuous, though such behavior may be its most direct forerunner. The urge toward competence is inferred specifically from behavior that shows a lasting focalization and that has the characteristics of exploration and experimentation, a kind of variation within the focus. When this particular sort of activity is aroused in the nervous system, effectance motivation is being aroused, for it is characteristic of this particular sort of activity that it is selective, directed, and persistent, and that instrumental acts will be learned for the sole reward of engaging in it.

Some objection may be felt to my introducing the word *competence* in connection with behavior that is so often playful. Certainly the playing child is doing things for fun, not because of a desire to improve his competence in dealing with the stern hard world. In order to forestall misunderstanding, it should be pointed out that the usage here is parallel to what we do when we connect sex with its biological goal of reproduction. The sex drive aims for pleasure and gratification, and reproduction is a consequence that is presumably unforeseen by animals and by man at primitive levels of understanding. Effectance motivation similarly aims for the feeling of efficacy, not for the vitally important learnings that come as its consequence. If we consider the part played by competence motivation in adult human life we can observe the same parallel. Sex may now be completely and purposefully divorced from reproduction but nevertheless pursued for the pleasure it can yield. Similarly, effectance motivation may lead to continuing exploratory interests or active adventures when in fact there is no longer any gain in actual competence or any need for it in terms of survival. In both cases the motive is capable of yielding surplus satisfaction well beyond what is necessary to get the biological work done.

In infants and young children it seems to me sensible to conceive of effectance motivation as undifferentiated. Later in life it becomes profitable to distinguish various motives such as cognizance, construction, mastery, and achievement. It is my view that all such motives have a root in effectance motivation. They are differentiated from it through life experiences which emphasize one or another aspect of the cycle of transaction with environment. Of course, the motives of later childhood and of adult life are no longer simple and can almost never be referred to a single root. They can acquire loadings of anxiety, defense, and compensation, they can become fused with unconscious fantasies of a sexual, aggressive, or omnipotent character, and they can gain force because of their service in producing realistic results in the way of income and career. It is not my intention to cast effectance in the star part in adult motivation. The acquisition of motives is a complicated affair in which simple and sovereign theories grow daily more obsolete. Yet it may be that the satisfaction of effectance contributes significantly to those feelings of interest which often sustain us so well in day-to-day actions, particularly when the things we are doing have continuing elements of novelty.

THE BIOLOGICAL SIGNIFICANCE OF COMPETENCE

The conviction was expressed at the beginning of this paper that some such concept as competence, interpreted motivationally, was essential for any biologically sound view of human nature. This necessity emerges when we consider the nature of living systems, particularly when we take a longitudinal view. What an organism does at a given moment does not always give the right clue as to what it does over a period of time. Discussing this problem, Angyal (1941) has proposed that we should look for the general pattern followed by the total organismic process over the course of time. Obviously this makes it necessary to take account of growth. Angyal defines life as "a process of self-expansion;" the living system "expands at the expense of its surroundings," assimilating parts of the environment and transforming them into functioning parts of itself. Organisms differ from other things in nature in that they are "self-governing entities" which are to some extent "autonomous." Internal processes govern them as well as external "heteronomous" forces. In the course of life there is a relative increase in the preponderance of internal over external forces. The living system expands, assimilates more of the environment, transforms its surroundings so as to bring them under greater control. "We may say," Angyal writes, "that the general dynamic trend of the organism is toward an increase of autonomy. . . . The human being has a characteristic tendency toward self-determination, that is, a tendency to resist external influences and to subordinate the heteronomous forces of the physical and social environment to its own sphere of influence." The trend toward increased autonomy is characteristic so long as growth of any kind is going on, though in the end the living system is bound to succumb to the pressure of heteronomous forces.

Of all living creatures, it is man who takes the longest strides toward autonomy. This is not because of any unusual tendency toward bodily expansion at the expense of the environment. It is rather that man, with his mobile hands and abundantly developed brain, attains an extremely high level of competence in his transactions with his surroundings. The building of houses, roads and bridges, the making of tools and instruments, the domestication of plants and animals— all qualify as planful changes made in the environment so that it comes more or less under control and serves our purposes rather than intruding upon them. We meet the fluctuations of outdoor temperature, for example, not only with our bodily homeostatic mechanisms, which alone would be painfully unequal to the task, but also with clothing, buildings, controlled fires, and such complicated devices as self-regulating central heating and air conditioning. Man as a species has developed a tremendous power of bringing the environment into his service, and each individual member of the species must attain what is really quite an impressive level of competence if he is to take part in the life around him.

We are so accustomed to these human accomplishments that it is hard to realize how long an apprenticeship they require. At the outset the human infant is a slow learner in comparison with other animal forms. Hebb (1949) speaks of "the astonishing inefficiency of man's first learning, as far as immediate results are concerned," an inefficiency which he attributes to the large size of the association areas in the brain and the long time needed to bring them under sensory control. The human lack of precocity in learning shows itself even in comparison with one of the next of kin: as Hebb points out, "the human baby takes six months, the chimpanzee four months, before making a clear distinction between friend and enemy." Later in life the slow start will pay dividends. Once the fundamental perceptual elements, simple associations, and conceptual sequences have been established, later learning can proceed with ever-increasing swiftness and complexity. In Hebb's words, "learning at maturity concerns patterns and events whose parts at least are familiar and which already have a number of other associations."

This general principle of cumulative learning, starting from slowly acquired rudiments and proceeding thence with increasing efficiency, can be illustrated by such processes as manipulation and locomotion, which may culminate in the acrobat devising new stunts or the dancer working out a new ballet. It is especially vivid in the case of language, where the early mastery of words and pronunciation seems such a far cry from spontaneous adult speech. A strong argument has been made by Hebb (1949) that the learning of visual forms proceeds over a similar course from slowly learned elements to rapidly combined patterns. Circles and squares, for example, cannot be discriminated at a glance without a slow apprenticeship involving eye movements, successive fixations, and recognition of angles. Hebb proposes that the recognition of visual patterns without eye movement "is possible only as the result of an intensive and prolonged visual training that goes on from the moment of birth, during every moment that the eyes are open, with an increase in skill evident over a period of 12 to 16 years at least."

On the motor side there is likewise a lot to be cumulatively learned. The playing, investigating child slowly finds out the relationships between what he does and what he experiences. He finds out, for instance, how hard he must push what in order to produce what effect. Here the S-R formula is particularly misleading. It would come nearer the truth to say that the child is busy learning R-S connections—the effects that are likely to follow upon his own behavior. But even in this reversed form the notion of bonds or connections would still misrepresent the situation, for it is only a rare specimen of behavior that can properly be conceived as determined by fixed neural channels and a fixed motor response. As Hebb has pointed out, discussing the phenomenon of "motor equivalence" named by Lashley (1942), a rat which has been trained to press a lever will press it with the left forepaw, the right forepaw, by climbing upon it, or by biting it; a monkey will open the lid of a food box with either hand, with a foot, or even with a stick; and we might add that a good baseball player can catch a fly ball while running in almost any direction and while in almost any posture, including leaping in the air and plunging forward to the ground. All of these feats are possible because of a history of learnings in which the main lesson has been the effects of actions upon the stimulus fields that represent the environment. What has been learned is not a fixed connection but a flexible relationship between stimulus fields and the effects that can be produced in them by various kinds of action.

One additional example, drawn this time from Piaget (1952), is particularly worth mentioning because of its importance in theories of development. Piaget points out that a great deal of mental development depends upon the idea that the world is made up of objects having substance and permanence. Without such an "object concept" it would be impossible to build up the ideas of space and causality and to arrive at the fundamental distinction between self and external world. Observation shows that the object concept, "far from being innate or ready-made in experience, is constructed little by little." Up to the age of seven and eight months the Piaget children searched for vanished objects only in the sense of trying to continue the actions, such as sucking or grasping, in which the objects had played a part. When an object was really out of sight or touch, even if only because it was covered by a cloth, the infants undertook no further exploration. Only gradually, after some study of the displacement of objects by moving, swinging, and dropping them, does the child begin to make an active search for a vanished object, and only still more gradually does he learn, at 12 months or more, to make allowance for the object's sequential displacements and thus to seek it where it has gone rather than where it was last in sight. Thus it is only through cumulative learning that the child arrives at the idea of permanent substantial objects.

The infant's play is indeed serious business. If he did not while away his time pulling strings, shaking rattles, examining wooden parrots, dropping pieces of bread and celluloid swans, when would he learn to discriminate visual patterns, to catch and throw, and to build up his concept of the object? When would he acquire the many other foundation stones necessary for cumulative learning? The more closely we analyze the behavior of the human infant, the more clearly do we realize that infancy is not simply a time when the nervous system matures and the muscles grow stronger. It is a time of active and continuous learning, during which the basis is laid for all those processes, cognitive and motor, whereby the child becomes able to establish effective transactions with his environment and move toward a greater degree of autonomy. Helpless as he may seem until he begins to toddle, he has by that time already made substantial gains in the achievement of competence.

Under primitive conditions survival must depend quite heavily upon achieved competence. We should expect to find things so arranged as to favor and maximize this achievement. Particularly in the case of man, where so little is provided innately and so much has to be learned through experience, we should expect to find highly advantageous arrangements for securing a steady cumulative learning about the properties of the environment and the extent of possible transactions. Under these circumstances we might expect to find a very powerful drive operating to insure progress toward competence, just as the vital goals of nutrition and reproduction are secured by powerful drives, and it might therefore seem paradoxical that the interests of competence should be so much entrusted to times of play and leisurely exploration. There is good reason to suppose, however, that a strong drive would be precisely the wrong arrangement to secure a flexible, knowledgeable power of transaction with the environment. Strong drives cause us to learn certain lessons well, but they do not create maximum familiarity with our surroundings.

This point was demonstrated more than half a century ago in some experiments by Yerkes and Dodson (1908). They showed that maximum motivation did not lead to the most rapid solving of problems, especially if the problems were complex. For each problem there was an optimum level of motivation, neither the highest nor the lowest, and the optimum was lower for more complex tasks. The same problem has been discussed more recently by Tolman (1948) in his paper on cognitive maps. A cognitive map can be narrow or broad, depending upon the range of cues picked up in the course of learning. Tolman suggests that one of the conditions which tend to narrow the range of cues is a high level of motivation. In everyday terms, a man hurrying to an important business conference is likely to perceive only the cues that help him to get there faster, whereas a man taking a stroll after lunch is likely to pick up a substantial amount of casual information about his environment. The latent learning experiments with animals, and experiments such as those of Johnson (1953) in which drive level has been systematically varied in a situation permitting incidental learning, give strong support to this general idea. In a recent contribution, Bruner, Matter, and Papanek (1955) make a strong case for the concept of breadth of learning and provide additional evidence that it is favored by moderate and hampered by strong motivation. The latter "has the effect of speeding up learning at the cost of narrowing it." Attention is concentrated upon the task at hand and little that is extraneous to this task is learned for future use.

These facts enable us to see the biological appropriateness of an arrangement which uses periods of less intense motivation for the development of competence. This is not to say that the narrower but efficient learnings that go with the reduction of strong drives make no contribution to general effectiveness. They are certainly an important element in capacity to deal with the environment, but a much greater effectiveness results from having this capacity fed also from learnings that take place in quieter times. It is then that the infant can attend to matters of lesser urgency, exploring the properties of things he does not fear and does not need to eat, learning to gauge the force of his string-pulling when the only penalty for failure is silence on the part of attached rattles, and generally accumulating for himself a broad knowledge and a broad skill in dealing with his surroundings.

The concept of competence can be most easily discussed by choosing, as we have done, examples of interaction with the inanimate environment. It applies equally well, however, to transactions with animals and with other human beings, where the child has the same problem of finding out what effects he can have upon the environment and what effects it can have upon him. The earliest interactions with members of the family may involve needs so strong that they obscure the part played by effectance motivation, but perhaps the example of the well-fed baby diligently exploring the several features of his mother's face will serve as a reminder that here, too, there are less urgent moments when learning for its own sake can be given free rein.

In this closing section I have brought together several ideas which bear on the evolutionary significance of competence and of its motivation. I have sought in this way to deepen the biological roots of the concept and thus help it to attain the stature in the theory of behavior which has not been reached by similar concepts in the past. To me it seems that the most important proving ground for this concept is the effect it may have on our understanding of the development of personality. Does it assist our grasp of early object relations, the reality principle, and the first steps in the development of the ego? Can it be of service in distinguishing the kinds of defense available at different ages and in providing clues to the replacement of primitive defenses by successful adaptive maneuvers? Can it help fill the yawning gap known as the latency period, a time when the mastery of school subjects and other accomplishments claim so large a share of time and energy? Does it bear upon the self and the vicissitudes of self-esteem, and can it enlighten the origins of psychological disorder? Can it make adult motives and interests more intelligible and enable us to rescue the concept of sublimation from the difficulties which even its best friends have recognized? I believe it can be shown that existing explanations of development are not satisfactory and that the addition of the concept of competence cuts certain knots in personality theory. But this is not the subject of the present communication, where the concept is offered much more on the strength of its logical and biological probability.

SUMMARY

The main theme of this paper is introduced by showing that there is widespread discontent with theories of motivation built upon primary drives. Signs of this discontent are found in realms as far apart as animal psychology and psychoanalytic ego psychology. In the former, the commonly recognized primary drives have proved to be inadequate in explaining exploratory behavior, manipulation, and general activity. In the latter, the theory of basic instincts has shown serious shortcomings when it is stretched to account for the development of the effective ego. Workers with animals have attempted to meet their problem by invoking secondary reinforcement and anxiety reduction, or by adding exploration and manipulation to the roster of primary drives. In parallel fashion, psychoanalytic workers have relied upon the concept of neutralization of instinctual energies, have seen anxiety reduction as the central motive in ego development, or have hypothesized new instincts such as mastery. It is argued here that these several explanations are not satisfactory and that a better conceptualization is possible, indeed that it has already been all but made.

In trying to form this conceptualization, it is first pointed out that many of the earlier tenets of primary drive theory have been discredited by recent experimental work. There is no longer any compelling reason to identify either pleasure or reinforcement with drive reduction, or to think of motivation as requiring a source of energy external to the nervous system. This opens the way for considering in their own right those aspects of animal and human behavior in which stimulation and contact with the environment seem to be sought and welcomed, in which raised tension and even mild excitement seem to be cherished, and in which novelty and variety seem to be enjoyed for their own sake. Several reports are cited which bear upon interest in the environment and the rewarding effects of environmental feedback. The latest contribution is that of Woodworth (1958), who makes dealing with the environment the most fundamental element in motivation.

The survey indicates a certain unanimity as to the kinds of behavior that cannot be successfully conceptualized in terms of primary drives. This behavior includes visual exploration, grasping, crawling and walking, attention and perception, language and thinking, exploring novel objects and places, manipulating the surroundings, and producing effective changes in the environment. The thesis is then proposed that all of these behaviors have a common biological significance: they all form part of the process whereby the animal or child learns to interact effectively with his environment. The word *competence* is chosen as suitable to indicate this common property. Further, it is maintained that competence cannot be fully acquired simply through behavior instigated by drives. It receives substantial contributions from activities which, though playful and exploratory in character, at the same time show direction, selectivity, and persistence in interacting with the environment. Such activities in the ultimate service of competence must therefore be conceived to be motivated in their own right. It is proposed to designate this motivation by the term effectance, and to characterize the experience produced as a *feeling of efficacy*.

In spite of its sober biological purpose, effectance motivation shows itself most unambiguously in the playful and investigatory behavior of young animals and children. Specimens of such behavior, drawn from Piaget (1952), are analyzed in order to demonstrate their constantly transactional nature. Typically they involve continuous chains of events which include stimulation, cognition, action, effect on the environment, new stimulation, etc. They are carried on with considerable persistence and with selective emphasis on parts of the environment which provide changing and interesting feedback in connection with effort expended. Their significance is destroyed if we try to break into the circle arbitrarily and declare that one part of it, such as cognition alone or active effort alone, is the real point, the goal, or the special seat of satisfaction. Effectance motivation must be conceived to involve satisfaction—a feeling of efficacy—in transactions in which behavior has an exploratory, varying, experimental character and produces changes in the stimulus field. Having this character, the behavior leads the organism to find out how the environment can be changed and what consequences flow from these changes.

In higher animals and especially in man, where so little is innately provided and so much has to be learned about dealing with the environment, effectance motivation independent of primary drives can be seen as an arrangement having high adaptive value. Considering the slow rate of learning in infancy and the vast amount that has to be learned before there can be an effective level of interaction with surroundings, young animals and children would simply not learn enough unless they worked pretty steadily at the task between episodes of homeostatic crisis. The association of interest with this "work," making it play and fun, is thus somewhat comparable to the association of sexual pleasure with the biological goal of reproduction. Effectance motivation need not be conceived as strong in the sense that sex, hunger, and fear are strong when violently aroused. It is moderate but persistent, and in this, too, we can discern a feature that is favorable for adaptation. Strong motivation reinforces learning in a narrow sphere, whereas moderate motivation is more conducive to an exploratory and experimental attitude which leads to competent interactions in general, without reference to an immediate pressing need. Man's huge cortical association areas might have been a suicidal piece of specialization if they had come without a steady, persistent inclination toward interacting with the environment.

Chapter 11

The Inherent Variability of Behavior

DONALD W. FISKE
University of Chicago

S UPPOSE we set out to describe the activity of a simple machine, such as a mechanical clock. We would find that its gears and other parts are in different positions at different moments of observation. If we attempted a full listing of these different states, we would produce a long list, the number of states being a function of the fineness of our units of description. We would also have to replicate this listing for each defined position of the hands and also for each degree of tension in the mainspring. Yet our catalogue of different states, however lengthy, would be finite.

Now let us try to describe the overt activity of a living higher organism, such as a rat. We immediately encounter the problem of selecting certain points on the rat's body for our observations, since the anatomy of the rat does not permit ready analysis into a small number of solid, separate parts. If we use the same fineness of measurement that we used with our clock, we will quickly find ourselves with a much longer list of observed states. But now we turn to a further complication: the location and orientation of the rat in physical space. While our hypothetical rat may be in a cage, there is still an exceedingly lengthy list of positions which the tip of its nose occupies and for each of these, there is a large number of discriminable orientations in three dimensions. Even if we limit our observations to a particular time of day, the variation in possible behavioral states will still be very large.

This discussion brings out a central feature of overt behavior—its almost infinite variety. To describe behavior, we must classify it into a limited series of categories. To understand behavior, we determine the association between specified conditions in the external situation (or in the history of the organism) and particular classes of activity which we label responses. Much of psychology is concerned with determining the response category associated with a particular set of stimulus conditions. The investigator is ordinarily interested in the modal response for a group of subjects, in the mean response of one type of subjects as compared to another type, or in the average response of one subject as compared to others. In each of these cases, he determines the central tendency of a set of responses, or compares two central tendencies. While the typical experimenter tries to set up conditions which will reduce the variation around the central tendency, he is rarely completely successful. Variation in behavior is almost inescapable if the behavior is coded in categories, each of which is sufficiently narrow to be reasonably homogeneous. Under rigorously controlled experimental conditions, variability can be reduced to a negligible amount. Under other conditions, it is a marked and significant feature of the activity of living organisms.

This chapter will be concerned primarily with one form of variability, the variation in the behavior of a given organism at different times but under the same external conditions. What is the amount of such variability around the organism's central tendency? Does this amount vary with the value of the central tendency? With what else is it related? Such questions will provide some evidence concerning the significance of variability in behavior.

It will quickly become apparent that the answers to these questions depend in part upon the response being considered. But what is a response? A response is an aspect of activity which an experimenter selects for study, on the basis of his interests and of his preconceptions. It may be a specific movement of a limb, it may be any action which produces a given change in the physical environment, or it may be a comparatively lengthy sequence of actions involving considerable locomotion and manipulation. In any case, two steps must be taken: first, the experimenter must select the aspect of behavior in which he is interested; second, he must identify at least two states, such as "turns right" *vs.* "turns left," "enters an alley" *vs.* "does not enter it," or "marks response alternative *a (b) (c)*" on a test. His delineation of the behavior to be observed must also specify the time and the external conditions under which he will make his observations.

In addition to selecting an aspect of behavior and a size of unit, the experimenter must decide on his rules for classifying a response as falling in a given category. A common and convenient practice is to define a response in overt physical terms: the rat causes the bar to be depressed a certain amount; the tip of the rat's nose passes over a line on the floor of the maze; the human subject makes a mark beside alternative *c;* he says "yes." Most of the evidence cited in this chapter uses such phenotypical, overt behaviors because it is easier to work with problems where there is no serious question whether two responses are the same.

The experimenter may, however, classify two responses as equivalent even though they are overtly different. Thus, if a subject gives the response "bat" to a Rorschach card on the first administration and says "bird" on a subsequent testing, the examiner may place these two responses in the same content category. Again, an uncooperative subject might check all the *a* alternatives on the first testing and all the *d* alternatives on the second testing; although every response has been changed, the experimenter may view the two series as having the same psychological implications for the subject's attitude toward the situation. These latter examples also suggest that the same responses can be studied at more than one level of analysis.

Classifications based on response equivalence typically utilize broader categories than those defining consistency in terms of overt characteristics. There is actually a continuum from the one extreme type of classification to the other, depending upon the relative emphasis on manifest similarity as opposed to psychological or functional equivalence. It is largely for this reason that we believe that the interpretations of variability offered below will be found eventually to hold for any approach to behavior, no matter how phenotypical or genotypical.

In the first steps toward the description and analysis of variability of behavior that will be taken in this chapter, the focus will be primarily on responses of human subjects to psychological tests. The testing situation is a convenient source of responses which can be readily identified and classified. However, our center of interest will generally not be the substantive, qualitative variables which may be measured in such a situation. Rather we shall view this situation as a microcosm, as a place in which we can identify fairly readily the main features determining behavioral tendencies and behavioral variability.

This situation has the additional advantage that there is ordinarily little or no obvious reinforcement of responses. The problem of variability can most readily be studied in situations where there is no monotonic trend over time. We shall assume not only that the external conditions are the same on each trial but also that no systematic changes have occurred in the organism: that is, we shall assume that no learning has taken place and that there is sufficient time between trials to avoid such effects as fatigue and boredom. As a consequence, the order of a pair of trials is immaterial. Furthermore, since there is no learning, the strength of any response tendency is considered to be constant. We are concerned not with the constitutional or experiential determinants of such strength but only its amount.

We shall define the response in which we are interested in conventional terms. For example, when presented with item X at time T, which of the several alternatives (potential responses) made available to him does the subject select? We shall be concerned with the following questions: Given standard testing conditions, how much variability of response occurs over trials separated in time? Does the extent of variability differ for different tests? Does it differ for different items? Do individual subjects show different amounts of variability? If so, with what are these differences associated?

Although test responses will be the behavior emphasized in this chapter, other kinds and classes of behavior will be considered. Within the limits of one chapter, it will not be possible to make a comprehensive analysis of even one of these other classes. Hence we cannot expect to convince the reader of our belief that the interpretation which we shall detail for variability in test response holds for most or all other behavior. The introduction of material about these various other approaches to behavior should at least demonstrate to the reader that the same questions can meaningfully be asked of behavior outside the domain of tests.

Finally, we shall offer a preliminary interpretation of variability. Over a series of separate occurrences of a given external situation, the behavior of a single subject is as variable as possible from occasion to occasion within the requirements which the situation imposes on the subject. The less the situation forces the subject to cope with it, to engage in a particular transaction with his environment, the greater is the variability of the subject's behavior from time to time in that situation. Conversely, the more the situation restricts the potential responses of the subject, the more consistent will be his behavior over occasions.

While the primary emphasis will be on responses defined in the usual way, we believe that the interpretation also holds for other conceptualizations of behavior, even to other classifications of the same set of responses. Thus a person may vary the location of his checkmarks on a test from one trial to another but he does make checkmarks every time because the situation induces him to cope with the situation by responding to each item.

THE FORMAL ANALYSIS OF VARIABILITY

This chapter is concerned with the extent to which different behavior is observed on two occasions. We shall assume that, as indicated above, the experimenter has rules for deciding when to make each observation or where to observe, and also has established a classification system for his observations. Thus he may observe the rat's location every minute or he may observe what the rat does at each choice point. With a human subject, he may note the alternative checked among those available for the given item. The classification system will ordinarily be one of two types: categorical or continuous. The experimenter records that the rat turned left and not right or that the subject chose alternative a and not b or c. On the other hand, he may record the time taken to complete a task (such as running a maze or finishing a test), the force exerted in pressing a bar, or the distance from one end of a rating scale to the subject's checkmark.

For these latter continuous variables, variability is measured as the absolute difference between a pair of responses. If a number of trials are given, we can compute the average of such successive differences. Where a number of observation points or items are comparable, it is appropriate to average the several differences for the same pair of trials. For categorical data, variability is the number of pairs of observations where the two observations are in different categories (for example, left and then right, c followed by b).

In both instances, the measure of variability can yield an estimate of the variance of the theoretical distribution, the distribution of an infinite number of observations of the given subject under identical conditions. It can be shown that an unbiased estimate of the standard deviation can be made from the mean of the absolute differences between successive observations (Keen, Page, and Hartley, 1953).

In parallel fashion, a two or more category system can be thought of as a binomial or multinomial distribution with a variance related to the relative frequency of dissimilar pairs. From this mathematical point of view, variability can be seen to be inversely related to response strength. For example, a person may select the "No" response to a two-choice item on 90% of a series of trials; his frequency of successive pairs of dissimilar responses will ordinarily be less for this item than it will be for an item to which he responds "No" only 50% of the time. But note that the same relationship holds for a large percentage of "Yes" responses and hence for small, complementary values of "No" responses. Psychologically, it is a matter of the relative strength of the predominant response tendency, which may be to choose one response or to avoid the other. In either case, the relationship between variability and strength is independent of the specific character or form of the response.

In contrast, the relationship between variability and the strength of a response which is measured on a continuum is not a clear-cut mathematical property of the distribution. It is mathematically possible to have a variance of zero, or nearly zero, and yet have a mean at any point on the scale. However, the typical psychological continuum for a response measure has some constraint: the scale is curtailed at one or both ends. Thus there is a lower limit to the time required for a rat to run a familiar maze, a limit set by the anatomy and physiology of the organism. Where there is such a constraint, there tends to be a reduction in variation as the mean approaches this limit. The running times of a rat with strong motivation will have a lower mean and also lower variability than those for a rat with weaker motivation.

The scales used for scoring ratings and tests are generally curtailed at both ends. In these instances, the distance between a mean score and the end of the scale which is nearer imposes an upper limit to the possible variance. Empirical data show that this limit on the variability is rarely if ever reached. We shall argue that any association between low variability and proximity to a scale's limit is best interpreted by the generalization that the stronger the predominant response tendency for the organism in a particular situation, the lower the variability of its responses. It is important to recognize that for this generalization, the specific nature or quality of the response tendency is immaterial. Certain qualifications or restrictions concerning the function and the adequacy of the tendency will be considered later.

Thus it is necessary to distinguish between the mathematical problem and the psychological properties. The determination of the direction of the association between a continuous variable and response strength must obviously be made on psychological grounds. When a subject is given a list of adjectives and asked to check those that describe him, the number checked may indicate a strong or a weak response disposition, depending upon the content of the adjectives: the more he checks favorable adjectives, the stronger his presumed desire to portray himself in a good light; on the other hand, the more unfavorable adjectives he checks, the weaker is the same tendency or the related tendency to avoid creating an unfavorable picture. In some instances, there are two functions with opposing directions: from some central point, response strength can be inferred to increase as the subject's mean moves away in either direction; for example, an attitude scale calling for relative preference for two political parties.

One final point must be made about a special categorical classification. In many instances, the psychologist counts the number of occurrences of a given response or, more precisely, the proportion of occurrences during a set of opportunities, trials, or observation periods. The result is a two-category distribution, A and non-A. Such an approach may lump several potential response tendencies together in the non-A class. Again, the class A may be defined in several ways: as one specific adaptive response; as a specific type of error; as all adaptive or right responses; or as all types of errors. While the mean and variance are directly related in such a two-category system, the experimenter must decide whether each category is psychologically homogeneous or whether it embraces a number of response tendencies so that the notion of response strength for the category is inappropriate and even misleading. Many of the infinite number of possible categories applicable to behavior cannot serve as useful indices of a single behavioral disposition. Thus a category including all errors on a free-response achievement test would usually not be a good direct measure of any response tendency, whereas the complementary category of all right answers could be considered to reflect certain motivational and cognitive dispositions.

BEHAVIOR WITH UNCHANGING STIMULATION

Before considering the variability of behavior as determined by placing the individual in the same situation on two different occasions, let us look first at behavior in the special case where the external conditions remain essentially constant for a considerable period of time. Under these extreme conditions, we may get some hints about behavior when the situation does not make specific demands upon the subject. In a previous chapter (Chapter 5), we have examined the effects of monotonous conditions upon performance. Here we shall be looking at behavior where no active task, no overt response is required of the subject. Consider the observations in the studies of restricted stimulation (also reported in Chapter 5). In these experiments, the subjects have nothing to do. They are usually instructed to stay in one position and not move around. External stimulation has minimal intensity and variation—its impact is reduced to the lowest possible point. While the subjects' motor behavior has not been systematically studied, their vocal behavior was recorded in at least one study; Goldberger and Holt (1958) encouraged their subjects to talk about their thoughts and feelings as they occurred. Through the kind cooperation of these investigators, it was possible to examine the protocols of these subjects. The contents were quite varied, both between protocols and within each protocol. Thoughts about the situation and about themselves, random associations, and such organized sequences as humming a tune were observed. As one might expect, there was almost no repetition of content during the several hours of each run. To be sure, one subject hummed the same tune twice, with a long period intervening. Another verbalized his concern with his appearance in the experimental equipment, using somewhat similar words on two occasions. But these are the exceptions. The other verbalizations showed no repetition at any time, and especially no consecutive repetition.

This general trend is supported by the reports of the subjects in the postexperimental interviews. However, some subjects did indicate continued or intermittent preoccupation with particular topics. In the earlier parts of the time period, there were attempts to think through particular problems, such as course papers, but the subjects experienced great difficulty in continuing such activity. The most common topic of preoccupation was the experiment itself: some subjects were concerned with how the time was passing, and with their ability to stay in the situation for the expected time. It is important to note that these more or less homogeneous thoughts were a reaction to the situation itself and were the only material which was common to several subjects.

The observations in the McGill experiments (Heron, 1957) appear to agree with this picture. While Heron (personal communication) indicates that the same visual image, such as an abstract pattern, might recur during a given brief period of time, such as a single hallucinatory period, it would not be repeated on a subsequent day.

These observations are cited to support the view that, under conditions with essentially constant external stimulation and with no set imposed by instructions, there is very little repetition in visual imagery or in the content of thoughts or associations. Although no protocols for control groups are available, we may hazard the guess that the extent of repetition under more normal conditions is also quite limited: in everyday conversation, the topic may be the same for a shorter or longer period of time, but each verbal response is typically a unique combination of words.

Sleep is another condition in which external stimulation is minimal in intensity and meaning, and is relatively constant for periods of time. (See Chapter 6.) How much variability is found in imagery during sleep? Kamiya and others have wakened subjects during each occurrence of rapid eye movement in periods of light sleep and asked them to report their dreams. These protocols also show preponderant variability: in the several dreams during a given night, and in the series for several nights, there is essentially no repetition of manifest content. Rarely if ever is a whole dream repeated, and even the plots and scenes are different. (While it might be argued that different dreams may have the same dynamic theme, each dream seems to develop the theme one step, rather than to repeat an earlier expression of the theme. See French [1952, 1954].) The one type of consistency which has been found is the dream about the experimental situation: an occasional subject will have two dreams with this topic. Note that here again, the consistency involves a reaction to the situation itself, and a reaction which is not idiosyncratic.

Introspective reports suggest that mental imagery shows a similar variability and constant flux in subjects who are awake and alert. Anyone can observe for himself how difficult it is to attend to a single thought or image for more than a few seconds, even when a strong effort is made to do so.

These observations suggest the speculation that imagery is always present in the human mind. Even when subjects are awakened from those deeper stages of sleep during which the connected series of images called dreams are less frequently reported, a high frequency of discrete images has been observed (see Chapter 6). Under waking conditions of minimal stimulation, this imagery is a flux with little or no repetition; when a person is trying to recall a fact or a name, or when trying to decide between courses of action, his imagery may show greater homogeneity from moment to moment and greater repetition.

Such imagery must of course be a consequence of activity in the central nervous system, activity which is always present during life. The flux of imagery under reduced stimulation is presumably associated not only wtih the flux of neural activity from spontaneous firing of neurones but also from the diverse stimulation originating in internal organs.

Such mental imagery is not directly observable behavior. While one may object to calling it behavior at all, one must grant that such a substrate would predispose the organism to showing variable overt behavior. If, in the relative absence of stimulation, imagery is highly variable, under similar conditions we should expect overt behavior to show marked variability. And this seems to be the case. For example, even under conditions with explicit stimuli but minimal structuring from instructions, such as a sentence completion test, very few responses are repeated on a second administration (Fiske, 1959).

In the preceding pages, we have considered the variability of responses within a fairly long time period, and have ignored the time between the compared responses, except in the case of successive responses. In the following material, we shall consider experiments involving arbitrarily fixed time intervals between responses. For experimental purposes, the interval is ordinarily in the order of days, so that the effects of the preceding presentations are minimized; for example, the subject is unlikely to recall his previous response. The conditions are those for what has been called Type I variability (Fiske and Rice, 1955): the same stimuli are presented under the same conditions on two or more occasions, with no feedback of information to the subject after a presentation. The only differences between the two occasions are the number of preceding presentations of the set of stimuli (0, 1, 2 . . .) and the current state of the organism, especially as affected by more or less recent stimulation. The primary source of data is the responses of human subjects to psychological "tests," although there have been a number of studies of variability in the responses of animals (Fiske and Rice, 1955). It is believed that the general principles found to hold for test responses are applicable to behavior in other situations.

VARIABILITY OF RESPONSES AS A FUNCTION OF THE STIMULUS AND SITUATION

Suppose a group of subjects responds to the same stimulus items on two occasions and we determine, for each item, the number of subjects who give different responses on the two occasions. It has been found repeatedly that this response variability will differ from item to item (for further discussion and specific references on this and subsequent points, see Fiske, 1957b). Just as this variability increases with the number of alternative responses that are permitted, so the mean of the subjects' variability scores increases as a function of the group's dispersion on a single trial: the greater the differences between the responses of different individuals, the greater the number of individuals changing their response from one trial to the next. We may conclude that the degree to which the potential responses of an individual are constrained by an item is a function of the degree to which the group distribution of responses is constrained. Whenever a set of factors restrict the group distribution, they are restricting the responses of the typical individual and hence they reduce the variability of his responses.

It is necessary to point out that this tendency is not an artifact. There can be different degrees of group dispersion with little or no changing of individual responses—on a biographical questionnaire, for example. Moreover, the association between mean response variability and group spread, while often high, is rarely perfect. Finally, the mean variability is always less than that expected on a statistical basis from pairs of observations randomly drawn from the group distribution, because each response is not independent of the subject making it. Insofar as there are reliable differences between the response tendencies of different individuals, there are constraints which affect each individual in addition to those which affect all individuals.

As might be expected, the mean response variability is also a function of general aspects of the situation. Both the nature of the task (Fiske, 1957b) and the structuring of the instructions are factors: it is obvious that word associations will be more variable under free conditions than when opposites are called for. For different tests, that is, different types of items and instructions, the proportion of responses showing changes varies from almost none to almost all. Relatively few responses are changed on multiple-choice intelligence tests (defining change here as giving the right response on one trial and a wrong response on the other). Jarrett (1948) reports about 3% and Glaser (1949) found 12%. Glaser also found 16% of changed responses on both an interests test and a personality test, a figure close to that reported by others. In free word associations, 35% are changed when stimuli are repeated within a single series, but up to 50% are changed when the series is repeated after an interval of 15 minutes with a different activity intervening (Howard and Fiske, 1961). About half of the responses given to inkblots are changed on a second testing. On sentence completion tests, 64 to 80% of responses have different manifest content (see Fiske, 1959, for detailed references).

The above findings show that variability is clearly a function of the number of alternative responses which fulfill the instructions and are acceptable to the subject. On an intelligence test, the subjects agree with the examiner that there is only one right answer.

On interest and personality tests, the number of alternatives is typically very small; even though a subject is told that "there are no right or wrong answers," he will usually find only one alternative that is close to his view of himself. The range of possible associations to an inkblot is limited only by such factors as the effort of the subject and the strictness of his criterion of resemblance between the stimulus and his percept. Responses to incomplete sentences are almost unlimited: the instruction to make a complete sentence imposes little constraint. Thus the average amount of variability appears to decrease as the test becomes more structured, as the requirements of the task impose more restrictions upon the number of responses acceptable to the subject.

The absence of perfect consistency of response is also evident in most experimental studies of learning. Perhaps the extreme of invariability is observed in the pecking of a pigeon in a Skinner box under severe food deprivation. Such a bird can be made to do nothing but peck for long periods of time. The only observed variation is in the rate or temporal spacing of the pecks: while the bird may peck at a steady rate for short spurts, there will usually be breaks in the rhythm from time to time.

In experiments requiring more complicated and longer responses, such as running a maze, a slightly lower degree of consistency is characteristic. The criterion for learning is not a long series of errorless trials, but rather is more likely to be 3 consecutive errorless trials, or perhaps 9 correct runs out of 10 consecutive trials. In studies of discrimination in monkeys, it is commonly observed that a monkey who has mastered a particular problem will, every now and then, make an incorrect response. Such responses can be interpreted as adaptive: the animal may have learned previously that the environment is not completely stable and that such a "wrong" response may actually lead to a reward of equal or greater value than that following the right response.

Up to this point, we have been concerned with the content and direction of responses. Before turning to variability as a function of the subject, let us consider briefly the low variability in the form or style of actions regardless of the function they serve. As compared to the variable content of behavior, the consistency of an individual's well-practiced, essentially automatic acts is remarkably high. This consistency, together with differences in physical structure, metabolism, and motivation, produce a striking degree of individuality, even idiosyncracy, in such acts. We frequently recognize a voice by a single word over the telephone, and we can often recognize a person at a distance more confidently by his gait, posture, or gestures than by his appearance. The uniqueness of a person's signature is so great that large sums of money are risked on it in cashing bank checks or traveler's checks. Thus it would appear that acts which are repeated many times and which are relatively unimportant in themselves, as compared to the end which they serve, manifest a very extreme degree of consistency over time. Regardless of the frequency with which a given response follows a particular stimulus, regardless of the motive involved, the form or style of that response may be very consistent when it does occur. Congruent with this notion is the suggestion that formal aspects of affective functioning may show considerable consistency over stimuli and over time (Engel and Rechenberg, 1961) in contrast to the high variability of content in projective protocols.

The individualized quality of a person's instrumental acts appears to be in the patterning of the act as a whole, rather than in the consistency of the specific physical dimensions of the act. A signature may be large or small as the space suggests, but it is still characteristic and readily identified. The consistency over time of the physical properties of responses is high but far from perfect. Rimoldi (1951) reports test-retest correlations over several weeks in the order of .80 for a large number of measures of personal tempo, such as rate of tapping, writing, or drawing. The mean coefficient of stability was .62 in the study by Talmadge (1958) of such measures as pressure and time for copying figures. It seems likely that the apparent consistency of an individual's behavior is based in large part upon the consistency of expressive movements and the highly idiosyncratic patterning in instrumental acts.

It should be noted that there is a kind of biological value in high consistency of form and style of movements. The adaptation of the organism to its environment is facilitated by having certain acts take the same form repeatedly. Because strong habits are more rapidly executed and are economical of energy, they make adaptive responses more efficient. The particular way in which a person performs such an act as writing a "5" is, however, only one of a large range of possible patterns, as is evident from comparing the writing of different people.

Whatever their form, these actions are in the service of the organism's goals. Insofar as they are instrumental to the attainment of these objectives, they are being utilized by the organism in its efforts to meet the requirements of a situation. Hence, as part of coping activity, their relatively high consistency can be interpreted in the same way as consistency in the aims of behavior.

INDIVIDUAL DIFFERENCES IN VARIABILITY OF RESPONSES

Not only are responses in some situations typically more variable over time than those in other situations, but the degree of variability in responses to a particular situation also varies with the subject. Holding constant the general conditions and the specific stimuli, we can observe dependable individual differences in variability of responses. In almost every study in which appropriate analyses have been made, it has been found that individuals who change many responses to one set of stimuli also change many responses to a parallel set, and individuals making many changes between one pair of trials also make many between other pairs of trials. (In psychometric terms, measures of response variability for individuals show reliability of two kinds: internal consistency within a set of stimuli or items and stability over time.)

In one intensive study (Fiske, 1957a), a group of 25 college students were paid to take a set of tests once a week for nine weeks. The tests were given at the same hour on the same day of the week (with a few unavoidable exceptions). The battery included a questionnaire, a self-rating scale, and two projective instruments. Reliabilities of the variability scores, estimated from scores computed for the odd and the even items, ranged from .96 for a measure of variability of manifest content on a sentence completion test to .46 for one of several 10-item scales from a personality inventory. For other illustrative results, see Mitra and Fiske (1956), and Osterweil and Fiske (1956).

Dependable individual differences in response variability have been found for a wide variety of psychological instruments. As compared with test responses, however, the variability of ratings of behavior in a group situation may have limited dependability (Fiske, 1960; van der Veen and Fiske, 1960). Since these ratings by peers and by self were by untrained observers, and since the ratings by peers confound the variability of the behavior of the subjects with the variability of the raters in making ratings, these data are only suggestive. Consistent individual differences in variation of reported affective states were obtained by Wessman, Ricks, and Tyl (1960), but here again, the variability of actual or "true" mood and the variability in the act of reporting cannot be separated.

How can we account for individual differences in response variability? Since the external situation is essentially constant, at least in the studies involving paper-and-pencil instruments, the differences must obviously come from internal factors. These would include the past experience of the subject and his present motivational state. Most important of all is the meaning of the stimuli and the situation to the subject. Generally speaking, meaningful conditions structure the situation for a subject: they constrain his behavior by making some responses more probable and others more improbable. Two types of meaningfulness can be distinguished: the significance of the specific content of the stimulus items, and the significance of the rest of the situation, including such aspects of the measuring procedure as the range of responses permitted.

A relationship between variability of responses and mean response (conventional level score) has been found in a number of studies (Fiske and Rice, 1955; Fiske, 1957b). For multiple-choice ability and achievement tests, Glaser's rationale (1950) seems appropriate: individuals tend to change their responses to items at or near their threshold, especially from right to wrong or from wrong to right. Subjects give consistent responses to items which are well above or well below their level of ability, but are more likely to vary their responses to items near that level. Thus if a test is very easy or very difficult for a subject, his responses to each item will be more consistent (in terms of their being right or wrong) than they will be when a test is of moderate difficulty and he is able to pass about as many items as he fails.

The concepts of threshold and difficulty are, however, inappropriate for personality measures and for overt behavior. The consistency of the responses is a positive function of the strength of the response tendency elicited by the conditions. Thus for middle to high ranges of strength of interest, Mitra and Fiske (1956) found that variability decreased with level score. For these same ranges, a similar relationship has been shown for ratings by self and by peers on personality traits as manifested in a group problem situation (Fiske, 1960; van der Veen and Fiske, 1960). Schweiker (1959) reports that familiarity with a career field is associated with stronger and more stable career preferences. (There seems to be a parallel between strength of a personality trait and extent of a skill when such an ability is measured in terms of approximation to some fixed value: in archery, consistency of performance is associated with accuracy over all levels of performance [Lashley, in Crozier and Hoagland, 1934].)

On measures of personality and interests, the relationship is frequently reversed for the lower range of level scores, that is, of the conventional scores assigned to subjects. It would seem that within this range, the lower the level score or mean response tendency, the stronger the tendency to avoid certain behavior or to dislike certain activities.

In addition to the meaning provided by item content, the situation may have other meaning or significance for the subject. In self-report data, the tendency to avoid or to select certain response classes is related to variability (Fiske, 1957b). A subject who avoids the extreme positions on a rating scale and a subject who avoids attributing characteristics (especially unfavorable ones) to himself tends to be more consistent on retest. Consistency has also been found to be related to the tendency to describe oneself in favorable, socially desirable terms, and to the tendency to give popular responses. Each of these tendencies seems to contribute to the strength of responses to the several stimulus items. It does not appear to matter whether the tendency is most clearly seen as one to make or to avoid certain kinds of responses. This view is supported by the additional finding that on bipolar scales such as Agree-Disagree and Like-Dislike, the tendency to use middle categories ("?", "Uncertain," etc.) is associated with low consistency, presumably because items are at the individual's threshold and his responses have lower strength. Once again, we see variability inversely related to response strength.

Thus consistency is related to the relative strength of whatever predominant response disposition is evoked in a subject by the situation. The degree of consistency is a function of the interaction between the subject and the situation. Given this interpretation, it is not surprising to find that a person's consistency of response is relatively specific to the particular situation and does not appear to be a trait that characterizes his behavior in general. To be sure, variability scores can be expected to be correlated to the extent that they are obtained by similar means. Tests will tend to yield correlated variability scores when they use the same technique for obtaining responses and therefore permit the same response sets (Fiske, 1957a). This specificity has the same origin as that for level scores: diverse measures of a personality trait typically show low intercorrelations unless the methods of measurement have something in common (see Campbell and Fiske, 1959).

AN INTERPRETATION OF RESPONSE VARIABILITY

We are proposing a single general interpretation for the response variability associated with subjects and that associated with situations. Just as response variability is reduced in situations which are structured so that the range of acceptable alternative responses is reduced and the probability of certain responses is increased, so the variability in a subject's responses will be relatively less when the total situation evokes some strong response dispositions in him and constrains him to avoid other possible responses. The stronger the response tendency that a stimulus situation elicits in a subject, the greater the probability that he will give the same response on the next occurrence of this situation.

At an earlier point in the discussion, we suggested that less variability was found in situations that were especially meaningful or significant for the subject. We must now qualify this notion. Consistency does not necessarily increase with level of interest or motivation, and consequent increases in level of activation or arousal. (See Chapter 2.) Certainly at extremely high levels, performance is disrupted and responses may be quite variable or fragmentary.

Coping Behavior

The stronger the tendency to select certain definite types of responses, for example, the stronger the disposition to portray oneself in a favorable light, the more consistent the responses. Consistency increases with the strength of the disposition which the individual takes toward a particular stimulus in a context, or toward a particular situation as a whole. But not all dispositions or sets toward a test are necessarily reflected in the selection of responses: thus a person annoyed by taking a test for the second time might mark his responses with great force, but still change as many responses as someone less irritated by the situation. So the disposition must be one which increases the strength of one or a very limited number of responses at the expense of alternative responses. Ordinarily, it increases the probability of a single response to a value considerably higher than that for any other response. It should be apparent that, in this context, the term "set" is used to refer to the disposition to deal with a situation in a particular way. More completely, a set is a tendency to have a stable perceptual reaction to a situation, a reaction which strengthens one or more response tendencies and weakens others. The degree of consistency or stability in a person's responses to a situation is a function of the extent to which the situation elicits coping behavior. As Maslow (1949) has indicated, coping behavior (as opposed to expressive behavior) is means behavior which is not an end in itself; it is purposive, it is designed to cause a change in the environment.

The concept of coping involves a molar level of behavioral analysis. Coping behavior is an act or a sequence of acts which is interpreted as motivated by a specific goal. In contrast, a particular instrumental act may occur in different sequences of behavior, serving different ends. Still another approach is the expressive side of behavior discussed below. An act may be purely expressive, or it may be instrumental but with expressive features.

This discussion reminds us once again that the classification of behavior by an investigator depends upon his purposes. The same behavior may be studied from several different approaches, each with its own classification scheme. The classification of a response as coping or otherwise involves a genotypical approach. Two successive responses may be phenotypically different but genotypically similar, and therefore variable or repetitive, depending on one's approach. Yet in the present context, the coping behavior manifested on two different occasions will usually have the same phenotypical form: since we are comparing the behavior of the same person in the same situation, it is to be expected that the same overt response will ordinarily be used to achieve a given end.

Every effort to cope with the environment does not necessarily lead to consistent responses. Such an effort will be consistent when it is effective to some degree, when it is more or less successful. In a situation with which an organism cannot cope immediately, variable behavior is ordinarily observed until one response is found to be effective and learning occurs.

Most of the coping behavior of human beings is learned rather than innate. It typically consists of responses that the organism has acquired from previous exposure to the given situation, or to other situations. While some situations can be essentially identical with ones previously experienced, the similarity is a matter of degree. This observation seems to hold for most situations outside the experimental laboratory, and perhaps even for the conditions in many experiments on learning. Hence, in the usual case, the coping response has not been acquired in situations identical with the current one, but rather it occurs because the organism generalizes over stimulus situations. Thus the individual differences in response variability observed in a given situation reflect not only differences in the degree to which the organism generalizes across situations but also differences in the strength of the response which was acquired in or is evoked by the other situation. The variability of naturally acquired responses seems to follow the same principles as those which are implied in empirical generalizations about responses acquired in experimental situations, a major difference between the two types of response being in the recency of acquistiion. (See Howard and Fiske, 1961.)

One concept which has been proposed to account for the reduced probability that an act will be repeated immediately is that of action decrement: "Any psychological action is followed by an action decrement—a lowered capacity for [immediate] rearousal of the same event" (Walker, 1958, p. 130). Walker offers evidence that such a decrement is present even in conditions producing learning, and that its strength may be associated with speed of learning. Since action decrement is viewed as dissipating over time, it is relevant only to response variability in situations where the compared responses occur within a matter of minutes or perhaps an hour or so. (See the discussion of this concept in Chapter 8.)

.

While successful coping behavior will have high consistency, not all consistent behavior copes successfully with the situation confronting the organism. Stereotyped or fixated behavior in response to an insoluble task may represent the most effective reaction of which the organism is capable. But fixated behavior is also increased with incidence of punishment (Maier, 1949). In human psychopathology, we can observe fixations of response which cope to some extent with the stimulus situation by reducing tension, but are not optimally adaptive.

We have come to the conclusion that behavior is consistent when the organism seeks to remedy some disruption in its interaction with its environment, provided the organism has available a response tendency which serves to cope to some degree with the requirements of the situation. The coping response is ordinarily one which has been acquired from past experience in this or similar situations.

But if adaptive behavior is typically consistent, why is behavior so variable? Of course behavior varies with the situation: a response which is adaptive in one situation may be inappropriate in another. Yet even when the situation is held constant, there may be greater or smaller degrees of variability in responses. In general, behavior is consistent to the extent required by the demands of the situation and not to any higher extent. We are proposing that the consistency of behavior is entirely a function of the organism's interaction with its environment. If a given stimulus situation upsets the ongoing interaction between the organism and its environment and if the organism has a response which will modify the interaction in an adaptive direction, he will tend to make that response whenever the particular situation occurs.

From this point of view, it follows that the consistency of an organism's behavior is a function of the temporal consistency of the environment in which it is placed. The more similar the various situations confronting the organism, the more consistent his behavior, provided that the situations elicit coping behavior. Behavior is variable except when the organism must repeat a coping response to a recurring situation.

But in addition to this consistency stemming from repetition of the same coping responses to the same or similar situations, there is the important fact that the average degree of consistency is a function of the demands of the environment. In certain situations, consistent responses are observed. In others, behavior is more or less variable. The average consistency of response in a group of organisms varies with the situation to some extent, since the demands of a situation tend to be similar for all organisms of a given kind. However, not only in human beings but also in animals, there are individual differences in the degree of consistency in any one situation. These are less apparent in situations that strongly restrict the range of potential coping responses but are clearly evident in less demanding situations.

From the relationship between consistency and the availability of coping responses, we can infer that there is a polarity to some characteristics of behavior (see Jones, 1958). Consider archery performance (as in the Lashley study mentioned above): while both good and poor archers try to hit the bull's-eye, good archers have a complex response or sequence of responses which is more appropriate to this goal. Similarly, a person who reacts to a self-report instrument by portraying himself in favorable terms can be seen as having a goal which he is capable of approximating more or less successfully. But subjects who are low on this tendency ordinarily do not have the opposite goal of describing themselves unfavorably; at most, they simply have a weak tendency to describe themselves favorably. Again, a subject who sees himself as contributing many useful ideas to a group discussion (van der Veen and Fiske, 1960) apparently perceives the situation as calling for such responses on his part. In contrast, a subject who sees himself as contributing few ideas rarely has a need to contribute little. We are suggesting that many conceptual aspects of behavior are variables which have a specific orientation. At high values, they direct or control behavior, while at low values, they have little effect. The word which identifies such a variable ordinarily refers to the high end. It is for these variables that consistency is positively related to level score, especially when the level score reflects the strength of the variable.

Expressive Tendencies

The same behavioral act can be studied from different points of view: a response to an ink-blot has its adaptive aspect, its verbal characteristics, its content, and its determinants in the focal stimulus itself. Some aspects of behavior are not intended to produce a specific change in the organism-environment interaction. When a subject is instructed to respond to an ink blot, he can cope with the situation by making almost any response. In this sense, any response copes, whatever its content or determinants, and subjects are consistent from one test to another.

Approaching the behavior from a different orientation, we can ask what expressive tendencies does he manifest in his responses. But such tendencies as the utilization of color or seeing movement produce no specific modification in the subject's coping with the situation, that is, in his interaction with the task and the stimuli: for example, it makes no difference in his relationship with the testing conditions whether he sees a "man" or a "man dancing." These tendencies are called expressive in Maslow's sense of the term (1949): they are determined by the state of the organism, are often uncontrolled and even uncontrollable, are typically ends in themselves, rather than motivations to effect ends. These expressive tendencies are likely to be positively related to variability rather than to consistency.

Preliminary work by the author suggests that this relationship holds for a number of aspects of responses to ink blots. Subjects were given 55 blots from Holtzman's series; the instructions called for one response per blot and the scoring utilized Holtzman's categories and specifications of levels. For each scoring category, variability was measured in terms of change in score from one response to the next, a measure which is very highly correlated with the variance of the subject's distribution of scores on the dimension. (It will be noted that here we are measuring variability across a set of different stimuli, not across trials for a single stimulus. Since the same set was administered to each subject, we can determine relative variability, given these particular conditions.) High positive correlations between variability and level score were found for color, movement, shading, human, animal, anxiety, and hostility.

For any one of these dimensions, low levels are often characterized by consistent absence of the tendency, whereas higher levels involve the manifestation of the disposition some of the time. This finding suggests that in any given situation, an action stemming from a strong expressive tendency is likely to be more variable over trials. Note that for such a dimension, the level score typically reflects relative frequency of acts which are characterized by the tendency.

We have seen that when one's approach to behavior involves a classification related to ways of coping with a situation, variability is inversely related to the strength of the predominant response tendency. On the other hand, when one categorizes behavior in appropriate situations in terms of types of expressive tendencies, variability may be directly related to the amount of the manifested tendency. These two approaches to behavior differ in another respect. The tendency to cope with a situation in a particular way not only produces responses which are consistent over time for a given item, but also produces responses which tend to be homogeneous across items. Thus consistency of response is associated with tendency to give popular responses in word association and several other types of test (Fiske, 1957b). But the disposition to give popular responses is itself consistent across stimuli. This disposition imposes a general constraint on responses to all the stimuli and thereby increases the consistency of responses.

In contrast, the expressive tendencies which are positively related to variability are typically less closely tied to a single stimulus or class of stimuli. A movement response can be made to any ink blot, or color response can be made to any blot with color, etc. It seems as if these tendencies are latent, and appear from time to time in unpredictable fashion (see Fiske, 1959). They are more a product of the organism's internal state than a reaction to the constraints and demands of stimuli.

At this point, we have our general interpretation of variability based on the extent to which the situation evokes successful coping responses from the organism and the additional observation that the variability of an expressive tendency increases with its strength. Do we need separate, opposing generalizations for these different approaches to behavior? Although this may turn out to be necessary, the available evidence does not require it. Let us consider a resolution.

If we present a subject with the same situation a number of times and observe a single aspect of his behavior, we will typically find minimal variability of that aspect when its strength or frequency is very high or very low, and maximum variability at some intermediate point. A rat which always or never turns left at a particular choice-point is completely consistent, as is a subject who always or never chooses the "Yes" alternative for an item. Both organisms would be more variable if they made the particular response only some of the time.

However, if we consider variability not in terms of a single aspect of behavior but rather in terms of the range of possible responses to a given stimulus, variability is a function of the relative strengths of the several available response tendencies for the given subject. For example, if an item has five response alternatives and a subject selects each one fifth of the time, the variability of his responses to that item will be maximum. If our subject selects the fourth alternative most of the time, he will show little variability. If he never selects this alternative, we cannot predict the extent of variability in his responses beyond saying that there will be less than in the first case when he gave this response as frequently as each of the other possibilities.

This discussion suggests the following comprehensive account: with respect to any one category or dimension of behavior, its variability will tend to be low when it is very frequent or very infrequent, very weak or very strong, and will have a maximum at some intermediate point; when responses are classified into a set of discrete qualitative categories, variability will be maximum when no one response predominates and will decrease with increasing strength of the strongest category.

The latter statement provides an interpretation for situations which tend to elicit coping behavior. However the former statement also holds for the particular coping response manifested by a subject. Since this statement is in terms of a single variable, it is the more appropriate interpretation for the variability of a single expressive tendency, which has been shown to increase with the strength of the tendency, at least for the low to moderate ranges which are commonly observed. It will be seen that the two statements in this broad formulation are quite consistent with each other. They simply deal with two different ways of looking at a set of behaviors.

The Consistency of Personality

In this review, we have considered the relative consistency of many aspects of behavior: instrumental acts, expressive acts, responses to specific stimuli, and ideation. We have argued that behavior is inherently variable. If an individual is confronted with a situation which constrains his behavior, he will, if he can, engage in coping behavior and will tend to repeat this behavior when that situation recurs. The actions which he takes to execute his coping responses will ordinarily be highly consistent. Much of the consistency of behavior can be interpreted as consistency of form or style of action and as consistency in the coping responses to recurring situations.

It may have seemed to some readers that our picture does not account for the high degree of apparent consistency of personality over time. In spite of phenotypical variability, there may be high consistency in behavior when viewed genotypically. A man may seek for decades to reach the top in his business or profession. A woman may seem concerned with nothing but being attractive to others. A person may be characterized as persistently dominating or assertive. In the clinic or hospital, a patient may be labeled as abnormally suspicious or as obsessed by some thought. Surely people must be consistent with respect to such outstanding characteristics and also with respect to their primary unresolved conflicts and the major themes of their lives.

While clinical and casual observation appear to demonstrate such consistency of major personality trends, there is little empirical work on which to base definite statements. (See Baldwin, 1942; Bolgar, 1954.) Two points can be made. Scores on some psychological tests have been found to be remarkably stable over periods in the order of 20 years (for example, E. L. Kelly, 1955; Strong, 1951). Since such scores are derived from responses to specific, structured items, they can be interpreted as evidence that the manner in which subjects cope with this particular type of situation is highly stable over time. In like fashion, it is probable that observed consistencies in everyday behavior are consistent responses to specific kinds of situations. The classification of situations on the basis of consistency of response may be different for different individuals, but the consistency is found across those situations which the individual sees as equivalent.

In the second place, the limited evidence concerning ideation or fantasy suggests considerable variability. Earlier in the chapter, the variability of content in dreams and in ideation under constant stimulation was pointed out. When the author compared TAT protocols taken months or years apart, considerable differences were frequently observed between two stories told in response to the same stimulus picture. Kagan (1959) found little stability in needs and press manifested in the TAT stories of children. The needs for achievement and for physical aggression, the two themes consistent over a three-year interval (8 to 11, or 11 to 14 years), were ones which had the highest frequency in the group as a whole.

In connection with this problem, two speculations suggest themselves. The apparent stability of a conflict or theme that is observed in the clinic can be seen as the patient's persistent efforts to handle a large and enduring situation, such as adjustment to his immediate family—efforts which must be continued because his responses are far from adequate. The problem is aggravated to the extent that his neurotic reactions become stereotyped. We would also suggest that the persistence of a major theme is a matter of degree: a person who is characterized as assertive is assertive only a small part of the time, namely, in interpersonal situations. Even there, he is typically assertive only toward some kinds of people, and only some of the time. Hence the major themes, the most salient and idiosyncratic tendencies in a person's behavior may be manifested in only a small proportion of his waking hours. It is quite possible that careful experimental observations with constant external conditions would show that such behavioral tendencies are actually more variable at high and obtrusive levels than at lower, more modal levels. Manifestations of anger, for example, occur relatively infrequently in any given situation, and a quick-tempered person is actually more variable in this respect than one who is rarely angry. Thus the attribution of a major theme or a strong disposition to a person may appropriately describe him in comparison with other people, and yet a careful analysis would reveal that the tendency, though recurring, was highly variable. The consistency of a behavior in a person may be negatively related to its identifiability or deviancy, even within a given situation.

The Functions of Variability

What functions are served by the inherent variability of behavior? Such variability is highly adaptive. The greater the range of available responses, the greater the likelihood that the organism will make and learn (that is, be more likely to repeat later) the response by which he can cope most adequately with a given situation. A response cannot be reinforced until it occurs.

Another function of variability can be inferred from the thinking of Brunswik (1943). After pointing out the lack of univocality of the relationships between distal and proximal stimulus variables, he goes on to say: "Survival and its sub-units, which may be defined as the establishment of stable interrelationships with the environment, are possible only if the organism is able to achieve compensatory balance in the face of comparative chaos within the physical environment. Ambiguity of cues and means relative to the vitally relevant objects and results must find its counterpart in an ambiguity and flexibility of the proximal-peripheral mediating processes in the organism" (1943, pp. 257-258). In other words, the organism cannot function like a machine. There cannot be one-to-one relationships between particular stimuli and particular responses. Flexibility in response tendencies is necessary for optimal adaptation by an organism which cannot be absolutely certain of the meaning of the cues it receives from its environment.

Variability in responses, especially to the same situation, also serves the function of increasing the impact of stimulation and thereby sustaining the organism's level of activation. The impact of an external situation on the organism is reduced as a function of the frequency and duration of past exposures to the same or similar situations (see Chapter 2). In similar fashion, the impact of the stimulation produced by a response is reduced as a function of the frequency and recency of previous occurrences of that response. Hence, even if an external situation recurs or continues, the organism can minimize the consequent reduction of impact by varying its response. Such a change in response not only produces different interoceptive stimulation but also may produce a change in the environment so that external stimuli are altered.

An external situation that elicits a coping reaction ordinarily has greater impact on an organism than one which does not. For this reason, the greater variability in responses to situations which elicit little or no coping tendency serves to increase the amount of impact and to sustain the level of activation.

The behavior of an organism is characterized by variability of responses whenever the organism is not coping fairly effectively with a particular situation. This disposition toward variability is valuable in maintaining the organism's level of activation and consequent readiness to act effectively and also in making possible the acquisition of new ways of coping with an uncertain and changing environment.

Chapter 12

Complexity - Simplicity as a Personality Variable in Cognitive and Preferential Behavior*

JAMES BIERI
Columbia University

*G*IVEN objectively equivalent stimulus conditions, two persons may manifest markedly different degrees of response versatility. For one tourist, a castle perched upon a hill is just another ruin, while for another it is a particular type of architectural style, situated in a strategic setting, and embodying the social and political structure of a certain period of history. What could explain these differences in response? Why is it that one person can bring to bear upon a task or respond to a stimulus with a greater variety of alternative responses than can another person? Most personality theorists and researchers have advanced constructs to explain such individual differences; it is possible to identify three classes of these constructs. It should be emphasized that these are not independent categories, and each bears certain relationships to the others.

First, *developmental* differences may be of importance. Such factors as age differences, differences in the rate of biological maturation, and differences in learning opportunities must be considered. The older person, for example, has the advantage of having had more time and opportunity to learn skills, to acquire understanding and awareness of more aspects of his environment, and to integrate these acquisitions into his cognitive system. In general, however,

---

*The writer wishes to express his gratitude for the assistance of Robin Lobeck and Harold Plotnick in the preparation of this chapter.

these developmental characteristics can be subsumed under the other two types of constructs to be discussed next.

We may apply the generic term *cognitive abilities* to characterize the second class of constructs which has been invoked to explain individual differences in capacity for response variability. The person's capacity for discriminating accurately between aspects of his environment, for responding to nuances in social and nonsocial stimulus situations, and for bringing to bear a wider variety of fruitful solutions to a problem are some of the characteristics involved under this very broad heading of ability. As such, these ability constructs are of broader scope than just *intelligence* as ordinarily conceived and measured by psychologists. Certain formulations have attempted to place intelligence within a broader context of cognitive functioning and relate performance on intelligence tests to underlying structural constructs. For example, the work of Kounin (1941) in studying response satiation in normal and mental-defective subjects is an attempt to relate intellectual-structural variables to behavioral variability. The recent work of Guilford (1956) on various modes of intellectual functioning is also of direct relevance to response variability, especially his conception of *spontaneous flexibility* in relation to convergent and divergent thinking.

Other workers have attempted to relate these cognitive ability functions to motivational states. These characteristics have been described in the terms of psychoanalytic ego psychology as relatively autonomous "ego functions," that is, those aspects of personality which account for the processes concerned with the cognition and perception of the external world. Thus Klein (1958) and his co-workers have studied various "cognitive controls" as personality styles which regulate the expression of needs in relation to environmental demands.

A third class of personality variables related to capacity for response variability has to do with *motivational* characteristics of the person. Thus, the person's tendency to respond to an array of stimuli must be considered in relation to the "stimulus value" of these cues for the organism. Personality theories have conceptualized this relationship between internal motive states and external stimuli in various ways. Thus, psychoanalysis has the construct of "cathexis" to help explain the more intense response to certain stimuli than to others. Murray (1938) has conceived of environmental "press" in relation to the person's needs, so that the nature and variety of the person's behavior must be understood in terms of the relationship between his needs and the cognate press impinging upon him. Similarly, Lewin's concept of "valence" and N. E. Miller's conceptualization of the *drive* properties of stimuli in learning theory (1959) are further attempts to relate the motive states of the organism to its propensity to respond differentially to external cues. At a more gross level of analysis, we speak about such variables when we consider the *interests* and *preferences* which individuals have in a variety of activities. It is apparent that such interests and preferences relate not only to the underlying motivational characteristics of the person but also to his ability characteristics as discussed above.

The focus in this chapter is upon the last two types of personality constructs, ability and motivational, in relation to response variability in human behavior. In particular, we will be concerned with a *structural* characteristic of the person's cognitive system, its *complexity*, which we assume affects his ability to respond differentially to the environment. In addition, we will consider the motivational states which dispose the person toward the preference for more complex stimuli.

THE CONCEPT OF COGNITIVE COMPLEXITY

The importance attributed to cognition in personality theories ranges across a broad spectrum. Anchored at the more purely cognitive end of the continuum are such approaches as G. A. Kelly's personal construct theory (1955). Here the attempt is to build a system which emphasizes both the processes used by the individual in construing others and the manner in which the various type of organizations of these "constructs" lead to either more or less efficient anticipation and prediction of the person's social environment. Motives as we ordinarily consider them are not given a major role in Kelly's system; rather, a master cognitive motive is considered crucial, that is, the tendency for the organism to move in the direction of better prediction of others' behavior. Kelly has devised a method for assessing these constructs, the Role Construct Repertory Test (Rep Test). The various uses of this test in studying cognitive complexity will be presented subsequently.

Somewhat further away from the extreme cognitive end of the continuum, we find the system of Lewin. While Lewin's field theory placed strong emphasis upon the situational and environmental forces acting upon the person, this was done within the context of the structure of the personality, a structure which emphasized the relative differentiation of various segments of personality. In his rather detailed discussion of this theoretical problem, Lewin (1951) points out that the structure of a cognitive system has two aspects, the *complexity of its units* and its *hierarchical organization*. Differentiation in terms of the relative complexity of the system is directly related by Lewin to differences in the *variety* of behavior manifested. Thus, in speaking of the increased differentiation of the child as he grows older, Lewin considers this to be reflected in the increased variety of behavior in terms of motor skills, language, emotions, needs, knowledge, and social behavior.

Two further aspects of this differentiation process are important in Lewin's presentation. First, as increased differentiation is developed, there is increasing *distance* between the self and the environment, a notion also represented in Piaget's work and in recent psychoanalytic writing concerning ego development. We shall find what appears to be supporting evidence for this process of separation of the self from the environment in some of the empirical studies to be presented. A second aspect of the differentiation process mentioned by Lewin is what he calls *simple dependence,* by which he means to suggest a "spreading" from one part of the system to another. As the system becomes more differentiated this spreading effect decreases, and a change in one part of the system should have less effect on the entire system.

In addition to the complexity or differentiation of a system, we may also speak of its organization. Here Lewin speaks of a more complicated interdependence of parts of the system, in which hierarchical relationships are involved. Thus, one region may exert controlling influence over another region which is not necessarily contiguous to it. This idea of hierarchically organized subsystems is kept distinct, by Lewin, from the degree of differentiation of the system. Exactly how to conceptualize the relationship between these two major characteristics of a cognitive system has yet to be established. It should be noted, however, that Kelly is attempting a similar theoretical conception when he speaks of the relationship between subordinate and superordinate constructs.

Cognitive complexity is a concept which is intended to reflect the relative differentiation of the person's construct system. It will be recalled that this system is presumed to mediate the perception of others and the anticipation of their behavior. The cognitively complex person is assumed to have available a greater number of personal constructs to construe the behavior of others, while the cognitively simple person has available relatively few personal constructs. While this notion of cognitive complexity-simplicity is akin to Lewin's concept of degree of differentiation discussed above, a major difference should be pointed out. Lewin is concerned with a conception covering the whole range of human behavior, and discusses differentiation in terms of its effects upon many types of behavioral manifestations other than social behavior. In spite of this, both differentiation and cognitive complexity are constructs designed to cover similar behavioral phenomena. Thus it would be expected that the more complex or differentiated person would be more versatile in his response repertory in his social relations. Further, complexity implies that the person is capable of making finer discriminations between aspects of the social environment.

Cognitive complexity is associated with styles of response which have been studied by others. These cognitive or response modes all suggest cognitive processes characterized by the tendency to make finer discriminations in perception. In this regard, we may cite Klein's concepts of leveling and sharpening (1958), Mednick's finding of individual differences in stimulus generalization tendencies (1955), the work on repressors and sensitizers (Gordon, 1957), and the work by Pettigrew (1958) and by Wallach and Caron (1959) on categorizing style. It should be noted that while most of these workers stress the perceptual discrimination modes of response among their subjects, response variability is inherent in the behavioral differences they study: levelers maintain an earlier discrimination response, overgeneralizers fail to respond differently to a new stimulus configuration, and repressors tend to ignore different stimulus elements in a situation. While these various concepts appear to be related, the nature of their interrelationships is as yet unclear. Not only do they spring from such diverse theoretical systems as psychoanalytic ego psychology and learning theory, but their exact empirical measurement is yet to be attained. However, by a more detailed analysis of the research studies of cognitive complexity, we can perhaps begin to formulate more clearly some of these empirical and theoretical interrelationships.

STUDIES OF COGNITIVE COMPLEXITY

Because cognitive complexity is a measure of the degree of differentiation in the cognitive system for perceiving others, it is not surprising that the majority of studies using this concept have been concerned with various aspects of interpersonal or social behavior. In particular, cognitive complexity has been studied in relation to accuracy or effectiveness in predicting others' behavior, in relation to the tendency to perceive similarities or differences between oneself and others, and in terms of changes in attitudes and in impressions of others. Part of the difficulty in integrating the findings of these studies is to be found in the lack of common methods of measuring cognitive complexity. While this empirical heterogeneity may have certain advantages in terms of a multimethod approach (Campbell and Fiske, 1959), relatively little has been done to interrelate these diverse measurement approaches in order to determine to what extent they are measuring the same variable. We are, then, at only a beginning phase in terms of adequately assessing cognitive complexity.

The initial study using the concept of cognitive complexity (Bieri, 1955) stemmed directly from Kelly's theory of personal constructs and employed a complexity measure using the Rep Test. Because this measure has been central in many subsequent studies, a brief description of it is presented here. More detailed discussion of its use in diagnosis and research is given by Kelly (1955). Kelly's system for assessing personal constructs assumes a *triadic* process of concept formation, on which the form of his test is based. The subject is asked to list a series of individuals known to him personally, each of whom fits a role description provided by the examiner. These role descriptions sample a number of persons who are important in the life of the subject, such as mother, father, self, siblings, close friends, and spouse. The names of the persons fitting these role descriptions are entered by him along the top of a grid or matrix. He is then asked to consider three of these persons at a time in a series of triads selected by the examiner. The conceptual task given to the subject is to consider in what way two of these persons are alike in some important personal characteristics and different from the third in this respect. Thus, in a triad of the mother, father, and self, he may sort himself and his father as "dominant," and characterize the mother as relatively more "submissive." In this manner, a sequence of constructs is generated. On each sort, the subject checks the spaces in the grid under the columns headed by the names of the two persons whom he considers alike, and the name of the construct is entered next to the grid.

After all the sorts have been completed, the subject is asked to go through each construct row of the grid again and to check all the other persons, in addition to the two already checked, to whom he considers that construct also applies. No limit is put upon the number of checks a person may place in any construct row. This method results in a matrix of check patterns which represents how he perceives and differentiates a group of significant others relative to his own personal constructs. By considering how similar each construct row is to every other construct row in terms of the check patterns generated by the subject, a measure of the degree of differentiation among these constructs may be obtained. If two construct rows have identical check patterns, they are assumed to be functionally equivalent regardless of the verbal labels given these constructs. If the subject has many construct rows with highly similar check patterns, he is considered to have low cognitive complexity, or to be cognitively simple. Conversely, if he has a matrix in which the construct rows have check patterns markedly different from one another, then he is high in cognitive complexity. By weighting numerically the similarity of each row's check pattern with the check patterns in the other rows, a quantitative index of cognitive complexity is obtained.

The consistency of such a complexity measure over time has been determined by the writer: in two studies, the test-retest reliability coefficients were .78 and .82, respectively. Further evidence (Hunt, 1951) indicates a high degree of consistency in constructs formed by subjects over long time intervals. It should be mentioned that

in those studies in which the relationship between cognitive complexity and verbal intelligence has been analyzed, no significant
relationship has been found.

Predictive Behavior and Cognitive Complexity

In the first study on this measure of cognitive complexity,
the writer (1955) made two general predictions. The first of these
was that there should be a significant positive relationship between
degree of cognitive complexity and accuracy of predictive behavior.
The assumption underlying this prediction was that the person with
more variability in his perceptions of others would more likely have
available those perceptions which would provide an accurate appraisal of another's behavior. The second general prediction was
that there would be a significant negative relationship between degree
of cognitive complexity and the tendency, in one's predictive behavior, to engage in assimilative projection, that is, to emphasize
similarities in behavior between oneself and others. This prediction
rests upon the assumption that assimilative projection reflects the
cognitively more simple individual's lack of ability to discriminate
between others. For the predictive instrument, each of the 34 college
students in this study was asked to complete a Situations Questionnaire in which four response alternatives were provided for each
of the social situations. In addition, each subject had to predict the
responses of two classmates known to him who had also completed
the questionnaire. Predictive accuracy scores were obtained by summing the correct number of predictions he made for both persons he
predicted. An assimilative projection score was obtained for each
subject by totaling the number of accurate and inaccurate predictions which were identical to the responses given by the person
himself.

The results for the first prediction indicated that cognitive complexity did have a low but significant positive relationship with predictive accuracy. However, when the two component scores subsumed under predictive accuracy were considered separately, it was
found that cognitive complexity was not related ($r = .02$) to accurate
projection (that is, correctly predicting the other's response to be
the same as one's own), but was significantly related ($r = .35$)
to the other component, accurate perceived differences. Thus it ap-

peared that cognitive complexity might relate more to the accurate prediction of *differences* between oneself and others rather than to the accurate prediction of similarities.

The second prediction of this study was supported by the finding that cognitive complexity had a significant negative correlation with assimilative projection. Of the two components of assimilative projection, the tendency of cognitively simple persons to perceive unwarranted or inaccurate similarities between themselves and others was shown to make the major contribution to this relationship to complexity. The over-all results of this study, while supporting the relationship between complexity and predictive accuracy, also suggested that complex and simple subjects have differing modes of perception. Complex persons appear to stress the differences between themselves and others in their predictions. The cognitively simple subjects emphasized similarities, a tendency leading to unwarranted assumptions of similarity between oneself and others, perhaps reflecting the lack of that differentiation ability presumed to be measured by the complexity measure.

In a subsequent study investigating similar variables, Leventhal (1957) was concerned not only with the relationship between judges' cognitive complexity and predictive accuracy but also with the effects of the complexity of the objects being predicted and of varying amounts of stimulus information. With a total group of 253 male undergraduates, Leventhal employed the Rep Test procedures for measuring complexity that were used by Bieri (1955) and outlined above. A rather complicated design was used in which cognitively simple or complex judges made predictions about tape recorded interviews involving complex or simple interviewees.

In an attempt to reduce the effects of stereotyped accuracy in the predictions, Leventhal weighted his accuracy measure (based on a 38-item questionnaire) so that more popular responses and predictions would receive less weight. Complex judges tended to be more accurate than simple judges when the accuracy measure was weighted, but this relationship did not reach significance ($p < .10$). Furthermore, simple judges predicted significantly greater similarity between the interviewee's responses and their own responses than did complex judges. While simple judges were more accurate in predicting similarities, complex judges were more accurate in predicting differences (neither relationship was significant). These results tend to be consistent with those of Bieri (1955) reported above, both in terms of the relationship between cognitive complexity and predictive accuracy and in terms of the tendency for more complex judges to emphasize differences between themselves and others while simple judges emphasize similarities.

In a comprehensive assessment study which included an analysis of the predictive behavior of 129 social work graduate students, Plotnick (1961) has found evidence for a relationship between cognitive complexity and the ability to differentiate accurately between the behaviors of others. Using the Rep Test check-pattern system for measuring cognitive complexity, Plotnick had his subjects predict the attitude responses, on an acceptance of authority scale, made by three mental hygiene clinic clients; the three were respectively, high, medium, and low in terms of accepting authority. Complexity scores were found to be independent of the subjects' own authority scores. Cognitive complexity correlated positively with ability to predict accurately the two clients with low and medium degrees of acceptance of authority attitudes, the relationship being significant only for that client with a medium level of authority attitudes. For the client with high acceptance of authority attitudes, an insignificant negative relationship between accuracy and cognitive complexity was obtained. In this regard, Plotnick found that high complexity subjects predicted mean authority attitude scores which correctly differentiated the three clients in terms of the rank order of the clients' actual attitude scores. Low complexity persons, however, predicted the medium attitude client to be as low as the low attitude client.

Differences in predictive accuracy became more apparent when persons high on both complexity and intelligence (combined vocabulary and mathematics) are compared with those low on both these variables. The high complexity and high intelligence subjects had higher mean accuracy scores for all three clients than the low complexity and low intelligence subjects, two of these three mean differences being significant.

In a recent study relating to this same problem, Sechrest and Jackson (1961) have taken further steps to solve measurement problems in accuracy measures. In addition to an accuracy measure similar to that used by Bieri (1955) and Leventhal (1957), which

Sechrest and Jackson call "biased" accuracy, the latter writers developed a measure of "differential" accuracy which was intended to eliminate possible response sets in the biased accuracy measure. These accuracy measures were correlated with four measures of cognitive complexity: (a) the method developed by Bieri (1955) using the Rep Test; (b) the method of Bieri and Blacker (1956) for assessing number of determinants in ink blot responses; (c) the Barron-Welsh Art Scale; and (d) a measure of the complexity of stimuli afforded by one's family background. In addition, a measure of social intelligence based upon peer ratings was devised by Sechrest and Jackson.

All four complexity measures correlated positively with social intelligence, although these relationships were significant only for the art preference and family background complexity measures. A total complexity score was obtained by weighting each of the four complexity measures proportionally to their standard deviations and summing the individual scores across the four measures. This total complexity score correlated .54 (p<.01) with the social intelligence measure. In line with the results of Bieri (1955) and Leventhal (1957), the complexity measure derived from the Rep Test did relate positively to the biased accuracy measure ($r = .22$), but this relationship was not significant. The differential accuracy measure did not correlate significantly with any of the measures of complexity or with social intelligence.

In a study which broadens the scope of predictive accuracy, Ehart (1957) has approached the problem of the relationship between cognitive complexity and effectiveness as a teacher. She considers that cognitive complexity-simplicity should manifest itself in the tendency to differentiate pupils on personality traits, the tendency to associate traits in describing pupils, the tendency to describe pupils in evaluative terms, and the tendency to withhold judgment in rating pupils on traits. Comparing extreme groups of effective and ineffective student teachers who had made ratings of ten pupils on a personality rating scale, Ehart found that more effective teachers tended to withhold judgments and, contrary to her expectations, tended to be more evaluative in their judgments. The subjects who tended to differentiate pupils on traits also tended to associate traits and to make evaluative judgments. This study is noteworthy in that evidence is presented linking the degree of differentiation in one's perceptions of others with the degree to which these perceptions are organized.

Behavior Change and Cognitive Complexity

Several studies have been concerned with the relationship between behavior *change* and cognitive complexity. In the study noted above, Leventhal (1957) also was concerned with the effects of varying amounts of information on the judgments of simple and complex subjects. When more information was available, simple persons tended to improve their predictions more than complex persons, particularly in relation to the accurate prediction of differences. Leventhal suggests that the increased amount of information, because it included self-description material, served to correct the simple judges' tendency not to differentiate between self and other.

Mayo (1959) has presented results from a study in which she analyzed the relationship between cognitive complexity and the resolution of contradictory information in forming an impression. Her major hypotheses were that persons with high cognitive complexity would form less univalent impressions of others on the basis of limited information and would show less change in that impression upon the addition of conflict-producing information than would persons of low cognitive complexity. Mayo used a modification of the Rep Test complexity measure in which subjects generated as many constructs from each triad as possible, with the number of verbal constructs generated being the index of complexity. From an over-all group of 80 subjects, the upper and lower extremes in complexity were selected for the experimental treatment. These groups were matched for sex and intelligence. Mayo's results are in line with her predictions. Low complexity subjects changed their impressions significantly more than did high complexity subjects when presented with contradictory information, presumably because of the more univalent initial impressions of low complexity persons. However, direct comparisons of initial impressions were not reported.

In contrast, Lundy and Berkowitz (1957) predicted that high complexity persons would probably manifest more attitude change than would low complexity persons. They reasoned that new information must have relevance for existing constructs in order that it be seen in a new light. Subjects were administered attitude scales in three content areas before and after being given information regarding the attitudes of presumably influential others. Using the Rep Test method of comparing check patterns, Lundy and Berkowitz did an analysis of variance comparing level of cognitive complexity for four groups based on type of attitude change. An F value significant at the .05 level was obtained. While they found least change with those who were most simple, the most complex subjects were characterized by *negative* change, that is, they increased the level of their original attitudes. Those who were neither extremely simple nor complex included those who were variable in change on the different subtests, as well as those who were consistently susceptible to change.

Probability Preferences and Cognitive Complexity

In addition to the need for more empirical research to clarify the relationship between behavior changes and cognitive complexity, it is apparent that problems of theory must be more adequately resolved. The more complex individual may or may not vary his behavior when presented with new stimulus information about a previously judged person or issue. Such factors as the nature of the original judgment, the relationship of the new information to the original information (for example, complementary versus contradictory), and the nature of the over-all judgment situation must be taken into account. Certainly, one key factor could be the degree of *probability* attached by a person to his judgment. Thus it is reasonable that a more complex individual may attach different levels of certainty to his judgments than a more simple individual.

Higgins (1959) has conducted an initial investigation into this problem in a study relating cognitive complexity to probability preferences. If the more complex person is able to respond with more sensitivity to the nuances of his environment, Higgins reasoned that he should be more reluctant to advance extreme or definitive solutions to events involving indeterminant probabilities. Probability estimates were made by subjects on a series of items concerning events whose frequency of occurrence was unknown to them. Confidence ratings of these estimates were also made. He predicted that cognitive complexity should be related to the preference for *moderate* probability preferences and to the expression of *less* confidence in these judgments. A modified version of the Rep Test was used in deriving a measure of cognitive complexity. In place of the usual persons to be sorted, Higgins presented triads from six activity or value concepts: social service, science, religion, business, politics, and the arts. The measure of complexity was the number of different verbal constructs generated, a measure previously employed by Bieri and Blacker (1956). The major findings of this study strikingly support the predictions that were made. Thus, cognitive complexity was significantly correlated with both moderate probability preferences and lower confidence ratings ($r = .70$ and $.57$, respectively). These results are the more striking because of the insignificant relationship between probability preferences and confidence ratings. Higgins also calculated the tendency for subjects to be variable in terms of which value concept they sorted as "different" from the two which were alike, and found a significant correlation with cognitive complexity. For cognitively simple persons, the same concept is more repeatedly chosen as different in a variety of triads. It was noted that complex persons tended to single out religion and the arts more in their concept formation, suggesting that these two areas are perhaps more salient for them. Also, Higgins reports that females were significantly more complex than males in his sample, a relationship that has not received attention in other studies.

The Assessment of Cognitive Complexity

The use of value concepts instead of persons in Higgins' complexity measure raises the issue of the *generality* of cognitive complexity across different stimulus realms. This problem has been studied by Bieri and Blacker (1956) and involves both a theoretical and a methodological issue. The methodological aspect of this problem is the question as to whether a concept such as cognitive complexity can be assessed by more than one empirical measure. If not, it is likely that whatever is being measured is markedly affected by so-called method variance. Theoretically, the issue is whether the cognitive system of the individual is characterized by relatively enduring modes of cognitive schematization manifested in consistencies in conceptual behavior across stimulus situations, or whether these cognitive styles must be delimited in terms of the specific stimuli present.

Genetic considerations suggest two major types of stimulus situations, one that deals primarily with the nonhuman environment, and one that deals primarily with the social environment. Thus Piaget's discussion (1954) of the development of *schemata* relates to the cognitive development of children particularly in terms of the perception of the physical environment. Psychoanalytic theory, especially as modified by Sullivan, places emphasis upon various cognitive stages of development which have particular relevance to interpersonal relations. However these cognitive patterns of development are conceptualized in theory, we assumed that these patterns are to some extent trans-situational in terms of the particular realm of stimuli involved. Hence this study was concerned with degree of generality between the complexity of the individual's cognitive system in the perception of people and that in the perception of nonpersonal stimuli. To assess complexity in the latter realm, a modification of the Rorschach ink blot test was used, in which complexity was equated with response variability in the content and the determinants of responses. The Rep Test measure of cognitive complexity was the number of different *verbal* constructs elicited, a procedure subsequently used in the work of Mayo (1959), Higgins (1959), and Ehart (1957).

For four different indices of determinant variability and two different measures of content variability, significant correlations (ranging in magnitude from .27 to .50) were obtained on all indices with the measure of cognitive complexity. Interestingly enough, the only Rorschach determinant that correlated significantly with cognitive complexity was M, the human movement response. These findings suggest that some degree of generality in the complexity of behavior can be demonstrated for two perceptual tasks involving personal and nonpersonal stimuli.

In another study designed to determine the relationship between cognitive complexity and Rorschach performance, Bieri and Messerley (1957) predicted that subjects with a predominantly introversive experience balance on a modified Rorschach would have higher complexity scores than those with a predominantly extratensive experience balance. On two different samples of female subjects, significant differences in complexity scores were obtained in the direction *opposite* from that predicted, that is, extratensive persons were higher in complexity than introversive persons. These results appear to run counter to those reported above for the study by Bieri and Blacker, in which M production on the ink blots was associated with cognitive complexity for their all-male group. However, a subsequent study by Bieri, Bradburn, and Galinsky (1958) indicates that M production on the Rorschach may indeed reflect different cognitive functions in men and women.

A final area of research is concerned with alternative methods for the measurement of cognitive complexity. Most of the studies described above have either used the method of comparing similarity between check patterns on the Rep Test, or have used a measure of the degree of verbal or semantic similarity between the constructs generated on the Rep Test. Kelly (1955) has suggested a sort of nonparametric factor analysis method for measuring the relative factorial complexity of a Rep Test protocol. Utilizing the Thurstone multiple group method of factor analysis, Levy and Dugan (1956) have described how the Rep Test matrix of an individual may be considered in terms of its factorial complexity. Complexity may be equivalent to the number of factors derived from a given protocol. Further, one could perhaps approach the problem of the *organization* of the cognitive system by an analysis of the number of constructs having significant loadings on a given factor. Thus, Levy and Dugan suggest that the larger the number of constructs significantly loaded on a given factor, the more important that construct dimension is for the individual.

Another possible method for measuring cognitive complexity is advanced by Hutchins and Fiedler (1958), who analyzed two social perception scores in relation to a group's relative acceptance of the group leader. One component of the assumed similarity scores with which they were dealing indicated the diversity of the perceptions of the other and reflected the magnitude of person-by-item interaction variance scores. Considering this measure to be conceptually analogous to cognitive complexity, Hutchins and Fiedler report that formal group leaders who were accepted in both leadership and therapeutic roles had greater perceptual complexity. They conclude that the leader whose perceptual schema is complex is better able, in the eyes of his co-workers, to handle the conflicting roles of task-oriented leader and therapeutic figure than is the leader who is not aware of trait variations within his individual group members.

From the diversity of the studies reported above, it is apparent that cognitive complexity has been considered by researchers to be a possible explanatory concept related to a wide range of behavioral manifestations. As such, its heuristic value seems to be demonstrated. It is perhaps equally apparent that unambiguous conclusions are not forthcoming from these studies. However, the total impression left by this review of investigations should encourage further research with this variable. At this juncture, perhaps most crucial from a methodological viewpoint is the need for more careful assessment of the comparability of various methods for measuring cognitive complexity. The essential requirement of such methods is that they contain a finite set of stimulus elements permitting variable discrimination responses that can be judged in terms of their relative similarity or dissimilarity.

As a theoretical construct, cognitive complexity needs to be more critically developed in at least three aspects. First, more careful consideration must be given to its generality beyond the realm of the perception of people. More precise conceptualization, for example, may be needed in relating complexity of response in social and nonsocial stimulus situations. Second, it is unclear whether cognitive complexity is a differentiation concept exclusively, or whether it relates to organizational properties of the cognitive system as well. Methods of assessing these organizational properties certainly seem more difficult to develop. Finally, we must deal with the problem of whether cognitive complexity as one characteristic of the structure of the underlying cognitive system is necessarily equivalent to behavior tendencies which produce variability in response. Stated differently, we may ask to what extent the same behaviorial measure of complexity may represent in different persons differing interactions of cognitive structural characteristics and transitory or pervasive motive states. For example, the relationship between cognitive complexity and the tendency to perceive differences between oneself and others suggests such an amalgam of cognitive and motivational characteristics. As one illustration, Lundy (1956) found that, following social interaction, the same subjects showed more projective assimilation in their perception of the other when their interest during interaction had been on revealing themselves to the other, and more self-other differentiation when their interest had been on finding out about the other. Certainly, future empirical studies cannot ignore a more searching analysis of these and other theoretical problems.

THE PREFERENCE FOR COMPLEXITY

Another approach to the study of behavior variability deals with those motivational characteristics of the personality which dispose the individual to select out, choose, or prefer stimulus situations characterized by greater lack of structure, more ambiguity, and less balance or symmetry. The attempt here is not to define or isolate one personality attribute which reflects this tendency but rather to bring to bear a more multidimensional analysis of those factors which interact to result in the preference for more complex stimuli. An example of the pitfalls encountered in assuming a more unidimensional approach to this problem can be found in the work on tolerance for ambiguity, growing in large measure out of the work on the authoritarian personality. Researchers assumed an underlying trait of rigidity, or intolerance for ambiguity, and proceeded to develop tests to measure this variable. The result of this labor was that each method for assessing rigidity was relatively independent of the others, and the search for a common underlying dimension of personality came to naught.

Perhaps a more fruitful approach is exemplified in the series of studies, reviewed below, concerning the preference for complex stimuli. Such preferential behavior can be viewed as the result of different motivational factors interacting within the personality; we can deal not with a trait or disposition as such, but rather with a response tendency reflecting a variety of dispositional characteristics of the person. This analysis of the problem recalls the previous discussion of cognitive complexity as a response measure which perhaps reflects other underlying cognitive structural characteristics in addition to differentiation, and which may also have certain motivational concomitants.

As in so much psychological research, the development of the concept of preference for artistic complexity evolved from origins not immediately recognizable from the current scene. Welsh (1949) was originally concerned with the development of a figure preference test which would discriminate between groups with various psychiatric diagnoses. Three hundred ruled or freehand line drawings were constructed and given to 64 patients and 79 normals, with instructions to sort these drawings according to those which were liked and those disliked. A factor analysis of the sorts indicated that most of the variance in this choice task was accounted for by a general acceptance or rejection factor, and by a tendency to sort in terms of either the simple-symmetrical or complex-asymmetrical qualities of the drawings. It was observed that artists in both the patient and normal groups preferred the complex figures, and that those subjects preferring simple symmetrical drawings were judged to be more conservative, conventional, organized, and optimistic personalities, while those preferring complex-asymmetrical drawings were considered to be more antisocial, psychopathic, creative, with more "good taste." In a subsequent study, Barron and Welsh (1952) were concerned with the further development of the preference test in terms of its ability to discriminate between artists and nonartists. With another 100 items added, the test was administered to a group of 37 artists and 150 nonartists. On the basis of an item analysis, they made a new scale, the Barron-Welsh Art Scale, which contained the 40 items disliked (.01 significance level) more frequently by artists than nonartists, and 25 items liked (.05 significance level) more by artists than by nonartists. The 40 items disliked by the artists were all simple-symmetrical drawings while most of the 25 items liked more by artists were complex-asymmetrical. Weighting complex items higher than simple items, the over-all scores obtained on this test separated the original groups of artists and nonartists at the .0001 level of significance. When administered to new samples of 30 artists and 30 nonartists, this scale discriminated between these groups below the .001 level of significance. The odd-even reliability of the Barron-Welsh Art Scale on a group of 80 nonartists was .96.

Personality Correlates of Preference for Complexity

At this point, then, a scale had been developed which discriminated significantly between artists and nonartists, but the question remained as to whether preferences were more related to aesthetic appreciation of art composition or to underlying personality characteristics.

To explore this problem in more detail, Barron (1952) studied

a group of graduate students, of whom 20 had been rated by faculty
as high in originality, personal soundness, and potential success,
and 20 had been rated low on these characteristics. Although these
subjects' scores on the Art Scale were distributed bimodally, this
distribution did not correspond to the initial discrimination of the
groups on the basis of originality and potential success. Barron
then selected the 18 subjects with the highest scores and the 18
subjects with the lowest scores, two groups which were separated
by a 20-point gap in scores. These persons were given 105 reproduc-
tions of paintings by European artists, and asked to sort these in four
piles from most to least liked. It was found that those with high
scores on the Barron-Welsh Art Scale preferred modern abstractions,
nudes, primitivism, expressionism, impressionism, and cubism, while
low-scoring subjects preferred formal portraits of nobility, religious
themes, and landscapes. In their responses to the Gough adjective
checklist, the highs more often checked such items as gloomy, unstable, bitter, cool, dissatisfied, pessimistic, emotional, and pleasure-
seeking, while lows more frequently checked contented, gentle, conservative, unaffected, patient, and peaceable.

In a further attempt to relate preference on the Art Scale to personality variables, Barron (1953a) hypothesized that the person who
prefers complex figures is an oral character with feminine tendencies.
He conjectured that such a person has had an early complicated
relationship to the maternal source of supply and comes to view
his environment as complex and problematic, to be mastered without
the aid of repression or dependence on the environment. With subjects choosing the preferred drawing from randomly paired complex
and simple figures, a number of personality characteristics appeared
to differentiate complex and simple subjects on the Barron-Welsh
Art Scale. These could be grouped into four general categories.
The first of these might be called feminine-aesthetic, and included the
following characteristics for complex persons: a high rating on
effeminacy; low masculinity on the Strong Vocational Interest Blank;
and high scores on artistic good taste measures.

A second set of personality characteristics could be labelled *ex-
pansive-impulsive-unrepressed*. The complex person was rated as
having high personal tempo, verbal fluency, and impulsiveness; he
had higher scores on the MMPI scales of schizophrenia, psychopathic

deviate, and anxiety; and he characterized himself on the Gough adjective checklist as more gloomy, pleasure-seeking, spendthrift, pessimistic, dissatisfied, and demanding. The simple person was rated as being more constricted and rigid; he had higher scores on the MMPI hysteria scale; and on the checklist he described himself as more contented, gentle, timid, serious, thrifty, dreamy, and stable.

A third personality configuration, *independent-nonconforming-original*, was characterized by the preference of the complex person for modern, primitive, and unstructured art; by low political-economic conservatism scores; and by high ratings on originality. Particularly important in this configuration of dispositions is the finding that preference for complex drawings is related to independence of judgment. Barron (1953b) has found that subjects who were "independents" in the Asch judgment situation, that is, did not yield to the group pressure to respond incorrectly as most other group members did in a perceptual discrimination task, had significantly higher scores reflecting preference for complex drawings than did those who were "yielders" in the Asch situation. In this regard, it is to be noted that the adjectives with which independent subjects described themselves, such as artistic and original, reflect qualities which in other samples have been related to the preference for complex drawings.

A fourth set of personality characteristics discriminating between complex and simple figure preference we shall term *unadjusted-distrustful*. Particularly discriminating here were the adjective checklist responses of unstable, dissatisfied, and temperamental for those who preferred complex figures, in contrast to responsible, stable, and foresighted for those preferring simple figures.

Further evidence for the relationship between one of these four clusters, independence, and the preference for complexity is provided by a study done by Bieri, Bradburn, and Galinsky (1958). The Barron-Welsh Art Scale was administered with a variety of other cognitive tasks to groups of 50 male and 60 female subjects. One of the tasks, the Embedded Figures Test, has been found to reflect a personality disposition called field-dependence (Witkin, Lewis, Hertzman, Machover, Meissner, and Wapner, 1954). Persons who are field-dependent (that is, whose perception is greatly affected by stimulus field-forces) have difficulty in discerning a simple figure embedded in a complex field; more field-independent subjects quickly perceive the figure. A significant relationship was found by Bieri, Bradburn, and Galinsky between the preference for complex drawings and field-independence for the male subjects, while no relationship was found between these variables for females. Here again, we find evidence suggesting caution in the generalization of findings across sexes in relation to cognitive behavior. The fact that much of the work is likely to have been done with samples of one sex, usually males, underscores this caution.

A somewhat different perspective upon the personality correlates of preference for complexity is provided by the study of Sechrest and Jackson, described above. While they found no relationship between predictive accuracy and preference for complexity on the Barron-Welsh Art Scale, they did find a significant positive correlation between complexity preference and a measure of social intelligence. This measure of social intelligence was independent of academic intelligence in their sample of student nurses. In addition, social intelligence correlated very significantly with sociometric judgments that the person was typical of the group, most pleasant in the group, and the best nurse. Such characteristics appear to be somewhat contradictory to Barron's findings that the more complex person may be more deviant and antisocial. Again, it should be borne in mind that the sex differences in these studies may be crucial, and that for women, personality characteristics related to complexity preference are more typical of the feminine role. In terms of the possible developmental determinants of complexity preference, Sechrest and Jackson entertain the idea that the complexity of the person's family background experience could be important. They find that such a measure of the complexity of developmental stimuli afforded by family background does correlate significantly with social intelligence. Their variable is similar to the idea of degree of complication of early developmental experiences which Barron feels is characteristic of those who prefer complexity.

The development of another drawing preference test, the Design Preference Inventory, is reported by Christensen (1960). This test consists of 177 pairs of abstract, nonrepresentational designs. An initial cluster analysis of responses of 231 subjects provided 23 cluster scores which had low correlations with scores on the Edwards Personal Preference Schedule and the MMPI.

The Specification of Complexity

It would seem important in the development of art preference scales to determine the various stimulus characteristics which can enter into the over-all designation of a drawing as either complex or simple. For example, on the Barron-Welsh Art Scale, two such characteristics are the amount of *detail* contained in a drawing and the *shading* effects which might be present. Potanen (1959) has studied some of the personality correlates of preference for these stimulus characteristics, utilizing Rorschach interpretations relative to the relation of dependency and anxiety to various shading and depth response to ink blots. Drawings of geometric shapes were prepared which varied in the degree to which they contained detail and three-dimensional depth characteristics. For a group of 148 males Potanen found that the preference for detail in drawings was significantly related to a measure of awareness of dependency needs. Such an approach would perhaps be helpful in delineating more exactly what constitutes complexity or simplicity in a stimulus. It will be recalled that originally Welsh was inclined to characterize the drawings of his test as differing in their degree of symmetry. It is apparent that very complicated designs may be very symmetrical, and the equation of asymmetry with complexity is misleading.

What is needed, then, in studies of preference for complex stimulation is a more rigorous definition of what constitutes a complex stimulus. Once this can be established, it will be possible to determine the consistency of these preferences across a range of stimuli which might differ considerably in kind. As long as studies are restricted to the rather ill-defined concept of preference for complexity in drawings or designs, it is difficult to establish to what degree these preferences reflect personality correlates associated with differences in aesthetic taste alone, or whether these are personality dispositions associated with preferences for complex stimulation in a variety of situations. To date, it is the writer's judgment that the personality characteristics associated with preferences for complexity are too closely tied to stimuli reflecting aesthetic tastes. These tastes could reflect little more than socially acceptable preferences of a "sophisticated" nature.

A step in the direction of extending the range of stimuli that might be preferred in terms of relative complexity-simplicity is found in a scale originally used by Barron (1953b) in his study of personality correlates of independence judgments. This scale was modified and used by Berkowitz (1957) in relating the complexity-simplicity dimension to the leveling tendency (the forgetting of many details in recalling a stimulus). The complexity attitude scale used in this study was a mixture of some of Barron's independence items and items developed by Berkowitz. Several of the items referred directly to the degree of preference for the whimsical, unbalanced, or asymmetrical in art. Other items dealt with the preference for straightforward reasoning rather than metaphors or analogies and with preferring finished to unfinished problems. Using figure drawing and a written paragraph, Berkowitz predicted that the leveling tendency to forget or leave out details in both the drawings and the story would be associated with lower scores on the complexity attitude scale. Over three degrees of leveling tendency among the subjects, it was found that leveling was inversely related to attitudes on the complexity scale. While the complexity attitudes were also significantly associated with scores on the ethnocentrism scale, the latter scale did not relate significantly to leveling tendencies. It should be noted that the items on the complexity scale are heterogeneous, and that many of them refer to a high valuation of independent and unconventional behavior. Once again the legitimacy of construing these diverse types of behavioral stimuli as complexity may be questioned.

CONSIDERATIONS FOR THE FUTURE

Perhaps the common core of all the studies reviewed in this chapter is the inquiry into how individuals differ in terms of their responses to the same range of variation in stimulus conditions. These differences may be considered either in terms of the assumed underlying cognitive structure, and how the degree of differentiation or relative complexity of this structure influences behavior, or in terms of how different motive states of the person affect his relative attraction to the diverse stimuli present. There is no reason to expect that cognitive complexity, as a measure of the degree of differentiation of cognitive structure, should be associated necessarily with the preference for complex stimulation. We have discussed several theoretical considerations which suggest caution in this regard.

Certainly it is necessary to be more precise than researchers have been to date in defining the term complexity; there is a tendency to be somewhat overinclusive in imputing similar meanings to concepts with semantic similiarities. Cognitive complexity refers primarily to the structural differentiation of the cognitive system, and as such *may be* one precondition for preferring complex stimulation. However, as we have seen, the motivational dispositions of the person are perhaps equally, or more important in determining preferences. Here we meet an unsolved problem in personality and behavior theory: how to conceptualize adequately the interrelations of cognitive and motivational variables. It may be that, as future research on complexity more fully takes into account some of these conceptual ambiguities, our knowledge of these interrelations will increase. For example, as we have seen, a common developmental bond between more complex differentiation and the preference for complex stimulation may be the range of stimulation provided by parent-child relationships. (See Chapter 4.) It seems most reasonable, however, to emphasize that future research must consider more closely whether the empirical methods used to measure such a concept as complexity adequately represent the nature of the concept itself.

Chapter 13

Unexpectedness, Affective Tone, and Behavior

SALVATORE R. MADDI
University of Chicago

$\mathcal{R}$ ECENT theorizing and experimentation have stressed the increment in approach behavior produced by novel stimulus situations. However, some of the available findings suggest that different degrees of novelty have different behavioral effects. Moderately novel situations, such as those in which a moderate proportion of the elements differ from those of immediately preceding situations, do produce approach behavior (see Chapters 7 and 9). For example, Berlyne (1955) reported that the exploratory activity of rats increased when small objects, such as cubes, were introduced into the already familiar animal box. Similar phenomena have been reported for the monkey and chimpanzee (Butler, 1954a; Welker, 1956b). Berlyne (1957b) found that when human subjects were presented with a number of visual stimuli, they attended to those which included incongruous details more than they did to those which were ordinary.

In contrast, extremely novel situations, such as those in which a large proportion of the elements differ from the ones of immediately preceding situations, or those including elements which are unique in the life history of the organism, appear to produce avoidance behavior (see Chapters 7 and 9). For example, Bindra and Spinner (1958) found that exposure to a greatly changed form of a familiar stimulus situation produced grooming in rats, while exposure to an only moderately changed form produced sniffing and locomotion. While the latter behaviors resemble approach in that they are directed toward the stimulus situation, the former is perhaps more reasonably considered avoidance since it is not directed toward the situation. Hebb (1958a, p. 114) has reported that events which were unprecedented in the lives of his chimpanzees (for example, the model of a human head without a body) produced flight and fear, but similar, although less unprecedented events (such as the head of a man whose body was hidden behind a partition) did not produce this reaction. Perhaps a similar phenomenon in humans is the avoidance of stimulus ambiguity, even to the point of resolving it prematurely. By resolving actual stimulus ambiguity, the close correspondence between expectation and occurrence is maintained. The situation is simply not perceived as unusual or unclear.

Finally, there is evidence that situations lacking in novelty, such as those in which a negligible proportion of the elements differ from those of immediately preceding situations, also produce avoidance behavior (see Chapter 5). In a relevant study, Denny (1957) found that, following a number of forced, rewarded choices of one side of a T maze, rats chose the other side on each of two consecutive free trials. On the second free trial the commonly observed tendency to alternate responses broke down. This breakdown is particularly noteworthy in the light of Montgomery's demonstration (1952b) that rats ordinarily explore the least recently experienced portion of the maze. Denny's results suggest that the rats were actively avoiding the side of the maze which had lost all its novelty during the forced trials. Karsten (1928) reported that the effects upon humans of prolonged repetition of the same activity included an increase in emotional outbursts, in the tendency to vary the task and concentrate on something else, and in the attractiveness of other activities. These behaviors cannot be considered approach produced by novelty because there was no more novel alternative to the repetitive task in this experimental situation. It does not appear that the findings of Denny and Karsten can accurately be considered approach produced by novel situations. Rather, they suggest that situations lacking in novelty produce avoidance behavior.

Although the evidence is far from conclusive, it seems reasonable to suggest that moderately novel situations are associated with approach behavior but that extremely novel and minimally novel situations are associated with avoidance behavior. In this chapter, an examination will be made of the ability of some current theories to explain the behavioral effects of all three degrees of novelty, and one of these theories will be modified with a view toward increasing its comprehensiveness.

SOME RELEVANT THEORETICAL VIEWPOINTS

There are a number of conceptual schemes which have been utilized to explain the effects of novelty upon behavior. One such viewpoint involves response inhibition caused by repeated exposure to a stimulus situation. Hull's *reactive inhibition* (1943) and Glanzer's *stimulus satiation* (1953a) are of this variety. These concepts have been used to explain spontaneous alternation (see Chapter 8). The Hullian position is that each time one arm of a T maze is entered (response A), an increment in reactive inhibition occurs, reducing the likelihood of the occurrence of that response on a subsequent trial. Glanzer's behavioral prediction is the same, but for the reason that there is an increment in satiation to the stimuli associated with response A. Strictly speaking, neither of these notions explains the *alternation* of response at all, because the manner in which a reduction in the likelihood of response A increases the tendency to enter the other arm of the maze (response B) has not been stated. The inadequacy of this type of approach as an explanation of alternation stems from the assumption that response B is the only possible alternative to response A. Even if this were true (and it excludes the possibility that neither maze arm would be entered, or that the subject would not leave the starting box), response B cannot be predicted by theories dealing solely with response A. Indeed, as they are concerned with response decrement, such conceptualizations might explain sleep more easily than the occurrence of another response. The implication of the present discussion is that reactive inhibition and stimulus satiation are most appropriately used as explanations only of avoidance produced by situations lacking in novelty.

A conceptualization focusing upon the tendency to approach novel stimuli features the curiosity drive (Berlyne, 1957c; Montgomery, 1951b, 1952b). A novel stimulus is believed to increase drive level, which is then reduced by exploration of the novel object. Adherents to such a point of view are in the position of asserting that the subject typically approaches that which produces drive. This seems a paradox for those, like Berlyne, who suggest that the curiosity drive is based on the conflict caused by the incompatible response tendencies evoked by a novel stimulus. This is in the Hullian tradition, and carries with it the implication that increases in drive are punishing. Thus, it would seem that the subject should typically avoid, or at least not approach, novel stimuli, because they produce conflict, which is a drive state. Berlyne's form of this general position seems to be more compelling as an explanation of avoidance produced by extremely novel situations, than as a theory of curiosity and exploratory behavior. (For a more complete discussion, see Chapter 9.) In any event, this viewpoint, even as used by Berlyne, applies only to one of the three degrees of novelty mentioned previously.

In his subscription to the drive-producing properties of novelty, Montgomery has stressed stimulus factors more than response factors. Having defined increases in novelty as rewarding (see Glanzer, 1958a), he avoided the contradiction found in Berlyne's approach. However, this means that increases in drive should be reinforcing, and hence, that extremely novel situations should produce the most vigorous approach behavior. The findings presented earlier indicate that frequently this does not occur, and therefore suggest that the range of appropriateness of this viewpoint is restricted to approach produced by moderately novel situations.

An alternative to the approach described above is the postulation of an innate propensity to explore or manipulate. For Harlow (1953), the tendency to manipulate or explore is innate and at least equals the viscerogenic drives in importance. Novel or interesting stimuli function as releasers for such behavior. In comparison, White's position (Chapter 10) is an unusual instinct theory. He believes that there are no real consummatory acts in exploratory behavior, and that this behavior takes place most actively in the absence of strong viscerogenic needs. Although these theories are rather different, they are both limited in scope to the explanation of approach produced by moderately novel situations. Of course, in an attempt to explain the effects of extremely novel situations, reference can be made to some other instinct which operates in opposition to the exploratory propensity. Perhaps even a third instinct can be named to account for the effects of events lacking in novelty. It is not long before this approach leads to long, rather arbitrary lists of instincts. Instinct postulation is an easy, but hardly parsimonious, game to play.

Still another approach, exemplified by the positions of Fenichel (1945), G. A. Kelly (1955), and Sullivan (1954), involves the cognitive processes. According to these writers, the unexpected is anxiety-provoking. Because novel events are usually difficult to anticipate accurately, they should be associated with anxiety. Sullivan and Fenichel believe that anxiety is vigorously avoided. Kelly is less clear on this point, but unless the corollaries of his theory are to be painfully elastic, they seem to imply that people structure not only behavior but also perception, in a manner consistent with the avoidance of anxiety. According to this general approach, then, novelty should be associated with avoidance. The range of applicability of these positions is restricted to the effects of extremely novel situations. That these writers developed their thinking through observation of human beings is particularly surprising! Even rats are considered to be more venturesome and hardy than is this image of man.

This brief treatment of relevant viewpoints, although incomplete, will serve to demonstrate the limited scope of most theorizing in this area. Quite aside from questions of logical consistency and implicit assumptions, each of these approaches is not appropriately applied to the behavioral effects of more than one of the degrees of novelty which have been differentiated. Judged, then, on the basis of their comprehensiveness, most theories dealing with the effects of novelty are found wanting.

The Discrepancy Hypothesis

One point of view, the *discrepancy hypothesis* of McClelland, Atkinson, Clark, and Lowell (1953), has the advantage over the other theories that it accounts for the behavioral effects of both extremely and moderately novel situations. The explanation of these behavioral effects involves the assumption that the two degrees of novelty produce different affective states. In turn, it is affective tone which influences the direction of behavior.

These writers first concerned themselves with the effect of a stimulus impinging upon a sense organ. They postulated that a small discrepancy between a stimulus and the adaptation level of the sense organ involved produces positive affect, while a large discrepancy arouses negative affect. In this context, adaptation level refers to the hypothesized characteristic of the sense organ which defines the range of stimuli which are ineffective. No affective arousal should result when the stimulus matches the adaptation level completely. Under ordinary circumstances, the "natural adaptation level" of a sense organ was considered to be very near its threshold. In their usage, the term *affect* is roughly synonymous with feeling or emotion, and refers to a physiological state. Positive affect is experienced as pleasant, while negative affect is an unpleasant feeling. The affect construct was utilized because data existed which convinced McClelland and his collaborators of the afferent control of behavior, and the important role played in this by pleasant and unpleasant feelings.

The decision to postulate that small discrepancies from the natural adaptation level produce positive affect, while larger discrepancies from this level produce negative affect, was made on the basis of results such as the following. Human subjects, though indifferent to water containing no salt, judge the taste of water with increasing amounts of salt as pleasant up to a certain concentration. Beyond this level of concentration, the judgments of pleasant give way to judgments of unpleasant (McClelland *et al.*, 1953, p. 43). Similarly, Marx, Henderson, and Roberts (1955) have demonstrated that an increase in illumination up to a certain intensity will produce approach behavior (bar-pressing) in rats, while others have found that light of much greater intensity is avoided. The discrepancy hypothesis was an attempt to provide an adequate explanation of results of this type.

McClelland *et al.* also surmised that the natural adaptation level could be shifted somewhat by stimuli impinging upon the organism. Thus, following Helson (1948), the adaptation level concept also serves to account for the cumulative effects of past stimulation. In order for this aspect of the position to be tenable, it had to be demonstrated that discrepancies from a temporary adaptation level produced by immediately preceding stimulus conditions have effects similar to those of discrepancies from natural adaptation levels. An experiment performed by Alpert (McClelland *et al.*, 1953, p. 51) provided results only partially consistent with this aspect of the discrepancy hypothesis. Having produced sensory adaptation to a low light intensity, he found that small increases in the intensity level were judged to be pleasant, while larger increases were considered unpleasant. However, when adaptation to a high light intensity was produced, the results did not follow the same pattern: all increases in intensity tended to produce negative affect, while all decreases tended to produce positive affect. Although it was argued that the latter situation was not an entirely adequate test of the discrepancy hypothesis (due to technical problems), it must be concluded that the tenability of this position is more or less an open question.

Now that the nature of the reasoning behind the discrepancy hypothesis has been presented, however briefly, the aspect of this position most related to the behavioral effects of novelty can be more meaningfully discussed. McClelland *et al.* considered their notions important not only at the level of particular sense organs and the stimuli impinging upon them but also at a more broadly defined perceptual level. The construct *expectancy* was utilized because it seemed difficult to describe the effects of past experience at this more complex level in terms of sensory adaptation. They stressed the conviction that the expectancy, like the adaptation level, would eventually be described in physiological terms, and chose Hebb's conceptualization (1949) as the most likely to serve this function. Although the two terms summarizing the effects of past experience have rather equivalent functions in the discrepancy hypothesis, it may be argued that their physiological implications are too different to warrant this usage. An adaptation level may be considered primarily an afferent phenomenon, while an expectancy suggests central nervous system functioning. However, recent evidence concerning "gating" (Bruner, 1957a) indicates that even so-called sensory adaptation may be partially determined by central nervous system processes, by way of a feedback system involving previously unrecognized efferent pathways associated with the afferent ones.

McClelland *et al.* assign affect the role of determining the direction of behavior. Positive affect produces approach, and negative affect produces avoidance. Thus the discrepancy hypothesis at the cognitive level can be stated as follows: Small discrepancies between expectancy and occurrence arouse positive affect leading to approach behavior, but large discrepancies arouse negative affect leading to avoidance behavior. When expectancy and occurrence match completely, there will be no affective arousal and no behavior which can be characterized as approach or avoidance, unless that behavior is caused by some other affect-arousing property of the situation. It must be cautioned that this formulation is most appropriately applied in situations where rewards and punishments, as usually conceptualized, are at a minimum.

For the discrepancy hypothesis to be relevant to the explanation of the data previously discussed, it must be assumed that size of discrepancy and degree of novelty co-vary. If small discrepancies are likely to occur in moderately novel situations, and large discrepancies are more likely in extremely novel situations, this formulation can account for the effects of two of the three degrees of novelty. It cannot, however, provide an explanation of the behavioral effects of situations lacking in novelty, as it makes no specific predictions about such conditions. Nonetheless, the discrepancy hypothesis has a greater range of applicability than do the other positions which have been discussed.

Explanations of the effects of novelty which stress expectancies have been utilized infrequently, and have been restricted to experiments involving stimulus change preceded by a period of stimulus repetition. This usage may be overnarrow, as Dember (1960b) suggests. Expectancies can serve in the explanation of the results of virtually all of the experiments purporting to study the effects of novelty. The typical study in this area has included a period of habituation to a stimulus situation prior to the change of that situation. The habituation period may well be sufficient to produce an expectancy. Further, the effects of stimuli with incongruous elements may involve expectancies learned outside the context of the experiment. In any event, the present application of the discrepancy hypothesis presumes that size of discrepancy is the crucial variable, with degree of novelty being either superfluous or unimportant. This assertion is strengthened by the apparent inability to define novelty as an inherent attribute of stimuli. What has been called novelty is most adequately defined with regard to the subjective representation of past experience.

A word of caution is necessary. In generalizing to this wide range of phenomena we must take care to keep in mind that, in typical usage, the expectancy concept refers to sequential relationships among successive events or stimuli. Expectancies permit anticipation of what is coming next.

A well-known experiment by Dember (1956) provides the basis for comparing the ability of a number of the theories previously discussed to explain the same set of results. Rats were permitted to look into both arms of a T maze but could not enter them. During this exposure period, the arms were different in brightness (one was black and the other was white). The subjects were subsequently permitted a free choice, under conditions where both arms were the same in brightness (that is, both black). Thus, during the free choice, both arms were equally "satiated" and "inhibiting." As Dember points out, proponents of reactive inhibition and stimulus satiation would expect the responses of subjects to be randomly distributed. Although a change took place between the exposure and free choice periods, the changed arm was actually more similar to the other arm during the free choice period than it had been during exposure. Thus Montgomery, whose theory tends to stress the peripheral sensory effects of novelty, and who has demonstrated that the amount of exploratory behavior that occurs in a second maze is inversely related to the similarity of the second maze to the first (Montgomery, 1953a), would have little basis for expecting subjects to prefer the changed arm. The free choice period was the first opportunity afforded the rats to enter an arm of the maze, and hence it is difficult to conceive of the manner in which any responses could have become conditioned to the arms. Since the changed arm could not increase conflict by arousing incompatible response tendencies, Berlyne also would not have much reason to expect subjects to prefer the changed arm.

Dember, of course, found that 17 out of 20 subjects entered the changed arm when given a free choice. The discrepancy hypothesis can readily provide an explanation of these results. Having a view of the entire maze during the exposure period, the rat formed an expectancy concerning "what leads to what" in the maze. The portion of the maze that was changed prior to the free choice period could not have been anticipated accurately, and was therefore discrepant from expectation. As this portion constituted only approximately one third of the maze, and no more than half of the part of the maze actually traversed during the free choice trial, it is perhaps appropriately considered to have produced a small discrepancy. After all, at least one half and most likely more (especially if extramaze cues are considered) of the stimulus situation during the free choice trial was consistent with the expectation which had been formed during the exposure period. The small discrepancy aroused positive affect leading to approach behavior, that is, choice of the changed portion of the maze.

This is not the place to reargue the wisdom of imputing cognition to rats and other subhuman species. However, that this assumption is warranted in the present context is suggested by the work of Sutherland (1957), who found that the alternation tendency was decreased when the two goal arms led to a common goal box rather than to separate and distinct goal boxes. He argued that alternation occurs not only with respect to choice point stimuli but also, and perhaps even more so, with respect to "the rat's expectancy of the stimuli it will receive beyond the choice point."

In its present form, the discrepancy hypothesis, although plausible and imaginative, is neither sufficiently elaborated nor unambiguous enough to provide precise explanations and readily testable hypotheses. The treatment of Dember's results, for example, is so general that it can only be considered promising. The idea of discrepancy must be interpreted and expressed in a manner which leads to its quantification. Aspects of cognitive functioning relevant to the development of expectations should be detailed. Perhaps most crucial is the development of some objective basis for distinguishing small and large discrepancies. In addition, as was mentioned earlier, this position in its present form does not permit explanation of the avoidance of situations lacking in novelty. The next section of this chapter is an attempt to extend the discrepancy hypothesis so that it can apply to all degrees of novelty, and to interpret and state it in more testable form.

MODIFICATION OF THE DISCREPANCY HYPOTHESIS

Series Unexpectedness and Affective Tone

The discrepancy hypothesis emphasizes the degree of difference between what is expected and what actually takes place, or the unexpectedness of the stimulus situation that occurs. As the expectancy is based upon temporal or sequential relationships among events, the more precise term *series of events* will be substituted for *stimulus situation.* A series is a group of two or more events which have an order, each event leading to the next according to some definite temporal principle. The series may be a causal one, as in the rainstorm which follows the accumulation of clouds into a thunderhead, but it need not have a causal reference. An example of a noncausal series is the alphabet—it cannot be said that the occurrence of B is literally caused by the prior occurrence of A.

Repetitions of a series lead to the development of an expectancy, that is, a memory trace of the order and content characteristics of the series involved. The expectancy permits anticipation of the events which constitute the series. Once an expectancy is formed, each event in the series serves as a cue for the next and later events. In order to be repetitive, a subsequent series must be composed of events which are similar to, and ordered according to the same principle as, those of the original series.

Focusing upon the series as a unit of analysis suggests a method of quantifying unexpectedness. A series is unexpected to the degree to which its events were not accurately anticipated. In a given series, the proportion of inaccurately predicted events to the total number of events is an index of the unexpectedness of the series.

It is assumed that the organism has the capacity to experience bodily sensations, called affective, which can be characterized as pleasant (positive affect), or unpleasant (negative affect). Possible measures of affect have been discussed by others (Bousfield, 1950; McClelland *et al.*, 1953; Schlosberg, 1952). Affective tone varies along a bipolar continuum from the extreme of maximal negative to that of maximal positive intensity (Young, 1959).

The First Proposition

The modified version of the discrepancy hypothesis being developed in this chapter is embodied in two propositions. The first concerns the effects of series unexpectedness upon affective tone, and the second concerns the effects of affective tone upon series-oriented behavior. Taken together, the propositions permit prediction of the behavioral effects of unexpectedness.

Proposition 1: If series unexpectedness is plotted on the abscissa, and affective tone on the ordinate, the relationship between these two variables is described by a nonmonotonic function; as unexpectedness increases from a minimal value, affect is initially in the negative range, slopes upward to a peak in the positive range, and then slopes downward into the negative range again. Hence, relatively small and relatively large degrees of unexpectedness should be associated with negative affect. The mathematical function which generates this curve cannot be be determined from available data. In any event, the proposition in its present form avoids premature definition of the size of discrepancy between expectation and occurrence which shall be considered large or small, and, as will be discussed presently, provides a basis for generating hypotheses which can be readily tested.

A word of qualification is important. There are a number of sources of affective tone. In addition to degree of unexpectedness, there are others such as food, success or failure, and shock. This suggests that the effects of unexpectedness will be most clearly observed in situations in which rewards and punishments, as usually conceptualized, are at a minimum. (The interaction between a situation's reward value, and its unexpectedness, will be discussed later.)

A recently reported experiment (Maddi, 1961) tested two hypotheses following from the proposition stated above. The subjects, who were college students, experienced a number of series of visual stimuli in succession. Each series was composed of some numbers and a sentence completion stem, presented in succession, with the stems always being the last event in the series. For two of the groups the initial series (which was: number, number, sentence stem) was repeated seven times. These first eight series constituted environmental regularity. Following this, the various subgroups within each of these two groups experienced different versions of a final series of events. In each group, the final series was repetitive (no change) for one subgroup, and nonrepetitive (environmental change) for two subgroups. Of the latter two subgroups, one experienced a relatively large degree of change (for example, number, number, number, number, sentence stem), and the other experienced a relatively small degree of change (for example, number, number, number, sentence stem). For both subgroups, the change was in the order of the events in the final series. A control group received the same number of series in the course of the experiment as did the other two groups, but did not experience regularity because the order of events in each successive series was different from that of the preceding series.

In choosing sentence stems and instructions, an attempt was made to minimize rewards and punishments. The subjects were instructed to complete the sentence in whatever manner they wished whenever they encountered a sentence stem. The completions were used as indicants of affective tone, a procedure which seems reasonable in the light of Bousfield's demonstration (1950) that pleasant and unpleasant moods determine the affective value of word associations. Each completion was scored on a five-point scale of affective tone, the extremes of which were *strongly positive affect* and *strongly negative affect*, and group mean affect scores associated with each series were computed.

The members of one of the two groups experiencing environmental regularity were also asked to predict the occurrence of events in the series. This group was called the *prediction* group, and its predictions were used to determine the degree of unexpectedness associated with each series. The other group experiencing regularity was not asked to predict, and hence, was called the *no-prediction* group. The group which did not experience regularity, and also did not predict, was called the *no-regularity* group.

It was assumed that as a series is repeated, its unexpectedness decreases. Consistent with this assumption was the finding that the inaccuracy with which the prediction group predicted the events in each subsequent series decreased during environmental regularity. In both the prediction and no-prediction groups, the curve of mean affect score as a function of number of regular series thus far experienced was consistent with the hypothesis that as a series is repeated, affective tone is initially negative, becomes positive, and then becomes negative again. As expected, the curve of the no-regularity, or control, group was not consistent with this hypothesis. Further, in the prediction group, the greatest intensity of positive affect occurred in the third series, during which the group was inaccurate in 33% of its predictions. While inaccuracy of prediction decreased from 76% to 33% during the first three repetitive series, affective tone went from negative to positive, and while inaccuracy decreased from 33% to 6% during the last five repetitive series, affective tone went from positive to negative.

It will be recalled that the final series was repetitive for some subjects, but nonrepetitive for others. It was assumed that the larger the degree of change present in the final series, the more unexpected it would be. In keeping with this assumption, in the prediction group, the subgroups ordered in terms of increasing inaccuracy of prediction during the final series were as follows: the subgroup receiving no change, the one receiving the relatively small degree of change, and the one receiving the relatively large degree of change. A second hypothesis was that conditions of no change and of relatively large degree of change are associated with negative affect, but a relatively small degree of change is associated with positive affect. The results were consistent with this hypothesis in the no-change and relatively-small-change conditions, and there was a trend in favor of the hypothesis in the condition of relatively large change. It may be that the data would have more clearly substantiated prediction if greater degrees of change had been included in the experimental design. Taken as a whole, however, this experiment provides support for the proposition stated previously.

The Second Proposition

The relationship between affective tone and behavior remains to be discussed. Only the direction and intensity of behavior with respect to the series of events are of concern here. Consider a continuum of series-oriented behavior which extends from the extreme of maximal avoidance to that of maximal approach (Young, 1959): approach is behavior directed toward continued experience of the series, while avoidance is behavior directed toward discontinuation of the experience of the series. *Proposition 2* states that if affective tone is plotted on the abscissa, and series-oriented behavior is plotted on the ordinate, the relationship between these two variables is described by an increasing monotonic curve passing through the origin. In general, the stronger and more positive the affective tone, the greater the tendency to approach the series, but the stronger and more negative the affective tone, the greater the tendency to avoid the series.

This proposition might well hold in the case of affective tone determined by any of a number of factors besides unexpectedness. However, consideration of both propositions which have been offered indicates that our primary concern is with the behavioral effects of unexpectedness through the mediating affective process. These two propositions, which constitute the modified discrepancy hypothesis, are potentially useful in the explanation of such phenomena as exploratory behavior (see Chapter 9), and performance decrements in repetitive tasks (see Chapter 5).

It follows from the modified discrepancy hypothesis that as series unexpectedness decreases from a maximal to a minimal value, avoidance, then approach, and then avoidance should occur. This seems particularly applicable to studies such as Welker's (1956b), which demonstrated that exploratory behavior gradually increases and then decreases in intensity during the course of exposure to an initially novel stimulus situation. However, such studies cannot be considered a rigorous test of this hypothesis, because no index of unexpectedness is obtained. Perhaps some modification of the previously described procedure utilized by Maddi (1961) will provide a more appropriate test. Possible measures of approach and avoidance are discussed at length by McClelland *et al.* (1953).

An attempt has been made to clarify and modify the discrepancy hypothesis with a view to extending its scope and rendering it more accessible to test. The questions of the actual explanatory value of this position, and its relationship to other relevant conceptualizations, cannot be fully answered without the benefit of additional investigation.

FURTHER CONSIDERATIONS

Before proceeding further, a possible criticism of this and other similar conceptualizations must be discussed. It may be argued that the results of many stimulus generalization experiments are at variance with the proposed effects of unexpectedness upon behavior. These experiments indicate that stimulus change is associated with decrement in a trained response (Mednick and Freedman, 1960). Such findings might be construed as indicating that all degrees of change, and hence of unexepectedness, are associated with avoidance behavior. For this contention to be plausible, it would have to be assumed that decrement in a trained response was evidence of avoidance. However, while these studies show that a particular response can be conditioned to particular stimulus cues, they provide little information regarding approach or avoidance tendencies. Bindra (1959b) has suggested that decrement in a trained response occurs because change produces new behavior which takes the place of the trained response. It is precisely this new behavior which may indicate most adequately whether change is associated with approach or avoidance. Because stimulus generalization experiments do not involve a consideration of the full range of behavior associated with stimulus change, their results are not particularly relevant to the present formulation.

Biological Significance and Neurophysiology

What sense does the modified discrepancy hypothesis make in terms of the usual principles by which we understand phenomena in psychology? It certainly seems inconsistent with the idea that the sole biological significance of cognitive functioning and perception is to protect the individual from the potential dangers and shocks of the unanticipated. However, if at least moderate change in the environment is the modal state of affairs, then it is reasonable to consider a somewhat different approach to the question of biological significance. One implication of the present conceptualization is that with the accumulation of experience the typical individual begins to anticipate somewhat unexpected occurrences with pleasure, and completely expected or extremely unexpected events with displeasure. The individual will learn, under normal circumstances, to seek out situations of potentially mild unexpectedness because these have been associated with positive affect in the past. This implication is in keeping with models such as White's (Chapter 10), in which the preference for novel events is considered to contribute to the accrual of competence in dealing with the environment by stimulating the organism to seek a wide range of experiences. If the emphasis is put upon the advantages of learning to cope with a variable surround, then the present position makes sense in terms of survival value.

It may also make sense neurophysiologically. The following remarks are made tentatively, because they are dependent upon a conceptualization of the nervous system which has not been fully documented. The speculations will concern both the significance for affective tone of the level of activity in the activation system of the brain, and the contribution to this level made by unexpected occurrences. Building on the work of Hebb (1955) and others (such as Lindsley, 1951; Malmo, 1959), Chapter 2 suggested that levels of activation which are either above or below the characteristic, or normal, one are typically associated with negative affect. Levels of activation near the characteristic one were considered to be typically associated with mildly positive affect.

In addition to its function in emotionality, the activation system contributes considerable stimulation to the cortex. But Hebb (1955) has also stressed the contribution of the cortex to level of activation, by way of an extensive feedback system. He suggests that the psychological importance of this fact is in terms of the "immediate drive value of cognitive processes." The present speculations concerning the contribution made by series unexpectedness to the level of activation follow this lead. Consider the central nervous system locus of the expectancy to be the phase sequence (Hebb, 1949), or organization of cortical units. An unexpected event contributes stimulation to the cortex for which there are no fully appropriate phase sequences already established. Less of the "unusual" stimulation is bound up in organized cortical activity than would be the case with more usual stimulation, which would travel along already established channels. Series unexpectedness, then, is represented in the nervous system by the relatively diffuse, unorganized cortical activity engendered by an unusual type of stimulation. Such relatively diffuse activity may involve greater cortical area and make a greater contribution to the activation system, through the feedback channels spread out over the cortex, than would be the case with more organized activity.

Thus there would be a positive relationship between amount of diffuse cortical activity produced by afferent stimulation (this corresponds to degree of series unexpectedness), and level of activity in the activation system (this corresponds to, or determines, affective tone). Of course, the matter is not this simple, as it appears that the level of activation may determine whether organized cortical activity can occur at all. Nonetheless, these speculations suggest a manner in which the relationship between unexpectedness and affective tone can make neurophysiological sense. Holding other factors constant, minimal, moderate, and maximal unexpectedness are most likely to contribute to levels of activation that are, respectively, lower than normal, normal, and higher than normal.

Unexpectedness and Reward Value

Although previous discussion indicates that the effects of the unexpectedness factor are most clear when rewards and punishments, as usually conceptualized, are at a minimum, it need not be concluded from this that the former factor is trivial in determining affective tone. Results reported by Spector (1956) suggest that the positive affective tone produced by a rewarding event can be enhanced if the event is also relatively unexpected. Utilizing a procedure in which small groups were given a task to perform, he found that among the subjects who received "promotions," those who had perceived this rewarding event as low in probability responded with higher morale than did those who had perceived it as high in probability. The nature of the interaction between the affect produced by the situation's unexpectedness, and by its reward value, is likely to be complex and deserves further study.

This interaction should have significance for the direction and intensity of behavior. Indeed, results reported by Olds (1953) suggest that an increment in the unexpectedness associated with the occurrence of a reward produced an increase in the intensity of the approach behavior normally produced by that reward. In his study, children exerted more effort in turning a crank for chips (which could subsequently be traded for trinkets) when the number of turns necessary was unexpectedly increased during the test period over what it had been during the overlearning period. He interpreted these results as indicating that the delay in the occurrence of the secondary reinforcer increased its reward value because it was "wanted" for a longer period of time than had been usual during training.

If the interpretation of the results offered here is more reasonable than that of Olds, a decrease in the time interval preceding a reinforcer (over the time interval that had been usual during overlearning) should also increase its reward value. Olds' experiment does not permit comparison of these two explanations, even though he did include a group that experienced such a decrease in time to reward. During the test period, that group received a reward after the same number of crank turns on each trial, while the increase-in-time-to-reward group received rewards according to a variable schedule of crank turns. Hence, the two groups were not comparable in the extent to which the secondary reinforcer retained its unexpectedness throughout the entire three-day test period.

The Development of Enduring Orientations

The discussion of behavior has been limited thus far to that which immediately follows unexpected or expected occurrences. These reactions should be fairly uniform over individuals; avoidance should occur when the situation arouses negative affect, and approach should follow the arousal of positive affect. However, as an individual's past experience with unexpected situations accumulates, he will begin exhibiting behavior in anticipation of the possibility of unexpected occurrences. This learned, anticipatory behavior, which serves the function of regulating the emotional state of being, is considered by McClelland *et al.* (1953) to indicate the existence of a rather enduring orientation, or motive. In this usage, a motive is learned and constitutes a dispositional or directional tendency apparent in thought and action. A very important feature of this type of approach is that it stresses individual differences in orientation as a function of differences in past experience. The remainder of this chapter will explore the implications of such an approach for the development of enduring orientations toward the unexpected.

Two important factors to be taken into consideration are (1) the number of expectancies in the individual's expectancy system, and (2) the level of generality characteristic of the expectancies in that system. Assuming that the minimum conditions for learning expectancies are met, the number of expectancies developed by a person is directly related to the number of different series of events he has experienced. At any point in time, the greater the number of expectancies in the individual's system, the fewer the possible series of events which he will experience as unexpected.

Reference to the generality of the expectancy, or the number of possible cues which are sufficient to arouse it, indicates that there can be individual differences in the perception and memory of particular series of events. Suppose the series 15, 71, BOUNTIFUL occurs. If it is perceived and remembered very specifically, the subsequent occurrence of 32 (or any other number besides 15) will not arouse any expectancy, while the occurrence of 15 will lead to the anticipation of 71 followed by BOUNTIFUL. However, the series may be recorded in the memory at a higher level of generality as, for example, "a number, a number, and a word, in succession." In this case, the subsequent occurrence of 32, or 15, or any number will arouse the anticipation of another number followed by a word. The hypothetical series may also be recorded at a very overgeneral level as "three things in succession." It is clear that anything which occurred subsequently would arouse this expectancy.

To be sure, the generality of expectancy is not entirely independent of range of series experienced. The larger the number of different series the individual encounters, the more stimulated he may be to develop expectancies of above-minimal generality. However, even given a wide range of experience, people are likely to differ in the characteristic generality of the expectancies which they form. Other factors, such as intelligence and either momentary or more long lasting sets, may affect expectancy generality by sensitizing the individual to the perception of similarities or the discrimination of differences. A person sensitive to differences between series of events would tend to develop rather specific expectancies, while a person sensitive to similarities would develop rather general expectancies. The greater the characteristic generality of the expectancies in the individual's system, the fewer the number of possible series which will be experienced as unexpected in some degree, and the fewer the possible series which will be experienced as extremely unexpected.

Let us now consider three different orientations concerning the possibility of unexpected occurrences. Perhaps the most usual orientation is that in which the individual seeks out somewhat unexpected occurrences. This type of behavior will be fostered in an environment in which the typical degree of unexpectedness is moderate. Such an environment will be established by parents who encourage the child to experience a wide range of phenomena and to perceive the relatedness of events, while at the same time protecting him from encountering too many totally unexpected situations. Under such conditions, the child will develop many expectations about the course of events in the world. These expectations will presumably have a level of generality which is above minimum (due to the wide range of different series), but also below maximum (due to parental emphasis upon cognitive functioning which would belie meaningless overgeneralizations). These considerations and that of parental protection when it is necessary suggest that the child will most typically experience moderate degrees of unexpectedness. As he matures, he will come to regard the possibility of the unexpected as interesting, because, in the past, series unexpectedness had been of such magnitude as to arouse positive affect. He will either perform in a manner likely to produce unexpected results, or somewhat more passively seek out types of situations which had been associated with unexpected occurrences previously. Because the former, more active tendency would be likely to lead to the production of novel ideas and objects, it may be considered one factor contributing to creativity. In any event, the individual developing this type of orientation will be hardy enough to function effectively in a complex and changing world.

Another type of orientation relevant here is that in which the unexpected is categorically avoided. This type of behavior will develop in an environment in which the unexpected, when it does occur, is extreme in degree. Take as an example the sheltered environment in which the overprotected child is not permitted to accumulate a range of experience outside the home. This is in sharp contrast to the environment described above, in which the child is encouraged to encounter many diverse phenomena. Within the overprotecting home, not very much variety occurs (perhaps the parents are themselves wary of the unexpected). The general limitation of experience and the parents' restrictive attitudes permit the child to develop only relatively few expectancies. Also, such expectancies as are formed will tend to be rather specific. This means that he is likely to experience as extremely unexpected many of the unavoidable situations which are familiar to other children of the same age. For example, the necessary forays to school and the unannounced arrival of guests to the home may be real sources of discomfort. As he matures, the child will quickly come to regard the possibility of the unexpected as threatening and unpleasant. He will restrict himself with even greater determination to the well-known routines, and will not be venturesome or curious. In extreme form, this avoidance of potentially unexpected situations might make some contribution to the development of pathological states such as compulsivity and school phobia.

The next orientation is the most difficult to describe. It involves the avoidance of a very wide range of situations, because they are perceived as monotonous and boring. This type of orientation will develop in an environment which provides relatively little in the way of unexpected occurrences. In such an environment, the child is neither restricted from nor encouraged to experience a wide range of phenomena. Rather, he is neglected, or else a premium is put upon the development of other human potentialities to the exclusion of the thought processes. The range of experiences available to him is not especially limited, as it is for the overprotected child. But because of parental neglect or devaluation of cognitive functioning, the present child will not be stimulated to a very high degree to develop subtleties of thought requiring a fair amount of discrimination. To be sure, expectancies will have to develop in order for the child to function at all adequately, but these expectancies will tend to be so overgeneral as to appear vague and superficial. With such overgeneral expectations, the ordinary course of events in the world will be experienced as more or less expected and monotonous. The individual will come to regard a very wide range of situations as potentially boring. He will avoid such situations and constantly search for "kicks" in the form of radically novel experiences. In his attempt to avoid monotony he will exhibit great response variability and risk-taking. This formulation may be relevant to the development of juvenile delinquency. Many delinquents seem to be perpetually bored, and seem to break the law in an attempt to produce some excitement, or some unusual experience. It may not be coincidental that their home environment is often characterized by neglect and a devaluation of cognitive functioning.

These speculations have been of necessity quite brief and incomplete. Nonetheless, they suggest the significance for psychological development of the degree of unexpectedness which characterizes the child's early environment.

Chapter 14

Beauty: Pattern and Change

JOHN R. PLATT
University of Chicago

Poetry is a superior amusement: I do not mean an amusement for superior people . . . If we think of the nature of amusement, then poetry is not amusing; but if we think of anything else that poetry may seem to be, we are led into far greater difficulties . . . [Other classic definitions of poetry are] frigid to anyone who has felt the full surprise and elevation of a new experience of poetry.

*T*HIS cryptic aesthetic comparison is from T. S. Eliot's preface to the 1928 edition of *The Sacred Wood*. It is at first sight a puzzling statement, and those who regard Eliot's poetry as an obscure joke— an amusement!—may think this is cut from the same cloth. But I want to take it here as a kind of text whose meaning will become clearer as we examine the nature and evolution of perception, the role of change-in-stimulation for every complex stimulus-response system or organism, and its newly discovered relation to such peculiarly human responses as amusement and aesthetic appreciation in the highly developed human organism. I hope to show that Eliot's statement, even from a scientific and psychological point of view, is a serious and important insight, and that when we do think about the nature of amusement and surprise as indicated by various theoretical and experimental studies today, the statement ceases to be cryptic and becomes natural and even obvious, and can be applied not only to verbal arts like poetry but also to the musical arts and the arts of design.

Actually only a part of the aesthetic problem of art will concern us here, but it is the most curious and difficult part. Most critics agree that art has two aspects, a formal aspect and a representational aspect. It is easy to see why we may be pleased and satisfied by the representational elements in art—by the moment of prayer in "The Angelus" or the thunderstorm in the Pastoral Symphony. They resemble our own moments of heightened experience. It is not so easy to see why a full-grown and intelligent adult is deeply satisfied by the formal elements in art. That is, by space and time patterns and the deviations from them, as in the development of the theme in a quartet or in the balancing of the painting by a touch of red in the opposite corner. This problem of formal beauty is the one to which Eliot and the other formal theorists have addressed themselves.

This problem has recently begun to yield to analytical examination from two sides: first from the side of aesthetic analysis, particularly in the field of musical aesthetics, assisted by some general ideas from "information theory" (Meyer, 1956, 1957); second from the side of biophysics or the physics of perception (Platt, 1958). It now appears that the requirements for aesthetic enjoyment are simply the requirements for perception itself, raised to a higher degree; and the essential thing in each case is to have *a pattern that contains the unexpected*. This seems to be the heart of what we call beautiful, and it is no exaggeration to say that men need it as they need food.

I hope to justify this view here not by means of rigorous deductions from accepted premises nor by experimental proofs (although I hope that experimental tests for these assertions may be devised in the near future); but rather by a sort of ramble through a number of fields, from natural science on the one hand to aesthetic criticism on the other. To outline the argument briefly, I want to show that the mind's grasp and enjoyment of the external world rest on two complementary neuropsychological principles: the principle of response to novelty or change-in-stimulation, and the principle of response to repetition or pattern. We will begin by noting that response to changes-in-stimulation, and specific and patterned changes at that, is fundamental to life and goes back to the beginnings of organic evolution and even before. Moreover, the physiology and structure of the brain suggest that its function is to select patterns for response out of a tremendous flux of information inputs. We will go on to the recent archaeological evidence, which demonstrates that the human brain has evolved almost explosively under the stresses of the postglacial world so as to cope selectively with patterns of the highest complexity.

We will then turn to the psychophysical evidence on the role of pattern in the brain's organization of external experience, as given by a current theory of visual perception or "how we see straight lines"; in vision at least, the experimental evidence seems to confirm the theoretical conclusion that neither a steady flux nor an unpatterned random flux can be organized into experience. Taken all together, this evidence from different fields for the central role played by pattern and by change-of-pattern in the functioning of a central organ such as the brain strongly suggests that these features of the input flux may have an affective as well as an informational significance, not only in the representation of external objects but as pattern *qua* pattern; and in fact that the affective and the informational aspects of response to pattern may be indissoluble.

This conclusion seems to be confirmed by examining what critics have said about the role of patterns or symmetries in the visual arts, where the symmetries can play simultaneously not only a formal role but also a representational role because of the presence and "naturalness" of symmetric patterns in the biological world. Finally our ramble will turn to the role of pattern-expectations, and of surprise and randomness and the unexpected, and their humorous or pleasurable affect, in current aesthetic theories of music and the other arts; and this will bring us back again with renewed understanding to the poetic problem we have posed here at the beginning.

In these times of defiant analysis or defiant opposition to analysis in the humanities, a word of justification may be needed for this kind of wandering back and forth among the analytical sciences, psychology, and poetry. The justification lies in the fact that the study of patterns and how the brain responds to them is necessarily an interdisciplinary subject. Anyone interested in a full account of the peculiarities and powers of the human brain must be prepared to discuss it in several languages. We see the brain at various times from the inside or from the outside, emotionally or historically or by dissection, as a piece of watery tissue, or as a weapons system, or as the creator of philosophy. All the disciplines are needed, and evidence from several different ones will be introduced here. With such an approach, there is a danger of being found superficial by specialists; but in searching for the central elements in so extensive a problem, it is not as important at first to go deep into the different kinds of description as it is to be sure that they are mutually consistent and that the general picture is complete.

What is particularly likely to offend many persons is an apparent "reduction" of humanistic appreciation to mere mathematics and biology. It smacks not only of pedantry, which we always excuse, but of dissection, which we do not. It looks like the work of a calculating and joyless mind, one that would pull the wings off a bird in order to analyze flight. But I think an unwillingness to converse in both types of language is part of the breakdown in communications between the humanities and the sciences that C. P. Snow has discussed in *The Two Cultures and the Scientific Revolution* (1960).

The truth is that we need both types of language, and easy translations between them. The situation is like the problem of whether to discuss the physiological basis of love. For the intelligent mind, love is not belittled but enlarged by physiological understanding. This is what guarantees that the emotion is a yes-saying of the whole organism and not just a disembodied sentimentality. Likewise with the appreciation of beauty: In music or art or poetry, an understanding of the physiological and physical basis of our aesthetic response is what can guarantee that it is consistent with civilized intelligence and judgment and is not merely a rationalized jungle dance. If someone says it is absurd to drag in the language of evolution and science to discuss the poetic experience, I reply, Who told you to compartmentalize? The human mind is *one;* it is absurd not to.

THE NEURAL DEMAND FOR STIMULUS, PATTERN, AND CHANGE

The Primitiveness of Response to Stimuli

Let us begin our ramble toward the aesthetic problem by bringing out a number of paradoxes about the physics and physiology and evolution of perception. One paradox is that our response system demands new information or novelty, and yet at the same time demands regularity or pattern. A second paradox is that these properties of the response system are both very old in their evolutionary origins and yet very new in their recent and sudden elaboration in the human brain.

In higher animals, the nervous system is a device for responding with great discrimination to the environment. Its response involves a selective double amplification system (Platt, 1956). For example, in the visual process, the light images carrying information from the environment strike the rods and cones of the retina and are amplified first into electrical-chemical nerve pulses that travel back along the neurons. At any instant, there are about 100 million of these input pulses passing into the processing centers of the retina and the brain. What happens to them then is still obscure, but somehow all the visual and nonvisual inputs become collated into either a memory or a new "decision," a kind of self-consistent order to the oculomotor and other muscles, about every twentieth of a second. Each decision may be proliferated into millions of motor impulses which are then amplified a second time as the individual muscles make the ordered response to the changing environmental situation. It is a beautiful thing to watch such a system operating at maximum capacity. The most complex continuous performance in the whole animal kingdom may be that of a skilled pianist sight-reading Bach.

It is obvious that such a sophisticated type of response did not develop out of nothing. Its roots must go back, at least in some form, to the very beginnings of organic evolution. A little consideration shows that the response to stimulation and the demand for information from the environment must have been coeval with life itself. Before there were networks of neurons, before there were single neurons, there was selective response. At a sufficiently early stage, in fact, there was probably no distinction between nervous and muscular response, or between chemical and electrical transmission of signals. In an ionic medium such as the living cell, every chemical signal has an electrical component, and vice versa. Muscle and nerve cells are alike in many of their electrical and contractile properties, and at the level of the flatworm they are even said to stain alike. The flatworm probably does not care whether his signal is propagated by a twitch or a pulse, so long as it is adequate.

And even within a single-cell organism there can be a network of communications fibrils, as biologists know from the delicate neuromotor fibrillar network inside a *Paramecium*. (Such micronetworks within a cell might also be important in higher brains.) Still lower down the scale, in precellular systems, there must have been some elementary kind of response organization. In fact, the simplest imaginable self-reproduction, whatever the chemical types of the molecules involved, requires the acquisition by the reproducing system of suitable "food" molecules and no others, and so must show some selectivity of response. When the molecules in the solution around such a growing and self-reproducing system are of the wrong kind or touch it at the wrong place or time, nothing happens. But when the right molecule touches the system at the right place, presto! There is a release of chemical energy, and a new bond is formed, carrying the system one step farther toward completed reproduction. This is a selected amplification of the input contact "stimulus" into a "response." At this level the specification of such a response is usually regarded as being in the province of chemistry or biochemistry, but it would be meaningless to debate whether it is primarily a change of chemical structure or of mechanical shape or of electrical charge. All these aspects will be involved in the elementary act.

And I would say that this kind of chemical selectivity and amplification and response even enters into the still earlier selective chemistry of "inorganic evolution," from which we believe the first living or self-duplicating molecules were built up. We pride ourselves on our own mental abilities in manipulating the environment. But any selective response to a stimulus does the same. Mind developed out of selective response; and selective response goes all the way back to the origin of life and, quite possibly, even before.

Structure and Function of the Brain

Let us consider next the gross structure and physiology of our brains, a subject as important to our discussion as their pre-Adamite ancestry. The brain makes up only about 2 per cent of our body weight, but is now provided with about 20 per cent of the resting oxygen consumption and blood supply. It is the organ most sensitive to oxygen deficiency. Even if we knew nothing about what the brain does, this oxygen demand would prove that it is an organ designed for complete and rapid processing of something.

I think there is no doubt about what it is processing. It is input information. The flow and volume of the signals are so prodigious that one can easily see why they add up to this great physiological demand for blood and oxygen. With those 10^8 visual inputs or perhaps 10^9 inputs of all kinds fresh every millisecond, and those 20 decisions to be made every second, the brain consumes information as a stomach consumes food, only more continuously and with more imperious demands both for fresh information and for the energy needed to process it.

What is demanded is not merely information-signals but variations in the signals, as has been shown experimentally quite conclusively in the case of visual perception. In the last few years, it has been found that "scanning"—motion of the eyeball over the visual field— is necessary in order to have any sensation of vision at all. Riggs, Ditchburn, and their co-workers measured the motions of the eyeball by a photoelectric detector (Riggs, Ratliff, Cornsweet, and Cornsweet, 1953; Riggs, Armington, and Ratliff, 1954; Ditchburn and Fender, 1955). They found that when a person is trying to fixate a point of light, his eyeball is oscillating all the time through a range of about one half minute of arc and at a frequency of the order of 100 cycles per second. This motion is of course too delicate and rapid to be detected visually by the visual process which it mediates. The eyeball not only trembles in this way, but it also changes direction suddenly from time to time and drifts, somewhat more slowly, so that the image wanders about continually over the fovea.

Both groups of workers have compensated these motions of the eyeball by using electronic-optical feedback devices and corneal lens devices to form a "stabilized image" on the retina (Riggs *et al.*, 1953; Ditchburn and Fender, 1955). They made the curious discovery that, as soon as such a stabilization begins, vision ceases within a fraction of a second. The edges of patterns appear to blur out and the perceptual field becomes a uniform gray. The subject has a sensation of stress, and his eyeball makes wilder and wilder excursions. It is said to be a great relief if the eyes overshoot the stabilization limits of the apparatus so that vision reappears for a second. (Perhaps the origin of this relief is similar to that of the relief produced in other stimulus-deprivation experiments when the deprivation ends.)

What this dependence of vision on movement means is that our perceptual system is not equipped to detect really steady inputs, but only fluctuating inputs, and that its own motions are normally used to produce these fluctuations. Such "reafferent stimulation" or "stimulation that changes as a consequence of movements of the recipient organism" may always play a vital role in perception, as Held (1961) and others have emphasized. It may be that perception without participation is impossible.

To put it another way, the visual system is not a d.c. or "direct-current" detecting system, but an a.c. or "alternating" system, as Ditchburn says. Sharpness of boundaries is an important factor in maximizing the alternations or fluctuations of input, and the automatic focusing mechanism of the eye is operating all the time to make the image boundaries as sharp as possible. The sharp or the highly contrasting object draws our immediate attention, and we follow it, perhaps because it offers us sharper fluctuations. The now-famous two-color illusions of Edwin Land (1959) depend critically upon sharpness of focus, which may be evidence that fluctuations play an important role in color perception also.

Conceivably fluctuation is as necessary for hearing as for vision. It is true that in a steady tone, the sound pulses always represent a pulsating physical stimulus (just as in a steady light the single photons represent a pulsating physical stimulus), but lower-frequency variations of pitch or intensity are probably necessary for effective stimulation. We cease to notice a continued steady tone, and warbling notes are used for warning. It is said that even persons with absolute pitch have difficulty in identifying the pitch of a perfectly pure sine wave input.

Therefore, if we say that the brain consumes and demands information, we are not using these words lightly. The nervous system oscillates for information, that is, for the variable, the contrasting, and the least expected; it tracks it down; and if none is to be had, perhaps it invents it (Held, 1961). I think this is the simplest way to summarize the meaning of curiosity and attention and boredom, and of the aberrations and hallucinations of the stimulus-deprivation experiments, phenomena which have all been discussed at length by many authors. (See Chapters 5, 7, and 9.) And I am no longer using the word "information" to mean merely stimuli or light images from the external world. I am using it in the full technical sense of information theory, a sense which Warren Weaver (1953) has explained very well:

> Information is . . . a measure of one's freedom of choice in selecting a message. The greater this freedom of choice, and hence the greater the information, the greater is the uncertainty that the message actually is some

particular one. Thus greater freedom of choice, greater uncertainty, greater information go hand in hand (1953, p. 273).

The mind seeks to escape from the certainties of the diffuse light that remains during stimulus-deprivation. It is bored by the certainties of any humdrum job or routine entertainment. It seeks out the single moving spot on the landscape or the tiny squeak in the engine. It plays the slot machine to exhaustion, hoping for the rare and unpredictable payoff when the three lemons turn up. What it seeks in the variable light signals, and what it processes and responds to on all levels, is information—the changing, the novel, the surprising, and the uncertain.

Nevertheless, having emphasized this need for novelty, we must turn around and consider the other branch of our first paradox, namely, the need for regularity or pattern in our input information. The mind demands pattern, and it is easy to show that this must also be a primitive and essential need. For consider what kind of connections are required to make a response network efficient. A human being has of the order of 10^9 input channels from all his senses. He may have a similar number of output channels, or possibly somewhat fewer. It would obviously be fruitless to have each input matched up with only one output, like a billion reflex arcs laid side by side; because with a billion different inputs at each instant, we should then have a billion uncoordinated and conflicting outputs also. It follows that if we are to have a unique and self-consistent set of outputs without internal conflict between them, cross-connections are necessary between these arcs; and extensive ones, too, so that essentially every input signal can be collated with every other one before the unitary output decision is made.

But cross-connections mean that the response is not to any single input alone, but to the whole array or pattern of inputs. A single input would give only one alternative, on or off, and only one output behavior, on or off; making the other inputs unnecessary. It is therefore a fundamental axiom that any many-element receptor system, any organism with more than one sensory input spot (even *Paramecium*!) is necessarily a pattern-selecting or pattern-perceiving system. Pattern perception must be almost as primordial as response itself, and must have a role that has grown to vast importance in a brain with 10^9 inputs.

It is an amusing exercise to try to schematize our many-channel input-output system by drawing on a sheet of paper a dozen parallel input-output lines (since 10^9 is too many to draw). If we then try to add to these lines a distinguishable set of cross-connections, and cross-connections of the cross-connections between and around them, we can see immediately how the three-dimensional physical pattern would almost necessarily swell into a "great raveled knot," which is what the brain has been called. Possibly the convolutions of the brain have just this kind of physical necessity, as being a physically efficient way of packing an indefinitely growing number of cross-connections; just as the quite differently shaped convolutions of the intestines have a kind of physical necessity, in providing a large surface-to-volume ratio for a continuous tube in a small space. If this is so, the shape of the convolutions of the brain is a sort of visible proof of cross-connections and therefore of a mode of operation based on pattern perception.

Recency of Evolution of the Brain

And now, having emphasized the antiquity of the nervous response to stimuli and to pattern, we must also turn around to the other branch of the second paradox and emphasize exactly the opposite, namely, the astonishingly recent evolution of the highly developed brains that we have. Several papers on this subject were given at the 1959 Darwin Centennial Celebration at Chicago. The anthropological evidence presented by Washburn (1960) and Washburn and Howells (1960) shows that our brains have roughly tripled in size since the discovery of fire and tools and speech. Our thumbs seem to have moved around to the opposed position in the same period. The internal and external changes occurred together, and apparently we have a newly developed tool-using brain to operate the new tool-using thumb.

In another paper at the same symposium, Emiliani (1960) gave radioactive dates for this development of the brain: although the exact figures are still being debated, he found that it may have occurred in much less than 500,000 years. On an evolutionary time scale, this is an absolutely explosive development of a new species or a new capacity. To paraphrase some older writers, if the two-billion-year history of life is represented by the height of Rockefeller Chapel at the University of Chicago, the time since our brains began to develop in this way is represented by a stick a half inch thick lying on top of the chapel roof, and the time since the development of agriculture is represented by the mere thickness of a postage stamp on top of that. Our brains and our powers have enlarged with spectacular rapidity, and there is no reason to suppose that they are not still enlarging at the same rate!

There must have been a reason for this enlargement, a challenge which brought it forth. The anthropological evidence shows what it was, and what kinds of situations these brains were evolved to cope with. The external problem for pre-man and early man was the problem of coming down from the trees into a new environment and of manipulating tools, fire, and speech so as to survive during the ice ages. We know from geological evidence that ice ages were essentially unprecedented within the experience of mammals. So were tools and fire. One suspects that upon this daring species of primates—using tools and weapons and fire not only against the cold and the other animals but against each other—novel situations of all kinds may have crowded in at a rate faster than any species had ever experienced before and survived. In every generation, in every year, and sometimes every day, they had to search over and over again for the crucial regularities in the flux of strangeness. It was learn or die. What our brain was evolved to deal with was continuous novelty of pattern. It should therefore be no surprise to find that that is what it is prepared to deal with and demands to deal with today.

PATTERNS IN VISUAL PERCEPTION

Functional Geometry and the Necessary Symmetries of Perception

The second phase of my argument comes closer to the actual aesthetic problem. It deals with the basic role of patterns in our visual perception. Certain problems of perception are peculiar to big brains with vast numbers of sensory elements. A beginning has been made on these problems (Platt, 1958, 1960), and some of the results can be summarized here.

Consider what it means to have the enormous number of 10^8 elements packed into a biological mosaic receptor such as the human retina. Since this is a piece of tissue which has been subject to all the accidents and irregularities of biological growth, and since the arrangement of the receptor cells looks random under the microscope—very different from the orderly arrangement in the little insect eye—it seems almost a certainty that this great number of elements could not have been individually prelocated, say on the basis of genetic information, with any great precision. It is then hard to see how the brain can "know where the cells are" or can make any visual discriminations that depend on their precise location. If the cells have a microscopic uncertainty of location, one would suppose that a line appearing straight to one man would appear full of little wiggles to his twin brother; the amplitude of the wiggles would indicate the limits of accuracy of the genetic specification.

Yet our actual discrimination and precision in certain visual observations is fantastic. Our "vernier acuity," or ability to detect a lateral break in a straight line, and our "stereoscopic acuity," or ability to detect the nonequivalence of a pair of angles seen with both eyes, are both known to be about 2 seconds of arc, which corresponds to $1/10$ of a cone diameter, or about 1,600 angstroms distance on the retina. Simply as an achievement in mechanical construction, such a precision would be astonishing, for a distance of 1,600 angstroms is not measurable in the finest machine shops except by optical methods. But biologically, the prelocation of every tissue cell in the eye to such an accuracy, 10 times finer than the size of the cell, would be absolutely unbelievable.

I was puzzled by this for a long time, until I finally began to wonder if we were not looking at the problem in the wrong way in emphasizing the precision of location of individual cells. Could there not be some very high-precision physical method that a 10^8-element system could use in making discriminations without having to know exactly where the individual sensory elements are located? And I found that there is at least one such method; that it is closely related to the very high-precision methods used in optical work; and that it would permit us to make precisely those pattern comparisons that we make most accurately. It involves moving the eye over a field and comparing the signals received at one time with those received at another. I have called this method "functional geometry," since it is the geometry generated by a mosaic or areal system undergoing its normal functional motions, and is not the static point-by-point location of images. The requirement of motion is not unreasonable since this motion is experimentally necessary for perception in any case.

The way the method works is as follows. Consider the array of light signals from all the rods and cones. (By "array," I mean a set of signals with no specified relationships between them; by "pattern," a set containing some relationship.) If this array is the same after some particular rotation of the eyeball—if the array is then "congruent" to an earlier array—this means there is some pattern, something in the external field which is congruent to itself after such a displacement of the array, resulting from the rotation. The brain can then perceive such a something if it can only detect the "sameness" of the array before and after the displacement—which is about the weakest requirement one could impose on a network. And the perception can be made without "knowing" where any of the receptor cells are individually located.

A straight line is such a self-congruent something, since it is congruent to itself and the array remains unchanged under any displacement along it. The array of signals from parallel lines would also be self-congruent under any displacement along the lines. Note that the images on the retina or on the cortex can be as crooked as you please without destroying the self-congruence, since all that is required is that the image fall on the same locus after displacement, and it makes no difference what that locus is. The discrimination is for straightness or parallelism in the *external* field. A circle is also self-congruent, but under rotations—which the eye can in fact perform. Concentric circles are likewise. Equidistant repeated patterns —"periodic" patterns—are self-congruent for unit displacements (discrete translations) in the direction of the repetition.

Congruence is also possible in the time dimension. Any space or sound array which is repeated after an interval or is repeated periodically is self-congruent in time. Audition may also have its own "stationary" self-congruent patterns similar to those of vision. One can imagine that octave or harmonic relationships between tones involve congruent excitation patterns on the basilar membrane of the ear. (It would be interesting to know whether changes of tension in this membrane could be used for "scanning" the excitation patterns.)

One advantage of the self-congruent method of perceiving patterns is that it is invariant to damage or loss of the receptor cells, or to blind spots. This method therefore makes it easier to understand psychological "closure" and also the extrapolation of patterns, which on a deeper level is called induction.

Another advantage is that the precision of discrimination is not limited by the coarseness of the retinal mosaic but only by the time taken in observation, that is, the time to look for small discrepancies in the congruences of the input signal array. This makes it possible to account for the high precision of the visual acuity judgments mentioned above. This approach to infinite precision is typical of functional geometry and is the central concept in high-precision optical work. Spherical and plane mirrors and precision screws are brought to perfection by being polished with a matching tool until they are self-congruent under certain types of displacements. In biology, this is the principle that generates perfectly helical elbow joints, spherical hip joints, and eyeballs in spherical sockets.

For the experienced adult eye, it might not be necessary to scan every new straight line afresh to determine its approximate straightness. Certain retinal elements may have been associated so often in past straight-line perceptions that when these elements are excited again and give off the same chorus of signals, we are satisfied of the straightness of the new object without further scanning. A single high-speed flash of light permits an adult to read all the writing in his 1-degree foveal circle; so retinal elements may be associated in letter relationships as well as straight-line relationships. After learning many such association patterns, the brain knows all it needs to know about the location of the individual receptors (although it might forget under retinal damage or stimulus deprivation).

Nevertheless this method of pattern perception would require that an infant or a visually naive adult (after removal of a congenital cataract, for example) might require long scanning and study to determine the straightness of a line; and this is in fact the case. This is consistent with the Hebb doctrine (1949) that perceptual organization even of such apparently primitive relationships as straightness or triangularity is only acquired — learned — through visual experience.

Arthropods can learn almost nothing, and birds can learn only certain things. It follows that much if not all of their pattern-perceiving system is prelocated and preconnected, from genetic information alone. This involves a great limitation on an individual animal's responses and powers in the presence of any situation completely new to his species. To escape this limitation it is necessary to develop a new type of pattern perception, one capable of jumping conceptual gaps and of learning, perhaps by using methods such as fundamental geometry that permit the learning of regularities that go beyond the genetic information. Such an escape is obviously needed for a really big brain with a billion inputs. These considerations add weight to our earlier anthropological conclusion that pattern learning may be the faculty that grew most rapidly in the sudden evolutionary expansion of our own brain capacity.

There is one even more surprising aspect to the discrimination of pattern by functional geometry: certain kinds of patterns will always be selected out as unique or primitive patterns by any mosaic system, whether biological or artificial. While a mathematician of curved spaces might say that an S curve in one curved space is a straight line in another and that these are equally good descriptions, a functional mosaic will accept as straight only those Euclidean lines that satisfy self-congruence under displacement. (It accepts uniformly curved arcs, too, but the error can be discovered by putting two identical arcs back to back.)

This selectivity means that an external characteristic called straightness is a primitive and unique category of perception to all such mosaic systems. Likewise something called parallelism (and self-congruent parallels never meet!). And something called equidistance, and so on. There are other important categories of perception such as continuity and discreteness which contribute to "thingness" but which will not concern us here; in part they involve the local self-congruence of small areas of the input pattern rather than the larger symmetry. It is interesting to see that these various categories are the "synthetic *a priori*" categories of Kant, and some of them are the "unprovable axioms of science" of Bertrand Russell—unique categories that impose themselves on all minds regardless of particular experiences and yet cannot be learned without particular experiences and comparisons.

I suspect that there is only a small number of these unique symmetry categories for a visual mosaic receptor, and that these are just the complete set of "group-theoretical" operations involving the three rotations of the eyeball. (The "group theory" referred to is the mathematical theory of the rotations and other operations about a point center that transform a symmetrical pattern from one configuration into another one identical to it.) If so, every visual pattern relationship that can be perceived is some combination of these rotation operations associated with the group theory. To take an example, consider three lines that are not equidistant but are separated by distances in the ratio $1:\pi$. One might ask whether such a set of lines could ever form a natural or primitive pattern category for all minds—perhaps to be distinguished and identified by a sophisticated self-congruence of the intervals under some queer combination of motions. I think the answer is that a *genetic* system might be evolved to select such a pattern, or any other; but that such a pattern would not satisfy self-congruence for any imaginable mosaic receptor whatever. "God made the integers, man made all the rest" is the remark of a big mosaic receptor that looks for sharp boundaries and self-congruence.

In the one dimension belonging to time, there is only one self-congruent pattern element. It is repetition or periodicity, like that of a rhythmic beat or, on a finer scale, that of the successive waves in a steady tone. We know, of course, that very complex rhythmic patterns can be combined, but it will scarcely be denied that the pattern variation available to composers is far less than that available to the painter or sculptor.

These remarks on the physics of perception can be reduced to two main points. First, time and space fluctuations of input stimuli are probably necessary in order to perceive pattern, at least in the learning stage. Second, a big mosaic detector preferentially selects as unique just those few pattern elements that have the self-congruence property in space or time.

I think we can extend both principles from the area of perception to the area of appreciation. There is a physiological component in all satisfaction: one can't enjoy anything with a stomach ache. The brain is a physiological organ. It would be hard to believe that any physiological process that goes as far back in evolution as does the acquisition and ordering of new information should not have the strongest affective overtones in our daily lives. The functional satisfaction of this large organ doing its job and doing it well may be a major element in our feelings of pleasure and aesthetic satisfaction.

If this is so, then at the root of enjoyment must lie the same factors that perception itself depends upon. If fluctuations are basic to perception, we may suspect that they will play a large role in enjoyment. If the self-congruent patterns are basic for perception, we may suspect they will be basic for enjoyment. And perhaps a combination of the two, a flux in which we can find a pattern, or a pattern that contains unexpected fluctuations, will give the greatest satisfaction of all. The child is pleased and laughs when, in his random scanning up and down a line, he discovers straightness or, in his manipulation of the block, he discovers that it just fits the hole in the box. Perhaps the intellectual satisfaction of the adult has the same roots. This could help us understand why all the students in a mathematics class are pleased by an elegant proof, a proof that uses the full reasoning and inductive powers of the brain to discover a new order in a maze of complexity.

Art and the Symmetries of Animals

The mathematician and group theorist, Hermann Weyl, has a classic essay on "Symmetry" which has recently been reprinted (1956), and which discusses the translational and rotational symmetry groups used by artists. He pays especial attention to the symmetry forms found in the biological world, forms which are basic points of departure for painters and sculptors. In fact, all of us are accustomed to certain symmetries throughout our lives just because of our experience of the animal world.

In these forms, only certain symmetry classes are found. For example, many single-cell animals, spores, blood cells, and other free-floating creatures which seem indifferent to propulsion in one direction rather than another, are spherical or quasi-spherical, with a shape indifferent to direction in space. They are self-congruent under rotation. We are immediately in the presence of art as well as geometry. This is exactly the reason why the Greeks spoke of the sphere and the circle as the most perfect shapes, although the classical geometry that defines these shapes by points and fixed radii tends to obscure the self-congruence property.

Angular shapes have a lower symmetry. They have some self-congruence under directional changes, but of a more limited kind. An angular figure that can be converted into itself only by certain discrete rotations has the symmetry of a polygon; or, in three dimensions, of a polyhedron. This lower, but still very great, symmetry is seen in the beautiful star polyhedra of the radiolarians. It is also seen in the art of Christmas ornaments, which are free-swinging if not free-floating, and are therefore free to have space symmetry rather than flat symmetry. In animals where one might expect rotational indifference, the choice between round and angular forms probably depends on whether their mode of life requires minimum surface area or maximum surface area for survival.

Moving up the scale of life, the sessile animals or plants that are attached to a surface tend to have cylindrical symmetry, with a shape indifferent to rotation about an axis perpendicular to the surface, and therefore self-congruent under this rotation. We see this in sea anemones and sand dollars and in the general shapes of trees and their trunks. A few moving forms with directed motions, especially swimming or burrowing forms, are also relatively indifferent to rotation about the axis of motion and have cylindrical symmetry, like that of roundworms and the roots of plants. Self-congruence under discrete rotations about an axis gives us the polygonal forms of the starfish and of flowers.

For plants climbing on vertical surfaces, gravity and light give a preferred direction in the surface and the cylindrical symmetry is lost. The same is true for animals having a directed motion over a surface, that is, having a head end and a tail end. For such forms, there is only one possible symmetry left, bilateral symmetry, which means indifference to right and left, or to reflection in a plane perpendicular to the surface and containing the head-tail axis. Reflection is a group-theoretical operation not available to the rotating eyeball, so we are not terribly sensitive to right-left differences or to deviations from symmetry in our friends' faces. As a result, familiar faces look strange when seen in a mirror. But we are sensitive to equidistance; and perhaps it is the equidistance of the right and left sides of an object from the median line that accounts for whatever abstract appreciation of bilateral symmetry we have.

In nature we also find the symmetry of equidistant segments, periodic translational self-congruence. It is everywhere in the lower animals and plants, in the segments of the bamboo or the worm, in the legs of the millipede and in the nipples of the pig. A similar symmetry is the helical translational-rotational periodicity, found at the molecular level in long-chain protein and nucleic acid molecules, and higher up, in helical plant stems and spiral shells, as emphasized by D'Arcy Thompson in his seminal book *On Growth and Form* (1959). But these translational and helical repetitions of form do not grow out of the symmetry relations to the environment as the rotation symmetries do. Our own bodies have no helical periodicities, I believe, except in kinky hair, and no translational periodicities except in hidden or small parts such as ribs and vertebrae, fingers and toes, eyelashes, and fingerprints.

The strange and interesting thing about self-congruence relations is that there are no other symmetry classes than those we have mentioned. One can say with mathematical certainty that the Martians or creatures from any other world must have either some of these symmetries, or none!

(Psychologists might consider adding other symmetry groups to the Rorshach ink blot test. The monotonous bilateral symmetry of these tests necessarily tends to lead to interpretations involving animal forms. If subjects were presented with fivefold symmetries, or translational periodicities, or representations of three-dimensional circular symmetries, the variety of the interpretations might be greatly increased.)

To summarize these remarks on pattern, there is evidently a happy coincidence between many of the physiological symmetries imposed by evolution and the primitive pattern symmetries involved in perception. Weyl emphasizes this agreement. Both of these symmetries have a common geometrical explanation. The reason is that they are both derived from the limited set of group-theory symmetries of the "translation groups" and "rotation groups" in three dimensions. We can go on to see that this coincidence of the two sets of forms makes them doubly significant for us as elements of artistic organization, because they now have *both* a referential and a formal meaning, and in art they satisfy us on two levels at once, the biological and the abstract. That is to say, the bizarre fascination of fences and lattices and the repetitious windows of Italian palaces is related on the one hand to the familiar biological repetition of the centipede and the spinal column and on the other hand to the importance of equidistance in our own visual organization of space.

Similar remarks would apply to the time dimension. Repetition and time-periodicity, which are the self-congruent categories of temporal perceptual organization, are also the categories of biological sounds and rhythmic biological movement. We perhaps should recognize that they also can satisfy us on two levels and can have some referential meaning as well as a formal meaning when they appear in the temporal arts of music and the abstract screen. The biological and emotional meaning of a fast tempo is necessarily different from that of a slow one, even if the formal pattern is exactly the same.

The intention of this discussion of symmetry has been to show that there could reasonably be within us a physiological basis for calling certain geometrical symmetry relations beautiful. It is now time to go further and to emphasize that the connection between mathematical pattern and aesthetic excellence has been, in fact, a central part of aesthetic criticism since the dawn of history. In all our languages, the technical terms that indicate geometrical or physical regularities are also the terms of artistic praise. Ever since the Greeks, the words balance, symmetry, and harmony have had both meanings.

A symmetrical picture is well balanced. Musical harmonics are harmonious. Harmony in the laboratory is a numerical relation between frequencies; outside, it is a larger aesthetic satisfaction. Rhythm is even used occasionally in the larger sense, as in describing smooth and skillful movements, or the good life. I mention these linguistic identities not as an argument, but as a deep psychological summary of many arguments. For 2,000 years, mathematical regularities have been inseparable from the aesthetic dialogue.

THE NEED FOR DEVIATIONS IN PATTERNS

Humor and Emotion in Music

Modern aesthetic theory says, nevertheless, that formal beauty is more than pattern: what is beautiful is pattern that contains uncertainty and surprise and yet resolves them into the regularity of a larger pattern. I believe that this view can easily be understood in the light of our physiological need for novelty as well as pattern. Long-lasting aesthetic satisfaction is produced not by one pattern by itself, for this soon becomes boring, but only by a pattern developing into patterns of patterns, continually full of new information drawing attention to itself (Platt, 1959).

This is a change from older ideas. Weyl admits, for example, that ". . . occidental art, like life itself, is inclined to mitigate, to loosen, to modify, even to break strict symmetry" (1956, p. 676). But he then asserts, "Even in asymmetric designs one feels symmetry as the norm from which one deviates under the influence of forces of non-formal character" (p. 676). As part of a thesis on symmetry, this is excellent, but as criticism, it is incomplete. In current theory, the deviation is as important to art as the norm, and we may have formal statistically random forces as well as nonformal ones.

Again, Weyl says, "All musicians agree that underlying the emotional element of music is a strong formal element. It may be that it is capable of some such mathematical treatment as has proved successful for the art of ornaments" (p. 703). True. And we have seen how the emotion might be generated. But a more complete statement would include the strong emotions produced by formal randomness, like the emotions of gamblers or of children playing peek-a-boo, and would also include the possibility of a mathematical treatment of randomness or information content as well as of order. We want a theme with variations; and the variations are as important as the theme.

In the word "attractive" there is another double meaning that illustrates this point. The attractive (from *trahere*, to draw) signifies not only an aesthetic judgment but also a physical pull: that which draws us, that which our eyes "trace" and follow; the unusual, the information-full. A moving spot on the landscape, a memorable design, or a strange perfume draws or attracts us through basic feedback mechanisms of great importance for survival and therefore of great emotional importance. It is a question of the singular case. Put one fly in a classroom and the whole class watches it. Put a hundred in, and no one bothers. Everyone remembers the audience-rousing blare that precedes the "Hymn to Joy" in the Ninth Symphony, because it is so singular and unexpected; and later on, so triumphantly resolved. The classic aesthetic formulations are incomplete: What is memorable is not the perfect but the perfect that contains the unexpected. "There is no excellent beauty that hath not some strangeness in the proportions," said Bacon. He was the first of the moderns.

Several critics have described this link, in music and poetry, between aesthetic emotion and new information. Among the humanists, Leonard Meyer probably comes closest to thinking in terms of quantitative information theory. He says:

> At one time I subscribed to I. A. Richard's statement that "the two pillars upon which a theory of criticism must rest are an account of value and an account of communication." However it has seemed increasingly clear that these two are as inextricably linked to each other as are means and ends. When you discuss one, you are of necessity implying the other (1959, pp. 486-7).

And he stresses elsewhere "the importance of uncertainty in musical communication, the probabilistic nature of musical style" (1957, p. 412). In his book on *Emotion and Meaning in Music* (1956), he shows how composers manipulate our expectations and thereby surprise us in order to achieve an aesthetic effect. When we listen to music, he says,

> Under certain conditions we expect change, under others continuity, and under still others repetition . . . expectation is always ahead of the music, creating a background of diffuse tension against which particular delays articulate the affective curve and create meaning (1956, p. 59).

A detailed musical analysis along these lines would not be easy to describe here. But it is easy to see what Meyer means if we apply his ideas to the development of a simple visual pattern, the kind of thing we might watch developing in a television advertisement. Suppose I draw an incomplete circle for you, thus:

You watch it and wait for me to finish it, in a sense completing it in your mind. There is a hesitation and a sense of tension in you while waiting, like the sense of tension in waiting for the second shoe to fall in the apartment overhead. When the circle is finally completed there is at least a little sense of satisfaction.

But suppose I start over and draw only part of the circle:

and then while you are waiting for me to complete it, I draw instead a similar part of another circle, a mirror image, a little distance away so that the two gaps face each other. As the second circle is begun, there is a moment of confusion and then the expectation of

the first is postponed. There is a reassessment. You think, Aha! Maybe he will stop at the same point on the second one; then there would be some symmetry. And when I do stop at that point, you feel that expectation satisfied; but the other expectation of completion now reappears more intensely than before, because there are now two circles to be completed.

Yet if I simply do complete them, I am sure you will feel a let-

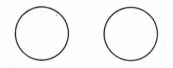

down. That would simply satisfy your old expectation; and you have now begun to like this game of having a little uncertainty at every step about what the new development will be.

So the situation of the two circles with gaps cries out for a different solution, for a third entity to be developed, a third movement in musical terms. And if we do not want to build up great contrapuntal designs—which would be interesting and which might be the great abstract screen art of the future—then a simple solution is to draw a third complete circle symmetrically between the other two, touching and so closing the four open points.

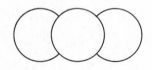

This last addition to the two circles with gaps surprises us in a certain sense, by not fulfilling the initial expectations at all. Yet it satisfies the expectation of closure as well as that of novelty by producing closure in another way. And the closure is particularly satisfying because it is a closure in several senses at once. As the last circle is just being completed, it restores the symmetry which has been temporarily disrupted during the drawing of it, it closes itself, and it closes the first two, all at the same time. It brings them all together in a larger architectonic unity, to use the grand musical terminology. We have a feeling of completion, a feeling that any further pencil stroke would necessarily have to be a starting off of some completely new idea.

The completed pattern I have drawn is a rather standard design motif, suitable perhaps for a beer advertisement or for a new Olympic flag. As a television ad, of course, the final architectonic triumph would turn out to be the manufacturer's trademark. People get paid for composing this kind of game; and millions watch, so it must be aesthetically satisfying to somebody, perhaps for some of the reasons just outlined.

The same teasing game can be found in music, if one looks for it. Anyone can work out for himself the similar structure of an immortal nursery tune like "Three Blind Mice," with its expectations, little fulfillments, surprises, and so on. By the time you reach the end of it, you are astonished to catalog how many different kinds of chromatic and rhythmic expectation are satisfied by the concluding descending phrase.

Meyer (1956) emphasizes that our expectations in a given art medium are built up culturally. If the playing of "Three Blind Mice" were interrupted at one point or another, a Western 6-year-old child with a good ear and some musical experience could probably pick out many of the next fulfillment-notes on a piano, even if he had not heard the tune before (if such a combination of experience and musical naivete is possible in our society). But a comparable Senegalese child or a Chinese child, from a different culture with a different musical scale, probably could not do this nearly as well, except perhaps for the identification of the universal keynote at the end. On the other hand, these other children would have expectations for their own music that we would be unable to guess. This is what makes Oriental and African music difficult for Westerners to understand or enjoy. It violates our expectations at almost every note, so that our perception of the organization is slow and difficult, like the attempt of a visually naive adult to perceive a triangle.

Meyer (1959) illustrates the aesthetic necessity for variation of pattern by comparing two similar themes with a similar basic melody, one by Bach (the introductory bars of the Prelude and Fugue for Organ), and one by Geminiani. The first is better, Meyer says, because Bach introduces unexpected variations, where Geminiani simply descends straight down the scale, so that there is less delay in our expectation, and less satisfaction when we reach the end. The circle is completed, but too easily. He loses our attention because he plays no games with us.

This may be a good place to mention the relation of these notions to games and amusement. It is music, I believe, that proves the fundamental nature of humor more conclusively than all the books that have been written explaining humor. For it is an experimental fact that the formal patterns of music and their variations can be not only amusing in the sense of being entertaining but amusing in the sense of being laughable. Whole audiences can be made to laugh on cue at the Surprise Symphony or at Mozart's off-key violin. This is not referential humor; no external clown is being pointed to and the amusement is not produced by funny glubbing noises from the oboe or tuba. It is formal internal humor having to do with the syntax of the musical sentence, with some combination of delay-and-fulfillment or doubt-and-reassurance as the shocking gaffe is found to be part of a larger plan. Not pattern, but surprise-in-pattern. The explosion of breath is the physiological proof of our tension and relief. It might help our understanding if we called this pattern-game "wit" and made a sharp distinction between it and "humor." Wit is syntactic, humor referential.

What has complicated the interpretation of laughter is the referential character of most humor: the conceited man who slips on a banana peel. But this has formal humor also. Surprise, that an adult should fall; satisfaction, that his conceit has fallen also, to where it belongs. We say that man is the only animal that laughs. This means he is the only animal that plays games with patterns. The child will laugh at patterns that give only a gentle pleasure to adults. Perhaps all the child's games are such a mixture of formal patterns and surprise. But the roots of the adult's pleasure are in the child's laughter.

Music is a good field in which to study this interaction between the regular and the unexpected, the shock and the reevaluation, with their resultant aesthetic—or humorous—effects. It is a one-dimensional form, so that a complete analysis is easier than for the multidimensional forms of the colored visual arts with their tremendous information inputs. Reproduction and playback are simple, and the investigator could stop a musical piece and determine, as Shannon did for language, the precise statistical expectations of an audience, thus actually measuring quantitatively the information conveyed by the next notes. And the investigator can examine easily the aesthetic effect of various alternatives.

Pseudomusic is already being written by computing machines (Hiller, 1959; Hiller and Isaacson, 1959). The machine chooses random notes for its compositions, imposing on them only the rules of harmony and those short-range correlations between successive notes which are typical, say, of a culture or of a particular composer. It is rather startling to find that by this simple means, the machine produces a crude but recognizable imitation of the style in question. Eventually such an experimental approach will permit the effects of randomness and pattern choices, both long-range and short-range, to be studied in detail. Perhaps a computing machine, if it knew enough about what to expect, could even write a surprise symphony. It would be interesting to find out whether it could be programmed to have a sense of humor! At any rate, work with computing machine compositions should enable music teachers and composers to get a clearer understanding of the ground rules of their craft. Music may soon become, if it is not already, the most sophisticated field of aesthetic criticism.

Excellence in Poetry

I will conclude with a few quotations that show the same ideas running through modern poetic criticism. The first is a very explicit statement by Gerard Manley Hopkins, who influenced so many later poets. In a kind of undergraduate manifesto, "On the Origin of Beauty: A Platonic Dialogue," he applies to poetry his own theory of natural and visual beauty, which is summarized in these words:

"Then the beauty of the oak and the chestnut-fan and the sky is a mixture of likeness and difference or agreement and disagreement or consistency and variety or symmetry and change."

"It seems so, yes."

"And if we did not feel the likeness we should not think them so beautiful, or if we did not feel the difference we should not think them so beautiful. The beauty we find is from the comparison we make of the things with themselves, seeing their likeness and difference, is it not?" (House and Storey, 1959, p. 90.)

Hopkins then applies this to rhythm in poetry.

". . . Rhythm therefore is likeness tempered with difference . . . And the beauty of rhythm is traced to the same causes as that of the chestnut-fan, is it not so?" (House and Storey, 1959, p. 101.)

And he extends this to other aspects of poetic beauty in considerable detail.

It is also instructive to note this passage from Aristotle on rhythm in prose, which Hopkins singles out for quotation in his later lecture notes on rhythm and rhetoric:

The shape (or figure) of the diction must not be metrical nor yet unrhythmical. The first of these breeds distrust: it seems artificial and moreover it stands out and catches the ear, making the hearer on the watch for resemblances, when the chime will come again. . . On the other hand what is unrhythmical is unbounded. Now it should be bounded . . . (Aristotle, *Rhet.* III viii, quoted in House and Storey, 1959, p. 275.)

I think that this requirement that art should "not be metrical" is an insight unusual in Greek criticism. But it is coming to be common in modern poetic theory, as shown in the following quotation by Meyer from Robert Penn Warren (1943):

. . . a poem, to be good, must earn itself. It is a motion toward a point of rest, but if it is not a resisted motion, it is a motion of no consequence. For example, a poem which depends upon stock materials and stock responses is simply a toboggan slide, or a fall through space (Meyer, 1959, p. 489.)

One thinks of the fall through space of the Geminiani theme.

In the same vein, someone else has said of Longfellow's style: "If you try to write poetry in the regular meter of 'By the shores of Gitche Gumee, by the shining Big-Sea-Water,' you might as well write prose." The audience becomes bored; and something variable, some new information, has to be introduced just to maintain attention, even before one can begin to achieve any emotional response.

John Crowe Ransom says, in *The World's Body:*

It is not merely easy for a technician to write in smooth metres; it is perhaps easier than to write in rough ones, after he has once started; but when he has written smoothly, and contemplates the work, he is capable actually, if he is a modern poet, of going over it laboriously and roughening it (1938, p. 12).

Naturally, what is rough and what is smooth depends upon our expectations. "A rose is a rose is a rose" is a repetition, but far from smooth or expected. What we expect is a predicate definition. The most interesting predicate could not be such a surprise. Each "rose" means something different—in the sense of formal, not referential, meaning—because each satisfies or surprises with respect to a different expectation. The second "rose" is rare but possible, a blunt, factual emphasis; we do "call a spade a spade." But the third one builds it up into the easy pattern of a child's chant; which for an adult is a linguistic outrage. The trivial repetition is so incredible that it becomes immortal, and changes every "rose" forever after.

T. S. Eliot explicitly compares poetic organization to musical organization. In an essay on *The Music of Poetry*, he says:

There are possibilities for verse which bear some analogy to the development of a theme by different groups of instruments; there are possibilities of transitions in a poem comparable to the different movements of a symphony or a quartet; there are possibilities of contrapuntal arrangement of subject matter (1957, p. 38).

So a theory which accounts for the aesthetic satisfaction of the one form may be applicable to the other also.

Another passage of Eliot's describes particularly clearly the need for both pattern and change in poetry. He says in his early essay, "Reflections on *Vers Libre*":

. . . the most interesting verse which has yet been written in our language has been done either by taking a very simple form, like the iambic pentameter, and constantly withdrawing from it, or taking no form at all, and constantly approximating to a very simple one. It is this contrast between fixity and flux, this unperceived evasion of monotony, which is the very life of verse (1953, pp. 88-89).

This brings us full circle, back to the text from Eliot that I quoted at the beginning. I hope it is now less of a riddle. Poetry is like "amusement," because of its "surprise" and abstract "elevation." It is amusing because it is like wit or humor, which, as we saw for pure musical wit, depends on surprise combined with fulfillment. Our highest mental organization is a continual search for patterns and surprises.

This modern insistence on pattern variation may go beyond anything the Greek critics demanded of their art. In poetics as in music and architecture and science today, we may be reaching out for organizational complexities not dreamed of earlier. We are realizing that it is amusement in this larger sense that is the present intellectual and aesthetic demand.

"But if we think of anything else that poetry"—or wit, or any other art—"may seem to be, we are led into far greater difficulties."

Chapter 15

An Appraisal of the Proposed Conceptual Framework

SALVATORE R. MADDI and
DONALD W. FISKE
University of Chicago

B Y now the reader can appreciate the wide variety of topics included in this book. In spite of their diversity, these sets of empirical phenomena share certain fundamental similarities. The conceptualization presented in Chapter 2, which drew upon a number of ideas already available in the literature, was an attempt to provide a set of concepts with which some of these phenomena could be explained. It is time now to appraise the adequacy of that conceptualization, to ask how useful it actually is for interpreting the various topics from a common viewpoint. In this appraisal, we shall stress the fairly well established empirical phenomena rather than the fragmentary observations and isolated findings. We shall not attempt a critique of alternative explanations and suggestions. This, then, is the appraisal of a particular conceptual scheme at this point in its development, and at this stage of our research knowledge.

The well-documented phenomena described in this book break down into those which can and those which cannot be readily explained by our conceptualization. Among those we can explain are exploratory behavior, alternation behavior, play, some reactions to restricted stimulation, and performance decrement during monotonous tasks. Not within our theoretical grasp at this point are the developmental effects of restricted and enriched environments, individual differences in one or another of the topics of the book, and dreaming. The major sections of this chapter will indicate the nature of our explanation of the first group of phenomena, and will discuss the implications of the second group for the possible revision and extension of our conceptual scheme.

PHENOMENA EXPLAINED BY OUR CONCEPTUALIZATION

Exploratory Behavior

In a wide variety of organisms, exploratory behavior is elicited by the occurrence of a stimulus providing greater variation than was previously characteristic of the surround with which the organism has become familiar (Chapters 7 and 9). Such behavior, which orients the organism toward that stimulus, can take many forms, including visual fixation, manipulation, and play. Although a number of writers favor characterizing the stimuli capable of eliciting exploration in terms of novelty, complexity, or other concepts, we have considered them to embody variation (Proposition 3 in Chapter 2, p. 22). Our concept is broadly defined to include simple change, spatial and temporal unexpectedness, and novelty, all of which have been shown to elicit exploration.

It is important that a strong interest in increments of stimulus variation is found in organisms with low levels of specific motivation, such as hunger. In the typical experiment in this area, the environment with which the animal becomes familiar is composed of stimuli of limited intensity and meaningfulness. Under such conditions, according to Proposition 6 (Chapter 2, p. 38), activation will tend to fall below the normal level unless there is sufficient variation in stimulation to offset this trend. Such a discrepancy is especially likely during the long middle portion of the wakefulness period when normal level is highest. As the usual experimental period of familiarization prior to the introduction of the test stimuli involves little variation, the conditions for a decline in activation level are met.

According to Proposition 7 (Chapter 2, p. 42), the organism should engage in impact-increasing behavior aimed at sustaining normal level of activation. It is in this vein that exposure of the sense receptors to the subsequently introduced test stimuli can be understood. Exploration of the different and perhaps novel or unexpected stimulus is a reactive form of impact-modifying behavior which nonetheless contributes to the maintenance of activation level. The gradual decrease in concern with the new stimulation as it becomes more familiar is also understandable in terms of our viewpoint: after presentation, an initially explored stimulus is typically unchanging, and hence it does not retain its ability to contribute to an increment in activation level. After a period of time, the organism must find some other means of increasing impact. It follows from our approach that the introduction of a continually changing stimulus should elicit exploratory behavior which does not diminish as rapidly as is the case in the typical experimental situation.

Proposition 7 is broad enough to predict that the organism in the typical exploration experiment should orient toward more intense or meaningful stimuli, as well as ones constituting an increment in variation. Certainly all three stimulus properties are considered to contribute to activation. But this consideration raises a problem: Any more intense or meaningful stimulus will also constitute an increment in variation because it constitutes a change from previous stimulation. In order to justify the conceptual distinction between the three properties, it should be possible to achieve at least partial separation of them in practice. We believe this differentiation is possible, and that it might be achieved by comparing the effects on activation of each of two stimuli. One of these stimuli would have more intensity (or meaningfulness) than was characteristic of the surround, while the other would not. Both, of course, would constitute an increment in variation when they were presented to the subject. According to Proposition 3, both stimuli should raise activation level but the one combining an increment in intensity (or meaningfulness) with an increment in variation should make the larger contribution.

Just such a combination of factors contributing to activation level may be important in understanding the observed aversive effects of extremely novel stimuli (see Chapters 7 and 13). Extremely novel stimuli also tend to be either intense or quite meaningful. According to our formulation, such stimuli can actually produce higher-than-normal levels of activation. If they do, then we would expect, on the basis of Proposition 7, that the organism would engage in impact-decreasing behavior in order to reduce level of activation. Avoidance would be an example of such an attempt. It is important for our position that such extremely novel stimuli as the model of a human head clearly without a body (Hebb, 1958a, p. 114) produced not only flight, but also rather clear-cut evidence of fear and high arousal in adult chimpanzees. The occurrence of such negative affective states when activation becomes very high is predicted in Proposition 8 (Chapter 2, p. 46).

The explanation of exploratory behavior given above assumes the initial period of familiarization which is typical of experimental settings in this area. We believe that the course of familiarization is accompanied by a decline in activation, and that this decline is important in understanding exploration of subsequently introduced test stimuli. If this initial period were not to be utilized, if a major portion of the situation were novel, exploratory behavior in the sense of interest in the test objects for their own sake might not occur. Welker's procedure (1957, 1959b) for studying free and forced exploration is relevant here. He found that when rats are placed in a rectangular box lined with objects of various types, their initial response is to leave this environment for a smaller, darker, plainer area if they are given the opportunity to do so. This result suggests that exploratory tendencies are temporarily reduced by employing a procedure which does not involve a period of familiarization with the surround prior to the introduction of the test objects. Whatever exploratory-like behavior occurs in situations of the type used by Welker may actually be instrumental to escape. To check this interpretation, evidence of the emotionality of the rats, perhaps indexed by defecation and urination (Hall, 1934b), would be pertinent.

We have maintained that the aversive effect of extremely novel stimuli is explained on the basis of concomitant increases in intensity or meaningfulness. But contrary to our viewpoint that variation by itself makes little contribution to the higher ranges of activation (Chapter 2, p. 29), it may be found that a very great degree of novelty, of perhaps an absolute rather than a relative nature (Berlyne, 1960, p. 19), can contribute to above-normal activation. If this were the case, our formulation would require modification.

Alternation Behavior

The most thoroughly investigated form of alternation behavior is the tendency of rats that first entered one arm of a **T** or **Y** maze to choose the other arm on the next trial (Chapter 8). In alternating, the rat seems to be seeking stimulation which is different from, and hence provides more variation than, that to which it initially exposed itself. In our terminology, alternation and exploratory responses are both considered impact-increasing behavior. The procedures typically used in studying the two phenomena are similar in that both involve an initial period of familiarization prior to the test period. In the alternation procedure, the first trial serves to familiarize the rat with most of the maze. The major difference between the two procedures is that, on a test trial, no environmental change takes place in the alternation experiment, while such a change does occur in the exploration experiment. In alternating, the rat increases the variation in stimulation he receives by entering the portion of a stable environment with which he is least familiar, while in exploring, a similar increment is achieved by attending to a changed or new portion of the surround. Conceptually, the two behaviors would seem to be quite similar, even though procedural differences make alternation appear more active, and exploration more reactive.

Most of the recent alternation studies have involved animals with low levels of specific motivation. In such conditions, activation will tend to fall below normal level unless there is ample variation in stimulation (Proposition 6). In order to sustain normal activation, the organism will engage in impact-increasing behavior (Proposition 7), which in the present instance involves exposure to the portion of the environment not recently encountered. To re-enter the previously chosen maze arm on the second trial would be inconsistent with sustaining normal level of activation. Thus we explain alternation and exploratory behavior in a similar fashion.

Our position implies that it should be possible to decrease the alternation tendency by utilizing rats with specific motivation (for example, hunger) of sufficient intensity to produce well above the normal level of activation and by providing reward (such as food) on the first trial. On the subsequent trial, the task of finding the goal object would require response repetition, rather than alternation. Response repetition would also be consistent with a reduction in the above-normal level of activation. Although there are some relevant data available, the picture is by no means clear enough at this time to permit evaluation of this implication of our position. We know that alternation does occur in specifically motivated rats that have been rewarded on the first trial (see Estes and Schoeffler, 1955). Yet, if our position is correct, there should be some intensity of specific motivation beyond which the alternation tendency would be reduced if the first trial was rewarded. Although the results of one study (Fowler, Fowler, and Dember, 1959) are consistent with this expectation, only additional research will permit a clear-cut evaluation of our viewpoint.

In the typical alternation experiment, the maze is not changed from the first to the second trial. But it has also been fairly well established that if one arm is changed following visual exposure to both arms, the changed arm will be chosen on the subsequent trial (see Chapter 8, pp. 244–45). This different form of the alternation experiment is subject to the same explanation given above, as our definition of variation incorporates such instances of environmental change.

The response variability examined in Chapter 11 might at first seem to represent a phenomenon at the human level which is similar to that of alternation behavior in the rat. However, it must be noted that the bulk of Chapter 11 deals with conditions under which the subject cannot convincingly be construed as seeking or preferring responses which are new and therefore provide variation in stimulation: the typical situation involves too many responses and too long a period between trials for the subject to recall many of his previous responses at the time of the second trial. Chapter 11 suggests that behavior tends to be as variable as the requirements of the organism's adaptation permit and that such variability has utility.

On the other hand, humans do show response alternation when the trials are contiguous or close in time (see Chapter 8; Fiske and Rice, 1955, p. 235; Denny and Allen, 1959). These conditions do not typically involve strong, specific motivation. With repeated trials close in time, level of activation should fall, unless there is sufficient variation to sustain it (Proposition 7). As the stimuli comprising the second trial are the same as those of the first one, the experimental procedure provides rather minimal variation. Hence, in order that activation not fall below normal level, the subject may engage in impact-increasing behavior, which in this case takes the form of giving different responses than those previously given to the same stimuli.

By now this explanation must be something of a familiar refrain, and the reader will be spared any additional details except one. Conceptually, the situation in which there is no time interval between trials should have the greatest potential for decreasing activation level, and all intervals greater than this up to the limits of immediate memory span should have less. Hence, if we are correct in interpreting human and rat alternation as impact-increasing behavior, extending the interval between the first and second trial from a minimal value to a fairly small one should at least not increase the phenomenon. There is evidence at both the human and rat level that alternation occurs with greater frequency at shorter intertrial intervals (see Fiske and Rice, 1955; Heathers, 1940; Telford, 1931; Weitz and Wakeman, 1941). Of course, this explanation cannot account for all response variability, especially when the intertrial interval is very large.

Play

A final example of behavior aimed at increasing the variation in stimulation supplied by the environment is a type of play which does not seem to be merely exploratory behavior of the kind previously discussed. Such play is not elicited by the occurrence of a stimulus having more variation than was previously present in the surround; rather it appears in what seems to be a spontaneous fashion, particularly when the organism is relatively free of specific motivation. This kind of play occurs in a wide variety of species, especially during childhood (see Chapters 7, 9, and 10), and can appropriately be considered a very active form of impact-increasing behavior. Our explanation of this phenomenon would be the same as that offered above. However, no further discussion will be attempted, as the conditions antecedent to its occurrence are not very precisely known. If our interpretation is adequate, this type of play should occur most frequently when the child is exposed to a familiar situation with limited intensity and meaning.

Effects of Monotonous Tasks and Restricted Stimulation

Research involving monotonous tasks and restricted stimulation has ordinarily involved greater and more prolonged reductions in variation than any of the areas of study thus far discussed. For this reason, the two topics are discussed in the same section of this chapter, even though they involve somewhat different kinds of data.

In monotonous tasks which supply repetitive or unchanging stimulation but require considerable attention, performance becomes less effective as a function of time (Chapter 5). According to Proposition 4 (Chapter 2, p. 31), there is a range of activation which is optimal for the performance of any given task. If performance is initially effective on the monotonous task, we may assume that activation is within the optimal range for the task. However, as time goes on, the repetitive stimulus conditions provide little in the way of variation in stimulation. In the typical task which has been studied, large or varied movements are not compatible with adequate performance. In short, what little variation in stimulation there is at the beginning of testing decreases rapidly as a function of familiarization. Unless the meaningfulness and intensity of the monotonous condition can be kept rather high throughout the testing period, activation may well fall below the level necessary for maximally effective performance. If it does, performance will suffer.

The usually observed decline can be partially offset by utilizing very intense test stimuli. In addition, the introduction of extraneous stimuli, usually of a motivational nature, during the course of testing can boost performance to the initial level (see Chapter 5). These findings are quite understandable from our point of view, as the dimensions of meaningfulness and intensity contribute to activation level (Proposition 3).

Thus far we have attributed decrement in performance on monotonous tasks to decline in activation to a point below the level which is consistent with maximal effectiveness. However, in such a situation the individual may attempt to maintain activation within the optimal range for the task by entering into impact-increasing behavior (Proposition 5). He may hum, tap his foot, become angry at the task, or daydream. If he is unsuccessful in his attempts, then performance will lose effectiveness as indicated earlier. But he may be successful in maintaining activation level and still be less than maximally effective in performing the task. This condition will occur when the impact-modifying behavior engaged in is incompatible with task performance (for example, daydreaming while watching a radar screen). However, if optimal activation level is maintained by means which are not inconsistent with the task, then performance should not suffer at all. It is not feasible at this time to check upon these various possibilities, although the last one may help to explain why some subjects do not show any performance decrements (McGrath *et al.*, 1959).

A number of experiments have been performed in which the impact from external and kinesthetic stimulation is severely curtailed for a period of some hours (Chapter 5). Usually, the nature of the situation and the instructions are such as more or less to limit the forms of impact-modifying behavior available to the organism to that of thinking. Although differing results have been reported by various investigators, a few consistent lines of evidence seem to be emerging. First, subjects typically dislike the situation, experience considerable discomfort and negative affect as time progresses, and terminate their participation in the study. Second, most subjects experience difficulty in maintaining a consistent train of thought concerning a topic or problem they had wished to consider during the experimental period. Third, many participants go to sleep rather soon after the beginning of the study. Fourth, some investigators report that a number of subjects show temporary impairment of perceptual and cognitive functioning as a result of comparatively long periods of restricted stimulation. Fifth, mental imagery of varying type and quality seems to be universally experienced, and hallucinations occur in some subjects.

As the variation, intensity, and meaningfulness of the external and kinesthetic stimulation available in the typical experimental setting is low, a decline in level of activation during the first stages of the study should occur (Proposition 3). This decline is probably offset to a certain extent by an increase in ideational stimulation, but this source of impact alone is apparently not sufficient to maintain normal level of activation. The increasing discomfort and negative affective tone which occur are understandable if activation can be considered to fall considerably below the normal level (Proposition 8). That restricted stimulation does lead to very low activation levels is indicated by the fact that subjects often fall asleep at some point (before their usual time for going to bed). The inability to maintain a train of thought suggests that activation is below the level required for continued effort on mental problems.

It may be that sustained thinking about a single topic is facilitated by the presence of such pertinent stimuli as notes, which repeatedly start new chains of relevant associations. If these speculations should be borne out by empirical work, they might lead to some corollary to Proposition 4 such as: orientation to a task or problem occurs only when the impact from task-relevant stimuli is sufficiently greater than the impact from any other source of stimulation.

The impairment in perceptual and cognitive functioning observed in some studies seems to fall outside our conceptualization. A long period of greatly reduced sensory input may produce a breakdown of normal functioning involving a peculiar temporary condition free of drives and tensions which interferes with the maintenance of a high level of activation (see Shurley, 1960, p. 543). This possibility suggests the importance of determining whether subjects who have just terminated a period of restricted stimulation can handle stress effectively.

The frequency of reported imagery and hallucinations seems to vary with the conditions, especially with the duration and extent of restriction. Little is clearly established about these subjective phenomena. The imagery appears to be a product of ongoing neural activity and perhaps also of the very weak stimulation from both exteroceptive and interoceptive receptors. While similar imagery can be experienced at least momentarily under natural conditions of reduced stimulation (for example, when comfortable and relaxed in a quiet place, with closed eyes), the imagery in these experimental conditions has marked salience because it is the major source of impact. Our conceptualization can account for the relative importance to the subjects of this imagery but not for its existence. The hallucinations, less common and appearing later in the period of restricted stimulation, are beyond the present scope of our interpretive framework. We are unwilling to attempt an explanation until further research specifies their characteristics and the variables associated with their occurrence.

OTHER RELEVANT TOPICS

This book includes relevant discussions of affective tone (Chapter 13) and aesthetic preference (Chapter 14). As the empirical features of these topics have not yet been clearly established, no attempt will be made to appraise our conceptualization with regard to them.

There is a bit of experimental evidence in Chapter 13 that both negligible and fairly large degrees of stimulus unexpectedness are associated with negative affect. The stimuli involved were of rather low intensity and meaningfulness. The results are generally consistent with Proposition 8 since the impact values of small and great unexpectedness are most likely to be associated with low and high levels of activation, respectively.

Chapter 14 presents a point of view which can be similarly interpreted. It is argued that unexpectedness is an important determinant of preference for works of art. Aesthetically valued products provide unexpectedness of a mild degree which is subsequently resolved by the emergence of a larger pattern or regularity. Objects or works which are completely expected, or very unexpected in the sense of providing minimal experience of regularity or pattern, are typically not preferred. If affective experience is considered the basis for the development of preferences, then the argument presented in Chapter 14 is consistent with Proposition 8. Should subsequent investigation confirm the expectations expressed in that chapter, our conceptualization will have to be elaborated to include the statement of some mechanism, presumably involving learning, for the development of preferences.

In providing what is an alternative explanation of exploratory behavior and related phenomena, Chapter 10 stresses effectance and competence motivation. The organism is considered to transact with its environment because of the pleasure to be derived from producing effects by virtue of its own responses, and because of the biological utility of such transaction for the development of competence in coping with a wide variety of situations. While this approach and ours agree on the importance of behavior as a source of what we call stimulus variation, the one discussed in Chapter 10 places little emphasis on environmental change which is independent of the organism's activity. The explanation of exploratory behavior in terms of biological utility involves a different level of analysis than we have employed. Although we certainly have not stressed the value of acquiring competence, our approach is not incompatible with this concept.

PHENOMENA NOT EXPLAINED BY OUR
CONCEPTUALIZATION

Developmental Effects of Restricted or Enriched
Environments

In studies of early restriction, the typical conditions involve limited variation, both in range and moment-to-moment change in stimulation. The intensity of stimulation is also frequently curtailed. There is evidence suggesting that children reared under unusually severe conditions of restriction are relatively inattentive, impulsive, limited in cognitive ability, and deficient in ability to relate to others (Chapter 4). In a variety of lower animals, adverse and enduring effects upon emotionality, learning ability, activity level, social behavior, and perception result from conditions of early restriction (Chapter 4). These empirical phenomena cannot be explained by our conceptualization in its present form. We have not concerned ourselves thus far with the formulation of developmental propositions. However, there are at least two lines along which our approach might be extended in order to subsume the effects of early restriction in stimulation.

Chapter 3 provides evidence that complete or severe deprivation of certain aspects of stimulation in early life can lead to impairment in the development of fairly complex sensory-sensory, sensory-motor, motor-sensory, and motor-motor integrative functions. It would seem that the young organism requires certain types of experience so that various capacities can develop normally. But there may be another important aspect of early restriction. During such a period, activation would tend to be at a low level. In such a state, the young organism would not be able to perform well those learning tasks requiring fairly high levels of activation. Thus, the restricted early environment may have a double-barreled effect: it limits or prevents the occurrence of crucial types of experiences, and it reduces the ability to learn from whatever experiences are available. This outlines one approach to the understanding of the fairly gross deficiencies in cognitive, perceptual, affective, and motor functioning discussed in Chapter 4.

Another possible approach to the explanation of these deficits involves the effects of early stimulus restriction on the development of the characteristic level of activation. Perhaps the low day-to-day levels of activation under such conditions produce a comparatively low characteristic activation curve in maturity. A habituation mechanism could be invoked to explain such a phenomenon. In the absence of tasks to be performed, such an organism would exhibit impact-reducing behavior more often than an organism reared under more ordinary stimulus conditions. It would also avoid tasks requiring substantial levels of activation. Perhaps this second approach would help to explain the durability of the effects produced by restricted early environments.

The effects of an enriched early environment are rather complementary to those of early restriction. However, results are most striking with animal subjects, probably because conditions of normal laboratory rearing are themselves somewhat restricting. In animals, enriched stimulus conditions in childhood lead to comparatively high growth rate, intelligence, and ability to withstand stress (Chapter 4). Such enriched conditions seem to involve greater variation, intensity, and meaningfulness of stimulation than is characteristic of the usual early laboratory environment. The same two possibilities outlined above are applicable here. An enriched early environment may lead to improved cognitive, affective, and motor functioning because it facilitates the development of the complex integrative capacities necessary to adequate performance. The other alternative is that the enriched early environment may, through habituation, result in a comparatively high characteristic curve of activation in maturity. An organism with such an activation curve would perform hard tasks more adequately and would exhibit impact-increasing behavior more often than if it had been reared under more ordinary circumstances.

Individual Differences

There may very well be stable individual differences in all of the empirical phenomena thus far considered. At present our conceptual scheme provides no explicit basis for dealing with such differences. But the previous discussion of developmental effects of restricted and enriched early environments certainly indicates the lines along which relevant individual differences could be explained. Consider the variable of preference for complexity as an example. There is evidence that individuals differ in the degree of stimulus complexity to which they are attracted (Chapter 12). As indicated in the discussion of Proposition 3, we would consider a complex stimulus to have greater potential for variation than a less complex stimulus. Hence, the degree of complexity preferred would give us an indication of the degree of variation to which the person is most attracted. It may be that the persons who characteristically choose high degrees of stimulus complexity also have high characteristic curves of activation, and hence are most frequently seeking increased variation. The converse would be the case for individuals showing preference for low levels of complexity. Of course, it may be that differences in preferred complexity level are better explained in terms of the effects of early environments differing in degree of variation, intensity, and meaningfulness on the development of cognitive, affective, and motor capabilities. This possibility would seem more likely if subsequent investigation discloses a high direct relationship between the disposition to construe complexly and preference for complex stimuli.

Any further consideration of the possible existence and meaning of individual differences in exploratory behavior, performance decrement in monotonous situations, and the like, would take us too far from our primary purpose of evaluating our conceptualization. However, discussions of individual differences are included in a number of the chapters of this book, and there certainly seems little question concerning the usefulness of additional investigation along these lines. In conclusion, note that there may be individual differences in the preferred levels of stimulus intensity and meaningfulness, as well as variation.

Sleep and Dreaming

Since our conceptualization deals only with the period of wakefulness, it cannot at present explain any phenomena occurring during sleep. Yet any further development of our point of view should consider sleep, because it is a natural state of restricted stimulation. During sleep, the intensity, meaningfulness, and variation of external stimuli are markedly reduced. Among the types of interoceptive stimulation, the kinesthetic is greatly curtailed and other forms are somewhat limited.

Our concept of characteristic level of activation can probably be extended to the period of sleep. However, no complete interpretation of the periodic fluctuations is currently available. A topic needing systematic investigation is the interrelationships among the segments of the total diurnal activation function: is the average level of activation during wakefulness related inversely to that during sleep, or to the length of time in the light sleep phase? Perhaps high average waking activation is balanced by low average activation during sleep so that more depleted energy reserves can be adequately replenished.

It is well established that the several periods of light sleep are accompanied by what is usually known as dreaming (Chapter 6). But there is also evidence of mental content during the stages of deeper sleep. Although the nature and frequency of such imagery and thought processes have not been definitely established, the findings permit the tentative speculation that such imagery occurs during much if not all of the sleep period. This assertion would seem to be consistent with the notion of an active organism in which there is continual neural activity.

While this imagery is highly varied and nonrepetitive, it is also realistic, and close to the content of waking experiences, as if it were derived from their residues. On the other hand, subjects' immediate reports of dreams during the light sleep phases have the well-known fanciful and unreal qualities. The function of dreams is still an unsettled problem. They may serve to protect sleep, to keep us from waking, as both Freud (1956) and Foulkes (1960) have suggested, but for different reasons. Dreams seem to be related to current problems (see French, 1952, 1954). Perhaps dreams preserve and promote sleep by dealing with problems in a manner that reduces the impact of the cortical stimuli associated with the representation of the problems, thus permitting the level of activation to decline again. If dreams are more or less successful attempts to cope with conflicts or to reduce the associated tensions, then Proposition 4 might conceivably apply: the level of activation during these light sleep periods of dreaming is better for this task than the lower levels during deeper sleep.

CONCLUDING REMARKS

Our conceptualization is an attempt to use one set of propositions to interpret a number of topics and thereby to identify their essential interrelationships. Although it can hardly be said that we have fully succeeded, progress has been made. The conceptual scheme provides what we believe is the framework from which a more precise theory can emerge. To us, the preceding pages indicate explanatory potential which is ample to justify further development of the approach. At the least, we hope that this volume will succeed in stimulating the theoretical efforts of others.

The comprehensiveness of our conceptualization should make it useful. However, a major aspect of the value of any theory is its ability to stimulate additional research, to lead the investigator to look for empirical results he might not otherwise have thought about. The accuracy of these expectations is, of course, an important way of evaluating the adequacy of the theory. Some general predictions following from our approach have been included at appropriate places throughout this chapter, and from these it can be seen that the scheme has potential for generating research. Many other general predictions could be listed. Those likely to be most characteristic of this conceptualization as opposed to others will probably follow from our broad definition of impact and its sources, and from the concept of normal level of activation.

We must add a note of caution at this point. It is not yet time for detailed lists of very specific predictions. In order to be most useful in the evaluation of a theory, predictions following from it should be precise enough to refer to observables in an unequivocal fashion, and should be more or less unique to it. Such predictions from our conceptual scheme can occur only when our variables have been defined in terms of concrete procedures. Greater precision can best be gained through investigation of the type suggested in the section of Chapter 2 on measurement. We are convinced that any attempt to increase precision without additional empirical investigation would involve too great a risk of missing the essential features of the constructs we have somewhat intuitively posited. The irrelevant surplus meaning of these constructs must be sifted out through the process of measuring them and relating them to the behavioral phenomena they are supposed to influence.

An important aspect of attaining greater precision is quantification. Until we can answer questions like, "How much stimulus variation (or intensity or meaningfulness) is sufficient to maintain activation at the characteristic level?" and even more basically, "How much of an increment in activation level does a certain increment in variation (or intensity or meaningfulness) produce?" we will not be able to make very precise predictions. Although the answers to questions such as these can be ascertained, we are a long way from them at this time. In this initial stage of our conceptualization, the explanations must be mainly *post hoc* and rather general.

Let us suggest two final speculations concerning the implications of our approach for the understanding of learning and sensation. Simple learning usually requires response repetition in the context of either unchanging or repetitive stimulation. Yet if we assume that the individual's general behavior is variable to a certain degree, and that this variability helps to maintain normal level of activation, then the process we call learning should be associated with a decreasing level of activation. As we have stated them, the requirements of learning and of maintaining normal activation are at least somewhat incompatible. It is perhaps for this reason that high specific motivation facilitates learning. Such motivation orients the individual toward a specific goal, and produces a level of activation which will continue at or above that which is normal until the goal has been attained. Strong specific motivation makes impact-increasing behavior, such as response variability, unnecessary.

The unchanging stimulus conditions maintained in empirical investigations of simple learning are not representative of behavioral environments outside the laboratory. In its normal existence, the organism may be able to acquire adaptive responses when its level of specific motivation is relatively weak because the typical degree of variation in external stimulation makes a significant contribution to activation level.

Here and in Chapter 2 we have considered variation to be one property of stimulation. At least at a molar level of analysis, there are other properties, namely, intensity and meaningfulness. But if we adopt a more molecular approach, we are struck by the possibility that all sensation may require a change in the physical energy impinging on the separate receptor cells. Thus, variation of this kind may be the basis of sensation. It is certainly well known that the beginning and the end of a stimulus are critical points for the acquisition of specific responses (Mowrer, 1950, pp. 278-287), and that a changing stimulus is more readily discerned than a fixed one. As indicated in Chapter 14, visual perception may require continual change in stimulation of the sense receptors, and the small but rapid eye tremor may provide the mechanism for this change. Similar mechanisms for other sense modalities have not been established. However, it is perhaps relevant that the kinesthetic receptors in the joints respond only to changes in the position of the limb. Presumably, sensation in this case is a function of change in energy. Similarly, a stimulus applied to the skin produces sensation only initially. When the pliable skin tissues relieve the tension produced by the object, the sensation of pressure disappears (Geldard, 1953).

At the specific point of contact between the physical world and the organism, a change in energy may well characterize the conditions of sensation. While the rate of this variation in stimulation may, for some modalities, be much higher than that which we have construed to be a source of impact, both are manifestations of temporal change in the interaction between organism and environment. Both the more molar level of analysis employed in our conceptualization and the molecular one considered here must take into account the fundamental contribution of variation.

These speculations are, we believe, only illustrative of the potential implications of our approach. With subsequent revisions and development, its relevance and usefulness in a number of other traditional areas of psychology will, we trust, become apparent.

Bibliography

Aarons, L., Kitsui, H., & Riesen, A. H. Retention and interocular transfer of intensity discriminations in dark-reared kittens after ablation of visual cortex. *Amer. Psychologist*, 1960, **15**, 500-501. (Abstract)

Adams, H. B., Carrera, R. N., Cooper, G. D., Gibby, R. G., & Tobey, H. R. Personality and intellectual changes in psychiatric patients following brief partial sensory deprivation. *Amer. Psychologist*, 1960, **15**, 448. (Abstract)

Adams, J. A. Vigilance in the detection of low-intensity visual stimuli. *J. exp. Psychol.*, 1956, **52**, 204-208.

Ader, R. The effects of early experience on subsequent emotionality and resistance to stress. *Psychol. Monogr.*, 1959, **73**, No. 2 (Whole No. 472).

Adey, W. R., Merrillees, N. C. R., & Sunderland, S. The entorhinal area; Behavioral, evoked potential, and histological studies of its interrelationships with brain-stem regions. *Brain*, 1956, **79**, 414-439.

Adlerstein, A., & Fehrer, E. The effect of food deprivation on exploratory behavior in a complex maze. *J. comp. physiol. Psychol.*, 1955, **48**, 250-253.

Adrian, E. D. Afferent areas in the brain of ungulates. *Brain*, 1943, **66**, 89-103.

Aldous, S. E. Notes on a black-footed ferret raised in captivity. *J. Mammal.*, 1940, **21**, 23-26.

Allen, J. The associative process of the guinea pig. *J. comp. Neurol.*, 1904, **14**, 293-359.

Allport, G. W. *Personality: A psychological interpretation.* New York: Holt, 1937.

Allport, G. W. Effect: A secondary principle of learning. *Psychol. Rev.*, 1946, **53**, 335-347.

Almquist, J. O., & Hale, E. B. An approach to the measurement of sexual behavior and semen production of dairy bulls. *Proc. III int. Cong. anim. Reproduction*, 1956. London: Brown, Knight, & Truscott. Pp. 50-59.

Altmann, M. Social integration of the moose calf. *Animal Behav.*, 1958, **6**, 155-159.

Andrew, R. J. Fear responses in *Emberiza*, Spp. *Brit. J. animal Behav.*, 1956, **4**, 125-132.

Angyal, A. *Foundations for a science of personality.* New York: Commonwealth Fund, 1941.

Ansbacher, H. L., & Ansbacher, Rowena R. (Eds.) *The individual psychology of Alfred Adler.* New York: Basic Books, 1956.

Appel, J. B., & Hurwitz, H. M. B. Studies in light-reinforced behavior. IV. Effects of apparatus familiarization. *Psychol. Rep.*, 1959, **5**, 355-356.

Arbit, J. Two early reports on the effects of sensory deprivation. *Amer. J. Psychiat.*, 1960, **117**, 467-468.

Armington, J. C., & Mitnick, L. L. Electroencephalogram and sleep deprivation. *J. appl. Physiol.*, 1959, **14**, 247-250.

Aserinsky, E., & Kleitman, N. Two types of ocular motility occurring in sleep. *J. appl. Physiol.*, 1955, **8**, 1-10.

Atkinson, J. W. (Ed.) *Motives in fantasy, action, and society,* Princeton: Van Nostrand, 1958.

Azima, H., & Cramer, Fern J. Effects of partial perceptual isolation in mentally disturbed individuals. *Dis. nerv. System*, 1956, **17**, 117-122.

Azima, H., & Cramer-Azima, Fern J. Studies on perceptual isolation. *Dis. nerv. System* (Monogr. Suppl.), 1957, **18**, 80-85.

Azima, H., Vispo, R., & Azima, Fern J. Observations on anaclitic therapy during sensory deprivation. In P. Solomon *et al.* (Eds.), *Sensory deprivation.* Cambridge: Harvard Univer. Press, 1961. Pp. 142-160.

Bain, A. *The senses and the intellect.* (3rd Ed.) London: Longmans Green, 1868.

Bakan, P. Discrimination decrement as a function of time in a prolonged vigil. *J. exp. Psychol.,* 1955, **50,** 387-390.

Bakan, P. Extraversion-introversion and improvement in an auditory vigilance task. *Brit. J. Psychol.,* 1959, **50,** 325-332.

Bakan, P. Response-tendencies in attempts to generate random binary series. *Amer. J. Psychol.,* 1960, **73,** 127-131.

Baker, C. H. Attention to visual displays during a vigilance task. II. Maintaining the level of vigilance. *Brit. J. Psychol.,* 1959, **50,** 30-36. (a)

Baker, C. H., Toward a theory of vigilance. *Canad. J. Psychol.,* 1959, **13,** 35-42. (b)

Baker, C. H. Observing behavior in a vigilance task. *Science,* 1960, **132,** 674-675.

Balaban, M. Attenuation of differences in visual problem solving ability between visually deprived and non-deprived cats. Unpublished doctor's dissertation, Univer. of Chicago, 1959.

Baldwin, A. L. Personal structure analysis: a statistical method for investigating the single personality. *J. abnorm. soc. Psychol.,* 1942, **37,** 163-183.

Bard, P., & Rioch, D. McK. A study of four cats deprived of neocortex and additional portions of the forebrain. *Bull. Johns Hopkins Hosp.,* 1937, **60,** 73-147.

Barmack, J. E. Boredom and other factors in the physiology of mental effort: an exploratory study. *Arch. Psychol., N.Y.,* 1937, No. 18.

Barnes, G., & Kish, G. Behavioral effects of the cessation of weak light energy. *Amer. Psychologist,* 1957, **12,** 411. (Abstract)

Barnett, S. A. Behavior components in the feeding of wild and laboratory rats. *Behavior,* 1956, **9,** 24-43.

Barnett, S. A. An analysis of social behavior in wild rats. *Proc. Zool. Soc. Lond.,* 1958, **130,** 107-152. (a)

Barnett, S. A. Experiments on 'Neophobia' in wild and laboratory rats. *Brit. J. Psychol.,* 1958, **49,** 195-201. (b)

Barnett, S. A. Exploratory behaviour. *Brit. J. Psychol.,* 1958, **49,** 289-310. (c)

Barron, F. Personality style and perceptual choice. *J. Pers.,* 1952, **20,** 385-401.

Barron, F. Complexity-simplicity as a personality dimension. *J. abnorm. soc. Psychol.,* 1953, **48,** 163-172. (a)

Barron, F. Some personality correlates of independence of judgment. *J. Pers.,* 1953, **21,** 287-297. (b)

Barron, F., & Welsh, G. S. Artistic perception as a factor in personality style: its measurement by a figure-preference test. *J. Psychol.,* 1952, **33,** 199-203.

Bartholomew, G. A. Mother-young relations and the maturation of pup behavior in the Alaska fur seal. *Animal Behav.,* 1959, **7,** 163-171.

Bartlett, F. C. Fatigue following highly skilled work. In E. L. Hartley, H. G. Birch, & Ruth E. Hartley (Eds.), *Outside readings in psychology.* New York: Thomas Y. Crowell, 1950.

Bartley, S. H. Fatigue and inadequacy. *Physiol. Rev.,* 1957, **37,** 301-324.

Bartley, S. H., & Chute, Eloise. *Fatigue and impairment in man.* New York: McGraw-Hill, 1947.

Bates, M. Notes on a captive icticyon. *J. Mammal.,* 1944, **25,** 152-154.

Battersby, E. Do young birds play? *Ibis,* 1944, **86,** 225.

Baxter, B. L. An electrophysiological study of effects of sensory deprivation. Unpublished doctor's dissertation, Univer. of Chicago, 1959.

Beach, F. A. Analysis of factors involved in the arousal, maintenance and manifestation of sexual excitement in male animals. *Psychosom. Med.,* 1942, **4,** 173-198. (a)

Beach, F. A. Comparison of copulatory behavior of male rats raised in isolation, cohabitation, and segregation. *J. genet. Psychol.*, 1942, **60**, 121-136. (b)

Beach, F. A. Current concepts of play in animals. *Amer. Naturalist*, 1945, **79**, 523-541.

Beach, F. A. Instinctive behavior: Reproductive activities. In S. S. Stevens (Ed.), *Handbook of experimental psychology*. New York: Wiley, 1951. Pp. 387-434.

Beach, F. A., & Jaynes, J. Effects of early experience upon the behavior of animals. *Psychol. Bull.*, 1954, **51**, 239-263.

Beach, H. D. Effect of morphine on the exploratory drive. *Canad. J. Psychol.*, 1957, **11**, 237-244.

Bech, K. Classification and functional changes in the basophilia of the retinal ganglion cells. *Anatomiske Skrifter*, 1955, **2**, Univer. Aarhus, Denmark, 59-73.

Benchley, B. J. *My friends the apes*. Boston: Little, Brown, 1942.

Benchley, B. J. *My animal babies*. Boston: Little, Brown, 1945.

Benoit, J., & Ott, L. Effect of irradiation with different wave-lengths on the mechanisms of photostimulation of the hypophysis and on testicular growth in the immature duck. *Yale J. Biol. Med.*, 1944, **17**, 27-46.

Berkowitz, L. Leveling tendencies and the complexity-simplicity dimension. *J. Pers.*, 1957, **25**, 743-751.

Berlyne, D. E. Novelty and curiosity as determinants of exploratory behavior. *Brit. J. Psychol.*, 1950, **41**, 68-80.

Berlyne, D. E. Attention to change. *Brit. J. Psychol.*, 1951, **42**, 269-278.

Berlyne, D. E. A theory of human curiosity. *Brit. J. Psychol.*, 1954, **45**, 180-191.

Berlyne, D. E. The arousal and satiation of perceptual curiosity in the rat. *J. comp. physiol. Psychol.*, 1955, **48**, 238-246.

Berlyne, D. E. Attention to change, conditioned inhibition (sIR) and stimulus satiation. *Brit. J. Psychol.*, 1957, **48**, 138-140. (a)

Berlyne, D. E. Conflict and information theory variables as determinants of human perceptual curiosity. *J. exp. Psychol.*, 1957, **53**, 399-404. (b)

Berlyne, D. E. Uncertainty and conflict: A point of contact between information-theory and behavior-theory concepts. *Psychol. Rev.*, 1957, **64**, 329-339. (c)

Berlyne, D. E. The influence of complexity and novelty in visual figures on orienting responses. *J. exp. Psychol.*, 1958, **55**, 289-296. (a)

Berlyne, D. E. The influence of the albedo and complexity of stimuli on visual fixation in the human infant. *Brit. J. Psychol.*, 1958, **49**, 315-318. (b)

Berlyne, D. E. The present status of research on exploratory and related behavior. *J. indiv. Psychol.*, 1958, **14**, 121-126. (c)

Berlyne, D. E. Supplementary report: complexity and orienting responses with longer exposures. *J. exp. Psychol.*, 1958, **56**, 183. (d)

Berlyne, D. E. *Conflict, arousal, and curiosity*. New York: McGraw-Hill, 1960.

Berlyne, D. E., & Slater, J. Perceptual curiosity, exploratory behavior and maze learning. *J. comp. physiol. Psychol.*, 1957, **50**, 228-232.

Bernstein, L. A note on Christie's "Experimental naivete and experiential naivete." *Psychol. Bull.*, 1952, **49**, 38-40.

Bernstein, S., & Mason, W. A. The role of age and stimulus characteristics in the emotional responses of young rhesus monkeys. Unpublished Report, Univer. of Wisconsin, 1960.

Bexton, W. H., Heron, W., & Scott, T. H. Effects of decreased variation in the sensory environment. *Canad. J. Psychol.*, 1954, **8**, 70-76.

Bibring, E. The development and problems of the theories of the instincts. *Int. J. Psychoanal.*, 1941, **22**, 102-131.

Bieri, J. Cognitive complexity-simplicity and predictive behavior. *J. abnorm. soc. Psychol.*, 1955, **51**, 263-268.

Bieri, J., & Blacker, E. The generality of cognitive complexity in the perception of people and inkblots, *J. abnorm. soc. Psychol.*, 1956, **53**, 112-117.

Bieri, J., Bradburn, Wendy, M., & Galinsky, M. D. Sex differences in perceptual behavior. *J. Pers.*, 1958, **26**, 1-12.

Bieri, J., & Messerly, Susan. Difference in perceptual and cognitive behavior as a function of experience type. *J. consult. Psychol.*, 1957, **21**, 217-221.

Bills, A. G. The influence of muscle tension on the efficiency of mental work. *Amer. J. Psychol.*, 1927, **38**, 227-251.

Bills, A. G. Blocking: a new principle of mental fatigue. *Amer. J. Psychol.*, 1931, **43**, 230-245.

Bills, A. G. Fatigue, oscillation and blocks. *J. exp. Psychol.*, 1935, **18**, 562-573.

Bills, A. G., & Shapin, M. J. Mental fatigue under automatically controlled rates of work. *J. gen. Psychol.*, 1936, **15**, 335-347.

Bindra, D. What makes rats hoard? *J. comp. physiol. Psychol.*, 1948, **41**, 397-402.

Bindra, D. *Motivation: a systematic reinterpretation.* New York: Ronald, 1959. (a)

Bindra, D. Stimulus change, reactions to novelty, and response decrement. *Psychol. Rev.*, 1959, **66**, 96-103. (b)

Bindra, D., & Seely, J. F. Response decrement, induced by stimulus change, as a function of amount of training. *J. exp. Psychol.*, 1959, **57**, 317-322.

Bindra, D., & Spinner, N. Response to different degrees of novelty: The incidence of various activities. *J. exp. Anal. Behav.*, 1958, **1**, 341-350.

Bingham, H. C., Sex development in apes. *Comp. Psychol. Monogr.*, 1928, **5** (1), 1-165.

Bingham, W. E., & Griffiths, W. J. The effect of different environments during infancy on adult behavior in the rat. *J. comp. physiol. Psychol.*, 1952, **45**, 307-312.

Birch, H. G. The relation of previous experience to insightful problem-solving. *J. comp. Psychol.*, 1945, **38**, 367-383.

Bjerner, B. Alpha depression and lowered pulse rate during delayed actions in a serial reaction test: a study in sleep deprivation. *Acta Physiol. Scandinavica*, 1949, **19**, Suppl. 65, 1-93.

Blake, H., Gerard, R. W., & Kleitman, N. Factors influencing brain potentials during sleep. *J. Neurophysiol.*, 1939, **2**, 48-60.

Blewett, D. B. An experimental study of the inheritance of intelligence. *J. ment. Sci.*, 1954, **100**, 922-933.

Blohmke, A. Über das Verhalten des Dunkelnystagmus beim Hunde nach zentraler Vestibularausschaltung. *Ztschr. f. Hals, Nasen, u. Ohrenheilkunde*, 1927, **18**, 427-433.

Bolgar, Hedda. Consistency of affect and symbolic expression: a comparison between dreams and Rorschach responses. *Amer. J. Orthopsychiat.*, 1954, **24**, 538-544.

Bolles, R. C. The usefulness of the drive concept. In M. R. Jones (Ed.), *Nebraska symposium on motivation.* Lincoln, Neb.: Univer. of Nebraska Press, 1958. Pp. 1-33.

Bond, R. M. Development of young goshawks. *Wilson Bull.*, 1942, **54**, 81-88.

Bostock, J. Exterior gestation, primitive sleep, enuresis and asthma: A study in aetiology. Part I. *Med. J. Austral.*, 1958, **45(2)**, 149-153.

Bousfield, W. A. The relationship between mood and the production of affectively toned associates. *J. gen. Psychol.*, 1950, **42**, 67-85.

Bovard, E. W. The effects of early handling on viability of the albino rat. *Psychol. Rev.*, 1958, **65**, 257-271.

Bowlby, J. *Maternal care and mental health.* Geneva: World Health Organization. Monogr. No. 2, 1951.

Bradley, P. B., & Elkes, J. The effects of some drugs on electrical activity of the brain. *Brain*, 1957, **80**, 77-117.

Brattgård, S. O. The importance of adequate stimulation for the chemical composition of retinal ganglion cells during early post-natal development. *Acta Radiologica*, Suppl. 96, 1952, 1-80.

Breder, C. M., Jr. On the habits and development of certain Atlantic synentognathi. *Papers Tortugas Lab; Carnegie Inst. Wash.* (No. 435), 1932, **28**, 1-35.

Breder, C. M., Jr. *Field book of marine fishes of the Atlantic coast from Labrador to Texas.* (Revised) New York: G. P. Putnam's Sons, 1948.

Breder, C. M., Jr. Factors influencing the establishment of residence in shells by tropical shore fishes. *Zoologica*, 1950, **35**, 153-158.

Breder, C. M., Jr. Further studies on factors influencing the reactions of tropical shore fishes to shells. *Zoologica*, 1954, **39**, 79-86.

Breder, C. M., Jr., & Halpern, F. Innate and acquired behavior affecting the aggregation of fishes. *Physiol. Zool.*, 1946, **19**, 154-190.

Bremer, F. The neurophysiological problem of sleep. In J. F. Delafresnaye (Ed.), *Brain mechanisms and consciousness.* Oxford: Blackwell Scientific Publications, 1954. Pp. 137-162.

Broadbent, D. E. Classical conditioning and human watch keeping. *Psychol. Rev.*, 1953, **60**, 331-339. (a)

Broadbent, D. E. Noise, paced performance and vigilance tasks. *Brit. J. Psychol.*, 1953, **44**, 295-303. (b)

Broadbent, D. E. Some effects of noise on visual performance. *Quart. J. exp. Psychol.*, 1954, **6**, 1-5.

Broadbent, D. E. *Perception and communication.* New York: Pergamon Press, 1958.

Broadhurst, P. L. Determinants of emotionality in the rat. I. Situational factors. *Brit. J. Psychol.*, 1957, **48**, 1-12.

Brooker, H. The effect of the amount of early handling on weight gain in the albino rat. Unpublished master's thesis, Univer. of Toronto, 1955.

Brooks, C. McC., Hoffman, B. F., Suckling, E. E., Kleyntjens, F., Koenig, E. G., Coleman, K. S., & Treumann, H. J. Sleep and variations in certain functional activities accompanying cyclic changes in depth of sleep. *J. appl. Physiol.*, 1956. **9**, 96-104.

Browman, L. G. The effect of optic enucleation on the male albino rat. *Anat. Rec.*, 1940, **78**, 59-77.

Brownlee, A. Play in domestic cattle in Britain: An analysis of its nature. *Brit. Vet. J.*, 1954, **110**, 46-68.

Bruner, J. S. On perceptual readiness. *Psychol. Rev.*, 1957, **64**, 123-152. (a)

Bruner, J. S. Neural mechanisms in perception. *Psychol. Rev.* 1957, **64**, 340-358. (b)

Bruner, J. S., Matter, J., & Papanek, M. L. Breadth of learning as a function of drive level and mechanization. *Psychol. Rev.*, 1955, **62**, 1-10.

Brunswik, E. Organismic achievement and environmental probability. *Psychol. Rev.*, 1943, **50**, 255-273.

Buckner, D. N., Harabedian, A., & McGrath, J. J. *A study of individual differences in vigilance performance.* Los Angeles: Human Factors Research, Inc., 1960.

Bühler, C. The reality principle. *Amer. J. Psychother.*, 1954, **8**, 626-647.

Bühler, K. *Die geistige Entwicklung des Kindes.* (4th Ed.) Jena: Gustav Fischer, 1924.

Butler, R. A. Discrimination learning by rhesus monkeys to visual-exploration motivation. *J. comp. physiol. Psychol.*, 1953, **46**, 95-98. (a)

Butler, R. A. Satiation of responses by rhesus monkeys to visual incentives. *Amer. Psychologist*, 1953, **8**, 329. (Abstract) (b)

Butler, R. A. Curiosity in monkeys. *Scient. Amer.*, 1954, **190**, 70-75. (a)

Butler, R. A. Incentive conditions which influence visual exploration. *J. exp. Psychol.*, 1954, **48**, 19-23. (b)

Butler, R. A. Discrimination learning by rhesus monkeys to auditory incentives. *J. comp. physiol. Psychol.*, 1957, **50**, 239-241. (a)

Butler, R. A. The effect of deprivation of visual incentives on visual exploration motivation in monkeys. *J. comp. physiol. Psychol.*, 1957, **50**, 177-179. (b)

Butler, R. A. Exploratory and related behavior: A new trend in animal research. *J. indiv. Psychol.*, 1958, **14**, 111-120. (a)

Butler, R. A. The differential effect of visual and auditory incentives on the performance of monkeys. *Amer. J. Psychol.*, 1958, **71**, 591-593. (b)

Butler, R. A., & Alexander, H. M. Daily patterns of visual exploratory behavior in monkeys. *J. comp. physiol. Psychol.*, 1955, **48**, 247-249.

Butler, R. A., & Harlow, H. F. Persistence of visual exploration in monkeys. *J. comp. physiol. Psychol.*, 1954, **47**, 258-263.

Butler, R. A., & Harlow, H. F. Discrimination learning and learning sets to visual exploration incentives. *J. gen. Psychol.*, 1957, **57**, 257-264.

Cambareri, J. D. The effects of sensory isolation on suggestible and non-suggestible psychology graduate students. Unpublished doctor's dissertation, Univer. of Utah, 1958.

Campbell, B. A. Absolute and relative sucrose preference thresholds for hungry and satiated rats. *J. comp. physiol. Psychol.*, 1958, **51**, 795-800.

Campbell, B. A., & Sheffield, F. D. Relation of random activity to food deprivation. *J. comp. physiol. Psychol.*, 1953, **46**, 320-322.

Campbell, D. T., & Fiske, D. W. Convergent and discriminant validation by the multitrait-multimethod matrix. *Psychol. Bull.*, 1959, **56**, 81-105.

Campos, G. B., & Welker, W. I. Some physiological and anatomical comparisons between brains of Capybara (Hydrochoerus) and guinea pig (Cavia). *Physiologist*, 1960, **3** (3), 35. (Abstract)

Cannon, W. B., & Rosenblueth, A. *The supersensitivity of denervated structures.* New York: Macmillan, 1949.

Carlson, A. J. Changes in the Nissl's substance of the ganglion and the bipolar cells of the retina of the Brandt Cormorant *Phalacrocorax pencillatus* during prolonged normal stimulation. *Amer. J. Anat.*, 1902/3, **2**, 341-347.

Carmichael, L. The onset and early development of behavior. In L. Carmichael (Ed.), *Manual of child psychology.* (2nd Ed.) New York: Wiley, 1946. Pp. 60-185.

Carpenter, C. R. A field study of the behavior and social relations of howling monkeys. *Comp. Psychol. Monogr.*, 1934, **10**, 1-168.

Carpenter, C. R. Behavior of red spider monkeys in Panama. *J. Mammal.*, 1935, **16**, 171-180.

Carpenter, C. R. A field study in Siam of the behavior and social relations of the gibbon *(Hylobates Lar).* *Comp. Psychol. Monogr.*, 1940, **16**, 1-212.

Carr, R. M., & Brown, W. L. Manipulation of visually homogeneous stimulus objects. *J. genet. Psychol.*, 1959, **95**, 245-249. (a)

Carr, R. M., & Brown, W. L. The effect of sustained novelty upon manipulation in rhesus monkeys. *J. gen. Psychol.*, 1959, **61**, 121-125. (b)

Carr, R. M., & Brown, W. L. The effect of the introduction of novel stimuli upon manipulation in rhesus monkeys. *J. genet. Psychol.*, 1959, **94**, 107-111. (c)

Carr, R. M., Overall, J. E., White, R. K., & Brown, W. L. The effects of food deprivation and restricted activity upon exploratory behavior of the rat. *J. genet. Psychol.*, 1959, **95**, 321-328.

Chance, M. R. A., & Mead, A. P. Competition between feeding and investigation in the rat. *Behaviour*, 1955, **8**, 174-182.

Chang, H.-T., Woolsey, C. N., Jarcho, L. W., & Henneman, E. Representation of cutaneous tactile sensibility in the cerebral cortex of the spider monkey. *Fed. Proc.*, 1947, **6**, 89.

Chapman, R. M., & Levy, N. Hunger drive and reinforcing effect of novel stimuli. *J. comp. physiol. Psychol.*, 1957, **50**, 233-238.

Charlesworth, W. R. The effects of electrical stimulation during pregnancy on behavior of rat offspring. Unpublished master's thesis, Wesleyan Univer., 1958.

Cho, J. B., & Davis, R. T. Preferences of monkeys for objects other than food. *Amer. J. Psychol.*, 1957, **70**, 87-91.

Chow, K. L., Dement, W. C., & Mitchell, S. A., Jr. Effects of lesions of the rostral thalamus on brain waves and behavior in cats. *EEG clin. Neurophysiol.*, 1959, **11**, 107-120.

Chow, K. L., & Nissen, H. W. Interocular transfer of learning in visually naive and experienced chimpanzees. *J. comp. physiol. Psychol.*, 1955, **48**, 229-237.

Chow, K. L., Riesen, A. H., & Newell, F. W. Degeneration of retinal ganglion cells in infant chimpanzees reared in darkness. *J. comp. Neurol.*, 1957, **107**, 27-42.

Christake, A. Conditioned emotional stimuli and arousal from sleep. *Amer. Psychologist*, 1957, **12**, 405. (Abstract)

Christensen, C. M. Dimensions and personality correlates of abstract design preferences. *Amer. Psychologist*, 1960, **15**, 453. (Abstract)

Clark, A. W. A reinvestigation of the habituation of exploratory behavior. *Austral. J. Psychol.*, 1958, **10**, 151-162.

Clark, W. E. L. A morphological study of the lateral geniculate body. *Brit. J. Ophthal.*, 1932, **16**, 264-284.

Clark, W. E. L. The anatomy of cortical vision. *Trans. Ophthalmol. Soc. United Kingdom*, 1942, **62**, 229-245.

Clayton, F. L. Light reinforcement as a function of water deprivation. *Psychol. Rep.*, 1958, **4**, 63-66.

Cofer, C. N. Motivation. *Ann. Rev. Psychol.*, 1959, **10**, 173-202.

Cohen, B. D., Rosenbaum, G., Dobie, Shirley I., & Gottlieb, J. S. Sensory isolation: hallucinogenic effects of a brief procedure. *J. nerv. ment. Dis.*, 1959, **129**, 486-491.

Cohen, W. Color-perception in the chromatic Ganzfeld. *Amer. J. Psychol.*, 1958, **71**, 390-394.

Colby, K. M. *Energy and structure in psychoanalysis.* New York: Ronald, 1955.

Coleman, P. D., Gray, F. E., & Watanabe, K. EEG amplitude and reaction time during sleep, *J. appl. Physiol.*, 1959, **14**, 397-400.

Cook, W. H., Walker, J. H., & Barr, M. L. A cytological study of transneuronal atrophy in the cat and rabbit. *J. comp. Neurol.*, 1951, **94**, 267-292.

Coombs, C. L. Theory and methods of social measurement. In L. Festinger & D. Katz (Eds.), *Research methods in the behavioral sciences.* New York: Dryden, 1953.

Cooper, J. B. An exploratory study of African lions. *Comp. Psychol. Monogr.*, 1942, **17**, 1-48.

Cooper, R. M., & Zubek, J. P. Effects of enriched and restricted early environment on the learning ability of bright and dull rats. *Canad. J. Psychol.*, 1958, **12**, 159-164.

Courts, F. A. Relations between muscular tension and performance. *Psychol. Bull.*, 1942, **39**, 347-367.

Coxe, W. S., Hirsch, J. F., Benjamin, R. M., Welker, W. I., Thompson, R. F., & Woolsey, C. N. Precentral and supplementary motor areas of *Ateles. Physiologist*, 1957, **1** (1), 19. (Abstract).

Cronbach, L., & Meehl, P. E. Construct validity in psychological tests. *Psychol. Bull.*, 1955, **52**, 281-302.

Crozier, W. J., & Hoagland, H. The study of living organisms. In C. Murchison (Ed.), *Handbook of general experimental psychology.* Worcester, Mass.: Clark Univer. Press, 1934. Pp. 39-49.

Danziger, K., & Mainland, M. The habituation of exploratory behavior. *Austral. J. Psychol.*, 1954, **6**, 39-51.

Darchen, R. Sur l'activité exploratrice de *Blatella germanica. Z. Tierpsychol.*, 1952, **9**, 362-372.

Darling, F. F. *A herd of red deer.* London: Oxford Univer. Press, 1937.

Darrow, C. W., Vieth, R. N., & Wilson, J. Electroencephalographic "blocking" and "adaptation". *Science*, 1957, **126**, 74-75.

Dashiell, J. F. A quantitative demonstration of animal drive. *J. comp. Psychol.*, 1925, **5**, 205-208.

Davis, D. R. *Pilot error.* Air Ministry Publication (3139A). London, H.M.S.O., 1948.

Davis, H., Davis, P. H., Loomis, A. L., Harvey, E. N., & Hobart, G. Human brain potentials during the onset of sleep. *J. Neurophysiol.*, 1938, **1**, 24-38.

Davis, J. D. The reinforcing effect of weak-light onset as a function of amount of food deprivation. *J. comp. physiol. Psychol.*, 1958, **51**, 496-498.

Davis, J. M., McCourt, W. F., & Solomon, P. The effect of visual stimulation on hallucinations and other mental experiences during sensory deprivation. *Amer. J. Psychiat.*, 1960, **116**, 889-892.

Davis, R. C. Somatic activity under reduced stimulation. *J. comp. physiol. Psychol.*, 1959, **52**, 309-314.

Davis, R. T., & McDowell, A. A. Manipulation of a 6-unit mechanical puzzle by monkeys under spaced practice. *Proc. S. D. Acad. Sci.*, 1953, **32**, 143-146.

Davis, R. T., McDowell, A. A., & Deter, C. W. Performance of rhesus monkeys on selected laboratory tasks presented before and after a large single dose of whole-body x-radiation. *J. comp. physiol. Psychol.*, 1956, **49**, 20-26.

Davis, R. T., Settlage, P. H., & Harlow, H. F. Performance of normal and brain operated monkeys on mechanical puzzles with and without food incentive. *J. genet. Psychol.*, 1950, **77**, 305-311.

DeCoursey, P. J. Daily activity patterns in the flying squirrel, *Glaucomys Volans.* Unpublished doctor's dissertation, Univer. of Wisconsin, 1959.

Deese, J. Some problems in the theory of vigilance. *Psychol. Rev.*, 1955, **62**, 359-368.

Deese, J., & Ormond, E. Studies of detectability during continuous visual search. *USAF WADC tech. Rep.*, 1953, No. 53-8.

Dell, P. C. Some basic mechanisms of the translation of bodily needs into behavior. In Ciba Foundation Symposium, *Neurological basis of behavior.* Boston: Little, Brown, 1958. Pp. 187-201.

Dember, W. N. Response by the rat to environmental change. *J. comp. physiol. Psychol.*, 1956, **49**, 93-95.

Dember, W. N. A comment on "Studies on 'response by the rat to environmental change'". *Psychol. Rep.*, 1958, **4**, 242. (a)

Dember, W. N. Stimulus alternation in peripherally blinded rats. *Canad. J. Psychol.*, 1958, **12**, 219-221. (b)

Dember, W. N. Replication report: Alternation following exposure without choice. *J. exp. Psychol.*, 1960, **60**, 64. (a)

Dember, W. N. *The psychology of perception.* New York: Henry Holt, 1960. (b)

Dember, W. N., Brodwick, M., & Roberts, W. W. Alternation and exploration in rats with hippocampal lesions. Paper read at Eastern Psychol. Ass., New York, April, 1960.

Dember, W. N., & Earl, R. W. Analysis of exploratory, manipulatory, and curiosity behavior. *Psychol. Rev.*, 1957, **64**, 91-96.

Dember, W. N., Earl, R. W., & Paradise, N. Response by rats to differential stimulus complexity. *J. comp. physiol. Psychol.*, 1957, **50**, 514-518.

Dember, W. N., & Fowler, H. Spontaneous alternation behavior. *Psychol. Bull.*, 1958, **55**, 412-428.

Dember, W. N., & Fowler, H. Spontaneous alternation after free and forced trials. *Canad. J. Psychol.*, 1959, **13**, 151-154.

Dember, W. N., & Millbrook, Barbara A. Free-choice by the rat of the greater of two brightness changes. *Psychol. Rep.*, 1956, **2**, 465-467.

Dember, W. N., & Roberts, W. W. Alternation behavior in peripherally-blinded rats. *Percept. mot. Skills*, 1958, **8**, 91-94.

Dement, W. The occurrence of low voltage, fast electroencephalogram patterns during behavioral sleep in the cat. *EEG clin. Neurophysiol.*, 1958, **10**, 291-296.

Dement, W. The effect of dream deprivation. *Science*, 1960, **131**, 1705-1708.

Dement, W., & Kleitman, N. Cyclic variations in EEG during sleep and their relation to eye movements, body motility, and dreaming. *EEG clin. Neurophysiol.*, 1957, **9**, 673-690. (a)

Dement, W., & Kleitman, N. The relation of eye movements during sleep to dream activity: an objective method for the study of dreaming. *J. exp. Psychol.*, 1957, **53**, 89-97. (b)

Dement, W., & Wolpert, E. A. The relation of eye movements, body motility, and external stimuli to dream content. *J. exp. Psychol.*, 1958, **55**, 543-553.

Denenberg, V. H. The effects of critical periods and amount of early experience upon adult learning. Paper read at the Amer. Psychol. Ass., Washington, September, 1958.

Denenberg, V. H. Interactive effects of infantile and adult shock levels upon learning. *Psychol. Rep.*, 1959, **5**, 357-364.

Denenberg, V. H., & Bell, R. W. Critical periods for the effects of infantile experience on adult learning. *Science*, 1960, **131**, 227-228.

Denenberg, V. H., & Karas, G. G. Effects of differential infantile handling upon weight gain and mortality in the rat and mouse. *Science*, 1959, **130**, 629-630.

Denenberg, V. H., & Karas, G. G. Interactive effects of age and duration of infantile experience on adult learning, *Psychol. Rep.*, 1960, **7**, 313-322.

Dennis, W. A comparison of the rat's first and second explorations of a maze unit. *Amer. J. Psychol.*, 1935, **47**, 488-490.

Dennis, W. Spontaneous alternation in rats as an indicator of persistence of stimulus effects. *J. comp. Psychol.*, 1939, **28**, 305-312.

Denniston, R. H., II. Escape and avoidance learning as a function of emotionality level in the Wyoming ground squirrel *Citellus richardsonii elegans*. *Animal Behav.*, 1959, **7**, 241-243.

Denny, M. R. Learning through stimulus satiation. *J. exp. Psychol.*, 1957, **54**, 62-64.

Denny, M. R., & Allen, J. N. Alternation behavior in humans. *Amer. Psychologist*, 1959, **14**, 405. (Abstract)

Denny-Brown, D. Motor mechanisms. Introduction. The general principles of motor integration. In J. Field, H. W. Magoun, & V. E. Hall (Eds.), *Handbook of physiology*. Section I. Neurophysiology. Vol. II. Washington, D.C.: American Physiological Society, 1960. Pp. 781-796.

DeValois, R. L. The relation of different levels and kinds of motivation to variability of behavior, *J. exp. Psychol.*, 1954, **47**, 392-398.

Diamond, S. A neglected aspect of motivation. *Sociometry*, 1939, **2**, 77-85.

Ditchburn, R. W. Eye-movement in relation to retinal action. *Optica Acta*, 1955, **1**, 171-176.

Ditchburn, R. W., & Fender, D. H. The stabilized retinal image. *Optica Acta*, 1955, **2**, 128-133.

Doane, B. K. Changes in visual function with perceptual isolation. Unpublished doctor's dissertation, McGill Univer., 1955.

Doane, B. K., Mahatoo, W., Heron, W., & Scott, T. H. Changes in perceptual function after isolation. *Canad. J. Psychol.*, 1959, **13**, 210-219.

Dollard, J., & Miller, N. E. *Personality and psychotherapy*. New York: McGraw-Hill, 1950.

Dubkin, L. *The white lady*. New York: Putnam, 1952.

Duffy, Elizabeth. The conceptual categories of psychology: a suggestion for revision. *Psychol. Rev.*, 1941, **48**, 177-203.

Duffy, Elizabeth. The concept of energy mobilization. *Psychol. Rev.*, 1951, **58**, 30-40.

Duffy, Elizabeth. The psychological significance of the concept of "arousal" or "activation". *Psychol. Rev.*, 1957, **64**, 265-275.

Eagles, J. B., Halliday, A. M., & Redfearn, J. W. T. The effect of fatigue on tremor. In W. F. Floyd & A. T. Welford (Eds.), *Symposium on fatigue*. London: Lewis, 1953. Pp. 41-58.

Earl, R. W. Problem solving and motor skill behaviors under conditions of free-choice. Unpublished doctor's dissertation, Univer. of Michigan, 1957.

Eayrs, J. T. Spontaneous activity in the rat. *Brit. J. anim. Behav.*, 1954, **2**, 25-30.

Edinger, L. *The anatomy of the central nervous system of man and of vertebrates in general.* (5th Ed.) (Trans. by W. S. Hall, P. L. Holland, & E. P. Carlton) Philadelphia: F. A. Davis, 1899.

Edinger, T. Hearing and smell in cetacean history. *Mschr. f. Psychiat. u. Neurol.*, 1955, **129**, 37-58.

Ehart, Mary E. Cognitive complexity-simplicity in teachers' perceptions of pupils in relation to teaching effectiveness. Unpublished doctor's dissertation, Univer. of Illinois, 1957.

Ehrlich, A. Effects of past experience on exploratory behavior in rats. *Canad. J. Psychol.*, 1959, **13**, 248-254.

Ehrlich, A., & Burns, N. Exploratory behavior of the black-footed ferret. *Canad. J. Psychol.*, 1958, **12**, 235-241.

Eibl-Eibesfeldt, I. Über die Jugendentwicklung des Verhaltens eines mannlichen Dachses *(Meles meles* L.) unter besonderer Berücksichtigung des Spieles. *Z. f. Tierpsychol.*, 1950, **7**, 327-355.

Eldred, E. Posture and locomotion. In J. Field, H. W. Magoun, & V. E. Hall (Eds.), *Handbook of physiology.* Section I. Neurophysiology. Vol. II. Washington, D. C.: American Physiological Society, 1960. Pp. 1067-1088.

Eliot, T. S. *The Sacred Wood.* London: Methuen, 1928.

Eliot, T. S. Reflections on *Vers Libre.* In J. Hayward (Ed.), *T. S. Eliot: Selected Prose.* Harmonsworth, Middlesex: Penguin Books, 1953.

Eliot, T. S. *On poetry and poets.* London: Faber and Faber, 1957.

Elkes, J. Drug effects in relation to receptor specificity within the brain: Some evidence and provisional formulation. In Ciba Foundation Symposium, *Neurological basis of behavior.* Boston: Little, Brown, 1958. Pp. 303-332.

Emiliani, C. Dating human evolution. In S. Tax (Ed.), *Evolution after Darwin.* Chicago: Univer. of Chicago Press, 1960. Pp. 57-66.

Engel, Mary, & Rechenberg, W. The reliability of affective functioning in children—Further development of the Children's Insight Test. *J. proj. Tech.*, 1961, **25**, 158-163.

Erikson, E. H. *Childhood and society.* New York: Norton, 1952.

Erikson, E. H. Growth and crises of the healthy personality. In C. Kluckhohn, H. A. Murray, & D. Schneider (Eds.), *Personality in nature, society, and culture.* (2nd. Ed.) New York: Knopf, 1953, Pp. 185-225.

Escalona, Sibylle. Feeding disturbance in very young children. *Amer. J. Orthopsychiat.*, 1945, **15**, 76-80.

Essapian, F. S. The birth and growth of a porpoise. *Nat. His.*, 1953, **62**, 392-399.

Estes, W. K. Learning. *Ann. Rev. Psychol.*, 1956, **7**, 1-38.

Estes, W. K. & Schoeffler, M. S. Analysis of variables influencing alternation after forced trials. *J. comp. physiol. Psychol.*, 1955, **48**, 357-362.

Fantz, R. L. Object preferences and pattern vision in newly hatched chicks. Unpublished doctor's dissertation, Univer. of Chicago, 1954.

Fantz, R. L. Form preferences in newly hatched chicks. *J. comp. physiol. Psychol.*, 1957, **50**, 422-430.

Fantz, R. L. Pattern vision in young infants. *Psychol. Rec.*, 1958, **8**, 43-48. (a)

Fantz, R. L. Visual discrimination in a neonate chimpanzee. *Percept. mot. Skills*, 1958, **8**, 59-66. (b)

Fehrer, E. The effects of hunger and familiarity of locale on exploration. *J. comp. physiol. Psychol.*, 1956, **49**, 549-552.

Fenichel, O. *The psychoanalytic theory of neurosis.* New York: Norton, 1945.

Fenichel, O. On the psychology of boredom. In D. Rapaport (Ed. and Trans.), *Organization and pathology of thought.* New York: Columbia Univer. Press, 1951. Pp. 348-361.

Fichter, E. Watching coyotes. *J. Mammal.,* 1950, **31,** 66-73.

Fisher, A. E. Effects of stimulus variation on sexual satiation in the male rat. *Amer. Psychologist,* 1958, **13,** 382. (Abstract)

Fisher, E. M. Early life of a sea otter pup. *J. Mammal.,* 1940, **21,** 132-137.

Fiske, D. W. An intensive study of variability scores. *Educ. psychol. Measmt.,* 1957, **17,** 453-465. (a)

Fiske, D. W. The constraints on intra-individual variability in test responses. *Educ. psychol. Measmt.,* 1957, **17,** 317-337. (b)

Fiske, D. W. Variability of responses and the stability of scores and interpretations of projective protocols. *J. proj. Tech.,* 1959, **23,** 263-267.

Fiske, D. W. Variability among peer ratings in different situations. *Educ. psychol. Measmt.,* 1960, **20,** 283-292.

Fiske, D. W., & Rice, Laura. Intra-individual response variability. *Psychol. Bull.,* 1955, **52,** 217-250.

Fitzgerald, A. Rearing marmosets in captivity. *J. Mammal.,* 1935, **16,** 181-188.

Foley, J. P., Jr. First year development of a rhesus monkey reared in isolation. *J. genet. Psychol.,* 1934, **45,** 39-105.

Forgays, D. G., & Forgays, J. W. The nature of the effects of free-environmental experience on the rat. *J. comp. physiol. Psychol.,* 1952, **45,** 322-328.

Forgays, D. G., & Levin, H. Learning as a function of sensory stimulation of various intensities. *Amer. Psychologist,* 1957, **12,** 411. (Abstract)

Forgus, R. H. The effect of early perceptual learning on the behavioral organization of adult rats. *J. comp. physiol. Psychol.,* 1954, **47,** 331-336.

Forgus, R. H. The effect of different kinds of form pre-exposure on form discrimination learning. *J. comp. physiol. Psychol.,* 1958, **51,** 75-81.

Foulkes, W. D. Dream reports from different stages of sleep. Unpublished doctor's dissertation, Univer. of Chicago, 1960.

Fowler, H. Response to environmental change: A positive replication. *Psychol. Rep.,* 1958, **4,** 506.

Fowler, H., Blond, Joyce, & Dember, W. N. Alternation behavior and learning: The influence of reinforcement magnitude, number, and contingency. *J. comp. physiol. Psychol.,* 1959, **52,** 609-614.

Fowler, H., Fowler, D. E., & Dember, W. N. The influence of reward on alternation behavior. *J. comp. physiol. Psychol.,* 1959, **52,** 220-224.

Fraenkel, G. S., & Gunn, D. L. *The orientation of animals; kinesis, taxes and compass reactions.* Oxford: Clarendon Press, 1940.

Franz, S. I., & Layman, J. D. Peripheral retinal learning and practice transfer. *Univer. of Calif. Los Angeles Publ. in Educ., Philos., and Psychol.,* 1933, **1** (3), 65-136.

Franz, S. I., & Morgan, R. C. Transfer of effects of learning from one retinal area to other retinal areas. *Univer. of Calif. Los Angeles Publ. in Educ., Philos., and Psychol.,* 1933, **1** (5), 91-98.

Fraser, F. C., Fainstat, T. D., & Kalter, H. The experimental production of congenital defects with particular reference to cleft palate. *Études Néo-natales,* 1953, **2,** 43-55.

Fraser, F. C., Walker, B. E., & Trasler, D. G. Experimental production of cleft palate: genetic and environmental factors. *Pediatrics,* 1957, **19,** 782-787.

Freedman, S. J., & Greenblatt, M. Studies in human isolation. *USAF WADC tech. Rep.,* 1959, No. 59-266.

Freedman, S. J., Grunebaum, H. U., & Greenblatt, M. Perceptual and cognitive changes in sensory deprivation. In P. Solomon *et al.* (Eds.), *Sensory deprivation.* Cambridge: Harvard Univer. Press, 1961. Pp. 58-71.

Freeman, G. L. The facilitative and inhibitive effects of muscular tension upon performance. *Amer. J. Psychol.,* 1933, **45,** 17-52.

Freeman, G. L. The optimal muscular tension for various performances. *Amer. J. Psychol.*, 1938, **51**, 146-150.

Freeman, G. L. The relationship between performance level and bodily activity level. *J. exp. Psychol.*, 1940, **26**, 602-608.

French, G. M. A deficit associated with hypermotility in monkeys with lesions of the dorsolateral frontal granular cortex. *J. comp. physiol. Psychol.*, 1959, **52**, 25-28. (a)

French, G. M. Locomotor effects of regional ablations of frontal cortex in rhesus monkeys. *J. comp. physiol. Psychol.*, 1959, **52**, 18-24. (b)

French, G. M., & Harlow, H. F. Locomotor reaction decrement in normal and brain-damaged monkeys. *J. comp. physiol. Psychol.*, 1955, **48**, 496-501.

French, T. M. *The integration of behavior.* Vol. I. *Basic postulates.* Chicago: Univer. of Chicago Press, 1952.

French, T. M. *The integration of behavior.* Vol. II. *The integrative process in dreams.* Chicago: Univer. of Chicago Press, 1954.

Freud, Anna. The mutual influences in the development of ego and id: Introduction to the discussion. *Psychoanal. Stud. Child*, 1952, **7**, 42-50.

Freud, S. *Wit and its relation to the unconscious.* New York: Moffat, Yard, 1916.

Freud, S. Formulations regarding the two principles in mental functioning. *Collected papers.* Vol. 4. London: Hogarth Press and Institute of Psycho-analysis, 1925. Pp. 13-21. (a)

Freud, S. On narcissism: An introduction. *Collected papers.* Vol. 4, London: Hogarth Press and Institute of Psycho-analysis, 1925. Pp. 30-59. (b)

Freud, S. Instincts and their vicissitudes. *Collected papers.* Vol. 4. London: Hogarth Press and Institute of Psycho-analysis, 1925. Pp. 60-83. (c)

Freud, S. *The ego and the id.* (Trans. by J. Riviere) London: Hogarth Press, 1927.

Freud, S. *Beyond the pleasure principle.* London: Hogarth Press, 1948.

Freud, S. *An outline of psycho-analysis.* (Trans. by J. Strachey) New York: Norton, 1949.

Freud, S. *The interpretation of dreams.* (Trans. by J. Strachey) New York: Basic Books, 1956.

Fuller, J. L., & Thompson, W. R. *Behavior genetics.* New York: Wiley, 1960.

Furchtgott, E., & Echols, M. Locomotor coordination following pre- and neonatal X irradiation. *J. comp. physiol. Psychol.*, 1958, **51**, 292-294.

Galambos, R., Sheatz, G., & Vernier, V. G. Electrophysiological correlates of a conditioned response in cats, *Science*, 1956, **123**, 376-377.

Ganz, L., & Riesen, A. H. Stimulus generalization to hue in the dark-reared Macaque. *J. comp. physiol. Psychol.*, in press.

Garcia, J., & Kimeldorf, D. J. The effect of ophthalmectomy upon responses of the rat to radiation and taste stimuli. *J. comp. physiol. Psychol.*, 1958, **51**, 288-291.

Gardner, W. J., & Licklider, J. C. R. Auditory analgesia in dental operations. *J. Amer. Dental Ass.*, 1959, **59**, 1144-1149.

Gately, M. J. Manipulation drive in experimentally naive rhesus monkeys. Unpublished master's thesis, Univer. of Wisconsin, 1950.

Gates, W. H. Spotted skunks and bobcat. *J. Mammal.*, 1937, **18**, 240.

Gauron, E. F., & Becker, W. C. Effects of early sensory deprivation on adult rat behavior under competition stress. *J. comp. physiol. Psychol.*, 1959, **52**, 689-693.

Geldard, F. A. *The human senses.* New York: Wiley, 1953.

Gesell, A., & Ilg, Frances L. *Infant and child in the culture of today.* New York: Harper, 1943.

Gibbs, F. A., & Gibbs, E. L. *Atlas of electroencephalography.* Vol. 1. Methodology and controls. (2nd Ed.) Reading, Mass.: Addison-Wesley, 1950.

Gibby, R. G., Adams, H. B., & Carrera, R. N. Therapeutic changes in psychiatric patients following partial sensory deprivation. *A.M.A. Arch. gen. Psychiat.*, 1960, **3**, 33-42.

Gibson, Eleanor J., & Walk, R. D. The effect of prolonged exposure to visually presented patterns on learning to discriminate them. *J. comp. physiol. Psychol.*, 1956, **49**, 239-242.

Gibson, Eleanor J., & Walk, R. D. A comparison of depth-discrimination in dark- and light-reared cats. Paper read at the Eastern Psychol. Ass., New York, April, 1960.

Ginsburg, B. E. Genetic control of the ontogeny of stress behavior. Paper read at Amer. Psychol. Ass., Chicago, September, 1960.

Girdner, J. B. An experimental analysis of the behavioral effects of a perceptual consequence unrelated to organic drive states. *Amer. Psychologist*, 1953, **8**, 354-355. (Abstract)

Glanzer, M. Stimulus satiation: An explanation of spontaneous alternation and related phenomena. *Psychol. Rev.*, 1953, **60**, 257-268. (a)

Glanzer, M. The role of stimulus satiation in spontaneous alternation. *J. exp. Psychol.*, 1953, **45**, 387-393. (b)

Glanzer, M. Curiosity, exploratory drive, and stimulus satiation. *Psychol. Bull.*, 1958, **55**, 302-315. (a)

Glanzer, M. Stimulus satiation in situations without choice. *J. comp. physiol. Psychol.*, 1958, **51**, 332-335. (b)

Glaser, R. A methodological analysis of the inconsistency of response to test items. *Educ. psychol. Measmt.*, 1949, **9**, 727-739.

Glaser, R. Multiple operation measurement. *Psychol. Rev.*, 1950, **57**, 241-252.

Glees, P., & Clark, W. E. L. The termination of optic fibers in the lateral geniculate body of the monkey. *J. Anat.*, 1941, **75**, 295-308.

Glickman, S. E. Effects of peripheral blindness on exploratory behavior in the hooded rat. *Canad. J. Psychol.*, 1958, **12**, 45-51.

Gloor, P. Amygdala. In J. Field, H. W. Magoun, & V. E. Hall (Eds.), *Handbook of physiology*. Section 1. Neurophysiology. Vol. II Washington, D.C.: American Physiological Society, 1960. Pp. 1395-1420.

Goldberger, L. Individual differences in the effects of perceptual isolation as related to Rorschach manifestations of the primary process. Unpublished doctor's dissertation, New York Univer., 1958 *(Dissertation Abstr.*, 1959, **19**, 1816-1817.)

Goldberger, L. Homogeneous visual stimulation (Ganzfeld) and imagery. *Percept. mot. Skills*, 1961, in press.

Goldberger, L., & Holt, R. R. Experimental interference with reality contact (perceptual isolation): Method and group results. *J. nerv. ment. Dis.*, 1958, **127**, 99-112.

Goldberger, L., & Holt, R. R. Experimental interference with reality contact: individual differences. In P. Solomon *et al.* (Eds.), *Sensory deprivation*. Cambridge: Harvard Univer. Press, 1961. Pp. 130-142.

Goldfarb, W. Emotional and intellectual consequences of psychologic deprivation in infancy: A reevaluation. In P. H. Hoch, & J. Zubin (Eds.), *Psychopathology of childhood*. New York: Grune & Stratton, 1955. Pp. 105-119.

Goldman, A. E. Studies in vicariousness: degree of motor activity and the autokinetic phenomenon. *Amer. J. Psychol.*, 1953, **66**, 613-617.

Goldstein, K. *The organism*. New York: American Book, 1939.

Goldstein, K. *Human nature in the light of psychopathology*. Cambridge, Mass.: Harvard Univer. Press, 1940.

Goodenough, D. R., Shapiro, A., Holden, M., & Steinschriber, L. A comparison of "dreamers" and "nondreamers": Eye movements, electroencephalograms, and the recall of dreams. *J. abnorm. soc. Psychol.*, 1959, **59**, 295-302.

Gordon, J. E. Interpersonal predictions of repressors and sensitizers. *J. Pers.*, 1957, **25**, 686-698.

Gordon, K. The natural history and behavior of the Western chipmunk and the mantled ground squirrel. *Oregon St. Monogr. Stud. Zool.*, 1943, **5**, 104.

Grastyan, E. The hippocampus and higher nervous activity. *Second conference on the central nervous system and behavior*. New York: Josiah Macy, Jr. Foundation, 1959. Pp. 119-205.

Green, J. D., & Arduini, A. A. Hippocampal electrical activity in arousal. *J. Neurophysiol.*, 1954, **17**, 533-557.

Griffin, D. R. Sensory physiology and the orientation of animals. *Amer. Scientist,* 1953, **41**, 209-244.

Groos, K. *The play of animals.* (Trans. by E. L. Baldwin) New York: D. Appleton, 1898.

Groos, K. *The play of man.* (Trans. by E. L. Baldwin) New York: D. Appleton, 1901.

Grosslight, J. H., & Ticknor, W. Variability and reactive inhibition in the meal worm as a function of determined turning sequences. *J. comp. physiol. Psychol.,* 1953, **46**, 35-38.

Grossman, M. I. Integration of current views on the regulation of hunger and appetite. *Annals N. Y. Acad. Sci.,* 1955, **63**, 76-91.

Grunebaum, H. U., Freedman, S. J., & Greenblatt, M. Sensory deprivation and personality. *Amer. J. Psychiat.,* 1960, **116**, 878-882.

Grunt, J. A., & Young, W. C. Psychological modification of fatigue following orgasm (ejaculation) in the male guinea pig. *J. comp. physiol. Psychol.,* 1952, **45**, 508-510.

Guilford, J. P. The structure of intellect. *Psychol. Bull.,* 1956, **53**, 267-293.

Hagamen, W. D., Lance, E. M., & Ungewitter, L. H. Increased responsiveness to stimuli following lesions of the forebrain. *Anat. Rec.,* 1959, **133**, 387-388.

Halberg, F. The 24-hour scale: a time dimension of adaptive functional organization. *Perspectives Biol. Med.,* 1960, **3**, 491-527.

Hall, C. S. Drive and emotionality: Factors associated with adjustment in the rat. *J. comp. Psychol.,* 1934, **17**, 89-108. (a)

Hall, C. S. Emotional behavior in the rat. I. Defecation and urination as measures of individual differences in emotionality. *J. comp. Psychol.,* 1934, **18**, 385-403. (b)

Hall, C. S., & Whiteman, P. H. The effects of infantile stimulation upon later emotional stability in the mouse. *J. comp. physiol. Psychol.,* 1951, **44**, 61-66.

Hall, J. F. The relationship between external stimulation, food deprivation, and activity. *J. comp. physiol. Psychol.,* 1956, **49**, 339-341.

Halstead, W. C. *Brain and intelligence.* Chicago: Univer. of Chicago Press, 1947.

Hamberger, C. A., & Hydén, H. Transneuronal chemical changes in Dieters' Nucleus. *Acta Otolaryngol.,* Suppl. 75, 1949, 82-113.

Harker, Janet E. Diurnal rhythms in the animal kingdom. *Biol. Rev.,* 1958, **33**, 1-52.

Harlow, H. F. The formation of learning sets. *Psychol. Rev.,* 1949, **56**, 51-65.

Harlow, H. F. Learning and satiation of response in intrinsically motivated complex puzzle performance by monkeys. *J. comp. physiol. Psychol.,* 1950, **43**, 289-294.

Harlow, H. F. Mice, monkeys, men, and motives. *Psychol. Rev.,* 1953, **60**, 23-32.

Harlow, H. F. The nature of love. *Amer. Psychologist,* 1958, **13**, 673-685.

Harlow, H. F. Basic social capacity of primates. In J. N. Spuhler (Ed.), *The evolution of man's capacity for culture.* Detroit: Wayne State Univer. Press, 1959. Pp. 40-58.

Harlow, H. F., Blazek, Nancy C., & McClearn, G. E. Manipulatory motivation in the infant rhesus monkey. *J. comp. physiol. Psychol.,* 1956, **49**, 444-448.

Harlow, H. F., Harlow, Margaret K., & Meyer, D. R. Learning motivated by a manipulation drive. *J. exp. Psychol.,* 1950, **40**, 228-234.

Harlow, H. F., & McClearn, G. E. Object discrimination learned by monkeys on the basis of manipulation motives. *J. comp. physiol. Psychol.,* 1954, **47**, 73-76.

Harlow, H. F., & Zimmermann, R. R. Affectional responses in the infant monkey. *Science,* 1959, **130**, 421-432.

Harris, A. Sensory deprivation and schizophrenia. *J. ment. Sci.,* 1959, **105**, 235-237.

Harris, J. D. Habituatory response decrement in the intact organism. *Psychol. Bull.,* 1943, **40**, 385-422.

Harris, L. J., Clay, J., Hargreaves, F. J., & Ward, A. Appetite and choice of diet. The ability of the vitamin-B deficient rat to discriminate between diets containing and lacking the vitamin. *Proc. Roy. Soc., B.,* 1933, **113**, 161-190.

Hartmann, H. Comments on the psychoanalytic theory of the ego. *Psychoanal. Stud. Child,* 1950, **5**, 74-95.

Hartmann, H. Notes on the theory of sublimation. *Psychoanal. Stud. Child*, 1955, **10**, 9-29.

Hartmann, H. Notes on the reality principle. *Psychoanal. Stud. Child*, 1956, **11**, 31-53.

Hartmann, H. *Ego psychology and the problem of adaptation*. (Trans. by D. Rapaport) New York: International Univer. Press, 1958.

Hartmann, H., Kris, E., & Loewenstein, R. Notes on the theory of aggression. *Psychoanal. Stud. Child*, 1949, 3/4, 9-36.

Haslerud, G. M. The effect of movement of stimulus objects upon avoidance reactions in chimpanzees. *J. comp. Psychol.*, 1938, **25**, 507-528.

Hauty, G. T., & Payne, R. B. Behavioral and physiological consequences of thirty hours of sustained work. *Amer. Psychologist*, 1957, **12**, 405. (Abstract)

Havelka, J. Problem-seeking behavior in rats. *Canad. J. Psychol.*, 1956, **10**, 91-97.

Hayes, C. *The ape in our house*. New York: Harper, 1951.

Hayes, K. J. Exploration and fear. *Psychol. Rep.*, 1960, **6**, 91-93.

Heathers, G. L. The avoidance of repetition of a maze reaction as a function of the time between trials. *J. Psychol.*, 1940, **10**, 359-380.

Hebb, D. O. *The organization of behavior*. New York: Wiley, 1949.

Hebb, D. O. Drives and the C.N.S. (conceptual nervous system). *Psychol. Rev.*, 1955, **62**, 243-254.

Hebb, D. O. *A textbook of psychology*. Philadelphia: Saunders, 1958. (a)

Hebb, D. O. The motivating effects of extroceptive stimulation. *Amer. Psychologist*, 1958, **13**, 109-113. (b)

Hebb, D. O. Heath, E. S., & Stuart, E. A. Experimental deafness. *Canad. J. Psychol.*, 1954, **8**, 152-156.

Hebb, D. O., & Riesen, A. H. The genesis of irrational fears. *Bull. Canad. Psychol. Ass.*, 1943, **3**, 49-50.

Hebb, D. O., & Thompson, W. R. The social significance of animal studies. In G. Lindzey (Ed.), *Handbook of social psychology*. Cambridge, Mass.: Addison-Wesley, 1954. Pp. 551-2. (Ch. 15)

Hediger, H. *Wild animals in captivity*. (Trans. by G. Sircom) London: Butterworth's Scientific Publications, 1950.

Hediger, H. *Studies of the psychology and behavior of captive animals in zoos and circuses*. (Trans. by G. Sircom) New York: Criterion, 1955.

Held, R. Exposure-history as a factor in maintaining stability of perception and co-ordination. *J. nerv. ment. Dis.*, 1961, **132**, 26-32.

Held, R., & Hein, A. Adaptation of disarranged hand-eye coordination contingent upon re-afferent stimulation. *Percept. mot. Skills*, 1958, **8**, 87-90.

Held, R., & White, B. Sensory deprivation and visual speed: an analysis. *Science*, 1959, **130**, 860-1.

Helson, H. Adaptation level as a basis for a quantitative theory of frames of reference. *Psychol. Rev.*, 1948, **55**, 297-313.

Helson, H. Adaptation level theory. In S. Koch (Ed.), *Psychology: A study of a science*. Vol. 1. Sensory, perceptual, and physiological formulations. New York: McGraw-Hill, 1959. Pp. 565-621.

Hendrick, I. Instinct and the ego during infancy. *Psychoanal. Quart.*, 1942, **11**, 33-58.

Hendrick, I. Work and the pleasure principle. *Psychoanal. Quart.*, 1943, **12**, 311-329. (a)

Hendrick, I. The discussion of the 'instinct to master.' *Psychoanal. Quart.*, 1943, **12**, 561-565. (b)

Hernández-Péon, R., Guzmán-Flores, C., Alcaroz, M., & Fernández-Guardiola, A. Photic potentials in the visual pathway during attention and photic habituation. *Fed. Proc.*, 1956, **15**, 91-92.

Hernández-Péon, R., & Scherrer, H. "Habituation" to acoustic stimuli in cochlear nucleus. *Fed. Proc.*, 1955, **14**, 71.

Hernández-Péon, R., Scherrer, H., & Jouvet, M. Modification of electrical activity in cochlear nucleus during "attention" in unanesthetized cats. *Science*, 1956, **123**, 331-332.

Heron, W. The pathology of boredom. *Sci. Amer.*, 1957, **196** (1), 52-56.

Heron, W., Bexton, W. H., & Hebb, D. O. Cognitive effects of a decreased variation in the sensory environment. *Amer. Psychologist*, 1953, **8**, 366. (Abstract)

Heron, W., Doane, B. K., & Scott, T. H. Visual disturbances after prolonged perceptual isolation. *Canad. J. Psychol.*, 1956, **10**, 13-18.

Herrick, C. J. *Neurological foundations of animal behavior.* New York: Henry Holt, 1924.

Herrick, F. H. Life and behavior of the cuckoo. *J. exp. Zool.*, 1910, **9**, 169-232.

Herrick, F. H. *The American eagle. A study in natural and civil history.* New York: Appleton-Century, 1934.

Hess, A. Optic centers and pathways after eye removal in fetal guinea pigs. *J. comp. Neurol.*, 1958, **109**, 91-115.

Hess, E. H. Natural preferences of chicks and ducklings for objects of different colors. *Psychol. Rep.*, 1956, **2**, 477-483.

Hess, E. H. The relationship between imprinting and motivation. In M. R. Jones (Ed.), *Nebraska symposium on motivation.* Lincoln: Univer. of Nebraska Press, 1959. Pp. 44-77.

Hess, E. H., & Polt, J. M. Pupil size as related to interest value of visual stimuli. *Science*, 1960, **132**, 349-350.

Higgins, J. C. Cognitive complexity and probability preferences. Unpublished manuscript, Univer. of Chicago, 1959.

Hill, W. F. Activity as an autonomous drive. *J. comp. physiol. Psychol.*, 1956, **49**, 15-19.

Hiller, L. A., Jr. Computer music. *Sci. Amer.*, 1959, **201** (6), 109-120.

Hiller, L. A., Jr., & Isaacson, L. M. *Experimental Music.* New York: McGraw-Hill, 1959.

Hinde, R. A. Changes in responsiveness to a constant stimulus. *Brit. J. anim. Behav.*, 1954, **2**, 41-55. (a)

Hinde, R. A. Factors governing the changes in strength of a partially inborn response, as shown by the mobbing behavior of the chaffinch *(Fringilla coelebs)*. II. The waning of the response. *Proc. Roy. Soc. B.*, 1954, **142**, 331-358. (b)

Hinde, R. A. Unitary drives. *Animal Behav.*, 1959, **7**, 130-141.

Hines, M. The development and regression of reflexes, postures, and progression in the young macaque. Carnegie Inst. Washington. Publ. 541. *Contrib. Embryol.*, 1942, **30** (196), 153-209.

Hochberg, J. E., Triebel, W., & Seaman, G. Color adaptation under conditions of homogeneous visual stimulation (Ganzfeld). *J. exp. Psychol.*, 1951, **41**, 153-159.

Holland, J. G. Human vigilance. *Science*, 1958, **128**, 61-67.

Holt, R. R., & Goldberger, L. Personological correlates of reactions to perceptual isolation. *USAF WADC tech. Rep.*, 1959, No. 59-735.

Holt, R. R., & Goldberger, L. Research on the effects of isolation on cognitive functioning. *USAF WADC tech. Rep.*, 1960, No. 60-260.

Holt, R. R., & Goldberger, L. Assessment of individual resistance to sensory alteration. In B. E. Flaherty (Ed.), *Psychophysiological aspects of space flight.* New York: Columbia Univer. Press, 1961. Pp. 248-262.

House, H., & Storey, G. (Eds.), *The journals and papers of Gerard Manley Hopkins.* London: Oxford Univer. Press, 1959.

Howard, H. E. *The British warblers: A history with problems of their lives.* London: R. H. Porter, 1907-1914.

Howard, K. I., & Fiske, D. W. Changes in relative strength of naturally acquired responses as a function of intervening experience. *J. Pers.*, 1961, **29**, 73-80.

Hudson, B. B. One-trial learning in the domestic rat. *Genet. Psychol. Monogr.*, 1950, **41**, 99-145.

Hugelin, A., Dumont, S., & Paillas, N. Tympanic muscles and control of auditory input during arousal. *Science*, 1960, **131**, 1371-1372.

Hughes, K. R., & Zubek, J. P. Effect of glutamic acid on the learning of bright and dull rats: I. Administration during infancy. *Canad. J. Psychol.*, 1956, **10**, 132-138.

Hughes, K. R., & Zubek, J. P. Effect of glutamic acid on the learning ability on bright and dull rats. II. Duration of the effect. *Canad. J. Psychol.*, 1957, **11**, 182-184.

Hull, C. L. *Principles of behavior.* New York: Appleton-Century-Crofts, 1943.

Hull, C. L. *Essentials of behavior.* New Haven: Yale Univer. Press, 1949.

Humphrey, G. *The nature of learning in its relation to the living system.* London: Kegan Paul, Trench, Trubner, 1933.

Hunt, D. E. Studies in role concept repertory: conceptual consistency. Unpublished master's thesis, Ohio State Univer., 1951.

Hunt, H. F., & Otis, L. S. Restricted experience and "timidity" in the rat. *Amer. Psychologist*, 1955, **10**, 432. (Abstract)

Hurwitz, H. M. B. Conditioned responses in rats reinforced by light. *Brit. J. anim. Behav.*, 1956, **4**, 31-33.

Hurwitz, H. M. B., & De, S. C. Studies in light reinforced behavior. II. The effect of food deprivation and stress. *Psychol. Rep.*, 1958, **4**, 71-77.

Hutchins, E. B., & Fiedler, F. E. An analytic treatment of two interpersonal perception scores. *Amer. Psychologist*, 1958, **13**, 362. (Abstract)

Hymovitch, B. The effects of experimental variations on problem-solving in the rat. *J. comp. physiol. Psychol.*, 1952, **45**, 313-321.

Inhelder, E. Über das Spielen mit Gegenständen bei Huftieren. *Rev. Suisse Zool.*, 1955, **62**, 240-250. (a)

Inhelder, E. Zur Psychologie einiger Verhaltensweisen—besonders des Spiels—von Zootieren. *Z. Tierpsychol.*, 1955, **12**, 88-144. (b)

Iwahara, S. Studies in spontaneous alternation in human subjects: III. A developmental study. *Jap. Psychol. Res.*, 1959, **8**, 1-8.

Iwahara, S., Matsubara, R., & Washiyama, K. Response alternation after two forced turns on the same elevated alleys as a function of inter-trial intervals in the white rat. *Annu. anim. Psychol.*, 1958, **8**, 1-10.

Iwahara, S., & Soeda, N. The effect of electric shock on spontaneous alternation in the cockroach. *Annu. anim. Psychol.*, 1957, **7**, 43-51.

Iwata, K., & Watanabe, M. Alternate turning responses of *Armadillidium Vulgare:* III. Effect of preceding turning response. *Annu. anim. Psychol.*, 1957, **7**, 57-60.

Jackson, C. W., Jr. An exploratory study of the role of suggestion in research on sensory deprivation. Unpublished doctor's dissertation, Univer. of Michigan, 1960.

Jackson, M. M. Reactive tendencies in the white rat in running and jumping situations. *J. comp. physiol. Psychol.*, 1941, **31**, 255-262.

Jackson, M. M. Anticipatory cardiac acceleration during sleep. *Science*, 1942, **96**, 564-565.

Jacobsen, C. F., Jacobsen, M. M., & Yoshioka, J. G. Development of an infant chimpanzee during her first year. *Comp. Psychol. Monogr.*, 1932, **9**, 1-93.

Jaeger, E. C. *Denizens of the mountains.* Springfield, Ill.: Charles C Thomas, 1929.

James, W. *Principles of Psychology.* Vol. II. New York: Henry Holt, 1904.

Jameson, H. D. Behavior changes in monkeys following cobalt-60 lesions in the region of the amygdaloid nucleus. Unpublished master's thesis, Univer. of Wisconsin, 1956.

Jarrett, R. F. The extra-chance nature of changes in students' responses to objective test-items. *J. gen. Psychol.*, 1948, **38**, 243-250.

Jasper, H. H. Electrical activity and mechanisms of cerebral integration. *Twenty-seventh annual conference, Milbank Memorial Fund*, 1952. Pp. 226-240.

Jasper, H. H. Reticular-cortical systems and theories of the integrative action of the brain. In H. F. Harlow & C. N. Woolsey (Eds.), *Biological and biochemical bases of behavior*. Madison: Univer. of Wisconsin Press, 1958. Pp. 37-61.

Jenkins, H. M. The stimulus control of approach in the male rat. *Amer. Psychologist*, 1953, **8**, 373-374. (Abstract)

Jenkins, H. M. The effect of signal-rate on performance in visual monitoring. *Amer. J. Psychol.*, 1958, **71**, 647-661.

Jerison, H. J. Experiments on vigilance: Duration of vigil and the decrement function. *USAF WADC tech. Rep.*, 1958, No. 58-369.

Jerison, H. J., & Arginteanu, J. Time judgments, acoustic noise, and judgment drift. *USAF WADC tech. Rep.*, 1958, No. 57-454.

Jerison, H. J., Crannell, C. W., & Pownall, D. Acoustic noise and repeated time judgments in a visual movement projection task. *USAF WADC tech. Rep.*, 1957, No. 57-54.

Jerison, H. J., & Wallis, R. A. Experiments on vigilance: One-clock and three-clock monitoring, *USAF WADC tech. Rep.*, 1957, No. 57-206.

Jerison, H. J., & Wing, J. F. Human vigilance and operant behavior. *Science*, 1961, **133**, 880-881.

Jerome, E. A., Moody, J. A., Connor, T. J., & Ryan, J. Intensity of illumination and the rate of responding in a multiple door situation. *J. comp. physiol. Psychol.*, 1958, **51**, 47-49.

Johnson, E. E. The role of motivational strength in latent learning. *J. comp. physiol. Psychol.*, 1953, **45**, 526-530.

Jones, M. B. The polarity of psychological tests. *J. consult. Psychol.*, 1958, **22**, 25-29.

Jones, Mary C. The development of early behavior patterns in young children. *J. genet. Psychol.*, 1926, **33**, 537-585.

Kagan, J. Differential reward value of incomplete and complete sexual behavior. *J. comp. physiol. Psychol.*, 1955, **48**, 59-64.

Kagan, J. The stability of TAT fantasy and stimulus ambiguity. *J. consult. Psychol.*, 1959, **23**, 266-271.

Kagan, J., & Beach, F. A. Effects of early experience on mating behavior in male rats. *J. comp. physiol. Psychol.*, 1953, **46**, 204-208.

Kagan, J., & Berkun, M. The reward value of running activity. *J. comp. physiol. Psychol.*, 1954, **47**, 108.

Kalter, H., & Warkany, J. Experimental production of congenital malformations in mammals by metabolic procedures. *Physiol. Rev.*, 1959, **39**, 69-115.

Kandel, E. J., Myers, T. I., & Murphy, D. B. Influence of prior verbalizations and instructions on visual sensation reported under conditions of reduced sensory input. *Amer. Psychologist*, 1958, **13**, 334. (Abstract)

Kappauf, W. E., Payne, M. C., & Powe, W. Performance decrement in relation to task difficulty. USAF Contract No. AF 33(038)—25726. Univer. of Illinois, Memorandum Report H-6, 1955.

Kappauf, W. E., & Powe, W. E. Performance decrement at an audio-visual checking task. *J. exp. Psychol.*, 1959, **57**, 49-58.

Kardiner, A., & Spiegel, H. *War stress and neurotic illness*. New York: Hoeber, 1947.

Karsten, Anitra. Untersuchungen zur Handlungs—und Affektpsychologie: V. Psychische Sättigung. *Psychol. Forsch.*, 1928, **10**, 142-154.

Katz, J. J., & Halstead, W. C. Protein organization and mental function. In W. C. Halstead (Ed.), Brain and behavior: a symposium. *Comp. Psychol. Monogr.*, 1950, **20**, 1-38.

Katz, S. E., & Landis, C. Psychologic and physiologic phenomena during a prolonged vigil. *Arch. neuro. Psychiat.*, 1935, **34**, 307-316.

Kawai, M. On the relation between the exploring behavior in the strange place and the dominance subordination of rabbit. *Annu. anim. Psychol.*, 1954, **4**, 25. (Abstract in English)

Keen, Joan, Page, D. J., & Hartley, H. O. Estimating variability from the differences between successive readings. *Appl. Stat.*, 1953, **2**, 13-23.

Keller, F. S. Light aversion in the white rat. *Psychol. Rec.*, 1941, 4, 235-250.

Keller, F. S. *Learning: reinforcement theory.* Garden City, N. Y.: Doubleday, 1954.

Kelly, E. L. Consistency of the adult personality. *Amer. Psychologist*, 1955, **10**, 659-681.

Kelly, G. A. *The psychology of personal constructs.* Vol. 1. A theory of personality. New York: Norton, 1955.

Kendall, S. B., & Thompson, R. F. Effect of stimulus similarity on sensory preconditioning within a single stimulus dimension. *J. comp. physiol. Psychol.*, 1960, **53**, 439-442.

Kennedy, J. L., Some practical problems of the alertness indicator. In W. F. Floyd & A-T. Welford (Eds.), *Symposium on fatigue.* London: H. K. Lewis, 1953. Pp. 149-153.

King, J. A. Social relations of the domestic guinea pig living under seminatural conditions. *Ecology*, 1956, **37**, 221-228.

King, J. A. Parameters relevant to determining the effect of early experience on the adult behavior of animals. *Psychol. Bull.*, 1958, **55**, 46-59.

Kinsey, A. C., Pomeroy, W. B., & Martin, C. E. *Sexual behavior in the human male.* Philadelphia: W. B. Saunders, 1948.

Kish, G. B. Learning when the onset of illumination is used as reinforcing stimulus. *J. comp. physiol. Psychol.*, 1955, **48**, 261-264.

Kish, G. B., & Antonitis, J. J. Unconditioned operant behavior in two homozygous strains of mice. *J. genet. Psychol.*, 1956, **88**, 121-129.

Kivy, P. N., Earl, R. W., & Walker, E. L. Stimulus context and satiation. *J. comp. physiol. Psychol.*, 1956, **49**, 90-92.

Klein, G. S. Cognitive control and motivation. In G. Lindzey (Ed.), *Assessment of human motives.* New York: Rinehart, 1958.

Kleitman, N. *Sleep and wakefulness.* Chicago: Univer. of Chicago Press, 1939.

Kleitman, N. Biological rhythms and cycles. *Physiol. Rev.*, 1949, **29**, 1-30.

Kleitman, N., & Doktorsky, A. Studies on the physiology of sleep. *Amer. J. Physiol.*, 1933, **104**, 340-343.

Kleitman, N., & Ramsaroop, A. Periodicity in body temperature and heart rate. *Endocrinology*, 1948, **43**, 1-20.

Kling, J. W., Horowitz, L., & Delhagen, J. E. Light as a positive reinforcer for rat responding. *Psychol. Rep.*, 1956, **2**, 337-340.

Klugh, A. B. Ecology of the red squirrel. *J. Mammal.*, 1927, **8**, 1-32.

Klüver, H. Reexamination of implement-using behavior in a Cebus monkey after an interval of 3 years. *Acta Psychol.*, 1937, **2**, 347-397.

Klüver, H. "The temporal lobe syndrome" produced by bilateral ablations. In Ciba Foundation Symposium, *Neurological basis of behavior.* Boston: Little, Brown, 1958. Pp. 175-182.

Knapp, H. D. Taub, E., & Berman, A. J. Effect of deafferentation on a conditioned avoidance response. *Science*, 1958, **128**, 842-843.

Knott, J. R., Gibbs, F. A., & Henry, C. E. Fourier transforms of the electroencephalogram during sleep. *J. exp. Psychol.*, 1942, **31**, 465-477.

Knott, J. R., Ingram, W. R. & Chiles, W. D. Effects of subcortical lesions on cortical electroencephalogram in cats. *Arch. neurol. Psychiat.*, 1955, **73**, 203-215.

Köhler, W., & Wallach, H. Figural after-effects: an investigation of visual processes. *Proc. Amer. Phil. Soc.*, 1944, **88**, 269-357.

Kounin, J. Experimental studies of rigidity. I and II. *Charact. Pers.*, 1941, **9**, 251-282.

Krech, D., Rosenzweig, M. R., & Bennett, E. L. Effects of environmental complexity and training on brain chemistry. *J. comp. physiol. Psychol.*, 1960, **53**, 509-519.

Krechevsky, I. Brain mechanisms and variability. I. Variability within a means-end-readiness. *J. comp. Psychol.*, 1937, **23**, 121-138. (a)

Krechevsky, I. Brain mechanisms and variability. II. Variability where no learning is involved. *J. comp. Psychol.*, 1937, **23**, 139-163. (b)

Krechevsky, I. Brain mechanisms and variability. III. Limitations of the effect of cortical injury upon variability. *J. comp. Psychol.*, 1937, **23**, 351-364. (c)

Kritzler, H. Observations on the pilot whale in captivity. *J. Mammal.*, 1952, **33**, 321-334.

Kubzansky, P. E., & Leiderman, P. H. Sensory deprivation: an overview. In P. Solomon et al. (Eds.), *Sensory deprivation*. Cambridge: Harvard Univer. Press, 1961. Pp. 221-238.

Lacey, J. I. Psychophysiological approaches to the evaluation of psychotherapeutic progress and outcome. In E. A. Rubenstein & M. B. Parloff (Eds.), *Research in Psychotherapy*. Washington, D.C.: Amer. Psychol. Ass., 1959. Pp. 160-208.

Lacey, J. I., & Lacey, Beatrice C. Verification and extension of the principle of autonomic response-stereotypy. *Amer. J. Psychol.*, 1958, **71**, 50-73.

Ladd, G. T. Contributions to the psychology of visual dreams. *Mind*, 1892, **1**, 299-304.

Ladieu, G. The effect of length of delay interval upon delayed alternation in the albino rat. *J. comp. physiol. Psychol.*, 1944, **37**, 273-286.

Land, E. H. Color vision in the natural image, I, II. *Proc. Nat. Acad. Sci.*, 1959, **45**, 115-129, 636-644.

Lashley, K. S. The accuracy of movement in the absence of excitation from the moving organ. *Amer. J. Physiol.*, 1917, **43**, 169-194.

Lashley, K. S. Experimental analysis of instinctive behavior. *Psychol. Rev.*, 1938, **45**, 445-471.

Lashley, K. S. The problem of cerebral organization in vision. In H. Klüver (Ed.), *Visual mechanisms*. Lancaster, Pa.: Jaques Cattell, 1942. Pp. 301-322.

Lashley, K. S., & Wade, M. The Pavlovian theory of generalization. *Psychol. Rev.*, 1946, **53**, 72-87.

Lawless, R. H., & Engstrand, R. D. Alternation in the human stylus maze. *Psychol. Rec.*, 1960, **10**, 101-106.

Lehner, G. F. J. A study of the extinction of unconditioned reflexes. *J. exp. Psychol.*, 1941, **29**, 435-456.

Leiderman, H., Mendelson, J. H., Wexler, D., & Solomon, P. Sensory deprivation, clinical aspects. *Arch. int. Med.*, 1958, **101**, 389-396.

Leighton, A. H. Notes on the beaver's individuality and mental characteristics. *J. Mammal.*, 1932, **13**, 117-126.

Leighton, A. H. Notes on the relations of beavers to one another and to the muskrat. *J. Mammal.*, 1933, **14**, 27-35.

Lepley, W. M. Variability as a variable. *J. Psychol.*, 1954, **37**, 19-25.

Lepley, W. M., & Rice, G. E., Jr. Behavior variability in paramecia as a function of guided act sequences. *J. comp. physiol. Psychol.*, 1952, **45**, 283-286.

Leuba, C. Toward some integration of learning theories: the concept of optimal stimulation. *Psychol. Rep.*, 1955, **1**, 27-33.

Leventhal, H. Cognitive processes and interpersonal predictions. *J. abnorm. soc. Psychol.*, 1957, **55**, 176-180.

Levine, S. Infantile experience and resistance to physiological stress. *Science*, 1957, **126**, 405.

Levine, S. A reply to a comment by Dember. *Psychol. Rep.*, 1958, **4**, 433.

Levine, S., Alpert, M., & Lewis, G. W. Differential maturation of an adrenal response to cold stress in rats manipulated in infancy. *J. comp. physiol. Psychol.*, 1958, **51**, 774-777.

Levine, S., Chevalier, J. A., & Korchin, S. J. The effects of shock and handling in infancy on later avoidance learning. *J. Pers.*, 1956, **24**, 475-493.

Levine, S., & Lewis, G. W. Critical periods for the effects of infantile experience on the maturation of the stress response. *Science*, 1959, **129**, 42-43. (a)

Levine, S., & Lewis, G. W. The relative importance of experimenter contact in an effect produced by extra-stimulation in infancy. *J. comp. physiol. Psychol.*, 1959, **52**, 368-369. (b)

Levine, S., & Otis, L. S. The effects of handling before and after weaning on the resistance of albino rats to later deprivation. *Canad. J. Psychol.*, 1958, **12**, 103-108.

Levine, S., Staats, S. R., & Frommer, G. Studies on "Response by the rat to environmental change." *Psychol. Rep.*, 1958, **4**, 139-144.

Levy, D. M. Oppositional syndromes and oppositional behavior. In P. H. Hoch & J. Zubin (Eds.), *Psychopathology of childhood*. New York: Grune & Stratton, 1955.

Levy, E. Z., Ruff, G. E., & Thaler, V. H. Studies in human isolation. *J. Amer. Med. Ass.*, 1959, **169**, 236-239.

Levy, L. H., & Dugan, R. D. A factorial study of personal constructs. *J. consult. Psychol.*, 1956, **20**, 53-57.

Lewin, K. *Field theory in social science*. New York: Harper, 1951.

Liddell, H. S. Conditioning and emotions. *Sci. Amer.*, 1954, **190** (1), 48-57.

Liers, E. E. Notes on the river otter *(Lutra Canadensis)*. *J. Mammal.*, 1951, **32**, 1-9.

Lilly, J. C. Mental effects of reduction of ordinary levels of physical stimuli on intact, healthy persons. *Psychiat. res. Rep.*, 1956, **5**, 1-9.

Lindemann, W. Beobachtungen an wilden und gezähmten Luchsen. *Z. f. Tierpsychol.*, 1950, **7**, 217-240.

Lindner, I., & Umrath, K. Veränderungen der Sehsphäre I und II in ihrem monokularen und binokularen Teil nach Extirpation eines Auges beim Kaninchen. *Dtsch. Z. Nervenheilkunde*, 1955, **172**, 495-525.

Lindsley, D. B. Emotion. In S. S. Stevens (Ed.), *Handbook of experimental psychology*. New York: Wiley, 1951. Pp. 473-516.

Lindsley, D. B. Psychological phenomena and the electroencephalogram. *EEG clin. Neurophysiol.*, 1952, **4**, 443-456.

Lindsley, D. B. Physiological psychology. *Ann. Rev. Psychol.*, 1956, **7**, Pp. 323-348.

Lindsley, D. B. Psychophysiology and motivation. In M. R. Jones (Ed.), *Nebraska symposium on motivation*. Lincoln, Nebr.: Univer. of Nebraska Press, 1957. Pp. 44-105.

Lindsley, D. B. Attention, consciousness, sleep, and wakefulness. In J. Field, H. W. Magoun, & V. E. Hall (Eds.), *Handbook of physiology*, Vol. III. Washington, D.C.: American Physiological Society, 1960. Pp. 1553-1593.

Lindsley, O. R. Operant behavior during sleep: a measure of depth of sleep. *Science*, 1957, **126**, 1290-1291.

Linn, L., Kahn, R. L., Coles, R., Cohen, Janice, Marshall, Dorothy, & Weinstein, E. Patterns of behavior disturbances following cataract extraction. *Amer. J. Psychiat.*, 1953, **110**, 281-289.

Linsdale, J. M. *The California ground squirrel. A record of observations made on the Hastings Natural History Reservation*. Berkeley: Univer. of California Press, 1946.

Linsdale, J. M., & Tomich, P. Q. *A herd of mule deer. A record of observations made on the Hastings Natural History Reservaton*. Berkeley: Univer. of California Press, 1953.

Littman, R. A. Motives, history and causes. In M. R. Jones (Ed.), *Nebraska symposium on motivation*. Lincoln, Nebr.: Univer. of Nebraska Press, 1958. Pp. 114-168.

Liu, S. Y. The relation of age to the learning ability of the white rat. *J. comp. Psychol.*, 1928, **8**, 75-85.

Livingston, R. B. Central control of receptors and sensory transmission systems. In J. Field, H. W. Magoun, & V. E. Hall (Eds.) *Handbook of physiology*. Section I. Neurophysiology. Vol. I. Washington, D.C.: American Physiological Society, 1960. Pp. 741-760.

Loeb, M., & Jeantheau, G. The influence of noxious environmental stimulation on vigilance. *J. appl. Psychol.*, 1958, **42**, 47-49.

Loehlin, J. C. The influence of different activities on the apparent length of time. *Psychol. Monogr.*, 1959, **73**, (Whole No. 474).

Loomis, A. L., Harvey, E. N., & Hobart, G. Cerebral states during sleep as studied by human brain potentials. *J. exp. Psychol.*, 1937, **21**, 127-144.

Lorenz, K. Z. The human companion in the bird's world. *Auk*, 1937, **54**, 245-273.

Lorenz, K. Z. The comparative method in studying innate behavior patterns. Symposia of the Society for Experimental Biology, No. IV: *Physiological mechanisms in animal behavior*. New York: Academic Press, 1950. Pp. 221-268.

Lorenz, K. Z. *King Solomon's ring*. New York: Thomas Y. Crowell, 1952.

Lorenz, K. Z. *Man meets dog*. (Trans. by M. K. Wilson) London: Methuen, 1955.

Loukashkin, A. S. On the pikes of North Manchuria. *J. Mammal.*, 1940, **21**, 402-405.

Lowney, E. D. Characteristics of food-carrying behavior in the rat. *J. comp. physiol. Psychol.*, 1958, **51**, 565-569.

Lowther, F. deL. A study of the activities of a pair of *Galago senegalensis moholi* in captivity, including the birth and postnatal development of twins. *Zoologica*, 1940, **25**, 433-462.

Lubow, R. E. A spatial gradient for exploratory behavior. *Psychol. Rep.*, 1959, **5**, 293-296.

Luchins, A. S., & Forgus, R. H. The effect of differential post-weaning environments on the rigidity of an animal's behavior. *J. genet. Psychol.*, 1955, **86**, 51-58.

Lundy, R. M. Assimilative projection and accuracy of prediction in interpersonal perceptions. *J. abnorm. soc. Psychol.*, 1956, **52**, 33-38.

Lundy, R. M., & Berkowitz, L. Cognitive complexity and assimilative projection in attitude change. *J. abnorm. soc. Psychol.*, 1957, **55**, 34-37.

McBain, W. N. Arousal hypothesis and effectiveness in a monotonous work situation. Paper read at Western Psychol. Ass., April, 1959.

McClearn, G. E. The genetics of mouse behavior in novel situations. *J. comp. physiol. Psychol.*, 1959, **52**, 62-67.

McClelland, D. C. Personality: an integrative view. In J. L. McCary (Ed.), *Psychology of Personality: Six modern approaches*. New York: Logos Press, 1956.

McClelland, D. C., Atkinson, J. W., Clark, R. A., & Lowell, E. L. *The achievement motive*. New York: Appleton-Century, 1953.

McClelland, W. J. Differential handling and weight gain in the rat. *Canad. J. Psychol.*, 1956, **10**, 19-22.

McCormack, P. D. Performance on a vigilance task as a function of inter-stimulus interval and interpolated rest. *Canad. J. Psychol.*, 1958, **12**, 242-246.

McCormack, P. D. Performance in a vigilance task with and without knowledge of results. *Canad. J. Psychol.*, 1959, **13**, 68-71.

Macdonald, G. E., & Teghtsoonian, R. Weight gain in the albino rat as a function of early visual experience. Paper read at Canadian Psychol. Ass., Toronto, June 7, 1957.

McDougall, W. *Introduction to social psychology*. (16th Ed.) Boston: John Luce, 1923.

McEwen, P. Figural after-effects. *Brit. J. Psychol. Monogr. Suppl.*, 1958, **31**. New York: Cambridge Univer. Press, 1958.

McFarland, R. A., Holway, A. H., & Hurvich, L. M. *Studies in visual fatigue*. Cambridge: Harvard Graduate School of Business Administration, 1942.

McGrath, J. J. *The effect of irrelevant environmental stimulation on vigilance performance*. Los Angeles: Human Factors Research, Inc., 1960. (a)

McGrath, J. J. *Subjective reactions of vigilance performers*. Los Angeles: Human Factors Research, 1960. (b)

McGrath, J. J., Harabedian, A., & Buckner, D. N. *Review and critique of the literature on vigilance performance*. Los Angeles: Human Factors Research, Inc., 1959.

McGrath, J. J., Harabedian, A., & Buckner, D. N. *An exploratory study of the correlates of vigilance performance*. Los Angeles: Human Factors Research, Inc., 1960.

McReynolds, P. A restricted conceptualization of human anxiety and motivation. *Psychol. Rep.*, 1956, **2**, 293-312. Monogr. Suppl. 6.

Mackworth, H. H. *Researches on the measurement of human performance.* Med. Res. Council, Spec. Rep. Sci., 1950, No. 268, London.

Maddi, S. R. Affective tone during environmental regularity and change. *J. abnorm. soc. Psychol.*, 1961, in press.

Maddi, S. R., Charlens, A. M., & Maddi, Dorothy-Anne. The effects of a monotonous condition on fantasy productions. Unpublished manuscript, 1961.

Magoun, H. W. Non-specific brain mechanisms. In H. F. Harlow & C. N. Woolsey (Eds.), *Biological and biochemical bases of behavior.* Madison: Univer. of Wisconsin Press, 1958. Pp. 25-36.

Mahut, H. Breed differences in the dog's emotional behavior. *Canad. J. Psychol.*, 1958, **12**, 35-44.

Maier, N. R. F. Attention and inattention in rats. *J. genet. Psychol.*, 1930, **38**, 288-306.

Maier, N. R. F. Specific processes constituting the learning function. *Psychol. Rev.*, 1939, **46**, 241-253.

Maier, N. R. F. *Frustration.* New York: McGraw-Hill, 1949.

Malmo, R. B. Measurement of drive: an unsolved problem in psychology. In M. R. Jones (Ed.) *Nebraska symposium on motivation.* Lincoln: Univer. of Nebraska Press, 1958. Pp. 229-265.

Malmo, R. B. Activation: a neuropsychological dimension. *Psychol. Rev.*, 1959, **66**, 367-386.

Maltzman, I. On the training of originality. *Psychol. Rev.*, 1960, **67**, 229-242.

Marx, M. H., Henderson, R. L., & Roberts, C. L. Positive reinforcement of the bar-pressing response by a light stimulus following dark operant pretests with no after effect. *J. comp. physiol. Psychol.*, 1955, **48**, 73-76.

Maslow, A. H. Comparative behavior of primates. VI. Food preferences of primates. *J. comp. Psychol.*, 1933, **16**, 187-197.

Maslow, A. H. A theory of human motivation. *Psychol. Rev.*, 1943, **50**, 370-396.

Maslow, A. H. The expressive component of behavior. *Psychol. Rev.*, 1949, **56**, 261-272.

Maslow, A. H. *Motivation and personality.* New York: Harper, 1954.

Maslow, A. H. Deficiency motivation and growth motivation. In M. R. Jones (Ed.), *Nebraska symposium on motivation.* Lincoln: Univer. of Nebraska Press, 1955. Pp. 1-30.

Mason, W. A., & Harlow, H. F. Initial responses of infant rhesus monkeys to solid foods. *Psychol. Rep.*, 1959, **5**, 193-199.

Mason, W. A., Harlow, H. F., & Rueping, R. R. The development of manipulatory responsiveness in the infant rhesus monkey. *J. comp. physiol. Psychol.*, 1959, **52**, 555-558.

Max, W. L. An experimental study of the motor theory of consciousness: III. Action-current responses in deaf-mutes during sleep, sensory stimulation and dreams. *J. comp. Psychol.*, 1935, **19**, 469-486.

Mayo, Clara. The effect of cognitive complexity on conflict resolution in impression formation. Paper read at the Eastern Psychol. Ass., 1959.

Mednick, S. A. Distortions in gradients of stimulus generalization related to cortical brain damage and schizophrenia. *J. abnorm. soc. Psychol.*, 1955, **51**, 536-542.

Mednick, S. A., & Freedman, J. L. Stimulus generalization. *Psychol. Bull.*, 1960, **57**, 169-200.

Meier, G. W., & McGee, R. K. A re-evaluation of the effect of early perceptual experience on discrimination performance during adulthood. *J. comp. physiol. Psychol.*, 1959, **52**, 390-395.

Melzack, R. Irrational fears in the dog. *Canad. J. Psychol.*, 1952, **6**, 141-147.

Mendelson, J., & Foley, J. M. An abnormality of mental function affecting patients with poliomyelitis in a tank-type respirator. *Trans. Amer. Neurol. Ass.*, 1956, **81**, 134-138.

Mendelson, J., Kubzansky, P., Leiderman, P. H., Wexler, D., & DuToit, C. Catechol amine excretion and behavior during sensory deprivation. *AMA Arch. gen. Psychiat.*, 1960, **2**, 147-155.

Mendelson, J., Solomon, P., & Lindemann, E. Hallucinations of poliomyelitis patients during teratment in a respirator. *J. nerv. ment. Dis.*, 1958, **126**, 421-428.

Menzel, E. W., Jr., Davenport, R. K., Jr., & Rogers, C. M. Some aspects of behavior toward novelty in young chimpanzees. *J. comp. physiol. Psychol.*, 1961, **54**, 16-19.

Meyer, J. S., & Hunter, J. Behavior deficits following diencephalon lesions. *Neurology*, 1952, **2**, 112-130.

Meyer, L. B. *Emotion and meaning in music.* Chicago: Univer. of Chicago Press, 1956.

Meyer, L. B. Meaning in music and information theory. *J. Aesthet. Art Crit.*, 1957, **15**, 412-424.

Meyer, L. B. Some remarks on value and greatness in music. *J. Aesthet. Art Crit.* 1959, **17**, 486-500.

Miles, R. C. Learning in kittens with manipulatory, exploratory, and food incentives. *J. comp. physiol. Psychol.*, 1958, **51**, 39-42.

Miles, W. R. Eye movements during profound sleepiness. *Proc. Ninth Int. Congr. Psychol.*, 1929, 308-309.

Miles, W. R., & Laslett, H. R. Eye movement and visual fixation during profound sleepiness. *Psychol. Rev.*, 1931, **38**, 1-13.

Miller, G. A. The magical number seven, plus or minus two: some limits on our capacity for processing information. *Psychol. Rev.*, 1956, **63**, 81-97.

Miller, J. G. Information input overload. Paper read at Amer. Psychol. Ass., September, 1959.

Miller, N. E. Learnable drives and rewards. In S. S. Stevens (Ed.), *Handbook of experimental Psychology.* New York: Wiley, 1951. Pp. 435-472.

Miller, N. E. Central stimulation and other new approaches to motivation and reward. *Amer. Psychologist*, 1958, **13**, 100-108.

Miller, N. E. Liberalization of basic S-R concepts: extensions to conflict behavior, motivation, and social learning. In S. Koch (Ed.), *Psychology: a study of a science.* Study I, Vol. 2, New York: McGraw-Hill, 1959.

Mitchell, E. D., & Mason, B. S. *The theory of play.* (Rev. Ed.) New York: Barnes, 1948.

Mitra, S. K., & Fiske, D. W. Intra-individual variability as related to test score and item. *Educ. psychol. Measmt.*, 1956, **16**, 3-12.

Mittelmann, B. Motility in infants, children, and adults. *Psychoanal. Stud. Child*, 1954, **9**, 142-177.

Monnier, M., & Tissot, R. Correlated effects in behavior and electrical brain activity evoked by stimulation of the reticular system, thalamus and rhinencephalon in the conscious animal. In Ciba Foundation Symposium, *Neurological basis of behavior.* Boston: Little, Brown, 1958. Pp. 105-120.

Montagu, M. F. A. Constitutional and prenatal factors in infant and child health. In M. J. E. Senn (Ed.), *Symposium on the healthy personality.* New York: Josiah Macy, Jr. Found., 1950. Pp. 148-175.

Montagu, M. F. A. The sensory influences of the skin. *Texas Rep. Biol. Med.*, 1953, **11**, 291-301.

Montgomery, K. C. Spontaneous alternation as a function of time between trials and amount of work. *J. exp. Psychol.*, 1951, **42**, 82-93. (a)

Montgomery, K. C. The relationship between exploratory behavior and spontaneous alternation in the white rat. *J. comp. physiol. Psychol.*, 1951, **44**, 582-589. (b)

Montgomery, K. C. A test of two explanations of spontaneous alternation. *J. comp. physiol. Psychol.*, 1952, **45**, 287-293. (a)

Montgomery, K. C. Exploratory behavior and its relation to spontaneous alternation in a series of maze exposures. *J. comp. physiol. Psychol.*, 1952, **45**, 50-57. (b)

Montgomery, K. C. Exploratory behavior as a function of "similarity" of stimulus situations. *J. comp. physiol. Psychol.*, 1953, **46**, 129-133. (a)

Montgomery, K. C. The effect of activity deprivation upon exploratory behavior. *J. comp. physiol. Psychol.*, 1953, **46**, 438-441. (b)

Montgomery, K. C. The effect of hunger and thirst drives upon exploratory behavior. *J. comp. physiol. Psychol.*, 1953, **46**, 315-319. (c)

Montgomery, K. C. The role of the exploratory drive in learning. *J. comp. physiol. Psychol.*, 1954, **47**, 60-64.

Montgomery, K. C. The relation between fear induced by novel stimulation and exploratory behavior. *J. comp. physiol. Psychol.*, 1955, **48**, 254-260.

Montgomery, K. C., & Monkman, J. A. The relation between fear and exploratory behavior. *J. comp. physiol. Psychol.*, 1955, **48**, 132-136.

Montgomery, K. C., & Segall, M. Discrimination learning based upon the exploratory drive. *J. comp. physiol. Psychol.*, 1955, **48**, 225-228.

Montgomery, K. C., & Zimbardo, P. G. Effect of sensory and behavioral deprivation upon exploratory behavior in the rat. *Percept. mot. Skills*, 1957, **7**, 223-229.

Moon, L. E., & Lodahl, T. M. The reinforcing effect of changes in illumination on lever-pressing in the monkey. *Amer. J. Psychol.*, 1956, **64**, 288-290.

Moore, C. S. Control of memory images. *Psychol. Rev.*, 1903, **4**, Suppl. No. 17, 277.

Moreau, R. E. A contribution to the biology of the *Musophagiformes,* the so-called plantain-eaters. *Ibis*, 1938, **2**, 639-671.

Moreau, R. E., & Moreau, W. M. Do young birds play? *Ibis*, 1944, **86**, 93-94.

Morgan, C. T. *Physiological psychology.* New York: McGraw-Hill, 1943.

Morgan, C. T. Physiological mechanisms of motivation. In M. R. Jones (Ed.), *Nebraska symposium on motivation.* Lincoln: Univer. of Nebraska Press, 1957. Pp. 1-35.

Morgan, C. T. Physiological theory of drive. In S. Koch (Ed.), *Psychology: a study of a science.* (Study I. Conceptual and systematic.) Vol. 1. Sensory, perceptual, and physiological formulations. New York: McGraw-Hill, 1959.

Morgan, C. T., & Stellar, E. *Physiological psychology.* New York: McGraw-Hill, 1950.

Morgan, C. T., & Wood, W. M. Cortical localization of symbolic processes in the rat. II. Effect of cortical lesions upon delayed alternation in the rat. *J. Neurophysiol.*, 1943, **6**, 173-180.

Morris, G. O., Williams, H. L., & Lubin, A. Misperception and disorientation during sleep deprivation. *AMA Arch. gen. Psychiat.*, 1960, **2**, 247-254.

Mowrer, O. H. "Maturation" vs. "learning" in the development of vestibular and optokinetic nystagmus. *J. genet. Psychol.*, 1936, **48**, 383-404.

Mowrer, O. H. *Learning theory and personality dynamics.* New York: Ronald, 1950.

Mullin, F. J., & Kleitman, N. Variations in threshold of auditory stimuli necessary to waken the sleeper. *Amer. J. Physiol.*, 1938, **123**, 477-481.

Mullin, F. J., Kleitman, N., & Cooperman, N. R. Studies on the physiology of sleep. Changes in irritability to auditory stimuli during sleep. *J. exp. Psychol.*, 1937, **21**, 88-96.

Munroe, R. *Schools of psychoanalytical thought.* New York: Dryden, 1955.

Murphy, D. B., Kandel, E. J., & Myers, T. I. Influence of instructions on verbal report of visual sensations under conditions of restricted sensory input. Presidio of Monterey, Calif.: US Army Leadership Human Research Unit, Task ENDORSE, Research Notes 3. (Undated)

Murphy, G. *Personality: A biosocial approach to origins and structure.* New York: Harper, 1947.

Murray, E. J. The effects of hunger and type of manipulandum on spontaneous instrumental responding. *J. comp. physiol. Psychol.*, 1953, **46**, 182-183.

Murray, E. J., Williams, H. L., & Lubin, A. Body temperature and psychological ratings during sleep deprivation. *J. exp. Psychol.*, 1958, **56**, 271-273.

Murray, H. A. *Explorations in personality.* New York & London: Oxford Univer. Press. 1938.

Murray, H. A., & Kluckhohn, C. Outline of a conception of personality. In C. Kluckhohn, H. A. Murray, & D. M. Schneider (Eds.), *Personality in nature, society, and culture.* (2nd Ed.) New York: Knopf, 1953.

Myers, A. K., & Miller, N. E. Failure to find a learned drive based on hunger; Evidence for learning motivated by "exploration". *J. comp. physiol. Psychol.,* 1954, **47,** 428-436.

Myers, T. I., Forbes, L. M., Arbit, J., & Hicks, J. A preliminary study of the effects of controlled isolation. Fort Ord, Calif.: US Army Leadership Human Research Unit. 1 Feb., 1957.

Nealey, S. M., & Edwards, Barbara J. "Depth perception" in rats without pattern-vision experience. *J. comp. physiol. Psychol.,* 1960, **53,** 468-469.

Nice, M. M. Studies in the life history of the song sparrow. II. The behavior of the song sparrow and other Passerines. *Trans. Linnaean Soc.,* N.Y., 1943, **6,** 1-328.

Nissen, H. W. A study of exploratory behavior in the white rat by means of the obstruction method. *J. genet. Psychol.,* 1930, **37,** 361-376.

Nissen, H. W. Phylogenetic comparison. In S. S. Stevens (Ed.), *Handbook of experimental psychology.* New York: Wiley, 1951. Pp. 347-386.

Nissen, H. W. A re-examination of the concept of instinct as seen by a psychologist. *Psychol. Rev.,* 1953, **60,** 291-294. (a)

Nissen, H. W. Sensory patterning versus central organization. *J. Psychol.,* 1953, **36,** 271-287. (b)

Nissen, H. W. Development of sexual behavior in chimpanzees. In *Symposium: Genetic, psychological and hormonal factors in the establishment and maintenance of patterns of sexual behavior in mammals.* Amherst, Mass., 1954. (Mimeographed) Pp. 204-228. (a)

Nissen, H. W. The nature of the drive as innate determinant of behavioral organization. In M. R. Jones (Ed.), *Nebraska Symposium on Motivation.* Lincoln, Nebr.: Univer. of Nebraska Press, 1954. Pp. 281-321. (b)

Nissen H. W., Chow, K. L., & Semmes, Josephine. Effects of restricted opportunity for tactual, kinesthetic, and manipulative experience on the behavior of a chimpanzee. *Amer. J. Psychol.,* 1951, **64,** 485-507.

Noble, R. C. *The nature of the beast. A popular account of animal psychology from the point of view of a naturalist.* Garden City, N.Y.: Doubleday, Doran, 1945.

Ohm, J. Der Nystagmus bei Blinden. *Albrecht v. Graefe's Archiv für Ophthal.,* 1950, **151,** 293-326.

Olds, J. The influence of practice on the strength of secondary approach drives. *J. exp. Psychol.,* 1953, **46,** 232-236.

Olds, J. Satiation effects in self-stimulation of the brain. *J. comp. physiol. Psychol.,* 1958, **51,** 675-678. (a)

Olds, J. Self-stimulation of the brain. *Science,* 1958, **127,** 315-324. (b)

Olds, J., & Milner, P. Positive reinforcement produced by electrical stimulation of septal area and other regions of rat brain. *J. comp. physiol. Psychol.,* 1954, **47,** 419-427.

O'Leary, J. T., & Coben, L. A. The reticular core—1957. *Physiol. Rev.,* 1958, **38,** 243-276.

Ormiston, D. W. The effects of sensory deprivation and sensory bombardment on apparent movement thresholds. Unpublished doctor's dissertation. Purdue Univer., 1958. (*Dissertation Abstr.,* 1958, **18,** 2200-2201.)

Osgood, C. E. *Method and theory in experimental psychology.* New York: Oxford Univer. Press, 1953.

Osgood, C. E., Suci, G. J., &. Tannenbaum, P. H. *The measurement of meaning.* Urbana: Univer. of Illinois Press, 1957.

Osterweil, J., & Fiske, D. W. Intra-individual variability in sentence completion responses. *J. abnorm. soc. Psychol.,* 1956, **52,** 195-199.

Oswald, I., Taylor, Anne, & Treisman, M. Discrimination and response to stimulation during sleep. *EEG Journal,* 1959, **11,** 603.

Page, J. D. Kayak hunting and space flight. *Amer. Psychologist,* 1959, **14,** 655.

Pantin, C. F. A. The elementary nervous system. *Proc. Roy Soc., B.,* 1952, **140,** 147-168.

Patrick, J. R. The effect of emotional stimuli on the activity of the white rat. *J. comp. Psychol.,* 1931, **12,** 357-364.

Patrick, J. R., & Anderson, A. C. The effect of incidental stimuli on maze learning with the white rat. *J. comp. Psychol.,* 1930, **10,** 295-307.

Pavlov, I. P. *Conditioned reflexes.* London: Oxford Univer. Press, 1927.

Pearce, J. A captive New York weasel. *J. Mammal.,* 1937, **18,** 483-488.

Perky, C. W. An experimental study of imagination. *Amer. J. Psychol.,* 1910, **21,** 422.

Petrie, Asenath, Collins, W., & Solomon, P. Pain sensitivity, sensory deprivation, and susceptibility to satiation. *Science,* 1958, **128,** 1431-1433.

Pettigrew, T. F. The measurement and correlates of category width as a cognitive variable. *J. Pers.,* 1958, **26,** 532-544.

Piaget, J. *The origins of intelligence in children.* (Trans. by M. Cook) New York: International Univer. Press, 1952.

Piaget, J. *The construction of reality in the child.* New York: Basic Books, 1954.

Pillsbury, W. B. *Attention.* New York: Macmillan, 1908.

Platt, J. R. Amplification aspects of biological response and mental activity. *Amer. Sci.,* 1956, **44,** 180-197.

Platt, J. R. Functional geometry and the determination of pattern in mosaic receptors. In H. P. Yockey, R. L. Platzman, & H. Quastler (Eds.), *Information theory in biology.* New York: Pergamon, 1958. Pp. 371-398.

Platt, J. R. The fifth need of man. *Horizon,* 1959, **1** (6), 106-111.

Platt, J. R. How we see straight lines. *Sci. Amer.,* 1960, **202** (6), 121-129.

Plotnick, H. L. The relation between selected personality characteristics of social work students and accuracy in predicting the behavior of clients. Unpublished doctor's dissertation, N. Y. School of Social Work, Columbia University, 1961.

Pokrovsky, A. I. Development of visual perception and sensation in blind patients recovering vision after operation in light of Pavlovian theory. *Vestnik oftal.,* 1953, **32,** 6-17 (Rus.).

Pollack, I., & Knaff, P. R. Maintenance of alertness by a loud auditory signal. *J. Acoustical Soc. Amer.,* 1958, **30,** 1013-1016.

Potanen, Natalie. Perceptual preferences as a function of personality variables under normal and stressful conditions. *J. abnorm. soc. Psychol.,* 1959, **59,** 108-119.

Premack, D., Collier, G., & Roberts, C. L. Frequency of light-contingent bar pressing as a function of the amount of deprivation of light. *Amer. Psychologist,* 1957, **12,** 411. (Abstract)

Pribram, K. H. A review of theory in physiological psychology. *Ann. Rev. Psychol.* 1960, **11,** 1-40.

Prosser, C. L., & Hunter, W. S. The extinction of startle responses and spinal reflexes in the white rat. *Amer. J. Physiol.,* 1936, **117,** 609-618.

Rand, A. L. Notes on the development of two young bluejays *(Cyanocitta cristata). Proc. Linn. Soc. N. Y.,* 1937, **48,** 27-59.

Ranger, G. Life of the crowned hornbill. Part III. *Ostrich,* 1950, **21,** 1-14.

Ransom, J. C. *The world's body.* New York: Charles Scribner's Sons, 1938.

Rapaport, D. (Ed.) *Organization and pathology of thought.* New York: Columbia Univer. Press, 1951.

Rapaport, D. On the psychoanalytic theory of thinking. In R. P. Knight & C. R. Friedman (Eds.), *Psychoanalytic psychiatry and psychology.* New York: International Univer. Press, 1954. Pp. 259-273.

Rapaport, D. The theory of ego autonomy: A generalization. *Bull. Menninger Clin.,* 1958, **22,** 13-35.

Rasch, Ellen, Swift, H., Riesen, A. H., & Chow, K. L. Altered structure and composition of retinal cells in dark-reared mammals. *Exp. Cell Res.,* in press.

Raudnitz, R. W. Experimenteller nystagmus. *Wien. med. Wochenschr.*, 1903, **53**, 1401-1402.

Reed, J. D. Spontaneous activity of animals. A review of the literature since 1929. *Psychol. Bull.*, 1947, **44**, 393-412.

Remington, J. D. Food habits, growth, and behavior of two captive pine martens, *J. Mammal.*, 1952, **33**, 66-70.

Rheingold, H. L., & Hess, E. H. The chick's "preference" for some visual properties of water. *J. comp. physiol. Psychol.*, 1957, **50**, 417-421.

Rhodes, J. M., & Wyers, E. J. Effect of blindness on saccharine intake and manipulatory activity in rats. *Amer. Psychologist*, 1956, **11**, 445. (Abstract)

Ribble, Margaret A. Infantile experience in relation to personality development. In J. McV. Hunt (Ed.), *Personality and the behavior disorders.* Vol. 2. New York: Ronald Press, 1944. Pp. 621-651.

Rich, A. The bearing of structural studies on relationships between DNA and RNA. In R. E. Zirkle (Ed.), *A Symposium on molecular biology.* Chicago: Univer. of Chicago Press, 1959. Pp. 47-69.

Richardson, W. B. Wood rats *(Neotoma Albigula)*: Their growth and development. *J. Mammal.*, 1943, **24**, 130-143.

Richter, C. P. Some observations on the self-stimulation habits of young wild animals. *Arch. Neurol. Psychiat.*, 1925, **13**, 724-728.

Riesen, A. H. Arrested vision. *Sci. Amer.*, 1950, **183**, 16-19.

Riesen, A. H. Plasticity of behavior: psychological aspects. In H. F. Harlow & C. N. Woolsey (Eds.), *Biological and biochemical bases of behavior.* Madison: Univer. of Wisconsin Press, 1958. Pp. 425-450.

Riesen, A. H. Effects of stimulus deprivation on the development and atrophy of the visual sensory system. *Amer. J. Orthopsychiat.*, 1960, **30**, 23-36. (a)

Riesen, A. H. Learning. In R. H. Waters, Dorothy A. Rethlingshafer, & W. E. Caldwell (Eds.), *Principles of comparative psychology.* New York: McGraw-Hill, 1960. Pp. 177-207. (b)

Riesen, A. H. Excessive arousal effects of stimulation after early sensory deprivation. In P. Solomon *et al.* (Eds.), *Sensory deprivation.* Cambridge: Harvard Univer. Press, 1961. Pp. 34-40. (a)

Riesen, A. H. Studying perceptual development using the technique of sensory deprivation. *J. nerv. ment. Dis.*, 1961, **132**, 21-25. (b)

Riesen, A. H., & Aarons, L. Visual movement and intensity discrimination in cats after early deprivation of pattern vision. *J. comp. physiol. Psychol.*, 1959, **52**, 142-149.

Riesen, A. H., & Kinder, Elaine F. *Postural development of infant chimpanzees.* New Haven: Yale Univer. Press, 1952.

Riesen, A. H., Kurke, M. I., & Mellinger, J. C. Interocular transfer of habits learned monocularly in visually naive and visually experienced cats. *J. comp. physiol. Psychol.*, 1953, **46**, 166-172.

Riggs, L. A., Armington, J. C., & Ratliff, F. Motions of the retinal image during fixation. *J. Opt. Soc. Amer.*, 1954, **44**, 315-321.

Riggs, L. A., Ratliff, F., Cornsweet, J. C., & Cornsweet, T. N. The disappearance of steadily fixated visual test objects. *J. Opt. Soc. Amer.*, 1953, **43**, 495-501.

Riley, D. A., & Shapiro, A. M. Alternation behavior as a function of effortfulness of task and distribution of trials. *J. comp. physiol. Psychol.*, 1952, **45**, 468-475.

Rimoldi, H. J. A. Personal tempo. *J. abnorm. soc. Psychol.*, 1951, **46**, 283-303.

Roberts, B. B. Notes on the birds of central and south-east Iceland. *Ibis*, 1934, **4**, 239-264.

Roberts, C. L. A comparison of the positive and negative reinforcing effects of light on the albino rat. Unpublished master's thesis, Univer. of Missouri, 1954.

Roberts, C. L., Marx, M. H., & Collier, G. Light onset and light offset as reinforcers for the albino rat. *J. comp. physiol. Psychol.*, 1958, **51**, 575-579.

Robinson, E. S., & Bills, A. G. Two factors in the work decrement. *J. exp. Psychol.*, 1926, **9**, 415-443.

Robinson, J. Light as a reinforcer for bar pressing in rats as a function of adaptation, illumination level and direction of light change. *Amer. Psychologist*, 1957, **12**, 411. (Abstract)

Robinson, Mary F. The work decrement as affected by three kinds of meaningfulness. *J. exp. Psychol.*, 1938, **22**, 124-149.

Rogers, W. W. Controlled observations on the behavior of kittens toward rats from birth to five months of age. *J. comp. Psychol.*, 1932, **13**, 107-125.

Rosenbaum, G., Dobie, Shirley I., & Cohen, B. D. Visual recognition thresholds following sensory deprivation. *Amer. J. Psychol.*, 1959, **72**, 429-433.

Rosenblum, L. A. The development of social behavior in the rhesus monkey. Unpublished doctor's dissertation, University of Wisconsin, 1961.

Rosensweig, H. Sensory deprivation and schizophrenia: some clinical and theoretical similarities. *Amer. J. Psychiat.*, 1959, **116**, 326-329.

Rosvold, H. E. Physiological psychology. *Ann. Rev. Psychol.*, 1959, **10**, 415-454.

Rothballer, A. B. Studies of the adrenaline sensitive component of the reticular activating system. *EEG clin. Neurophysiol.*, 1956, **8**, 603-622.

Rothkopf, E. Z., & Zeaman, D. Some stimulus controls of alternation behavior. *J. Psychol.*, 1952, **34**, 235-255.

Rotter, J. B., Fitzgerald, B. J., & Joyce, J. N. A comparison of some objective measures of expectancy. *J. abnorm. soc. Psychol.*, 1954, **49**, 111-114.

Royer, F. L. The formation of concepts with non-verbal auditory stimuli. *Amer. J. Psychol.*, 1959, **72**, 17-31.

Ruegamer, W. R., Bernstein, L., & Benjamin, J. D. Growth, food utilization and physical activity in the albino rat as a function of extra handling. *Science*, 1954, **120**, 184-185.

Rueping, R. R. The effect of food reward on puzzle performance by year-old rhesus monkeys. Unpublished master's thesis, Univer. of Wisconsin, 1956.

Ruff, G. E., & Levy, E. Z. Psychiatric research in space medicine. *Amer. J. Psychiat.*, 1959, **115**, 793-797.

Ruff, G. E., Levy, E. Z., & Thaler, V. H. Factors influencing the reactions to reduced sensory input. In P. Solomon *et al.* (Eds.), *Sensory deprivation.* Cambridge: Harvard Univer. Press, 1961. Pp. 72-90.

Russell, E. S. Playing with a dog. *Quart. Rev. Biol.*, 1936, **11**, 1-15.

Sagara, M., & Oyama, T. Experimental studies on figural aftereffects in Japan. *Psychol. Bull.*, 1957, **54**, 327-338.

Samuels, Ina. Reticular mechanisms and behavior. *Psychol. Bull.*, 1959, **56**, 1-25.

Schachtel, E. G. The development of focal attention and the emergence of reality. *Psychiatry*, 1954, **17**, 309-324.

Schaefer, T. The effects of early experience: Infant handling and later behavior in the white rat. Unpublished doctor's dissertation, Univer. of Chicago, 1957.

Schaefer, T. Frequency, duration, and periodicity of voluntary absences of mother rats. Paper read at Amer. Psychol. Ass., Cincinnati, September, 1959.

Schiller, P. H. Innate constituents of complex responses in primates. *Psychol. Rev.*, 1952, **59**, 177-191.

Schlosberg, H. The concept of play. *Psychol. Rev.*, 1947, **54**, 229-231.

Schlosberg, H. The description of facial expressions in terms of two dimensions. *J. exp. Psychol.*, 1952, **44**, 229-237.

Schlosberg, H. Three dimensions of emotion. *Psychol. Rev.*, 1954, **61**, 81-88.

Schmid, B. Das Tier in seinen Spielen. *Natur u. Volk.*, 1939, **69**, 1-10.

Schneirla, T. C. An evolutionary and developmental theory of biphasic processes underlying approach and withdrawal. In M. R. Jones (Ed.), *Nebraska symposium on motivation.* Lincoln: Univer. of Nebraska Press, 1959. Pp. 1-42.

Schnore, M. M. Individual patterns of physiological activity as a function of task differences and degree of arousal. *J. exp. Psychol.*, 1959, **58**, 117-128.

Schoenfeld, W. N., Antonitis, J. J., & Bersh, P. J. Unconditioned response rate of the white rat in a bar-pressing apparatus. *J. comp. physiol. Psychol.*, 1950, **43**, 41-48.

Schreiner, L., & Kling, A. Behavioral changes following rhinencephalic injury in cat. *J. Neurophysiol.*, 1953, **16**, 643-659.

Schreiner, L., & Kling, A. Rhinencephalon and behavior. *Amer. J. Physiol.*, 1956, **184**, 486-490.

Schwartzbaum, J. S., Wilson, W. A., Jr., & Morrissette, J. R. The effects of amygdalectomy on locomotor activity in monkeys. *J. comp. physiol. Psychol.*, 1961, in press.

Schweiker, R. F. Stability of interest measures and their validation for selection and classification. *USAF WADC tech. Rep.*, 1959, No. 59-36.

Scott, J. P. *Aggression.* Chicago: Univer. of Chicago Press, 1958. (a)

Scott, J. P. Critical periods in the development of social behavior in puppies. *Psychosom. Med.*, 1958, **20**, 42-54. (b)

Scott, J. P., & Marston, M. Critical periods affecting the development of normal and maladjustive social behavior of puppies. *J. genet. Psychol.*, 1950, **77**, 25-60.

Scott, T. H. Intellectual effects of perceptual isolation. Unpublished doctor's dissertation, McGill Univer., 1954.

Scott, T. H., Bexton, W. H., Heron, W., & Doane, B. K. Cognitive effects of perceptual isolation. *Canad. J. Psychol.*, 1959, **13**, 200-209.

Sechrest, L., & Jackson, D. N. Social intelligence and accuracy of interpersonal predictions. *J. Pers.*, 1961, **29**, 167-182.

Segall, M. H. Curiosity motivated learning and anxiety reduction. *J. gen. Psychol.*, 1959, **60**, 201-204.

Seitz, A. Untersuchungen über angeborene Verhaltensweisen bei Caniden. *Z. f. Tierpsychol.*, 1950, **7**, 1-46.

Seitz, P. F. D. Infantile experience and adult behavior in animals. *Psychosomat. Med.*, 1959, **21**, 353-378.

Seton, E. T. *Lives of game animals.* Garden City, N. Y.: Doubleday-Doran, 1929.

Shadle, A. R. The play of American porcupines *(Erethizon D. Dorsatum* and *E. Epixanthum). J. comp. Psychol.*, 1944, **37**, 145-150.

Sharpless, S. K. Role of the reticular formation in habituation. Unpublished doctor's dissertation, McGill Univer., 1954.

Sharpless, S. K., & Jasper, H. H. Habituation of the arousal reaction. *Brain*, 1956, **79**, 655-680.

Sheffield, F. D., & Roby, T. B. Reward value of a non-nutritive sweet taste. *J. comp. physiol. Psychol.*, 1950, **43**, 471-481.

Sheffield, F. D., Roby, T. B., & Campbell, B. A. Drive reduction vs. consummatory behavior as determinants of reinforcement. *J. comp. physiol. Psychol.*, 1954, **47**, 349-354.

Sheffield, F. D., Wulff, J. J., & Backer, R. Reward value of copulation without sex drive reduction. *J. comp. physiol. Psychol.*, 1951, **44**, 3-8.

Shipley, T. E., & Veroff, J. A projective measure of need for affiliation. *J. exp. Psychol.*, 1952, **43**, 349-356.

Shorten, M. The reaction of the brown rat toward changes in its environment. In D. Chitty, & H. N. Southern (Eds.), *Control of rats and mice.* Vol. II. Rats. Oxford: Clarendon Press, 1954. Pp. 307-334.

Shurley, J. T. Profound experimental sensory isolation. *Amer. J. Psychiat.*, 1960, **117**, 539-545.

Sidis, B. An experimental study of sleep. *J. abnorm. Psychol.*, 1908, **3**, 1-32, 63-96, 170-207.

Siegel, A. I. Deprivation of visual form definition in the ring dove. I. Discriminatory learning. II. Perceptual-motor transfer. *J. comp. physiol. Psychol.*, 1953, **46**, 115-119, 249-252.

Siegel, P. S., & Pilgrim, F. J. The monotony effect in food acceptance. *Amer. J. Psychol.*, 1958, **71**, 756-759.

Simon, C. W., & Emmons, W. H. EEG, consciousness, and sleep, *Science*, 1956, **124**, 1066-1069. (a)

Simon, C. W., & Emmons, W. H. Responses to material presented during various levels of sleep. J. *exp. Psychol.*, 1956, **51**, 89-97. (b)

Simpson, G. G. The principles of classification and a classification of mammals. *Bull. Amer. Mus. Nat. History*, 1945, **85**, 1-350.

Singleton, W. T. Deterioration of performance on a short-term perceptual-motor task. In W. F. Floyd & A-T. Welford (Eds.), *Symposium on fatigue*. London: H. K. Lewis, 1953. Pp. 163-172.

Skinner, B. F. *Science and human behavior*. New York: Macmillan, 1953.

Skinner, M. P. The prong horn. *J. Mammal.*, 1922, **3**, 82-105.

Slonaker, J. R. The normal activity of the white rat at different ages. *J. comp. Neurol. Psychol.*, 1907, **17**, 342-359.

Small, W. S. Notes on the psychic development of the young white rat. *Amer. J. Psychol.*, 1899, **11**, 80-100.

Snow, C. P. *The two cultures and the scientific revolution*. Cambridge: Cambridge Univer. Press, 1959.

Snygg, D. Mazes in which rats take the longer path to food. *J. Psychol.*, 1936, **1**, 153-166.

Solomon, P., Kubzansky, P. E., Leiderman, P. H., Mendelson, J. H., Trumbull, R., & Wexler, D. (Eds.), *Sensory deprivation*. Cambridge: Harvard Univer. Press, 1961.

Solomon, P., Leiderman, P. H., Mendelson, J., & Wexler, D. Sensory deprivation: A review. *Amer. J. Psychiat.*, 1957, **114**, 357-363.

Solomon, R. L. The influence of work on behavior. *Psychol. Bull.*, 1948, **45**, 1-40.

Southern, H. N., The house mouse and its environment. In D. Chitty & H. N. Southern (Eds.), *Control of rats and mice*. Vol. 3. House mice. Oxford: Clarendon Press, 1954. Pp. 8-32.

Spector, A. J. Expectations, fulfillment, and morale. *J. abnorm. soc. Psychol.*, 1956, **52**, 51-56.

Spitz, H. H. The present status of the Köhler-Wallach theory of satiation. *Psychol. Bull.*, 1958, **55**, 1-28.

Stegeman, L. C. Notes on young skunks in captivity. *J. Mammal.*, 1937, **18**, 194-202.

Stein, L., & Ray, O. S. Self-regulation of brain-stimulating current intensity in the rat. *Science*, 1959, **130**, 570-571.

Steinkamp, G. R., Hawkins, W. R., Hauty, G. T., Burwell, R. R., & Ward, J. E. Human experimentation in the space cabin simulator. *USAF School of Aviation Medicine*, 1959, No. 59-101.

Stellar, E. The physiology of motivation. *Psychol. Rev.*, 1954, **61**, 5-22.

Stennett, R. G. The relationship of performance level to level of arousal. *J. exp. Psychol.*, 1957, **54**, 54-61.

Stone, C. P. The congenital sexual behavior of the young male albino rat. *J. comp. Psychol.*, 1922, **2**, 95-153.

Strong, E. K., Jr. Permanence of interest scores over 22 years. *J. appl. Psychol.*, 1951, **35**, 89-91.

Sullivan. H. S. *The psychiatric interview*. New York: Norton, 1954.

Sutherland, N. S. Spontaneous alternation and stimulus avoidance. *J. comp. physiol. Psychol.*, 1957, **50**, 358-362.

Svihla, A. Habits of the Louisiana Mink *(Mustela Vison Vulgivagus)*. *J. Mammal.*, 1931, **12**, 366-368.

Svihla, R. D. A family of flying squirrels. *J. Mammal.*, 1930, **11**, 211-213.

Symmes, D. Anxiety reduction and novelty as goals of visual exploration by monkeys. *J. genet. Psychol.*, 1959, **94**, 181-198. (a)

Symmes, D. Effect of cortical ablations on visual exploration in monkeys. *Fed. Proc.*, 1959, **18**, 155. (b)

Talmadge, M. Expressive graphic movements and their relationship to temperament factors. *Psychol. Monogr.*, 1958, **72** (12), (Whole No. 469).

Telford, C. W. The refractory phase of voluntary and associative responses. *J. exp. Psychol,.* 1931, **14**, 1-36.

Teplitz, Z. An electroencephalographic study of sleep and dreams. Unpublished master's thesis, Univer. of Illinois, 1943.

Thackray, R. I., & Michels, K. M. Externally-aroused drives in the raccoon. *Anim. Beh.*, 1958, **6**, 160-163.

Thiessen, D. D., & McGaugh, J. L. Conflict and curiosity in the rat. Unpublished study, San Jose State College, 1959.

Thistlethwaite, D. A critical review of latent learning and related experiments. *Psychol. Bull.*, 1951, **48**, 97-129.

Thomas, D. G., Appel, J. B., & Hurwitz, H. M. B. Studies in light-reinforced behavior: V. Effects of lever size, shift in lever size, and light position. *Psychol. Rep.*, 1958, **4**, 411-413.

Thompson, D'Arcy W. *On growth and form.* (2nd Ed.) Cambridge: Cambridge Univer. Press, 1959.

Thompson, W. D., Jr., & Sontag, L. W. Behavioral effects in the offspring of rats subjected to audiogenic seizures during the gestation period. *J. comp. physiol. Psychol.*, 1956, **49**, 454-456.

Thompson, W. R. Exploratory behavior as a function of hunger in "bright" and "dull" rats. *J. comp. physiol. Psychol.*, 1953, **46**, 323-326. (a)

Thompson, W. R. The inheritance of behavior: Behavioral differences in fifteen mouse strains. *Canad. J. Psychol.*, 1953, **7**, 145-155. (b)

Thompson, W. R. The inheritance and development of intelligence. *Proc. Ass. Res. Nerv. Ment. Dis.*, 1954, **33**, 209-231.

Thompson, W. R. Early environment—its importance for later behavior. In P. H. Hoch & J. Zubin (Eds.), *Psychopathology of childhood.* New York: Grune & Stratton, 1955. Pp. 120-139.

Thompson, W. R. The inheritance of behavior: Activity differences in five inbred mouse strains. *J. Hered.*, 1956, **47**, 147-148.

Thompson, W. R. Influence of prenatal maternal anxiety on emotionality in young rats. *Science*, 1957, **125**, 698-699.

Thompson, W. R. Motivational factors in development. *Austral. J. Psychol.*, 1958, **10**, 127-143.

Thompson, W. R. Early environmental influences on behavioral development. *Amer. J. Orthopsychiat.*, 1960, **30**, 306-314.

Thompson, W. R., & Heron, W. The effect of early restriction on activity in dogs. *J. comp. physiol. Psychol.*, 1954, **47**, 77-82.

Thompson, W. R., & Melzack, R. Early environment. *Sci. Amer.*, 1956, **114** (1), 38-42.

Thompson, W. R., & Solomon, L. M. Spontaneous pattern discrimination in the rat. *J. comp. physiol. Psychol.*, 1954, **47**, 104-107.

Thorpe, W. H. The learning abilities of birds. Part I. *Ibis*, 1951, **93**, 1-52.

Thorpe, W. H. *Learning and instinct in animals.* London: Methuen, 1956.

Thurstone, Thelma G., Thurstone, L. L., & Strandskov, H. H. A psychological study of twins. 1. Distribution of absolute twin differences for identical and fraternal twins. *Psychometr. Lab., Univer. of N. Carolina*, No. 4, 1953.

Tilney, F. Behavior in its relation to the development of the brain. Part II. Correlation between the development of the brain and behavior in the albino rat from embryonic states to maturity. *Bull. Neur. Inst., N.Y.*, 1933, **3**, 252-358.

Tilney, F., & Casamajor, L. Myelinogeny as applied to the study of behavior. *Arch. Neurol. Psychiat.*, 1924, **12**, 1-66.

Tinbergen, N. *The study of instinct.* London: Oxford Univer. Press, 1951.

Tinbergen, N. *Social behavior in animals.* London: Methuen, 1953.

Titelbaum, S. The electrical skin resistance during sleep. Unpublished doctor's dissertation, Univer. of Chicago, 1938.

Tolman, E. C. Purpose and cognition: The determiners of animal learning. *Psychol. Rev.,* 1925, **32**, 285-297.

Tolman, E. C. Cognitive maps in rats and men. *Psychol. Rev.,* 1948, **55**, 189-208.

Toman, E. P. Conditional features of sound-evoked EEG responses during sleep. *Fed. Proc.,* 1958, **17**, 163. (Abstract)

Travis, A. M., & Woolsey, C. N. Motor performances of monkeys after bilateral partial and total cerebral decortications. *J. physic. Med.,* 1956, **35**, 273-310.

Twitchell, T. E. Sensory factors in purposive movement. *J. Neurophysiol.,* 1954, **17**, 239-252.

Tyler, D. B., Goodman, J., & Rothman, T. The effect of experimental insomnia on the rate of potential changes in the brain. *Amer. J. Physiol.,* 1947, **149**, 185-193.

van der Veen, F., & Fiske, D. W. Variability among self-ratings in different situations. *Educ. psychol. Measmt.,* 1960, **20**, 83-93.

Vernon, J. A., & Hoffman, J. Effect of sensory deprivation on learning rate in human beings. *Science,* 1956, **123**, 1074-1075.

Vernon, J. A., & McGill, T. E. The effect of sensory deprivation on rote learning. *Amer. J. Psychol.,* 1957, **70**, 637-639.

Vernon, J. A., & McGill, T. E. Sensory deprivation and pain thresholds. *Science,* 1961, **133**, 330-331.

Vernon, J. A., McGill, T. E., Gulick, W. L., & Candland, D. K. Effect of sensory deprivation on some perceptual and motor skills. *Percept. mot. Skills.,* 1959, **9**, 91-97.

Vernon, J. A., McGill, T. E. Gulick, W. L., & Candland, D. K. The effect of human isolation upon some perceptual and motor skills. In P. Solomon *et al.* (Eds.), *Sensory deprivation.* Cambridge: Harvard Univer. Press, 1961. Pp. 41-57.

Vernon, J. A., McGill, T. E., & Schiffman, H. Visual hallucinations during perceptual isolation. *Canad. J. Psychol.,* 1958, **12**, 31-34.

Veroff, J. Development and validation of a projective measure of power motivation, *J. abnorm. soc. Psychol.,* 1957, **54**, 1-8.

Vincent, N. M. The effects of prenatal alchoholism upon motivation, emotionality, and learning in the rat. *Amer. Psychologist,* 1958, **13**, 401. (Abstract)

Volkart, E. H. *Social behavior and personality: contributions of W. I. Thomas to theory and social research.* New York: Soc. Science Research Council, 1951.

Volmar, F. A. *Das Bärenbuch.* Bern: Paul Haupt, 1940.

von Holst, E. Relations between the central nervous system and the peripheral organs. *Brit. J. anim. Behav.,* 1954, **2**, 89-94.

von Senden, M. *Space and sight: the perception of space and shape in congenitally blind patients, before and after operation.* Leipzig: Barth, 1932; Engl. transl., London: Methuen, 1960.

Wada, T. Experimental study of hunger in its relation to activity. *Arch. Psychol.,* 1922, **8**, 1-65.

Walk, R. D., Response of dark- and light-reared rats to stimulus change. *J. comp. physiol. Psychol.,* 1960, **53**, 609-611.

Walker, E. L. The duration and course of the reaction decrement and the influence of reward. *J. comp. physiol. Psychol.,* 1956, **49**, 167-176.

Walker, E. L. Action decrement and its relation to learning. *Psychol. Rev.,* 1958, **65**, 129-142.

Walker, E. L., Dember, W. N., Earl, R. W., & Karoly, A. J. Choice alternation: I. Stimulus vs. place vs. response. *J. comp. physiol Psychol.,* 1955, **48**, 19-23.

Walker, E. L., Dember, W. N., Earl, R. W., Fliege, S. E., & Karoly, A. J. Choice alternation: II. Exposure to stimulus or stimulus and place without choice. *J. comp. physiol. Psychol.*, 1955, **48**, 24-28.

Walker, E. L., Dember, W. N., Earl, R. W., Fawl, C. L., & Karoly, A. J. Choice alternation: III. Response intensity vs. response discriminability. *J. comp. physiol. Psychol.*, 1955, **48**, 80-85.

Walker, E. L., & Paradise, N. A positive correlation between action decrement and learning. *J. exp. Psychol.*, 1958, **56**, 45-47.

Wallach, M. A., & Caron, A. J. Attribute criteriality and sex-linked conservatism as determinants of psychological similarity. *J. abnorm. soc. Psychol.*, 1959, **59**, 43-50.

Warren, R. M. An auditory analogue of the visual reversible figure. *Amer. Psychologist*, 1960, **15**, 499. (Abstract)

Warren, R. P. Pure and impure poetry. *Kenyon Rev.*, 1943, **5**, 251.

Washburn, M. F. *The animal mind. A text-book of comparative psychology.* (4th Ed.) New York: Macmillan, 1936.

Washburn, S. L. Tools and human evolution. *Sci. Amer.*, 1960, **203** (3), 62-75.

Washburn, S. L., & Howells, W. W. Human evolution and culture. In S. Tax (Ed.), *Evolution after Darwin.* Chicago: Univer. of Chicago Press, 1960. Pp. 33-56.

Watanabe, M., & Iwata, K. Alternative turning response of *Armadillidium Vulgare. Annu. anim. Psychol.*, 1956, **6**, 75-82.

Watson, J. D., & Crick, F. H. C. Genetical implications of the structure of deoxyribonucleic acid. *Nature*, 1953, **171**, 964-967.

Wayner, M. J., Jr., & Zellner, D. K. The role of the suprapharyngeal ganglion in spontaneous alternation and negative movements in *Lumbricus Terrestris L. J. comp. physiol. Psychol.*, 1958, **51**, 282-287.

Weaver, W. Recent contributions to the mathematical theory of communication. *Etc: A Rev. of gen. Semantics*, 1953, **10**, 273.

Webb, H. Marguerite, & Brown, F. A., Jr. Timing long-cycle physiological rhythms. *Physiol. Rev.*, 1959, **39**, 127-161.

Webb, W. B., & Wherry, R. J., Jr., Vigilance in prolonged and repeated sessions. *Percept. mot. Skills*, 1960, **10**, 111-114.

Weill, G., & Pfersdorff, C. Les functions visuelles de l'aveugle-né opéré. *Ann. méd.-psychol.*, 1935, **93** (Pt. 2), 367-382.

Weininger, O. The effects of early experience on behavior and growth characteristics. *J. comp. physiol. Psychol.*, 1956, **49**, 1-9.

Weiskrantz, L. Sensory deprivation and the cat's optic nervous system. *Nature*, 1958, **181**, 1047-1050.

Weiss, P. Does sensory control play a constructive role in the development of motor coordination? *Schweiz. Med. Wschr.*, 1941, **22**, 406-407.

Weiss, P. Nervous system (neurogenesis). In B. H. Willier, P. A. Weiss, & V. Hamburger (Eds.), *Analysis of development.* Philadelphia: W. B. Saunders, 1955. Pp. 346-401.

Weitz, J., & Wakeman, M. L. "Spontaneous" alternation and the conditioned response. *J. comp. physiol. Psychol.*, 1941, **32**, 551-562.

Welker, W. I. Play and exploration in chimpanzees. Unpublished doctor's dissertation, Univer. of Chicago, 1954.

Welker, W. I. Effects of age and experience on play and exploration of young chimpanzees. *J. comp. physiol. Psychol.*, 1956, **49**, 223-226. (a)

Welker, W. I. Some determinants of play and exploration in chimpanzees. *J. comp. physiol. Psychol.*, 1956, **49**, 84-89. (b)

Welker, W. I. Variability of play and exploratory behavior in chimpanzees. *J. comp. physiol. Psychol.*, 1956, **49**, 181-185. (c)

Welker, W. I. "Free" vs. "forced" exploration of a novel situation by rats. *Psychol. Rep.*, 1957, **3**, 95-108. (Monogr. Suppl. 2).

Welker, W. I. Persistence of sniffing after bilateral ablation of olfactory bulbs in rat. *Physiologist*, 1958, **1** (4), 84-85. (Abstract)

Welker, W. I. Comparative study of physiology and morphology of somatic cerebral cortex of *Procyonidae*. *Physiologist*, 1959, **2** (3), 121-122. (Abstract) (a)

Welker, W. I. Escape, exploratory, and food seeking responses of rats in a novel situation. *J. comp. physiol. Psychol.*, 1959, **52**, 106-111. (b)

Welker, W. I. Factors influencing aggregation of neonatal puppies. *J. comp. physiol. Psychol.*, 1959, **52**, 376-380. (c)

Welker, W. L. Genesis of exploratory and play behavior in infant raccoons. *Psychol. Rep.*, 1959, **5**, 764. (d)

Welker, W. I., & King, W. A. Effects of stimulus novelty on growing and eating by rats. Unpublished manuscript, Univer. of Wisconsin, 1961.

Welker, W. I., & Seidenstein, S. Somatic sensory representation in the cerebral cortex of the raccoon *(Procyon lotor)*. *J. comp. Neurol.*, 1959, **3**, 469-502.

Welker, W. I., & Welker, J. N. Reaction of fish *(Eucinostomus gula)* to environmental changes. *Ecology*, 1958, **39**, 283-288.

Welsh, G. S. A projective figure-preference test for diagnosis of psychopathology: 1. A preliminary investigation. Unpublished doctor's dissertation, Univer. of Minnesota, 1949.

Wendt, G. R. Negative adaptation as an active positive antagonism. *Psychol. Bull.*, 1931, **28**, 681-682.

Wenzel, B. M. Tactile stimulation as reinforcement for cats and its relation to early feeding experience. *Psychol. Rep.*, 1959, **5**, 297-300.

Werboff, J. Developmental effects of prenatal drug administration in the white rat. Paper read at Midwest. Psychol. Ass., Chicago, May, 1959.

Wessman, A. E., Ricks, D. F., & Tyl, Mary Nel. Characteristics and concomitants of mood fluctuation in college women. *J. abnorm. soc. Psychol.*, 1960, **60**, 117-126.

Wetmore, A. *A systematic classification for the birds of the world*. Revised and amended. *Smithsonian Misc. Coll.*, 1940, **99** (7), 1-11.

Wexler, D., Mendelson, J., Leiderman, P. H., & Solomon, P. Sensory deprivation, a technique for studying psychiatric aspects of stress. *Arch. Neurol. & Psychiat.*, 1958, **79**, 225-233.

Weyl, H. Symmetry. In J. R. Newman (Ed.), *The world of mathematics*. Vol. I. New York: Simon & Schuster, 1956. Pp. 671-724.

Wheaton, J. L. Fact and fancy in sensory deprivation studies. *USAF School of Aviation Medicine*, 1959, Review 5-59.

White, R. W. Motivation reconsidered: the concept of competence. *Psychol. Rev.*, 1959, **66**, 297-333. (Reprinted as Chapter 10 in this volume).

White, R. W. Competence and the psychosexual stages of development. In M. R. Jones (Ed.), *Nebraska symposium on motivation*. Lincoln: Univer. of Nebraska Press, 1960.

Whiting, J. W. M., & Mowrer, O. H. Habit progression and regression—a laboratory study of some factors relevant to human socialization. *J. comp. Psychol.*, 1943, **36**, 229-253.

Whitney, L. F., & Underwood, A. B. *The raccoon*. Orange, Conn.: Practical Science Publ. Co., 1952.

Wikler, A. Pharmacologic dissociation of behavior and EEG "sleep pattern" in dogs: morphine N-allylnormorphine, and atropine. *Proc. Soc. Exp. Biol.*, 1952, **79**, 261-265.

Wilder, C. E. Selection of rachitic and antirachitic diets in the rat. *J. comp. Psychol.*, 1937, **24**, 547-577.

Williams, E., & Scott, J. P. The development of social behavior patterns in the mouse, in relation to natural periods. *Behavior*, 1953, **6**, 35-64.

Williams, H. L., Lubin, A., & Goodnow, J. J. Impaired performance with acute sleep loss. *Psychol. Monogr.*, 1959, **73** (Whole No. 484).

Windle, W. F., & Becker, R. F. Effects of anoxia at birth on central nervous system of the guinea pig. *Proc. Soc. Exp. Biol. Med.*, 1942, **51**, 213-215.

Wingfield, R. C. Some factors influencing spontaneous alternation in human subjects. *J. comp. physiol. Psychol.*, 1943, **35**, 237-243.

Wingfield, R. C., & Dennis, W. The dependence of the rat's choice of pathways upon the length of the daily trial series. *J. comp. Psychol.*, 1934, **18**, 135-147.

Winkelmann, R. K. The erogenous zones: Their nerve supply and its significance. *Proc. Staff Meetings, Mayo Clinic*, 1959, **34**, 39-47.

Witkin, H. A. "Hypotheses" in rats: An experimental critique. II. The displacement of responses and behavior variability in linear situations. *J. comp. Psychol.*, 1941, **31**, 303-336.

Witkin, H. A., Lewis, H. B., Hertzman, M., Machover, K., Meissner, P. P., & Wapner, S. *Personality through perception.* New York: Harper, 1954.

Wittenburg, J. A., Ross, S., & Andrews, T. G. Sustained perceptual efficiency as measured by the clock test. *Percept. mot. Skills*, 1956, **6**, 109-116.

Wolf, A. The dynamics of the selective inhibition of specific functions in neurosis. *Psychosom. Med.*, 1943, **5**, 27-38.

Wolfe, J. B., & Kaplon, M. D. Effect of amount of reward and consummative activity on learning in chickens. *J. comp. Psychol.*, 1941, **31**, 353-361.

Wolpert, E. A. Studies in psychophysiology of dreams: II. An electromyographic study of dreaming. *AMA Arch. gen. Psychiat.*, 1960, **2**, 231-241.

Woods, P. J. The effects of free and restricted environmental experience on problem solving behavior in the rat. *J. comp. physiol. Psychol.*, 1959, **52**, 399-402.

Woods, P. J., & Jennings, Sallie. Response to environmental change: A further confirmation. *Psychol. Rep.*, 1959, **5**, 560.

Woodworth, R. S. Reinforcement of perception. *Amer. J. Psychol.*, 1947, **40**, 119-125.

Woodworth, R. S. *Dynamics of behavior.* New York: Henry Holt, 1958.

Woolsey, C. N. Patterns of localization in sensory and motor areas of the cerebral cortex. In Milbank Symposium, *The biology of mental health and disease.* New York: P. B. Hoeber, 1952. Ch. 14.

Woolsey, C. N., & Fairman, D. Contralateral, ipsilateral and bilateral representation of cutaneous receptors in somatic areas I and II of the cerebral cortex of pig, sheep and other mammals. *Surgery*, 1946, **19**, 684-702.

Wyckoff, L. B. The role of observing responses in discrimination learning: Part I. *Psychol. Rev.*, 1952, **59**, 431-442.

Yerkes, R. M. The mind of a gorilla. Part I. *Genet. Psychol. Monogr.*, 1927, **2**, 1-193.

Yerkes, R. M., & Dodson, J. D. The relation of strength of stimulus to rapidity of habit-formation. *J. comp. Neurol. Psychol.*, 1908, **18**, 459-482.

Yerkes, R. M., & Tomilin, M. I. Mother-infant relations in chimpanzees. *J. comp. Psychol.*, 1935, **20**, 321-359.

Yerkes, R. M., & Yerkes, A. W. *The great apes.* New Haven: Yale Univer. Press, 1929.

Young, P. T. Reversal of food preferences of the white rat through controlled pre-feeding. *J. gen. Psychol.*, 1940, **22**, 33-66.

Young, P. T. Food-seeking drive, affective process, and learning. *Psychol. Rev.*, 1949, **56**, 98-121.

Young, P. T. The role of hedonic processes in motivation. In M. R. Jones (Ed.), *Nebraska symposium on motivation.* Lincoln, Neb.: Univer. of Nebraska Press, 1955. Pp. 193-238.

Young, P. T. The role of affective processes in learning and motivation. *Psychol. Rev.*, 1959, **66**, 104-125.

Zeaman, D., & Angell, D. A spatial gradient of alternation tendency. *J. comp. physiol. Psychol.*, 1953, **46**, 390-392.

Zeaman, D., & House, B. J. The growth and decay of reactive inhibition as measured by alternation behavior. *J. exp. Psychol.*, 1951, **41**, 177-186.

Zimbardo, P. G., & Miller, N. E. Facilitation of exploration by hunger in rats. *J. comp. physiol. Psychol.*, 1958, **51**, 43-46.

Zimbardo, P. G., & Montgomery, K. C. The relative strengths of consummatory responses in hunger, thirst, and exploratory drive. *J. comp. physiol. Psychol.*, 1957, **50**, 504-508.

Ziskind, E., Jones, H., Filante, W., & Goldberg, J. Observations on mental symptoms in eye patched patients: hypnagogic symptoms in sensory deprivation. *Amer. J. Psychiat.*, 1960, **116**, 893-900.

Zubek, J. P., Pushkar, Dolores, Sansom, W., & Gowing, J. Perceptual changes after prolonged sensory isolation (darkness and silence). *Canad. J. Psychol.*, 1961, **15**, 83-100.

Zubek, J. P., Sansom, Wilma, & Prysiazniuk, A. Intellectual changes during prolonged perceptual isolation. *Canad. J. Psychol.*, 1960, **14**, 233-243.

Index

This book has been set on the Linotype in 12 point Bodoni Book, leaded 2 points and 10 point Bodoni Book, leaded 1 point. Chapter numbers and titles are in Mandate. The size of the type page is 27 by 46½ picas.